Baltimore

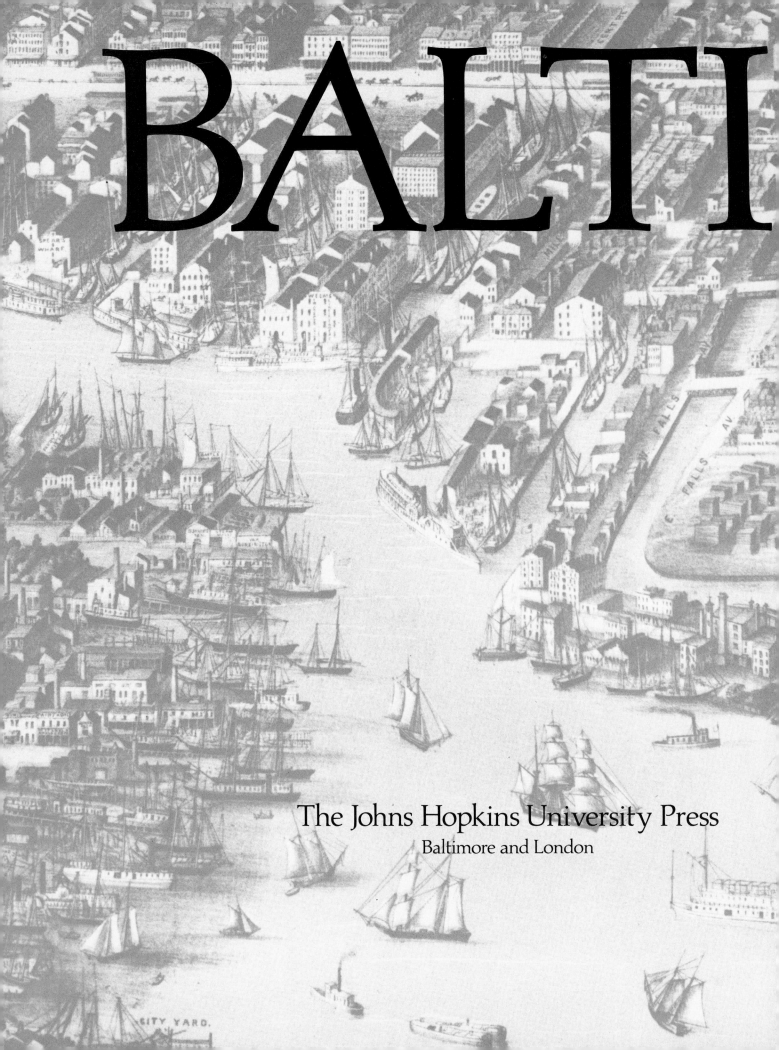

BALTI

The Johns Hopkins University Press

Baltimore and London

MORE

The Building
of an American
City

Sherry H. Olson

Publication of this book was generously assisted by grants from the National Endowment for the Humanities; the Maryland Arts Council; the Bernice L. and Albert D. Hutzler, Jr., Foundation, Inc.; Mr. and Mrs. Robert H. Levi; Lois and Philip Macht; the Harvey M. and Lenore P. Meyerhoff Fund; and James W. and Patricia T. Rouse.

The Johns Hopkins University Press, Baltimore, Maryland 21218
The Johns Hopkins Press Ltd., London

Library of Congress Catalog Card Number 79–21950
ISBN 0–8018–2224–6
Library of Congress Cataloging in Publication data will be found on the last printed page of this book.

ILLUSTRATION CREDITS. Archives of the B&O Railroad Museum (Chessie System): 108, 153, 157, 160, 351. Baltimore City Courthouse: 12, 23, 24, 31, 33, 39, 56. Baltimore City Microfilm Archives: 21, 54, 60, 77. Baltimore Department of Housing and Community Development: 116, 378. Baltimore Gas and Electric Company: 43, 84, 113, 167, 247, 248, 260, 261, 263, 265, 269, 288, 290, 296, 309, 313, 315, 317, 318, 322, 323, 327, 337. Baltimore Health Department: 376. Baltimore *News-American*: 205, 208, 236, 242, 255, 319, 334. Baltimore Sewerage Commission, annual report (1908): 256. Baltimore Sewerage Commission, annual reports (1911, 1912, 1913): 258. Baltimore *Sun*: 118, 241, 252, 310, 341, 348, 375. Baltimore Topographical Survey, atlas (1914): 87. Elinor B. Cahn: 385. Enoch Pratt Free Library, 150, 171, 174, 179, 213, 250–51, 332, 371. Harborplace Limited Partnership, 354. A. Hoen & Co.: 177 (left). Hughes Collection, Edward L. Bafford Photography Collection, University of Maryland Baltimore County Library: 75, 109, 114, 141, 201, 216, 267, 272, 303, 307, 312, 320. Conrad N. Lauer, *Engineering in American Industry* (New York: McGraw-Hill, 1924): 211. Library of Congress, Geography and Map Division: 78, 104, 106, 164. Maps, Inc.: 361. Maryland Bureau of Industrial Statistics, *Eleventh Annual Report* (1903): 229. Maryland Bureau of Statistics and Information, *Thirteenth Annual Report* (1904): 202. Maryland Historical Society: 19, 37, 65, 121, 227, 239. Maryland Mass Transit Administration: 253. National Archives, Records of the Office of the Chief of Engineers: 59. Oblate Sisters of Providence: 95. Julian Olson: 367. George Peabody Department of the Enoch Pratt Free Library: 73. Peabody Institute of The Johns Hopkins University: 192. The Peale Museum: 204, 293. Regional Management, Inc. (Hughes Co., photographers): 304. Linda G. Rich: 90, 223, 364. YMCA of the Greater Baltimore Area: 177 (right).

Contents

Acknowledgments

Without the collaboration of Phoebe Stanton in teaching and research, I would not have begun this book. At all the choice points Reds Wolman made me feel it was worth continuing. Over eight years Julian Olson photocopied maps, microfilmed archives, and printed photographs; he steadily reformed my punctuation and tempered my language. David Harvey shared his discovery of Baltimore for several years. Ronald Walters commented on an early draft of the manuscript, David Hanna another. Peter Holland read every word and insisted I say what I meant. David Boehlke thought out, collected, and prepared the illustrations and captions. Without David's energies, the book would not be finished.

Among the generous contributors of documents were the Baltimore City courts (land records division), the city's reference library and microfilm archive, the bureau of sewers, the mayor's office, the planning, urban renewal, and housing agencies, the Maryland Historical Society, the Maryland Room of the Enoch Pratt Free Library, the Peabody Library, the Peale Museum, the Johns Hopkins University libraries, the Library of Congress, the National Archives, the Jewish Historical Society, the Catholic Archdiocese, the Citizens Planning and Housing Association, the Baltimore Gas & Electric Company, the Union Trust Company, the Canton Company, and Maps, Incorporated.

In the course of this research, I have taxed the tolerance of more librarians than I can name personally, and the curiosity and endurance of six cohorts of undergraduate students at Johns Hopkins University. I cannot begin to name the splendid neighbors, friends, and allies, and some rather splendid adversaries, who have lit and focused my view of Baltimore since 1960.

Introduction

There is a tempo and a pattern to urban growth—a dance of larger sweep from generation to generation, as brick rows and marble steps extend over the landscape, as people do their social climbing or take a fall, and move around the corner or up the hill or out to the valley. This book is organized to reflect that rhythm as it was experienced in the neighborhoods of Baltimore. City growth is a boom-and-bust sequence of "long swings," with eighteen years or so separating the neighboring peaks. This applies equally to North America and Europe over at least two centuries, and to much of the world in the last hundred years.

The reader may not find here, therefore, all he wants to know about Baltimore. The outsider may find that this portrait does not match his private image of the city: baseball, softshell crabs, Eubie Blake at the piano, or Blaze Star on the Block. Some of Baltimore's choice gifts to the nation are not even mentioned: Harriet Tubman's underground railroad, Albert Fink's bridges, Babe Ruth, or Edgar Allan Poe. Others appear in the cast of the book, but not in their greatest roles: Frederick Douglass and Isaac Myers as national figures in the black struggle, Henrietta Szold in American Jewish scholarship or world Zionism, Charles Carroll as maker of the constitution or Judge Taney as its interpreter, H. L. Mencken adding to the American language and American literary criticism, Tom Winans building railroads in Russia, or the mark of The Johns Hopkins University on graduate education. Neglected utterly are the military exploits of the Maryland colonels and sea captains, and the eight thousand crosses in rows in the national cemeteries at Baltimore.

If these glories are neglected, what remains? This book is about city building, an internal dynamic of the city-state, and how Baltimoreans see themselves and their situation. In that sense, Baltimore is America, in its rhythm of building up and tearing down, swarming and dispersing, getting and spending, birthing and dying, sharing and competing. Just as the story of one farm or quarter-section of forest, a single square in the counterpane of America, lends an understanding of the processes that formed the landscape, so Baltimore is one square in the great cotillion of the cities.

Some dimensions of Baltimore life must remain understated because they are given their due elsewhere. Excellent modern histories focus on the party politics and political leadership of successive generations in Maryland. The generals and the jurists have their biographies, and there are new works each

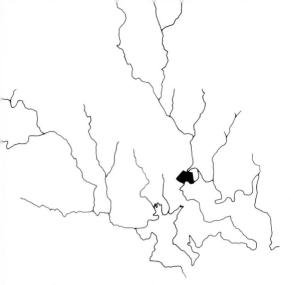

Original shoreline, drainage, and sixty-acre site of Baltimore Town, 1729.

Streets of Baltimore, Jones Town (Oldtown), and Fell's Point, as developed between 1745 and 1788.

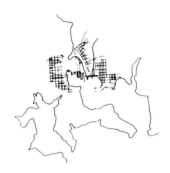

Streets developed from 1789 to 1801.

year on Baltimore clipper ships, locomotives, steamboats, or streetcars. The interested reader can turn to other books for such detail.

Other dimensions are understated because we know too little about them. The most serious gap is our ignorance of the lives of slaves and servants in Baltimore, the urban economy of servitude and its extinction. Another hole in written history is the transplantation of the Polish Catholic community—uprooted from the old world village, heeled in to urban squalor, then thriving in tidy rows of marble steps. A third missing link is an account of the strategies of landowners and real estate investors in each round. Here the reader can only be advised to look out the window and read the landscape. Baltimore possesses some magnificent sources for the books that must be written to fill these gaps. In addition to the resources of the Enoch Pratt Library, the Peabody collection, The Johns Hopkins University library, and the Maryland Historical Society—to all of which I am indebted—there are a barely scratched wealth of maps and surveys, and wonderfully indexed land records and legal archives. In the land-

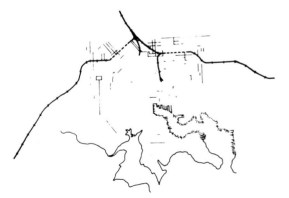

Streets opened between 1866 and 1877 and railroad tunnels connecting the Pennsylvania Railroad system, built ca. 1872 (Baltimore & Potomac Railroad to the west and Union Railroad to the east).

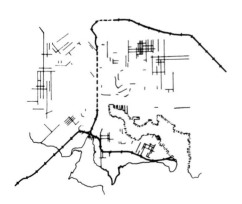

Streets opened from 1878 to 1899 and B&O Railroad tunnels and crossover, built ca. 1893.

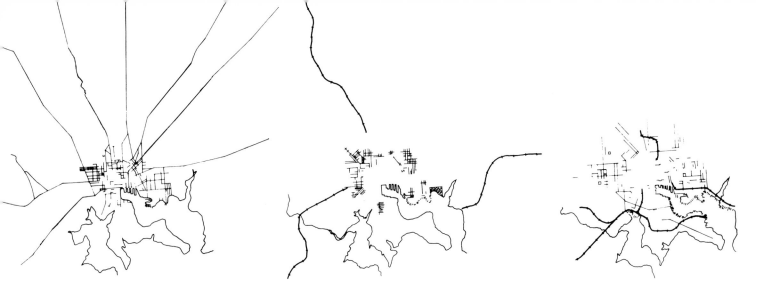

Streets and turnpike roads developed between 1802 and 1821.

Streets opened between 1822 and 1837 and railroads built by 1837 (B&O Railroad to the southwest, Baltimore & Susquehanna Railroad to the north, and Baltimore & Port Deposit Railroad to the east).

Streets opened from 1838 to 1864 and railroad extensions toward the waterfront.

scape itself, the city's social record is built into its dwellings, and its technological history is imprinted in the industrial buildings and engineering works.

Meanwhile, a twelfth generation of children of all colors of ribbons and races plays hopscotch on the sidewalks, correcting with chalk a "standard American" grid to match Baltimore tradition, hopping and giggling and waiting a turn, thinking not at all of grown-up games or the place of Baltimore in a hopscotch world.

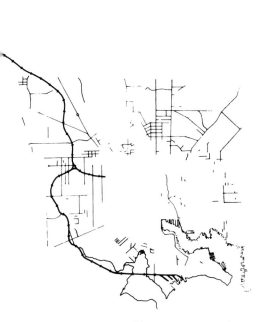

Streets opened between 1900 and 1918, chiefly in the territory annexed in 1888, and the Western Maryland Railroad, as developed ca. 1903.

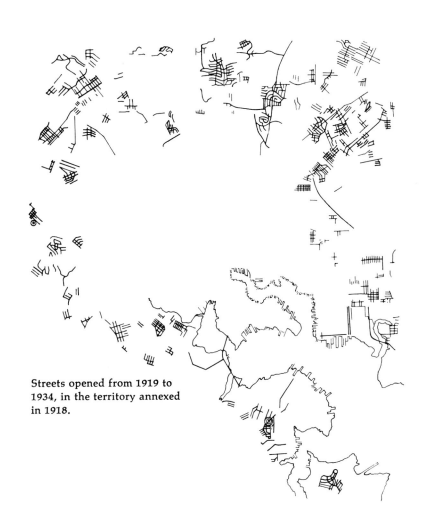

Streets opened from 1919 to 1934, in the territory annexed in 1918.

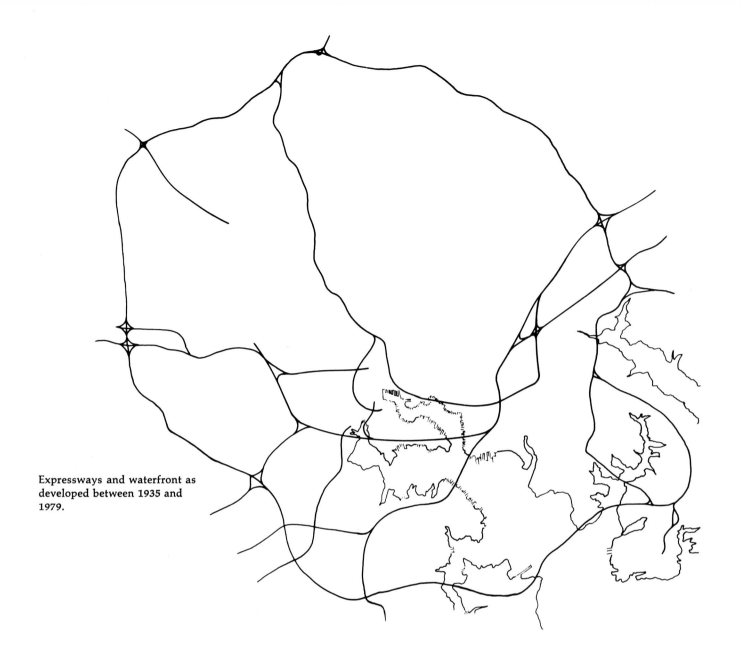

Expressways and waterfront as developed between 1935 and 1979.

Baltimore

The Empty Century

The streams were called *Felles* or *Fells* by Governor Smith of Virginia, who first explored the Chesapeake Bay, probably because the waters fell over rocks or precipices until they met the tide, where they became and are called Rivers. The points of land stretching into the Bay and divide them, have been and are still called *Necks.* Among us the West or upper part of the Harbor is called *Basin*, because it is a pond open on one side only and surrounded by hills which preserve much stillness on the surface of the water.[1]

The features belonged to a town site of magnificent potential. The place was a natural haven for ships. It possessed streams with plenty of fall for turning mills, and also admirable timber on the necks, a generous agricultural climate, a great variety of soils, an abundance of fine springs of water, and a long ridge of excellent red brick clays, called the bolus by John Smith, but later known as the minebank for its nuggets of iron ore.[2]

Yet for a hundred years no city grew. Unlike Boston, New York, Philadelphia, or Charleston, Baltimore was never a significant center of colonial trade, enterprise, government, or culture. Laid out in 1730, it was still a mere village of twenty-five houses in 1752, and at the onset of the Revolution it was a small town of six thousand persons and ten churches, and it had just acquired its first newspaper. The failure to develop a colonial city on the Patapsco cannot be blamed on a strong rival. Colonial Maryland had no truly urban life, and its economy required no system of market towns. The town of Annapolis revolved around the personal presence of the governor and the sessions of the assembly and general court; it was a political environment and a seasonal place of social life and leisure among the large landowners.

This long gestation has never been a particular source of pride for Baltimore, and its citizens have preferred to direct their attention to its sudden remarkable growth with national independence. Nevertheless, the empty century was formative. For a hundred years before the village was laid out, and for another generation of village life whose traces are all but gone, influences combined that would subsequently forge the identity of Baltimore. The citizens came to define themselves as a people struggling against the past, resisting the oppressive institutions of the state, surviving in a political environment hostile to cities. At times the struggle was clearly directed against some outside enemy—twice they repelled the British on the battlefield, and scores of times they renewed their demand for representation in the state legislature and for municipal powers of self-determination. In part, the struggle was internalized, built into conflicts of class, race, generation, and party within the city and its institutions. The struggle extended into the very conscience of the individual citizen. Conflicts arising from the economic and social system of Baltimore's empty century have continued to find expression, generation after generation, in the design and redesign of the city and in its monuments, symbols, and celebrations, in virulent journalism, pamphleteering, and electioneering, and in epidemics of arson and mob violence. Each new surge of growth, each new influx of strangers, reopened all the questions, revealed buried anxieties, and brought again and again to a focus the question of identity—how shall we come to terms with our past?

The Tobacco Economy

The Chesapeake Bay and its rivers had been explored by Captain John Smith in 1609, a colony had been organized by Leonard Calvert in 1634, and by 1650 the proprietor, Lord Baltimore, had issued to favored persons scores of patents or land grants averaging a thousand acres. With the land, these people received the privileges of local justice, collection of taxes and fees, and control over the further subdivision or resale of the land; thus, the essential developmental power of selecting and promoting sites of trade, mills, landings, tenements (for tenant farmers), and quarters (for slave labor). Early settlements were concentrated in the accessible tidewater region. The sandy soils of the plain were suitable for growing tobacco south of the Patuxent River, on the Western Shore, and on the Eastern Shore in Kent and Talbot counties. Purchase money, quit rents, and alienation fees were commonly priced and paid in tobacco.

The tobacco economy required no towns. Large planters produced foodstuffs for their slaves and made garments from imported "negro cloth." English middlemen lightered tobacco from the planters' river landings to ships in the bay. They also extended credit and supplied imports of necessaries such as nails and paper and luxuries such as glassware, wine, and furniture. The large planters retailed supplies and extended credit to small farmers, at high prices.

Agricultural settlement of the lands in the piedmont was even slower, and urban settlement was nonexistent. A number of patents were issued in Baltimore County in the 1650s, and the first on the present site of the city were carved out of the woods in the early 1660s: fifty acres on Whetstone Point and Mountenay's Neck, two hundred acres of bottom or glade along either side of Harford Run. At first, it was the practice, "while there were few competitors," to portion off a bit of the best land and take up but little "waste." But by the end of the decade the taking-up accelerated, and larger contiguous grants were made, with generous possibilities for fraudulent surveying, "overrun," and future litigation. The colony's legislative assembly instructed Baltimore County to build a courthouse and a record vault, then a jail and a road to the courthouse. The vast size of the territory, the sparseness of settlement, the absence of roads, and the limited navigable waterways into the rolling piedmont lands encouraged endless disputation over the location of a "county town."

Slow transport, communications, and settlement, as well as the beautiful, elegantly furnished manors now restored, lead visitors to imagine a conservative, traditional, and gracious way of life in colonial Maryland and to idealize it as a time of great stability. This is misleading. Baltimore's "empty century" was one of rapid transformations, reflecting the fast pace of change and development in the affairs of Europe and Britain.

The politics of religion was one area of swift change. The Catholic proprietors and circle of wealthy Catholic planters formulated the Toleration Act of 1649, for their protection in a society of accelerating Puritan immigration.

The Limits of Toleration

That noe person or psons whatsoever within this Province or the Islands Ports Harbors Creeks or Havens therevnto belonging professing to believe in Jesus Christ shall from henceforth bee any waies troubled molested or discontenaced for or in respect of his or her religion nor in the free exercise thereof.[3]

It was for the protection of varieties of Christians only, and ordered death and confiscation or forfeiture of lands and goods as the punishment for any person who blasphemed God, denied the holy Trinity, or profaned the Lord's Day. Toleration did not extend to the Jews. The only person reported sentenced to death under the act was a "Jew Doctor," Jacob Lumbrozo, in 1658, for blasphemy. (He was released in a general political amnesty of the mother country.) The immigration of Jews into Maryland was rare before the Revolution. Members of the Society of Friends were also persecuted in the years immediately following the Act of Toleration. In 1650 the governor and council accused "Idle persons known by the name of Quakers" of "diswading the People from Complying with Military Discipline in this time of Danger as also from giving testimony or being Jurors." Some dozens were fined or whipped.[4] In spite of persecution, there was a considerable development in Maryland of Quaker missions and conversions. Between 1665 and 1677 communities of Friends were established in the more populous tobacco counties. Smaller meetings were organized along the Great Falls of the Gunpowder and in Anne Arundel County. Some land was taken up in the Patapsco region by Quaker families, notably Gorsuch and Fell.

Religious disputes reverberated across the Atlantic. In 1689, at the time of the Glorious Revolution in England, Protestants deposed the Catholic proprietor. In 1702 the Catholics in Maryland were disfranchised. They were allowed to worship only in their homes. A special tax was laid on the importation of Irish servants "being Papists," and a test or oath of loyalty was required to determine tax liability. Religious tests were obstacles to the civil participation of Jews, Quakers, and Puritans, as well as Catholics. The transformation of the wealthy, landed Catholic elite into a self-conscious political minority persecuted for their religion encouraged their interest in foreign education, their refuge in a tight-woven circle of families, and their connections with French Catholic culture. In 1694, partly in order to separate the government from Catholic ties, Maryland's seat of government was removed from St. Mary's City to Annapolis, a more central location. Annapolis became the only town with urban amenities such as newspapers and theaters. It was "hailed, as the rising sun, as 'the bright particular star', of the state."[5]

Slaves and Servants

A second set of changes involved the settlement of a labor force to give value to the land grants. Small capital was needed to begin tobacco farming, and land was cheap, but the crop demanded much labor and close management. Consequently, the extension of tobacco farming could proceed only as the labor force expanded. There is very little information about servitude in Maryland before 1640, but the evidence is substantial that over the 1640s the distinction was being made between Negro slavery for life and white service for a term.[6] White servants were often indentured for a term of seven years for payment of their ship passage, while some were sold into servitude as penalty for crimes, including the crime of indigence. When his term was finished, the servant was given fifty acres to farm. Over a few years, he might even accumulate the price of one or two slaves, to extend his scale of operation. In contrast, it was extremely difficult for a black slave to obtain his freedom, and still more difficult for him to purchase land. Benjamin Banneker's was such a family; they managed to survive as independent tobacco farmers, to create and protect a family of free persons, and to get some education in a neighborhood of rural isolation at Oella, near Elk Ridge. Banneker was assistant surveyor to Major Andrew Ellicott in laying out the District of Columbia in 1791.[7]

The legal degradation of blacks became more definite over the years, as their numbers increased. Africans were imported at a high rate between 1698 and 1707. From contemporary estimates, in 1715 a quarter of the slaves in Maryland were imported in that decade. In that year the assembly formalized the status of their children: they should henceforth be *born* slaves. Blacks could not testify against whites, could not serve on a jury or in the military, and could not strike a white even in self-defense, so that they had no recourse whatever against a master. Over the eighteenth century it was gradually made more difficult legally to manumit or free slaves, although it was done, notably by Quaker masters in the 1760s and 1770s.

In 1715, Baltimore County still held only three thousand people all told, or fewer than eight hundred "masters and taxable men," in an area that today includes nearly the whole metropolitan region of five counties. Blacks were one-fifth to one-sixth of the population, as in the rest of the province. After the surge of slave importation, the slave population grew by natural increase, approximately doubling in each generation until about 1800. The proportion of blacks in the population probably peaked at 30 percent in 1754, then fell back to 20 or 25 percent as the importation of white servants and tenants increased. This demographic rhythm is characteristic of every major immigration, whether slave, indentured, or wholly voluntary, since the age groups of high mobility and high economic productivity are also the age groups of high fertility. It implies that at the time Baltimore began to grow rapidly, the black population of the state retained a vivid memory of the experience of enslavement, and its age structure was young, vigorous, and—to the race of masters—threatening. In 1665 a slave who murdered his master was convicted of petit treason. It is not possible to estimate how frequently such an event occurred, or how often slaves were caned to death, raped, or sold out of state, or how often they cut their own throats or burned their masters' houses. Nor is it possible to estimate how great was the proportion of decent masters, well-ordered plantations, or mutual care. However generous the estimate, at the heart there was always mutual terror— the inexorable nightmare of Maryland.

A third set of changes began twenty years before the actual layout of Baltimore in 1730 and continued twenty years afterward. It involved the increase and concentration of wealth, the diversification of enterprise, and the acceleration of investment—in other words, the process of economic development.

Grain and Iron

In 1732, the European tobacco market was entering a long period of depressed prices, severe enough in Maryland to cause rioting and the destruction of many acres of the crop.[8] New demands were developing in England for iron as a strategic material and for grain to feed the highly specialized sugar colonies of the West Indies. The changed market demands in the Old World shifted the relative advantages of differently endowed regions of Maryland. The stagnant tobacco economy of coastal plain Maryland and the growth economy of wheat and iron in the piedmont were politically and socially antagonistic. Contrasts in labor conditions in the two regions also generated conflicts of interest between Baltimore City and the state of Maryland. Hostility between regions and hostility between the city and state governments were most intense during the Civil War, but are evident to the present day.

Baltimore, situated on the fall line, at the junction of piedmont and tidewater, was an offspring of the growth economy of the piedmont. It was an economy of the north, of the Delaware, Brandywine, and Susquehanna valleys. Flour mills and iron furnaces were being built in Delaware and Pennsylvania, and a frontier of wheat farming was moving southward, in conjunction with the immigration and settlement of the Germans and the Scotch-Irish. In the Baltimore region, mill seats began to be established, such as Jonathan Hansen's mill in 1711, on the Jones Falls. The streams that ran down from piedmont Baltimore County—Jones Falls, Gwynns Falls, Gwynns Run, Great Gunpowder, and Little Gunpowder—offered numerous sites for water-driven mills. Such a "fall" or "run" provided several hundred feet of head before it reached tidewater. The oldest iron furnace in Maryland, Principio, on the Great Falls of the Gunpowder near North East, was producing iron in 1715. Because John Moale had hopes for developing ore on Locust Point, he withheld his land from a town-site venture, affecting the settlement of Baltimore.

In order to seize such opportunities to build mills and furnaces, for which the central piedmont of Maryland had the natural resources, capital was wanted. By the 1720s the planters had begun to accumulate large fortunes, which could be turned to the cause of further economic development. Families like the Carrolls, the Dulanys, and the Ridgelys had reached a point at which they could afford to hold large blocs of land long enough to profit from their gradually rising value.[9] They had assets of hundreds of slaves whose labor could be re-allocated. They recruited servants directly from Ireland and Germany to be tenant farmers on their back lands in Frederick County. In 1733 the assembly chartered the Baltimore Company, which acquired 100 acres and built a furnace and forge on Gwynns Falls. Dr. Charles Carroll of Annapolis had shares in the Baltimore Company venture; he also acquired the tract called Mount Royal for iron ore, the plantation Georgia between Gwynns Falls and Maiden's Choice Run, and a plantation at The Caves in the limestone region of Baltimore County. His letters to his sons evaluate the economy of the Baltimore region in 1752, when he was about to build Mount Clare mansion and to develop his surrounding Georgia plantation. He had sold an interest in an iron furnace at North East and lost by fire a warehouse and bakehouse. He had sent one son to London to study law and seek new capital, and another to Philadelphia to learn surveying and bookkeeping. His advice is revealing: "I cannot see that by making Tobacco I should better my own Yours or Your Bros Fortunes & that induces me to go upon the Iron Business and making Grain to Support it."[10] Dr. Carroll developed a merchant mill at Elk Ridge Landing with a bakery for ship bread. The mill utilized material from a furnace venture he had scrapped. The mill and bakery would create a market for wheat, which would allow settlers to pay off the back lands he had sold them near Frederick. He planned an iron furnace sixty miles away on several thousand acres of charcoal timber, a forge at a site twelve miles nearer, with another six thousand acres of woods, and close to Elk Ridge a quarter, or settlement, for the slave labor force. He figured he would need £700 for four or five years to put this scheme into operation, and that he could pay off the total capital and interest in another five years.

In conjunction with the attempt to develop farming and tillage, mills and iron exports, and also to control shipping more effectively, attempts were made to found towns. Most of them failed. The colonial legislature in 1706 had authorized the founding of ten riverine towns planned as public landings for seagoing craft and as markets with storehouses, ship repair, and provisioning. The extension of agricultural settlement contributed to the siltation of their harbors and to the eventual abandonment of several of the town sites, including Joppa and Elk Ridge Landing. In 1753, the assembly ordered an end to dumping earth and sand into the Patapsco and its tributaries. Persons digging ironstone were told to adopt erosion control measures.[11]

Corporate private enterprise, such as the Baltimore Company, did not differ greatly from corporate public enterprise at that time. The Baltimore Company obtained from the assembly a charter designating the persons who constituted the corporation, their purposes, and a limited period of time in which to operate. Most public enterprises, such as building a public road or jail or laying out a town, were authorized in the same manner and were directed to be carried out by a commission of persons designated in the legislative act.[12] A substantial landowner had the same range of management experience required for the "public" enterprises. The decisions and activities were the same—adjudication of disputes, surveying, valuing land, valuing crops, drawing up legal documents, managing a labor force, supplying the labor force with food and housing, negotiating sales, locating and cutting roads, and overseeing the construction of buildings. For public enterprises, the same set of persons was taxed for the cost of the improvements and received most of the benefits of the enterprise, roughly in proportion to the size of their land holdings. It is easy to understand, then, that these commissions should have consisted of the large neighboring landowners who together worked out the solutions to development problems that affected more than one person's property. The same landowners often served in other roles, such as judge or county surveyor. It is also natural that this system, in which the private and the public interest were so closely interwoven, should have resulted in a rather ingrown form of social control and in an enormous number of appeals to the courts in Annapolis. Lawsuits were also encouraged by the scarcity of cash (which meant that everyone did business on credit), by the problems of controlling an unwilling labor force in a near wilderness, and by the rising resale value of land as development proceeded. Despite its modern image as a genteel society, this was a property-conscious, speculative, and litigious society in which the courtroom was a political forum and a favorite spectacle.

The growth of Baltimore was knotted in this web of mutual debts and transactions in land, the process of private development on credit, the expectation of ever-rising land values, and the dependence upon public investment to generate land values. The city itself was to be the great speculation.

Baltimore grew, not by the regular enlargement of one focus of settlement, but by the seeding, rivalry, and coalescence of three nuclei—Baltimore Town, Jones Town, and Fells Point. The distinctive character of each was to prove stubborn.

On 12 January 1730, commissioners, appointed for life, laid off Baltimore Town: "Sixty Acres of Land, in and about the place where one John Fleming now lives." Its original site and shape were governed by natural features, that is, the extent of high ground near the waterfront. The water came up to present-day Water Street; the village was surrounded by water on the south, by a great gully on the northwest (toward Sharp Street), and by swamps on the east along the Jones Falls. The falls "swept round in a deep, horse-shoe bend"[13] as far as the corner of Calvert and Lexington streets, and then northeastwardly along the line of Calvert Street. The internal arrangements of the town resembled the design of a village of English plan. There were only two wide streets, sixty-six feet, or four perches. Long Street, later called Market Street and now Baltimore Street, was intended for business. Perpendicular to it, a short but potentially monumental street rose from the waterfront to the bluff overlooking the Jones Falls. It was given a more elegant name, Calvert Street, for the proprietor's family. Forrest Street, later Charles Street, was three perches wide, but all the other streets were mere "lanes" one perch wide. Sixty one-acre lots were laid out, more or less square. With one hundred years of hindsight, Griffith offered a critique of the original plan:

Creating a Town

From the small quantity of ground originally taken for the town, and from the difficulty of extending the town in any direction, as it was surrounded by hills, water courses or marshes, it is evident that the commissioners did not anticipate either its present commerce or population. The expense of extending streets, building bridges, levelling hills and filling marshes, to which their successors have been subjected, and which, unfortunately, increases that of preserving the harbour as improvements increase and the soil is loosened, have been obstacles scarcely felt in other American cities; but requiring immense capitals of themselves, against which nothing but the great local advantages for internal and external trade would have enabled the citizens to contend.[14]

The same kind of vision is evident in the original layout of Jones Town (Oldtown) and later Fells Point: the same keen sense of strategic location for trade and the same very modest expectations. The street plans were pragmatic and riverine, aligned to exploit the waterfront and the natural drainage. Jones Town was laid off in 1732, into half-acre lots on ten acres east of the Jones Falls. It consisted of three streets, "or one street with three courses, corresponding with the meanders of the bank of the falls." The only cross street was the eastern road, now Gay Street, redirected by a ford.[15] Rivalry between Jones Town and Baltimore Town was felt from the beginning, but the original plats gave no hint that they might grow together.

William Fell, a ship carpenter, had settled east of the Jones Falls in 1726 on a tract called Copus Harbor and had built a mansion on what is now Lancaster Street. The harbor potential there was distinctly better than at Baltimore Town. Depths of sixteen to twenty feet were normal at the point, while to the west the alluvions and shoals created problems, more or less severe from year to year. Nevertheless, nothing happened at the point for nearly forty years.

To "read" the original plans of Baltimore Town and Jones Town on the spot today is difficult. The street orientations remain, but only a few disjointed alleys near Water Street, along the old southern waterfront of the town, convey some feeling of the narrowness of the original lanes. Generation by generation, the relief has been softened, the grades lessened, the precipices blunted, the crowns lowered, the gullies filled. From the site of St. Paul's Church one still gets a distinct impression of the steep edge of the Jones Falls valley. The first parish church, situated on the highest lot in the village, was later described as a "barn-like edifice on the edge of a sand hill, with the graves of deserted congregations clustered around, their coffins at times being exposed by the violence of northeast storms." A walk through the changing courses of Saratoga Street, with glances down Liberty, Charles, and Light streets toward the harbor, and over the "hump" of Calvert Street, now much cut down, gives some sense of the original lay of the land.

The lots toward the river were all taken up within a few days of the survey, but those on Baltimore Street were not in demand. A number of lots eventually reverted to the owner, Charles Carroll, because they had not been improved within the prescribed seven years. As streets were graded, as structures were raised, as the woods were cut and the land farmed, man and nature conspired to scour the heights and muddy the low places.

As the wheat lands were slowly being settled, the road network began to be crudely defined. In 1745 York Road, Reisterstown Road, which branched to Westminster and Hanover, and the old Frederick Road could be traveled by wagons, but only under good weather conditions. That same year, the town of Frederick was settled, and German tenants and settlers were arriving from Pennsylvania. The Gay Street bridge brought the great eastern road linking Georgetown and Philadelphia through both Baltimore Town and Jones Town. The bridge gave value to the land between, and was critical to the process of uniting Baltimore. Thomas Harrison, who had arrived from England three years before, bought the lots nearest the water on each side of South Street and built a house near South and Water streets. In 1745 he, with William Fell, Captain Lux, and others, served as commissioner for joining the two towns. He bought from the Carrolls the twenty-eight-acre marsh lying between the two parts of the town. The legislature authorized adding to the town the part that was "fast land" west of the falls. Gay, Frederick, and parts of Second and Water streets were laid out through it. Further additions were made, fifteen or twenty acres at a time. A public wharf was built at the end of Calvert Street, and a tobacco inspection house west of Charles.

The acts authorizing the merger and addition also empowered the town commissioners to open and widen streets or alleys, to remove nuisances, and to oversee chimneys. One act promoted the "making of land" by allowing a person to claim land he had developed by dredging or filling. It was, however, specifically set down that neither the commissioners nor the inhabitants of the town should elect delegates to the assembly. "How different," says Griffith, "have the fortunes of Baltimore been in this respect, from that of all the other great cities of this continent."[16]

Rhythms of Growth
1745–1788

The second half of the eighteenth century saw a sudden take-off for Baltimore. From an insignificant way place of twenty-five wooden houses at midcentury, it grew to a brick-and-mortar town of thirty thousand inhabitants by 1800 and crystallized as the central place of Maryland. It became one of the most important nodes in the communication system of a new nation pushing its frontier inland, and it functioned as one of several dozen new pressure points in world trade. Most important, Baltimore came to define itself as a city.

Baltimore's rhythm of growth was determined by international war and peace. The town thrived on disorder and stagnated in years of calm. Its four major spurts occurred during the French and Indian War (1756 to 1763), the American Revolution (1775 to 1781), the wars of the French Revolution, Directory, and Convention (1789 to 1802), and the Napoleonic wars (1806 to 1815). Familiar to Americans only to the extent of their military participation, these were actually a long series of world wars of grand scope. Of great importance to Baltimore were the perennial naval warfare between England and France, which drove up flour prices, and the frequent changes of management in the sugar islands of the West Indies, major importers of wheat: Baltimore merchants profited from the interruption of European shipping and exploited the ups and downs of the price of flour.

The town received successive groups of refugees, including many daring, canny, and well-informed individuals. Repeated military threats stimulated a new civil organization for defense. The payoffs did not come until after 1800, but in this half century one can discern the development in Baltimore of a far-flung information network and a great flexibility and willingness to risk, to hustle, and to maneuver. Baltimore's magnificent little sailing vessels were symbolic of a new, truly Baltimorean style, distinct from what had gone before.

A Spirit of Fierceness

Between 1752 and 1774, the number of houses in Baltimore increased from 25 to 564. Much of this growth was compressed into the period of the Seven Years War (or French and Indian War) and its aftermath. Thomas W. Griffith claims, "the savages got within eighty or ninety miles of the town, in parties of plunder and murder."[1] Other writers comment that citizens of Baltimore were not enthusiastic about the war because of increased taxes but the war promoted the growth of the wheat and iron economy of the piedmont and the growth of Baltimore.

The demand for wheat and iron certainly increased because of the war. About 1761 the Ridgelys opened the Hampton, or Northampton, furnaces. The Mount Royal forge was developed on the Jones Falls, the Kingsbury furnace on Herring Run, Dorsey's forge at Avalon, and the furnaces in Frederick County at Catoctin and Tom's Creek.

Most famous of the successive groups of refugees who fostered the town's growth, were an estimated nine hundred Acadians, French-speaking Catholics expelled from Nova Scotia in 1756. They brought few resources with them, and survived by navigation, fishing, and picking oakum. They lived in huts in "French town" along the undeveloped waterfront of South Charles Street and formed the nucleus for the first Catholic parish, St. Peter's congregation. This was not an easy time for Catholics in Maryland, even for the earlier settlers with resources. War with the French encouraged anti-Catholic fanaticism, and with the need for revenues a double tax was laid on Catholics. Governor Horatio Sharpe apparently attempted to restrain the "indecent Reflections" of the assembly, but believed the Catholics should not appeal the double tax.[2]

Another small stream of wartime settlers was the Scots, who brought some capital for development. Among them were the Smiths, the Sterretts, the Spears, and the Buchanans, four Presbyterian families who had emigrated from Scotland to Ireland. In the late 1720s they had reemigrated from Ireland to Lancaster County, Pennsylvania, and prospered in flour milling. In 1750 they moved, together, to Carlisle, Pennsylvania, where they kept store and shipped wheat to Baltimore. Because the fighting was detrimental to business on that frontier, in 1759 they all moved to Baltimore, with considerable capital ($40,000 in just one of the families), which they invested in slaves, ships, and waterfront property. The slaves built wharves extending a thousand feet—the only ones that reached as far as the ship channel. The Scottish families then shipped wheat to Europe and the West Indies. They built warehouses on the wharves, a bakery, a brewhouse, and substantial dwellings and counting houses in the vicinity of Gay and Water streets, and, with others, a Presbyterian church. All of these families were to play major roles in the city's development over the next three generations. Their collective impact was unique, but in its elements their story is somewhat characteristic of a development pattern followed by hundreds of others: a close-knit intermarrying circle of people of high mobility and keen entrepreneurship, and a consistent and calculated strategy of seizing the advantages of location.

German settlers followed a similar path. They had moved into York and Lancaster counties, Pennsylvania, in the 1720s and '30s, and into Frederick County, Maryland, as tenants of Carroll and Dulany. They tended to compete in settlement with the Scotch-Irish and to locate in separate valleys and townships. Enterprising Germans began moving from these regions into Baltimore about 1748, and the trend accelerated in the 1760s.

The stimulus to milling and shipping wheat attracted English and Irish millers from Cecil County, Pennsylvania, and Delaware. Jesse Hollingsworth

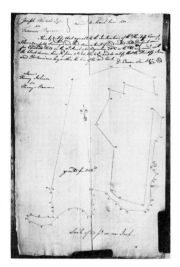

Nearly 350 acres were surveyed in 1761 for Edward Fell. This plat was used as evidence in the lawsuit of *Joseph Alender's lessee* v. *Terrence Byrnes*, amended *Henry Johnson* v. *Henry Manson* (March 1812).

came from Elkton, from a family associated with milling, shipping, and ship-building interests in the Brandywine Valley. William Moore, also from the Brandywine, redeveloped Fell's mills on the Jones Falls; Joseph Ellicott and Hugh Burgess developed mills on the Jones Falls opposite the jail. This stream of settlers was identified with the eastward expansion of the town, and with new congregations formed in the early 1770s, including the Baptists and the Quakers, and the Methodists in Strawberry Alley and Lovely Lane.

The arrival of Quaker millers coincided with a consensus among Friends to free their slaves, which implied leaving tobacco planting and developing an alternative economy. John Woolman, on horseback and on foot, traveled through Maryland in 1746, 1757, 1766, and 1767, pleading with each Quaker meeting and each Quaker slave holder personally to rid himself of slavery. He was "bowed down to tears," feeling that over twenty years he had seen the "gold appear dim, and much fine gold changed," as he watched his hosts "living in fulness on the labours of the poor oppressed Negroes" and their children growing up "without much labour." He observed the appearance of "a spirit of fierceness and the love of dominion . . . and an inward desolation."[3] Through Woolman's efforts some hundreds of slaves were freed, chiefly at the head of the Chesapeake.

The Quaker association of the Fells explains some of the choices of sites in Jones Town, Fells Point, and Fell's Addition. Toward the end of the war, Mr. William Fell, persuaded by Robert Long, laid off the town of Fells Point, corresponding, like the earlier townsites, with the lines of the waterfront—Philpot, Thames, and Fell streets. The plan had a wide respectable cross street (Bond), lesser lanes, and more or less square lots. Between 1765 and 1770, wharves, warehouses, and shipyards were erected on the Fells Point waterfront. Among the entrepreneurs, Captain Patton came from Ireland, and Nelson, Griest, and Vanbibber from Charlestown, Cecil County. These streams of migrants and the specific form of enterprise, based on access to deep water, set the pattern for development of the point over several generations.

Rivalry with Baltimore Town was immediate and persistent. "The first settlers were in fact at great loss to determine in which part to buy, as most likely to improve, and those who had sufficient means or enterprise, generally took lots both in town and point."[4] At the beginning of the American rebellion, a quarter of the houses but only 14 percent of the people of Baltimore were on the point. It is likely that most of the houses there were smaller than those in the town, that there were fewer slaves and servants, and that members of some households may have been at sea. The houses on the point, with the exception of those of the "gentlemen," were generally frame houses with shingle roofs. In Baltimore Town, frame construction was outlawed, although the roofs were still shingled.

The most important development in the last few years before the Revolution was the effort to conquer the lowlands between town and point. This was a slow process. Promptly at the end of the French and Indian War, Thomas Harrison and others were instructed by the assembly to drain and reclaim their "large miry marsh" on account of "noxious effluvia," and the town was authorized to annex, wharf out, fill, and lay out the land into at least eight lots per acre. In 1768 and again in 1770 the assembly gave Harrison more time. In 1779 it authorized Harrison's marsh to be surveyed and "laid out anew." To these sections were added a hundred acres of Steiger's former marsh and Moale's lowland between town and point. On the south and west were added Cornelius Howard's thirty-five acres, including Conway and Barre streets.[5] These additions represented the preparation of a large terrain for future expansion, but each was platted with no consideration for through traffic or any relation to other parts of the town.

The French and Indian War was the occasion for organizing the Ancient and Honorable Mechanical Company of Baltimore. Its early records, skimpy though unbroken, indicate that it existed as a club or society by 1763, and its earliest recorded functions were military drills for the defense of the town and turning out to fight fires and floods.[6] For that reason, it seems to have been a remarkably democratic institution, including young men and old, tradesmen as well as doctors and prominent merchants, and the German residents recently come from Pennsylvania. Certainly the Mechanical Company differed from the formal commissions and councils of government, which were selected from among large landowners. It called a meeting whenever there was a matter of importance to discuss in town. In 1769 it raised the money to buy a little copper ship's pump, Baltimore's first fire-fighting engine, and it built a frame lodge and engine house in East Lane (later Chatham, then Fayette) near Calvert Street, with a bridge to get over the twelve-foot gully in front.

That very flexible, informal, and creative organization was all the more important because Baltimore lacked the formal institutions and powers of self-government, and its modest urban services were fragmented. The town was not represented in the assembly of the province, and it had no locally elected council. In 1768 the functions of the county—court sessions, jail, and land records—were brought to Baltimore from Joppa Town after much invective and "some violence and outrage." (Dissatisfied residents to the north promptly separated themselves and formed Harford County.) Poverty grew alongside wealth. In 1773 the assembly created Trustees for the Poor of Baltimore County and authorized them to levy a new tax and to build near the edge of the town an almshouse "for the reception of the poor" and a workhouse for "vagrants, beggars, vagabonds, and other offenders."[7] The attempt to distinguish between the "deserving" and the "undeserving" poor was rooted in English practice and remained a permanent feature of public social services. In creating Trustees for the Poor the legislative assembly for the first time appointed representatives for the town separately from the rest of the county. The costs of the almshouse were to be shared in proportion to the numbers of poor sent from town or county. "An elevated and beautiful site" of twenty acres was purchased from one of the trustees.

Many elements combined to make the Revolution both popular and profitable in Baltimore.[8] The rhythm of political protest kept time with the rhythm of the economy. Maryland was still subject to the whims of the tobacco

Revolution and
Opportunity

market, and the mercantile economy of Baltimore was vulnerable because of its dependence on credit from the mother country. For several years at a time (1759 to 1762 and 1768 to 1773) Maryland imported—on credit—much more than it exported. Each such boom was followed by a panic, when English creditors, responding to financial crisis at home, demanded their money. To pay such massive debts, imports were cut in half, and merchants and mechanics and the people who took in their washing all felt the squeeze. The merchants of Baltimore responded to restrictions on colonial trade with the same outrage as New England merchants. The wealthier planters, whose capital was invested in iron furnaces and wheat lands, resented British attempts to stifle manufacturing in the colony. They were also concerned to preserve their authority as an elite among the rest of the population. The relatively high quality of legal practice in Maryland contributed to the attachment to fundamental principles of English law and gave rise to a philosophy for the rebellion. The concentration of the web of communication and political organization in the general court system at Annapolis made possible a rather swift and decisive revolutionary effort, in spite of the economy of rural isolation. There were differences of class interest and of tactics between the networks of Baltimore and Annapolis. Ultimately the Revolution thrust the Baltimore economy well ahead of that of Annapolis.

In the early stages of the war, the Baltimore Mechanical Company seems to have played a great part. It operated the chain of correspondence with the Sons of Liberty in other cities, from 1776.[9] The members constituted a Whig Club that met secretly. Governor Eden considered it the most rebellious and mischievous organization in the province. David Poe, the chairman, was subsequently quartermaster at Baltimore. Many Mechanical Company men, who were also members of the First Baptist congregation, followed Captain James Cox and distinguished themselves in the war. Quaker members, who would not bear arms, patrolled the town at night, maintained and worked the fire engine, and provided assistance to the poor. The Maryland Council of Safety, centered in Annapolis, was not always pleased by the zeal of the more radical and insubordinate Baltimore committee—as when Samuel Smith, son of a leading Baltimore merchant, led a party to prevent Governor Eden's sailing out of Annapolis.[10] Samuel Smith also superintended recruiting in Baltimore for several years, commanded the town battalion of the Maryland militia, trained eight hundred men, and handled the investigation and arrest of Tories. His activities demonstrate how money was risked and made by the patriots. He participated in the ownership of perhaps a dozen privateers, of which five were lost. In addition to capturing enemy ships as prizes, his own ships carried cargoes of wheat or flour to be sold at wartime prices. He was engaged in the other most important wartime operation of Maryland—the state had undertaken to supply Spanish forces in the West Indies with wheat and flour. It financed shipments at 50 percent of the profits. Smith contracted as the state's exclusive agent for purchasing flour and wheat, on 5 percent commission. He also rented vessels and had a contract for fitting and repairing gunboats.

As naval warfare was almost entirely a private enterprise operation, and Baltimore sent out 250 privately armed vessels, Samuel Smith's case was merely one among many. The privateers were owned by Baltimore merchants individually, in partnerships, or in shares, and the owners' names that appear in the letters of marque and reprisal—Sterrett, Yellott, Buchanan, Bowley, Jaffrey, Messonaire, Salmon, Zollickoffer, Ennels, Crookshanks, Pringle—also appeared in postwar newspaper ads for exports, imports, and shipping.[11]

The Revolution also stimulated manufacturing. Obviously, flour milling expanded. The Ellicotts alone were delivering 100 barrels a week to Baltimore in 1774 from their mills on the Gwynns Falls. Removal of colonial restrictions was enough to unleash new types of enterprise, such as dyeing, wool carding, and linen manufacture, a bleach yard, a slitting mill, and two nail factories. Two papermills were built on the Great Gunpowder Falls; the more substantial one had two hundred workers and produced paper money for the Continental Congress.[12]

The Revolution allowed the Baltimore region to make the most of its natural advantages over Annapolis. The new mills were built along the falls in the stretches where they crossed the "fall line," or geologic zone of contact between piedmont rocks and the coastal plain sands and gravels.[13] The state council explained to Robert Morris in 1782 its pessimism with respect to a tax levy to be paid in cash:

Our People are possessed of but very little Specie, and even that Little is chiefly confined to Baltimore Town, and the few upper Counties which are so situated as to have Intercourse with Baltimore or Philadelphia. The lower and most considerable Part of the State, has neither Specie nor the Means of getting it, for there is no Demand for any Thing the People make.[14]

Baltimore's social climate was as important in the development of manufactures as its physical setting. The limitations of the tobacco economy, and even of the prewar social environment of Baltimore Town, insofar as it resembled the old settled Maryland, lay in the attitude toward labor. When John Adams attended the Continental Congress in Baltimore in 1776, while Philadelphia was threatened, he found it "a very pretty town," "the dirtiest place in the world," and "full of good Whigs," but added, "They hold their Negroes and convicts, that is, all laboring people and tradesmen, in such contempt, that they think themselves a distinct order of beings."[15] A steady influx, during and after the war, of German and Scotch-Irish settlers from Pennsylvania, and others directly from Ireland, Scotland, and France, was a counterforce essential to the development of the crafts and manufactures. Baltimore and the mill villages north and west offered niches for new populations. Skills were transferred from one mill to another, and Philadelphia capital and business experience were brought in.

During the Revolution, the generation that had founded the town of Baltimore died out, according to Griffith, and the generation of young men who rose to leadership in the army, privateering, and manufacturing constituted a new set of leaders who retained ever after a certain glamor, national idealism, and keen appreciation of risk. Among those who led the Maryland troops were young men from established planter families, notably John Eager Howard. Others, like Charles Carroll of Carrollton, risked their fortunes in the patriot cause. As John Latrobe explained to Tocqueville years afterward, their daring reinforced their popularity with the people, including the members of the Mechanical Company in Baltimore, and made it possible for them to retain their leadership and a high degree of elite decision making for a generation after the war. They were involved in structuring the political institutions of the state as well as the new nation.

Maryland retained certain institutions virtually intact—the general assembly, the general court at Annapolis, the county courts, the use of ad hoc boards of commissioners for public enterprises, and the restrictions that reserved political participation and office holding to men of wealth. Two important changes were made in legal privilege—inheritance law and church "disestablishment." Their impact was felt, not immediately, but over a generation.

Before the Revolution, the large planters had used the estate tail to keep land in the hands of a few. By a clause in his will, a landowner could define the succession indefinitely, limiting it to a son, grandson, etc., and restricting forever their right to will, sell, or subdivide it among their children. The new laws of inheritance virtually abolished the tail, thus reversing the trend toward concentration of fortunes.[16]

Mission and Compromise

The zeal of the Church of England had never been great in Maryland. Effective "establishment" with a clerical presence had only lasted seventy-five or eighty years. In 1739 George Whitefield considered Maryland among "the dark corners of the earth . . . a place as yet unwatered with the true Gospel of Christ."[17] With the Revolution, the Episcopal Church lost even more of its clergy as well as the provincial tobacco tax for their support, although it retained its property.

Disestablishment was, however, a factor that released a surge of zeal among Catholics and Methodists. Religious impulses from France and England were transmitted to settlers on the American frontier through administrative networks centered in Baltimore. Catholics were assured full freedom of worship and could form corporations and schools; their "take-off" occurred in the 1790s (chapter 3), while a Methodist take-off began promptly after American independence was recognized. Early in 1784, John Wesley published his Deed of Declaration, reorganizing the 359 English Methodist chapels into a self-perpetuating annual conference independent of the Church of England. In the fall he decided to ordain and send ministers and a superintendent "to serve the desolate sheep in America." These shepherds (Thomas Coke, Richard Whatcoat, and Thomas Vazey), together with Francis Asbury, who was already in Maryland, succeeded in calling together sixty Methodist preachers for a Christmas conference in Baltimore. They adopted Wesley's articles, formed an annual conference, and ordained Asbury as superintendent. The superintendent had the power to lay out circuits and to deploy ministers and lay teachers on missions deep into Maryland and the Appalachian frontier. This organization, directed from Baltimore, kindled individual piety, and the Methodist "classes" were the buds of new congregations.

The Christmas Conference affirmed its opposition to slavery and resolved to press all preachers and members of the Methodist communion to contract within one year to free their slaves.

We view it as contrary to the golden law of God on which hang all the laws and the prophets, and the unalienable rights of mankind, as well as every principle of the revolution to hold in the deepest abasement, in a more abject slavery than is perhaps to be found in any part of the world except America, so many souls that are all capable of the image of God.[18]

This position was strongly influenced by Asbury and, through his epistles, by John Wesley. Wesley, in turn, had been influenced by the writing of Anthony Benezet and John Woolman, Quakers from Pennsylvania. Methodists and Quakers, Brethren and Mennonites, were in close touch and in sympathy on a number of matters of religious feeling. Asbury traveled in the '70s and '80s through the same Maryland territory that John Woolman had visited, and he was impressed with the extent to which Quakers had freed their slaves.

Asbury immediately made a new circuit of the chapels to explain the resolution to rid the Methodist Church of slavery. But within six months he was obliged to "suspend the execution of the minute" of the Christmas Conference. This was the beginning for the Methodists of a slow backtracking and compromising on the issue of slavery. The ambivalence was associated with a high growth rate of the Methodist Church, an inability to assimilate such large numbers of slave holders, and a desire to evangelize the slaves. These goals could not be reconciled with a consistent mission to eradicate slavery. In these respects, the Quakers differed sharply with the Methodists in Maryland in the 1780s and 1790s.

Nation Building and City Building

When the Revolution was won, Baltimore became a community of immense self-confidence and creativity, in spite of the expected postwar depression of trade. Opportunity was eagerly sought—in trade, manufacturing, and transport, and in proselytizing and self-improvement. American trade was now free of the former restrictions of marketing through Britain. The French had participated in the American struggle. Both these factors favored the settlement in Baltimore of foreign merchants and gentlemen with capital. Zacharie and Pascault were among the French merchants; Mayer and Brantz were German Swiss from Zurich. The export of grain to the West Indies continued, and sugar refineries were built in Baltimore to process the return cargo. Robert Oliver was undertaking new ventures each year, among them the importing of linens from Ireland and the exporting of tobacco to the Orient. Samuel Smith bought a safe-conduct from the piratical Barbary Powers in order to trade safely in the Mediterranean. He was a subcontractor in a deal to supply the French national monopoly with Maryland tobacco. French and Dutch consuls were assigned here, as both nations were substantial buyers of Maryland tobacco, and Baltimore became the state's central tobacco market.

The first comers and the best situated of the several nationalities created a pattern of assistance to newcomers. As early as 1783 the German Society of Maryland was founded "for the protection of the redemptioners and destitute immigrants who were sold into voluntary slavery."[19] Shipmasters advertised for craftsmen, such as rope makers, shoemakers, blacksmiths, bricklayers, carpenters, butchers, hostlers, tailors, and papermakers, in addition to a larger number of house servants and farm laborers. By the 1780s the Germans were numerous enough and diverse enough to begin splitting and hiving off churches, a process characteristic of each immigrant group. They built a Calvinist church at the east end of Baltimore Street, and the Otterbein church on Conway Street. Nevertheless, participation in the German Society, on both the giving and receiving ends, cut across religious lines. By including Catholics, Jews, and Protestants (both Lutheran and Reformed), they set a pattern for Irish, French, and other organizations that followed.

In every form of enterprise, the need was felt for more efficient and reliable transport and communications. These areas had occasioned complaint and debate for a century, but they were brought into constructive focus by the nation-building spirit. Here, above all, the distinction between private and public enterprise was blurred. It was assumed that if the benefits outweighed the costs, a project was justified and a reasonable profit could be made. Men of wealth and property along the route initiated the petitions, ceded the land, and subscribed the capital. In 1784, Charles Carroll of Carrollton was among Baltimore property owners who raised £40,000 to improve navigation on the Susquehanna River by blasting rocks from the channel. Development of the Susquehanna region would offer great commercial opportunities to Baltimore. In 1785 the Potomac Navigation Company was chartered, and a sailing packet line was opened to Norfolk.

The conception of a road network for nation building and regional development was connected with a city-building goal. In 1784 petitions urged delegates to the legislature to build bridges, the lack of which had caused many accidents. The grand jury reported the state of the roads as a "public grievance," and a plan was proposed to designate certain roads as "state roads." They were essentially radial roads from Baltimore. "Roads and highways are to the community, what veins and arteries are in the natural body, the channels and sources of general circulation. As these all lead to and from the heart, so ought those all lead to and from the great seat of commerce in a state.—As Baltimore is."[20] The three major roads—to Frederick, Reisterstown, and York—were, in fact, "laid out anew." The county erected toll gates, and these routes became the important entrances to Baltimore City, determining its principal commercial arteries. Howard Street skirted Colonel Howard's estate, and became a favored location for flour and country produce stands. Reisterstown Road led into Pennsylvania Avenue. Frederick Road led into West Baltimore Street. Roads from York, Harford County, Bel Air, and Joppa led into Ensor Street, and thence into Gay Street. The old Philadelphia Road led into Baltimore Street. At Gay Street and at Baltimore Street were the two important bridges over the Jones Falls.

Built for Trade and Convenience

With such growth, Baltimore's appearance was changing. The most visible change was the cutting of the woods during the Revolution: "Most of the timber fell a prey to the wants of necessitous inhabitants during the cold winters of 1779 and 1783."[21] For a generation afterward, travelers remarked

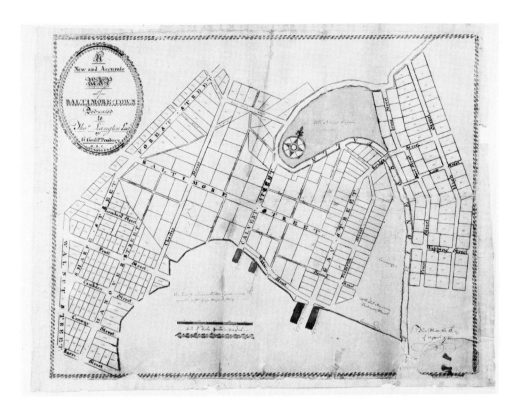

On G. G. Presbury's "New and Accurate Map of Baltimore Town" (1780), the harbor extends north to the present location of Lombard Street, and the Jones Falls flows as far west as Calvert Street.

on the barrenness of the surrounding countryside. Land was added to the town by an act of the assembly, upon request of landowners who wanted to subdivide into town lots. A number of additions were made during the Revolution: on the east, Roger's Addition, Parker's Haven, and Kemp's Addition; and on the west and south, Howard's Addition, Howard's Timber Neck, and Gist's Inspection. Construction reached a peak between 1783 and 1785. In 1783 some three hundred houses were said to have been built. A youthful visitor, Robert Hunter, commented in his diary for November 1785, "They are building away here in every corner of the town."[22]

The several parts of the town were not yet fully integrated. Communication between Baltimore Town and Jones Town was relatively easy, but the distance between town and point was considerable. The road to the point crossed marshes at the mouth of the Jones Falls and Harford Run. For want of agreement on a single market site, the town created in 1784 three market houses, each convenient to the waterfront but on rising ground to permit drainage. Each became the kingpin of a local economic system, speculative building, and a residential neighborhood.

The first market house was the Centre or Marsh Market in Harrison Street, which was "intended for a canal or dock." By 1800 the market space itself had become the location for taverns, boardinghouses, and services to farmers. Night life and casual labor were concentrated in the vicinity. The creation of Centre Market was part of a rapid construction of a whole district from Water Street south to the water, and from the market space west to South Street. The owners of this property were the inner circle of merchants who had built the wharves and acquired capital during the Revolution. William Buchanan, for example, sold off lots along both sides of Water Street, between Frederick Street (Buchanan's wharf) and the new market space. West of Frederick Street, on higher ground, the same merchants associated their personal residences with their locales for wholesaling, shipping, and financial dealing. This was the nucleus for the modern banking district.

The second site was the Hanover or Camden Market on Howard's Hill.

(The Howards owned several hills.) It developed into a produce market, primarily wholesale, which was leveled in the 1970s. Two-story houses, both brick and frame, were advertised opposite the new market house and in Camden, Pratt, Sharp, and Walnut streets. Forty-seven lots (nineteen acres) were sold in Ridgely's Addition, and leaseholds were offered in Rusk's Meadows, between Ridgely's Addition and Howard's Hill. Speculation in this district was promoted by a scheme, never carried out, for digging a canal from the basin across the neck to the Spring Garden or cove at the foot of Fremont Avenue.

The third site was the Fells Point or Broadway Market. Fell had set aside the site for a market, but the street was not yet built up. Bond Street was the respectable, well built-up street toward the point, while wholesale commerce was found along the waterfront. Construction of the new market house defined Broadway as a commercial street, which would combine services to farmers and boatmen and ease the contacts between dealers with landward and seaward orientations. Like the other markets and the country routes into town, the Broadway Market was soon ringed with shops to serve countrymen and their horses: taverns, lodging houses, stables, blacksmiths, and harness makers.

In an effort to make the town look less like a village, a paving act was approved by the legislature, with a tax on vehicles and limits on the extent to which steps and cellarways could encroach on the public streets and walkways. There was no real progress toward paving, but there was considerable regrading and widening of the streets. As Griffith noted for 1783, "the defects of the original plan of the town now became more burthensome." This was the experience in each successive wave of growth as the caterpillar several times shed its skin. The straightening and widening of Hanover Lane, Holliday Street, East Lane (now Fayette Street), and Light Lane were critical.

Most intriguing was the series of projects undertaken to unplug Calvert Street at the bluff overlooking the Jones Falls, to open a northward route along the west side of the stream. In 1783 Leonard Harbaugh succeeded in underpinning the courthouse, so that the street could be run right through the building. This was a favorite novelty for tourists, and regrading cut down twenty feet from the courthouse square, leaving "a row of houses like scraggly soldiers stepping down Calvert street."[23] In 1789 Englehard Yeiser cut a new channel for the Jones Falls, from the lower mill at Bath Street across the meadow to Gay Street bridge, and the old course of the falls by the courthouse was gradually filled up, allowing the northward expansion of the town and unleashing a long dispute over the ownership of the ground. At the same time, Colonel John Eager Howard built his mansion, Belvedere, at an angle in the line of Calvert Street, between present-day Eager and Chase. This would constitute the next obstacle to the extension of Calvert Street, and might be regarded as the limit of the urban expectations of the revolutionary generation.

New public improvements demanded new financial tools. The method used for turnpike and navigation improvements was applied to town street improvements. The costs, including damages for private land taken or injured, were determined by a board of commissioners and distributed among the landowners who would benefit from the improvements. Since the property owners fronting

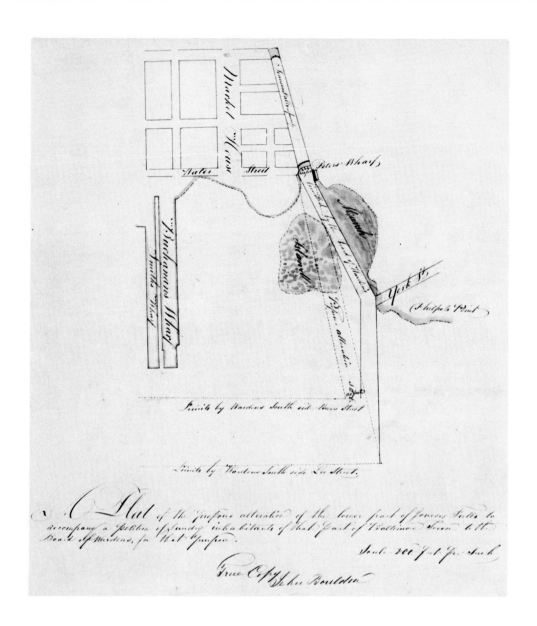

This plat of the lower Jones Falls (ca. 1784) describes the proposed alteration that accompanied a petition to the port wardens.

on a street would bear the principal benefits and costs of opening, grading, paving, widening, or repairing a street, it was assumed that it could be left to their initiative to petition for such improvements. However, the swift pace of growth and the reliance on private initiative produced a sense of confusion and chaos, which led, in turn, to a limited concept of planning. In 1782 the assembly created a board of port wardens—wharf owners and prominent merchants—and charged them with a survey of the harbor and with keeping the basin and channels clear.[24] At the same time, the town commissioners were authorized to hire a surveyor, G. G. Presbury, to produce a correct plot of the town, and the state council issued new rules and orders for the direction of surveyors. The logic behind the two surveys is useful for understanding the growth experience of the revolutionary generation and the modest limits that they now imposed on the form of growth for the succeeding generation.

The nature of Baltimore's economy and topographical site posed the basic problem of the interfingering of water and land. The critical economic function was the moving of country produce into markets and warehouses and out on ships. The vital spaces were the contacts between land carriage and vessels, and the growth of the economy required an increase of vital waterfront space. The site was swampy and the inner harbor shallow. The cutting of the timber and more intense traffic on unpaved streets aggravated erosion. Intense summer rainstorms and freshets swept silt into the harbor, and the lack of tide insured that much of the deposit would remain. A letter from "a Humble Citizen" suggested dragging the lower falls, walling it in to prevent "washings and moulderings," altering its course to carry it clear of the range of hills, or creating a current in the basin by means of a canal to Spring Garden (Middle Branch).[25] The latter scheme was preferred, supported by the brickmakers and property owners of South Baltimore. Agitation continued as shipping increased and merchants complained of sandbars and mudflats. But the humble citizen must have been dismayed at the inaction. He had warned that "a season should not be wasted in contending which solution should be preferred." The contention continued for 125 years.

The problems of developing both dock (water) and wharf (land) space had initially been handled by the inducement to private initiative in making land. The new port wardens created a line beyond which wharves could not be extended. Supported by new wharfage and auction taxes, they began regular dredging to keep the basin nine feet deep. In 1783, that is, about twenty years after the important wharf construction of John Spear and others, John and Andrew Ellicott extended a wharf on Light Street and filled it, using a drag and team of horses, iron scoops, and a windlass. Ellicott's became the flour merchants' wharf. The construction of the market space also expanded the waterfront, and in 1785 most of the private wharves were extended on piles.

The need to recognize ownership of "made ground" was one reason for ordering the town surveyed. As land became more valuable, litigation over property increased. The town commissioners were continually occupied with resurveying property lines to settle disputes. Several technical reasons contributed to this situation. First, there were no generally agreed-upon reference points from which to begin any survey. The witness trees from original surveys had been cut, houses rebuilt, and piers washed out. The port wardens and the surveyors were instructed to set durable markers or boundary stones that could be used thereafter as reference points. Second, many of the original surveys were inaccurate or inconsistent. A source of inaccuracy was the failure to take note of compass declination.[26] Maryland rules made no reference to any standards for instruments, nor to any attempt to keep track of errors or control the outline rigidly. "You are upon all Surveys & Resurveys, to describe your Beginning as well and as full as the Thing will admit of and then only Courses and Distance to the last Course, which is always to be thus expressed 'then with a streight Line to the first Beginning.' "[27] They did try to insure that one man's courses would match another's, ordering resurveys to be run first according to the original language of "ancient metes and bounds," and that surveyors should "make the Line or Lines of one Tract the Line or Lines of another that no small Parcel or Spots of Vacant Land may be left out."[28]

A further task assigned to the maker of the plot of the town was to try to integrate the numerous separate villages and additions that had been laid out independently. The surveyor was to function as a planner "authorized to make the streets correspond as nearly as may be." The survey was a corrective plan rather than a growth plan; it showed limited foresight and there was no real

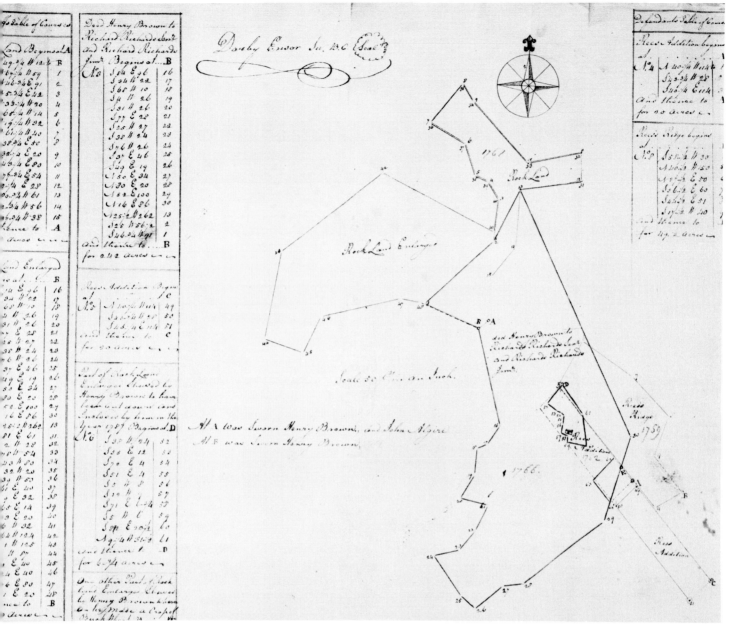

A plat of Rockland in 1808 shows the manor house tract with the additions of the 1760s and a section enclosed in 1787. It is an example of the litigation and difficulties of the survey. On the left is shown the plaintiff's table of courses, or compass indications, and on the right the defendant's table of courses. Witnesses were sworn at points A and B.

mechanism of control. The extent to which it operated was probably a result of the continuing personal influence of G. G. Presbury as city surveyor and later as one of the commissioners. Even after the survey, the various defects of past practice gave rise to dozens of situations that had to be resolved by legal recognition of past errors.[29]

The wave of building after 1747 was based on the ground rent, now rare in the United States but common in Baltimore. It was devised in Presbury's generation, when capital and hard currency were scarce and land was cheap. In order to give value to his town lots or to make his land produce some income, the landowner would contract to "rent" or "lease" the land, effectively forever, at a fixed annual sum, to someone who had the capital or the credit to build a house or warehouse on it, which he in turn rented or sold. "It became the practice to dispose of lots by leases, for long terms, mostly ninety-nine years renewable for ever." The leaseholder paid an annual ground rent to the original owner, his heirs, or buyers of the ground rent. This device was favorable to the upward spiral of rising population, rapid cons'ruction, and capital accumulation,

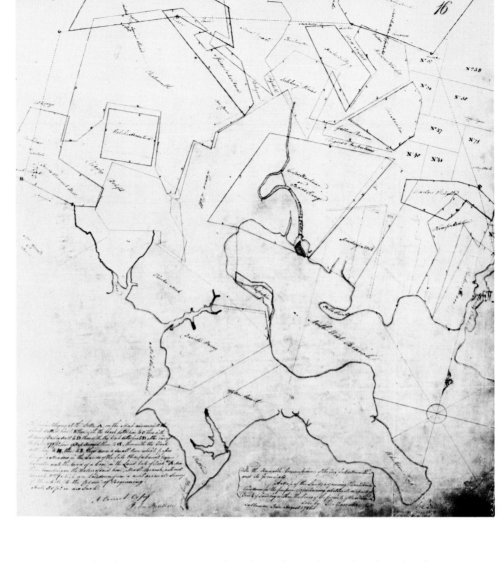

Thomas Maccubbin's map of 1786 shows the various original tracts of land lying within the precincts of Baltimore. Within the diamond shape of Coles Harbor/Todd's Range is the original bend of the Jones Falls, its cutoff, and the shoals or flats in its mouth.

but certain disadvantages were felt when the value of either land or money changed drastically. For example, from the middle of 1786 well into 1788 there was a postwar depression of trade. Flour and tobacco prices fell. British imports offered severe competition for the new domestic products. In Baltimore several substantial businessmen failed, notably the Purviance brothers. Others, among them William Patterson, sued their debtors. "The rents stipulated after the war were so high that, upon the depression which now took place, the lessees or tenants frequently abandoned the lots, and the town lost some valuable citizens who fled from persecution, though their only fault or error was an excess of enterprise."[30]

Despite the hazards, enterprise was the watchword of Baltimore. Many new undertakings of the years 1785–89 failed because of the recession and the persistent scarcity of capital, but many such schemes were revived or developed in the next generation. The principal merchants, including James Calhoun, Alexander McKim, and Richard Caton, formed a joint stock company, the Baltimore Manufacturing Company, to make linens, cottons, and woolens, but without immediate result. Christopher Cruse and his son Englehard built an early steam-powered gristmill near Pratt Street, but failed for want of capital to perfect it (1789). An attempt to form a water company failed.

Having freed themselves from the trade and shipping restrictions of the mother country, Baltimore's merchants were not above using their new government to further their interests. Under the new constitution, seven hundred mechanics, tradesmen, and artisans of Baltimore petitioned Congress for tariffs to protect American manufactures, and the city's shipwrights petitioned for a navigation act that would insure that American goods were carried in American ships.

The town was approaching 13,000 people, and a corporation or charter was several times proposed. A newspaper correspondent complained in 1784, "I know it may be said, that if the citizens at large are to be consulted about a corporation, they will never agree to one, so they ought not to be consulted. This way of reasoning . . . is very alarming."[31] Under the normal practice of private charters in the state, the power would have remained in the hands of a self-perpetuating few, "leaving the citizens but little share in their own government."[32] The nature of a "good corporation" was hotly debated, and basic issues of local government were aired in the newspapers of Baltimore (1784–87), somewhat in the manner of "the Federalist" papers, the articles that contemplated a new constitution for the Union. How would a town charter protect the general good in the face of private property interests? What checks could be devised for mob law? How could a balance be assured among the aldermen, between the rich and the poor? "The rich man should not lay at the mercy of the poor, nor the poor man at the mercy of the rich."[33] For want of a consensus, Baltimore remained unincorporated.

Order and Disorder

1789–1801

Visitors to Baltimore in the 1790s were impressed with the bustle of shipping and construction and recounted its impressive growth. The town doubled its population. Its merchants totted up record exports, pooled large capitals, and pulled down their storehouses to build greater. The houses numbered more than 3,000. Creeping up the hills and over the additions, the town extended a rough-woven fabric, a nubbly, thick-piled rug spreading over the gravels and bedrock. Nearly all dwellings were two stories high, with gabled shingled roofs, and chimneys on the kitchens and back buildings, as well as on the houses. Cobbled streets and dirt lanes formed the pattern, still in three distinct parts, and there were no significant monuments or monumental buildings to dominate the whole.

But without much outward change, the people of Baltimore in this decade began to see themselves as a city. Editors in their columns and merchants in their correspondence began to refer to Baltimore as a city rather than a town, and in 1796 it was incorporated by an act of the legislature. This transformation of the mind and the law in the 1790s was critical to the monumental conception of the years after 1800. The Baltimore of the '90s was still a brutal frontier boom town in an economy of slavery, yet some urban or civilizing process was under way. The sap was running that would make possible a cultural blossoming about 1820.

What makes a city? It can be looked at from two vantage points—from the outside, in its relation to the world, and from the inside, in its internal order and disorder. From either viewpoint one can see a transformation of Baltimore.

A Place on the Map

In the 1790s Baltimore became a knot in the world's web of shipping, finance, and communications. The world system was knitted together and dominated by Britain, France, and Holland, rivals in industrial take-off. Americans, thanks to their new sovereignty and federal constitution, were able to break into international trade, capture the middleman profits of other nations' wars, market American agricultural products despite the long costly hauls, and develop a ship-building industry. For Baltimore, the most important market was the West Indies, still the theater of naval warfare and commercial rivalry among France, Spain, and Britain. Not only was Baltimore well situated, but the momentum was there. Baltimore schooners were designed for hide and seek. The sailing experience and marketing connections of Baltimore ship captains, merchants, and insurance brokers provided a powerful edge in the West Indian market. But new markets were swiftly developed and abandoned, fortunes were touched and lost, in the kaleidoscope of trade.

Robert Oliver was a prime example of the talents required: a willingness to calculate dramatic risks and to roll with the punches. He started small, as a young immigrant with no capital, handling linens on commission from Belfast. During the 1790s he extended himself into new fields on his own account: he shipped tobacco to Lorient and flour to Brest, and imported coffee from Santo Domingo and reexported it to Amsterdam, Rotterdam, Leghorn, and Bremen. In spite of several losses to British capture and then several to French capture, wartime profits were grand, and Oliver's biographer estimates he was worth a quarter of a million dollars by 1797, when he began sending ships (at least fifteen) to Batavia to bring back coffee or sugar. Some stopped at Lisbon for wines. He also speculated in the medium of exchange (for instance, Spanish dollars and bank notes) as well as the goods, and earned freights on the vessels. He shared joint ventures with other Baltimore merchants, especially Robert Gilmor, Jeremiah Yellott (worth half a million dollars), and Henry Thompson. Oliver's operations, like those of Alexander Brown, illustrate the premium placed on the best possible intelligence system and shrewd appraisal of character. They still included family members as agents, but had strategic relationships with merchant bankers in London, Amsterdam, and Bremen. Oliver once sent a vessel out to intercept his earlier cargoes for Batavia and redirect them to a more profitable market.

Men like Oliver made no sharp distinction between politics, law, and economics. Their morality appears to have been one of honor among thieves. For example, Baltimore merchants were incensed to learn in January 1797 of the injustice done to Isaac McKim. McKim had sold his outbound cargo in a French port (against French law), bought coffee in Jérémie (British), was then captured by a French privateer, carried into a French port, and there condemned "without a hearing." Soon after, under an American embargo forbidding trade with French ports, including the West Indian colonial ports, Oliver wrote a shipowner: "we were obliged to give Bond at our Custom House to the amount of your vessel and cargo that she would not during her intended voyage go to any French Port. But we presume She is at liberty after landing her cargo at any neutral Island to take it on board again & go where she pleases."[1]

The expansion of trade and the high-risk multinational operations placed enormous strains on the financial system. New institutions of banking and insurance were created in Baltimore. In 1789 the Bank of Maryland was formed, in 1792 a branch of the United States Bank was established, and in 1797 the Bank of Baltimore was organized on a much larger scale by merchants who felt that the Bank of Maryland catered only to one circle.

The psychological impact of the new profits and far-flung connections was immense. At least half the population of the town was tied directly into the commercial sector—commission merchants, shopkeepers, and peddlers. They were hungry for information. The number of printers, publishers, and book-sellers rose from four or five to at least nineteen, a rate of increase greater than Philadelphia, New York, or Boston. The number of newspapers increased in the decade from two to six. They carried primarily foreign news except when Congress or the legislature was in session. They recounted revolutions in the West Indies and atrocities in Ireland; curious details of the geography and history of distant places like Mocha suddenly connected with Baltimore. Baltimore was vulnerable to bank failures in Hamburg and the financial ups and downs of the Spanish crown, as well as French naval courts and East Indian prices. This vulnerability, or at least the keen awareness of it, is a peculiarly urban phenom-enon. The inner circle of merchants was most sensitive to it, and they made communications their highest priority. They organized an exchange and a circulating library, and patronized European-style coffeehouses. About three hundred merchants subscribed to Captain David Porter's new observatory on Federal Hill, which ran up the owner's flag when a ship was sighted coming up the bay. This relatively small group of people developed their ability to cope, to maneuver, to exercise control. They became accustomed to decision, risk, and a sense of self-determination. They were operating on a stage much larger than the state of Maryland.

A large share of craftsmen were also dependent on the commercial sector—either on the demand for ships and shipfitting or on the consumption of luxury goods and services by the merchant elite. During the "undeclared war" with France (from 1794) the demand for private vessels and government naval vessels generated unprecedented activity on Fells Point. The United States had the *Constellation*, the *Montezuma*, the *Baltimore*, and the *Patapsco* built or fitted out, along with smaller gunboats. The number of craftsmen and apprentices increased. Numerous ropewalks were established.

The cosmopolitanism of Baltimore was enhanced not only by its long lines of trade and communications, but by the transfusion of new blood. The doubling of the population must be attributed chiefly to immigration. A low ratio of females to males—only 85 to 100 among whites in the town in 1800—is charac-teristic of pioneering, mobile, and turbulent populations. The cultural back-grounds and skills of the immigrants provide clues to the cultural growth of the city.

Immigrants continued to come from the British Isles, particularly Ireland, but their numbers are difficult to estimate, as they were quickly assimilated. Many stayed but a short time, or merely passed through. For example, a boat-load of Welsh immigrants was bought and sold by a Welsh tavern keeper on Fells Point, and transported by the flour wagoners for resale and resettlement as agricultural laborers three hundred miles inland.[2] A hundred Irish "redemp-tioners" were advertised for sale from the vessel, at Spear's wharf. They had fourteen days to arrange a bargain for years of labor service, to an employer who would pay the shipowner ten guineas for passage. The short-lived sugar-house imported workmen from London. Advertised runaways and jailbreakers included an Irish hairdresser and an Irish apprentice who played the flute, two seamen who spoke in Scotch dialect, two English convicts, a blacksmith, and a wagoner.

Germans continued to arrive, directly as indentured servants and indirectly from smaller settlements in Pennsylvania. Samuel Sower began publishing English and German books in Baltimore, and opened a type foundry. Dieter Cunz estimates that at least 10 percent of the households in Baltimore were German, on the basis of unmistakably German names in the directory of 1796.[3] They continued to enter skilled crafts and trades, particularly as brewers, bakers, soap and sugar boilers, and workers in metals, leather, and wood. They represented half the membership of the Manufacturing Society founded in 1789. The German Society was active in checking on conditions in arriving immigrant ships. Toward the end of the decade, the revival of trade in tobacco led to renewed ties with Bremen merchants and banking houses.

Unique in the 1790s was a potent French influence. The number of French immigrants was substantial, produced by events in France and the French colony of Santo Domingo. Their cultural impact was more substantial yet. At precisely the moment when John Carroll went to England to be consecrated as the first Catholic bishop of the United States—shepherd of perhaps fourteen Jesuit mission priests and a widely scattered flock—the Sulpician order was expelled from France in the wake of the French Revolution, and its superior, Father Nagot, went to England. The meeting of Father Carroll and Father Nagot represents the seepage of French Catholic tradition into the lives of Catholics in England and Maryland. John Carroll, like many other sons of the original land patent families, had been educated at Saint Omer (Flanders) and the Jesuit college at Liège. Carroll invited Father Nagot to found a seminary in Baltimore. The priests secured the money and began arriving in 1792. Carroll selected a site, the One-Mile Tavern just beyond the edge of town on the Hookstown Road (Pennsylvania Avenue), convenient as a choir and chapter for his episcopal seat, St. Peter's Church. Over the next generation Saint Mary's Seminary became a vital force in the development of education and the consolidation of Baltimore as the center of Catholic publishing and administration in the United States. The Catholic population of Baltimore was about a thousand in 1785 and ten thousand in 1815.[4] This would amount to as much as a third of the population. Many of the German immigrants were Catholics, and Father Carroll's invitation to a German priest to serve them resulted in an internal conflict over Father Reuter's demand for a German school, a German catechism, and a German bishop. Even in its first stages, the plan to build a cathedral worthy of the center of Catholic America was a symbolic step toward the vision of Baltimore as a city. A site was acquired in 1795 bounded by Granby, Exeter, Queen, and Stiles streets, on Philpot's Hill, a fast-growing and respectable neighborhood, convenient to all three sections—the point, the town, and Oldtown.

Meanwhile, hundreds of French settlers were arriving from Santo Domingo (Haiti). Refugees from bloody revolutions in Cape François escaped in a fleet of vessels that limped into Baltimore in July 1793.[5] Over two weeks fifty-three ships brought 1000 whites and 500 people of color and blacks. A Baltimore committee had raised $12,000 for their relief, and four hundred persons were being housed with private families. The outpouring of assistance to "our distressed French brethren" was magnificent. So was the impact. Such numbers would amount to a 10 percent increase in the town's population in one fell swoop. Not all stayed: some proceeded to France, some to Philadelphia. More continued to come in subsequent upheavals (notably 1796 and 1804), and some came from Philadelphia—such as the shipbuilder Despeaux—in order to retain their slaves. There were, in addition, an unknown number of emigrés from France itself. In 1804 there were perhaps 5 percent French households in the city.[6]

The French contributed many of the techniques and arts of a highly developed country, in particular, scientific, medical, and pharmaceutical advances and an enthusiasm for art and the trappings of culture. Most valuable were the doctors, trained in the clinically most advanced medical schools of the western world, and the several shipbuilders. A much larger number, perhaps a majority, were merchants, traders, and shopkeepers. For the most part, the French immigrants considered themselves "gentlemen," an ambiguous term in America. They were at least a rising bourgeoisie. In contrast to the Germans, whose self-respect and aspirations were frequently founded on their skilled crafts, the French self-respect was based on rubbing shoulders with the elite: they introduced a range of new skills, products, and services sought after by the wealthy. Thanks to them, Baltimore was "a place of many luxuries and no comforts."[7] In 1804 there were French hairdressers, perfumers, booksellers, upholsterers, milliners, goldsmiths, wine merchants, confectioners, cordial distillers, incredible numbers of dancing masters, French teachers, teachers of music, and even a chevalier de sculpture, a miniature limner, and a fencing master.[8] The French themselves provided enough of a market to insure the survival of French bakers and pastry cooks, several market gardeners to produce lettuces, and a Café du Commerce. Lewis Pascault, who had arrived about ten years earlier and was a successful merchant active in assisting the newcomers, arranged immediately to include a French section in the city's circulating library. Bookstores increased their stocks of French books, from Catholic works of piety to the revolutionary thinkers. Because of the timing of their arrival, the French introduced their political and religious ferment. This fostered interpretation of American nationalism in ideological terms.

The introduction of the free "people of color" and slaves of the French was significant for the development of new institutions among blacks, and of a more complicated set of attitudes. In sheer numbers, they may have added 30 percent to the colored population of the town. The impact was even greater in terms of the number of free persons and individuals schooled in the crafts, in reading, and in the Catholic religion. Newspaper advertisements indicate that many French slaves, African born, succeeded in running away soon after their arrival in Baltimore. The French Revolution had not only unleashed the turmoil of a society of slavery in Santo Domingo, but through the Code Noir (1794) had raised again the basic issues of the relations of race, slavery, and republicanism. In Baltimore, Father Dubourg at Saint Mary's Seminary organized regular cate-

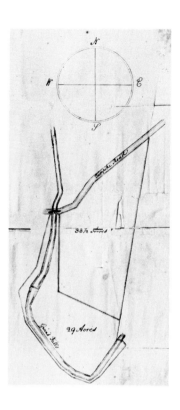

The Old Forge Tract, part of Georgia, belonged to Cornelius Howard. In 1797 it was described as "Part of Four Tracts of Land lying in Baltimore County, called Newton, Georgia, Howard's Discovery, and a Tract condemned for a Forge, laid out for James Carroll. Beginning at a Rock marked IC No. 5 and running thence N38°W 4½ perches to Gwinns Falls, then N82½°W 4½ perches to the end of the S by W line of Georgia then bounding on the S by W line of Georgia . . . 155 perches to the Turnpike Road, then bounding on the Turnpike Road the 4 following viz. S50°W 53 perches . . . to highwater mark of the Old Forge Pool . . . up the stream . . . to highwater mark of the Old Forge Pool on the West side of the Falls . . . down the stream, the three following courses . . . to a large Walnut tree . . . to a Post . . . to the Beginning; Containing 62½ Acres of Land more or less."

chism classes for colored children in 1794. In the same year Joseph Townsend and other Quakers and Methodists organized the Sharp Street school for children of free Negroes, "to elevate them from the degraded state into which they had fallen." In a few years Africans took over the management, and it "exceeded every expectation."[9] From among the people of African and French descent were formed a few years later near the seminary a day school and an order of teaching nuns, the Oblate Sisters of Providence.

Increasingly secure about their place in the sun and playing an ever more exciting role on the world stage, Baltimore's leading citizens had to cope with the internal problems of making a city work. Rapid growth produced problems of a new scale and complexity. Gambling in world trade produced dramatic losses as well as profits, and neither profits nor losses were shared equally. The overall climate of growth and prosperity generated impatience with the poor and the unsuccessful. The sense of mastery and action stimulated criticism of inaction and frustration at the intractable social and environmental problems at home.

The fast-developing city with soaring aspirations was caught in the squeeze of an undeveloped or backward region out on the margin of the world economy. The nation in general, and Maryland in particular, lacked capital, skills, and an adequate institutional framework for collective action. The underdeveloped condition was especially evident in agriculture. Baltimore's trade was based on the export of agricultural products—wheat, flour, and tobacco—and we are long accustomed to the notion that America is a great producer endowed with magnificent soils and climate. Reminiscences of epicurean guests and local gluttons of the late nineteenth century make Baltimore sound like a marvelous food market, and Sunday drives into Baltimore County suggest a rural landscape of horse farms, old stone houses, rolling green pastures, and lush woods. Nothing could be farther from the reality of the 1790s. The population was small, and no care had been lavished on the landscape. Grass and pastures were rare. Most of the forest was cut-over scrub. Slopes like Federal Hill and the bluffs along the streams were bleak and gullied. Isaac Weld described the landscape of the Patapsco valley as barren and depressing. Other travelers remarked upon the bare and untended look of the Maryland countryside along the main road from Havre de Grace into Baltimore and south toward Georgetown.

One must be wary of argicultural descriptions written as propaganda to

Making It Work

lure immigrants, and of some visitors' accounts biased by views of slavery. Most of them looked at the landscape of slavery with horror, although they accepted the slave owner's stereotype of the African as childlike, incompetent, or sub-human. Probably the most honest and complete account of the local agricultural economy was that of a disillusioned Englishman, Richard Parkinson, who leased Orange Hill Farm for a year, on the old Philadelphia Road three miles northeast of town. The fundamental problems, which Parkinson experienced personally and discussed with all the best farmers, were the scarcity of labor and the lack of efficient transport. The transport problem was regarded as a lack of capital, but it came to much the same thing—not enough labor had yet been applied. The transport problem produced the grim limitations of market. All profit in production was eaten away by the cost of getting the goods to a market. "If a man clips wool, there is no market for it. O'Donnel kept sheep only to grow wool for making his negroes' stockings." No farmer dared specialize in a single product, such as turnips, because of the small local market. They raised pigs "as a conveyance" to carry corn to market.

Under these conditions, even the superior and well-capitalized farmers lost money, like Mr. Gough at Perry Hall, Mr. Oliver, and Mr. Gittings. General Ridgely had a farm "of great note" nine miles from Baltimore, with fine race horses. "What enables him is his very extensive iron works." Mr. O'Donnel at Canton, Parkinson's neighbor, had brought between £60,000 and £75,000 from the East Indies into America and "could not live comfortably with it." O'Donnel had manured his land with dung from Baltimore and planted an orchard of red peaches, reckoned superior for making brandy. But after his orchard had grown to bear in great perfection, the profit proved so small, "he suffered the whole go to waste, and his pigs to consume the produce; and, in the winter, rooted up all those fine peach trees, and planted the ground with Indian corn." As O'Donnel had hundreds of acres of unimproved woodland (twenty-five hundred acres all told), the cause, Parkinson observed, could not be for want of land. His investments in Baltimore seem to have been more profitable, as he had wharves and houses "to an immense amount."[10]

Parkinson despaired of the Maryland soils and climate, "there being no spring and autumn, but all winter and summer." He commented on the erosive power of the summer rainstorms and the lightness of the soils, even in the bottomlands. "You cannot plow and harrow fine or deep, or the whole acre moves." He reckoned good only the limestone land, as at The Caves and the Green Spring and Worthington valleys. In fact, certain problems of soil and climate were closely related to the difficulties of transport and labor. For example, it was too hot to make cheese or butter, or to butcher meat. Fish could not be conveyed in summer. Parkinson used to get up at 2 a.m. to take his milk to market, while it was cooler, to French customers who wanted milk good enough to boil without souring. The high costs of transport and labor made it un-economical to bring manure, plaster, marl, oyster shells, or other fertilizers to the farm, and therefore soil improvement was rare, practiced only by the in-town grower of winter lettuces or by the gentlemen who made their money in trade

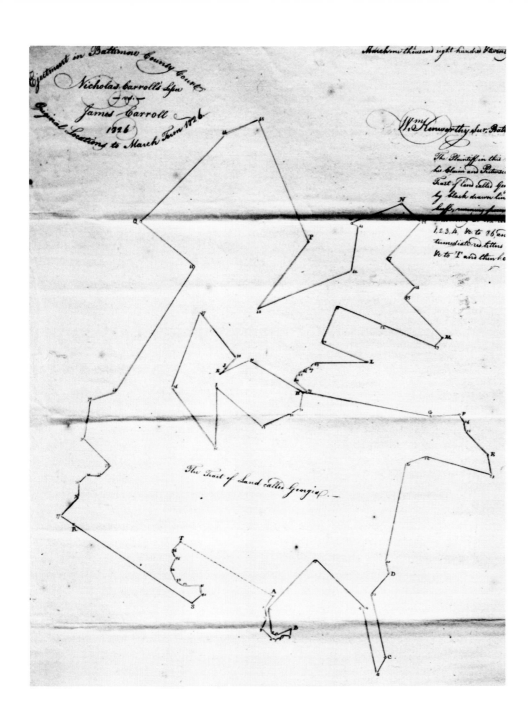

The documents of a lawsuit of March 1826 (*Nicholas Carroll's lessee* v. *James Carroll*) show Georgia and the surrounding areas, which included Gwynns Run, Anthony's Delight, Maiden's Choice, Wells's Chance, Cuckold Maker's Palace, Crowley's Contrivance, Seamore's Adventure, Fox Hall, Brotherly Love, and Rich Neck.

and could afford to lose it in farming. "The cultivation of one's own land, I was sure, would make any man poor."

The underdeveloped economy, paradoxically, has a scarcity of labor but little reward for it. From the viewpoint of employer or farmer, labor is dear, because little is produced per unit of labor. Wages for a mower, for example, were a dollar a day plus meat and a pint of whiskey, but a man could mow only an acre in a day, and the farmer was never sure his contracted laborer would show up at the critical moment. But from the viewpoint of the laborer the return was small. In spite of the apparently high wage, he was poor, as his labor was wanted only for a short season. Small farmers and farm laborers lived on cornmeal johnny-cake, and fed their horses on corn, which made them unfit for work. "They work barefoot, and the children run naked." There were few country churches or country schools. The more versatile, like Parkinson, managed to supplement their income occasionally as brewers, millers, or soap boilers.

Parkinson had refused an offer from George Washington for a farm at Mount Vernon, because he did not want to become involved in "the management of negroes," even though he considered the blacks expert at farm work, and much the best market men as well. It was not, therefore, a lack of capabilities that made slavery economically unworkable, but the system of incentives and the market limitations on all agriculture.

In every calculation made of the cultivation and produce it appears plainly that, if there be anything got, it is pinched out of the negro. . . . The idea of the negroes is, that as they work and raise all, they have a right to consume all. . . . "Massa does not work—overseer does not work."[11]

Of Ridgely and Carroll, the richest men in Maryland, he says, apparently quoting Washington, "What did their riches consist in? land and negroes? he compared them to dust and ashes."[12]

Parkinson's basic experience in farming—the high cost of transportation and of skilled and motivated labor, and the devastating effects of these scarcities on the marketability of farm products—applied also to manufacturing. Craftsmen took young boys and indentured servants as apprentices and helpers. Millers and weavers took young immigrants to board in their households. There was scarcely any take-home pay, and the working and living conditions depended on the temperament of the master. Slave labor was utilized in the iron works and brickmaking at outlying sites, but was even less appropriate to craft enterprise in town than to mixed farming. It became common in Baltimore at this time to hire out one's slaves on terms or to allow them to hire themselves out. They might also board out. The ambiguous status—free, slave for a term of years or for life, and slave but free to hire out—may account for the confusion of numbers in the local census. In 1800 blacks were a fifth of the town's population, and as many as half reported themselves as free persons. The ambiguities had bitter consequences, and state law presumed that all blacks were slaves unless they could prove otherwise.[13] Slaves were sometimes able to buy their freedom or negotiate a term of years, but sustaining such a right was difficult because they could not testify against a master or other white person. Such a case is mentioned in the biography of one of Maryland's star lawyers. In 1793 Nathan Harris had sold Cato to Jesse Harris for £65. At the end of seven years at the latest, Cato was to be freed, but Nathan "repossessed" him and sold him to a third person. Hearing this, Jesse recorded manumission papers, and Cato petitioned the courts. He was finally freed, it appears, in 1808.[14]

In the face of such injustices, Elisha Tyson, a Friend, retired from managing his merchant flour mills and devoted himself to the civil rights of blacks. He formed a society "to protect the colored population of this state in the enjoyment of their legal privileges."[15] Backers included some slave owners. The Protection Society obtained legal counsel, for example, for two Indian boys, aged ten and thirteen, who had been enslaved and brought to Baltimore about 1798.[16] Tyson was also the driving force behind the Society for Promoting the Abolition of Slavery, composed of "all the most respectable class in Baltimore." In 1789 the young William Pinkney led their first legislative battle to repeal the laws forbidding owners from freeing their slaves. "Are we not equally guilty? They strewed around the seeds of slavery; we cherish and sustain the growth."[17] Slave owners argued that freeing slaves would impoverish their heirs and render slaves turbulent, disobedient, and unruly. In 1796 the society's seventh legislative battle was successful in restoring the legal right to free one's slaves.

The great environmental hazards in this period were fire and yellow fever. Like the sufferings of the poor, these hazards were seasonal. As the seasons revolved, the threats waxed and waned. They influenced the physical growth of the town.

Fires were most feared in winter, but many other anxieties were translated into the fear of fire as a result of carelessness or reprisal. A stable burned due to the neglect of two boys with a candle, catching rats. A fourteen-year-old slave girl who set fire to her master's house said she was persuaded by a wench who belonged to his brother.[18] A fire in Light Street in December 1796 spread from a doctor's surgery, consumed the Methodist church and its new college, the tavern opposite, and a row of warehouses insured by the Baltimore Equitable Society. The society had to levy an extra assessment on its membership to pay for rebuilding; it then took the lead in introducing legislation and fire insurance rates calculated to favor slate roofs and parapet walls.[19] A person was designated to salvage and take custody of property at fires. A new fire company was formed, a new engine was acquired at Fells Point, and all the companies were ordered to meet and set rules and regulations.

Yellow fever was a late summer and autumn threat, severe in 1794 (344 deaths), 1797 (545 deaths), 1799, and 1800. Yellow fever determined that Baltimore Town, not Fells Point, would become the growth area and residential location of the wealthy and influential. In 1794 Moreau de Saint Méry, a French observer from Santo Domingo on his way to Philadelphia, admired the site and activity in Fells Point and took an optimistic view of its future: "The Point, its buildings much more modern than those of Baltimore, is increasing prodigiously." He remarked on the yellow fever, already bad on the point in 1793: "An interest stronger than love of life, however, anchors there all who believe the promises of fortune rather than the threats of inexorable death."[20] By 1800 his positive expectation was no longer expressed. The yellow fever had been dreadful several years in succession. "The disease, rising from the rank of a bilious, to that of a yellow fever, mounted its chariot of death, and spread dismay and mourning wherever it appeared."[21]

Baltimore's doctors debated the causes. They never accepted the principle of contagion, which implied quarantine and the total cessation of trade. The spread of the fever was attributed to local putrefaction and the gasses given off and carried by the wind. Dr. Davidge said, "The seeds of the remittent bilious and yellow fever are produced in putrid vegetable and stagnant water, and are quickened by heat and dryness."[22] The facts and the theories were brought out when a newspaper printed a letter from young Dr. Nathaniel Potter to a colleague in Philadelphia. He described the terror in Fells Point, and the local disadvantages that might explain it. He claimed that half the inhabitants were

Perennial Crises

"dead or fled," that people were buried "clandestinely" at night, and that some were infected merely by riding through the narrow, unventilated, unpaved streets.[23] Potter blamed the small wooden houses, "irregularly situated." "There are between the town and the point low fenny grounds, covered with putrifying vegetable substance, as well as certain unfinished wharves . . . where pestilential gasses were continually evolved." The city fathers were incensed at Potter's attack on the board of health: "Their conduct has never been marked by such peculiar vigilance or care, for an indefinite and temporizing policy has ever been their most prominent characteristic."[24] The point was temporarily evacuated. The dangers appear to have guided the merchant class in its gradual abandonment of Fells Point to the working class and its selection of new residential districts on higher ground.

John Hollins and James Buchanan built the first fine residences in Calvert Street north of Baltimore Street, in 1799. New demand favored the healthier hilltops, in particular, the neighborhood of the courthouse and the hills where Lexington Market and the cathedral were later located. Other merchants lived in the Gay Street area just south of Baltimore Street. The epidemics also confirmed the upper class in the tradition of maintaining summer residences or country seats, in the style of the older planters and landed wealth. About this time, Samuel Smith bought Montebello, Robert Oliver bought Green Mount, John Donnell bought Willow Brook, and Robert Gilmor, Sr., Beech Hill. Properties within a range of two or three miles of the city were being subdivided into estates of six to ten acres and advertised as country seats.[25]

Successive catastrophes provided a series of heroic tests for citizens of Baltimore. They intensified the sense of inadequacy of the town's internal initiatives and controls, and probably explain the decision to incorporate, as suggested in the preamble to the charter of 1796:

Whereas it is found by experience, that the good order, health and safety of large Towns and Cities, cannot be preserved, nor the evils and accidents to which they are subject, avoided or remedied, without an internal power competent to establish a police and regulations, fitted to their particular circumstances, wants, and exigencies. . . .[26]

The Mechanical Society had opposed incorporation in 1789 and again in 1793 "before such bill shall be published and approved by a majority of the citizens." They were afraid Fells Point would be taxed for deepening the basin. They also feared that the legislature would not provide adequate representation or powers for the town. Indeed, it did not. The city, approaching 25,000 people, was given no representation in the assembly, apart from the two already authorized delegates of Baltimore County, of which it was a part. Within the city, authority was divided among the elected mayor and council, the appointed port wardens, and the appointed town commissioners. The unusual fragmentation of Baltimore's local government was already assured. Trustees appointed by the governor managed the poorhouse, but any hard winter was marked by the appearance of "cases of humanity" in the newspapers and ad hoc collections of firewood and food. All farm work was suspended, the laborers and "vagrants" arrived in Baltimore, and the economy provided little employment in manu-

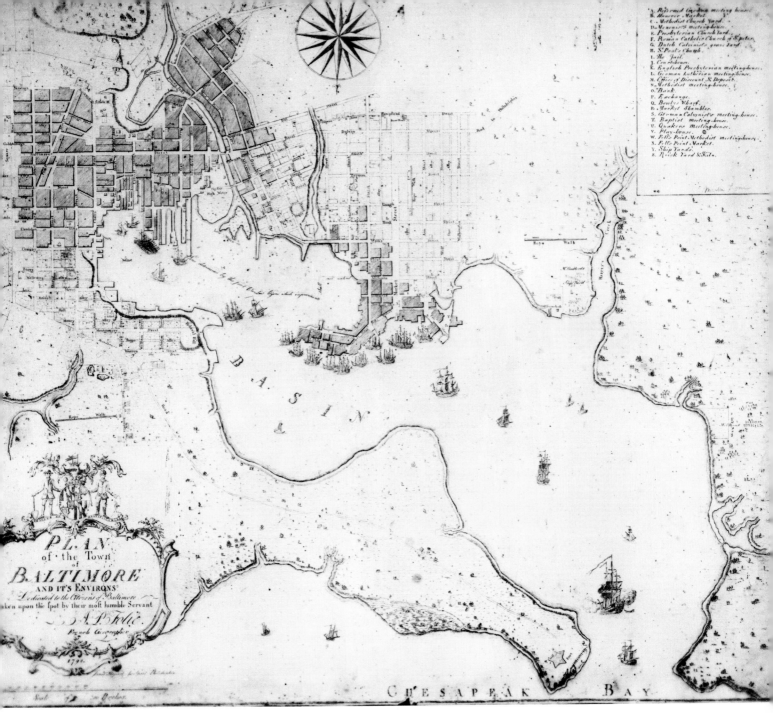

A. P. Folie published his "Plan of the Town of Baltimore . . ." in 1792. In little more than a decade, the course of the Jones Falls had been shortened, and significant filling and wharf construction constricted the harbor.

facturing. Class attitudes hardened responses. In 1797, for example, Baltimoreans gave $1,200 for their poor, where they had easily raised ten times as much for the bourgeois French refugees and again for the genteel victims of a fire in Norfolk.[27]

The early actions of the city government were concerned with sanitation and fire laws—the environmental hazards that required collective action. The private fire companies were subsidized by the city, and frame construction was outlawed. Sanitary policy was more variable. The degree of threat of yellow fever determined the amount of energy directed to collecting garbage, controlling pigs (the scavenger service) and dogs, and supervising the dumping of spoiled cargo or the emptying of privies. The city continued to rely on private individual self-interest to initiate major public improvements. Virtually every act, such as a street condemnation or purchase of property, had to have a special enabling act from the state legislature or it could be questioned on grounds of insufficient municipal powers or doubtful jurisdiction.

The major public improvements of the '90s were a continuation of the effort to increase the valuable fringe zone of land and water. There was agreement on the general scheme of building up the perimeter of the basin and making the market space its centerpiece. The channel could accommodate 500-ton ocean vessels, but coastal shipping took on new importance in unifying the nation, and the local trade of the Chesapeake Bay multiplied. A resident of North Point reported passing to Baltimore in 1796 over 5,000 bay craft, nearly ten times the number of ocean-going vessels. To make Centre Market accessible from the west, Fayette Street was opened into Calvert Street, Sharping Street was widened from Gay to South, and Second Street was extended from South Street to the market space. These east-west openings were intended to ease the congestion of Baltimore Street and were related to the development—at long last—of Harrison's Marsh. Dugan and McElderry built 1600-foot matching wharves extending south from the market space. The conception was that of the British docks of Bristol and Liverpool: ranges of three-story brick warehouses fronting on the enclosed water.

Meanwhile, development extended, pier by pier and block by block, darning in the west fringe of the basin. Charles Street was extended across two or three docks by filling between Camden and Barre streets. The legislature authorized filling and wharfing Light Street. A lawsuit records that the tide had originally flowed within one hundred feet of Charles and Pratt streets, but by 1802 most of the filling up was accomplished and a second generation of buildings was already under construction near Pratt and Charles.[28] Pratt was still not a through street, but it had been extended piecemeal and the intent was clear. The old docks (Cheapside and Hollingsworth's), so important in the midcentury development of the port, were decidedly obsolete. They were occupied by flour dealers, tanners and curriers, and paint dealers. Their owners, the Hollingsworths and the Ellicotts, seem to have moved from a progressive to an obstructionist posture. The city had outgrown them.

"Because these piers jut out in the water there are . . . marshes dented with wide inlets, while neighboring wharves are just so many breakwaters. All this gives an air of disorder."[29] That was the perspective of a French emigré passing through Baltimore. He argued for a "strict adherence to alinement." The wharves were symbolic. Order and disorder were a source of deep anxiety in Baltimore, evident in the polarization of class and party. Mechanics demanded a share of the profits reaped in the good years. The carpenters organized, and various strikes occurred in the building trades. A master builder who ordinarily had twenty to fifty men at work with several good teams of horses was "so perplexed by his men . . . as to be compelled to carry bricks and mortar up to the scaffold himself."[30] The mechanics organized a Republican society to lobby for an American navigation act and protective tariffs. Baltimore was moving toward a Republican (Jeffersonian) majority, although Baltimore citizens Samuel Chase and James McHenry were given important posts in the Federalist cabinet and judiciary in 1796. The tumultuous elections of 1798 made a Republican out

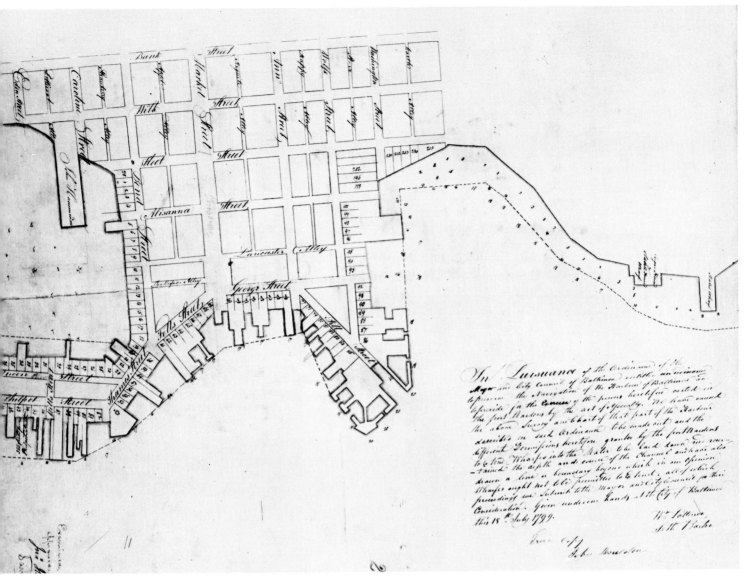

In 1797 the port wardens defined a line beyond which wharves might not extend. This plat shows the valuable character of the point, the interfingering of land and water, and the undeveloped state of the cove on the west and the Canton district on the east.

of merchant-congressman Samuel Smith and established a "permanent" Republican majority in Baltimore. These elections were "riotous," and Baltimore's conflict with the Federalist state government hardened into a more or less permanent battle line. Many issues were debated in this partisan context of Baltimore City—unrepresented—in the state of Maryland. Solomon Etting, an active Republican, made his first plea for the civil rights of Jews. The "Jew bill," defeated year after year for thirty years, became an issue symbolic of the oppression of Baltimore, as well as the oppression of Jews and blacks. Baltimore identified with the medieval merchant cities, fighting passionately for certain freedoms—the Jew's right to hold office and serve on juries, the black man's right to remain free unless proved a slave, and the slave owner's right to emancipate his slave.

Baltimore's participation in the affairs of Europe, its desire to project its own image on a backdrop of grand scale, and its ambivalence toward the French Revolution are illustrated by events of the summer of 1797. Hundreds of Baltimoreans trooped out to the pleasure gardens or taverns to celebrate the Fourth of July. At the observatory on Federal Hill, Porter offered fireworks, a 10 p.m. royal salute, a cold collation, and the best of liquors. The proprietors of Gray's gardens at Chatsworth prepared a band of music and illuminated life-size transparent pictures commemorating American independence, the destruction of the

Bastille, the downfall of monarchy, and universal peace. Bryden, at the Fountain Inn on Light Street, featured an optical machine in which "Buonaparte will be seen, conducted by an angel, and trampling upon tyranny." The spectacles and festivities recommenced on 14 July, Bastille Day. In September, however, the papers were full of anxiety. An episode of shooting and self-poisoning by laudanum involved several German families. A daring footpad was at large on the road to Ellicott Mills. Negro Lydia was sentenced to be hanged for burning the house of Sophia Allender, and revelations were published daily of a supposed conspiracy of French Negroes to set fire to the town of Charleston. The editor was moved to comment:

All the various enormities of the old world, during its late convulsions, have been more or less felt in the new. The revolutionizing phrenzy, the prostration of all law and order, and the total disregard of everything human and divine. . . . Robberies, murders, and assassinations are now becoming the order of the day.[31]

Commerce Is the Mainspring

1802–1821

The war-and-peace rhythm of Baltimore's eighteenth-century growth continued into the nineteenth century. Gold flowed in, gold flowed out. Wealth increased, poverty increased. The timing of mobs and strikes, prizes and bankruptcies, fires and epidemics corresponded to fits of growth or sudden arrest. Philadelphia editors and Virginia politicians accused Baltimore of a collapse into anarchy. Baltimore citizens, faced with successive crises and galled by the critics, began tinkering with their municipal institutions and trying to make sense of their urban experience.

Population doubled in the first decade as it had in the 1790s. It continued to rise until 1816, when growth slackened for several years. An accumulation of people required an accumulation of houses, and most of the house building was concentrated in bursts of a few years before and just after the War of 1812.[1] Intense building booms of a few years in a cycle of roughly twenty-year periods have been characteristic of American cities, and are related to international migration and to counterwaves of construction in Europe. This time Baltimore experienced a greater upswing and slightly different timing from other cities, notably its archrival, Philadelphia.

The accumulation of buildings—three hundred in the boom years—provided a showcase for the accumulation of wealth. As individuals piled up fortunes, they began to display their private wealth and to pool their capital for civic improvements and even civic grandeur. Society was projected on the landscape, as the variations of individual wealth were expressed in the site and scale of town dwellings. Homes were advertised for the genteel and respectable, and architects were employed to design the town residences of wealthy merchants, notably Lorman, Oliver, Gilmor, and Smith. The accumulation of wealth made possible construction on a larger scale. In this period the habit was acquired of building ordinary houses and warehouses in rows of six to twelve at a time. Financial intermediaries were present to organize this, such as Elkan Solomon, broker, who was ready to "raise money on brick houses in town." Financial pools were also created to insure them, since a single fire might destroy, as in 1822, a range of twelve dwellings and sixteen warehouses on McElderry's wharf. Wealthy merchants built distinctive terraces: Pascault's eight houses on Lexington Street, William Patterson's wharf, William Shipley's row on Pierce Street, George Grundy's on Richmond Street, Wales' and Clopper's warehouses on Bowley's wharf, an elegant four-story terrace on Saint Paul Street, and others on George Street and Sharp Street. Most elegant was the water company's "Waterloo row" on Calvert Street.

The rate of incorporations matched the rhythm of construction. A special act of the legislature was needed to form a corporation for either profitable or social purposes. Among the ventures for profit was the Union Manufacturing Company, incorporated in 1809, with both private capital and shares taken by the state. The company bought 300 acres from the Ellicotts on the Patapsco River and developed an elaborate hydraulic system that could supply numerous mill seats. By 1812 they were employing forty families and developing a third large cotton mill. The Washington Cotton Factory was built on the Jones Falls. On Gwynns Falls, Worthington, Jessup, Cheston, and others erected five mills known as the Calverton mills on a two-mile race with a fall of eighty feet. The Napoleonic wars, the War of 1812, and the Spanish-American revolutions stimulated the chemical industries. In 1810 Lorman's powder mills, capitalized at $100,000, were as large as the Brandywine powder mills.[2]

All of these were on a new scale in terms of capital, structures, water power, labor force, and production. The shift of capital into manufacturing and the transformation of merchants into manufacturers was a national process, but in Baltimore it represented a more decided break with the past than in New England or Philadelphia. Much credit must be given to the influence of the Quaker miller families as they diversified their interests, developed the hydraulics, and created instruments for cooperation. John McKim operated the big steam cotton mill on French Street (Oldtown) and started the Union Manufacturing Company; Benjamin Ellicott dominated the Union Bank; and Isaac Tyson manufactured drugs and chemicals on Pratt Street, explored the uses of chrome pigments, and acquired the chrome-bearing properties at Bare Hills and Soldier's Delight.

Collective enterprises were organized on a new scale and incorporated for public uses. Some of the new institutions were modeled on Philadelphia. Several nonprofit corporations were formed to promote the development of manfactures. In 1809 seventeen hundred persons subscribed twenty thousand dollars to the Athenian Society; they agreed to "wear American," and operated a warehouse and store in Market (Baltimore) Street for receiving and vending domestic dry goods. They became "a prosperous little society," although they limited dividends in order to achieve their long-run objective of decreasing prejudices against American-made goods. Churches began to rival one another in lifting up towers and steeples out of the mass of houses. Cosmopolitan Baltimore, in its pride, sought a scale and a style to rival the old-world cities of culture and history. Buildings would express meanings and impose order. The most impressive were the great domes—the Catholic cathedral, the Exchange, the Unitarian church, Saint Paul's Episcopal Church, First Baptist, and that "superb edifice," the Medical College. The ultimate was the conception of monuments with no function other than commemoration, above all, the Washington Monument, from which Baltimore claimed its nickname, "the Monumental City," and the Battle Monument, dedicated to those who died in the 1813 battle for North Point. The city council also authorized two large paintings as "monumental remembrances" of the defense and "second birth" of Baltimore.

For siting their monumental structures, the builders developed a new appreciation of the natural topography as a stage. Baltimoreans determined to build on a scale at once to rival and to exploit its piedmont setting. The original site for a cathedral, near Granby and Exeter streets, was abandoned in 1806 in order to fix it upon a hill. The Washington Monument, originally proposed for the courthouse square, was resited on Howard's Hill. The two structures together defined for Baltimore a unique skyline, and dominated it for a century. For a century, they also defined a locus of legitimacy. Tough men with a sense of a great future for Baltimore had founded a past, a rock of religion, a mythology of elegance and noblesse oblige exemplified by George Washington and John Eager Howard. The building of those two "great piles" (still standing) was the establishment of the Establishment.

Designed by Maximilian Godefroy, the Unitarian church was built in 1820.

Other new institutions were sited on the west or northwest of the city to obtain advantages of country air and drainage, cheaper ground, or because their presence might threaten a densely populated district. This was the case with the hospitals and colleges, remarkably creative in this period. The beautiful domed Medical College, founded by the doctors in the southwest, had a magnificent prospect of the Patapsco River. The doctors invited the Sisters of Charity, Mother Seton's order from Emmitsburg, to provide the nursing in their teaching hospital. The charter for the Medical College contained the concept of a state university, and David Hoffman taught law. William Sinclair and James Priestly built an $80,000 structure on Mulberry Street for their Maryland College. Within walking distance was laid out the Lexington Market, also on a hill. Together with Saint Mary's Seminary, the new cathedral, and the Washington Monument, these institutions—all fixed on ground of John Eager Howard—provided a scaffolding for the "genteel" development of the western perimeter of Baltimore in this construction boom and the next.

Citizens were determined to create symbols in the center of the city as well. The courthouse, admired as "an immense edifice," was built between 1805 and 1809, and after the war the square was regraded to locate the Battle Monument on the crest of the hill. Nearby was the Masonic Hall, which later served as a federal courthouse. Lawyers took possession of the district, and publishers and booksellers clustered at Calvert and Baltimore streets. Two blocks south and east, toward the waterfront, the merchants decided to build an Exchange, a collective palace that would outclass the country houses of the planter aristocracy such as Homewood and Mount Clare. In 1820 they occupied their newspaper reading room and stock exchange, and rented spaces to the federal post office, treasury, and customs offices, and to numerous brokerage and insurance offices. The construction of the Exchange was an attempt to create order, symmetry, and mass in the midst of a waterfront all disorder, bustle, brick, and rigging. Symbolic of the curious mixture of great vision and grudging implementation was the practice of financing all these magnificent structures by lotteries and taking for granted their future operation as self-supporting.

The search for meaning and the passion for imposing order on a complex world reached into every domain. The collection of grand semipublic works fixed in Baltimore for some years a number of remarkable architects, notably Benjamin Latrobe, Jr., Robert Mills, and Maximilian Godefroy. But they were recognized, sought after, and hired through the influence of a more fixed circle of local men who were thoughtful and sophisticated. All the innovations in institutions, in literature, building, mechanics, medicine, agriculture, and science, are traceable to a single network of gifted and articulate men whose ideas sprang up like mushrooms all over town.[3] Vital in this network were several editors of considerable persuasive powers, in person as well as in print. One was William Gwynn, publisher of the *Federal Gazette*, enthusiast of the theater and the Spanish-American revolutions. He was a member of the original committees to create a water company and a gas company. Gwynn backed Sower's type foundry. He held together the Hibernian Society and the important literary circle known as the Delphian Club.

Fielding Lucas, Jr., bookseller with Philadelphia connections, stocked hundreds of titles in French, published some of the finest made books in the nation, played the flute, and founded the Baltimore Harmonic Society central to the musical life and charitable efforts of Baltimore. After the war he was associated with Catholic publishing ventures and the zeal for Bolivar. He published a new-style Spanish grammar by a priest of Saint Mary's Seminary and a magnificent atlas of the West Indies, for which he drew many of the maps himself from information garnered from Baltimore sea captains. Lucas and Gwynn secured a loan to a Philadelphia theatrical company, to build the Holliday Street theater. As a manager of the Washington Monument project, Lucas was in close touch with Robert Mills. He had Mills design a new store front and interior for him, and published Mills's *Treatise on Inland Navigation* and his atlas of South Carolina.

Hezekiah Niles, through his weekly *Register*, of national circulation, helped formulate the "American System" of public works and protective tariffs for manufacturing.[4] He promoted the Athenian Society and the Economical Society, as well as vaccination and Spanish-American independence. Joseph Townsend, a member of the Society of Friends, was involved in nearly every social or institutional innovation—the African school, the Protection Society, and the potter's field. He was the manager secretary of the Equitable Society, a member of the board of health, commissioner of the Maryland Hospital, and a commissioner for the town plan. John Skinner's *American Farmer* was probably the nation's most important agricultural journal, and also reported on technical and medical devices beyond the realm of agriculture. Skinner was the secretary of the state agricultural society and personally imported new breeds of livestock.

Another key person in the network was Robert Goodloe Harper, congressional representative from South Carolina who came to Baltimore about 1800 to pursue his career as an attorney. Married to Carroll's daughter, and thus brother-in-law to Richard Caton, Harper was often the channel between wealthy patrons and impecunious men of ideas. He was an active member of the Delphian Club and a prime mover in the Library Company and in the construction of the Exchange. In these roles he figured as a patron of both Mills and Latrobe, despite their rivalry.[5] Mills dedicated his canal plan to Harper, who organized the subscription for the publication. Harper was a central figure in the new movement to free and resettle blacks in colonies on the coast of Africa, similar to the British experiments in Sierra Leone. He believed slavery was a curse and free blacks were destined for hopeless inferiority and consequent degradation. "You can manumit the slave," he argued, "but you cannot make him a white man."[6] Although his objectives now appear unrealistic and ambiguous, his reading of the British and French explorers of Africa is impressive, and he showed a grasp of the geographical and geopolitical requirements for a successful colony. He recommended the initial Mesurado River sites and the name Liberia for the Maryland colony.

Several other gentlemen played similar roles as channels of communication between men of capital and men of ideas. William Lorman, founder of the gas company and president of the Bank of Baltimore, had Latrobe build him a row of shops on Charles Street at Conewago. Robert Smith, a planter, played the role of model farmer and patron of prize livestock and agricultural inventions. James Mosher, variously identified as bricklayer, mason, architect, or builder, was often teamed with Robert Cary Long. Long was carpenter, architect, builder, and lumber merchant. Mosher and Long were spokesmen for the growing class of "mechanics," craftsmen whose economic and political importance increased in the period of intense construction. The mechanics demanded more democratic participation, but nevertheless accepted a certain paternalism in their institutions. Mosher was the president of an apprentices' library, and Long was the secretary of the Carpenters Society.

The intellectual network seems always to lead to a few "back lanes," particularly Chatham Street, which ran west from the courthouse. The original site of the Mechanical Company clubroom and engine house, it had become a residential street convenient to the new courthouse, the publishing corner at Baltimore and Calvert, and to the prestigious new residences along North Charles Street near the cathedral. In Chatham Street in 1804 were found William Gwynn; James Mosher; Mary C. Goddard, a remarkable old lady who had been a publisher, political gadfly, postmistress, and shopkeeper; the Baltimore General Dispensary; Horace Hayden, the dental surgeon and geologist; and Dr. James Smith, who spearheaded all organization against smallpox. There were Mrs. Coffey's dame school and Mrs. Lacombe's young ladies' seminary. The new Union Bank was on the corner of Chatham and Charles streets, and just around the corner on Saint Paul's Lane were James Priestly and William Lorman. Daniel Raymond set up his law office in Chatham Street. After Chatham Street was demolished to develop Fayette Street, Baltimore was never the same.

Circulation

Characteristic of this period was the recognition of the dynamic properties of great systems of circulation. The merchant city was part of such a circulatory system, and Baltimore grew off its levy on the circulation of goods, money, and information. The accumulation of wealth, visible in the new buildings, depended upon an acceleration of the flows of money and goods. The number of banks increased from two to nine, and the new ones had much larger capital.

As Niles said, "It is the great secret of banking to keep the bank bills in circulation with the least chance of a demand being made for their payment."[7] The extraordinary development of the international circulation of money through Baltimore is shown by two bizarre ventures of Robert Oliver, by means of which he became a millionaire.[8]

In the years 1801 to 1803, when a hundred Baltimore merchants had been ruined by "the disasters of the peace" (the Treaty of Amiens), Oliver noted, "We see so many people ruined by speculative and extensive operations that we intend to be very cautious."[9] Oliver had, however, a contract to supply cash for a British paymaster and purchasing agent in Martinique and later Barbados. For a 5 percent commission, he procured gold, had it melted down and recoined into Spanish joes by a Baltimore firm (Bedford and Morton), then captured additional profits on the charter of vessels, insurance, negotiation of the bills of exchange, and sales of return cargoes of sugar via Saint Croix. Oliver and his go-betweens redeemed notes of banks in Alexandria, Washington, Georgetown, and Wilmington, until "all the Banks within reach south of Philadelphia are drain'd of Gold."[10] The business was highly secretive because the banks did not like the reduction of their lending capacity, and the ship captains were not told they were carrying specie. Through his brother-in-law, John Craig, Oliver was able to obtain gold in Philadelphia to the extent of $100,000 in one year.

From mid-1806 through 1808, again through the collaboration of the same Philadelphia brother-in-law and *his* brother-in-law, who was in favor with the Spanish court, Oliver entered a still more amazing trade, which poured gold *into* Baltimore. As neutrals, Oliver and Craig obtained a coveted Spanish monopoly license to trade with the port of Vera Cruz. The Spanish king owed a vast tribute to Napoleon; a French banker paid Napoleon and arranged for a Dutch loan, secured by the Spanish treasure stores of gold and silver in Vera Cruz. The Dutch bankers negotiated with Craig and the Olivers for the movement of the gold in American—that is, neutral—ships, to be converted into American goods, which were shipped, again in American vessels, to Antwerp. Oliver was able to seize this opportunity in part through the exceptional sailing vessels and insurance facilities of Baltimore, in part through his carefully developed connections and correspondences. He "bought" half a million dollars worth of the Mexican gold stores at a 21 percent discount and nearly a million more at 17 percent. Thus, a million and a half was brought to Baltimore in Oliver's schooners in less than a year, and the gross profit was a quarter of a million. Much of the money was advanced to Baltimore merchants—Smith and Buchanan, Lemuel Taylor, John Donnell, Mark Pringle, and Isaac McKim—who handled the consignment of goods to Europe, to pay off the Dutch loan.[11]

The embargo of 1807 cut back trade, but the declaration of the War of 1812 unleashed new enterprise as daring as during the Revolution. More privateers were commissioned in Baltimore than any other port, and a third of U.S. Navy ships were built in Baltimore.[12] After the war, some of the unemployed vessels were refitted for the slave trade outside the United States, while other owners harnessed their energies to the cause of the Spanish-American revolutions. Baltimore became the principal world center for privateering and propagandizing in the service of the new republics. At least twenty privateers, carrying two thousand men, were outfitted in Baltimore.[13] The "respectable" Baltimore merchants publicly disapproved of this activity, which verged on piracy and required duping crews or kidnapping sailors. But a number privately participated in "the American Concern," an interlocking directorate of the operation. Legitimate merchant channels were essential to the disposal of the prize cargoes. Politically active Baltimoreans such as General William Winder, attorney William Pinkney, collector of the port James McCulloch, and postmaster John Skinner were involved in the legal defense of the concern. John O. Chase was one of the most successful captains. On one voyage in the spring of 1818, under flags of Buenos Aires and Uruguay, Chase plundered twenty Portuguese merchantmen. Three of the prizes he took in the *Fortuna* were estimated at $750,000. Chase came up the Chesapeake on a pilot boat to deposit $100,000 cash in the Union Bank and the Marine Bank in Baltimore before he rejoined his ship and sold off the rest of the cargo in St. Thomas. He brought the ship back empty to Baltimore to refit, and to face the legal challenges.

As Baltimore's international activities grew, it became evident that the facilities for inland trade were lagging. The circulation of money depended on circulating the goods, and an acceleration of trade through Baltimore required, in each generation, improvements in land transport to match ocean transport. In 1804, when the legislature failed to pass a road bill, a great clamor arose in the newspapers for road improvements to the wheat-producing regions westward. The farmer and wagoner complained of "the miery sloughs, the dreadful precipices, the often-times impassible streams, which would everywhere freeze him with horror-chills."[14] The advocates of road improvements shivered worse as they watched Alexandria's trade developing, the District of Columbia laid out, and Baltimore capital moving out of shipping into real estate: "One year we see them all running into the water like ducks. . . . Now they think of the water with as much horror as if they had the hydrophobia on them; and every man who can buy a lot, is building a house of some kind."[15] They suggested that Baltimore merchants "forego shaving on building a year or two" and spend the money paving a road across the Monocacy to Hagerstown or Cumberland. They entreated Baltimore to recognize,

whenever cities suffered their inland trade to depart from them, it required nothing but *the inexorable tooth of time* to dissect them into ruins, and to gnaw them into dust. Such, too, O Baltimore, will be thy fate, if thy perverse stars shall doom thee much longer to be so *unrepresented.*[16]

Within the year they obtained a turnpike incorporation bill and abandoned the convict labor system that had failed to maintain the old-style roads. By 1809 three great turnpike roads—Frederick, York, and Reisterstown—were completed twenty feet wide and stoned twelve inches deep, altogether about 150 miles in length, at a cost of $1.5 million.[17] The land was offered free because of the value the road added along its route. Freight could now be hauled year-round. Other turnpike companies were incorporated and built soon after: Falls Road, the Washington Road, the road to Havre de Grace, and Harford Road.

Meanwhile, the state legislature made an extraordinary move. Seeing that the Baltimore banks were the great pool of wealth (the popular intuition of their secret ventures was, after all, correct), the state would renew their charters in return for the banks' accepting a tax to establish a state system of country schools and a bank investment of half a million dollars to build a fifty-eight-mile turnpike road to Cumberland. The policy of transforming commercial capital into social overhead capital, such as public roads and schools, is the modern strategy of the national development banks created by European governments toward the end of the century and developing nations today. The road would benefit Baltimore and sustain the urban-centered commercial economy. It also turned out to be a profitable undertaking. The Cumberland Turnpike Company is said to have paid 20 percent on its stock for many years,[18] and, as shown in the next chapter, it stimulated thinking on a still grander scale of investment.

Fire and Flood

The circulation of money was one of the complex vital systems. The other was the circulation of water. Because of its new spread and height and its vast stone piles, the city was recognizable as a man-made or artificial system, in a special relation to nature. As great structures were raised and foundations sunk, earth and mud were moved and slopes were adjusted in ways that interfered with or corrected the existing system. It is in the hydrological system, or circulation of waters, that nature imposes system thinking. In this period, by the intense aggravation of everyday problems and by successive catastrophes, Baltimore citizens were disciplined to consider systematic planning.

The need for water to put out fires was the incentive to create a water company. The matter was always discussed after a serious fire—cisterns on the housetops, cisterns under the street—and the fire of 1804 finally stimulated the formation of a water company. Philadelphia was already embarked on developing a supply from the Schuylkill River, in a similar "fall line" environment. The chief problems were not technical, they were the problems of mobilizing resources. On 5 May 1804, the commissioners for the water company expressed disappointment with stock subscriptions. The editor of the *Federal Gazette* confessed no great surprise: "Every enterprise of this kind, in a city so devoid of public spirit as ours, must depend upon a few." Charles Carroll of Carrollton subscribed 200 shares to set an example, and three days later 1,000 shares were subscribed (chiefly by the Maryland Insurance Company, the Marine Insurance Company, John O'Donnell, John McKim, and the Equitable Society), sufficient to "secure an influence over fire plugs." Once the enterprise was assured, the stocks were subjected to a "bubble" of speculation.[19]

The technical debates turned on how diversion of water from the Jones Falls, Gwynns Falls, the Gunpowder, or the Patapsco might affect the existing mills or future development of mill seats. Industry was developing swiftly, and water power was its prime source of energy. On the Jones Falls there were already a dozen mills developed along a fourteen-mile stream with a fall of 350 feet. The Baltimore millers were involved in the water company, not only to protect their interests, but because they had the experience with hydraulics and engines. The plan adopted was simple: buy off the rights of the five or six mills nearest the mouth of the Jones Falls, take water by a race at Keller's dam (east of the present Guilford Avenue bridge), and raise the water by means of pumps driven by a water wheel (near the present Sun Papers building) to reservoirs at the present intersections of Calvert and Centre streets and Cathedral and Franklin streets. A second pumping station, with reserve steam pumps, was created near the Belvidere bridge, and the water company race supplied the Salisbury mill at that location.

A supply of drinking water was a secondary matter, for convenience and for defraying the costs of the fire-protection system. "A Citizen" figures that "genteel families" able to pay $12 to $20 a year would include three thousand out of five thousand households in the town, for water conducted to the house: "all those who know how much time is consumed, and how many servants are spoiled, in sending to the pumps for water."[20] In fact, thirty years later, the corporation was only supplying four thousand households, and service was not yet available to all parts of town. Meanwhile, the city continued to supply drinking water by sinking shallow wells wherever eight property owners offered to pay for their installation. By 1816 the town had 290 such pumps, and 59 were out of repair. The shallow wells were contaminated from surface drainage and from the privies "dug to water" in spite of regulations. Germ theory was undiscovered, and the water of the most dubious wells was particularly celebrated, as the Green Tree Pump in Oldtown.

The water company was more important as a developer and agent of development than as a supplier of water. The company's works formed the structure for a large new section of town, and its engineers applied their talents to a larger domain of environmental problems. The company managed to lure John Davis away from the Philadelphia waterworks to supervise the construction and operation of the Baltimore works. On the side he consulted on nearly every hydraulic undertaking in the region. His fee was 10 percent of the construction costs. When the stone arch bridge over the Jones Falls fell in, Davis built a new bridge. As consultant engineer for the city, he redeveloped several valuable old springs as fountains in ornamental squares, with cupolas and shade trees. The first was the "City Spring" in the bank of the Jones Falls near Saratoga Street.[21] Similar plans were adopted for Clopper's and Sterrett's springs. He led water from the water company's spring in the bank of the Jones Falls near Centre Street to supply water to the Centre Market. Davis located many of the new cotton mills on the Jones Falls. He supervised the erection of the Lanvale cotton factory on water company property, and a large flour mill six miles out. On Gwynns Falls he "surveyed, leveled and attended" the building of Calverton mills and millrace. He supervised the location of Cumberland Road and the renewal of the Susquehanna Canal. Davis was proudest of his deep well at Fort McHenry, finished in time to supply the troops during the Bombardment.[22]

When Robert Mills of Philadelphia was chosen architect for the Washington Monument, the water company hired him as consultant, then as superintendent.[23] During his association with it, he was a commissioner for laying out North Street through water company property.[24] He designed and built on water company land a terrace of twelve houses known as "Waterloo Row" fronting on

North Calvert Street. This project capitalized on the site of the monument, the company reservoir, the new road, and the Howard image, to create an elegant residential row along the new axis of legitimacy.[25] Mills also managed the works of the new gas company, on North Street at Bath, adjoining the city mill. He designed homes in the Mount Vernon area, notably John Hoffman's on the northeast corner of Franklin and Cathedral streets opposite the other reservoir. He designed and installed warm air furnaces for churches and elegant homes. The web of idea men sustained him, but it was his association with the Jones Falls water supply that allowed Mills to influence the development of the city.

Mills's most ingenious renewal plan was never carried out. He offered a remedy after the catastrophic 1817 flood. The useful millstreams of Baltimore had certain perennial inconveniences. Every thirty years more or less, a torrential summer downpour caused flash floods of this magnitude. The Jones Falls was ordinarily confined by stone walls and houses to a width of sixty feet, its depth "nowhere above a horse's knee." But on 9 August 1817, toward midday it swelled suddenly to twenty feet above its normal height and swept away all its mill dams and wood bridges. Bridge timber, tree trunks, and hogsheads lodged against the stone arch bridge, and water overflowed the streets, particularly Harrison Street and the old "Meadow," to depths of six to ten feet. Several lives were lost. By sundown all the water had drained away.[26] Robert Mills proposed to remove all nuisances situated on the banks, open a street on either side of the falls, scour the bed, and cover it with a sheet of water deep enough for navigation as far as Madison Street. Self-interest would guide property holders to contribute to the opening of the new streets, "as they obtain by this means an additional front, and that upon a street of business." The bend between Madison and Bath streets would be straightened, and low wharves between the streets and the stream bed would give a greater width for runoff, "a second bed to the stream" in time of high water. The falls would become an "embellishment," instead of a menace. The Jones Falls was the ideal location for a promenade: "Its central situation, the romantic scenery and waterfalls, which present themselves as you proceed up, and running North and South, giving every advantage of air and shade, all contribute to make this spot preferable to any other."[27] The vision was new but consistent with the way Davis was redeveloping the springs. The need for recreation and refreshment was evident in an age when everyone, including the wealthy, walked. The city council opined that Mills's plan might be of considerable importance to the city, but it was "of such infinite extent and magnitude" that they preferred to postpone spending any money.[28] The first bridges were rebuilt conforming to Mills's suggestion of a single wide span, and the council eventually paid him some city stock for his advice. Meanwhile, they paid Benjamin Latrobe $500 for an alternate plan. He proposed to divert the entire stream of the Jones Falls into Herring Run, by tunneling under Gallows Hill. It was a still more ambitious engineering scheme with great impact on the lower mills.[29]

Floods recede quickly from memory. A rare event, seen in a generation as an act of God, perhaps should not be expected to govern the organizing of an everyday system of hydrology. Both of these elegant plans nevertheless represented a new grandeur of conception—systematic and integrating—and an earthy calculation of the costs and benefits of a multipurpose plan. They provided fuel for a century of debate. Mills's conception of the storm drainage problem on the falls was intelligent, conformed to the common view, and indeed was essentially the same plan proposed *de novo* and carried out after the flood of 1868— widening, straightening the bend, and walling. But the public promenade and the development of the private property values in this district were opportunities missed once for all.

"Foul and Filthy Spots"

Death rates were exceptionally high in the years 1818 through 1822. Although estimates are less reliable before 1812, there appears to have been also a wave of deaths in the years 1799–1801.[30] Long swings in the death rate are thus the inverse of the building cycle. There are several possible elements of explanation. A likely factor is the exposure of "a newly collected people"; mortality rose following a period of heavy immigration, wartime mobility, and the European migrations and epidemics following the treaty of 1815. Depressed construction and high death rates coincided with increases of homicide, pauperism, begging, and vagrancy. The intense population growth and uncontrolled construction created sanitation problems of new dimensions, whose handling depended on the habits and whims of thousands of individuals as well as the whims of nature.

Specific diseases have cycles in their natural history that are not fully understood. They vary in their frequency of attack and in their virulence. There were notable outbreaks of measles in 1802, 1808, 1813, 1819, and 1823; whooping cough in 1816 and 1819; and membranous croup (diphtheria) in 1812. These diseases entered Baltimore as epidemics, more or less widespread and fatal, but after several episodes they became endemically established in the population, and later, over several generations, they tended to become less fatal. Other major causes of death were tuberculosis, pneumonia, and infant cholera. Each reached death rates as high as two persons per thousand for the specific disease in a single year. They tended to concentrate their fatalities among the poor, the very young, and the old, and they were ignored by the city fathers as essentially personal, medical, and theological problems.

In sharp contrast was the attitude toward smallpox and yellow fever, catastrophes more terrifying than flood or fire. They were hideous, and they were no respecter of persons. Civic leadership could not ignore them. Baltimore had a more progressive and thoughtful collection of doctors than most American cities at the time, with backgrounds from both France and Scotland, the most advanced medical centers of the western world. Over this period I detect a learning process at work, and the creation of new institutions of collective response. Although yellow fever and smallpox were "as generically distinct from each other, as the sheep and the hog; or the oak and the pine,"[31] and the strategies to combat them differed, both diseases were clearly identified as system failures, susceptible to some reengineering of the city or reorganization of its life.

Smallpox flourished in the cold season. It had appeared in Baltimore numerous times in the eighteenth century. As early as 1755, Dr. Henry Stevenson was inoculating people with "vaccinia" or kine pox and nursing them through a generally mild illness that reduced their susceptibility to smallpox. During an outbreak in 1800 Dr. James Smith obtained smallpox vaccine from London and introduced Dr. Jenner's practice of vaccination. Dr. Smith performed his first vaccinations on persons in the almshouse, then set up a Vaccine Institution in his front room in Chatham Street, vaccinated his own children, and exposed them to the smallpox.[32] Local doctors became ardent protagonists of his method, although the public responded cautiously. The state approved a lottery to help finance free distribution, and a Jennerian society was formed, but lapsed. The outbreak of a serious epidemic in 1812 produced a new acceptance. The upper class had its children and slaves revaccinated. Niles accused those who neglected the duty of "murder of the first degree."[33] When the smallpox began to rage in 1821 and the death rate again approached two per thousand, a Vaccine Society was again formed. Its five young men vaccinated seven hundred persons unable to pay, and physicians paid by the city council vaccinated thirty-two hundred more.[34] Although it seems doubtful whether vaccination had any effect on the scale of these epidemics, Baltimoreans believed vaccination could protect the individual and arrest the epidemic. In spite of this conviction action was always proportionate to the immediate threat.[35]

There was considerable controversy over whether the various fevers—remittent and intermittent, bilious and yellow—were the same or distinct diseases, and the diagnosis seems to depend sometimes upon the degree of "malignancy," that is, whether the patient died. In 1819, 350 died of the true "yellow fever," characterized not only by yellowness of skin and eyes, but by horrifying last stages:

A black vomiting or purging, hemorrhages from every part of the body, especially the stomach, uterus, bowels, nostrils, and the incisions made by the lancet in bleeding; carbuncles and numerous little biles . . . deafness, excitability to touch, a considerable degree of delirium, and small purple spots.[36]

In terror five thousand residents temporarily moved out of Fells Point. A thousand with small resources were forcibly encamped for weeks in a ropewalk on Hampstead Hill (Patterson Park).[37]

It is now known that in the life cycles of the organisms that are the agents of malaria (remittent) and yellow fever, essential vectors are species of mosquitoes that breed in standing water. The mosquitoes and the diseased human hosts were repeatedly introduced through commerce with the West Indies, but the mosquitoes did not survive Baltimore winters, and the disease did not become endemic to Baltimore. However, the theory prevailing in Baltimore since the 1790s was putrefaction of vegetable matter.[38] Variations on it stressed the role of damp air, decaying wood, or spoiled cargoes of hides and coffee. The theory, combined with new outbreaks of the disease in the same locations, fostered observation of meteorological conditions and local environments. It was generally agreed that the difference between conditions on high ground and low held the key to health or sickness. The low ground and swamps on the necks, inlets, and creeks of the Patapsco were the environment of fevers. The natural swamps were regarded as unhealthy, but the most vigorously debated question was the effect of human intervention in changing the environment. A published self-criticism, consisting of letters from the doctors to the mayor after the 1819 epidemic, pointed to the problem of land fill: "Those who have suffered most from Fever, dwell on a soil made with their own hands."[39] The doctors disagreed about the effects of construction of the City Block and reconstruction of the old cove at the mouth of the Jones Falls. In 1819 there still remained twenty acres of marsh and water between town and point, and several doctors opined it was "a foul core in the heart of the City."[40] A larger number pointed to the improvement as evidence that intelligent public works could remove the local tendency to yellow fever. Not a solitary case was traced in 1819 to the blocks most deadly in 1800 and since drained. "It belongs peculiarly to foul and filthy spots, and from the experience had, it is also evident that those spots may be divested of their destructive qualities."[41] The doctors' demand that the section of "made ground" at Fells Point be reengineered laid the basis for the next round of public improvements.

Coupled with environmental theories of disease were social theories. Doctors, public officials, clergy, and laymen, brought face to face with the ultimate question, all framed their own rationalizations. As tension mounted, each individual projected into the situation his own fears and guilts and his own conception of society, what it was and ought to be, problems of social class differences and private virtue. The victims were carefully recorded as temperate or intemperate; doctors and publishers took for granted that the lower classes were intemperate, the craftsmen respectable, and the genteel irreproachable. The wealthiest class was generally able to escape yellow fever by leaving or avoiding the district. Each epidemic provided new revelations of poverty, as nuisances were inventoried, the sick were succored, and those still healthy were relocated. Disease was concentrated in the pockets of poverty, the lanes of both the outskirts and the center. In 1799 Dr. Davidge noted, "The skirts of most cities are occupied by the poorer class of inhabitants—their houses are exposed to the first and most violent assaults of all endemical epidemicks."[42]

In 1819 poverty and congestion had reached new dimensions, as business depression deepened and construction declined. During the yellow fever season, an anonymous physician begged to commend to the mayor's attention the poor east of Harford Run:

Commerce is the main spring of this City. Fells Point is as it were the key thereof— it is therefore important to all. But this same business which diffuses life, vigor and activity to the whole City, brings down upon this part of the City most of these poor. They have all been, more or less, directly or indirectly engaged in commerce, and have felt its depressed spirit comparatively speaking, a thousand fold more than the merchants.[43]

The vaccine physicians reported in 1821, "we found the smallpox confined almost entirely to such of the streets and alleys of the city as were inhabited by the greatest numbers of poor people."[44] And Dr. G. S. Townsend described a slum behind the lower end of Frederick Street, between Pratt and Water streets:

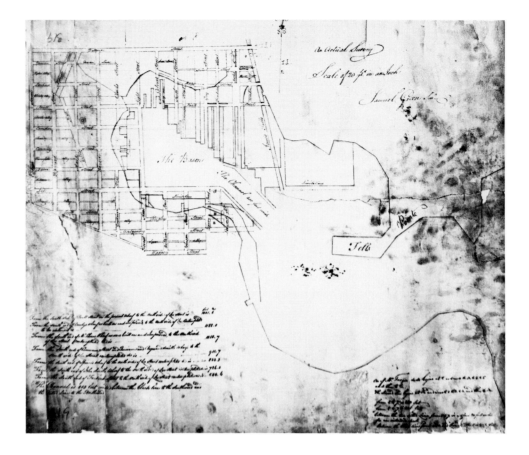

The basin of Baltimore, as surveyed by Samuel Green, was recorded as of 27 January 1812.

a nest of houses, tenanted by Negroes, and divided by an alley, very appropriately called "Squeeze Gut"! If I may be allowed to judge from the quantum of excrementitious matter and stench with which it abounds! . . . Disease and death have year after year, luxuriously rioted among the miserable and abandoned victims, who have there nestled together.[45]

A Plan for the City

Epidemics called attention to certain foul and filthy spots and spurred the increase of regulatory power, but it was the everyday nuisances in the physical environment that created an awareness of the need for system in the layout of streets and led to Baltimore's first serious attempt at a city plan.

Because physical growth had always outstripped the pace and powers of municipal management, it was customary for the town to accept street beds laid out by private persons. The layouts of the three original sites and several early additions did not match. Attempts to connect them created problems of traffic movement and—more serious—drainage problems. The streets themselves were the storm drainage system; the footways and stepping stones were pedestrian bridges. Imperfect grading of the streets created the perennial nuisances of stagnant water, gullying, and deposits of sand and manure.

As growth rose to a high pitch about 1808, the town began to look toward annexing a large surrounding territory called the precincts, already subject to certain urban taxes and fire regulations.

The parts which are not built up, but remain in the hands of rich proprietors, derive all their high value from their proximity to the commercial parts, to the markets, to the navigation &c., and consequently ought in justice to contribute to the maintenance and support of these important objects.[46]

The legislature authorized special commissioners, one board for the eastern precincts and one for the western precincts, to lay out streets and establish their building lines and grades. On receiving a petition, the commissioners published a notice that they would meet on the site to make a survey and receive testimony; at their next meeting they recorded the decision in their minutes. The commissioners were about equally occupied with boundary disputes between property owners and with storm drainage problems.

The western precincts commissioners seem to have been more formal and legalistic. They proceeded block by block. The owners of large tracts were frequent petitioners, sometimes in groups. The process was evidently a speculative platting and turnover in advance of building. The mixed public/private character of town making persisted. Lewis Pascault, for example, was at one time or another a commissioner for development of the Lexington Market, a western precincts commissioner, the developer of a range of houses on Lexington Street, and the subdivider of a tract.

In Oldtown, the eastern precincts commissioners were more pragmatic, concerned mainly about connecting the streets. Their alignments framed in the development of East Baltimore for a generation. They located the Bel Air Market and ran the line of McElderry Street, and Aisquith Street from Belair Road north to intersect Harford Road on Gallows Hill. James Sterling and Thomas McElderry were landowners whose decisions to sell, lease, or develop were important in the layout of this district.

The commissioners found that every establishment of a grade in one street segment forced them to reexamine the grades of all streets nearby. The streets had to be level enough for travel but steep enough to drain properly. When they did drain well, they washed down silt. For example, the wash from Hampstead Hill (west side of Patterson Park) down Washington, Wolfe, and Ann streets caused filling in the cross streets. The commissioners ordered Ann Street rebuilt in a concave form with a one-foot rise, creating a storm drain channel directly into the harbor. On the southern end of town the principal developer was Christopher Hughes, who planned an enclosed dock with quays on both sides. The gradual cutting down of "Hughes Street" at the base of Federal Hill caused continuous erosion into the harbor.[47]

Since all the drainage of Baltimore found its way into the active portions of the harbor and channel, anxiety again arose about silting. In the 1780s filling was accelerated by the clearing and cultivation of the hills; in the 1790s the harbor was made smaller by the extension of wharves and filling of the borders. Now the rapid urban construction on the perimeter of the town was the main source of sedimentation. Shoals tended to form at the mouth of the Jones Falls.

The war drew attention to the military and commercial importance of Baltimore harbor, and in 1816 the port wardens authorized a map of the harbor. Lewis Brantz, merchant and sea captain, was employed, and his was the first scientific survey of the Patapsco River harbor. The charts were used until the U.S. Coast and Geodetic Survey sheets were published in the 1840s. The triangulations, sightings, and the ranges of depth soundings in the harbor were made along the lines of house fronts, "all the measurements on Shore perfectly agreeing with the Triangulations on the Ice." Brantz also developed historical information about the sedimentation of the harbor. He consulted Mr. Burton, who had resided at the point since 1778, and who made a profession of grappling

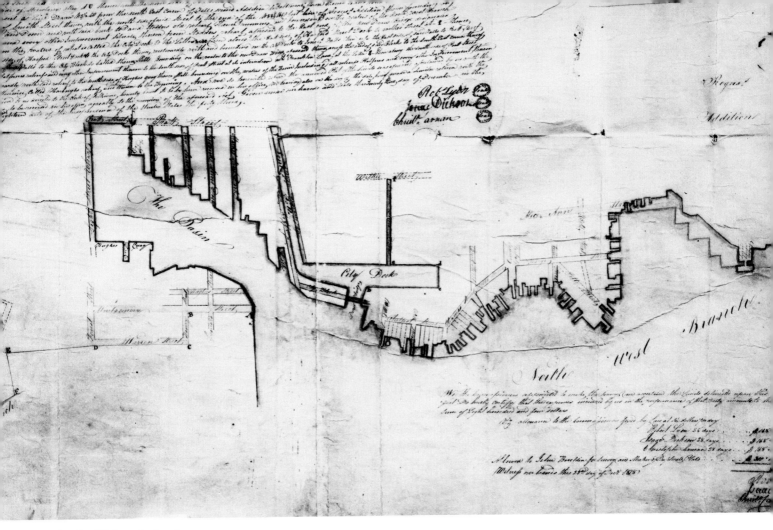

Jehu Bouldin's waterfront survey of 1818 reflects the progress of development toward both the cove and the Canton district.

for and raising things from the bottom, "which naturally made him intimately acquainted with its depth throughout a long course of years." Brantz concluded that the "mud machines" were laboring in vain, and that the mean depth of the inner harbor was now only eight or nine feet, formerly ten or eleven.[48]

In the same year as Brantz's survey, the annexation was authorized, tripling the acreage of the city and increasing its municipal powers and representation somewhat. A board of commissioners was authorized to employ an engineer-surveyor, T. H. Poppleton, and a secretary, Joseph Townsend, to survey the new boundaries, lay out streets in the annexed territory, select lots for public uses, and harmonize street names.[49] For the first time the legislation specified that they should establish a true meridian and durable landmarks. The city paid two thirteen-year-olds twenty-five cents a day to take part in locating the boundary stones, so that they could transmit the information to a later generation.[50]

"It was never the intention of the Board to interfere . . . with the old part of the City." But rapid growth of the city as a whole always put pressure on the central district. The need to connect all parts of the perimeter of growth and to handle a greater circulation of goods through the city forced changes in the old parts. As the turnpike roads were built and wharves extended, the city's street network had to accommodate increased traffic between them. Several breakthroughs were made to the north, where the controlling factor was the crossing of the Jones Falls. Cathedral Street was extended, angled to cross the falls and connect with the new Falls Road. North Street and Aisquith Street were laid out in Oldtown to York Road (Greenmount Avenue). Charles and St. Paul streets could be extended only as far as the Howard estate, but Calvert was connected by Belvidere or North Street (now Guilford Avenue), to cross the falls by the Belvidere bridge, a timber structure of 170-foot span.[51] To the south, Forest and Goodman streets were extended to intersect the road to the ferry, and Green Street was opened leading from Pratt Street to the Washington turnpike.

Crosstown routes were always a difficult problem because of the high value of property in built-up areas. Centre Street was authorized to cross the falls. It was found possible to connect the segments of Saratoga Street by twists, but proposals for through routes below Saratoga were bitterly fought, despite congestion. Lombard Street was authorized between Hanover and Calvert, but not put through. There was litigation over a private property obstructing Water Street. And the opening of Pratt Street across Hollingsworth, Cheapside, and Ellicott docks provoked debate for twenty-two years: "The question was agitated until 1818." Every move was contested in both the council and the legislature.

A constant, irregular and absurd interference in our local affairs by the legislature, renders everything attempted to be done by the city authorities, either as regards improvement, revenue or order, uncertain in its continuance, and consequently of little avail.[52]

The obstructions of wharf owners, the interference of the legislature, and the interruptions of the War of 1812 created a crisis in 1818, when several costly, long-delayed projects had to be undertaken at once, just as depression set in: the $150,000 loan for opening Pratt Street, and the $100,000 loan for opening and extending North Street and the Belvidere bridge. The Jones Falls flood had occurred in 1817; the timing helps to explain the council's reluctance to embark on a major engineering effort in the Jones Falls.

Late in 1821 the commissioners displayed Poppleton's plan for public examination and invited corrections. Admitting that there were some unavoidable "deformities," they claimed that a glance at the plot would show that

a striking regularity as a whole, pervades the plan.—And that the disjointed settlements which before made up the city, are interwoven and connected together in a manner which, we flatter ourselves, could not be improved. The combination exhibits the metropolis of Maryland in an aspect of great beauty . . . entire accuracy. *All is certainty.*

It ought never to be forgotten, that it is a great system which must be preserved in all its parts.[53]

Poppleton's plat was preserved entire to a surprising degree, in its best and worst features. It was the basic framework for the development of Baltimore until 1888, within the boundaries of the present North Avenue, Edison Highway, East Avenue, and, on the west, a line just beyond Monroe Street south to the mouth of the Gwynns Falls. The standard Baltimore block that Poppleton selected differed from New York, and his hierarchy of street widths—front, side, and alley—created a pattern for future construction and for differentials in social structure that persist to this day. Poppleton's solutions for stitching together the several preexisting street grids along the seams of through streets produced the modern traffic engineer's nightmare and the pedestrian citizen's delight. Dozens of Baltimore streets jogged, or met in intersections of five streets. A street vista was often visually closed by an angled terrace, a steeple, chimney, or turret.

Sometimes triangular points of land were left, better suited to a statue, fountain, or garden than a house.

The chief limitations of the plan stemmed from the fact that it was not a topographical survey. In order to save money, topographical survey was rejected, and the final plan was two dimensional. Its "striking regularity" was achieved at the cost of ignoring variations of terrain. This feature, too, contributed to the character of inner-city Baltimore: straight rows of houses step up and down the hills, and vistas surprise the driver at each rise or dip. But much of the costly bridging, filling, tunneling, storm sewering, and regrading for a century must be attributed to a cavalier attitude toward the relief. A two-dimensional plot, as some citizens realized at the time, would not produce order in the hydrologic system, correct the nuisances, or minimize future public investments. It did, however, make possible the continuation of subdivision and private speculative development. Ads began appearing immediately that suggest why the plot met with the "entire approbation" of all the large landowners. Christian Mayer's estate was offered for sale: "In the late plan of the city a public square is laid out on it, with Baltimore street extended running through the estate, with a front of about 240 feet." Part of Edward Ireland's estate was subdivided along the newly plotted Chatsworth Street front.[54] City planning of this kind was an essential tool for efficiency in the private exploitation of urban land. Public control of the proper sort stimulated the speculative system. Facilitating the circulation of money took precedence over facilitating the circulation of water.

The Social Environment

The contradictions were glaring. The means of developing and controlling the physical environment increased, yet, as I have shown, environmental problems loomed larger than before. The same thing was happening in the social environment: the resources were greater, but so were the disharmonies. The dimensions of poverty seemed to increase. Like smallpox and yellow fever, violence threatened to break into mob rule or anarchy. Everyone saw the visible signs of success and failure all around, and everyone experienced the pressures of boom and collapse. For the rich and the poor, both vulnerable, these experiences intensified the sense of disorder and produced a yearning for order. Each struggled in his own way to make sense of his world.

The most common and perhaps easiest interpretation to make was frankly partisan. Property qualifications for voting and holding office were reduced, opening up roles for home owners and master mechanics who owned their shop and tools. Jefferson came to the presidency in 1801, and Baltimore voters, especially the mechanics, were his enthusiastic supporters (Democratic Republicans), while the state government and many members of the bar in Baltimore were firm Federalists, among them Samuel Chase, Luther Martin, James McHenry, Robert Goodloe Harper, and merchants Robert Oliver and Robert Gilmor. Political rhetoric was taken from national politics: the "war against property and rags versus houses and land."[55] The "rags" were inflationary notes issued by banks. Tension ran high during the "disasters" of the peace of Amiens (1801) and again in the doldrums of trade embargo (1807–9). Episodes of party feeling in Washington produced tremors in Baltimore, in particular, the impeach-

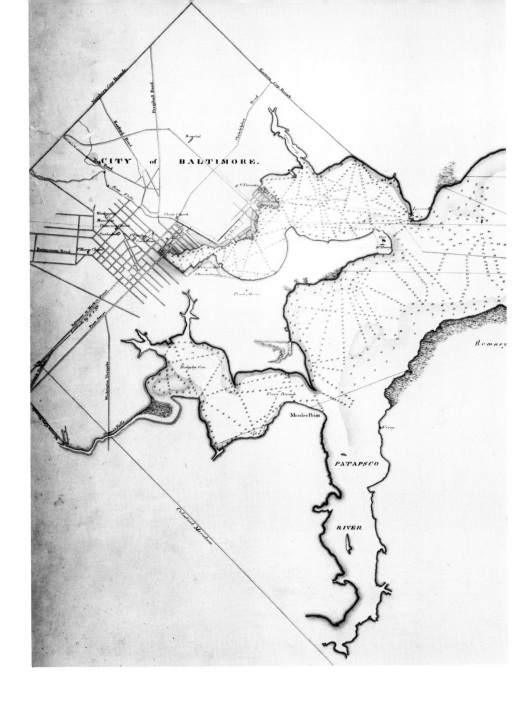

The Patapsco River survey by
Lewis Brantz for Marine
Insurance Companies (1819)
was performed on winter ice.
(Note that north is at the
upper left corner.)

ment of Samuel Chase, Federalist justice from Baltimore, and the alleged conspiracy of Aaron Burr. A mob of fifteen hundred "made up at Fells Point" set
out to hang Burr's associate, Blennerhasset, when he passed through town. (They
didn't find him.) Baltimore supported, indeed demanded, the embargo, but it
caused losses and unemployment, making the political splits more intense.
During that debate a mob burned Holland gin on Fells Point, while the crowd
made off with all it could from the gutters.[56] The journeymen cordwainers went
on strike, and the grand jury indicted three dozen. Even the Fourth of July was
a partisan affair. "A numerous and respectable company of Federal Gentlemen
from the city celebrated the day with great glee, harmony, and pleasure at
Govanstown," toasting "the Virtuous Minority," John Eager Howard, the governor, the judiciary, the navy, and the flag of Maryland. Meanwhile, the Democratic Republicans organized a spectacular parade from Fells Point through
Baltimore Street to Howard's Park. Each association, from the biscuit bakers to
the students of medicine, the barbers, and the cordwainers, had a workshop
drawn by horses. An eighteen-gun ship, the *Union*, saluted at the cross streets.

This plat, filed on 21 August 1818, illustrates a disputed section of the proposed opening of Pratt Street across the old docks. Rows of warehouses had been developed on the more recent docks below Pratt Street, but the frontage on High Street was still undeveloped. (Note that, due to the unusual orientation, Hughes Street, to the south, is at the top of the map.)

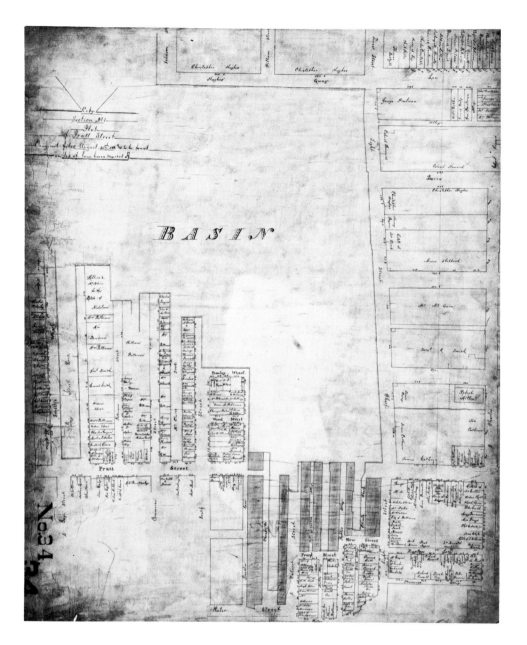

Republicans toasted the president and Congress, the fall of faction, universal suffrage, jury trial, "a free but pure press," American seamen, and "the independence of the poor, the security of the rich, the happiness of all."

The occasion was gay, but feelings ran deep. The trend toward war with England and the oncoming presidential election of 1812 touched off more sinister mob action in Baltimore. A press was destroyed, and the Federalist editor and his backers, including merchants Mark Pringle and George Winchester, were lynched. The mob stormed the jail, killed one, and dreadfully beat and abused eleven others.[57] Investigations were launched, and the violence drained away like a flash flood, but a certain tension remained through the summer. The Federalists urged an "association of all men of property, & all men of principle." As Ben Stoddert stated in a letter to McHenry, "Our Union is worth saving, so is civil liberty—so is the prosperity of those who possess it."[58]

The need to defend the city after the burning of Washington restored a degree of unity. "A view of the enemy has made the people's eyes sparkle. The word is Union."[59] The banks agreed to lend up to half a million dollars for the defense (actually $100,000 was borrowed), and the Committee of Vigilance and

Safety was broadly representative. Samuel Smith again took charge of defense.[60] Baltimoreans acquitted themselves splendidly and recovered their pride, but the legislature refused to grant the city funds for its defense or the right to tax itself to repay the defense loan. Instead, they sought to punish the city for the mob and for its Republicanism.

Year after year, the city failed to obtain adequate representation.[61] By the legislation of 1816 it was given two delegates in the legislature, while each county had four: "A fortieth part of the power of legislation, and a fifth, if not a fourth, of all the white persons,"[62] and half the value of real property in the state. Partisanship between factions in the city died down after the war, but resentment of the oppressive treatment of the legislature solidified. Niles, whose paper was read throughout the nation, directed frequent barbs at the Maryland state constitution, "the most uncouth thing of its sort that ever appeared."[63] He mourned the death of the state chancellor, Mr. Kilty,

who, it is said, is perhaps the only person in Maryland, who can readily decide what is the constitution of the state—which, originally composed of the very worst materials, has been tinkered over and over again so often. . . . Its most disgusting feature is, that it provides no way by which the people can destroy it and make another.[64]

Potentially united in the face of outside oppression, Baltimore became more and more divided in dealing with its own underclass of paupers. Pauperism was described as "a luxuriating plant yearly increasing in size and fruitfulness." Poverty was a crime, and the poor, especially the black poor, were frequently referred to as an infestation. Who were the poor? how many? where did they live? One can only piece together fragments of misery. About half the people admitted to the almshouse were recorded as suffering from acute diseases, and an inventory in a winter appeal for rags for bandages mentions numerous cases of frostbite and cuts or burns that had become infected or gangrenous. In 1806 the mayor sought to make provision for the protection and maintenance of "unfortunate helpless maniacs" who were appearing on the streets. In 1810 he noted a great increase of idle and wandering poor.[65] Individual cases of humanity were publicized, chiefly "women left with children and without husbands, and old men, both destitute and helpless—without work, and every year increasing." Among them, for example, was a poor family in a wretched upstairs tenement at the head of Frederick Street. The father, a rigger, and two sons had died. The fourteen-year-old was trying to provide for his mother and three smaller children by crabbing. A certain Thomas Paul died leaving seven children; the mother, living in Harrison Street, was making umbrellas.

From these and other fragments, patched together and dated, one cannot escape the conclusion that poverty had its rhythm. It was seasonal, as in earlier years, and its dimensions were sensitive to the ups and downs of trade and to the longer-period building cycles. Poverty was most intense in all its manifestations for several years after the Peace of Amiens, more briefly during the embargo and the war, and acutely in the five or six years after 1816. The *American*, in October 1817, seeing a depression deepen, an increase of rents, a high grain price, and winter setting in, commented, "Misery could not be exhibited in a more condense form than it is in the suburbs, lanes and alleys—the huts, hovels, and dens of Baltimore."[66]

Financial upheavals among the wealthy produced misery at the bottom of the heap. Bank runs occurred in June 1819. Revelations of embezzlement and speculation by James Buchanan, respected citizen and merchant, were part of a national scandal that broke the Baltimore branch of the Bank of the United States[67] and ruined Buchanan's partner, General Samuel Smith, who was bankrupted overnight and lost his Montebello estate.[68] By 1821, 350 persons had applied for insolvency.[69] In 1822 Niles calculated from the observatory pennants that half the ship owners and importers had failed within four years:

It is sickening to the heart to see the lists of persons who are published weekly in the Baltimore papers, as making application for the benefit of the insolvent laws of Maryland. The amount of debts due by them is enormous. . . . They who were a little while since the "tip of the ton" and residing in palaces, are thus engaged in settling their debts, and dragging many sober and discreet mechanics and tradesmen along with them.[70]

Manufacturers were reported "some of them at the lowest ebb, and others but heaps of mouldering ruins."[71] A woman and several children were in want, among hundreds laid off from the cotton mills. References were made to multitudes of arrivals, especially Irish, who flock to the town, to worn-out Negroes, and infant beggars.

I live in a part of the city particularly exposed to the interruptions and importunities of street beggars. . . . A new set lately appeared. Wounds, legless, eyeless, ague-shook visages, little flaxen-haired, dirty-faced apprentices to mendicity, young blackies greased to elbows gnawing on a bone. . . . To have every feeling of your soul harrowed up by a sight most shocking to humanity, age in rags, in want, in pain, homeless, friendless, penniless. To have this is unacceptable in our State, and an infinite inconvenience to its citizens.[72]

That writer, who ends by asking for enforcement of the vagrant laws, exposed the ambivalence of the leadership class toward poverty. When unemployment rose, new societies were formed: in 1792 a Corporation for the Relief of the Poor and Distressed of every Sect or Religious Denomination whatsoever; in 1804 the Friends of the Poor, who wanted a "permanent" solution;[73] and in 1822 a Society for the Prevention of Pauperism in Baltimore, P. E. Thomas, President.[74] Their interpretations of the problem, strongly influenced by English debates on the poor law and the Irish question, revolved around the moral value of work. They attempted to distinguish the deserving from the undeserving, the afflicted from the corrupt. Griffith, for example, a trustee for the poor, believed provision must be made for the afflicted

not only because it is commended by heaven and imposed on our feelings by nature, but because the title to superior wealth, when most legally acquired, might be shaken, if a state of suffering was permitted to arise, which by accumulation, in numbers or degree, might render doubtful the disadvantages of the savage state or the benefits of civilization.[75]

The inquiry of 1822 was sparked by rising costs of welfare. A report of the Society for the Prevention of Pauperism cited Thomas Malthus, recommending schools to deal with ignorance and regulations to restrict intemperance. The price of whisky had been cut by half, and domestic consumption nearly doubled since 1810. "Cheerfully conceding" the need for benevolence, the report focused, nevertheless, on the ethic of work: "Idleness is the very core of the disease."[76] The society feared a system of benevolence that might "nurse the crime," and posed the question

Whether the relief of some has not excited the sanguine, but unjustifiable expectations of others, and decoyed them from those industrious efforts they were compelled to make under the pressure of many necessities. . . . Such a stimulus seems to be absolutely necessary to promote the happiness of the great mass of mankind.[77]

Its lead was followed by the city council, who acknowledged "serious doubts, whether by legalizing poverty we do not hold out strong inducements for its increase."[78]

What kind of public policy results from a philosophy that asserts that poverty is a crime and that the misery of the poor promotes the happiness of the mass? The basic policy recommendations of the Society for the Prevention of Pauperism were accepted in 1822 by the mayor, the council, and the trustees for the poor: the expansion of institutions mixing relief with repression. They recommended the creation of a "house of industry" as part of a larger almshouse on a new site at Calverton, overlooking the Gwynns Falls. The trustees expected to accommodate eight hundred or nine hundred paupers. "Pauperism has always kept pace with the utmost efforts of philanthropy to relieve and cure it."[79] Development of the farm surrounding the almshouse would permit more strenuous enforcement of the vagrant and begging laws. Chronic drunkards, vagrants, and prostitutes could be forced to work off the costs of their keep.

This scheme was the most coherent formulation of a policy, but in practice it did not differ substantially from the policies of the previous twenty years, or the years following. It was merely one episode in the uneven growth of public institutions. The institutional population of Baltimore—jail, state penitentiary, almshouse, hospital—rose dramatically over a few years, but still amounted to only about 1 percent of the population. Just as with houses and warehouses, Baltimore in this period also pulled down its human warehouses and built greater. The new structures were "better appropriated to the use," they were monumental, and they were relatively isolated. The combined effects of their increased population, their walled isolation, the mixed feelings of taxpayers toward the inmates, and the political struggle between state and city meant that every reform degenerated immediately. In 1801, for example, legislation was passed to substitute a state penitentiary for the old wheelbarrow gangs on the roads. The criminal code was revised, eliminating the death penalty except for murder, rape, arson, or treason. Prisoners were set to work at weaving, brush making, oakum picking, and nailing, and the penitentiary was expected to pay its way, as well as to rehabilitate the criminals through labor. Numbers promptly rose from the 51 transferred from the roads in 1812 to the design capacity of

This T. H. Poppleton plat,
dated 1823, describes Baltimore
as it had enlarged in 1816.

360. They were mostly male, and although they are often described as "perfectly comfortable, quite contented, and having no symptoms of shame,"[80] mutinies and riots occurred every few years.

The new city jail housed a hundred, a much larger capacity than the old courthouse cellar, and it was designed to separate men from boys, witnesses from accused, and blacks from whites. The jailed blacks were chiefly presumed runaways or slaves lodged "for safekeeping" by their masters. Prisoners were issued wood, raw meat, and cornmeal, and made their own fires for cooking.[81] Half the white prisoners were there for small debts, while the insolvent laws offered a bankruptcy and trusteeship procedure for the rich.

The Maryland Hospital was built east of town by state loans and lotteries. It was owned by the city and leased back to the doctors who had initiated the plan. Maniacs and diseased persons were sent by the city at fixed rates for long-term care. The university's new hospital treated acute cases.

The catchall institution was always the almshouse. Its population had averaged 250 persons, but it doubled during the four years of depression, plus one hundred out-pensioners, or persons on home assistance. Such averages meant the reception of 1150 individuals in a year, rising to 3000 or even 4000. About a fifth were children. As their numbers rose, the costs rose, from $14,000 to $20,000 a year. However, the level of spending matched a small town like Lancaster, Pennsylvania, and bore no comparison with the other large seaboard cities; 1818 was the first year in which Baltimore's spending exceeded the amount spent for relief *before* the Revolution.[82]

Misery was still "condense," but the movement to prevent pauperism was perhaps not as fruitless as it might seem from the warehousing of the dependent. Doctors, teachers, editors, and clergy introduced ideas from many sources for helping the "deserving poor." Poor people were likely to be considered deserving if they were young and malleable, and the institutions were straightforwardly paternalistic. The Dispensary, an outpatient clinic and pharmacy on Chatham Street, in 1803 had 234 patients; by 1822 it had 6000. "The honest poor are dreadfully afraid of a doctor's bill." Dispensaries were later opened in Fells Point and Eutaw Street. The Savings Bank of Baltimore was organized in 1818 on models from Boston and Scotland. Active among the founders were Friends: Isaac Tyson, Evan Ellicott, and Moses Sheppard. The "industrious poor" were invited to save, and the rolls were occasionally purged of individuals too wealthy. The bank was mutually owned, that is, profits were distributed among the depositors, so that overall interest averaged 6 percent. Management remained in the hands of the founding trustees of the merchant class, and the funds were kept in the Farmers & Merchants Bank of Baltimore. Employers often opened accounts on behalf of their apprentices and employees, black and white, and oversaw their management. Employers such as James Mosher, a builder, participated in the establishment of an apprentices' library, brainchild of the city's booksellers.

The Sunday school movement was another new institution oriented to promoting literacy and a Protestant ethic of thrift, decency, self-reliance, temperance, and order. Its missionary effort was toward the children of the lower

class. By 1825 over 4000 were enrolled. Most of the full-time "free schools" were organized through churches and reflected a philosophy of noblesse oblige, or a responsibility of the fortunate for the children of misfortune. Saint Peter's Protestant Episcopal School in German Lane, endowed with ten thousand dollars by Jeremiah Yellott and James Corrie, was a model Lancastrian school of rigid mass discipline. A new African school was organized, associated with the African society of the Methodist Episcopal church. On Fells Point, St. Patrick's Church organized the first Catholic parish school. John McKim endowed a free school in Oldtown. At the Orphaline Charity School "thirty little innocents"—that is, girls—were fed, clothed, and instructed, and would be bound out as apprentices. The two philosophies of self-help and noblesse oblige were combined in the Pay Soup House, a kitchen opened in the hard winter of December 1819: cheap soup and bread tickets could be purchased by the working poor *or* purchased for individuals by their charitable patrons.

The Conscience of Baltimore

A city is a projection of society on the ground. The changes in the physical structure of Baltimore reflected the deep contradictions of American society: an economy based on war in a nation committed to the pursuit of happiness; a monument to the sober virtues of George Washington, built by public lottery; extremes of wealth in a republic of equals; the coexistence of slavery with an ethic of dignity through labor and craftsmanship; periodic unemployment absorbed by a workhouse where the idle poor would pay for their keep; a "want of good laws" felt in a nation "under a government so happy and free." All these ironies of human society could be seen in the new shape of Baltimore. From the windowed dome of a new and magnificent palace of commerce, seat of the banks, brokers, insurance companies, and the U.S. treasury agent, one might look west toward the dome of the new school of surgery; north toward that great dome of glory to God, set on a hill, and beyond it to the monument; northeast past a Greek temple of justice to the Tudor fortress of a jail, its gallows and whipping yard, and the factorylike penitentiary; or east over the new city block, the lumberyards, and shipyards. Snuggled around the Exchange were the elegant townhouses of several millionaires, the masts of their ships in the docks, and the back buildings of an alley called Squeeze Gut.

Elisha Tyson and Daniel Raymond, two men very different in temperament and style, made heroic attempts to resolve the contradictions of public policy toward the poor and the black. They were the conscience of Baltimore.

Tyson walked the Friend's tightrope between law and justice, in a society where the laws were, in Niles's words, "palpably unjust." His family recorded a rare account, as Tyson told it to them, of the tragic dimension of Maryland law. A man of Anne Arundel County came late one evening to Mr. Tyson. His master had promised him his freedom, provided he would pay $500 within six years. The slave had earned and paid his master half of the money, and the six years had not expired, yet he was about to be sold to Georgia. Tyson asked whether he had any receipts. The man had none. Any witness? None but the master's wife. "Then the law is against thee, and thou must submit. I can do nothing for thee." The man rose and clenched his fist to heaven. "I will die before the Georgia man shall have me." Then he melted into tears. "I cannot live away from my wife and children." Said Tyson, "This is no common man, he will do what he has resolved." Soon after, a man was found drowned in the basin. Tyson went to see the body. It was the same man.[83]

On other occasions, Tyson, the stalwart of the Protection Society, was able to obtain some legal point or some gain in public awareness. "Well knowing that all laws in a republican country are founded upon public opinion, his great object was to work a change in that regard." In 1812, Tyson obtained writs of habeas corpus for five blacks who had been arrested on suspicion of being escaped slaves, but had not been claimed by any master. Such persons, after languishing in jail for several months, were usually auctioned off by the state at the jail door to slavers to pay the jail fees. In this test case Judge John Scott released the five, and in 1817 the legislature acknowledged that unclaimed persons should be eventually released.[84] The 1817 laws also made it illegal to sell out of state persons who had only a term of years to serve. By this means "the jail was rid of the crowds of negroes with which it was heretofore infested," but the dealers created private jails. One night Tyson, informed that two boys and their mother, free blacks, were being held in one of these dens, went alone to the tavern and took the keys from the three men drinking there. "Shoot if thee dare," he said, "but thee dare not, coward as thou art, for well does thee know, that the gallows would be thy portion." He found six people chained in the cellar and released the woman's gags to hear her story. By waking up a judge and giving his personal bond, Tyson was able to have a constable remove the three free persons.[85] In all likelihood, this occurred at Slater's, on Pratt Street near Howard, just a block from Tyson's home and the Friends meetinghouse.

Tyson had always mistrusted the Maryland Colonization Society, because of the participation of slavers who sought ultimately to banish all free blacks, clamp down on slaves, and abolish all manumission. But a privateering incident brought him into collaboration with the colonizationists. A Colombian privateer commanded by that same Captain Chase of Baltimore (lately naturalized in Colombia) captured a Spanish slave ship returning from the coast of Africa to Havana with forty-two slaves. The captain selected eleven strong and able-bodied men for the service of the privateer, disposed of the rest in the West Indies, then made for Baltimore to be refitted. Although it was illegal to import slaves, the men appeared to be part of the crew and spoke no English. By the time they docked, Tyson, whose information system stirs admiration, had filed a petition for their freedom on the presumption that they were held involuntarily. They were brought to the jail for safekeeping. Elisha Tyson, Robert Goodloe Harper, and Dr. E. Ayres, agent of the African Colonization Society, together went through the legal maneuvers involving the president, the navy department, and the federal marshal in Baltimore. The chief justice of the city court decided he had to release the men, and they could go with whomever they wished. With much difficulty, Tyson located an interpreter. The Colombian captain managed to grab three boys, but ultimately eight were returned, "much emaciated, and reduced almost to a skeleton," to their hometowns and kin near Sugary.[86]

Where Elisha Tyson was a man of exceptional moral courage and perception, Daniel Raymond was a man of intellectual honesty and scathing tongue and pen. His pamphlet, *The Missouri Question*, expressed his position on slavery:

And can the idea be for a moment endured, that for countless ages this poisonous plant is to infest our soil, blasting as with mildew, the beautiful tree of liberty? Can we endure the thought that millions and millions of our fellow creatures for ages to come shall be born to drag out wretched lives of slavery! Shall we leave our posterity to grapple with this monster of iniquity, and possibly if not probably be finally overcome in the struggle? Or shall we not rather if it be possible, labour to eradicate it ourselves . . . ?[87]

Raymond opposed slavery, not only on moral grounds, but on the grounds of its practical consequences. "The footsteps of an angry God, are plainly visible throughout a state where slavery abounds."[88] His basic argument, much discussed, was the demographic experience of Maryland and the other slave states. He used census figures to show that slave populations grew faster than free black populations, and faster than the free white populations of slave states.

Raymond also believed that the colonizationists were deluding themselves. His pamphlet directly countered Harper's letter, published the year before, which described the manumitted as an "idle, vagabond, and thieving race" destined for degradation. Raymond claimed that the character of manumitted slaves tended to change in the course of one or two generations: "The industrious thrive and increase,—their offspring, accustomed to liberty, acquire the habits of the whites, and make equally as good citizens, that is, the laboring class. . . . The worthless come to naught."[89] Raymond belonged to the Colonization Society and expected it to do some good, but as a means of solving the problem of slavery in its massive dimension, it was chimerical. "The African race is effectually planted in this country, and will remain here until the last day. . . . They are here, and have as much right to remain here as the whites."[90] He favored encouraging manumission, and opposed extension of slavery to new states. "Diffusion is about as effectual a remedy for slavery as it would be for smallpox."[91]

But Raymond cut deeper into the contradictions, elaborating an interpretation of poverty relevant to both black and white. He disagreed fundamentally with Adam Smith and Thomas Malthus, and contrasted the peculiar conditions of the American economy with those of England and Ireland. He arrived at a thoroughly modern labor theory of value: "Labour is the cause, and the only cause of wealth."[92] As a lawyer, he defined a nation as a corporation or unity of all its citizens, and regarded national wealth as something quite different from individual wealth. Individual wealth or property is a capital or stock. But national wealth, Raymond said, is not an accumulation, but a productive capacity. The laws of property govern the distribution of the stock of wealth among a few individuals and families, who thereby control the product of all the earth and have the right to determine whether the rest of the people shall be allowed to labor and obtain any share of the product. "The rich and powerful have established a system, which has thrown all the property in the kingdom into the hands of a few; the necessary consequence of which is an immense number of paupers in the kingdom."[93] More astonishing, the rich managed to blame the paupers for their lack of industry and frugality:

If a man were to plant his field with trees, and then complain of the corn for not growing under them, it would not be more unreasonable. . . . The laws of justice, as well as the laws of the land, require the rich either to furnish the poor with labour, or support them without labour.[94]

If, indeed, pauperism was the consequence of an unequal division of property, the remedy was obvious: "such modification of the laws of a country, as shall produce a more equal division of property."[95] In Baltimore's interminable discussions of putting an end to poverty, this is what no one else dared to print. It was unpopular. Mathew Carey offered $500 to endow a chair of political economy for Raymond at the university, but received no reply from the doctors.

Raymond's ability to put his finger on numerous other contradictions of the economies of England and Ireland reveals close observation of events in Baltimore: "It is a singular fact, that while multitudes of people were starving; cargoes of potatoes were imported into Baltimore from Ireland, and sold for a fair profit. . . . There is food enough in the country, but it all belongs to a few."[96] His *Thoughts on Political Economy* must be considered the first comprehensive American theory of political economy. While he had much in common with Mathew Carey of Philadelphia, and Hezekiah Niles, in arguing tariff protection for manufacturers and opposing the paper credit system, Raymond was more coherent and systematic. Every argument recalls the viewpoint of a Baltimore resident and the intense conflicts of Baltimore in the depression years after 1818. Especially modern are his interpretations of war, public works, and monetary policy as stimulants to the economy, and the need in times of unemployment to force consumption to "tread hard upon the heels of production."[97]

The body politic like the natural body is liable to fall into a state of comparative lethargy and torpor. It then becomes necessary to arouse its dormant energies, by administering stimulants. The expenditure of public money, in public works, will often produce this effect.[98]

If, for example, the Susquehanna Canal—a live issue in Baltimore in 1820— could be built without diminishing the agricultural or manufacturing product of the country, it was worth doing regardless of the value of the completed structure. The banks he also regarded as a potential stimulant, but, unregulated and working on a wrong theory of wealth, they tended to store or hoard up wealth instead of forcing the money to circulate.

Every available shred of Raymond's work shows it to be the result of reflection upon Baltimore as a model of political economy and a mirror of the human condition. Baltimore provided the example of the effects of war on the economy. War stimulated industry by furnishing a demand for labor, "but as war cannot be permanent or lasting, that demand may be suddenly withdrawn, and then distress is produced. . . . All fluctuations are unfavourable to national wealth and happiness."

The entire network of men of ideas, as well as the whole apparatus of municipal leadership, met in an extraordinary moment of truth the night of 28 December 1819. Tyson, Harper, and Raymond, working together in spite of their differences, sought to demonstrate that although Maryland was counted among the slave states, Baltimore City did not favor the admission of Missouri as a slave state. According to custom, they advertised a public town meeting at the courthouse and solicited speakers. Mayor Johnson presided over a tense and prolonged session of two hundred of the "most respectable" men in Baltimore. Niles and Bishop Kemp took part in the committee, and several slave holders (John Hoffman and Thomas Kell among them) spoke for the resolution, "Resolved, That in the opinion of this meeting, the future admission of slavery into the states which may be hereafter formed, west of the Mississippi, ought to be prohibited by Congress." Daniel Raymond acted as secretary and wrote the memorial they agreed upon: "We know that *we are*, and we fear that our posterity *may be cursed* with slavery; but, as lovers of our country, we would not willingly see this evil extended."[99] Two thousand Baltimore citizens signed the petition within hours, and it was forwarded to Congress. Astonishment produced "a very strong effect" in the House of Representatives, but the issue was compromised. In Baltimore itself, the proslavery forces now became relatively quiet, and the number of slave dealers was reduced and "hid themselves in the very skirts of the city." In July 1821, advertisements headed "cash for negroes" were excluded from Baltimore newspapers, and a "dealer in and stealer of negroes for the southern market" was sent to the Maryland penitentiary for five years. Still the trade continued. In spite of the politicking and pamphleteering, in spite of the courage of Tyson and the logic of Raymond, the poisonous plant still grew. In that same month, this incident occurred on a public wharf in Baltimore—the black man's moment of truth.

Liberation: A miserable black man, brought from one of the lower counties of Maryland to Baltimore, and sold to a dealer in human flesh for transportation, cut his own throat and died at the moment when he was about to be delivered over to the blood-merchant, through his agent, a peace officer![100]

The Grand Civic Procession

1822–1837

And, as it is in prosperity, that success in one branch of business enlivens and benefits many others—so in adversity, a pressure upon any particular class of persons is felt by all. The connection is so intimate and delicate between the parties to a community, that every material or valuable part may be said to have a common profit or a common loss to enjoy, or suffer.[1]

A new prosperity, a new excitement, a new speculation took hold of Baltimore in the 1820s. It focused on capturing the western trade, and its most powerful city-making effect was the layout of the railroads. But no sooner had fundamental decisions been reached, resources mobilized, and the common profit glimpsed than adversity set in. "Pressure" began to be felt. In the '30s the city was again buffeted by flood and fire, epidemic disease and epidemic violence. Under pressure, the apparent harmony of the great civic celebrations of the '20s splintered into fears and hostilities of party, race, and class.

The city's energies from 1822 through 1836 were bent on "public improvements," based on a geopolitics peculiar to the time. Where in an earlier generation each person for himself had focused on his role in the international web of trade, now attention was directed to the national market, particularly the new trade beyond the Alleghenies. Baltimore's strategy was governed by rivalry with other American seaports for this trade, and its survival depended on collective effort.

In any scheme for heavy hauling, vertical movement requires far more energy than forward motion. Topography is, therefore, a crucial factor governing the costs, the feasibility, and the relative attractiveness of various routes and modes of transport. This generation of Baltimoreans, consequently, became keenly aware of the lay of the land, and placed value on accurate leveling, that is, the topographical survey, which they had till now neglected.

From the general topography of the United States, George Washington had discerned that the prime trans-Allegheny routes must be through the valleys of the Potomac and the Susquehanna rivers, and corporations had been organized in Maryland for the improvement of their navigation as early as the 1780s. The other great routes would be the Ohio-Mississippi system and the Erie-Mohawk-Hudson route. As steamboat navigation developed on the Ohio, the Mississippi, and the Hudson, and as the state of New York undertook the Erie Canal, New Orleans and New York City grew and prospered. Watching them, Philadelphia and Baltimore and the legislatures of Maryland and Pennsylvania were able to agree that the Susquehanna and the Potomac routes must be developed. Their collaboration had its ups and downs, but Baltimore's problem remained—to funnel the trade of the Susquehanna and the Potomac to itself, in competition with Philadelphia and the federal city. Throughout the period, these twin objectives were kept firmly in mind.

In 1820 Robert Mills published, by subscription of the city's traditional patrons—Harper, Carroll, Caton, Patterson, Oliver, and others—a grand scheme for opening a water communication from the city to the Potomac and Susquehanna rivers. The Potomac River would feed water from above Harper's Ferry (310 feet above tide) across a summit to the Susquehanna River at Conewago Falls (160 feet). From the summit, between Westminster and Gettysburg, another canal would branch toward Baltimore, the great tidewater port of the whole network. "Baltimore is destined to become the emporium of the eastern section of the union—provided proper exertions are made to secure the advantages offered. . . . Shall we remain passive spectators? . . . Shall our energies sleep?"[2] The proper exertions Mills estimated at an appalling $2 million, and the problem that he had so brilliantly integrated was again split in two: the state appointed two sets of commissioners, one for the navigation from Baltimore to the Susquehanna, and one for the navigation from Baltimore to the Potomac. In 1823 they published their reports. The proposed million-dollar connection to Conewago was a thirty-six-mile system of canals with 335 vertical feet of locks.[3] Again the expense "created a degree of alarm in the people."[4] Therefore, the city of Baltimore appointed still another set of commissioners to devise a cheaper plan. Early in 1825 this set recommended that a "stillwater" navigation go from Port Deposit to Havre de Grace as already improved, then to Swan Creek, with a double row of piling to protect the passage against wind and waves of the bay, and then to Baltimore by "through cuts" across the necks of land, with no locks. "The trade of the Susquehanna is the great prize for which the cities of Philadelphia and Baltimore are calling into requisition all their talents and ingenuity to secure. . . . But they appear to be influenced by very different views as to the best means."[5]

The Philadelphians were now concentrating on the Chesapeake and Delaware Canal "for the exclusive accommodation of themselves," while Baltimoreans were "straining every nerve" to improve the upstream navigation of the Susquehanna. They invested $50,000. Meanwhile, the Maryland legislature, to the rage of Baltimore, committed itself to the construction of the Chesapeake and Ohio Canal along the left bank of the Potomac, from Georgetown to Harper's Ferry and on to Cumberland. To pacify Baltimore, a "cross-cut" or extension, known as the Maryland Canal, would come to Baltimore from Georgetown. The surveys for a direct cut from Harper's Ferry to Baltimore proved unfavorable, and even the prospects for the cross-cut were discouraging. Particularly devastating was the 1826 report of General Simon Bernard of the U.S. Army Board of Engineers on Internal Improvements. Meanwhile, Pennsylvania had already begun its expensive system of state works, combining canals with inclined planes.

This view of the Thomas Viaduct by Michel Chevalier (ca. 1834) shows the B&O Railroad as it crossed the Patapsco River.

Caught in the squeeze play between Philadelphia and Georgetown, Baltimoreans had visions of grass growing in the streets. But through the imagination of Evan Thomas, who had seen an English mining railroad, and his influential brother, Philip Thomas, Baltimore resorted to a scheme that turned out to be the wave of the future: "The railroad was seized upon by the citizens of Baltimore as the very thing to redeem them from their embarrassments, and restore them to their original rights and inheritance."[6] At a public meeting in February 1827, William Patterson presiding, a committee of twenty-five was created to contemplate a railroad. It supported the canal to the Susquehanna, but looked toward the "immense commerce which lies within our grasp to the West."[7] The members of this committee were identified with the earlier plans; many were Mills's subscribers in 1820 or commissioners for the Susquehanna projects.

Within a few weeks, the Baltimore and Ohio Railroad was incorporated by the legislature; its charter was modeled on the turnpike charters. While the legislature granted half a million dollars for the Chesapeake and Ohio Canal and another half million for the Susquehanna Canal, Baltimore closed ranks behind the railroad. The city council agreed to take half a million dollars of Baltimore and Ohio Railroad stock. Among the private backers were Alexander Brown, Robert Oliver, Philip Thomas, and William Patterson. They expected the venture to turn a profit, but more important, they expected it to promote their merchant trade: "The treasures of three millions of enterprising people will flow into your lap, and Baltimore will yet become the first city of the union."[8] The backers sought the best technical advice they could get. The U.S. Army engineers were asked to do the surveys, and the board of engineers functioning in April 1828 included Dr. William Howard (a son of John Eager Howard), Lieutenant Colonel Stephen Long, Captain William Gibbs McNeil, Isaac Trimble, and George Washington Whistler. Jonathan Knight, a Friend and graduate of West Point, was particularly requested; he, Whistler, and Ross Winans were sent to England to examine the state of the art. As soon as Baltimore promoters grasped the new technology, they applied it to the twin goal, and a railroad to the Susquehanna was promptly incorporated. "They knew well their points of attack. The Ohio river and the Susquehanna, were to be made tributary."[9]

The Railroad at Home

Baltimore citizens found it easy to agree on overall railroad strategy. The first twelve miles of the B&O would follow the Patapsco valley, an easy grade, to Ellicott's mills, the nearest major freight source, and thence to Harper's Ferry and Cumberland, the coal region. But they found it impossible to be decisive about the railroad's course into and through the city of Baltimore. Justification for the enormous investment lay in the expectation of powerful effects on commerce and property values. The railroad itself was the basis for all land speculation in this era of city building, and these rich benefits were the stakes in the struggles of the generation. As John Latrobe described it later, each person saw the railroad as "the rose of a vast watering pot" that would irrigate his property.[10] From April to September 1828, the major problem for the engineers was the manner in which the railroad should be connected with the city of Baltimore. On 28 May, the board of directors ordered the engineers to find the route "best calculated to distribute the trade throughout the town as now improved."[11] This represented an abandonment of any notion of long-range planning and an attempt to soothe the agitation of vested interests in the several parts of town. From this directive "the Board of Engineers have experienced great relief."[12] By 23 June, they had gone far enough with their surveys and developed certain principles of location, so that the decision could be reached on where and at what elevation to lay the first stone, on the Fourth of July.

Because the bulkier traffic for many years would be descending toward Baltimore, the main line must avoid uphill grades toward the town. The railroad would be horse drawn at first, but it would be expensively built, to avoid inclined planes and grades greater than a steam engine might manage. In a very broken landscape, the critical levels to be determined were the most favorable passes across the ridge (140 feet) dividing the waters of the Gwynns Falls from those of the Patapsco, across the broad valley of Gadsby's Run (20 feet), and across the Jones Falls. "If the level be *low*, the quantity of excavation will be greatly increased; on the other hand, if the level be *high*, the cost of the embankments and bridges will become very formidable."[13] The engineers also assumed that the main line should be "remote from places of bustle and business." Any thickly settled street, such as Pratt Street or Baltimore Street, would be "utterly inadmissible." The controversy was skirted by choosing an elevation of 66 feet, which would leave options open to enter Baltimore by any of several routes, to serve the several parts of town and to approach tidewater at nearly any point without steep grades. In September, the engineers proposed that the main line come in north of the more improved parts of town, from a point on Lexington Street and Chatsworth Run.[14] Branch lines would connect the main depots outside the town with warehouses and wharves in the city near tidewater. In May 1829, James Carroll offered the Mount Clare site, a "hickory hill" 19 feet above the level of the road, and it was decided that it would fit into the conception of a main line running north of the town. Mount Clare proved well situated for entry of the line to Washington, under construction by 1833.

Exactly the same set of problems was now posed for the location of the Baltimore and Susquehanna Railroad. McNeill and Whistler were transferred by the army in June 1829 to make surveys for the B&S. Their strategy of keeping options open was the same. By late August the company and the city council agreed that the B&S would commence at the north boundary near the turnpike gate west of the Jones Falls (where the Pennsylvania Railroad produce terminal still is), at an elevation of ninety feet above tide. "From this commanding posi-

After the crucial decision in 1831 to run the B&O Railroad through Pratt Street, horse carts, wagons, streetcars, trains, and cabs all contested for street space near the docks.

tion the whole city is overlooked, and the railroad may be carried on in any direction."[15] The alternatives were much the same as those proposed for the B&O, and they represented an effort to conciliate all parts of the city. Winchester's argument shows how the rhetoric of competitive development of the natural advantages of the various regions of the nation reechoed as a mini-problem in the development of the various parts of the city: "By these various approaches to the city, each portion of it will derive a peculiar advantage from that which reflects a general benefit upon the whole."[16] In 1830 the B&S obtained three acres for a city depot on Calvert Street, and later prepared "a costly viaduct" over the Jones Falls from Belvidere Street. This was the Madison Street viaduct.

Once those tentative decisions were reached on main lines and main depots, a clamor arose for branches to wharves and warehouses. "Everybody wanted it at his alley gate."[17] The city council's priorities were to give value to the city's two undeveloped properties at the city dock east of the mouth of the Jones

Falls and the old almshouse site near Biddle and Madison streets and to insure connections between the railroads at these two points. Early in 1831 the council authorized branch lines along Pratt, Fremont, Saratoga, Chatsworth, and Biddle streets, so that the B&O could run branches from Mount Clare to the two city properties. Virtually all the main streets of Baltimore were conceived as railway branches by one railroad or the other, and in December, at the request of Howard Street property owners, the state legislature acted to force the city council to approve a branch track in any street where a majority of property owners desired it. It was becoming apparent that, regardless of the original conception, the Pratt Street rail line was going to be a major connecting link, the city's streets of "bustle and business" were going to have freight cars in them, and the almshouse site would not become a union depot.

The debate over the railway in Pratt Street was resumed in 1834 and agitated feverishly in March 1835, as council members James Carroll and James Peregoy tried to have it removed. Their discussions resound with appeals to unemployed draymen, laborers, and mechanics. "The rail tracks, we believe, do now infringe the right of property, and the right of labor."[18] At least 2,000 persons signed petitions, including hundreds of draymen, many Irish. In fact, underlying this split was the old issue as to which part of town would profit. The B&S was seen as a measure favoring East Baltimore, and the B&O as a measure favoring West Baltimore.

If the trade acquired by these improvements is to increase the size of the town, all parts ought equally to enjoy the advantages which nature has given them. This can only be accomplished by terminating the B&O railroad at a distance from tide water in the west, and the Susquehanna railroad at a distance from the tide water in the east. Then will the labouring classes find employment in conveying the trade through your streets.[19]

The new development that actually triggered the alarm was the creation of the Baltimore and Port Deposit Railroad (later part of the Philadelphia, Wilmington, and Baltimore). The Canton Company had a site for the B&PD depot, and was planning to join all three railroads at a great tidewater terminal outside the eastern city limit on Boston Street. Vested interests in the city basin, as well as property owners in the southwest and northeast of town, felt threatened by this development in the southeast.

The agitation waned, and the council allowed the B&PD to run a branch from Canton along Fleet Street to the city dock. The basic railway entries into the city were now fixed. Later generations would have to grapple with the problems of developing efficient waterside terminals, cross-town hauls, and the mutual accommodation of trains, wagons, pedestrians, and drainage in "the streets of bustle."

By the end of 1835 the Baltimore and Susquehanna was operating horsecars to Timonium. This section was already obsolete. Ill-adapted British locomotives ran the next twenty-eight miles to Hise's mill, and the roadbed was nearly completed to York, Pennsylvania. An eight-mile side branch ran horsecars through the Green Spring Valley to Reisterstown Road and Owings Mills. The

Port Deposit Railway operated between Canton and Wilmington with a steam ferry crossing at the Susquehanna, and the B&O ran to Washington and eighty-two miles up the Potomac valley to Harper's Ferry. Turnpikes were extended or rebuilt as feeders to the railroad. New post offices were established in western Maryland, and the population of the tributary region increased. The city that had sent its engineers to study English track and imported English engines was now exporting locomotives to Leipzig and receiving delegations of Austrian and French engineers to borrow its know-how. The speed of movement and communication had taken a dramatic leap in fifteen years, with the development of the railroad, the clipper, and the steamboat. By 1835 Baltimore was only 2 hours from Washington and 9½ hours from Philadelphia. Letters came back answered from Norfolk in 41 hours and Jamaica in 37 days.

At this point, the city closed ranks again, fearing that in the economic pressure Baltimore would be outdistanced. "Your day of prosperity is gliding by, and the streams of your power are stealing from you. Is it not time that Baltimore was at work?—Not to make piddling efforts to creep ten miles and then rest."[20] John Pendleton Kennedy published three letters from "a man of the times" in the *American*, exhorting citizens to make a new effort to reach the Ohio River in three years. His geopolitics are reminiscent of William Howard and Robert Mills in their plans for roads and canals. "Baltimore should imitate the spider; spread her lines towards every point of the compass, and lodge in the centre of them."[21] Baltimore must find $3 million, Kennedy argued, the state legislature $3 million, and Pittsburgh and Wheeling must find $1 million each. Within the year, the legislature appropriated $8 million to finance the advance of the C&O Canal and the cross-cut canal. And Baltimore City subscribed $3 million to the B&O to reach Cumberland.

The enormous city-making potential of the railroad, and, therefore, its potential for land speculation, was illustrated at Canton, probably the nation's earliest, largest, and most successful industrial park. In 1830 three New Yorkers, including Peter Cooper, formed a corporation and acquired O'Donnel's 2500-acre estate for $320,000. It was known as Canton because of the profitable China venture that had allowed him to acquire the land and plant his peach trees. The Canton Company lands formed a suburban tract a third the size of Baltimore, astride the city limits. "All their privileges, appurtenances and energies, also, form a part of the capacity of the whole city, so that their destiny being inseparably interwoven, must rise or fall together."[22] Peter Cooper salvaged the operation from the two other speculators, who disappeared. His plan, which bears the mark of William Gwynn, was elaborate, and the kingpin was the tidewater freight depot for the several railroads, just outside the city limits. These depots, as shown on the survey and plat laid out by Caspar Weaver (once superintendent of construction for the B&O), would also provide the critical junction of the several lines. By means of the B&O, the Susquehanna, and the Port Deposit railroads, they calculated that Baltimore would become a great market for coal and iron and other heavy and bulky products, which would take up the whole "Canton Sea Shore." The waterfront was to be commercial and industrial, the landward lots residential. Among the early lots sold were waterfronts between

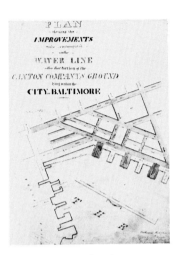

This rendering details contemplated improvements to Canton Company holdings at the waterfront, as projected on 17 March 1833.

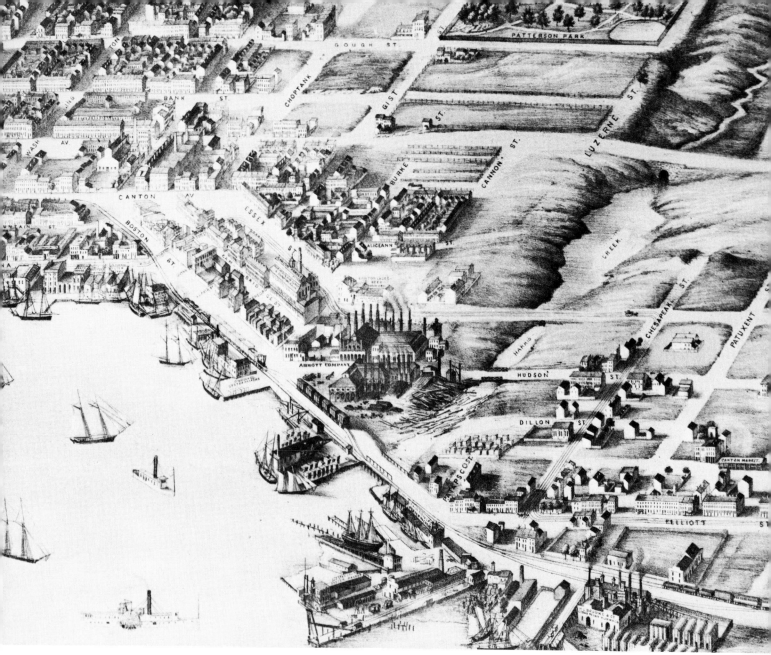

The Sachse bird's-eye view reflects Canton in 1869. Boston Street parallels the waterfront and Patterson Park is on the north. Harris Creek is on the east and the Abbot Rolling Mills are at the mouth of the creek.

the city and Harris Creek—seven warehouses to a New Yorker, sites for a steam sawmill, a steam forge and trip hammer works, and a mechanics' shop to operate by steam power. Cooper created the steam ironworks himself, then sold them to Horace Abbott.

The company contrived to raise capital from the sale of lots in order to build the public improvements that would give value to the land. The block size Weaver selected was based on New York City, with avenues 70 feet wide, streets 60 feet, blocks 458 x 204 feet, or 10 to the mile north and south and 20 to the mile east and west. This produced a favorable ratio of two-thirds of the land saleable and one-third in street area. In 1833 the company sold off 200 lots (20 x 60) averaging $100, and retained the ground rents. It spent the money leveling, filling, opening streets, and building wharves. In 1835, about the time Baltimore City subscribed its $3 million for the B&O, there was considerable speculation in Canton stock in Boston, and lots were sold averaging $350 each, the highest along Boston Street running up to $875.

Similar planning initiative was shown in the western part of town. James

Carroll, nephew and heir of barrister Charles Carroll, offered Mount Clare depot site to the railroad. He carried on a debate with the railroad over the viaduct at the Gwynns Falls; he claimed it was angled in such a way as to disturb the normal flow of the stream and injure his millrace. In addition to several mills, he leased concessions for brick clay on the low lands surrounding his mansion on the hill. The most important was to Jameson, for brick to build a shot tower. When James Carroll died, his heir, the second James Carroll, through an act of the legislature, changed the Poppleton plat of streets and alleys on his entire one hundred acres, bounded by the B&O Railroad, the western city limits, and Washington Boulevard. The new layout was designed to accommodate the street plan to the B&O Railroad line and expected future development along the railroad and Spring Garden waterfront. This is further evidence of the fact that the B&O Railroad was laid out with a sensitivity to topographic levels that had not governed Poppleton's plat, the achievement of the last generation.

The city-building style of this era was captured in John Pendleton Kennedy's satire of 1840, in which he described the growth of the village of Quodlibet. The scheme of Nicodemus Handy, cashier of the Copperplate Bank, can be interpreted as a combination of operations of Evan Ellicott's Union Bank and the Canton Company. As Mr. Handy said, "We must all make our fortunes."

We start comparatively with nothing, I may say, speaking for myself—absolutely with nothing. We shall make a large issue of paper, predicated upon the deposites; we shall accommodate every body, as the secretary desires—of course not forgetting our friends, and more particularly ourselves:—we shall pay, in this way, our stock purchases.—You may run up a square of warehouses on the Basin; I will join you as a partner in the transaction, give you the plan of operations, furnish architectural models, supply the funds, et cetera, et cetera. We will sell out the buildings at a hundred per cent advance before they are finished; Fog here will be the purchaser. We have then only to advertise in the papers this extraordinary rise of property in Quodlibet— procure a map to be made of our city; get it lithographed, and immediately sell the lots on the Exchange of New York at a most unprecedented valuation. My dear sir, I have just bought a hundred acres of land adjoining the Borough, with an eye to this very speculation.[23]

Speculation was not limited to individuals or private corporations. It became the strategy of the public corporation. Since the property tax was the only substantial local tax, and since nearly all property except street beds was privately held, the prime goal of the city council was to protect and enhance the value of individually held property. The objective of the town as a corporation was to make collective improvements. Only insofar as it succeeded in creating private property values could it increase the taxable "basis" or capacity of the corporation to do more. Any distinction between public and private enterprise was meaningless, although there was continual debate and litigation over whether the costs and benefits of a particular improvement were equitably shared among individuals.

Since the objective of improvements was to increase property value in the future, it seemed logical to postpone costs until those benefits could be realized. As individuals might borrow (or sell in advance) in order to build, so the corporation mortgaged the city. In 1827 Mayor Jacob Small, himself a builder, argued that the present holders of property in the city were heavily taxed. They were bearing the expenses of numerous improvements, the costs of the war, the interest on the city debt, and the sinking fund to diminish the principal; "under all these circumstances it may appear wise and equitable to lighten their burdens by the expedient proposed, and to transfer a portion of the load to their successors."[24] The rising value of property in the city would make it easy for the successor generation to discharge the debt, and meanwhile, taxes could be reduced by "at least one per cent."

Kennedy took the same position in his 1836 pamphlet urging the swift completion of the B&O to Wheeling: "It must be completed, no matter at what cost. The city has credit, and that resource must be used liberally:—the present generation are able to pay interest; let the next generation pay the principal."[25] He figured that an investment of $3 million in B&O stock, at 3.5 percent interest would mean paying $100,000 interest a year, or a dollar a head, and would double city property value. Between 1828 and 1844 the city increased its debt tenfold. Like any developing nation that invests borrowed money, the city began to run high debt-service costs. From 1835 on, interest on loans represented between a third and a half of the net annual outlay of the city.[26] The state also accumulated a very large debt for public works, "under the pressure of which the credit of the state reeled and tottered," and it imposed a property tax.

Meanwhile, Baltimore was slow to capitalize on the earlier increases of property values because of constraints by the legislature, always controlled by the large land holders. Only in 1831 was the city allowed to extend the line of direct taxation to include the belt that had been improved or developed since the line was fixed in 1817. "Ripening" as the city grew outward, this property had increased in value. By the act that made it taxable, the legislature put a ceiling on the total amount of taxes the city could collect each year ($220,000) and a ceiling on the total amount that it could borrow ($1.1 million). In 1834 Baltimore was finally allowed to reassess all property for the first time since 1813. The results were spectacular. The taxable basis increased more than tenfold—from $4 million to $43 million—and it was possible to reduce the *rate* of taxation from $4.78 to 0.67 on $100.[27] State restrictions on city finance and city improvements, and state manipulation of the great public works of national significance exasperated Baltimoreans throughout the years 1822 to 1837. Baltimore still had only two representatives in the legislature. "Country gentlemen have had, always, in all countries, a most preposterous fear of city influence, accompanied with a most insatiable desire to make the cities contribute, without return, to the prosperity of the country."[28]

Nonimprovement

Since canals and railroads were the priority of the generation, they diverted resources from other local improvements. A large number of contemplated projects were postponed or reduced in scope. They form an intricate jigsaw of expectations in the development of property values. When the jigsaw puzzle is pieced together, one can discern the perennial problems of the hydrologic system. Residential expansion of the city on the east and the west flanks gave the development problems of Harford Run and Chatsworth Run, respectively, greater importance in this period than those of the Jones Falls. Improvements to the Jones Falls and the water supply were among the projects contemplated and then postponed for a generation.

A severe drought, at its worst in 1826, made the deficiencies of the water company apparent, because the supplemental wells dried up or their pollution became more noticeable. The council's Water Committee of 1829, seeing that neither Fells Point, and most of Oldtown, nor the improving northwest was supplied, and that the quality had deteriorated to "a muddy substitute," enlisted the volunteer help of Captain Lewis Brantz. The committee recommended a million-dollar program equal to the city's total debt ceiling. They estimated that the Gwynns Falls, if tapped at Calverton mills, would serve half a million people, but opposition came from the ten mills downstream. An alternative was to acquire the Hockley mill on the Patapsco River. Another was to acquire Tyson's millrace, three miles out on the Jones Falls, along with ten mills downstream from it.[29] Under the threat of purchase or competition by the city, the water company made some effort to expand. It stayed with the Jones Falls supply, but simply bought the Salisbury mill, the next one upstream.

A succession of serious fires revived the issue, and in 1835 a new council committee recommended buying out the water company. "Experience has shown what indeed might have been foreseen . . . ; it could not be expected that a private corporation would consult the public good when the benefit of the community could only be had by the sacrifice of Corporate interests."[30] Municipal acquisition was also proposed for the gas company and the B&O Railroad. It was part of the nationwide agitation of the Jackson era against the "money power" and against monopolies in banking. The delightful feature of the water proposal was that "it requires no money, but only the issue of a stock."[31] The half million dollars in corporation stock would bear 5 percent interest and be paid off over ten years from water rents on all improved properties proportionate to the front footage of the lots. The plan did not, however, face the basic question of how to expand the system, and an engineer, John Randel, was next employed to make a topographic and hydrologic survey and estimate the investment required for an adequate future supply. The progress of leveling experience for locating canals and railroads and the new sensitivity of Baltimore leaders to topographical questions made possible a clear evaluation of the alternatives. Randel's recommendation to go to the Great Gunpowder Falls is the one adopted several generations later. Neither the Gwynns Falls nor the Jones Falls, he stated, could be relied on in a dry season.[32] Nevertheless, the high cost of new investment plus the purchase price of the old works stymied the program, and the council scrapped the entire survey.

New flood-control plans were introduced every time the water rose in the Jones Falls. The Mills plan to redevelop the lower falls and the Latrobe plan to divert the creek into Herring Run had been set aside as too costly. All that was accomplished was an ordinance requiring adjoining property owners to build walls along the falls.[33] After a freshet in 1831, a council committee suggested diverting the Jones Falls west to strike Chatsworth Run and flow into Spring

Garden. Nothing was done. In July 1837, the rampageous stream drowned seventeen persons, carried away its stone walls, and washed out most of the mill dams. "All the scenes of devastation of the former freshet of 1817 were again repeated; with this difference, that the city, being now larger, and more improved, the destruction of life and property was far greater. . . . At our house the water was 18 inches deep in the dining room."[34]

In the valley of Harford Run one sees the intricate relationship of the various improvements, as well as the limited approach to hydrologic problems. The mouth of the stream was slowly developed by filling the swampy cove to form a "city block." The wash from Hampstead Hill was diverted from Harford Run into Ann Street, east of Fells Point. By 1824 a "bold shore" had been made around the cove, and French drains were made in Eden and Bank streets, with the "happiest effects" in the view of the health commissioners. In the mid '30s, fill continued east of Harford Run as the easiest way to dispose of one hundred thousand tons of mud from dredging a seventeen foot channel in the harbor to implement the Brantz plan. The city continued to press the President Street site upon the railroad companies. (It eventually became the depot of the Philadelphia, Wilmington, and Baltimore Railroad.) Meanwhile between Baltimore Street and Wilks Street (Eastern Avenue), Eden Street was filled, and Harford Run itself was walled in as a canal or drain, known as Harford Street, now Central Avenue. It was tunneled—that is, covered over—at major cross streets. In this way, Oldtown and Fells Point were soldered together.

But each local improvement produced unforeseen consequences. In his state-of-the-city message of January 1823, the mayor attributed current complaints of sedimentation at the foot of Ann and Washington streets

to the want of foresight in having imprudently collected into Ann Street . . . all the waters of the surrounding hills, thereby producing a torrent sweeping by its impetuosity thousands of loads of sand and gravel into the boldest and deepest and consequently most valuable part of our Harbor.[35]

New gullies and washings continued, and in 1828 the affected wharf owners were suing the city for damages.

The problem on the west side of town was much the same, involving the drainage of Chatsworth Run from the vicinity of Biddle Street and George Street. In the early '20s wood bridges were built across it, as at Mulberry Street, and, like Harford Run, the stream was confined in walls. In its lower course a causeway was developed north of Three-Pronged Branch from Ostend Street in the line of Ridgely Street. They began covering the run in 1827. The extension and regrading of streets on the west side allowed the city to spread across the valley of Chatsworth Run onto the high ground of west Baltimore. Of greatest importance were the westward extension of Fayette, Baltimore, and Lexington streets and the northward extension of Division and Pine streets. The area just north of St. Mary's Seminary was developing rapidly. The seminary itself subdivided and sold off a substantial piece of property in 1833. Numerous street openings were associated with the subdivision of G. W. Moore's estate. Part of the almshouse property was at last taken for the Bolton depot of the Susquehanna Railroad, and the rest was laid out into lots.

The peripheral growth of the city produced, as always, strains at the center. Congestion increased in the central parts of Baltimore and Oldtown, and new thoroughfares were put through. With Pratt Street under construction, the opening of Lombard Street became the chief controversy. German Street was widened, and the buildings were moved. Ruxton Lane, the focus of the cholera epidemic of 1832, was widened as a slum clearance operation. Hillen Street was carried across the Jones Falls to connect Oldtown and Bel Air Market with the center. As the railroad and the water company expanded, Madison Street was opened, and a viaduct built east of Aisquith Street.

B altimore's economy grew more complex, interconnected, and well buffered. The shape it took in the '20s defined its structure till the Civil War. Its successes vindicated the "American system" promoted so energetically by McKim, Patterson, Niles, and Raymond in the early years of the century. As they had projected, commerce and manufacturing were not rival forms of enterprise any more, but woven together. By 1827 Baltimore no longer traded primarily in reexports; far more substantial were the home-grown and home-processed materials of the region and impressive quantities of local manufactures. The protective tariff had succeeded in nursing new industries that now supplied the American market more cheaply and were beginning to compete in the world market. In one week, twelve thousand chairs of Baltimore manufacture were shipped to South America, and a single ship cleared with $160,000 worth of Baltimore-made cotton goods. The heavy investments in transportation had given Baltimore an exceptional efficiency for several lines of reciprocal trade. Costs were lower and service better because of the reliable return cargoes. For example, in spite of the rise of New York in foreign trade, Baltimore merchants retained a major share of American imports of Brazilian coffee by exporting the flour of the Baltimore region, selected for its good keeping quality for the Brazilian market. Baltimore's exports to Brazil and Chile grew to dimensions rivaling its exports to Liverpool and Bremen. Baltimore and Bremen merchants, linked in family, and social clubs, such as the Concordia, operated a reciprocal trade: they took tobacco into Bremen and brought German immigrants to Baltimore.

The excellence and speed of Baltimore-built vessels contributed to the growth of trade. Coffee and wheat were carried in a coffee fleet built and owned in Baltimore by Hugh Jenkins, Thomas Pierce, and William Whitridge. Even the vessels were exported. "A beautiful and powerful ship, of 64 guns, built at Baltimore by Mr. Beacham, completely fitted, has sailed for Brazil, to serve the emperor."[36] Tied in with shipbuilding was the manufacture of cotton duck for sails. Charles Crooks, Jr., and his brother were employing fifty families (two hundred persons) on a $500 to $600 payroll, in French Street, Oldtown. Baltimore shipowners and captains testified to their canvas. The navy in 1826 ordered a supply for sails of the *Constellation*. In 1828 Baltimore profited from labor stoppages in the rival mills of Paterson, New Jersey, and the Baltimore mills became a national monopoly and a principal world supplier.

Creations in the Back Shops

This 1924 photograph records Mount Vernon Mill No. 1, a cotton mill.

Cotton duck was only one of several products in this line, and the cotton mills represented a new scale of employment and a much greater value added than the grist mill operations they replaced. Good mill sites with a developed mill race and machinery were rather easily converted from flour to weaving, sawing, or paper making. The cotton mills were, however, sensitive to the business cycle in their capital valuation and the income they generated. The Warren factory, for example, cost $180,000 to build and sold in 1820 for one-sixth the value, but by 1825 had again expanded and was employing nine hundred persons. It produced the first American calicoes finished from first to last in one establishment. It was typical of seven or eight that were incorporated in this period; others were still family owned or partnerships. The village of eight two-story stone dwellings at Warren, since inundated by Loch Raven reservoir, was one of the first of several dozen such villages, strung out along the streams of the Baltimore region in New England mill-town style. When a fire destroyed the calico printing works at Warren in 1830, the flour mill at Rockland was converted into a calico printing factory.

Experiments with steam became more significant. Besides Crooks's mill, other important steam-powered firms were a sugar refinery, a flour mill, two woolen factories, two planing and grooving mills, a glass-cutting operation, a plaster mill, and a mill for grinding chocolate, ginger, mustard, and castor oil.[37] In all these lines of work, the steam-powered factories competed with other large firms operated by water power or even, as in rope making, by horse power. Foundries in Baltimore evolved from blacksmith work, ship fitting, and block making to supplying machinery for the first railroads and steamships. Charles Reeder built a steam dredge for the harbor. Canton iron works produced walking beams for steam engines. Stockton and Stokes had a hundred hands building railroad coaches.

The new chemical industries employed fewer people, but were innovators and were linked to other new metallurgical and mechanical industries. McKim, Sims & Co. made alum at half the price of the imported chemical, and also epsom salts, blue vitriol (copper sulfate), yellow and green chrome, tartaric acid, and rochelle salts. Isaac McKim, Jr., built a chrome factory near the new City Block, and Tyson manufactured a wide variety of chemicals at the foot of Fremont Avenue. The powder mills were at a distance, but their owners built three towers in town for the manufacture of lead shot. Among the shot tower entrepreneurs, Lorman, Gwynn, and Alexander were also incorporators of a gas company and a coal mining company, the first in the state (1829).[38] Their concept and timing indicate the interlocking of ideas and promoters in railroad building and industrial technology.

New manufacturers created an economic base for new neighborhoods, and the braiding of trade and manufactures into such chains of enterprise meant also a weaving together of the various neighborhoods. The connections between the various districts of the city became more "intimate and delicate." New prosperity at Fells Point reflected the expansion of the shipbuilding industry.

The yards and shops are filled with cheerful men, and the hum of industry continually greets the ear. The countenances of the citizens,—nay, the very appearance of the houses and the streets, have delightfully changed. Three or four years ago, we never left the Point without gloomy feelings.[39]

The cotton mill villages hummed in unison, making sailcloth. The margin between Federal Hill and the inner harbor became a zone of industry. In addition to the foundries of Reeder, Watchman & Bratt, the chemical works of McKim, Sims & Co., and the expanded glass works, the Bellona copper works had a large plant on Smith's wharf, and Berry developed a factory for firebricks for furnaces. This halved the price of a producer good formerly imported from England. The manufacture of common building brick increased hugely, as in every building boom, and occupied large areas of Federal Hill and Locust Point, and began surrounding Mount Clare.

Industrialists, prominent among them the Quaker entrepreneurs (McKims, Tysons, and Ellicotts), sought to bring the railroad to their mills or docks. But there is little evidence of industry's coming to the railroad. Baltimore was gradually defining certain tidewater districts of the south, southwest, and southeast as its industrial backyards, and certain streets as work streets—Pratt Street, Fremont Avenue, Pennsylvania Avenue, Howard Street, Central Avenue, and Fleet Street. New industries were also developing in a welter of back lanes. "The passing bales of goods up Market street are seen by everybody—But the creations in the back shops, or small alleys, are known only to a few."[40] Niles estimated that the city's $8 million in foreign imports "returned whence they came," leaving only "a tythe" for profits, drayage, and rents. But the new factories, he reckoned, were producing $5 million worth, of which the city retained and recirculated four-fifths.

The New Order of Things

Daniel Raymond had been outraged by the English laws of inheritance—primogeniture and entail—that tended to accumulate property in the hands of a few.[41] In 1825 Raymond involved himself in certain lawsuits that turned on the issue of inheritance of land rights through persons in England at the time of the Revolution. He was the attorney for a suit against Charles Carroll of Carrollton and Charles Ridgely of Hampton. Other large prerevolutionary patentees joined them in the defense. Raymond's party lost, but the gradual

The topographic map of the Jones Falls Valley shows
mill no. 1 and its village, with "Brick Hill" in the upper
left. The Northern Central repair shops and Mount
Royal Reservoir are in the lower center, and the Belt
Railroad (B&O) "crossover" appears on the right.

effects of time and the postrevolutionary law of division of property were operating to diminish the great estates and transform the structure of society.

The state of Maryland was moving to limit more strictly the right of entail, that is, the right of a man by his will to restrict the transmission of property to the male line or to the eldest in successive generations. Charles Carroll of Carrollton in the mid-1820s created an uproar by re-creating a "tail" to transmit Doughoregan Manor to his eldest son and his eldest male descendant, etc.[42] He sought to avoid inventory and probate, and even stipulated that any relative who contested the will would forfeit all rights. His estate included Homewood, Oakland, Brooklandwood, Carrollton, extensive lands in Frederick County, and thousands of acres in Pennsylvania and New York State. In contrast, at the same moment his distant cousin James Carroll had by his will "docked the tail" his uncle, barrister Charles Carroll, had attached to his estate during the Revolution. James Carroll's property included Mount Clare (Georgia plantation), mill sites on the Gwynns Falls and Gwynns Run, The Caves in Baltimore County, and property in Annapolis and Anne Arundel County.[43] His action opened the way for the division and alienation of the property and its urban subdivision.

About the time those wills were drawn, John Eager Howard died, and his will divided the estate equally among the families of his eight children. His property was so extensive as to require several years of survey and legal work, but because it formed a belt around the very core of the city, it was ripe for immediate subdivision, and the estate requested the city promptly to open all the streets through it. Their family surveyor was, conveniently, T. H. Poppleton, who certified that the street plans conformed to his city plan of 1822.[44]

Alexis de Tocqueville, who visited Baltimore in the fall of 1831, recorded his conversation with John Latrobe on the changes in Maryland since the founding of the colony:

Until the Revolution, Maryland showed the face of an English province; birth was as prized as on the other side of the Atlantic; all power was in the hands of the great families.

What changed this state of affairs?

The law of succession. With equal sharing of inheritances, fortunes were rapidly divided. A few families, like that of Charles Carroll, for instance, having only one heir for several generations, have conserved their fortune, but in general the great estates were fractioned into a thousand parts.

The "nobles" of Maryland, Latrobe said, had embraced the Revolution and led the people on the battle field, and then many of them adopted the Jeffersonian party, which favored greater power to the several states. By these circumstances, Latrobe argued, "through love of power and the desire to keep their local importance," they retained favor with the people. Nevertheless,

In two or three generations they will have disappeared.

Do you not regret it?

Yes, in some ways. This class was generally a seed bed of men distinguished in the legislature and the army. They made the best statesmen, the finest characters. All the great men of the Revolution came, in the South, from this class. Yet I am led to think that, all things considered, the new order of things is better. The upper classes

now among us are less remarkable, but the people are more enlightened; there are fewer distinguished men but a more general happiness. In a word, we are becoming every day more like New England.

Tocqueville raised this question wherever he went. Evidently Charles Carroll, at ninety-four, regretted the decline of the aristocratic institutions, but James Carroll spoke for the popular role. The question was recognized throughout society as a fundamental political issue.

A series of civic processions in 1824, 1826, and 1828 also reflect the passing of an era, the self-conscious end of a generation, and a shift in the relative weights of the various classes of society. The first was Lafayette's three-day visit. Lafayette's steamboat, the *United States*, was escorted by four more steamboats, "all beautifully dressed, with flags and streamers flying." The party landed at Fort McHenry, and the governor conducted Lafayette to Washington's tent, where he was received and embraced by the Society of Cincinnati, the patriarchs of the Revolution. "All were convulsed into tears, but they were tears of joy and gratulation." Lafayette was escorted by seven or eight hundred horses past Federal Hill to the crowd in Baltimore Street. In the evening fifty thousand enjoyed the "illumination" of the streets. The general was most delighted at the beauty and order of the scene: "He felt the last especially as coming from the heart, a compliment that money cannot buy or wealth confer." The lighted decorations were marvellous in their eclecticism—civil arches with Greek orders and wreaths of laurel, radiating well-polished bayonets, the golden eagle, and the ensign of Hibernia. On the Baltimore Street bridge over the Jones Falls were erected thirteen arches, one with a transparent painting fifteen feet by ten feet representing the father of our country on a rock amid foaming billows and royalty dashed to pieces.

The general received an honorary degree at the University of Maryland, reviewed the school children, visited his Masonic brethren in their "chaste and beautiful hall," visited the museum, attended divine worship at the cathedral, and received a venerable delegation of the French inhabitants of Baltimore as well as the clergy of the Methodist church, "ministers of a peaceful gospel." The Society of the Cincinnati gave him a splendid dinner at James Buchanan's mansion in Monument Square—"a brilliant line of the richest plate and glass, and the characteristic hospitality of Baltimore." For the ball, the theater was converted into a ballroom. The decorations, superintended by Mr. Finlay, featured mottoes from Shakespeare and a twelve-foot diameter chandelier ornamented with twenty-four glittering stars for the twenty-four states. With a flourish of trumpets and "Lafayette's March," "the gas light flashed like magic into a blaze almost equal to day."[45]

On the Fourth of July 1826, John Adams and Thomas Jefferson died, exactly fifty years after signing the Declaration of Independence, leaving Charles Carroll as the last survivor of the signers. In honor to the illustrious dead, a funeral procession was contrived, from Baltimore Street up Howard and Madison streets to Howard's Park. A troop of mounted cavalry was followed by a long line of carriages of the clergy. Six noble black horses drew the funeral car bearing two black-shrouded coffins, on it "the winged globes of the Egyptian mausoleum." As chief mourners, Charles Carroll of Carrollton, Colonel Howard, and General Smith rode in a barouche; four generations marched behind.[46]

That event was elaborately planned, but in the same year a plainer man died, whose passing also represented a shift from an older form of paternalism. A few days before he died, Elisha Tyson called an unprecedented meeting of the colored population in a church. (There were now several black churches, each of which held a thousand persons.) After a Quakerly silence, he said, "I know not who will befriend you after I am gone, unless you become friends to one another. . . . I feel that the Arm of Omnipotence is stretched out for your enlargement."[47] The crowd wept and organized a mutual assistance fund. For two days after his death, crowds of mourners thronged the whole of Sharp Street and Baltimore Street for half a mile. That, too, was a compliment money could not buy.

Funeral followed upon funeral—Charles Ridgely of Hampton, Robert Goodloe Harper, John Eager Howard, Robert Oliver, James Carroll, James McHenry, Alexander Brown, and Isaac McKim, Jr. As a new generation took the reins, the processions showed a turn toward a different participation of the masses, reminiscent of the mechanics' politics of 1809, but now harmonized with the goals of the entrepreneurs. On the Fourth of July 1828, as the first shovel was turned for the Chesapeake and Ohio Canal at Georgetown, Baltimore created a spectacular for the laying of the first stone of the Baltimore and Ohio Railroad, where the Carrollton viaduct now crosses the Gwynns Falls. The Declaration of Independence was read, and Carroll, a "relic" at ninety-one, turned earth. Masonic grand masters from Virginia, Pennsylvania, and Maryland measured the stone, poured wine and oil, and scattered corn. But the engaging feature of the occasion was the procession of the trade associations. The blacksmiths and whitesmiths presented the pick, spade, hammer, and trowel; the stonecutters escorted the stone. In the course of the parade, the hatters manufactured beaver hats for Mr. Carroll and General Smith, the weavers and tailors presented to Carroll a coat made on the way, the bookbinders an engineers' report, and the cordwainers a pair of green morocco slippers, their lining ornamented with a view of the railroad.[48]

The Union Manufacturing Company had a huge carriage bearing 102 females belonging to the factory. Other trades carried Biblical motifs and labor slogans recalling the Democratic Republican parade. The millers and flour inspectors marched, as did the bakers, and the victuallers in their butchers' aprons bearing pole axe and meat cleaver. A smith's shop with furnace and bellows was in full operation, while 160 united Sons of Vulcan followed under the motto, "American manufactures—internal improvements." The bleachers and dyers carried a banner saying "Ye were naked and we clothed ye," with a circle of gold around the shuttle, the sheaf, and the ship on the other side. Britannia was portrayed in an attitude of grief, as an eagle bore a golden treasure across the ocean to Columbia. Underneath was the motto: "A wise and just distribution of labor and its reward, is the foundation of national prosperity."

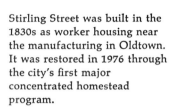

Stirling Street was built in the 1830s as worker housing near the manufacturing in Oldtown. It was restored in 1976 through the city's first major concentrated homestead program.

The carpenters, lumber merchants, and plane makers carried a miniature Greek temple seven feet square. The cabinet makers, riding on a "bedstead," built a patent rocker cradle. The cedar coopers built a barrel churn, churned five gallons of cream, ate the butter, and drank the buttermilk. The tinplate workers manufactured tin tumblers and threw them to the spectators; the printers published the ode and address of the day, handing them up to ladies at the windows with long poles. The printers also carried refreshments, bantered back and forth, and drank toasts with the pilots and shipbuilders, who "sailed" a twenty-seven-foot model ship, the *Baltimore,* drawn by six horses.

The sense of harmony, order, and solidarity was characteristic of the revival of prosperity and construction at the rate of five hundred houses a year between 1824 and 1829.[49] The population of Baltimore, as shown in the census of 1830, had a more settled character than earlier, due to a somewhat slower rate of growth. For the first time, the white population showed a slight excess of females over males, concentrated in the servant age group under twenty and among the elderly. Young men (fifteen to forty), only 18 percent of the population, were concentrated in the waterfront wards. Among free blacks there were far more females than males at all ages above ten, as slave owners tended to retain males in the agricultural counties or sell them south. The city directory shows half the city's population in skilled and semiskilled craft work: mechanics or tradesmen. The next largest group was in commercial occupations. Less than a thousand persons were listed as professionals or in other occupations requiring formal education and conferring status. All those classes of jobs were controlled by whites. Among blacks, the men were chiefly laborers, drivers of carts, stable hands, and wood sawyers. One in five or six had skilled jobs representing steadier income, chiefly seamen, barbers, waiters, and blacksmiths, and in smaller numbers ship caulkers, shoemakers, musicians, cigar makers, and painters. Both black and white were found among seamen and drivers. A fifth of the listings were women. Nearly all of the black women listed were laundresses, but only a third of the white women had occupations listed, chiefly in sewing trades (seamstress, milliner, silk button maker), or as keepers of shops, boarding houses, or taverns.[50]

That age and caste structure represented an increase in the more stable, more docile, and more respectable classes and a relative decrease of the more turbulent elements. But the situation was beginning to change. Railroad construction and the new prosperity contributed to speculative enterprise and attracted both mechanics and unskilled laborers. Nationwide expansion of public works (the C&O Canal, the Pennsylvania line of state works, and the Ohio state canals were also under construction) was associated with an enormous immigration beginning in 1830, including many poor people from England and Ireland, and after 1834 a very large share from Germany. As always, the bulk were young men. Arrivals of foreigners in the port of Baltimore doubled in the year 1830 and doubled again in 1832, from two thousand to four thousand to eight thousand per year. Some of the immigrants, along with local farm laborers, moved on toward the midwest. Baltimore did a brisk trade in fitting out Conestoga wagons. Another share of immigrants was contracted for work on the C&O Canal or the B&O Railroad and was quartered in labor camps at construction sites in the piedmont. Bavarian Jews were settling in Oldtown—on High, Lombard, Exeter, and Aisquith streets—and a number became peddlers in Virginia and western Maryland.

As immigration rose, so did the building boom. "Foundations for new buildings, and the demolishing of old houses to be replaced by new, are to be seen in most streets of our city." Niles recalled the pancake flatness and hundreds of vacant houses of 1820 to 1823 as a contrast to the new scarcity of vacant houses: "No house, fit for persons to live in, is without its tenant." Construction could not keep up with the demand, and the immigrants took the hindmost. "The large amount of labor employed in our various workshops . . . and on our great public works have packed the people too thickly. We want many houses."[51]

Massive immigration also produced intense problems of assimilation and adaptation, and one observes a mixture of humanity and brutality in the effort to control epidemic and violence. The average population of the almshouse rose to five hundred.[52] The trustees for the poor attributed the increase of paupers to the arrival of outsiders and the use of liquor. Virtually all the inmates are described as intemperate, children of intemperate persons, or "of unknown habits." Of people admitted to the almshouse in the 1830s it was usual to find that a tenth had been in the city less than a week and a quarter less than six months. About 30 percent were foreign born, mostly Irish.[53] In 1832 the trustees asked the council, who in turn asked the legislature, who in turn asked the federal government, to curb the importation of English paupers that parishes "shovelled upon us." They were contrasted with arrivals from Bremen, "hardy, healthy and evidently industrious," bringing lots of hearty children and their own wagon and harness.[54] A $1.50 head tax was placed on immigrants, which was allotted to the almshouse, the Hibernian Society, and the German Society for their relief activities, and a $4 tax was imposed on liquor dealers for support of the jail.[55]

Death, as well as dependency, followed hard on the swell of immigration. A drop in death rates had occurred after 1822, as yellow fever and malarial fevers slackened their hold, evidently due to the drainage improvements and the relative

Containing Disorder

decline of commerce and privateering in the West Indies. The new threat was intestinal disease—dysentery, cholera, and infant cholera. Added to a new wave of respiratory diseases (tuberculosis, pneumonia, and whooping cough) and outbreaks of typhus, these diseases accounted for a new high death rate in the early 1830s. Two-fifths of all deaths in each year were of children under five.[56] This reflects both a high rate of infant mortality and a large proportion of young people in the population characteristic of American cities in this generation.

The intestinal diseases had several common features. All were most threatening in warm weather: death rates were highest in July and August, and infant cholera was also known as summer diarrhea. All were spread chiefly through the contamination of foods, especially water and milk, by human excreta. They were the scourge of European cities, too, and their extension was later understood to be caused by increased pollution of urban water supplies from human sewage. Baltimore's water supply was only about a third "external," that is, two-thirds of the population relied on wells and springs in town. The sewage of the entire populace was disposed of either through privies draining directly into surface or ground water, or vaults that were periodically emptied: the contents were removed to night-soil depots on the edge of town, where the untreated waste was open to flies and surface drainage. Much of the city's milk was supplied from cows living in the city and fed on garbage.

The strategy of Dr. Jameson, consulting physician to the city, as he observed the spread of cholera across Europe in 1832, was to clean the city and exhort citizens to temperance and moderation. They should avoid an excess of alcohol and cold water, all fruits, certain vegetables, and, above all, watermelons, green corn, green apples, peaches, and crabs. Intemperance and gluttony were identified as sins that God might choose to punish and as lower-class habits. The specific prohibited foods were the summertime indulgences known to bring on colic or intestinal upset, regarded as warning symptoms of cholera. The horrifying feature of cholera was sudden and total prostration. Individuals collapsed cold and almost pulseless or rolled in agony on the sidewalk or in the market, unable to reach home.

In the city of Baltimore there died of cholera, during the summer of 1832, eight hundred and fifty three persons, a very great majority of whom were the most worthless; but a few of our best citizens were its victims. Here then is a mortality of about one in 96; and, of persons of respectability, one, we believe, in a thousand.[57]

Treatments were strenuous: copious bleeding and calomel (mercurous chloride). One young Irishman, for example, "rallied from cholera, is now perfectly salivated and raving mad." He died. Injections of salt water were tried, presaging the modern treatment, but the patients still died. The records of the three emergency hospitals provide a register of the poor, recognized for the first time as a great mass. Few can be identified in directories. Many were immigrants, living in the alleys, back buildings, and upper stories above shops in the center of the city. Irish names are especially common, and five or six had arrived from Germany within a few weeks. Some twenty patients were reported as having slept the night before in a vacant lot, market house, or lumberyard. "Much emaciated. Has been sleeping in the woods for three weeks." Others are described as having been "out on a frolic" or "on a debauche" for days or weeks. The small children brought to the hospital had to be treated for worms as well as cholera.

The diary of a Methodist minister, Reverend T.H.W. Monroe, reveals the cholera among a broader class of persons.[58] Just as the individual survivor went through stages of anxiety, crisis, and convalescence, the city experienced a collective emotional binge. Among those who died and were regarded as martyrs were two Sisters of Charity who nursed at the temporary hospitals, one of the Oblate Sisters of Providence who nursed at the almshouse then nursed the archbishop and his housekeeper through cholera, a doctor in Oldtown, and Lewis G. Wells, "a colored man who had devoted several years to the acquisition of medical knowledge, under favorable circumstances."[59]

Strong attempts at repression, at tightening up a barbarous system, did not suffice to control violence. Repeated thoughtful reforms and reorganization did not manage to curb the violence of the law. Of a hundred persons in the jail on an average day, half were committed for economic crimes. In 1831, for example, of twenty-three hundred committed, a thousand were jailed for debt (half for less than ten dollars) and another four hundred for various labor offenses, such as suspicion of runaway slave, "safekeeping" of slaves, desertion or mutiny (seamen), and participating in a railroad labor riot. An attempt was made to rationalize the jail by introducing cost accounting and group cooking of food. The limit for debtors was raised to thirty dollars, and the creditor had to pay a week's jail fee in advance.

The Maryland penitentiary, adjoining, continued to develop along the line of thinking of the Philadelphia Quakers and the model penitentiary at Auburn, New York. Its population was more or less stable at 350 to 400 prisoners; 85 percent were convicted of stealing and the average sentence was three years. A new men's prison was built with 325 single cells, so that prisoners could sleep in separate cells. Silence and isolation were regarded as curative. The older building became the dining hall, infirmary, laundry, and women's prison: five beds to a room, straw pallets on planks, and in each bed two or three women.[60]

Maryland was determined to make the prison system entirely self-supporting, and French observers considered it the best model in the United States for the conduct of labor. Robert Cary Long designed the workshop buildings on a radial plan, with a central control point and slits from which the guards in galleries could observe the work below without being seen. Blacks and whites were partitioned into two shops operated by contractors, with a hundred looms for weaving, equipment for shoemaking, brush making, and stone cutting. The penitentiary labor was paying off the construction loans as well as making a profit for the contractors. After the shops were built, the prison managers introduced a stricter rule of silence and the lock step, and described the prisoners as "relatively subdued." "The convicts received are thoroughly scrubbed and purified; one half of their hair is shaven close to the skin and they are clothed in stout garments, striped horizontally."[61]

The Difficulty of Our
Situation

The jail and penitentiary were also part of a larger system of repression of the black population. The law made distinctions in the judicial and penal treatment of three classes of people: persons with property, persons without property, and black persons, who were themselves treated as property. For example, to rid the penitentiary of blacks (varying between a third and two-thirds), the state provided that second offenders should be sold into slavery and shipped out of state. Without any judicial proceedings, masters could privately take their black servants and slaves to the city jail to be whipped. Urban public opinion had the effect that slaves in Baltimore were generally better treated than on the plantations. They were more often reasonably well fed and less often beaten. But neither opinion nor law prevented brutal exceptions, such as the two girls in Aliceanna Street whom Frederick Douglass described as always half starved, contending with the pigs for offal in the street, and covered with festering sores from the whip. Douglass had been brought to Baltimore in 1825, about nine years old, to run errands and mind Hugh Auld's little boy. Mrs. Auld began teaching him the alphabet and basic spelling, but Master Auld found it out and forbade her: "Now if you teach that nigger (speaking of myself) how to read, there would be no keeping him. It would forever unfit him to be a slave. . . . From that moment, I understood the pathway from slavery to freedom."[62] Douglass cajoled and bribed little white boys in Philpot Street with bread to teach him further. A few years later he was returned to the Lloyd plantation on the Eastern Shore for a division of the estate. But the taste of freedom and the conception of the pathway were part of the Baltimore experience, not only for Frederick Douglass but for many.

Free blacks were exploring additional pathways of self-help and education. Founded in 1821, the Union Female Society may have been the first of their beneficial societies. Each member paid an initiation fee plus 12½ cents dues per month, and was eligible for sick benefits of a dollar per week for six weeks, 50 cents during the next six weeks, 25 cents indefinitely thereafter, and a paid funeral. The constitution designated annual elections and a bonded treasurer. They kept their money in the savings bank. The bylaws fixed fines of 25 cents for missing a monthly meeting, 50 cents for interrupting, and a dollar for missing a funeral.[63] Several other beneficial and burial societies were formed among the people of color in the 1820s, including the Tobias Society among Catholics. By 1835 there were thirty-five or forty such societies, each with 35 to 150 members.[64]

State laws barred the public schools to blacks, although they paid the school tax, but several independent schools flourished. The Sharp Street school was managed by blacks and attended with success "beyond any expectation." At least five large churches had black preachers, including St. James Episcopal. In 1824 a pastor was called to an upper room at Park and Marion streets, and a "very neat church" was built soon after at Saratoga and North (Guilford) streets. It was incorporated in 1829. The pastor, William Livingstone, insisted that those in bondage could be members, to the dissatisfaction of some free members. Even in the penitentiary, two hundred black convicts learned to read in the Methodist Sunday school.

The Oblate Sisters of Providence were instrumental in educating the children of the black community. In periods of economic decline their orphanage would swell in numbers, but it always remained exclusively black.

The Santo Domingo colored, Catholic and French-speaking, had retained a strong identity, nurtured by the Sulpician fathers at St. Mary's Seminary, first Father Dubourg, then Father Tessier. In 1828 Father Joubert, who had been a tax agent in Santo Domingo and was ordained at St. Mary's, encouraged Mary Elizabeth Lange to form an order of nuns, the Oblate Sisters of Providence, so that the children of the community might learn to read, and thus profit from their catechism classes.[65] Soon there were a dozen, some from Fells Point families, some from Delaware or Georgetown, some with savings or dowries of several hundred dollars, and some with nothing. They gave lessons in French, English, arithmetic, catechism, embroidery, and sewing. At first, two-thirds of the children had French names. Their physician was Dr. Chatard, one of the French from Santo Domingo. When the sisters made their vows, each received with her habit a chain as a token of their Association of the Holy Slavery of the Mother of God.[66] A favorite hymn was "O Victime de tous les crimes." Visits to the sisters made a decided impression on the American bishops who attended councils in Baltimore in 1829 and 1833. Blacks were being converted every day in Baltimore, and several hundred received communion each month in the Sisters' small chapel in Richmond Street. (In the cathedral as in other churches there was a separate gallery for blacks.) The delicacy of their position is illustrated by the soul searching involved in their agreement to manage the household of the Sulpician fathers. They took care of mending and nursing, with a cook, another woman to work, and a man to serve the table:

We do not conceal the difficulty of our situation. As persons of color and Religious at the same time, we wish to conciliate these two qualities in such a manner as not to appear too arrogant on the one hand and on the other, not to lack the respect which is due to the state we have embraced.[67]

In contrast to the Oblate Sisters' near-seclusion, foreign visitors often remarked on the gaiety and manners of the Baltimore blacks among themselves, especially the stylishness and chic of the young women in the markets and the cheek and impudence of the younger waiters and drivers. However dated their accounts, they leave hints of the vitality and richness of black life in Baltimore.

Among whites, an Anti-Slavery Society was organized in 1825 through the efforts of Benjamin Lundy. As in Tennessee, North Carolina, and Virginia, the society was strongest in the communities where there were fewer slaves and a strong witness among Friends. Baltimore supporters included John Needles, cabinet maker; Gerard T. Hopkins; A. Mathiot, chair maker; Jonathan S. Eastman, agricultural implement maker; John and Thomas Berry, brickmakers; and Henry Mankin. Lundy produced his first edition of *The Genius of Universal Emancipation* for the Fourth of July: "We hold these truths to be self-evident: that all men are created equal, and endowed by their Creator with certain inalienable rights; that among these are life, liberty, and pursuit of happiness." He documented regularly the purchases of slaves by Austin Woolfolk and others, sales in the Orphans Court, kidnappings of blacks, and the droves or coffles of slaves his informants met on the roads going west to Alabama. The society embarked several hundred freed slaves for emigration to Haiti, started a store to sell goods made by free labor only, and nominated an antislavery candidate to the legislature. The campaign platform coupled abolition with removal of Negroes to Haiti or Africa.

"The master and the slave are alike bound in the fetters of fear, distrust and danger. . . . And are we to sleep in quietness upon a volcano?"[68] The society's candidate, president, and attorney—Daniel Raymond—proposed gradual emancipation by freeing at the age of twenty-one all persons born after next Fourth of July. "Such a law will infringe no man's rights, because no man can have a right to a human being not yet created. Where is the audacious man that shall dare to claim as his inheritance the future workmanship of the Deity?"[69] His views were consistent with his position in the lawsuit against entail or class inheritance. The law of 1715, he said, declaring that children of a certain class should be born slaves, was "the most iniquitous" ever passed, visiting the sins of the fathers upon their children unto the third and fourth generations. Raymond finished last in the election.

The already difficult situation of blacks in Baltimore took a turn for the worse in the summer of 1831, after the Nat Turner uprising. A rumor ran through Baltimore of a vast slave conspiracy to "kill the damnd whites." The beneficial societies were accused of holding midnight military drill. Baltimore apparently returned to normal without violent reprisals, but in November John Latrobe told Tocqueville, "I am afraid the next Legislature will make some unjust and oppressive laws against the blacks. They want to make staying in Maryland unbearable. One must not hide it, the white population and the black population are at war. They will never mix. One must cede the place to the other."[70] On the same day, Tocqueville's personal observation of one black man's nightmare was prophetic of the coming repression:

Today 4 November, we saw at the Alms-House a negro whose madness is extraordinary: there is in Baltimore a celebrated slave merchant who, it seems, is much feared by the black population. The negro I am speaking of imagines that he sees day and night this man attached to his footsteps, and pulling off pieces of his flesh. When we went into his cell, he was lying on the floor rolled in a cover which was his only clothing. His eyes rolled . . . and the expression of his face was one of terror and rage.

From time to time he threw off the cover and raised up on his hands crying: "Get out, get out, don't come near me."[71]

In March the legislature's Brawner Commission, acknowledging intense disagreement in the memorials presented to them, recommended a legislative package to remove the colored population, estimated at fifty thousand free, largely in Baltimore, and one hundred thousand slave, largely outside the city. The commission considered them all injurious to the prosperity of Maryland; their "remedy" was colonization as an instrument of state policy.[72] Funds were provided at thirty dollars a head to transport blacks to Liberia. Free volunteers would be sent first, then individuals manumitted for the purpose. The question was postponed as to the purchase of slaves for resettlement. At the same time, the law restricted manumission (Elisha Tyson being in his grave) and assured a black the "choice" of consenting in open court to remain a slave if by reason of family ties he did not want to remove to Liberia. A second act codified police regulations: no free Negro could buy powder, lead, or whiskey, nor sell agricultural staples without written testimonials of whites. Religious meetings could be held only by permission of whites. Any free Negro who moved into or returned into the state was liable to be sold into slavery. For any criminal punishment except hanging by the neck until dead, a judge could substitute deportation to a foreign country.

What was the attitude of Baltimoreans in this debate? Certain memorials for abolition had doubtless come to the Brawner Commission from Baltimore. Baltimore newspaper reporters remarked cautiously on the peculiar details of the acts relating to manumission and assembly of "free" blacks. They grasped opportunities to comment on the bravery of many persons of color at a waterfront fire, or the colored sisters nursing cholera victims. Baltimore's white leadership regarded the extremism of the legislature as one more aspect of state oppression of Baltimore by the agricultural, land-holding, and slave-holding interests. The slave-holding interest of Maryland, meanwhile, hardened its position, sensing new vigor in the antislavery movement in northern states of the Union. Under these conditions of political conflict, the mood of Baltimore was an almost passionate search for compromise. Baltimoreans both for and against slavery embraced resettlement schemes. The *Gazette*, for example, was enthusiastic about the arrival of 342 persons of color in Liberia via the *James Perkins*. The editor looked forward to the day when the whole colored population "will have transferred themselves, by our assistance" from slavery here to independence in the land Providence gave them.

There let them go onwards, as we have done here. Let them subdue the forest, and bring the wild soil into cultivation, and civilize the poor native, and become a powerful and happy people. And, instead of being forever a reproach to us, when we breathe the name of freedom, let them prolong the chorus, on the other side of the Atlantic.[73]

Projects were dampened when the free blacks flatly refused to volunteer, and news from the colonies was unpromising. Certain Quaker colonizationists, such as Moses Sheppard, despaired of peaceful abolition, but noted the incongruities of colonization, such as sending lumber across the Atlantic to be carried into the woods of Africa.[74] Abolitionist views were no longer published in the daily papers. Men in authority, business, and the churches continued to place hope in the resettlement scheme. English visitor James Silk Buckingham was surprised to find that Baltimoreans did not defend or excuse slavery as New Yorkers did, but seemed to mix great tolerance of opinion with a certain silence. "In all our intercourse with the people of Baltimore, and we were continually out in society, we heard less about slaves and slavery than in any town we had yet visited."[75]

The willingness of prominent men to acquiesce in the degradation of the blacks, and their eagerness to go after a chimera left a vacuum. In 1833 several Negroes were convicted of crimes "in the most horrid circumstances," under the handicap of white-only testimony: a man for raping a white orphan girl, a cook for poisoning her mistress "by means of arsenic given in a bowl of soup," and two female slaves for conspiracy to rob and murder the family and set fire to the premises. As violence increased in society, in 1834 and 1835, white mobs began to direct more of their attacks on blacks—knocking out windows or ransacking a colored home. Yet convictions were rare. The way in which the law, the climate of violence, and the lack of leadership combined to permit outrages can be seen in Douglass's account of his second sojourn in Baltimore in 1836. This time Auld apprenticed him to William Gardner, shipbuilder. Whites and blacks were working side by side, but all at once the white carpenters knocked off, saying they would not work with free colored workers. The spirit spread to the apprentice boys. "My fellow-apprentices very soon began to feel it degrading to them to work with me. They began to put on airs, and talk about the "niggers" taking the country, saying we all ought to be killed."[76] When "hectored around," Douglass defended himself, and the whites combined with sticks, stones, handspikes, and half-bricks to beat him up in the sight of fifty white ship carpenters. The Aulds nursed his eye injury and took him to their lawyer, who said that nothing could be done unless some white man would come forward and testify. "Even those who may have sympathized with me were not prepared to do this. It required a degree of courage unknown to them to do so; for just at that time, the slightest manifestation of humanity toward a colored person was denounced as abolitionism."

Epidemic Violence

Douglass's experience was only one incident in an epidemic of violence in Baltimore. About 1834, as economic conditions worsened, labor trouble became more frequent on the public works. The general level of violence increased in the city, including an exceptional number of suicides.[77] Violence followed a course that can be observed at other cities and in other generations: a wave of rumors and arson over several months, a weekend of mob action that ceased as abruptly as it had begun, followed by six to twelve months of juvenile disorder and terrorism.

The labor force on the C&O Canal and on the various railroads was quartered in large construction camps by the several contractors. Whiskey was often part of the pay. Disputes arose from cuts in wages or from contractors' attempts to pay in scrip, to postpone payment, or to manipulate the value of money. These evolved into riots between rival groups over "scab" labor. On a Friday in August 1829, a man was killed and several wounded in "dangerous and disgraceful riots" among the laborers employed on the B&O section adjoining the city.[78] Several of the supposed ringleaders were committed to prison. In August 1831 a riot occurred between Irish and black laborers at New Market (Frederick County). Twenty "ringleaders" were taken prisoner, and four hundred Irish rallied to rescue them. At Sykesville Irish workers struck because the contractor owed them nine thousand dollars in pay. John Latrobe and others distributed two thousand dollars and sought to negotiate a return to work, then took out a riot warrant. A posse consisting only of William Patterson and a sheriff was repelled, but a hundred of the state militia arrived by train at dawn and arrested fifty workers. The contractor was replaced. In January 1834 five died on the C&O Canal in a conflict between rival gangs of Irish laborers.[79] President Jackson sent regular army units from Fort McHenry. In the fall a mob killed a superintendent on the Washington branch of the B&O "in a peculiarly violent and brutal way" and beat up two others of the contractor's men. This time the militia brought back three hundred prisoners. In another incident on the Washington branch, five or six Germans were wounded. Eleven Germans and one Frenchman were taken "with arms in their hands." They were alleged to have "made assault on those who were content with the wages paid to them." Negro laborers were attacked in Georgetown.

The economic pressure was severe by New Year's Day 1834. When the Warren cotton mills burned, seven hundred persons were thrown out of subsistence, "and they are, generally, very poor."[80] The Union Manufacturing Company stopped both their great cotton mills and discharged several hundred persons. Another large mill was doing "half-work."[81] Half the journeymen printers were reported unemployed, and many other mechanics out of work. The seamstresses, as in 1822, published their prices to show how widows "and others who have sickly or worthless husbands" were earning only fifty cents to a dollar a week.

Meanwhile, a banking scandal with a bizarre resemblance to that of 1822 provided targets for popular frustration. The issue of insolvent or bankruptcy laws had never died out. "WHAT IS JUSTICE?" asked Niles. While small debtors were jailed and small creditors lost their savings in bank failures, large debtors could declare insolvency, "walk the streets of our cities at large, and roll their chariot-wheels over the widows and orphans whom they have plundered, without ever having made restitution."[82] Niles, ever an opponent of paper credit, provides an account from the point of view of the Republican majority. The City bank, the Bank of Maryland, the Susquehanna Bank, the Maryland Savings institution, the United States Insurance Company "and two or three other rag-shops" all went bankrupt. Alexander Brown succeeded in using his personal credit to sustain the credit of certain other individuals, and to float a half-million-dollar loan for the state of Maryland. But there were many losers. "The people have been plundered of more than two millions of dollars." The case of the Bank of Maryland, "the weakest bank in the city," was most deeply resented.[83] According to Richard Townsend, it had become the private property of Evan

Poultney, stockholder, director, and controller of its affairs. He borrowed large sums. "Both interest and principal vanished. . . . A shade from the cloud of public stigma came upon the Society of Friends."[84] The Bank of Maryland stopped payment in March 1834, and anxiety and political unrest were expressed at numerous meetings in courthouse square. On 23 April such a meeting was broken up by violence. "As decency begets a respect for decency, so does violence beget a spirit of violence, and the end is anarchy unrestrained."[85]

In February 1835 the three-month wave of arson began.[86] There was no apparent political motive, and no reason to believe that a single individual or conspiracy was responsible. Yet every Saturday paper included accounts of fires or discovery of "firebrands." The chair factory burned. The Athenaeum burned, with its law offices, organ, the library, and "beautiful and costly philosophical apparatus" of the Mechanical Institute. "Worse and worse": the courthouse burned. Attempts were made to set fire to Mr. Duncan's church in Lexington Street, the female orphan asylum, the Friends Meeting in Lombard Street, and the office of the *Gazette*. A range of stables burned, and a wall fell, killing four fire fighters. While the bell was tolling their interment, arson was attempted at the watch house and again at the *Gazette*. Fires were set at two engine houses, and during another stable fire the hoses of the two companies were cut. Two "old offenders" were arrested as they were burying the tap screws of thirteen fire plugs.

In April a pamphlet war agitated the banking issue. No information was offered to the public by the trustees of the Bank of Maryland, and by August seventeen months had elapsed "obstructed by the law's delay." On Thursday and Friday night, 6–7 August, attempts were made to destroy the houses of the trustees into whose hands the affairs of the bank had been placed. Niles was incensed: "The state of society is awful. Brute force has superseded the law, at many places, and violence become the order of the day. The time predicted seems rapidly approaching when the mob shall rule."[87]

In view of the "feverish or fidgetty state of Baltimore," the mayor deputized six hundred citizens and supplied them with strips of muslin to be worn on the left arm and with sticks of turned poplar. Thirty were mounted on horses. They tried to cordon off Monument Square, but on Saturday night multitudes assembled, and the crowd made frequent rushes on the guard. Brickbats and stones were showered. Reverdy Johnson's splendid residence on Monument Square was destroyed, with all his furniture and his ten-thousand-dollar law library. The losses of John Morris in South Street included 171 dozen bottles of wine, of John Glenn in North Charles, a twelve-thousand-dollar law library and 4000 bottles of wine. Others whose possessions were heaped into bonfires in the street were Evan Ellicott, Mayor Jesse Hunt, and Captain Bentzinger, a paving contractor. "More than fifty others were marked." It was supposed that eight or ten persons were killed, including one in the watch house. "The receptacle for the prisoners was the scene of incessant din and commotion." Fifty-seven prisoners were confined at daybreak on Sunday. The mayor had resigned as the situation slipped out of control, and the officers of the militia were out of town for the weekend. "On Sunday, the people, *without a head*, had nothing to do but to look on and tremble. No one felt himself safe—as everything was given up. Anarchy prevailed."

But on Monday there was "a general, but gloomy, resolution" to restore order. Eighty-three-year-old Samuel Smith was elected by a great assemblage at the Exchange, took command of the people at an assembly in the park, met with the city council, and issued appeals for the people to stay home. John Spear Smith returned and succeeded in collecting the militia. Recalling the mob of 1812, Niles commented upon this one:

The *ostensible* ground of the late riots in Baltimore was in the affairs of the bank of Maryland, though we believe that other things were more at the bottom of them; together with that *general* disposition to violence that prevails at so many places. We shall not pretend to account for it. Whether the effect is *periodical*! or belongs to certain accidental causes—the foundations of which are deeply laid, to produce the elements of confusion and end their record in blood: and then, perchance, to be followed by a reaction that is peaceful and remarkably kind.[88]

Over the next eight or ten months, Baltimore experienced a series of juvenile disorders. On the surface they appear unconnected with the August riot. The mayor complained of assemblages of unruly boys from ten to eighteen or nineteen years old. "When dispersed and driven from one place, they assemble in another." There were several cases of stabbing. The mayor sent the council several Bowie and Spanish knives taken from suspicious persons, and urged fines for carrying dangerous concealed weapons. There were also complaints that the fire companies encouraged youths and apprentices to "assemble and carouse at the engine houses, causing fires or giving false alarms for mere diversion."[89]

The state legislature held an investigation of the riot of 1835 in Baltimore, and as in 1812 punished the city, whose citizens were already deeply resentful of their lack of representation.[90] A memorial of the council argued that while the city had two delegates, a group of counties of comparable total population had twenty-six. Annapolis, they said, "the 'bright particular star of the state', has long since paled her fires, and sunk beneath the splendour of the monumental city." Without wishing to insult the framers of the state constitution, "we state the plain fact, that they were not gifted with the spirit of prophecy—that they could not look into the womb of time and see what seeds would grow and what would not."[91]

A Lifelike Energy
1838–1865

As a great building and industrial boom rose to its peak from 1848 to 1852, Baltimore journalists burbled over each new and beautiful piece of Baltimore mechanism. The Vulcan Works of Murray & Hazelhurst built an engine for the new steamship *Republic*. John Rodgers exported a handsome fire engine. Lapsley devised a valve for extinguishing fire by steam, and Collier, Shaney built gas meters for the White House and Capitol. Most magnificent were the trial trips of the new locomotives. Two hundred were built in Baltimore in those five years, and each was an event. With suitable talent in their design and skill in their manipulation, they represented power, speed, and control. The *Lion*, a twenty-one-ton coal burner, "a really noble specimen of American mechanism" built under the direction of Thatcher Perkins for the B&O, could be "handled with the ease of the valves of a trumpet."[1] Energy involved risk and daring. The boiler explosion on the trial trip of the *Medora*, a steamboat built by Watchman and Bratt, killed twenty-five people, including "an extraordinary aggregation of mechanical talent of South Baltimore."

Baltimoreans celebrated the victories of the Mexican War with fireworks. German residents hailed the revolution of 1848 with torchlight parades. They also enjoyed the fireworks of the glass blowers, the copper smelters and iron-rolling mills "hammering, blowing, and beating away with a life-like energy."[2] At the Vulcan works, the pouring of nine tons of molten iron "emitted the most brilliant corruscations, variegated stars, and figures of dazzling brightness."[3] Thomas Lovegrove patented a process for casting iron pipe through centrifugal force: "suddenly, but noiselessly, with a discharge of flame, the metal has taken its place at the surface of the mould. . . . The time occupied from the tapping of the furnace to the lifting the perfect pipe from the mould, was precisely two minutes."[4]

Radical transformations of the city as a living space took place with all the suddenness and intensity that those industrial descriptions convey. The drama lay in the grand sweep of international, national, and local events. From Britain came the technological momentum of the shift to iron, coal, and steam. The U.S. national economy slowly recovered from the crisis of 1837. Prolonged agricultural depression in Europe produced waves of immigration from Ireland, which peaked in 1847, and from Germany, in 1854. These spectacles were played on different stages, but were mutually reinforcing. For example, each push to extend the B&O to Cumberland (1842) and then to the Ohio River at Wheeling (1853) depended on a favorable capital market in the national economy, and stimulated technological change in Baltimore. Transatlantic migrations rose and fell, depending on the relative states of European and American economies in the grip of reciprocal long swings in construction and public works.[5] The waves of immigrants provided labor for construction of the railroads and the city itself.

The net effect in Baltimore was a rhythm of recovery and prosperity toward 1845, rising to euphoria in 1852, then anxiety and ambivalence, severe problems in 1857, and a brief renewal of industrial activity in 1858 and 1859. In the late '30s construction levels were under 400 houses a year, and the year 1842 was still "shrouded in the darkness of general gloom." By 1845 construction reached 600 houses a year, by 1851 2,000 a year. An "excitement" of property values was remarked upon. Violence and sanitary problems intensified. Great urban projects were proposed and discussed on all sides. Construction was reduced during the commercial crisis (1857), but rose again in 1858 and 1859 to 2,000. It came to a halt toward the end of 1860, as related political crises gripped Baltimore City, then the state of Maryland, and then the Union. Over the full swing, 1837 to 1860, Baltimore doubled its population, its work force, the number of houses, its built-up area, and its street mileage. As I shall show, the changes of scale required reorganization.

The passion for mechanism stimulated new ways of looking at the city. The factory itself was perceived as a mechanism, and so was the residential neighborhood. Public services and institutions of government were viewed as complex pieces of mechanism requiring skillful design. Properly manipulated, there was order and harmony in all their working, but they, too, harnessed terrifying energies and explosive powers.

The steam locomotive was a model for the factory, and the factory was the model for the modern dwelling, the public institution, and the social structure. Knabe's piano works was an example of the kind of factory organization introduced in Baltimore about 1850. There was no distinction among entrepreneur, manufacturer, wholesaler, and retailer: the enterprise was integrated from start to finish, from earliest manufacturing stages to the retail customer. A multistory work space, a volume, was organized for an elaborate division of labor, a flow of goods through the factory, and a flow of customers through the store. In the first story was a powerful steam engine for sawing and planing. The lumber was hoisted to the second story, where workers made the piano cases and tops, which were transferred to the third floor to receive sounding boards, strings, plates, and keys. The fourth floor was used for polishing and varnishing the instruments and preparing them for the salesrooms. The sales space on Baltimore Street included a music store, a department for the sale of foreign pianos, a basement for rentals and repairs, a ladies' parlor, and upstairs "a musical sanctum for professors and gentlemen."[6]

Curlett's carriage factory had a similar layered organization: heavy work was displayed on the ground floor (coaches, cabriolets, chariots), lighter equipages were displayed on the second floor (buggies, hickory wagons, sulkies, family

The Factory As
Mechanism

The Sachse bird's-eye view illustrates the Spring Garden district in 1869. The Timber Neck tract is apparent in the patchwork of streets west of the new Camden Station. At the lower center can be seen Knabe's five-story piano factory and the Maryland Glass Works. John Boyd, owner of a five-story malt-house and wharf, built eleven two-story dwellings with back buildings for his workers. Shaum, the glass house proprietor, and his thirty blowers, who had combined their capital, all lived in the vicinity before the war. As late as 1837 there was fine fishing from Mud Bridge across the mouth of Chatsworth Run.

carriages), painting and polishing were done on the third floor, and trimming was on the fourth.[7] Mathiot, furniture maker, had manufacturing operations in various parts of town, but in a six-story building in Gay Street he coordinated the sequence of finishing, polishing, upholstery, display, and boxing.

The Stein Brothers' ready-made clothing enterprise on Baltimore Street carried even farther than Mathiot a system of flows of goods and movement of people. On the fifth floor, thirty employees cut out the work. On the fourth floor work was given out to two thousand hands employed to sew at home. The lower three floors were devoted to the display of ready-to-wear merchandise. In the basement were stored bolts of woolens. New internal mechanisms improved the flow of goods and connected all parts of the plant: hoisting machines, bells, speaking tubes, and gas from the basement to the roof. Other industries devised ingenious systems for moving goods. At Whitman's farm tool factory in Canton a "fall" extended through the four buildings; work was lowered on carts as they drove through. Under the two-story copper smelter at Canton, 230 feet long, ran "a perfect labyrinth" of vaults and arches leading to a 100-foot stack.[8] At the Mason bakery on McElderry's wharf, bread passed through a steam-powered revolving oven thirty feet long, with iron plates forming an endless chain, and the furnaces underneath. The loaves baked and dropped into baskets for packing. Numsen's pickling and preserving works consisted of a pier and dock where the oysters were received. On the second floor, the oyster packers dropped the shucks through trap doors into a trough that carried them away.[9]

The spatial elaboration of these factories was necessary because of the simultaneous increase in the scale of enterprise and the complexity of tasks. At their peak the B&O shops employed 1,000,[10] A. & W. Denmead and Sons (Monumental Locomotive Works) employed 350, Poole and Hunt at least 250, Bartlett Hayward 350, and most of the other foundries 100 to 150. They were all large family firms or partnerships.

The B&O Railroad was the head of steam for all this industrial activity. Its line reached the Cumberland coal region in 1842, and in 1849 there was an important change of management. Thomas Swann became president, and Johns Hopkins and George Peabody were involved in obtaining municipal and state financing to push the B&O westward to Wheeling, on the Ohio River. Continuing rivalry with the C&O Canal and the railroads of Pennsylvania goaded them on: "The fact is, that Philadelphia is gathering the cream of the rich trade of the West, whilst Baltimore and New York must content themselves with the blue milk."[11] The city once more poured $3 million into improvements conceived as tributaries to the B&O and B&S.[12] Five million dollars was raised for the B&O itself, first in the form of a municipal guarantee, then as a direct loan. At a meeting to boost stock subscriptions for the Cumberland Valley tributary to York, someone objected that millions had been sunk already. But others pointed out that the city property assessment had increased from $15 million to $85 million. "And what would the city be worth if these railroads were torn up?"[13] As they put it that night, it was, over and over again, "a question of Death or Go-ahead."[14]

Like any other city or nation, Baltimore sought to insure the greatest possible multiplier effect. To recapture the purchasing power from local investment, the B&O did its shopwork, manufacturing, purchasing, and subcontracting in Baltimore. Although we think of railroad building in terms of gangs of Irish and German laborers in the mountains of Virginia, the impact of the construction effort on Baltimore was startling. It was intensely concentrated because it involved equipping the whole western division in four years (1848–51). The shops adjoining Mount Clare built 190 locomotives for the B&O, at eight thousand to nine thousand dollars each. (Another fifty were built in Philadelphia.) The B&S built or bought at least ten more locally, and Ross Winans, contractor to the B&O, also sold some to the Reading and other lines outside Baltimore. The B&O bought thirteen hundred railroad cars, the B&S at least two hundred. Every machine shop in the city had railroad orders. Poole and Hunt built gondola cars, Watchman cast car wheels for the B&S, Abbott shifted from ship anchors to car axles. The wire weavers built spark catchers, and the locksmiths manufactured padlocks for all the B&O freight cars. The penitentiary contracted a hundred men, at fifty cents a day, to make railroad spikes.[15]

Of great value was the B&O's ability to attract and develop talent. Ross Winans, Henry Tyson, Benjamin H. Latrobe, Jr., Mendes Cohen, Thatcher

The Impact of the Railroad

This segment of the Sachse bird's-eye view details the
Union Square and Mount Clare district in 1869. Mount
Clare mansion stands surrounded by trees at center left,
and the B&O Railroad shops are at the upper right.
Spring Garden and Long Bridge are in the foreground.

A LIFELIKE ENERGY
1838–1865

107

Perkins, Wendel Bollman, Albert Fink, and John Tegmeyer were all mechanical
or civil engineers of this generation on the B&O. James Milholland, A. Denmead,
and George W. Fulton played similar roles on the B&S, and I. R. Trimble on
the PW&B. All made valuable contributions in terms of mechanical innovation
and the hiving off of enterprise.

In addition to rolling stock, there were the bridges. The B&O built sixty
bridges for the Cumberland-Wheeling section, all at its Mount Clare shops under
the direction of Wendel Bollman.[16] The company shops built a huge chain
pump for the coffer dam at Wheeling. In 1857 Bollman started a firm of his
own that obtained considerable B&O work. The B&S was laid out with an
incredible number of bridges, eighty of them in the fifty-eight miles to York.
Most were hasty trestle work, and James Milholland, master mechanic, in 1845
began replacing the larger ones with iron plate structures of his own design,
probably the first of their type in the world.[17] They were built in the B&S
Bolton shops.

Each railroad also built its most substantial shops, offices, operating structures, and stations in Baltimore. The B&O Camden Station, designed by Niernsee
and Nielson, cost two hundred thousand dollars.[18] In 1848 the B&O began developing its Locust Point coal piers. In 1850 the B&S finished Calvert Station, in
a "neo-Italian" style, and an adjoining plain and practical freight station,[19] and
the Philadelphia, Wilmington and Baltimore built its President Street Station, to
a Trimble design.[20] Four years later the Northern Central Railroad (formed by
consolidation of the Baltimore and Susquehanna with other lines from Harrisburg, Pennsylvania), developed carshops and an engine house on the site the
Canton Company had long reserved. All of these stations involved redevelopment of the surrounding district to widen streets and provide housing for employees.[21] Near Camden Station, a site was developed for a hotel. In the vicinity
of Calvert Station seven express companies built warehouses. The railroad supplier industries chose sites next-door to the railroads' own shops, or on the line:
Denmead near Calvert Station, Bartlett-Hayward next to Winans at Mount Clare,
Poole and Hunt on the Northern Central at Woodberry, and Wells & Miller at
President Street.

If those jobs represented a second round of effects of railroad construction,
there was also a third round—the impact of the construction of buildings for
the supplier industries. Construction was based on the expectation of contracts
or income over several years to come. Incestuous local credit allowed these investments to "crank up" the Baltimore economy. For example, among the heavy
machine shops, Denmead and Murray & Hazelhurst supplied castings for
Abbott's new rolling mill. Murray & Hazelhurst provided the steam engines for
bringing the Oregon and Ashland iron furnace back into production. Wells &
Miller fitted out the new copper smelter.[22]

In the larger realm of city building, the railroad boom and expectations of
railroad-related commerce created an immense demand for brick and iron. The
iron and steam technology of the railroads was related to breakthroughs in other
forms of architecture and engineering. The railway engineers played important

The Bartlett-Hayward Company, which was active in many areas of iron working, built this engine for the Philadelphia, Wilmington, and Baltimore Railroad in the 1860s. It was formally photographed at the B&O's Mount Clare Station, located adjacent to the Bartlett-Hayward shops.

roles in public debate and provided the imagination in municipal engineering in this generation and the next, notably the design of iron bridges[23] and proposals for sewers and flood control. The railroad suppliers played a role in other construction sectors. For example, Bartlett-Hayward made Latrobe stoves, cast-iron shutters for the new warehouses, storage tanks for the gas company's new works at Spring Garden, Oldtown, and Canton, iron fronts for downtown warehouses, iron balconies for Barnum's hotel, and a portico for the cathedral.[24] Denmead built engines for the waterworks (1850), and Fulton made plans for the reservoir. Brick production rose to meet the demand for two thousand houses a year and five-story warehouses. Brick kilns were enlarged, and patents developed for molding machines. The 1850 census lists fourteen hundred brickmakers in Baltimore City and County, mostly black workers.

Falling Behind

But while Baltimore seemed to be enjoying remarkable growth, other American cities were growing still faster in population and in diversity of enterprise and ingenuity. After 1852 the city's economic climate was anxious. The city was not holding its own. Why did Baltimore's new industrial mechanism run down?

First, the railroad core industry collapsed. The immense B&O demand for equipment was a one-shot affair. Even repair work was not all done in Baltimore, once the Martinsburg and Wheeling shops were developed. The western division began to operate independently. In the intensive drive to build the B&O, market development was neglected. Baltimore had bought little from the Philadelphia railroad manufacturers, and subsequently Baltimore manufacturers received few orders from the Philadelphia railroads. Milholland moved to Reading. When Ross Winans and Henry Tyson disagreed, Winans shut down his shops. Winans and his son began selling their talents elsewhere, and derived personal fortunes from their important work for the Moscow–Saint Petersburg Railway on the same buy-at-home policy: they created company shops and manufactures in Russia. Baltimore investors in the Georges Creek Coal and Iron Company helped to develop Cumberland and Lonaconing with relatively prosperous mines, furnaces, and integrated enterprises; Baltimore owners and investors prospered, but they did not produce many permanent jobs in Baltimore.

Second, Baltimore capitalists were old-fashioned. Some authors claim that Baltimore had less capital than other cities. It had fewer millionaires than

Boston or New York and a smaller bank capital relative to its population than most big cities. But there is also evidence that the city followed a very conservative banking policy, recirculating within a small circle. The Savings Bank of Baltimore expanded magnificently in this period (1836–1860), from $1 million to over $6 million in assets "by purely conservative management."[25] They made loans on real estate only within the city limits. They made very few industrial loans and accepted only local securities: city stock, stock in the B&O, gas and water companies, or local banks. Their borrowers were local people, "the tip of the ton." In the years from 1832 to 1844 they lent primarily to John S. Gittings, and from 1845 to 1866 the largest borrowers were Johns Hopkins and George Brown (of Alex. Brown & Co.). Although the Savings Bank, a depository for workers' savings, might be expected to be the most conservative, its policies were nevertheless characteristic of the city's entire banking style. For example, the cotton duck mills were at their peak in innovation and market acceptance. They sold to the U.S. Navy and the foreign merchant marine. McMullen's netting machine, their machine that would "tie a fisherman's knot," was exhibited at the London Crystal Palace. But they were outside the city limits, and had great difficulty finding capital in Baltimore.

Those conservative policies reflect the strikingly commercial nature of Baltimore industrialists. Just as Stein's clothing factory and Knabe's piano factory showed a basic retailing orientation, commercial interests dominated every industrial sector in Baltimore. The machinists were involved in shipbuilding, and shipbuilders were dependent for capital on shipowners and shippers. Hugh Jenkins owned an iron furnace as well as a coffee fleet. Another large shipowner built the copper smelter. The largest industrial promoter, the Canton Company, was still basically a real estate venture owned elsewhere. Johns Hopkins shipped oysters and coffee by wagon to Wheeling before he got the B&O finished. In addition to B&O stock, he invested in building warehouses on Light and Lombard streets. Enoch Pratt, a hardware merchant, had an iron yard at Canton, and was worth three quarters of a million dollars by 1850. John Gittings had an interest in cotton mills at Warren, but he invested more in building fine houses in the Mount Vernon area. In his business life he was concerned with the mechanisms of money and trade rather than the machinery of production. He became a stock exchange and commission agent, and the president of the Northern Central Railroad.

A large part of any economy consists of taking in each other's washing, and it is a relatively dependable or stable sector. But this kind of back scratching does not generate growth and innovation. Hezekiah Niles would likely have seen the problem. He conceived of manufacturing as an "export base" with outside markets to support a productive local labor force. The Baltimore merchants of the 1850s, in contrast, conceived of manufacturing merely as a means of building an infrastructure for their mercantile operations. Therefore, the same multiplier that allowed Baltimore to pump up its economy so quickly also allowed it to deflate swiftly.

Third, there were severe limits on the potential of Baltimore's commercial markets in this period. The direct commercial advantages of the railroad were

This photograph, ca. 1920, records earlier proportions of the towers at Camden Station. The main tower will be replaced in a $170 million development begun in the 1970s. The proposal emphasizes office, retail, and residential uses but little of the original transportation functions.

overrated. Coal was a large item. The B&O brought down a hundred thousand tons a year and took one-fifth of the haul for its own use; a thousand tons a year supplied the gas company at its expanded level, and much of the rest was exported directly from the B&O piers, contributing little to the Baltimore economy except the meager livelihood of immigrant coal heavers on Locust Point. Westward shipments of coffee and oysters increased, but there were no sizeable new markets to be found in the Maryland-Virginia region. There were no new tributary areas filling with population such as the midwestern cities—Cincinnati, Pittsburgh, St. Louis, Kansas City—were contending for when they built railroads.

Where, then, did Baltimore merchant princes see a commercial frontier? What was their market strategy? Toward the end of the 1850s there was a definite orientation toward market frontiers of four widening circles: a local trade, a bay trade, a Southern trade, and a South American trade. All four were destroyed by the Civil War, but provided at least a scheme for postwar development. The first was a local luxury market, which can be seen in the "residential mechanism." The second was the bay trade. Truck gardening and shellfish were sectors of growth.[26] Daily steamboat service to Norfolk, a new bridge to Anne Arundel County, and a large number of bay craft brought strawberries, cabbages, watermelons, and the crabs and oysters to Baltimore. There was no increase of population in the tidewater region, but agricultural development was possible because of the size of the Baltimore market itself and because of the Baltimore-built transport facilities. Baltimore canners took out a succession of extremely promising patents for hermetically sealing oysters, for canning peaches in syrup, and for cutting down the cooking time of corn.

The third frontier was the Southern market. Baltimore merchants were well placed to cater to its special tastes and political sensibilities. Thomas Swann at the opening of the Maryland Institute emphasized "the peculiar relation of Maryland to the whole South" owing to the presence of slavery in the state. Boston, the center of abolitionism, had offended the South, and Baltimore had already profited by "this unnatural strife."[27]

The fourth market frontier was ocean trade in the hemisphere. There was a sizeable increase in exports of flour to Brazil, in exchange for coffee. Trade with west-coast South America shifted from gold and silver to copper and Peruvian guano.[28] (Guano was bird manure imported from the truck farming region; racketeers even bagged a guano-colored earth from Hampstead Hill for this market.) Two large sugar refineries were (re)established in 1855, and the Baltimore and Cuba Smelting Company introduced Cuban copper ores. Ships were built for the Rio trade. Several carpenters shipped prefabricated frame houses, shops, and sawmills to San Francisco during the gold rush. Bollman built some bridges for Cuba and South America, and James Bruce some portable gasworks for Cuba and Ecuador.

The older businesses of farm tools, mills, seeds, and the new fertilizers looked promising in the markets of the bay, the South, and South America, while the peddlers, notion counters, dry goods merchants, and ready-to-wear clothing businesses adopted the Southern market orientation. Small-scale enterprise still allowed newcomers to get a foothold. William Rayner, for example, once an immigrant peddler on the Eastern shore and now a large dry goods merchant and real estate investor, sent Simeon Hecht, an immigrant goatskin trader from Hessen-Cassel, as a peddler to Kent Island. Once he was able to set up his own store, Hecht brought to Baltimore his four brothers, his mother, an aunt, five uncles, and a grandmother. He set up ten persons in business, first as notions peddlers in the Shenandoah, on the Eastern Shore, or on the Cumberland Road, then as storekeepers in Baltimore neighborhoods. But merchandising operations were now placed on a much bigger scale, and through the peddlers and storekeepers Baltimore suppliers were reaching out to larger markets. Merchandising was a piece of Baltimore mechanism that provides insight into this generation's renewal of the downtown area.

A Downtown

Baltimore saw itself as a wonderfully central location, the hub of "great arteries of travel" and a "political pulsating center."[29] Communications were revolutionized. A. S. Abell founded the *Sun* as a new-style "penny-paper" in 1837, and he prided himself on using every means of speeding the news.[30] In 1841 horse relays were organized to bring news of a court case in Utica, New York. Abell and John P. Kennedy maneuvered to get the Maryland legislature to appropriate money for Samuel Morse to build his experimental telegraph line between Baltimore and Washington. On 25 May 1844, in the B&O station, Alfred Vail received Morse's first message. The *Sun* commented on his "complete annihilation of space," and began using telegraph dispatches. In 1845 Abell organized an elaborate mechanism for hastening European news. A "horse express" met mail steamers at Halifax, crossed the 150 miles of Nova Scotia, then took steamers to Portland and the railroad from Boston to Baltimore. In April 1849 the *Sun* received news of the fall of Vera Cruz by special overland express a thousand miles long, and telegraphed the news to the president in Washington.[31] The Sun Building at Baltimore and South streets was itself a five-story marvel of mechanism symbolizing the nerve center of the nation. Its new-fangled eight-cylinder Hoe presses and their steam engines were in the basement, with business offices on the street floor. The second floor was occupied by telegraph companies—the Magnetic, the Western, and the Southern.[32] It was elaborately lit up at night with gas light. As Baltimore's first iron-front building, it was a model for a whole generation of downtown buildings.

The downtown area was rebuilt for higher throughput. German Street (Redwood), "a squalid place," was widened and redeveloped with a continuous row of five-story structures. In 1851 construction centered on Baltimore and Hanover streets, with iron fronts described as imitation brownstone. A block of five was built from the brick of the Eutaw shot tower. In breadth and depth the new "warehouses" were not much larger than before; they occupied the same blocks and lots. But they were taller. Inloes' was typical. For a $1 million a year commerce, they built a five-story building, 30 feet wide by 175 deep, with a steam air furnace, dumbwaiters, and an elegant iron front by Hayward Bartlett.[33] The greater volume of such buildings allowed for the new scale and intensity of activity, but required ingenuity to circulate light, heat, air, goods, and people into the interior. They introduced gas light, steam heat, hoists, bells, Venetian slats, and speaking tubes. Fickey's notion house offered customers baskets on wheels with portable desks.[34] At Hamilton Easter's, light was introduced by a skylight twenty feet long and six feet wide, "the openings of which on each successive floor are encircled with cast-iron railing, of handsome pattern, and bronzed in the most admirable style of work."[35]

Just as each of the new factories and warehouses had to have more elaborate internal communication systems, the industrial-commercial city as a whole had to improve its internal flows. In 1845 the first horse-drawn omnibus lines were organized. There were two round trips a day to Towson, and hourly departures on the line between Fells Point and Canton, with "gay and stylish vehicles" like the *Neptune*, the *Isabel*, the *Flora*, and the *Mars*—built in Baltimore, of course. On the waterfront, piers and channels had to be enlarged to handle the swell of trade. In 1853 the federal government dredged the four-hundred-thousand-dollar Brewerton Channel, 22 feet deep and 150 feet wide. (The steam dredges were built in Baltimore.) The port wardens' line was extended to allow longer wharves at Fells Points, Canton, and Locust Point, to handle a new generation of larger vessels, up to 200 feet long.

As in each downtown reconstruction, the higher buildings, their higher throughput, and the higher level of business activity and property values resulted in traffic congestion. Baltimore, Lombard, and Pratt streets were "occupied constantly, mostly to their utmost capacity." The railroads worked horsepower in Pratt Street, and were allowed steam engines at night in Preston Street, Cathedral Street, and Guilford Avenue. In 1847 Fayette Street was at last put through; it was heavily used for herding cattle and swine through town. Iron bridges over the Jones Falls increased capacity for heavy traffic. The drawbridge was rebuilt across the mouth of the falls, and a steam ferry was put into operation between there and the foot of Federal Hill. Fort Avenue was graded and paved eighty feet wide, at the request of Federal Hill interests. "The boys there are far-seeing; and they know that everything which tends to bring remote portions of our city closer together, tends also to the general good."[36]

The Residential Mechanism

The new warehouses replaced the old merchants' homes. In the vicinity of the present custom house, mansions like John Donnell's gave way to business. "The whole place is now nearly filled with extensive warehouses."[37] Sol Etting's family mansion was torn down for a four-story shoe, hat, and straw firm. The commercial specialization of the downtown area had a reciprocal in the emerging residential "uptown." The new complexity of the industrial and commercial mechanism produced a new kind of residential mechanism, with neighborhoods sorted out by social class.

James Silk Buckingham in 1841 described Baltimore's newest and finest houses around the cathedral as being handsome and commodious "without the least attempt at display,"[38] but as the building boom set in and the upper class reaped the harvest of industrial boom and real estate speculation, their houses became decidedly more showy. John S. Gittings's row of eight mansions, "the handsomest row of buildings in the city," displayed flues of Maryland soapstone

This 1935 aerial view of Spring Garden shows the gasholders and illustrates the extensive sedimentation.

and mantels of elegant Italian marble. They were of "chaste design, in fine ornamental brickwork, painted dove color."[39] On Franklin Square, Waverly Terrace had iron verandas and another set of townhouses consisted of four-story dwellings with porticoes and Ionic columns. For interior decoration, American-made wallpaper was available in twelve colors. Sewing machines were introduced for home use, and the new scale of production of pianos and rocking chairs in Baltimore factories found its market in such homes.

Each elegant townhouse was worth the price of a locomotive. Three stories tall, they had twenty-two- and twenty-four-foot fronts, double the width of the workers' homes built at the time and six times the volume. Twenty such "princely dwellings" were under construction on the four Mount Vernon squares.[40] Others were under construction on Charles Street and Madison Avenue, Bolton, Hoffman, and Preston streets, and Lexington Street near Pearl. As late as 1840 only 10 percent of new houses were three story; by 1857 a majority of new homes were three or three and a half story. The three-story building ran back about forty-eight feet, with a two-story "back building" that extended another forty-eight feet.[41] Fire regulations of 1834 required "parapet walls" extending above the roof line, and roofs sloping back to the alleys. Because of the reach of fire ladders, the height restriction encouraged the practice of

The cast-iron elegance on Baltimore Street before the fire of 1904 was copied on a less grand scale elsewhere in the city. The Oldtown site still stands today.

developing the basement as a lighted half-story. Therefore, the new building boom broke with the tradition of gable roofs and dormer windows. Older houses were rebuilt by raising the roof line to the new standard.

This generation of townhouses became complex residential mechanisms. In the spring of 1850, the Devries house on Washington Place was described as having "the most complete bathroom we ever saw,"[42] and patent water closets were reported "very general in the better class homes." A row on Madison Street had sliding doors, inside shutters, patent force pumps, a hot water system and central furnace, and, of course, speaking tubes and bells in every room and gas light throughout.

All these functioning systems within the upper-class home implied new exchanges with the surrounding community. A townhouse was not a self-sustaining plantation: it was dependent on its elaborate connections like so many umbilical cords. An important one was gas light. In 1838 gas was not used in residences, and there were only two miles of mains in the city, but it now became the distinguishing characteristic of wealthy homes. Because it depended upon the extension of the gas company mains through the streets, it implied the concentration of elegant homes in select neighborhoods on a select street network: "As the company look to this solely as a source of profit, their outlay in laying pipes is confined to such parts as will pay an interest of six per cent on the extension."[43] In fact, the gas company in the early '50s was paying 9 or 10 percent dividends. The extension of gas mains to Broadway in 1849 meant that a new class of construction would begin. Those who could pay interest also demanded company water, at reliable pressures to supply the complete bathrooms and put out fires that threatened these ten-thousand-dollar investments and their furnishings.[44] The attractions of carriage roads and the need for building carriage houses became evident. In 1832 there were only sixty-five carriages registered in the city, a tenth of the number of carts and drays. But Curlett's display rooms have given some idea of the wide range of private family vehicles by 1850. The elegant residential districts like Mount Vernon and Bolton Hill were located on hilltops, sixty to a hundred feet above downtown places of business and entertainment. The owners of the townhouses also had country houses for summer, on hills at elevations of up to 350 feet and twelve miles from the center of town. The hilltop locations were, of course, chosen for their healthfulness. The 1853 estimate that a seventh of the population lived at elevations above 100 feet is a measure of the size of an upper class, together with its servants, live-in help, and washers and laundresses in nearby alleys.[45]

The creation of "squares" supplied a nucleus for the joint effort of public and private enterprise in defining and planning such elite neighborhoods. Baltimoreans were embarrassed at the lag with respect to New York. The *American* and the *Sun* in the late '30s both complained of the want of open squares.[46] The Canton Company proposed to lay out four elegant squares "on the Commanding Eminences" in imitation of the great squares of Manhattan, and to preserve the forest trees on them. In 1839 the *Sun* gave sanitary, esthetic, and economic arguments for squares, and complained of "the indescribable irregularity" of new streets in East Baltimore, "intersecting each other at all degrees of angles," producing a crop of small tenements on small parcels of small value. The Mount Vernon squares were the unique local model. Poppleton submitted his plat for the division of the Howard estate in 1832 with the unusual feature of a cross shape centered on the Washington Monument. Subdivision proceeded swiftly, and its success as a speculation, combined with its attraction as a social summit, contributed to the demand for making more squares and terraces. By 1860 half a dozen new squares on hilltops beyond the built-up city had become center-pieces for small webs of development. Among them were Franklin Square,[47] Union Square, Ashland Square, Jackson Place (east of Broadway at Monument), Madison Square, Lafayette Square, and the Battery. Squares were planned in Broadway, Eutaw Place, and Park Avenue.

Buckingham described a class of small shopkeepers, mechanics, and trades-people "who appear to be better informed, more industrious, and in better condition as to circumstances than the same class of persons in England."[48] He attributed this to the fact that labor was better paid, and provisions of all descriptions more abundant and more cheap. Toward the end of the period the health commissioners described roughly the same group:

Paternalistic Landscapes

There is, perhaps, no city in which the industrial and laboring classes are better housed and fed, than in Baltimore. In some of these families may be seen the highest degree of social and domestic enjoyment, in connection with great moral worth, and the sternest integrity. But the improvident and thriftless are less comfortable, and pro-portionably less happy.[49]

It does not seem to have been a large class of people, and in both cases refers to skilled workers born in the United States. It was definitely a class to which immigrants and free blacks aspired and occasionally attained. It was a market for new housing. One can distinguish three types of workers' habitats: the mill villages, urban industrial neighborhoods, and a belt of modest rows. The common feature of demand was the need to live within walking distance of work places, but in family dwellings.

The mill villages grew in size but did not change in their traditional social organization. The labor force was all white, native born, and English speaking. Whole families worked in the same mill. The mill owners also owned the land and the houses. They excluded alcohol and introduced religion, temperance and beneficial societies, primary schools, and the company store. On the Jones Falls at Woodberry by 1847 there were at least forty dwellings for the operatives of Carroll's and Gambrill's cotton mills. Two to a block, three stories high, they exhibited "the appearance of prosperity and taste." "They occupied the face of the hill which is divided from the factory by the Baltimore and Susquehanna railroad. . . . The summit is ornamented with the beautiful mansion of Mr. Gambrill. Centrally situated among the dwellings is a handsome Gothic church."[50] Adjoining them, their machinists, Poole and Hunt, developed two acres of shops and twenty dwellings on Brick Hill for their own operatives. On the Gwynns Falls, Wetheredsville had a population of six hundred and was laid out on 300 acres, with a school, church, Oddfellows Hall, and two company-

A once grand residential row, Waverly Terrace was rehabilitated in the 1970s by the city of Baltimore for use as apartments.

owned stores.[51] Other mill villages had reached roughly the same scale at Calverton, Franklin, Ashland, and Rochdale, at Washington factory and Phoenix.[52]

In contrast to the mill village operated by a single firm, the strategy of the Canton Company was to develop a complete industrial neighborhood with a number of different enterprises. In 1845 the company rebuilt the wharves between Fells Point and Boston Street and located a four-story warehouse at Chester and Aliceanna. It was sustained by fifty-six massive columns of iron and had iron doors, shutters, sashes, and frames. The investment may have been premature, but the company continued to work eastward, confident that "Canton in the progress of time and things, indicated by a cycle of twenty years, has ceased to be 'Out of Town.' "[53] By 1850 it was finishing the Atlantic Wharf at the mouth of Harris Creek, with 752 feet fronting on the railroad and 1221 feet fronting on the water. The company contracted to build private wharves jutting out from it for lumber and coal yards and shipbuilders. The company bridged the creek and continued to grade and pave streets to the east: Hudson, Chesapeake, Elliott, O'Donnell. There were 350 brickmakers at work. The corporation received roughly equal thirds of its income from sales of brick clay, ground rents, and the sale and lease of industrial property. The ground rents assured a relatively steady income, while the other sources augmented cash flows during high-investment periods, for the development process. It was a strategy of balanced investment and balanced land use. Residential and semipublic facilities were provided to encourage industrial growth. Workers could purchase homes, subject to the ground rent; they did not need to purchase the land. A village of more than a hundred neat two-story brick homes for workers extended along Aliceanna Street and down Clinton Street. Population was estimated at twenty-five hundred, while a thousand more workers commuted to Canton to work at the three blast furnaces, forge, steel-rolling mill, two copper smelters, bridge factory, cotton duck mill, or distillery. The several chapels and the "pretty little schoolhouse" opposite the copper smelter filled and overflowed.

Employers closer to the center of town could depend on the private housing market. Any concentration of labor provided a market for mass rental housing. For example, the B&O workers at Mount Clare shops lived in the neighborhoods roundabout. Entrepreneurs occasionally managed to make a neat speculation of housing their workers. Several blocks west of the Mount Clare shops, properties bought for $33,000 in 1835 were resold in 1851 for $127,000.[54] Charles Keener and John Garrett, associated with the B&O, bought and resold them within a few weeks as 267 house lots for another 30 percent markup. Homes were built and rented to employees of the B&O. Those who earned more and those who earned less than $1.25 a day were separated not by districts, but by local variations in elevation, width of street, and height and breadth of the houses.[55] They did not have servants, and these neighborhoods had few blacks.

On the speculative frontier of the city, a new belt of housing was built, much of which was also destined for the class of employees, mechanics, and shopkeepers. Because of the diversity and smaller scale of enterprises in Oldtown, along the Jones Falls, and out Gay Street, Pennsylvania Avenue, and Frederick Road, these districts did not have the character of company towns. The roles of developer and speculator are more apparent, at a scale of scores of houses. On the west side the process continued to be more orderly, as estates were subdivided.[56]

Essential to the construction of new houses for the working class were the financial innovations that allowed them to purchase homes. The ground rent remained important; as at Canton, the home owner did not need to buy the land. The new device of the generation was the building and loan association. In the 1840s several German Catholic societies, in particular St. James parish, served by the Viennese Redemptorists, sponsored the first savings societies for building.[57] The mechanism became much more important in the building booms of the 1880s and 1900s, and remains an important institution in Baltimore today.

Previous generations had depended on a patriarchal household of apprentices for industrial labor. The mill villages were a paternalistic landscape at a different scale; they allowed a degree of family privacy. The Canton Company landscape offered the worker even greater autonomy through the purchase of a dwelling. In the new belt built up around the city, the distinctive neighborhoods were a landscape of paternalism blown up to the scale of the whole city. Owners, entrepreneurs, and managers lived together on the hills, and a stable core of skilled workers lived together close to the enterprise, within call of the factory fire alarm and dinner bell.

While the wealthy extended a tracery of elegant streets onto certain hilltops and squares and rebuilt the downtown commercial core, while new industrial activities and worker housing spread over the low-lying districts, and while modest respectability girdled the old city, other sections of brick and dormers looked much the same. But the old city, refilled with new populations, had swelled and changed. In the ring built in the last generation there was secreted a lining or interfacing four miles long, of narrow streets and alleys less than twelve feet wide. Additional small lanes, courts, and alleys were privately developed and owned. Some were known only as X Alley, Y Alley, or Painter's Court. In this lining lived, half-hidden, the masses of the poor and casual workers. It represented 4 percent of the length of paved streets. Most of the remaining length was the standard thirty-nine feet.[58] The dual system of streets and alleys was laid out by Poppleton, but it took a generation of building on his model to discover the social implications.

The same health officers who spoke of the comfort of the industrious mechanic sought to distinguish between "a very large class" of virtuous poor who were "compelled to practice the most rigid economy" and below them "the great horde of the idle and the dissolute, the immoral and the depraved." But they suffered the same housing problem:

The necessities of these people induce them to huddle together in houses greatly disproportioned in size to the accommodation of such numbers. . . . A necessity is thus

The Genius of Poverty

Little Rock Street, which extended from Lexington Street to Saratoga Street, was one block long and only six feet wide for one-third of its length, yet the street contained thirty-five houses and a stable.

created for obtaining rooms at the lowest possible rates, and there has been in many instances an attempt to meet this want by building small, unventilated, and inconvenient houses, in narrow and blind courts. . . . These houses are badly constructed and crowded upon small side or back portions of lots.[59]

In these lanes were played out the demographic dramas of this generation—the arrival of new immigrants, the competition for jobs, the crowding to make the rent, the winnowing of death. The essential features of the immigration were a swelling rhythm that matched the building cycle, the predominance of Germans (half) and Irish (over a third), of men over women (three to two), and of persons in their twenties. At their peak, arrivals at the port reached twelve thousand a year, well beyond the peak of the 1830s.[60] These simple facts produced complex changes in the balance of the several ethnic groups in the labor force.

Any effort to compare the rise and assimilation of the several groups is hampered by the ambivalence of public opinion as expressed in newspapers. In 1837 and 1838, despite the business depression and the poverty of many Irish immigrants, they are reported to have sent home at least $30,000 to parents and brothers in Ireland, through Alex. Brown & Sons.[61] The moment of deepest crisis in European departures was at the onset of the boom in Baltimore. In 1847 200 "poor" were shipped from Hesse via Bremen, and landed at Baltimore.[62] In the same summer, three ships arrived from Ireland "freighted with human misery and death."[63] The captain wanted to discharge the sick and dying on shore, but Father Dolan had them put on scows for the Lazaretto at lower Canton. Carpenters hired to build a temporary hospital fled. Some of the immigrants staggered into the woods to die, and Dr. Donovan had the rest removed to the hospitals. Father Dolan set up a house for orphans, while the Hibernian Society supervised the "binding out to trades" of others. The number of persons the society relieved with cash increased from 105 in 1838 to 700 in 1852. The society was also placing 25 Irish immigrants a month on railway jobs. The boom made possible effective action to absorb immigrants into the local labor force and to move others on toward the agricultural frontier. The German Society had an Intelligence Bureau, which in 1846 placed 3500 laborers in Cumberland, York, Pittsburgh, and Washington. By 1856 large proportions of Irish and German names appear on B&O payrolls, including scores of cases of brothers and relatives, and many were already doing skilled jobs.

Because German and Irish immigrants were arriving in such large numbers, competition was aggravated for unskilled and dirty jobs. Incidents of intimidation were frequent in 1858 and 1859, as employers tried to cut wages following a bank and business crisis. Episodes recall the depression sequels to heavy immigration in 1832–36. When a German crew was hired to unload barges at Fells Point for seven dollars a boat, "the Roughs," a gang of fifty, assaulted them and forced the captains to hire their gang at the old wage of nine dollars. When coal dealers brought in new hands for a lower wage, "collusion occurred between the two gangs," and their "mutiny" was celebrated over a quart of whiskey. At the end of a week the old employees were reengaged.

Black workers felt the fiercest pressure.[64] Formerly, no white men were employed as stevedores on Fells Point or as laborers in the coal yards.[65] A gang of twenty-five drove black workers from Canton brickyards. At Thomas's and Donnely's brickyards near Federal Hill they were driven off by rioters with guns.[66] A mob displaced black laborers on horsecar construction in the city and stopped all work until $1.25 was offered.[67] The most vicious attacks were, as in the '30s, directed at the caulkers. At Federal Hill they traditionally worked for $1.75. J. T. Fardy & Sons hired on a white gang at $1.25. The whites promptly sought to displace black caulkers at Hooper's yard adjoining, but Hooper refused to discharge them. As quitting time approached, a crowd gathered, the police suddenly disappeared, the bell rang, and the mob stoned the black caulkers. Some jumped into the harbor and were rescued by ship captains "at their peril." Demands were extended to other yards, one by one, until William H. Skinner "positively refused to comply at any risk." Taking two revolvers, one in each hand, Skinner got into the boat with his colored caulkers to protect them from an armed gang on a schooner alongside. Skinner shut down his yard and sued the city for police protection. All the shipbuilders in South Baltimore were hiring white caulkers, who next extended their tactics to Fells Point. There several black caulkers were beaten up. One had a facial artery cut and his jawbone fractured: a seventy-year-old man died of head wounds. "There were no white witnesses" until the shipyard owner himself, Hugh O. Cooper, was beaten and kicked in the abdomen. The law then intervened, and the black caulkers continued at the point.[68]

Irish and German laborers were also frequently pitted against each other. On the C&O Canal between Hancock and Cumberland, ethnic rivalry depressed wages. On 11 August 1839, a hundred Irish laborers reportedly assaulted sections being built by German contractors and German laborers. The German priest gave names of "Irish villains" to the management. Federal troops shot eight or ten rioters in the presence of the company engineer, destroyed numerous worker shanties and two unlicensed taverns, and took twenty-six prisoners. Wage rates fell from $1.25 to 87½ cents a day.[69]

The violence in the white community and the vulnerability of the black community were associated with the changed ratios of age and sex. Throughout the censuses of 1840, 1850, and 1860, the free colored population of Baltimore had more women than men in every age group, with the greatest difference among persons in their teens, twenties, and thirties. People over fifty were a sizeable proportion. The slave population was even more lopsidedly female. The case was quite the opposite in the white population: men exceeded women by a large margin in their twenties and thirties, and persons over fifty were few.

Forms of violence are familiar from the 1830s. On New Year's Eve 1838, a fire engine was thrown off the dock. The *Sun* referred to rivalries among gangs from different parts of town, and blamed "five or six dozen of flash fellows,— fancy rattlers—tie and jewelry, who drink liquor enough to make it necessary either to go to bed or do something to work off the excitement."[70] Beginning in 1847 there was a notable increase of fires and false alarms; by 1851 the city averaged one of each per day. A new sport was to insult religious congregations and to disturb evening services. From about 1850, riots were associated with elections as well as fires, and German immigrants as well as blacks were victimized. "The subject of conversation, the themes of ambition relate to broils and rowdyism, everywhere."[71]

The case of the black community is most difficult to evaluate because of the political rhetoric that overwhelms fact. The *Sun*, a young firebrand paper with respect to many issues, mixed occasional sympathy with low wit. It recounted how a "crooked little lump of humanity of ebony hue"[72] resisted arrest, how two colored women fought and one scalded another. "When their cart wheels locked, a German milk man beat a poor negro slave driver over the head. Such gusts of passion and their bloody sequels should not be allowed."[73] Three slaves of Gorsuch escaped to York in 1850. When he tracked and cornered them, they killed him. The incident led to new attacks on the free blacks, who still had no right to carry weapons or give court testimony against whites. A gang of youths attacked passers-by nightly in Baltimore Street. "They are especially unpleasant to the unprotected Africans."[74] A gang stoned the house of a "most respectable, worthy, and inoffensive colored woman."[75] Rowdies attacked a colored man leaving Lexington Market with his few groceries.[76] Two men accused of a "vicious murder of an estimable colored man" were freed because no white testimony was brought.[77] There were wide differences of class among the free colored, but all were vulnerable to the racism of the law. The grip of tidewater slave holders over the legislature was complete. The constitutional convention of 1851 prohibited any change in "rights and liberties" of slave holder and slave.

In spite of the pressures, the black community managed to cultivate a degree of freedom and solidarity and to consolidate families, some institutions of mutual assistance, and sometimes property. Throughout this period, the black population of Baltimore did not increase in numbers, but the proportion who were free approached 100 percent. Blacks maintained or improved their positions in water jobs, such as oystermen and seamen, and as hucksters and brickmakers because of types of local experience with which immigrants could not compete. A larger proportion of free blacks occupied domestic or personal service trades—barbers, cooks, waiters, laundresses, and porters—in spite of immigrant domestic workers. Market conditions did not favor slave labor in Baltimore or its agricultural region, and some slave owners were satisfied to sell out.

The instance of Noah Davis shows how little by little the proportion of free persons increased. Raised in slavery in Virginia and licensed as a Baptist preacher, in 1847 Davis obtained from his master a pass to go to Baltimore to serve a colored church and earn the money to pay $500 for his own freedom. He then raised $800 to buy his wife and two youngest children, and had to pay another $100 because the children increased in value while he saved. His salary was $300 a year, his wife took in washing and did daywork, and they put their daughter "in service" to pay off the last of the loan, bond, and life insurance on the other children. To prevent his twenty-year-old son from being sold south, he had to raise $700 in haste: the boy was already in a trader's jail in Richmond. For two others he paid $560 and $570, but a daughter, offered at $990, was "run up by a trader who agreed to let my friend have her for $1100." To raise money to buy the last of seven born in slavery, he published his life story.[78]

Before the Civil War, Baltimore achieved an intensity of construction that did not depend on buildings of great height. The Washington Monument and the cathedral define the skyline.

Nelson Wells, a free drayman employed by Charles Crooks, managed to save twenty dollars a month in the Savings Bank of Baltimore. About 1830 he began investing in property—first a ground rent on Ruxton Lane, then the leasehold, then a house on South Charles Street. When he died in 1843, he left several thousand dollars to provide for Negro education. The Savings Bank of Baltimore directors used it to found the Baltimore Normal School.[79]

The social layout of Baltimore is nowhere adequately described for this period, because the segregations of ethnic groups occurred at a fine scale below the size of wards and because they were in constant flux. A reshuffle of population occurred as those who could afford new housing and urban services moved out, and as immigrants scrambled for the smallest spaces. Job competition, combined with the need to live near the job, sharpened competition for housing. Fells Point had the boardinghouses for receiving arriving immigrants. Starving Irish arrived at Thompson's Sign of the Harp on Ann Street near Thames in 1847. By the early '50s the point swarmed with German immigrants, and the black population, which had been numerous in the north-south narrow streets such as Happy Alley and Star Alley, tended to move out, consistent with job pressures on shipyard and dock labor. They occupied alleys in other parts of the city, chiefly the middle ring. In West Baltimore, convenient to the new neighborhoods of the wealthy who used laundresses, porters, cooks, and waiters were Union Street, Biddle Alley, Greenwillow Street, and, running east-west, Sarah Ann, Pierce, and Raborg streets and Chestnut and Cider alleys. In 1850 many of these alleys were jointly occupied by Irish, German, and free colored householders.[80] The pattern continued in South Baltimore: Dover Street, Wayne Street, Welcome Alley, York Street, Little Hughes and Little Montgomery streets, and Sugar Alley. In Oldtown, blacks and some Germans occupied the irregular lanes along the axis of Bel Air Market: East, Chestnut, French, Low, Stirling, and Mott streets, and to the South Douglas Street, Necessity Alley, Half Moon Alley, Comet Alley, and Forest Street. All of these linings were growth tissue for postwar black neighborhoods, although they were hidden from the "respectable streets," like a reverse side of the urban fabric.

Draymen, carters, and other "horsey" trades were increasing also in cheaper housing and shanties farther out in the northwest and northeast. The Irish were particularly numerous along the axis of Harford Road and the Germans along Pennsylvania Avenue, as butchers, tanners, harness makers, and grain handlers, while the blacks were decidedly absent from the fast-growing outer ring of the city.

As tenants, the poor were at the mercy of their landlords, and had to move out to make room for commercial expansion. As second-class citizens, they were at the mercy of public improvements aimed at creating "decent" residences and a better tax yield for the city. The widening of Ruxton Lane and the rebuilding of Balderston Street, for example, were undertaken to destroy the rookeries and places of gambling and vice.[81] "Several fine warehouses have been built, others erecting, now respectable and business-like." Because the demolitions merely dispersed "foul deeds," *Sun* editors recommended that work be extended to Guilford Alley, Liberty Street, Brandy Alley, and Perry Place, "to pull down the old tottering buildings, which were inhabited by the most degraded and vicious part of our population." Redevelopment coincided with the appearance of "a new system of grinding the faces of the poor."[82] During the winter of 1839 landlords raised the rent, asking for a month in advance. "Every hovel" was rented.[83] In Oldtown a poor widow with three children had her stove and furniture taken from her for a rent of $3.50 "run up with costs to $5.26."[84] The continuation of a tight housing market for the poor was shown in the fall of 1843 by the appearance of squatters and resistance to ejectments.[85] But each wave of construction produced another wave of evictions. In 1850 the elegant improvements in Centre Street, between St. Paul and Charles, replaced a "half dozen little shanties, pigpens and stables," former residences of black workers and porters. The population of the city's central ward declined 10 percent in the '50s. When the B&O acquired the land for Camden Station, they tore down five squares occupied by "rude and dilapidated tenements."[86] The bricks were to be used in the new depot, but there was no such plan for recycling the tenants. The *Sun* editor was led to question the value of cities:

They harbor, as it were, the genius of poverty; accustom the masses to privation; and expose them to the wrongs of the oppressor. And that oppressor is found, wherever the use of capital is active, under the discipline of men indifferent to the rights of their fellow men, and unscrupulous about the invasion of them.[87]

The "personal" crises of the poor continued to occur chiefly in winters of business depression, every three or four years. Seasonal variation of casual labor was so great that the penitentiary released prisoners only between April and August, or they would be forced to steal to live. The crises of the poor were characteristic of certain parts of the city. As surely as the floods in the Jones Falls, they perennially victimized certain classes of neighborhoods. An epileptic woman ragpicker was found with marks of burns all over her. A policeman sent to the almshouse "a family of destitute negroes, some of whom were impregnated with loathesome diseases." In the upper room of a small hovel in Aetna Lane a poor widow who had lost her husband in the Mexican War was huddled on sacking, with her child. They had no furniture, no food, no fire.[88] In 1858 Mrs.

Thomas Winans organized a soup kitchen in her mansion in West Baltimore Street: she was feeding six hundred persons a day.

The several forms of discrimination in the labor market were reflected in the structure of wage rates, which in turn reinforced the vulnerability of the several classes of people. The black laborer generally earned $1.00, where the white on the same job earned $1.25. The inequality of wages between male and female labor was more extreme. The *Sun* commented, in July 1839, that where a brother and sister were both house servants, tailor and tailoress, or agricultural workers, "the one is earning more in one day than the other in seven. How shameful. Are not the labors of each class as necessary in their respective spheres?"[89] Instant destitution was often the fate of the woman whose husband died, fell ill, abandoned her, or simply could not earn enough for a household. She was reduced to "the grinding poverty of the widow of avaricious man," as the *Sun* called it. "From every view we take, we find injustice staring us in the face, like the eyes of a family portrait."[90]

Church and School

In this generation, church and school became neighborhood institutions, and the base was laid for an ideology of neighborhood integrity. In Baltimore both the public and parochial school systems took root, and their roles were defined in relation to religion, ethnic identity, and class.

At the end of the 1830s churches and schools were still concentrated in the downtown area and three subcenters—Fells Point, Oldtown close to the falls, and the southwest near Hanover and Lombard streets. But the number of churches and chapels tripled—from 50 in 1837 to 100 in 1845 and 150 in 1860. As the city grew, sheer distance forced the hiving off of new congregations. Parents demanded schools and Sunday schools spaced over the city's much greater area. At the same time, the increase in population made it possible to support a greater variety of movements, and with the immigrants came a transfusion of new ideas and fresh zeal. At least twenty-five of the new churches were of German language, and there was some duplication for linguistic reasons: a second New Jerusalem church, a tract society of colporteurs to the German speaking, a second Catholic parish on Fells Point. Disagreement over the cultural adaptations to be made to American conditions gave rise to five new synagogues and a rich variety of Lutheran and Reformed churches, with varying degrees of emphasis on English or German in worship and schooling. The fear that loss of language threatened faith was important among the Germans—Lutheran, Catholic, and Jewish alike. In Germany it was a period of intense revival of religious tradition, personal piety, and controversy, entwined with Romantic literature and music and a language-conscious nationalism. It was through German religious connections that Baltimore in this period was most intensely in touch with Europe.

The greatest growth was shown by the Catholics and the Methodists. Consistent with the past, Baltimore remained their national center of management and publishing, and Catholics and Methodists continued to make the greatest evangelizing efforts in the city. Small Methodist chapels were a quarter of the total of 1860. About half of the eighteen new colored churches were Methodist independents, and a number of the German churches were "Methodizing" groups, such as the Evangelical Society.

The Catholic church had to create new parishes and new orders of priests and teaching nuns to cope with ethnic differences. Jealousy occurred between immigrant Irish and German elements, as in the labor market. Most distinctively Irish, St. Patrick's Church on Fells Point grew rapidly, and its pastor, Father Dolan, was a key figure in services to immigrants. The parish school expanded to 250, and the Brothers of St. Patrick were imported to teach them. Small missions were started, St. Bridget's in Canton and Our Lady of Good Counsel and St. Laurence O'Toole at Locust Point. The Brothers of the Christian Schools had 500 pupils at the new St. Vincent de Paul's school, 180 in the cathedral school for boys in Calvert Hall, and 550 at the parish school of St. Peter the Apostle, convenient to the railroad shops.

The development of German Catholic activity in Baltimore in the 1840s was based on runners of thought that grew from Baltimore and Cincinnati into France, then Bavaria and Vienna, and back to Baltimore. Several of the exiled Sulpicians who had traveled widely in America, in particular Father Dubourg, had returned to France as bishops. Their connections with lay persons, refugees from the West Indies (such as Madame Petit) and émigrés, resulted in the founding of the Society for the Propagation of the Faith, at Lyons (1822). It rapidly became an international organization with strong participation in Belgium. Organized on a decimal basis, ten persons pledged a penny a week and a daily prayer for the missions; one of them forwarded the money and accounts to a central steward for ten cells. The society forwarded the gifts to the bishops nearest to mission frontiers, and their newsletter reported back to contributors. Similar mission societies were organized in Vienna (the Leopoldine Foundation, 1828) and Munich (the Ludwig Society, 1838).[91] The Congregation of the Most Holy Redeemer, which had its important bases in Vienna and Belgium, decided to send missionaries to America to convert Indians on the frontier. They found this exceedingly frustrating, and seeing everywhere en route German settlers "already of the fold" but without pastors or schools, they moved into a role of serving the German Catholics in America. The combined effects of the infusion of money, German-speaking personnel, and excellent communications resulted in a remarkable exchange of ideas within the American church and at the international level. From 1840 Baltimore was the American headquarters of the Redemptorists, as well as the home of the nation's archbishop, and a major port for travel from Germany and Belgium. Consequently, Baltimore—more precisely St. Alphonsus Church—was the center of this information system.

The Redemptorists organized a headquarters and seminary at St. James Church, Eager and Aisquith streets, and new German churches, St. Michael's on Fells Point and Holy Cross on Federal Hill, with parish schools at each location for some two hundred children, and an orphanage, St. Anthony of Padua.[92] The Redemptorists had lay brothers who assisted with the schools, and they developed a close working arrangement nationwide with the School Sisters of Notre Dame, introduced into America from Munich. Tireless travelers, the Redemptorists radiated out of Baltimore into its hinterland of railroad and mining towns, and even into areas of new settlement. In 1843 Father Alex Czvitkovicz attempted to salvage a pioneering venture in Elk County, Pennsylvania. A dozen families from Baltimore and a dozen from Philadelphia had contracted for thirty-five thousand acres at seventy-five cents an acre, and formed a German Catholic Brotherhood for a refuge from persecution. Father Alex surveyed the virgin forest for them, platted the townsite of St. Mary's, designed a church, prepared rules for the community, and arranged for them to receive German immigrants who might arrive at Baltimore. He finally suggested they send for German Benedictines: "They are farmers."[93] Not only were the Redemptorists great preachers and builders, but they were also known for their orderly reports and organizational skills.[94] There is reason to think they created the first building and loan societies in Baltimore in their parish of St. James. The mission societies themselves were the model of decimal organization, weekly saving, and accounting.

Catholic work in the black community was also renewed by the Redemptorists. By the time Father Joubert died, the Sisters of Providence were reduced to twelve sisters, ten free scholars, ten orphans, and a mortgage. "By degrees it appeared that everything was falling."[95] Archbishop Whitfield suggested they ought to return to the world, and his successor, Archbishop Eccleston, despaired that he could not even take care of his overwhelming immigrants, much less the blacks. But in 1847 Father T. Anwander from St. James begged to be allowed to serve as chaplain and confessor to the Sisters of Providence. Regular masses were again held, new buildings were bought for St. Frances Academy, and by 1853 there were 135 children in the school, with 30 to 50 boarders, a group of orphans, and a school for boys. Each Easter season 40 or 50 persons were baptized and confirmed. The impression that this institution made on visitors to church councils was considerable, and influenced the conviction nationwide that a separate colored parish was the best way to organize missions for Negroes.

The Jewish community was nearly all German, many from Bavaria, some via Holland and the West Indies. It may have numbered two hundred families in 1840, seven hundred families in 1850.[96] They were found in the three older subcenters of the city. Except for the Sephardic temple, Beth Israel, all of the new synagogues grew out of the original Baltimore Hebrew Congregation, known as Stadt Schul. From a rented room over a grocery in Fells Point, the congregation moved to a one-story dwelling in High Street, then to a three-story house on the corner of Harrison Street and Etna Lane, and in 1845 they built the Lloyd Street synagogue. Their rabbi, Abraham Rice, represented strict orthodoxy. Har Sinai Verein broke away to experiment with Reform. They built a temple in High Street, and in 1855 called Rabbi David Einhorn from Germany. He became a national spokesman for Reform Judaism. The other new synagogues represented middle paths between these two positions. Hebrew Friendship was created at Fells Point and later chartered and rebuilt as the Eden Street synagogue. When Rabbi Rice retired from Baltimore Hebrew Congregation to attend to his dry goods business, he officiated at a small service on Howard Street, uncompromising in its orthodoxy; the members eventually formed the congregation of Shearith Israel (Remnants of Israel). Oheb Shalom (Lovers of Peace) was founded in the southwest part of the city, first in a home, then in the third floor of a coach factory, and finally on Hanover Street. The rabbi, Benjamin Szold, was a conservative.

The German-language community was complex, ranging from the merchants of the Germania Club to the poorest immigrants. Among the Germans, religious divisions cut across class divisions, and there were numerous possibilities for communication among the different elements. Pastor Scheib, who arrived in 1835, developed a school at Zion Lutheran Church, and the Singeverein and Liederkranz performed a Beethoven symphony in 1837. The '48ers were less important in Baltimore than in Cincinnati or Milwaukee, but several liberal figures nevertheless played a role. George Fein founded the Concordia Club, which developed German music and theater, and Carl Heinrich Schnauffer wrote songs popular in the working-class Turner movement. He founded *Die Wecker* (1851), the German newspaper that stubbornly opposed slavery and promoted the Republican vote. When Emerson visited Baltimore in 1843, he complained that he could not "hear of any poets, mystics or strong characters of any sort."[97] If Emerson had spoken German, he might have discovered the strong characters in Baltimore.

In the architectural and artistic arrangements of the new churches of the 1850s can be seen the greatest extremes yet displayed. External sobriety hid the interior impression of warmth, ecstasy, comfort, or order in which each group made itself at home. Class differences produced surprising contrasts with ancient tradition, and with their relative status today. The Catholics, who had recently finished their magnificent cathedral for the whole nation, now built some of the plainest chapels. The Baltimore Hebrew Congregation in Lloyd Street built a synagogue whose sun-splashed and whitewashed pews and railings are reminiscent of New England meetinghouses or the eighteenth-century Anglican churches of Maryland. The Methodists built the Charles Street Church, while they continued to hold camp meetings under the tent and to erect frame chapels in the mill towns and factory settlements. The Presbyterians, raised in the austerity of John Knox and John Calvin but grown rich in Baltimore, ordered cushioned pews and stained glass.[98]

The new neighborhoods of elegance and respectability are most apparent in the older denominations of affluence, Presbyterian and Episcopal. First Presbyterian moved to Madison Street and Park Avenue, and numerous congregations grew from it: Westminster Church and the churches in Aisquith Street and Franklin Street. Its Sunday school missions developed into Franklin Square Church, Green Street Church, and Central Presbyterian. St. Paul's Episcopal Church was rebuilt in 1844 and again in 1856 as Italian Romanesque. There emerged from it in this generation five new congregations: Ascension, St. Stephen's, St. Mark's, Emmanuel, and All Saints Zion. St. Luke's, on Carey Street, was undertaken adjoining Franklin Square. Each congregation reflected and enhanced a conception of neighborhood and status.

The colored churches, associated with a sponsoring white congregation to meet the legal requirements of permits for gatherings, also seem to have developed some differentiation of class. Among those that moved uptown were

Pennsylvania AME Zion and Madison Avenue Presbyterian.[99] Particularly handsome were Union Baptist, First Baptist, and the Methodist Protestant. But most of the colored churches were still clustered in the center of town on Saratoga and Courtland streets, or in the three emerging black neighborhoods: in East Baltimore in narrow north-south streets such as Dallas, Wolfe, Spring, and Chestnut; in West Baltimore on Tessier and Orchard streets; and in South Baltimore on Sharp and Montgomery streets.

The proliferation of churches and their new architectural visibility offered an illusion of health and energy, but all of the churches were deeply threatened by rivalry and internal division. The visible differentiation of congregations by class, race, language, and attitudes toward religious tradition was a framework within which the passions of the nation were working. In the church as in national political life, Baltimore was a pivotal location, a fulcrum with respect to hostilities between Protestant and Catholic, conservative and reformer, and proslavery and antislavery factions.

In spite of the separation of church and state, the rhetoric of religion and the rhetoric of politics were hard to distinguish. Both political and religious leaders fostered "gusts of passion" and have some responsibility for "their bloody sequels." Reverend Robert Breckinridge, pastor of Second Presbyterian Church, accused the Irish keeper of the almshouse of operating a papal prison, and was sued for libel. Five hundred Baltimoreans crowded the Criminal Court for eight days, listening to all the distinguished lawyers and senators "in the finest effort of oratory" directed to the "agitation of the public mind." The jury, James S. Buckingham observed, seemed more and more puzzled the longer the case lasted. When they could reach no verdict, both Catholics and Protestants were enraged.[100]

As early as 1835 dozens of abolition societies were springing up in the North under Protestant evangelical leadership. In response, southern states curtailed freedom of the press. In Baltimore, caught in the middle, a vociferous rhetoric of union meant silence with respect to abolition. National splits within Presbyterian, Methodist, and Baptist churches involved alliances between an "old school" theology and a southern faction seeking to silence abolitionists. Critical national conferences were held in Baltimore, and Baltimore clergy played important roles in compromise, postponement, and extreme legalism.[101] Breckinridge was a major figure in the Presbyterian split, Stephen Roszel among Methodists. The Methodist general conference held in Baltimore in 1840 ruled out the testimony of black against white in states where it would not be allowed in trials at law. Two black congregations of Baltimore protested the "soul-sickening" decision, but their memorials were suppressed. The Baptists, convened in Baltimore in 1841, voted "not to deny any courtesy to a Christian brother because he is a slaveholder." The Society of Friends urged its members to avoid agitation as counterproductive. The Catholic councils and pastoral letters made no statements whatever on the abolition of slavery, and the editor of the semi-official *Catholic Mirror* contended, "It is fanaticism or hypocrisy to condemn slavery as in itself opposed to the law of God." The churches of Baltimore were morally paralyzed.

The public schools, founded in 1828, began developing rather suddenly ten years later. In a miniature building boom between 1838 and 1855, enrollment rose from a thousand to ten thousand,[102] the number of teachers from ten to two hundred, and the annual budget from ten thousand dollars to a hundred thousand dollars. The swift growth of clientele and political and financial support involved a definition of the institutional role: what groups in the society would be served? The public schools were grounded on ideas of religious neutrality (King James and Douai Bibles were authorized), individualism, and egalitarianism. Yet their growth took place in an age of widening class differences, divergent ethnic and religious identities, and a rigid color line. They were located and built in a context of social reshuffle and neighborhood segregation. A permanent gap appeared between ideology and practice in the Baltimore public schools.

The ideas upon which the city's public schools were founded and justified were expressed in a *Sun* editorial of 1843, when the state legislature was trying to withdraw the school fund and apply it to the public debt.

In the first place they are purely democratic institutions. It is the glory of the constitution that we recognize no privileged ranks or classes, or State religion. Notwithstanding these public provisions, however, society is much disturbed by the contests of political parties, the rancor of religious strife, and distrust and jealousy between the rich and the poor. These sever the bonds of a common brotherhood, and segregate society into divisions which become hostile in proportion to their isolation. It is the necessary tendency of a system of public instruction to heal these divisions.[103]

But even at that moment, who would control and benefit was being settled. The sudden popularity was associated with the creation of a high school for boys (1839) with a distinctive middle-class curriculum. Likewise, when the high schools for girls, Eastern and Western, were founded (1844), female enrollment in the system immediately rose from a third to half the total, and more women teachers were employed. Primary schools were distinguished from grammar schools, and school teachers, like garbage contractors, were reorganized as part of the new ward politics and patronage.

By 1854 there was a wide variation in the proportion of school-age children who were actually enrolled in the various wards, from none to half. Enrollment was lowest in the richest and poorest areas of the city; the public school had become a mechanism of social promotion of classes in the middle. Of the fathers of girls in the high schools, half were merchants and professionals, minor officials and clerks, and the other half were mechanics or skilled craftsmen such as plasterers, bricklayers, or upholsterers. A unique "floating school" was organized in 1857, and half the parents were in seagoing or shipbuilding occupations; a third were decidedly among the mercantile and professional class, the other two-thirds were mechanics. Only a handful had possibly Irish or German names.

As the budget rose, economy enforced a compromise that widened the gap between a small number of advanced pupils and a terminal education for the great majority. The Baltimore delegation managed to save their school fund in 1843 by arguing the efficiency of mass schooling "productive of the greatest good to the greatest number at the least expense." Rigid economy was evident in the ratio of fifty pupils to each teacher, and the investment in the average schoolhouse of five thousand dollars, or twenty dollars per pupil. The thirty school buildings were small, usually forty-three by sixty-five feet or fifty by seventy-five, on lots about double their size, with a main story and a basement beneath, "either on a level with the ground, or more or less sunk beneath the surface." The schoolrooms were heated by stoves, without flues except "a few holes perforated in the ceiling." Ventilation was so poor that teachers complained of headaches after two or three hours' confinement.[104] Contrasting with these were the new buildings for Eastern Female High School on Mullikin Street and Western Female High School on West Fayette Street near Paca. Conceived as monuments to learning and respectability, they merited the employment of an architect, and the interior arrangements were those of a far more complex mechanism.

The public schools were only a part of a still larger mechanism. They had two-thirds of the total number of children in school, and emerged as a white Anglo-Saxon Protestant institution. Twelve hundred black children were in schools, all private and church sponsored. They were not admitted to the public schools, although colored citizens paid the school tax. In 1852 the archbishop failed in a vigorous bid to obtain state funds for the parish and orphan schools of the Irish and German Catholics. All of those "free schools," parochial and charitable, had plain schoolhouses much like the public primary schools. German Protestants, however, developed private schools on a more elaborate model; the most important were Knapp's Institute and Pastor Scheib's at Zion Lutheran, under Pestalozzi influence. Other high schools were founded as private institutions, to serve the most respectable class, but they took the exceptional talented pupil on scholarship: Loyola College, the Academy of the Visitation, Mount Washington Female College, and Lutherville Female Seminary.

The most popular view of Baltimore in the 1840s was one imitating Constantinople. Buckingham had lectured here on the architecture of Turkey, and the comparison of the cathedral dome on the hill, its towers like minarets on the skyline, had an exotic appeal. In 1850, photographs began to show the city as a sea of brick and chimneys, punctuated by its steeples. The clustering of communities around their steeples reinforced the segregation of communities of race, language, origin, and social class, as well as of religion. The churches stimulated new kinds of societies, new institutions, a great organizational ferment. Yet the fragmentation of ideas, identities, and social responsibilities meant a loss of a sense of *civitas*. Common purposes were splintered, and great issues were set aside. Ethnic identity and status were structured by the churches, in worship, education, and welfare, from the cradle to the grave.

The Municipal Mechanism

The builder, the school superintendent, the city council, and the church extension society were alike prepared simply to develop more of the same in the new districts—another pump, another chapel, another 180 feet of cobbles. New watch houses were built at Fells Point and Federal Hill. New markets were built in Richmond Street, Cross Street, and Hollins Street, and the older ones expanded with gas lighting and cast-iron columns. Rigorous adherence to Poppleton's plat made the extension of streets and rows appear orderly. Each year's street extensions provided the warp and woof of a new bit of the urban tapestry. But the very defects of Poppleton's plan were thus built into the landscape. His two-dimensional regularity was imposed at the cost of ever more serious defects of grades and drainage. His layout of streets and alleys developed into a schizoid social landscape of rich and poor, native and foreigner, white and black, in back-to-back rows. The problems of physical and social engineering were interwoven. The development of new neighborhoods of the wealthy meant the abandonment of waterfronts, lowlands, and central districts to the poor and the concentration of new stresses in these environments. Hostilities of class and ethnic origin were reinforced by the scarcity of good environments.

Organisms do not grow merely by accretion, and overloads were produced on the city's metabolic system and its vital organs, particularly the hospitals and prisons. At the high tide of construction, the recognition that people were dying and killing each other at a higher rate stimulated examination of the mechanism and new attempts to reengineer the city. With the same rhythm observed earlier, a relatively healthy period in the early 1840s was followed by a frightening increase in death rates as the building boom hit its stride. The city was experiencing the highest infant and child mortality in its history. Half of all deaths were of children under five. The proliferation of churches, the advance of evangelical religion, and the introduction of cherubim in stained glass coincided with Baltimore's contribution between 1837 and 1860 of forty-four thousand little angels.

This was also the only time in Baltimore's history that death rates among whites rose to match those of blacks. This is what one might expect, knowing that the Irish and German immigrants were competing for the same kinds of ill-paid jobs and the same dwellings in alleys and courts. In every year consumption (tuberculosis) was a leading cause of death. With heavy immigration, European epidemic diseases were reintroduced.[105] In 1847 two hundred cases of smallpox were received by ship, but were successfully confined to the new marine hospital. Medical students were able to observe there a case of simultaneous smallpox and typhoid, and an Irish mother and daughter had typhus and typhoid fever at once. Scarlet fever was epidemic and exceptionally deadly from August 1847 to May 1848, followed by infant cholera in July and August. The next summer eighty-three cases of typhus were sent to the almshouse, "invariably from filthy and unwholesome localities." According to Buckler, in rows of houses occupied by Germans, Irish, and free blacks, it would single out the blacks, seizing an entire family.[106] The evidence suggests differences in levels of immunity in the several populations, rather than differences in living conditions. The manner in which typhus was transmitted was not yet recognized, but the presence of "the loathesome disease" in Louse Alley was not a coincidence. The physician at the marine hospital, noting the origin of cases of smallpox, questioned whether "the alley system" ought to be continued.

Next, the fever diseases reappeared in their usual locations. In 1851 a grave epidemic of intermittent and remittent fevers occurred at the penitentiary and on both sides of the Jones Falls north of Centre Street. In 1853 yellow fever appeared on Thames Street, traversed one block, and suddenly stopped. Eighteen died. The next year a malignant fever occurred in Will, Block, Philpot, and Canton streets, and in 1858 "a very malignant fever" occurred at Fort McHenry and Spring Gardens, where standing water in the extensive brick clay pits was favorable to the breeding of mosquitoes.

A sense of crisis rose to a peak along with the building boom. The search for explanations was based on the old theory that the putrefaction of solid wastes produced noxious gases that generated disease. Therefore, the effort to regain control involved improvements to solid waste collection and ventilation, and only later to water supply and drainage.

The city street was the physical framework for removing wastes as well as supplying goods. Garbage, street manure, and night soil had to be carried ever greater distances to rid the city of them. But street paving, repairs, cleaning, and garbage collection were all services in which the city had been holding the budget line since 1835, when it began to feel the pinch of debt service on its railroad investments. The garbage contract system, for example, initiated in 1845, degenerated quickly. Spending had gone down from twelve thousand dollars to five thousand dollars a year. Comparison of 1848–50 mortality figures with those of 1845–47 showed that July deaths had doubled. The health officer figured that a monthly economy of six hundred dollars was costing fifty to one hundred lives. More important, ran his cost-benefit argument, the hazard would cost Baltimore its economic future: "A tenacity for life is inherent in all, and just in proportion as the cancers of mortality are increased in any given place, in the same ratio will capital and enterprise contract or expand."[107] Therefore, in 1852 a public service corps of garbage cart drivers and street scrapers was created. They were paid a dollar a day, hired and assigned to their own ward, and enjoined to "strict sobriety and a becoming degree of politeness." The policy change was characteristic of the main lines of debate for the next seventy-five years: a seesaw between the demand for service and the demand for economy, and between the contract system and the public service corps.

In street cleaning the problem of social class was highly visible. The cancers of mortality were not the same in all parts of the city. The filth was found where the poor dwelled, and interpretations were various. "The narrow lanes, inhabited by the poor, although more liable to become filthy, receive less attention than the more public thoroughfares, and are always in a more dirty condition."[108] The small lanes and courts were private property, and there was little pressure on property owners to provide services. In years of epidemic, thousands of sanitary notices were issued, but only a score of police actions followed. Fells Point was described as an "augean stable . . . a mountain mass of nuisance,"[109] but a council member who owned property there pleaded that the alleged nuisance had been tolerated for at least ten years.

The dirtiness of the city also contributed to concern about its ventilation. Rising summer mortality reinforced the feeling of everyone in a Baltimore heat wave, that hot stagnant air was unhealthy. A bad smell was believed dangerous, and Baltimore had plenty of bad smells. Seafood consumption was rising, and there were new noxious fumes from industry. Twenty thousand privies drained illegally to the Jones Falls. When the wind was from the south, it wafted sewer odors through the city.[110] Experiments were made with "stench traps." New studies of human and animal physiology attracted attention to respiratory circulation. The role of the lungs in the human organism was easily extended: a city, too, needed to breathe. As early as 1839 the *Sun* made the analogy and attributed the "summer disease" of infants to the effects of "undue heat and vitiated atmosphere."[111] The atmosphere of cities, the editor argued, tended always to deteriorate. The houses retained heat at night, and to restore equilibrium he recommended squares numerous and exact in proportion to the height of houses and narrowness of streets. Dr. Wynne was explicit about the volume of air required per person for ventilating schoolrooms and public buildings, and he extended his notion to the mechanism of gas exchanges of the entire city.

While solid waste, heat, and foul smells were most easily perceived, we know from the vantage of hindsight that the critical problem was still the invisible pollution of the water supply by human sewage, compounded by grave difficulties of personal cleanliness without adequate water. The increase in deaths from intestinal diseases should be attributed to this cause. The differentials of death between rich and poor neighborhoods were the result of the geography of water pollution.

Water supply was a dual system, class structured. The elegant residential districts and the central business district used the piped water of a private corporation for an annual fee. The company extended its service somewhat, in order to postpone threatened municipal takeover. To protect its right to the flow of the Jones Falls, it acquired several valuable mill properties north to the city limits: Lanvale factory, Mount Royal mill, Rock mill, and the Eagle works. The company built one reservoir at 135 feet elevation (later the site of Belvedere Hotel at Chase and Charles streets) and a larger one at 67 feet elevation (near the east end of the present Pennsylvania Station). The lower reservoir filled directly from stream flow, and its capacity was expanded to 25 million gallons, to improve its function as backup supply in summer low flow.[112] Despite these improvements, by 1850 only half the city's built-up area was serviced by water mains, and about a quarter of its households were consumers. Builders of fine homes were encouraged to drain bathrooms and water closets "to water," in spite of legislation requiring that privies be sealed and emptied regularly. The poor and most of the middling population east of the Jones Falls had to carry their water from the eight hundred city pumps, that is, they depended on the shallow wells polluted from surface drainage, privies, and defective sewers or covered streams.[113] There were no free hydrants and no public baths, and the nearest public swimming place was at Ferry Bar.

The city's efforts at storm drainage had also lagged. Both surface grades in the streets and underground drains were makeshift. Problems were handled piecemeal, so that little was accomplished for the money spent. After twenty-two years (1829 to 1850), the cutting down of Hughes Street at the foot of

Federal Hill was still imperfect. The docks were filled at the southeast angle with mud washed from adjoining streets, "owing to a bad grade and the want of paving."[114] The ordinance of August 1837 ordering the bend in the Jones Falls at Centre Street to be straightened had not been implemented fifteen years later. Meanwhile, a new drain from Centre Street discharged so much water that it modified the channel and made a sandbank across three-fourths the width of the stream.[115] Such accumulations contributed both to stagnation in time of drought and to the risk of destruction in time of flood. Downstream, the old meadow remained the perennial flood district, and in 1858 "the usual people" were forced to remove.

The fundamental problem was that no overall engineering concept or system was applied to grading. The city surveyor complained of the defective system of establishing grades "one, two and several squares at a time."[116] Wyeth and Walker streets had "a vertical step" of over three feet where they joined St. Peter's Street. The Northern Central Railroad was located without presenting a topographic profile or any study of how it would affect the crossings of future city streets. Baltimore, the surveyor complained, possessed the most favorable ground for proper and economic grades of any city in the union, but "probably her grades are the worst." He urged a systematic topographic survey, which would make possible a rational organization of storm drainage. By planning all the grades at once, millions of dollars could be saved, and property owners could build and excavate efficiently.

At the same time, the board of health commissioners urged attention to underground storm drainage:

It appears that no survey of the sewers has ever been made. We are informed by the proper officer that there is not now, and apparently there never has been, a plat of the sewers prepared or recorded in his office. No one can now tell the forms, sizes, grades of decent [sic], connections nor directions of the sewers.[117]

Urban growth increased the load on the system, and the alternation of summer storms and summers of drought produced periodic crises, each worse than the last, of stench and disease. July or August storms produced freshets, followed by fill during the following winter. "We stood yesterday and watched the liquid mud running into Jones Falls. . . . It is nothing but mud, mud, mud, almost knee deep."[118] The low summer flow of the falls was reduced by the expanded reservoirs and aggravated in years of drought.[119] The water in McClure's dock was less than eight feet deep; a sewer emptied under it, and privies were built over it. When it was dredged in 1853, the stench was unbearable. In 1855 and 1856, at Smith's dock and Frederick Street dock, "the beds of the docks were deeply covered with a foul sediment, which, in the process of decomposition, was constantly emitting volumes of offensive gas."[120] By 1861 the bed of the Jones Falls was filled with smelly black mud nearly to the surface of the water as far up as Gay Street, and by 1862 the shores of Spring Gardens and Harris Creek were in the same state.

Conditions in the almshouse illustrate what was happening in the city as a whole, in terms of the relation between drainage and water supply, the impact of congestion, and the differential impact on various classes of people. Dr. Thomas Buckler's investigation of crisis in the almshouse furnished the medical profession with a model of the engineering mechanism of municipal public health. It was built for five hundred. The management was considered respectable, and reports of 1843 were congratulatory of improvements in both sanitary and social engineering.[121] They sought to separate "the virtuous poor from the dissolute vagrant," and the white from the colored women. Each group used its own stairway and dining rooms. There was a new mill and apparatus to lift water from Rutter's Run. An experiment with steam heat did not work, and the iron pipes were readapted for effluent. Water closets were introduced instead of buckets. Eight medical students lived on the premises, as well as an apothecary, an overseer with his family, and several hired hands. Attendants for the insane were chosen from among other inmates of the house. All the work on the improvements was done by inmates, rewarded by "a separate table."

But in 1844 and 1845 every lying-in woman died of childbed fever. In the history of the establishment no foundling had lived to the age of three years. Population rose to 750 persons, and in July 1849 86 died in a cholera epidemic.[122] The spatial arrangements of the almshouse not only reflected a social order, but offered clues to the order of dying. In the main building, the basement was occupied by dining rooms, kitchens, and small rooms for "the more refractory class of maniacs." The ground floor contained the matron's office, diet kitchen, sewing room, dormitory for working hands, and a schoolroom. Upstairs, the men's hospital occupied the east wing, and the west wing contained the lying-in ward and the hospital for colored women. In the attic were sleeping rooms for the aged colored women. Few from this building died.

A two-story building known as the black hospital was on lower ground than all the rest. Male surgical cases were on the lower floor, female surgical cases on the upper. In this building more men died of the epidemic than women. The water closets opened outside the east wall. Through another opening in this wall the pigs were fed. On higher ground opposite, a new four-story building contained on the top floor "the most respectable aged women"; on the next floor a room for children, foundlings, and their nurses; in the ground floor and basement were cells for lunatics. In the lower cells all fourteen lunatics and their three attendants died of cholera, while above none caught it. A few feet from the north basement entrance was a "ley-hopper" connecting the water closets above with an underground drain and discharging through the north wall.

When Buckler inspected the premises beyond the wall he found on the east side the overflowed cesspool from the black hospital, and along the north side dead pigs floating in a pond several feet deep, "a pestilent fermentation," the overflow of the men's privy, the piped outfall from water closets of the men's wing of the main building, and also washings from the dead house (which averaged one postmortem a day), and a foul ditch from the linen wash house. Buckler blamed the contagious air from the piggeries that came into the buildings through the drainage openings. His analysis of the mechanism was incorrect, but his actions were effective. He hired three free Negroes, two night-soil men and a hodcarrier, to fill the pond and clean out the ley-hopper. Two of the laborers fell sick with cholera (they recovered), but the disease then ceased.

The Political Mechanism

In facing its crises of growth, Baltimore was handicapped by its relationship to the state and the county. The city's chartered powers and its representation in the state legislature had not grown in proportion to population or needs. For certain purposes of representation, taxation, and criminal justice, the city was merely a part of Baltimore County. The act for rebuilding the courthouse and record office after the fire of 1835 explicitly recognized the possibility that the city and county might be separated. The jail visitors recommended separation, as overcrowding became acute in the obsolete structure. In 1841 when the city modernized tax assessments, a clamor arose over tax evasion by wealthy persons who claimed their summer homes in the county as residences. In 1845 the city council objected to the legislature's interference in the reorganization of wards, and compared a "special, unjust and onerous tax upon the city of Baltimore" with the Stamp Act.

All of those issues contributed to the calling of a constitutional convention in Maryland in 1851. Political alignments in the convention appear sectional. The tidewater counties resisted constitutional reform and sought to guarantee property rights of slave holders. Eastern Shore delegates tried to reserve an option of eventual secession from the state.[123] A complete description of the constitution is beyond my scope, but its importance to the transformation and self-consciousness of Baltimore should be underscored. Baltimore obtained some increase of representation, although it was not satisfied, and was still outvoted by rural and hostile interests in the legislature. The new constitution strengthened county governments, increased the number of elected officials, and divorced Baltimore City from Baltimore County.

Like the incorporation in 1796, the crucial impact of the divorce was psychological. The separation of the city from the county gave Baltimoreans a new conception of the meaning of the city boundary, and the territorial integrity of the city was essential to a new conception of the urban mechanism. Divorce was attended by the usual unpleasantness over division of joint property: the almshouse, the jail, the courthouse, the tobacco warehouse.[124] The inventory itself suggests how weak were the collective instruments. Boundaries were reexamined, and Poppleton's plat was "corrected" and updated. The county proceeded to build a courthouse and jail at Towson, while the city built a grand new jail on the old property and selected sites for a bigger almshouse and a city hall. These were all of symbolic importance. That much might be expected. But there was beyond that a startling appearance of new initiative, a new sense of system, and a new long-range horizon in the plans proposed in Baltimore City beginning in 1851. As I shall discuss, most of the grand plans arose from problems of properties, boundaries, and powers of the city, rooted in the divorce proceeding.

The mayor appointed a Boundary Avenue Commission in 1851 to develop a plan for extending the benefits of squares and open spaces to the city as a whole, by surrounding the city with a parkway 250 feet wide.[125] The width between house fronts would allow a 20-foot walkway with a row of trees, a 40-foot carriageway (as in Broadway), a 130-foot median of trees, shrubs, walks, and benches, then a second carriageway and footway. The plantations would relieve the eye from glare and diminish the dust. It was a city-building scheme, just as Franklin Square and Broadway were neighborhood-building schemes. Its circumference would attract taxable improvements. The plan also reflected the concern with breathing spaces. The accumulated deficiency of places of recreation "caused us to look to our outskirts for what should have existed in our midst." Part of the stimulus came from South Baltimore interests who wanted to make Federal Hill a park "ere it be too late." Opportunities would have to be seized quickly, or property values would place the entire program out of reach. At the rate the city was being built up, they reckoned the territory within the boundaries would suffice for ten or twelve years.

John Latrobe was president of the commission and wrote their report. Other members were James Carroll, Fielding Lucas, Jr., Mayor Jerome, and the presiding officers of the city council. The city surveyor, Captain Thomas Chiffelle, prepared plats, profiles, and cross sections with the help of Augustus Faul, and the commission obtained free engineering advice from Latrobe's brother, B. H. Latrobe, Jr. Poppleton had reserved an easement along the city boundary for such an avenue, but it was a purely geometrical design, and the commission recommended certain departures in the interest of esthetics and economy. These departures were adaptations to the natural topography. "The noblest would be level," but there were perspectives to be included, and developed sites to be avoided, such as Mount Hope asylum. On the northern boundary alone there were seventy-five intersections that would have to be met at grade or rebuilt. Crossing the Jones Falls and the railroad would require a viaduct whose cost would increase with height. The estimate for the whole project was $675,000.

The plan foundered on the elegance of its conception. Because it was strikingly sensitive to terrain and vista, the departures from Poppleton's plat would require city-county cooperation, or the legislature would have to adjust the city boundary again. Both solutions were unrealistic in 1852. "Under the present system the work cannot be done."[126] Once again the city was hampered by the flaw of the original Poppleton plat. Adequate for the speculative concept of exploiting flat raw space, block by block, acre by acre, it proved hard to restructure into a working mechanism in a real three-dimensional landscape.

Water, Parks, and Horsecars

The political growth and self-consciousness of the city after 1851 led to a new debate on water supply. It was resolved by a politically ingenious scheme, which joined together the mechanisms of water supply, green spaces, and horsecars. The first step was public acquisition of the water company, for $1,350,000. The arrangement was completed in July 1854. The new city water board promptly doubled the length of distributing mains and the number of users, to half of all households.

Expansion of supply was more difficult. The board and council commissions of the '50s reviewed all the alternatives considered twenty years earlier. Engineering consultants were instructed to contemplate the needs of a future city of five hundred thousand and a per capita use of thirty gallons a day. One team, headed by James Slade, gauged the Patapsco River by night with floating candles to estimate velocities, and made the most elaborate topographical surveys so far done in the city.[127] He ran the 100-foot contour line, to evaluate what portions of the city could be served from reservoirs at elevations of 125 feet or higher. A second corps under Chiffelle surveyed the topographical problems associated with the Gunpowder supply and a conduit to Mine Bank Run.[128] Virtually all the engineering consultants recommended the introduction of water from Gunpowder Falls, a much larger supply, but at greater capital cost. The bold plan of T. E. Sickels called for a seven-mile "air line tunnel" through rock 50 to 270 feet below the land surface. Opponents muttered about a Gunpowder Plot: the "Know-Nothing" mayors, Samuel Hinks and Thomas Swann, favored expanding the Jones Falls supply to reservoirs upstream beyond the city limits. Looking back, Buckler attributed their reservoir schemes to "hydraulic rings, each having some plan of personal or general aggrandizement for the parties interested."[129] It was touch and go from month to month, but the final decision to develop the Jones Falls supply represented a failure of nerve. The difference was a question of vision, as one can see in Mayor Hinks's argument for it: "I am inclined to believe that the youngest male child of the present day would be an old man, before the city of Baltimore will number 600,000 souls, hence the utter folly of incurring now, for our posterity, such a debt as recent projects would entail."[130] Baltimore had made another compromise between Death and Go-Ahead.

Work was started in 1858 on Lake Roland (or Swann Lake), a four-mile Jones Falls conduit, Hampden Lake (Roosevelt Park), and a new Mount Royal Reservoir above North Avenue. All these works were outside the city boundary. Expenditures ran over the maximum ever seriously discussed, and the works immediately proved inadequate. By 1862 plans were under way to add another reservoir on Nicholas Rogers's hill, Druid Lake.

The reservoir plan was grafted onto a vision of Mayor Swann's that compensated for his earlier failure. Druid Lake would be not only a reservoir, but an ornament to Baltimore's first large park. To finance the development of Druid Hill Park, a boundary avenue, and parks for other sections of the city, a tax would be levied on the new horsecar system: a penny park tax on a nickel fare. Most cities, eager to grasp the benefits of the new mode of transport, missed the opportunity to cut in the city collectively on the profits. Swann's plans were stalled by negotiations with the omnibus proprietors, objections in the legislature, an uproar over the sellout of the franchise to a Philadelphia capitalist, and disputes over wages for construction labor. Nevertheless, service began on the first line in July 1859, and other lines were under construction. The horsecar itself was a simple device—a boxlike car for twenty-two passengers, much like the omnibus, and far cruder than the railroad Baltimore had built thirty years earlier. But from the first, horsecar service was conceived as an elaborate mechanism. Its network of rails would connect all parts of the city, including the several railroad stations. Swann's reasons were his own. The horsecar debates, like the water debates, revolved around the credibility of cost estimates, and allowed behind-the-scenes manipulation of participation in corporations and contracts. Baltimore was way behind in water, parks, and horsecars, and Swann had introduced his share of the delays. But his stroke of genius was to put it all together, to see the mechanism as a whole.

Drains and Dredges

In this era of grand thinking, problems of drainage and development also came together into a grand scheme. In 1859 Thomas Buckler, who analyzed the epidemic at the almshouse, extended to the city as a whole his solution of filling the pond—he proposed shoveling Federal Hill into the basin. He argued that it would produce a vast level building area "of the best description,"[131] solve at once the problems of drainage and dredging, and improve air quality. Buckler and Thomas Winans privately hired Benjamin Latrobe, Jr., for $1200 to devise engineering estimates and a system of storm sewers for the new land. Augustus Faul mapped the topography. Latrobe figured that the enormous mass of clay and sand that would be removed from Federal Hill to reduce its "inconvenient height," undo its "beetle brow," its "ragged edge and winding gullies," would correspond nicely to the 3 million cubic yards required to fill the basin and docks. Otherwise, Federal Hill would continue to stand, "an unhealthy looking tumour upon the lower limb of the city, covered with mean dwellings and unsavoury manufactories."[132]

There was widespread agreement on the inconvenience of the inner harbor, but the project was blocked by two considerations. First, the estimate of $750,000 over three or four years seemed enormous at a time when the city was deeply indebted. A third to a half of the city's annual budget was already interest on its debts. Second, there was resistance from Light Street property owners fronting on that "pampered and cherished puddle." These "mysterious busybodies," whom Buckler later referred to as "the House of Piers," included Johns Hopkins.[133] They were presumed responsible for the disappearance of the printed engineering reports from the desks of city council members moments before they met to consider the issue.

The city did, however, create a sewerage commission to study both storm drainage and sanitary drainage. It was a commission of honor, that is, unpaid: Henry Tyson, John Dukehart, and J. Morton Saunders. They reviewed sewerage practices in London, Paris, and certain U.S. cities. Their engineering conception took into account three types of hydrological variation. The first was the normal seasonal variation. They recommended against connecting water closets and privies to the sewers, for fear that they would turn the inner harbor into a vast cesspool dangerous to health in the summer months. (In fact, it was, with over 20,000 illegal connections.) The second type of variation was the rare occurrence of extreme rainfall and flashfloods, say two or three inches in an hour. "Such occurrences do not take place once in ten years; if the sewers were made to carry off this excessive amount of water, their cost would be greatly increased."[134] They undertook to calculate the sizes of the drains in a systematic manner, taking into account the size of the drainage area and the gradient, for rainfalls up to one inch per hour. The third type of variation was the trend toward greater flow to be expected from further urban construction:

In the extended growth of most large cities, many difficulties have arisen on account of an improper appreciation, during the early stage of improvements, of the quantity of water which it would become necessary to void through them, after the cities became paved and compactly built.[135]

The commission members figured that the difference between natural soils and urban terrain would at least double runoff. They recommended main drains of brick set in hydraulic cement, of circular form and diameters up to eight feet. All would function by flow of gravity, with only two or three small siphons of a standard still reasonable today.

Their 1862 report served as a guide for the city commissioner's office for location and construction standards for storm sewers for the next thirty years. For example, when the B&O built a sewer from Camden Station, it was instructed to conform to the plan. The older lines of storm sewers in the city today follow the lines of drains constructed under this plan. They did not, however, suggest any priorities of construction or estimate the costs, and there was no immediate action taken for orderly implementation. An accurate topographical survey would still be needed for actually building such sewers. In municipal engineering, Baltimore habitually chose neither Death nor Go-Ahead.

As at the almshouse, problems of physical and social engineering were interwoven. The fire riots and gang activity reflected to some degree the intensified spirit of neighborhood, the ethnic rivalries, the hell raising of the remarkably youthful population, and the concentrations of males in waterfront wards. To get control of the volunteer fire companies, the mayor and council, who paid for their equipment, repeatedly set forth new regulations. In 1856 they were "nationalized" like the water system. Fire fighters became paid professionals. The city appointed a fire chief and inspector and appropriated money for modernization. The new mechanisms were the fire alarm telegraph—a wonderfully rickety affair carried over the housetops—and seven steam-powered pumpers. It was a symbolic finale for the age of mechanism, and fire-fighting efficiency was greatly improved.

Waves of crime and violence were far more difficult to control. Numbers jailed for arson and murder were especially high in 1844–45 and 1850–52. Homicide and suicide taken together doubled. In 1857, 11 percent of deaths were from "other than natural" causes. The penitentiary population by 1853 had reached the level of 1835, and a quarter were serving terms for killing. The messages of Mayor Jerome in 1850 indicate the tendency to associate the poor, the unproductive, the violent, and the criminal with the foreigner. In January, after congratulating the city on its unparalleled prosperity and the police on a momentary improvement in quiet and good order, he expressed disgust at new forms of depravity: "A few years ago, and scarcely a beggar was to be seen. . . . Now every steamboat landing, every railroad depot, the doors of hotels, the post

Social Engineering

office, places of amusement, and our most public streets are literally crowded with filthy vagabonds."[136] He complained of women thinly clad or wretchedly dressed in rags, seated on the ground, on steps, or in corners, with a child at the breast, imploring relief. "These scenes ought not to be tolerated—they are not the growth of the United States or legitimate offspring of our government or institutions."[137] On 20 November the mayor reported a fearful increase of crime, disorder, and bloodshed for the past several weeks. He recommended gun control, law and order, an increase in the police force, and more street lighting. The identification of a foreign threat became more explicit throughout the fifties.

Violence both came from and was directed at the repression of Baltimore's second-class citizens. If one adds together the fifth black, the fifth foreign born, and their children, at least half the population was defined from the outset as a nuisance or threat, to be repressed in some measure. The traditional mechanism for processing healthy dependent young persons was binding out to trades. In a case of destitution, the "interesting looking" four-year-old was adopted, and the mother was "placed" in domestic service. But this mechanism failed, now that a great pool of labor was available. Industrial employers preferred to manage their labor force by hiring and firing at will, not by long-term contract or by the whip. And there was no "place" for the weak, the sick, or the intractable. The hospitals, asylums, or prisons that would accept the social refuse were overwhelmed. New mechanisms of social engineering were devised that might reform, cure, or render productive these troublesome elements, or at least remove them from the public streets.

The penitentiary population rose. Built for 256, it held 450 when in 1857 Dr. Charles Frick publicized its condition. In the penitentiary throughout the 1850s one finds about 25 percent foreign born and 43 percent black. Two-thirds were under thirty. The 100 most productive were contracted out to work in the day, the rest included a half-idiot girl, a number of old and infirm persons, and several insane who had to be watched closely. A third were in such bad health they could perform no more than "half labor," that is, sew carpet rags or pick wool. The overflow was housed in damp basement cells and given cod liver oil. The prison hospital ward was close packed; a third of its deaths were from tuberculosis.[138]

The city jail, of course, had a much greater turnover. The number jailed rose from fifteen hundred in 1844 to thirty one hundred in 1854. The new jail was designed by one of the fine church architects of the city in Gothic style, with plenty of fashionable ironwork. It had three hundred cells for solitary confinement, about three times the capacity of the old jail. The numbers jailed continued to increase: in 1860 there were ten thousand, plus ten thousand more who were mere "lodgers": tramps, drunks, or homeless persons who spent a night in the watch house to keep warm.

The creation of new institutions for the insane and for juveniles illustrates the trend toward specialization. It is difficult to distinguish new hopes for therapy and reform from new forms of repressive removal and attempts to shift the costs on to the state government. The state opened Mount Hope Hospital in 1842. It was operated by the Sisters of St. Vincent de Paul (Sisters of Charity).

The city jail was a massive, castlelike structure of stone and metal built near the Jones Falls. Designed by Niernsee and Nielson, architects, it was dedicated in 1858 with a grand banquet of the city leaders in the galleries of the prison block.

Twenty of the personnel were supported by the church, seven by the city. Its capacity was 220, at least half in the insane department. In 1845 the Maryland Hospital began receiving state support and was restricted to cases of insanity. Its capacity was also about 200. In 1852 the state chose Spring Grove as a site for the Maryland Insane Asylum. It was high, healthy, and distant from the city. In 1857 Moses Sheppard founded a private asylum at Towson. There were also 73 insane in the almshouse, including some "subject to fits" who were kept chained, ad some "old and harmless." The city committed itself to build a new almshouse and hospital that would be larger and healthier. It selected a property from the Canton Company, called Bay View, now City Hospitals.

A joint effort of the city and George Brown was the House of Refuge for delinquent youth, the prize example of a mechanism of social engineering. Brown subsequently left the largest fortune thus far probated in the state of Maryland: it paid for the building of Brown Memorial Church in Bolton Hill. His role was characteristic of a new form of personal philanthropy, very different from the days of his grandfather, Alexander Brown. Instead of a circle of the wealthy getting together to back a public effort for the common good, one sees the single individual who applied his personal wealth, whim, organizing skill, and his own theory of society. A fifty-five-acre site was chosen on

Frederick Road beyond Gwynns Falls. At the laying of the cornerstone the speeches associated crime with foreigners. "The cities of the old world, it is well known, are casting upon our shores, to a terribly fearful extent, the vilest, and most reckless, and desperate of the population that swarm in their deepest and darkest purlieus." Brown blamed foreigners for "rendering the night hideous in parts of our own cities" and for the "horrible multiplications of robberies, and drunkenness and murders." Social ills and dependency he attributed to individual weakness, and the cure was an individual moral battle, in which the House of Refuge would play a role. "Its object is to save, not to punish. . . . It aims directly at the intellectual and moral culture of the poor, friendless and vicious children . . . growing up . . . to be pests and curses upon communities and the body politic."[139] The refuge was promptly filled to capacity. Statistics were compiled to show that indeed, of 350 inmates, white and between ten and sixteen years old, 60 percent had foreign-born parents. Most had lost one parent or both, and three-quarters were described as "offspring of intemperance."[140]

In spite of his logic of work, order, and discipline, Brown, too, participated in the rhetoric of violence. Like Mayor Swann of the Know-Nothing (American) party,[141] Brown preached a racism directed against the foreigner, in particular German Catholics. His opponents (Democrats) preached a racism directed primarily against the free blacks. One form of racism vied with another. Violence was part of the politics of the age, as well as the demographic structure of the city.[142] The election riots from 1855 through 1859 became ever more outrageous. The ballots were striped, so one's vote was public, and the polls were crowded. The parties bought votes and let the whiskey flow. Mayor Swann recommended increasing the police force and a penalty for carrying concealed weapons such as ice picks. He also complained of gangs in vacant abandoned houses and of permissive parents. The Democratic governor intervened in the election season of 1857, but the militia refused to support him. At last, in its finest tradition of 1812 and 1835, the state legislature reasserted partisan political repression. The Democratic legislature, on the last day of the session, to "free the city" and "protect the ballot," unseated the Know-Nothing delegation from Baltimore. It empowered the governor to take over the city's police force, liquor licensing, and elections. He appointed state boards of control over these vital municipal powers, and the city was required to pay all costs. The state has kept these controls, an anomaly in American politics, for over a hundred years.

In spite of the stability of political parties and political rhetoric in Maryland from the early '50s through the Civil War, real and important changes took place in the operation of the municipal mechanism. One key to this political puzzle lies in the fact that Baltimore City had such limited powers of self-government. Given a degree of freedom from Baltimore County, after 1851, Baltimore City bestirred itself to face its environmental problems. But new limits were quickly reached. The city could not emancipate itself from the state of Maryland. It could operate only at the whim of a legislature of slave owners. The deep divisions of American society were already present, on the eve of civil war.

In June 1860 the first Japanese embassy to the United States was conducted to Baltimore. A certain freshness of eye and foreignness of translation reveal features of the city that were new, and in which Baltimoreans took as much delight as the visitors: "On both sides of the street there were buildings of seven or eight stories like great mountains. . . . Ships come up to the very entrance of the doors of the buildings."[143] The Japanese delegates manipulated, drew, and marveled at each piece of Baltimore mechanism—the water closets, radiators, and bathing facilities, the gas lights and fireplace stoves. They were entertained, along with thousands of Baltimoreans, by a display of the new steam fire engines and the seventy-eight-foot folding firemen's ladder.[144] Unaware of the deep social divisions, the embassy was impressed by the wonderful new connections— gas mains, water mains, horsecar tracks, fire alarm telegraph. Still a primitive apparatus, these connections tied the neighborhoods, rich and poor, commercial, residential, and industrial, into an intricate urban mechanism.

Baltimore had always lived on an emotional roller coaster of passionate rhetoric, courtroom drama, election tumult, and turbulent town meetings. The blow-by-blow pace of wartime meshed with that traditional style to make life a succession of urgent personal crises.[145] Each summer Baltimore entrenched itself for an invasion—in 1862 a whiff of gunpowder from Antietam, in 1863 the arrival of the wounded from Gettysburg, in 1864 the raids of Jubal Early. In the off season there were the commercial blockade, federal arrests, and draft lotteries.

The mob reaction at the outbreak of the war was characteristic of the city's ambivalence throughout. President Lincoln ordered northern troops to Washington. They had to pass through Baltimore by train. On 19 April 1861, Baltimoreans stoned a Massachusetts regiment as it crossed the downtown area to transfer from the President Street Station to the Camden Station to continue to Washington. Four soldiers and twelve citizens died. The railroad bridges were burned to prevent northern troops passing through Maryland.[146] The German community of Baltimore had already secretly sent volunteers to Washington, and on 20 April the symbols of their Republican and Union sentiments were mobbed. The Turnverein hall and the presses of the *Wecker* and the *Sinai* were destroyed. Rabbi Einhorn retreated to Philadelphia. On 24 April John Pendleton Kennedy wrote with regret, "Maryland has found herself impelled into opposition (to the Union) by a popular sentiment no man can withstand."[147] But four days later Henry Winter Davis wrote, "A great reaction has set in. If we (of Union sentiment) now act promptly, the day is ours and the city is safe."[148] The British consul wrote to England, "The character of the people of Baltimore is decidedly impulsive, and many who a week ago advocated the most violent measures, now confess it would be madness on the part of Maryland to precipitate herself into a combat with the North."[149] The struggle of impulse and realism went on throughout the war. As in other wars, Baltimore was a stage for the sublime, the ridiculous, and the sordid, but this time it could not develop the continuity of purpose, the solidarity, or the daring of its wars before or since.

Both impulse and realism were responses to the city's strategic location,

A Position the Most Delicate

which required a wholly different posture from wars with Britain or Europe. Over ten years the city changed its perception of its location. What in 1851 seemed to Thomas Swann a site of opportunity, a pivot of trade between North and South, profiting from the "unnatural strife" of sectional division, he now perceived as a site of alarming vulnerability.

Maryland of all her sister states occupies a position the most delicate. Situated upon the borders of Pennsylvania, exposed upon an extent of coast beyond her ability adequately to protect—drawing her supplies mainly from the West by a line of intercommunication which has cost her more than $30,000,000, she may well look to her safety in the event of the severance of the Union.[150]

Baltimore was, naturally, subject to that heartbreak of situation between North and South, complicated further by self-interest and class interest. The governor urged a neutral position. The wealthy tobacco men of the Germania Club were "sesesh," while the Turnverein were antislavery and pro-Union. Samuel Harrison claimed that the manufacturers tended to northern sympathy, the landed gentry to southern.[151] As in other parts of the nation, families were divided, with sons fighting on either side. But specific to Baltimore was the vise that gripped its history in earlier generations: the political geography of Maryland. Baltimore, with its preference for free labor and its mercantile pragmatism, was embedded in a state founded on the economy of tobacco and slavery. The state's traditional landed leaders, shored up by archaic voter representation, were unable to come to terms with economic, social, and political reality. They postponed each decision, grasped at straws, and allowed themselves to be carried away by the oratory of blood, race, and states' rights. Marylanders were, in turn, embedded in a nation moving rapidly away from their life style and experience, and they were but a tiny element of the nation. They had an old powerful legal claim and eloquent voices, but only a handful of votes. Successive constitutions in Maryland (1851, 1864, and 1867) increased the representation of Baltimore and simultaneously allowed new powers to the several county governments. But such readjustments could not resolve the problems of Baltimore so long as war continued. Any compromise with political forces in the state moved Baltimore away from compromise with the political forces of the nation. The tug of war between state and federal powers took place in the unwilling city. Governor, mayor, police commissioner, and railroad president shuttled anxiously around the Baltimore-Annapolis-Washington triangle.

Baltimore's situation, its extensive border and its railroad lifeline meant that the city would be occupied. Abraham Lincoln's suspension of the right of habeas corpus was directed at Baltimore, to assure the passage of troops through Maryland. On 14 May General Butler ostentatiously camped the Union army on the "beetle brow" of Federal Hill, and began a series of arrests. He refused to bring those accused of treason to court. John Merryman's friends appealed to Chief Justice Taney, a Marylander, who said the power of the constitution and the law "has been resisted by a force too strong for me to overcome." The passions of Baltimore that drove it again and again into impasse and contradiction during the war were passions at the core of the American political ideal—

individual civil rights. The conservative outrage of Justice Taney and the progressive insolence of Henry Winter Davis were part and parcel of that ideal. The apparent caprice of Baltimore was rooted in tough convictions.

The city's delicate position also explains the uneven advance of Baltimore's economy during the Civil War, a case very different from other American cities. The War between the States was a period of little physical or material change in Baltimore, though it was one of intense changes of feeling and activity. Washington, only forty miles away, grew rapidly, and real estate prices rose in its suburbs and along the rail lines into Washington. The Baltimore papers began carrying daily columns of Washington local news. But in Baltimore itself, construction dropped to a hundred dwellings a year, and foreign immigration nearly ceased. Northern and inland cities such as Pittsburgh and Cincinnati, more secure from a strategic point of view, developed new industrial muscle. But because of the perennial threat of invasion as well as the reputation of impulsiveness, Baltimore's industrial development was limited. Its only growth sectors were closely tied to its role as a strategic transportation center. The railroad stations and shops expanded, handling massive troop movements. The Northern Central enlarged Calvert Station, dug great drive-in cellars, expanded the Bolton shops, and double tracked the line north to York and extended it toward Elmira. The B&O shops at Mount Clare kept busy rebuilding the rolling stock and bridges repeatedly destroyed by the Rebels. This was the nation's essential rail line, and Baltimore's essential military role was to keep the B&O Railroad operating. Hayward-Bartlett expanded into the Winans shops adjoining Mount Clare. Its heavy machine and casting operations now covered four acres. It cast round shrapnel for the Union. The shipyards were busy, too. On the south side of the basin the city filled and developed five hundred feet of waterfront at the old city yard, and began filling the marine hospital property. On the north side, the Abbott iron works cast iron plate for the first sixteen Monitors—foreshadowing a postwar decline of the wood shipbuilding industry in adjoining yards of Canton and Fells Point. Oyster and vegetable packers expanded, selling tinned food for the armies, and the garment industry produced uniforms in fits and starts.

Trade was exceedingly volatile. Fortunes were both made and lost. Prices for coffee, flour, and sugar rose, but naval warfare increased the risks. Baltimoreans slipped easily into the wartime commercial style of the white-haired "Old Defenders," quick to recognize shortages and short-term opportunities. The exposed position was convenient for purchases "across the lines"; merchants such as Hamilton Easter and manufacturers like Moses Wiesenfeld were arrested —rightly or wrongly—for selling to the enemy.

Maryland, like other border states and the Confederate states, had passed a "stay law" to try to keep money in the state. The Maryland courts would not enforce payment of debts to outsiders. The ruin of Simeon Hecht was an example of the ethical conflicts implicit in such public policy. Relatives whom he had set up in business refused to pay their New York and Boston creditors. Hecht himself, as intermediary, felt obliged to pay them off ($60,000), while his local creditors in Baltimore sued him. When Hecht was bankrupted, the chain of credit was broken, and with it the bonds of family and ethnic solidarity, the relation of trust on which business in the '50s still rested. His son and biographer noted bitterly, "Fortunes were made quickly in those days. . . . There were a great deal of speculators, notably among our leading coreligionists. . . . Some men arose from obscurity and became multimillionaires in a very short time."[152] Hecht started over again with his former energy and $2000 goods on credit from John Hurst, bought a boat and went down to scavenge old metal from the James and York rivers. This speculation lasted only eighteen months before competition became too severe. William Wilkens was another enterprising German immigrant of the '40s. In the '50s he had sent agents to the battlefields of the Crimea, and now he followed the Army of the Potomac to Richmond and Petersburg, to clip the tails from dead horses. Wilkins himself was a confirmed pacifist. Horsehair was essential for hospital mattresses as well as horsehair sofas and carriage upholstery. At his "curled hair factory" on the Frederick Road, horsehair and hog bristles were spread out like hay over the hillsides to dry. The smell was less sweet.[153]

Those risky and distasteful ventures were nothing compared with the thoroughly sordid commerce in manpower. Maryland supplied its share of the cannon fodder and more than its share of the officers to the Union army. As the war went on, the pool of volunteers dried up. The hospitals filled. Local industrial and farm labor became scarce. During the summer of 1863 the pressure became evident. A federal conscription law was passed, and a confiscation law that empowered the army to free, employ, or induct any Rebel's slave who came to army lines. In May, Maryland planters protested that their slaves were fleeing to Washington. In mid-June as Baltimore prepared for Confederate attack, slaves of suspected Confederate sympathizers were conscripted to build entrenchments. In July, Secretary of War Stanton sent Birney, son of a famed abolitionist, to recruit among them. Birney went farther. He freed sixteen shackled blacks from a slave pen on Pratt Street—pledged to enlist. His boats began slipping into Maryland rivers at night to receive "contraband." After Gettysburg, hospitals, schools, and warehouses were filled with freightcar loads of wounded soldiers. Women of the city nursed them. "That was all Baltimore saw of the war."[154] The largest convalescent hospitals, over a thousand beds each, were in Patterson Park on the east and at George Stewart's residence at the west end of Baltimore Street.

As the labor squeeze continued, Negro recruiting stations were organized in Maryland. City dwellers threatened by conscription saw them as "the poor man's substitute." Free blacks in Baltimore met to demand equal pay from the army.[155] Bounties were bid up to encourage enlistment of Maryland slaves whose masters were presumed loyal to the Union: the slave would be freed, receive $50 on mustering in and $50 on mustering out, while his owner would be compensated $300 to $400 from federal and state governments. These activities produced a collapse of the market for slaves, and Maryland moved toward an emancipation constitution. The constitutional convention spent two months debating a Declaration of Rights. Baltimore City ultimately voted five to one for the "free constitution and free labor," the state's Union soldiers ten to one by absentee ballot, while the other northern counties were touch and go, and southern Maryland and the Eastern Shore opposed it four to one.

In September 1864, the announcement of new draft quotas unleashed new anxieties. The city and the several counties were competing in the bounties they offered to persuade men to enroll. In each ward of the city exemption clubs were formed. They put the arm on wealthy citizens to raise money to buy recruits from outside the ward. They pressed the men eligible for the draft to put $100 in a pot, to be divided among those drafted. The eligibles of the fourth ward agreed to pay a $200 bonus to any man who would put in a substitute to the credit of the ward, to reduce their draft quota. Throughout the month of September, the price of such substitutes rose. The second ward club had a list of eighty-seven substitutes "who could be got for $1000 each." Businesses were advertising in the newspapers, "36 Alien or Contraband Substitutes. . . . Quotas filled. Satisfaction guaranteed. Bond for security. . . . Greenbacks! Greenbacks! Greenbacks!" while the editors fretted, "The material for volunteer recruits really appears to be in limited supply as compared with the demand, and, though there may be ever so much money collected, it is difficult to see where all the men which will be wanted are to come from."[156]

When the lotteries were finally held, about a third of the conscripts were able to supply substitutes. Some skilled workers were sent to the navy yard. Of those unable to finance substitutes, a large proportion were black or Irish. The colored churches had raised a pot for their draftees, but as in all other economic sectors their reward was smaller. On 1 November 1864 Maryland celebrated statewide emancipation under the new constitution with ringing of churchbells, cannon salutes, and prayers, while "freedmen" were being drafted.

The system of substitutes and incentives naturally provoked resistance, frustration, and innumerable dramas. To discourage attempts to escape induction, bounties were withheld till the men arrived at "Camp Cattlegrounds."[157] A Canadian substitute in Baltimore swallowed his four $100 greenbacks, but they gave him emetic powders till he vomited up the notes. "Slightly disfigured with the tomatoes, they were cleaned and placed to his credit."[158] The soldiers were kept under guard on their way to the camps. "Bounty jumpers" were shot running up Eutaw Street out of Camden Station yard.

A deserter who left the ranks and went into a fruit store was court-martialed and shot at Fort McHenry. "He died a penitent man, and thus the awful majesty of military law and discipline was satisfied."[159] The railroad stations were surrounded by taverns, lunch rooms, and street vendors of cakes and pies. A Delaware soldier shot a Baltimore boy over the price of his lemonade. The soldier was arrested that evening while he stood guard duty outside the Soldiers Rest Rooms, the Conway Street houses adjoining Camden Station, where twelve hundred to fifteen hundred soldiers were herded. He was hanged at Fort McHenry, a punishment less majestic than being shot. Another deserter suffocated in a trunk as his lover was bringing him to Baltimore to make his escape.

Government detectives or military police were everywhere. Near the President Street Station a government detective shot the proprietor of a lager beer saloon. On another occasion men rushed out of the taverns, beat the government detective, and took his soldier prisoner from him. The police then closed the tavern for selling liquor to soldiers. On Christmas Eve, while Maryland's soldiers in their camps were eating 1450 Christmas turkeys donated and prepared in Baltimore and three thousand pies donated by the Gilmor House, the provost guard shot a soldier in the snow outside the central police station for failing to halt and identify himself.

The war aggravated the city's old deep-seated problems. The principal cause of death was not battle, riot, or murder; it was smallpox. Eleven hundred cases were reported in 1864 and 1865, adding urgency to the usual litany of urban drainage complaints—the defective sewers, the private dumping of night soil, and the worsening stench from the Jones Falls and the "fetid swamp" at Spring Garden. Druid Hill Park, the city's pride and joy, offered a fresh-air diversion, and pick and shovel work began on Druid Lake. No other major works were undertaken, due to the extra costs of defense works every summer and the irritability of taxpayers in a time of inflation and business risks. The mayor made a habit of overestimating tax collections, overrunning the budget, and relying on short-term loans. His "floating debt" reached $2 million, setting a pattern for slovenly municipal finance in the '70s.

Such was the war Baltimore saw firsthand. The rest depended on the press (somewhat cowed) and on the thousand little gossip networks of a war of movement transmitting currents of human emotion. Campaign and convention oratory alternated from May to October with camp meeting preachers in the tents. At McKim's mansion (Howard's), three hundred disabled of the colored troops sang hymns together daily. While Grant's army was digging and mining and fighting in front of Petersburg, and the gunboats were shelling Mobile, "A large and very fashionable assembly of ladies and gentlemen in Baltimore attended the auction of a rich and elegant collection of glassware formerly belonging to Charles Carroll of Carrollton. . . . Every article offered sold at most extravagantly high prices."[160] Alongside the lists of Maryland soldiers captured in front of Richmond and those wounded at Cedar Creek were published the outcomes of the billiard tournament among Baltimore gentlemen.[161] Wounded soldiers continued to pour through the "distributing hospital" in West's buildings on Union dock: first the Union wounded, then the Rebel wounded. In April 1865, four years after the mob at the railroad station, the funeral train of Abraham Lincoln passed northward through Baltimore, and the hospital on Union dock received a boatload of released prisoners from Richmond, "living skeletons, covered with filth."[162]

A Rent
in the Social
Fabric

1866–1877

It is happy for the world that war, its greatest scourge, is not an unmixed evil. It has its compensations. The fact that war comes at all, proves the existence of some stumbling block to progress, which cannot be removed except by violence. . . . The processes of war are destructive, but they develop energy.[1]

The editors of the *American* shared their end-of-the-war optimism with others in Baltimore. The energy they mentioned was already at work. The city had not benefited from a wartime boom, but neither did it now suffer from a postwar depression. Construction rose swiftly to a peak in 1870–72 of thirty-five hundred houses a year. Speculative and industrial activity were also on the rise. Baltimore was now a city of some three hundred and fifty thousand people or fifty thousand buildings. These were the seven fat years of Pharaoh's dream. A sharp national business crisis in 1873 signaled the beginning of the seven lean years. Changes in the economic and social structure of Baltimore in this generation depended upon the relative growth of the various sectors, classes, and enterprises during the seven fat years, and upon how they weathered the seven lean years.

The editors proceeded to lay out Baltimore's opportunities on the basis of new markets in the South:

The laboring people of the south will live in real houses, with glass windows, a stove and fixtures, bedsteads and mattresses instead of mud sill, single iron pot, bed of leaves or husks. . . . Gourds will give way to crockery ware. . . . Buttons and pins will be needed for garments of cloth or calico, when a single string was all that was needed to tie the neck hole of the domestic smock frock. They will eat something else beside hog meat and hominy.[2]

And supposing that the southern laborers, black and white, would become "subject to the wants of civilized men," they proposed a strategy: "Who is to supply their wants? Why the merchants and manufacturers of the North. Baltimore, if she is true to herself, will at once set about supplying them."[3] And so she did. Baltimore began making more furniture and stoves, then added overalls and underwear, boots and shoes. Baltimore fed them canned corn and catsup

Portions of this chapter, in an earlier form, appeared in the *Annals* of the Association of American Geographers (December 1979).

In 1874, sixty years after the defense of Baltimore, a commemorative celebration brought together the veterans of the war.

and pickles and jam. To complete the circuit of exchange, Baltimore continued to process and market the South's cotton. To fill the "civilized" needs of the city's own successful merchants and manufacturers, the oyster packers and piano makers pulled down their sheds and built greater.

Growth strategy was coupled with a transport strategy. The people in charge were the merchants, whose object was to increase the turnover of goods, taking a profit on an ever greater circulation and accumulating more capital. It was done by more efficient harnessing of steam power. The B&O built sixty new heavy-duty locomotives at Mount Clare. In September 1865 there were reported eighteen first-class steamers from Baltimore in the coastal trade, and the first regular trips were made to Havana and Liverpool, with one ship on each line. The largest was sixteen hundred tons burthen, 250 feet in length, about double the size of the first-class ships before the war. By spring 1872 the largest was twenty-five hundred tons, and the city boasted eighteen steamships in the foreign trade alone, forty thousand tons aggregate. A steamer of oysters was shipped live to Liverpool in a tanker hold, to be fed on the voyage "by continued inhalation of seawater." The twenty smaller steamships continued to operate in the coastal trade as before, serving Boston, New York, Philadelphia, Savannah, Charleston, Wilmington, and New Orleans. New regular steamboat services connected the city with points on the Chesapeake Bay.

Steam was more than a transport technology. It offered advantages of greater speed, dependability, and larger batches for all kinds of industrial processes. The cotton mills and sugar refineries acquired steam pumps and steam engines. The construction materials for the building boom were manufactured in steam-powered mills. A steam-powered brickmaking machine dropped a hundred bricks a minute on a moving band as fast as half a dozen workers could pile them in a kiln, while two other workers fed dirt from the clay bank into the bucket loader. Steam sawmills sawed stone or lumber faster. At Beaver Dam Run near Cockeysville, a huge smoking, rumbling derrick was worked by steam with wire ropes. "A large two-acre hole resembles the crater of a volcano."[4] Prewar railroad engines were retired to quarrying there. Scores of men were at work on ledges 50 to 100 feet down. Each of several steam engines held upright bundles of sharp-pointed steel drills, and each long steel drill was fitted with half a dozen rough diamonds and was fed by a stream of water. In five minutes such a machine could drill a hole an inch in diameter and two feet deep—the equal of three men with hammer and drill for two or three hours. Downtown near Calvert Station, Hugh Sisson had seven gangs of steam saws to perform the next phase in processing marble into mantels and stoops.

The huge block of marble is lifted upon a truck by a crane, and run under a frame by means of a railroad. In these frames, the saws, which are thin pieces of fine soft iron, are fixed at a distance of one, two or three inches apart . . . which in their motion under the soft saw blade perform the part of teeth.[5]

They cut nine to thirteen inches a day, while before the war, two-man teams "of Hibernian or African descent" might manage an inch a day.

Steam power in the boom summer of 1872 produced an epidemic of industrial accidents.[6] In six months 150 were killed or mutilated and permanently disabled. There was at least one fatal work-related accident a week, not including the heat strokes. Other than falls, the most common types were related to steam technology—high-speed trains of machinery tended by young rural or immigrant labor. At the pipe factory an employee was mangled to death in belting. An identical accident occurred at the Northern Central machine shop, while at the B&O machine shop a man had his fingers cut off. In the sugar refinery a man was caught in the belting and wounded by his scraping tool. A German worker at a chemical factory had his hand severed. A lad at the steam box factory had his right hand split up the wrist. At Bartlett-Hayward a boiler head fell on a man's knee and hands. The only state regulation of safety in work was the licensing of steam boilers. Nevertheless, boiler explosions caused multiple deaths. At the McCullough rolling mill at North East three were killed and six severely injured. "I have often seen men run from this boiler," said a roller.[7]

The opportunities and the buoyant aims of the fat years encouraged head-long speculation. Faster circulation of goods stimulated land values. The city's growth in population, purchasing power, and bank deposits stoked the construction boom. Big lumps of public investment accelerated the process, while municipal and state franchises created private empires. Everybody bought a piece of the action. Each businessman divided his capital and his risks among a variety of ventures, but in the tradition of Robert Oliver and Samuel Smith he coupled up his ventures to profit from each round of value added. The *American* described how this worked, in making the argument that the management of the new steamship lines should be concentrated in few hands, because of the experience of stockholding corporations in Baltimore: "One man will take stock if he can supply the concern with stores. Another takes shares enough to control the supply of coal. Another must demand the privilege of furnishing meat." By the time the steamer was supplied by its interested shareholders at a generous profit, there was only a small margin left for profit to other shareholders, "and they, for lack of dividends, retire in disgust."[8] This style could be observed elsewhere, but it was the pattern in Baltimore, where the class of entrepreneurs was tightly knit and the commercial style was retained among manufacturers. The Merchants and Miners Steamship Company, organized before the war by William Jenkins, Captain William Kennedy, and Benjamin Deford, operated between Baltimore and Boston. They were all in the leather business and the boot and shoe trade with New England. Kennedy also owned cotton mills. George S. Brown (grandson of Alexander) was the founder of the Baltimore and Havana steamship line; he also had an interest in two large sugar refineries supplied from Cuba. Enoch Pratt developed the Maryland Steamboat Co. or "Bay Line."

The most remarkable strategist and one of the most richly rewarded was John Work Garrett, president of the Baltimore and Ohio Railroad Company and Hopkins's heir apparent. Promptly at the end of the war Garrett, with much fanfare, started steamship service to Liverpool by buying war surplus vessels from the government. The service was superseded by long-term agreements with the Allen line and the North German Lloyd line, which brought immigrants from Bremen to Baltimore. At Locust Point the B&O built special piers to off-load the immigrants directly into its passenger trains to the prairies. The steamships took on coal at Locust Point as well. Either personally or through his control of the B&O, Garrett owned coal lands around Cumberland and in West Virginia. The B&O built grain elevators, and the city's exports of grain to Liverpool expanded. During the seven fat years the revenues of the B&O tripled. Garrett was frequently lauded for these contributions to the development of the city, but they were largely limited to ventures that entrenched his geopolitical control, with his railroad as the backbone of the empire. The new state of West Virginia was "a military necessity of the war and really a westward extension of Maryland to the Ohio." Garrett's operation of the B&O as a loyal effort for the Union was repaid by his obtaining strategic control of that new state. "As Virginia had provoked the railroad company in its early struggle to get to the great river (the Ohio), the railroad retaliated during the war, and the new State was so shorn off that not a foot of the main stem of the railroad now runs on its soil."[9] Garrett's protégé, a poor lad who worked his way up as brakeman, conductor, and storekeeper on the B&O, was made the senator from West Virginia; the senator also had interests in timberland and the lumber trade.

Such financial ingenuity supported a whole network of allies. In Maryland, Garrett was a close ally of bosses Gorman and Rasin in the "regular" Democratic political machine. He influenced appointments to many judgeships in the state. Understandably, no important court cases were decided against the B&O in Maryland. In West Virginia, Garrett acknowledged no obligation to pay taxes: "There was nothing the President of the Company was so averse to as the payment of taxes; it really hurt him." Until his death (1873), Hopkins worked closely with Garrett; he lent large sums to the B&O "but exacted a quid pro quo." Hopkins once told Keyser on receiving such a commission, "The receipt of commissions earned affects me exactly as I imagine a drink must affect a toper; it exhilarates."[10] The Savings Bank of Baltimore had a $1 million loan secured on its B&O stock (1870). The boards of Hopkins University and hospital were set up to insure that the voting control of their large endowments of B&O stock bequeathed by Hopkins remained in Garrett's hands. The city had

This panoramic view of the B&O Railroad's Locust Point terminus illustrates the interrelationships of railroad and port. Arriving immigrants would witness a complex of grain elevators and coal trains. Note that many steamships were still fitted with masts, which are visible in the background.

minority representation on the board of directors of the B&O, in the amount of $3.25 million. The B&O was paying 10 percent dividends to the city in this period, more than enough to pay the 6 percent interest on its municipal bonds (it had borrowed the money in order to invest in the B&O), but the city could not obtain its stake in the accumulated "surplus." The city's share of the surplus was another $8 million, which the B&O reinvested elsewhere.

Meanwhile, Garrett's son, T. Harrison Garrett, managed the family investment banking house, which held stock in Consolidated, the coal mining subsidiary. He brokered the Consol's crude oil, which the B&O hauled from West Virginia, and on percentage commissions he handled the B&O's major loans—$4 million in 1868, $5 million in 1872, consolidation of the $4 million in 1875, and several millions more in 1877 and 1878—all in close conjunction with J. P. Morgan's London house.[11]

The lesser millionaires of this generation pursued the same strategies as Garrett, sometimes meshing with his projects, rarely confronting him directly. Their strategies all confirm the importance of manipulation of stocks and bonds to siphon off the increases of productivity and the higher land values associated with urban growth. The impressive financial expansion of the Canton Company, for example, in the seven fat years involved mortgaging first the ground rents, then the entire operation, through Alexander Brown and Co. and the company's London house.[12] The Canton Company used part of the new capital to build the Union Railroad and to promote development on its land by contributing to the capital stock of enterprises such as Gardner's grain elevator, the Baltimore Car Wheel works, the Chesapeake Dredging Company, and the Baltimore Warehouse Company. These operations were as wonderfully incestuous as the steamship companies. At the car wheel works, for example, a former superintendent for Winans and the B&O shops patented a process for making chilled iron car wheels, then sold the wheels to the B&O and other railroads in which Baltimoreans had a financial interest.

The mini-city at Canton expanded, as in earlier booms. The overall growth of Baltimore raised land values at Canton. The company sent an agent to Europe to sell its bond issue and promote immigration from German-speaking parts of Europe. It offered development sites for working-class housing and complained bitterly of the B&O for shipping immigrants west. "Even he who earns only $480 a year may own a home," by spending a quarter of his earnings over seven years. He would continue to pay an annual ground rent to the Canton Company. The company conceived of its property in the '70s as twenty-five hundred city lots (twenty by one hundred feet) on avenues already graded and paved or shelled, with water, gas, and service of seventy-two horsecars a day. Farther east, it held nineteen thousand more building lots, and beyond that 900 acres "yet of small value." In the zone of small value the company extended its holdings eastward by buying 235 acres at prices from $350 to $1000 an acre. It relocated 200 acres of brickyards to more distant clay lands and doubled the rents. Overall, income growth was not as impressive as the apparent capital growth. The real importance of the rise in land values lay in the development of capital. The Canton Company, on the strength of the prices paid for a few hundred lots a year, could sell stock and bonds and borrow long-term to a vast extent—$2.3 million in 1873 and $5 million in 1874—with the "future" land values as security. In other words, it was a pure speculation. Canton still resembled Quodlibet.[13]

The Seaboard pipeline, a short-lived scheme, shows how the largest entrepreneurs kept the lid on new enterprise. In 1875 and 1876 Pennsylvania oil producers, seeking to break John Rockefeller's control of their oil markets, secured and surveyed a 230-mile right of way from the Titusville oil region to tidewater near Baltimore. It passed near Catonsville, down the south side of Middle Branch, and through the land of the Patapsco Company at Brooklyn. A pipeline, they figured, would halve the cost of hauling oil. They planned a refinery and barrel factory on Curtis Creek. Rockefeller, however, reached an understanding with both B&O and Northern Central to continue bringing oil to Baltimore by railroad. He would pay five times the proposed pipeline rate, but less than the published railroad rates. By controlling the hauling of oil, he acquired control of all eight Baltimore oil refineries, through J. N. Camden's United Oil Company. The last holdout was Sylvia C. Hunt, a widow who rebuilt her refinery after it burned in the summer of 1877 and would not sell to Camden. Starved of oil, she was finally forced to lease it for five years. "They crushed her business and her spirit as remorselessly as they would have killed a dog."[14] That first long-distance pipeline was never built. But convinced by the engineering logic, Rockefeller quietly set out to create his own pipelines, and the scene of the struggle shifted to Philadelphia. Baltimore's exporters, refiners, and real estate speculators had been mere pawns in the game of the New York monopolists who aimed to control the national market.

The Trust and the Swindle

About the time the *American* published its glowing preview of economic opportunities, the *Sun* was fulminating against opportunists: "The country is filled with the spirit of speculation. It is infectious, and all professions and occupations seem to be affected by it. Men's minds are filled with vicious schemes of extravagant gains."[15] *Sun* editors complained of the gambler and horse fancier, shoddy and sharper, taking over the springs and summer places formerly frequented by respectable invalids. They tended to blame paper money and end-of-the-war inflation. "The poor become poorer, the rich grow richer. Money flows in streams; waste and extravagance and parade and ill-taste and bad manners obtrude their random and graceless forms everywhere."[16] In fact, the moral crisis was fundamental. It was not a matter of any basic difference of outlook of the two newspapers. The editors of both papers shared an enthusiasm for enterprise and a horror of speculation, never quite realizing that these were two sides of the same coin. They were at once urging the horse on and reining him in. The development of new wants and the spirit of speculation were part of the same growth process and the same buoyancy. Kirkland, Chase, a long-established firm dealing in sugar and coffee, was owed large sums in the West Indies, while it had advanced something like $2 million to other firms in Baltimore—grocers, lumber merchants working timberlands along the B&O, manufacturers of barrel staves and shook stuff for the West Indies. This enterprise illustrates the long-cycle behavior of many large firms: in 1870 the company had just finished paying off its debts from the crisis of 1857, as agreed upon by its creditors, seventy-five cents on the dollar, and in the fall of 1872 it again suspended payment, dragging numerous firms into financial reorganization.[17]

Another figure, John L. Crawford, was caught up in a succession of speculations characteristic of the seven fat years—chrome, coal and iron, oil, silver, and fertilizer. All his ventures involved a small tangle of Baltimore investors and informants, but resources as distant as Colorado. When dividends did not materialize and he lost money on margins in gold and a fire in a bottling establishment, he could not pay his debts. He had to refinance, borrowing at 15 and 18 percent a year interest, besides commissions. So he went "deeper in," developing each new venture to salvage the losing ones: he added West Virginia coal lands to his iron company, a railroad to open the mine, and a nail factory to provide a market for the iron. To build five miles of railroad from the B&O to his West Virginia coal lands, he proposed a stock lottery—offering additional stock in the coal lands as prizes. He was one of the first to go bankrupt.[18]

Through such experiences, the capitalists became obsessed with the problem of trust. Enoch Pratt, together with Henry Walters, S. M. Shoemaker, and Albert Schumacher, had organized the Safe Deposit Company, with an ingenious and magnificent vault, in 1864. By 1876 they had amended it to a "trust company." The object was to lodge "trust" in a corporation and to make relations of trust into objects of profit. The investment and management of the money of widow and orphan, lunatic and prodigal son, formerly handled by the merchant friend and overseen by the Orphans Court, would be handled by a corporation whose life was more permanent than a human being. The corporation's incentive to protect and amass capital would be insured by a rising rate of commission on all accretions to a trust fund. Pratt was also associated with the National Farmers and Planters Bank in Baltimore. He later reorganized his Safe Deposit and Trust Company as a complete financial department store, now part of the

Mercantile Trust Company, one of Baltimore's three largest banks. He was an incorporator of the National Trust and Guarantee Company (1882) and the Maryland Life Insurance Company, which had a remarkably broad charter allowing it to issue bonds and seals, sell at auction, buy and sell real estate and securities, and collect interest. These charters and "instruments of trust" offered breath-taking prospects for the strategic deployment of other people's money.

Meanwhile, the popular press became obsessed with the "swindle." The news columns were full of the alleged Tammany manipulations in New York, and the Baltimore police blotter was full of well-dressed, fast-moving, fast-talking "con men" and shoplifters from Washington and Philadelphia. A Baltimore preacher summed it up:

The swindler is everywhere—on the curbstone, in society, in church, in State, in your parlor. . . . There are genteel swindlers, masculine and feminine; pious swindlers, philanthropic swindlers, splendid swindlers and very mean ones. Every man feels that his gas bill is a swindle, and many think the same of the tax bill.[19]

The preacher's reference to the tax bill and the gas bill as swindles stated squarely the problem of municipal growth. What was the relation between municipal enterprise and private speculation? between mercantile morality and the public trust?

Municipal Enterprise

To compete with other cities, Baltimore's growth strategy was to boost the city's external exchange by new investments in steamships and railroads. But as the city multiplied its exchanges with the outside world, there had to be a comparable boost in internal communications. Within the very center of the city there was once again an intensification of exchange and communications, generating capital values—land values, built capital, corporate capital, and bank capital. In each form of intensification, one must examine the role of public investments.

Public enterprise decidedly grew in scale and complexity in this generation. The growth of the municipal corporation was essential to the growth of the other great corporations, such as the railroads and horsecars. The object of each private corporation was to capture exclusive, legally defensible rights of some kind that would insure it a competitive advantage. Such monopoly rights might be patents, franchises, exclusive rights of way, or ownership of land. Baltimore's businessmen were least effective in using patents. Only the canneries and a few foundries generated significant patents or technological advantages; the other industries depended on patents and machinery developed elsewhere. Their preferred devices were legally defensible rights to advantageous locations. Thus, each entrepreneur was a geographical strategist, and business competition rested upon competition for advantageous sites or routes. Public investments, public franchises, and the public law of real property protected or created values at particular sites, favoring one entrepreneur over another.

External Exchanges

As in former times, channel improvements were public investments, while waterfront land was private property. Private investments in warehouses, wharves, and elevators welded the railroads and steamship lines into an effective

This inner harbor view of post–Civil War Baltimore shows how the old merchant houses had been replaced by larger commercial structures to service the increased port activity.

system of external exchange, at the same time converting the benefit from public investments into private corporate income. The city itself appropriated $200,000 in November 1872 to deepen the channel. J. Hall Pleasants, John Garrett, and the mayor constituted a commission to lobby Congress for $1 million more. The engineer, Colonel Craighill, located a new channel to avoid a rocky bottom formation.[20] The lobbyists sought money to develop the new Craighill channel and also to deepen the older Brewerton Channel to twenty-four feet, to accommodate the largest type of steamship—three to four thousand tons—that entered New York. They argued that because of the great increase in railroad shipments of grain, coal, and beef from the West for export from Baltimore, it was proper that the West should assist in procuring adequate appropriations for the Baltimore harbor. A tenfold increase in the customs revenue of the city (now about $10 million a year) made a million-dollar investment appear worthwhile from the federal standpoint. The lobbyists were doubtless correct in this, and they got their million. Garrett in particular was in a position to reap a substantial portion of the yet greater private gains. By 1878 the B&O on Locust Point, Winans at Ferry Bar, the Canton Company, and the Patapsco Company were all reinforced in their monopoly locations by recommendations of Craighill and the Coast Survey. These planners, for sound technical reasons, recommended that no more pier or wharf permits be issued for development along Light Street, Locust Point, or Fells Point, but that development should be allowed on the south side of the basin and in Canton Hollows.

Rivalries for waterfront sites at the key junctions in the new steam transport system explain the railroad development strategy of this period, in particular, the two great tunnel projects. Virtually all the investments were concentrated in 1872 and 1873. They can be simplified somewhat by regarding them as a struggle between Garrett's B&O and the others. The only change in land and lines of the B&O was the acquisition of another forty acres on Locust Point and the Camden "cutoff," which allowed a more direct routing of passenger trains between Baltimore and Washington. But the B&O made massive investments in its properties to take full advantage of its established situation. By agreement with the PW&B it could transfer freight cars across the harbor from Locust Point to Canton, and save drawing them through Pratt Street.

The privileges of the tax-free, coal-owning B&O Railroad were much resented by major coal users and other waterfront land holders. In 1868 the B&O was charging $2.58 per ton of coal carried from Cumberland to Locust Point. "The B&O railroad carries coal from Cumberland, at a fixed rate and ample volumes. But it has drawn the utmost farthing."[21] The Western Maryland Railroad was a Baltimore strategy to create a line to compete with its earlier creation, the B&O, for the coal trade. The city endorsed $500,000 worth of bonds, contingent on only $150,000 of private subscriptions; it was to control the board of directors. The line would come in by Owings Mills, cross into the Gwynns Falls valley, then the Jones Falls valley, and reach tidewater at Canton. Progress was exceedingly slow, and private capital did not materialize. The city issued another $500,000 worth of bonds to finish the road, and two years later it appeared that it would require yet another $1 million. Local businessmen were annoyed with the B&O for blocking the project and with the "city directors" of the Western Maryland itself: "The city's interests have been carelessly compromised. The road has emphatically become a city work, the city being left to hold the bag pretty much by herself."[22] The *Sun* thought it would be better if the city would sell the road, "but—nobody bids." This time the city issued $1 million of city stock as backing. Altogether, Baltimore in the early '70s invested $3 million in the Western Maryland Railroad. By 1898 it had paid out on these bonds another $3.1 million of interest (6 percent), which the railroad had failed to reimburse. The Western Maryland main line was built and a depot was opened on Fulton Street, but it did not yet have its own downtown depot or the tidewater outlet essential to a coal road. It played a role in local real estate development, but it was not yet competitive in the railroad duel.

As the Western Maryland Railroad limped along, it was clear that the "Union tunnel," which would connect with tidewater at Canton, was critical to its overall strategy. The Union Railroad Company reorganized several times, but did not succeed in unifying all the railroads. The Canton Company, interested in creating real estate values and industrial opportunities, picked up the ball. In 1871 it subscribed $590,000 worth of stock to the Union Railroad and endorsed issuance of $873,000 in twenty-four-year bonds, secured with their own Canton ground rents. This amounted to nearly the whole cost, and the Canton Company took a mortgage on the entire franchise and rights of the Union Railroad. The $\frac{5}{8}$-mile tunnel was laid under Hoffman and Greenmount avenues, between Cathedral and Arch streets. The line cut off Belvedere Street and took the old water house and millrace. Together with the Northern Central's work, this represented once again railroad redevelopment of an earlier generation of water supply installations. The company announced in June 1873, "The Union Railroad with its noble tunnel is now completed."[23]

One can now see how the noble tunnel fit into place in the more aggressive strategy of the third major railroad, the Northern Central. At this time, the Northern Central was in the hands of the Pennsylvania Railroad, whose nationwide game was a rude competition with the B&O. Among the geographical advantages that would give the Northern Central an edge in through-passenger and long-haul freight traffic were access to tidewater at Baltimore and entry to Washington. Like the B&O, the Northern Central entrenched itself in its strongholds in Baltimore on land already acquired, raising its productivity and lacing itself into the redevelopment of the Jones Falls valley from Calvert Station to Druid Lake. It bought the city's old stock in the Baltimore & Susquehanna and made $2 million worth of improvements. It built an uptown depot on the Lanvale mill property (close to the present Pennsylvania Station), laid a new line on the east side of the falls, built a "powerful stone wall" along the Jones Falls as far south as Eager Street, and regraded land in front of the jail for freight yards. The city cooperated by diverting flood control money to street extension and bridges over the falls. The bridges at Charles Street and Decker Street (Maryland Avenue) were a second generation of iron bridges, the height of elegance. They were designed by Charles Latrobe.[24] Mount Royal Avenue and its park terraces were intended to join in a most attractive manner the two districts of wealth, Mount Vernon and Bolton Hill. As part of that scheme, the city wanted the Bolton locomotive shops removed. Therefore, it contributed $100,000 to a land exchange, and the Northern Central located its shops and repair works in a new Bolton yard north of North Avenue. The city also built bridges over the Northern Central at Madison, Monument, Fayette, and John (Preston) streets, further subsidizing the railroad's use of the valley.

The Northern Central was bringing down half a million tons of freight during the war, a million in '67, and over 3 million in '69. In 1873 it finally reached tidewater through the Union tunnel. All railroad companies could use the tunnel, subject to the same rates of toll. Oil shipments, by agreement with Standard Oil, doubled instantly. The Northern Central invested half a million dollars at Canton in a large grain elevator, warehouse, and coal pier. Thus, the Pennsylvania Railroad achieved the greatest advantages from the "Union" tunnel without investing its own capital and without any real threat from rivals.

The Pennsylvania's other *coup* was the construction of the Baltimore and Potomac Railroad. Organizers in Anne Arundel, Prince Georges, and Charles counties had been unable to raise the money during the war, so the president, Governor Oden Bowie, went to the Pennsylvania Railroad for capital. The ninety-mile line south from Baltimore to Pope's Creek on the Potomac would open up the coastal plain woods of Anne Arundel County, apparently barren, for truck farms and fruit. It would have a spur from the Bowie junction to Washington. What the B&P offered the Pennsylvania was, in fact, a right of way for a main line between Baltimore and Washington. To enter Baltimore, the B&P built a 1.5-mile tunnel into the Jones Falls valley.[25] There the B&P connected with the Northern Central tracks and new depot. It agreed to build bridges across all turnpikes leading into Baltimore to avoid the congestion of crossings at grade. There was quite an outcry when the company evaded the agreement. These points were outside the city limits, beyond the easy reach of city police and

The Baltimore and Potomac Railroad tunnel was in fact the gateway through Baltimore for the Pennsylvania Railroad's connection to Washington, D.C. The view here is of the eastern entrance to the tunnel, at the site of the present North Avenue bridge.

courts. The *Sun*, friendly to the B&O, accused the B&P of "working like an invading force, stealthily entrenching itself by night, so as to be ready for the attack which it anticipates with the dawn. Why should the city allow itself to be choked and blocked, dwarfed and confined?"[26] It also accused the B&P and the Northern Central of the same strategy of encircling and beseiging the city in order to secure permanence to themselves: "They are both daughters of the same mother."[27]

All the railroads laid financial siege to the city. B&O property was virtually tax free by its original charter. The new tunnels were also given a tax break: state legislation of 1876 provided that railroad tunnels in Maryland would be assessed, not at their capital cost or appraisal value, but at a rate "no higher than any other equal portion of said road," even a portion through piney woods or old sedge fields.[28] Thus, the profits of improved access and centrality were captured for private enterprise, and to a great extent by Philadelphia stockholders.

Internal Exchanges

New urban technologies offered opportunities, and the franchise insured not merely the protection of capital invested, but the protection of any larger stream of future profits. A well-secured geographical monopoly meant that more stock could be sold. It was possible locally, in gas, horsecars, and waste disposal, just as it was nationally in railroad, telegraph, and pipeline companies, to sell stock worth much more than was needed for actual construction. An inner circle of financial agents or managers could then skim off windfall gains before the overcapitalized company even began operating.

The several types of local franchise were smaller arenas than the railroads, and so there appeared a circle of smaller capitalists and engineers involved in many different ventures, often dependent on Philadelphia or New York for financial backing, patents, and construction contracts. They stirred the animosities between city and state, since the state through its chartering power could always overrule the city by facilitating or obstructing its franchises.

Issues of monopoly versus competition were debated. How should prices be set, and who should receive how much profit? All municipal fixtures were "natural" monopolies, that is, competition offered no long-run solution for the consumer because the larger distributor had lower costs. But each new technical option (borrowed from elsewhere) suggested a possible economy for the consumers, and the city council and the legislature were perennially persuaded to create "competition" to obtain the new technology. The competition was always short lived. The People's Gas Company was built at the foot of Scott Street (1871), but promptly reached a secret agreement with the older Baltimore Gas Company to split the territory along Eutaw and Pennsylvania avenues and to raise the price of gas streetlighting to the city. There were thirty-four hundred gas streetlights and more than eleven thousand customer households. Both companies made profits. In 1877 a new Consumer Gas Company had a $2.4 million works built on Lancaster Street on land leased from the Canton Company. Frank Hambleton was the engineer, and Thomas Hambleton & Co., bankers, were trustees for the mortgage. The Baltimore interests possessed nothing of value but the franchise, but they managed to take control of it and put it into operation without having paid the New Jersey contractors and patent holders anything.[29]

Horsecar lines were a feeble imitation of the steam railroad—low-grade power and technology, low-paid labor, inefficient operations, erratic profits. Their real appeal was for use in the development of suburban land values or as adjuncts to railway strategy, connecting the several railway station and steamboat lines. For such aims, the scramble for franchises offered an arena for modest local capitalists who were politically connected; the cast of characters is reminiscent of other public works contracts and public franchises. In 1872 City Passenger was the largest, with 800 horses; among the participants were Henry Tyson, who ran it in the red, Enoch Pratt, and Oden Bowie, who developed it to steady dividends of 10 to 12 percent. Its principal rival, Citizens Railway, had 215 horses and ran between Druid Hill Park and Patterson Park, by way of the Pratt Street wharves and the President Street Station. James L. McLane was the principal in the Frick Lines, whose Park Railway allowed the Western Maryland Railroad to connect its suburban depot (at Fulton and Laurens streets) with the Northern Central Station and the Broadway ferry. Its Baltimore, Peabody Heights, and Waverly line and its Edmondson Avenue line were geared to suburban real estate ventures. A dozen other suburban lines had 15 to 40 horses each. T. E. Hambleton organized the People's Passenger Railway in 1878, about the time the Hambletons launched their gas company.

An epidemic disease of horses, the "epizootic,"[30] in the fall of 1872 suggests the extent to which horse-drawn services integrated the circulation system of the city. The Board of Health estimated that there were fifty thousand horses in the urban area. The bronchitis and "hacking cough" of the horses stirred up more attention and concern than the smallpox epidemic a few months earlier. The newspapers were filled for weeks, first with preventives, then remedies, then weekly mortality estimates from Horner's glue factory. "Many poor animals are kept at work, staggering under heavy loads. The smell of burned tar, carbolic acid and other disinfectants about the stables is almost universal." The draymen and carters were sorely distressed, despite the prices they could suddenly command. Theaters held benefits for the car drivers. The livery stables suffered losses. With the near disappearance of horses from the streets, handcarts and wheelbarrows were in demand around the docks. Men and boys toted bundles on their heads, and milk was delivered by two-wheel pushcarts. The residents of Waverly arranged an hourly street railway car drawn by ten men. "Colored men appeared on the streets regularly hitched to vehicles of different kinds. . . . Such loaded wagons were followed by crowds of volunteer bipeds, to the great amusement of the crowds on the sidewalks." Firefighters, police, and citizens drew the steam fire pumps, "suggestive of the old volunteer days," and the B&O was allowed to use steam locomotives in the streets. At last, after a month-long crisis, "convalescing animals appeared, well wrapped up in blankets, and attended by grooms."

Hydrologic Circulation

Baltimore was suffering in drainage and water supply from the cumulated effects of growth, a lag in public works behind private enterprise, and thinking small in previous years. Nothing much had been done about the basin or about implementing the sewerage plan of 1862. In the absence of civic leadership and collective action, individualism ran rampant. The public wells still in use in Fells Point and other older neighborhoods were often polluted by sewage. The city council had become very lax in issuing all kinds of permits. There were now twelve hundred wooden sheds and stables adding to the fire hazards. Stray dogs could be counted by the thousands. Permits were issued for cellar drains, to many of which were attached water closets, "the drainage of which passes into the basin." Those fortunate enough to have private drains and interior closets now discovered the risk of deadly sewer gas in their homes.

These effects were noticed only in seasons of crisis, when natural variation swung to one extreme or the other—too little or too much water. In 1858, 1866, 1868, and 1869 there were serious floods in the Jones Falls. Most occurred in the thunderstorms of July. July was also the season of prolonged heat waves and drought. Droughts were severe enough in 1866, 1868, 1876, and 1878 to cause shallow wells to dry up. Fells Point was most often affected. Groundwater pollution was aggravated by the lack of rain to flush the streets. In July 1876 150 cases of typhomalarial fever occurred in one block of Fells Point. A week unbroken by storms could result in dozens of deaths from heatstroke and hundreds of cases of heat prostration. During one week in July 1876, for example, deaths reached double the seasonal norm. Heat deaths show the way environmental stress was associated with occupational risk and social assignments. Many of those who died were construction laborers—street pavers, cellar diggers, stone cutters. Most deaths occurred on the job about 5 p.m.—a seventy-year-old man digging at the bottom of a well, a man of fifty heaving coal on the pier, a man of seventy digging dirt in Wilkins Avenue, a sixty-eight-year-old man in the coke pit at the gashouse. There were also young men of twenty—stowing ice in a steamship hold, digging at the ore bank, or firing his father's brick kiln. An Irish man died in the smithy, an Italian fruit vendor on the street, a German cigar maker on the factory floor, a colored woman doing washing. Even the horses collapsed—three car horses and several "Irishmen's horses."

Such crises occurred once or twice in nearly every year, usually in July. But only the exceptional year, the twenty- or fifty-year record event, could wrench public opinion to demand civic action. The events of this generation, which focused attention on the Jones Falls and the basin, were the flood of 1868 and the drought of 1872.

On 24 July 1868, a record "waterspout" washed out all the bridges on the Jones Falls except the one at Eager Street.[31] Water rose to the top of the lamppost at Harrison Street and filled two thousand cellars to the ceilings. A horsecar was carried along Gay Street by the current, and two of its passengers were lost. The owners of millraces demanded compensation. Investigations were ordered, consultants hired, and the city's bevy of railroad engineers resurrected the schemes proposed after the floods of 1817 and 1837. They calculated that it had rained seven inches in twenty-four hours. A plan for diverting the Jones Falls through a tunnel and canal to Back River was estimated at $5 million to $6 million. An alternative proposal was a $3 million urban renewal scheme: the city would borrow the money to buy the entire flooded district, straighten the falls, raise the streets and bridges, and pay off the bonds by reselling the property.

Before any flood control work could start, the other catastrophe struck. The drought of 1872 surpassed all records for twenty-six years. On 13 May the water ceased to flow over the Lake Roland dam. The city was consuming 9 million gallons a day, and extreme conservation measures were taken. "Jones Falls is a failure. This stream, although capable, as the past has proven, of being rampagious and uncontrollable during the rainy season, now turns out to be equally unreliable during the dry season . . . an insignificant little brook hardly three feet wide."[32] The wells dried up. A heavy toll of smallpox in 1872 and 1873 may not be sheer coincidence. And the stench from the basin could no longer be ignored: "Every steamboat and little tug that moves about the harbor stirs up the nasty puddle." The newspapers reported its condition daily, and the grand jury undertook to investigate it.

The two events—flood and drought—crystallized a determination in Baltimore citizens to do something. But nobody agreed what to do or how much it should cost. The financial drought of 1873 postponed action, and ultimately nothing much was done. The walls of the Jones Falls were raised, the lower falls was dredged again, and the long-debated curve near Pleasant Street was straightened. Most of the flood control money was spent on fine iron bridges, contracted to the Baltimore Bridge Company and W. Bollman.

With respect to the basin nuisance, old schemes were also dusted off and new imagination was unleashed. F. H. Hambleton, the city engineer, recommended a sewer to intercept the sewage going into the falls and conduct it to a point downstream in the Patapsco River. Mayor Vansant wanted to fill the Pratt Street docks, extend Camden Street across them on a heavy stone wall, run a railroad on it, and then deepen the remainder of the basin.[33] Others suggested a

This segment of the Sachse bird's-eye view (1869) details the mouth of the Jones Falls and the harbor.

canal or drain toward Spring Garden, with aerators. Henry Tyson favored a "propelling pump" to create a current in the basin.[34] A consulting engineer who had worked on deepening the Danube and irrigating the borders of the Nile was hired from New York to arbitrate, but his proposals for the basin were ignored.[35] In fact, little was done for the basin except cheer in 1876 when the fish came back. It was observed that the sugar refineries had closed since the depression of '73. The financial drought had, for the moment, compensated for nature's drought. Federal Hill, having escaped cutting down, was at last acquired for a public park, and the topographic mapping, shoring up, and "greening" were undertaken by Augustus Faul, who had done the topographic survey for the Boundary Avenue Commission in 1851 and the survey for Buckler's plan in 1859.

Asked to comment on the basin, Buckler wrote back from Paris that while he loved the dear old city of Baltimore and its people, "past experience has taught me that, in their collective or municipal capacity, they are the most silly, unreflective, procrastinating, impracticable, and perverse congregation of bipeds to be found anywhere under the sun." He claimed they listened to no advice or common sense. "The result is that City improvements are never, or next to never, done as they should be at first, and consequently are required often to be done at great cost, again, and sometimes over and over again."[36]

The waterworks was clearly one of those projects that required redoing at great cost, again. Each new effort bequeathed another lake to the city, and this might be called the generation of lake makers. The Jones Falls water supply was completed as Swann had intended. Lake Roland was finished and began silting up, and the Hampden "high service" reservoir was in operation. Druid Lake was finished soon after the war. At Druid Lake the water engineer, Robert K. Martin, sought "to connect utility to beauty." His dam, 119 feet high, was the largest earth dam built in the country. Mount Royal Avenue was built from the dam, to curve around the new circular Mount Royal reservoir and connect the new terraces facing the new Pennsylvania Railroad Station and bridges with that older kernel of monumentality at Mount Vernon Place. Druid Lake showed an appreciation of topography and monumentality that recalls the 1820s or the 1851 plan for a boundary avenue. It was a success. Yet the Jones Falls was a failure as a water supply. The drought of 1872 convinced the public to approve loans for a new supply, the more generous Gunpowder Falls system recommended by the engineers of the 1830s and 1850s. The magnitude of the new waterworks compared with the new railroad tunnels. They cost $8 million and were not finished till 1881: Loch Raven Dam and Reservoir, Lake Clifton,[37] and Lake Montebello, and connecting them a great tunnel six miles long and seven feet in diameter.[38] All the lakes bore the mark of Robert Martin, connecting utility with beauty. Most of the elements are still part of both the water and park systems today.

The massive water projects introduced the city to a new plane of labor management and new opportunities for contractors and politicians. The work was concentrated during the lean years, especially 1877-78. While the city was building the Loch Raven reservoir and the tunnel from Gunpowder Falls to Lake Montebello, two thousand workers were employed on contract, night and day, for more than two years. The stream bed was excavated, and ten miles of roads were built around the reservoir. The principal contractors were L. B. McCabe and John and Charles Donoghue. "Colored men and mules do all this work," except for the building of bridges and a city force of bricklayers to arch the tunnel. "The huts of the laborers are thickly scattered along the riverside, built of logs and mud." The mining crews were also colored. They performed a dynamite demonstration for reporters, three hundred feet underground. These were Baltimore's John Henrys.

One man holds the drill while another strikes, and never misses. Both are stripped to the waist, and dripping with perspiration, and soaked with water, which percolates through the crevices of the rock continually. . . . The miners don't mind that sort of thing. They get their bread out of the wet, hard rock.[39]

As on the railroad tunnels, some died. When a rope broke, an Irish foreman had his neck broken and a member of his black labor gang was severely injured. Another Irish laborer was permanently disabled when a timber slipped the rope.

The city's routine labor force increased along with its construction labor, and much of the hiring was in the control of the health commissioners. After a snowstorm the health commissioners hired as many as six hundred laborers to clear crossings and drains. Night soil was regularly hauled out of town by two hundred to three hundred private contractors, while a force of over one hundred city employees hauled cartloads of garbage and ashes about two miles out. Volumes of garbage, street dirt, and night soil increased 40 percent over the seven fat years, and a new system was devised, combining the approaches to these problems and establishing new bases for political power. The health commissioner hailed a patent scheme called the Odorless Excavating Apparatus, "one of the greatest blessings of the age,"[40] with which privies could be suctioned in the daytime. By a plan of C. A. Leas, the various waste products could be mixed in suitable proportions and sold for fertilizer. The absorbent coal ash had a deodorant effect on the night soil from the OEA. The biggest problem was finding sites for the dumps.[41]

The Irish, who in the 1850s were the stablemen, draymen, common laborers, and haulers, continued to monopolize the occupations concerned directly with horses, including horse railway work, night-soil contracting, and garbage carts. All city streetcleaners and garbage collectors were white. But their humble participation in the city's fast-growing circulatory system allowed entrepreneurs and technical men to get a foothold. By 1872 Irish-owned livery stables and transfer companies employed up to 100 horses. The fifteen well-recognized horse doctors were mostly Irish. The Irish paving contractors hired black men with their mules and carts. When the city council gave George Padgett's OEA an exclusive municipal franchise, it created a vested interest for the next generation.

All of these systems—gas, horsecars, water, garbage, night soil—involved the use of the streets for collection or distribution. The street provided more and more specialized services, operated by private or public monopolies, and thus the streets themselves were trammeled with servitudes—poles, drains, signs, and tracks. From 1870 on, the mayors complained steadily of the constant breakup of paving, as each company needed to dig up the streets for its own purposes. The first experiments were made with patent asphalt in South Street, and with Belgian block. The cobbled street itself was the classic case of what required to be done over and over again, up to a million square feet a year.

The city's financing practices were defective. The mayors overestimated tax collections and made low-rate campaign promises, while the 1867 constitution restricted the city's borrowing power. The "floating debt" was used: perennial borrowing to meet end-of-the-year overruns. Then "funding" loans were approved to turn short-term debt into long-term debt. All in all, the city borrowed about $13 million in long-term loans in this period, primarily for the water system, the Jones Falls, and the harbor. By 1875 political and financial reform had become a major campaign issue. The *Sun* complained that the press performed the labor of Sisyphus, to interest people in municipal elections: "Each year the same dead weight of indifference and apathy has to be moved, and the cause of municipal reform, like a heavy stone, rolled uphill."[42]

Iron bridges, designed by Wendel Bollman, provided relatively secure links across the Jones Falls. The Falls often appeared this placid, but spring freshets were recurring problems.

Real Estate Momentum

In contrast to the dead weight of apathy toward municipal reform was the momentum developed in real estate. As the tide of urban optimism rose, the city built up a new ring, and beyond that subdivided another ring of real estate. Land values rose a notch. Two features distinguished this new tide, the impact of passenger railways and the constraint of the municipal boundary. For the first time since the annexations of 1816 the city filled its bounds. In 1874 the line of direct taxation and urban services became coextensive with the city limits. The boundary in this generation sharply distinguished the dense urban environment from the rural environment. But a variety of new experiments and small installations spilled beyond the city line and prefigured massive transformations of the next generation and a new conception of an in-between suburban zone.

Filling the City

As the city filled, not every square inch was built upon, but its layout was wholly structured—in particular, the four "corners" of the city and the northern edge. The new police stations, parks, and depots defined these corners of the city: Druid Hill Park on the northwest, Riverside Park on the south, an extension of Patterson Park on the east. Streets were opened to make them accessible. To connect the new Western Maryland depot, the city opened Fulton Street northward and Stricker Street southward, and improved North Avenue. Horsecar routes that joined the parks and depots also traced in a framework for whole districts. The handsome three-story dwellings that fronted on Franklin Square and Lafayette Square and many of the connecting axes had horsecar service, wide planted streets, and relatively good drainage and ventilation. In Bolton Hill, builders were putting up "first-class dwellings" in groups of five or six—for example, twenty-two-foot fronts along the Eutaw Place squares near McMechen Street, with mansard roofs, bay windows in the rear, and fronts of white marble and finest pressed brick. "The stairways are easy of ascent and massive." The development of the elegant northwest axis of Madison Avenue was attributed in large part to the Citizens Passenger Railway.[43]

Farther west, the Frick lines served Edmondson Avenue and Fulton Avenue. Dr. Edmondson's heirs donated Harlem Square, also on a height, as part of their subdivision. They owned all the surrounding land and had high expectations.

Jackson Square, in the east, was developed in much the same way.[44] The hill called Fairmount was leveled off to the building lines on Broadway and Hampstead (Fairmount Avenue), and wide dwellings were built facing the square or facing Broadway. Two were "on the New York plan," of "imitation brownstone" (a local sandstone), with a circular stairway in the center with ventilator and skylights. The horsecars went as far east as Patterson Park. The Union Railroad viaduct and tunnel laid the curious pattern of crossings and neighborhood distinctions for more modest houses in the northeast. Washington, Chester, and Choptank avenues were the new edge of the built-up city.

The southwest was predominantly a working-class section, where three thousand employees of the B&O lived. Ross Winans took out permits for a row of four-story brick "tenements" on Parkin Street between Pratt and McHenry. His innovation was modeled on the London schemes of dwellings for workers, probably upon George Peabody's pilot projects. But Baltimoreans were determined on single-family housing, and the experiment was not a financial success. More popular in Southwest, South, and Southeast Baltimore were the building associations, which advertised "ready to lend," with weekly dues twenty-five cents a share.

South Baltimore was rapidly built up as working-class housing, even in the lean years.[45] When the B&O roundhouse for freight locomotives was built next to new Riverside Park, a hundred families of enginemen and conductors moved from Mount Clare to this vicinity. Developers such as Gittings, Frederick, and Cardelin built two-story blocks for working-class home buyers, and a smaller number of three-story houses with rental dwellings over stores. They built rows east of the park along Fort Avenue for laborers and mechanics at the coal oil wharves. J. N. Camden, consolidator of the Baltimore refineries for John Rockefeller, invested $100,000 to fill marshland and build warehouses. He had several hundred employees working in "the Vineyard" near Ferry Bar. This was an advantage for Thomas Winans, who owned most of the land south of the B&O to Ferry Bar, the southern tip of the peninsula. Winans privately graded and paved several streets through his property, added a dock, and began to build dwellings.

The construction boom was financed by the advance mortgage, vigorously debated in the legislative session of 1872.[46] Nearly all buildings in 1870 and 1871, over 3000 a year, were built on advances. That is, the landowner sold a leasehold interest to a builder and agreed to advance him working capital in installments as the work progressed. The advances usually amounted to half the cost of the building. This mechanism promoted construction, but captured a lion's share of all profits for the landowner. He or she received an annual ground rent (as in the past), but more important, was able to charge more for the land: "It is a well known fact among builders that when they lease ground and build on advances, they have to pay a much higher rate for the ground, sometimes double what they would have to pay if they would lease without advances being made." The higher land price was passed on to the consumer, and required building for higher-income people. That helps explain why most of the construction was of three-story houses. "What is the present system doing? It is building all large houses, larger than most people can afford to live in." In addition, the landowner was protected by a mortgage on the property as of the date of the land sale. (The advances came later.) If the builder failed, the landowner foreclosed, getting the whole property for the value of the prior claim, or about half its cost. The mechanics and materials men were left without any security for their outlays, although their investment of labor and materials had supplied the other half of the working capital. "The present law makes the rich man richer and the poor man poorer."

The city remained compact because of the services it could provide directly—paving, water, fire, police, and schools—and indirectly, through franchises for horsecars and gas. Outside the city limits, lesser corporations tried to offer these services in integrated packages, but their success varied. Most proved to be small enterprises, but they had large pieces of land and large ambitions. The horsecar idea was seized upon in the counties by the old turnpike companies and by real estate owners who wanted to develop residential "parks." The village-like nuclei of Baltimore's important inner suburbs were all developed in this era. Waverly is an example. Near the old tollgate on York Road at the end of the Civil War there was a cluster of fifteen dwellings called Huntingdon, "dignified with a post office." On Harford Road opposite that spot, a village scheme called Homestead had failed in the '60s for want of transportation. It was still forested, and on Thanksgiving the sportsmen came out to shoot sparrows. A group of "enterprising gentlemen" purchased all the land between Huntingdon and Homestead, and laid it out in avenues—Huntingdon, Waverly, Washington, Baltimore, Gorsuch. Frame houses were built cottage-style with bay windows and ten to twenty rooms. By 1872 it was described as a neat country town of 250 to 300 dwellings or 2000 persons, spread over thirty or forty acres. It was served by the Peabody Heights and Waverly horse railway via Charles Street. Another line ran double-decker horsecars along the York turnpike from city hall to Towson, and the Hall's Spring line ran out Harford Road and Homestead Avenue. Contemporary estimates of the land values in Waverly give some idea of the mainspring of this process. In 1866 land could be bought at $450 to $600 an acre; once the avenues were built (1869) it cost $4000 an acre, and with the horse railway service (1872) it was $16,000 an acre. The total property value, including improvements, increased over the seven fat years from $600,000 or $800,000 to $3 million or $4 million.[47]

Land values rose likewise along other suburban railways. Before the Powhatan Railway was built, land between the Baltimore, Liberty, and Franklin turnpikes could not find a purchaser at $500 an acre, but George Appold now bought 144 acres at $1500 an acre, another sale was made at $2000 an acre, and these buyers in turn sold building lots at $2 a front foot, or over $8000 an acre.[48] The development corporation for Highland Park resembled the steamboat enterprises—a cut for the landowner, the loan company, and the savings bank.

Suburban Nuclei

Two miles of avenues were graded and planted, a gasworks built, and a dozen villas sold before the bubble burst. Walbrook, served by several horsecar lines, was more successful. Suburban horsecar lines permitted growth spurts in Highlandtown, Catonsville, Pimlico, Arlington, Pikesville, and Hampden. Country seats about the same distance out of town (seven or eight miles) not part of villages or on horsecar lines continued to bring only $350 to $1000 an acre. Consequently, development schemes were rampant in Baltimore County. A narrow-gauge railroad was projected along Stony Run, through the property of the Hampden Association, past Lake Roland, out to the Sheppard Asylum beyond Towson. The landowners signed free rights of way and subscribed $35,000 to extend Green Spring Avenue six miles from Rogers Avenue to the Green Spring Valley and Rogers Station on the Western Maryland Railroad.

Suburban industrial development also depended on the new transport. The cotton mill villages grew but remained rural in character. Industries began to come to the railroads. Among them were the slaughterhouses, responding to competition from western stockyards (Chicago, Cincinnati, Kansas City) and western railroads. The B&O purchased a piece of land on the Gwynns Falls from Ross Winans, and another group of investors bought a nearby site on Gwynns Run and the B&P Railroad. The by-product industries developed close by (Wilkens' hair factory, Lipps's glycerine and soap works, and Appold's new location for hide, oil, and leather works). Still another group of slaughterhouses expanded at the junction of Pennsylvania Avenue, North Avenue, and Fulton Street. They were at their most prosperous in this era, and all the owners were involved in suburban residential speculation. All these industries drained into Gwynns Run, Gwynns Falls, or Chatsworth Run, and eventually into Middle Branch. They illustrate the significance of the city boundary in defining a locus for dirty industries outside the city. The old city boundary, where it touched waterfront or stream valley, was marked out on the landscape in ways that could not be erased after later annexations—by the siting of the slaughterhouses and the horse barns of the street railways. The car lines were either city or county franchises, not both, and their operating logic placed barns at the ends of the lines, that is, near the city boundary. Once organized, these sites have persisted, even though the boundary has been removed twice, the corporate identity of the car lines has disappeared, the transit vehicles have been converted to electricity and then diesel fuel, and the barns have been rebuilt of concrete and steel.

As construction proceeded, inside the city and out, people gradually adjusted to a sense of inexorable movement toward annexation of a belt around the city. The mayor complained that the "disgraceful condition" of North Avenue was owing to joint party ownership. The city's inability to implement its boundary avenue plan still rankled. In this period the city had to buy land in the county for its parks and water system. Druid Hill Park, Lake Roland, the Bay View almshouse, Loch Raven, and the right of way for the new water tunnel were all outside the city proper. The purchases did not produce much conflict, but there were complications, such as the inadequate horsecar service to Druid Hill Park because of the different jurisdictions for franchises. The city had trouble, as I

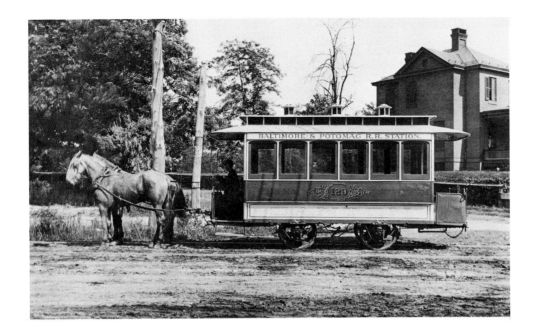

The horsecar was a key element in the rapid suburban growth of Baltimore in the 1870s, as it allowed a radical increase in the available residential building space. The Canton line was one of the last to continue in use.

have said, exercising its contract rights over the B&P Railroad grade crossings, which choked city-bound traffic. It had to make a complicated deal to rebuild and subsidize the Long Bridge from Ferry Bar into Anne Arundel County, to get rid of a toll on goods coming to Baltimore. Baltimore County resisted the city's attempt to find new depots for garbage and night soil. County citizens succeeded in 1874 and 1875 in getting injunctions to close all four dumps that the city had leased.

In addition to those immediate problems, the city saw annexation as inevitable and recognized the problems it would inherit from a want of planning in the counties. It therefore sought to impose a planning process on the surrounding belt. In 1868 the mayor ordered the city commissioner to prepare a map in relation to extending the line on the north "to promote the architectural beauty and symmetry of future improvements." A survey and a map were made showing the future locations of streets and building lines. Over five years (1871–76) the Baltimore County commissioners, under an act of the legislature, planted and recorded hundreds of stones to mark the corners of future streets, most laid out as extensions of the city's street grid. In November 1874, the city passed an ordinance for a trigonometric survey of "the interior topography of the city, and that part of the county which must at some time, not far distant, be absorbed in the limits of Baltimore," a district six miles on the north and two miles to the east and west of the city. Council members argued that this was the zone of "metropolitan" dimensions, and the city ordinance offered to pay up to $2000 a square mile in the city and $1000 a square mile in the county. The proposed map would show topographic contours at five-foot intervals, widths of streets and sidewalks, the direction of flow of surface drainage, and elevations of street corners. It would establish the grades of streets not yet open "with a view to the establishment of a general and uniform system of underground sewers . . . and water supply." It would be consistent with the topographic work of the U.S. Coast Survey, which was preparing new maps of the harbor and channel improvements.[49] The objectives were rooted in the city's own experience of its growth onto higher ground and the deficiencies of Poppleton's plat.

The outcome also recalls 1816. The plan did not go forward because of the costs. Maps were finally ordered from William Shipley, but instead of topographic maps, these were mere location surveys like Poppleton's. The sections returned in 1876 were "regularizing." Like Poppleton's, they tended to disregard natural relief. From buildings or fixed features, the surveyors fixed streets.

Sometimes they straightened them slightly, as in the case of Woodberry Avenue. Where there were as yet no buildings, they redesigned odd grids, as in Waverley and Homestead, to conform to an overall rectangular grid of north-south alignment.

There was so little initiative in Baltimore County government that the proposed through streets approved by the street commissioners were never developed. Some would have been difficult over hilly land. For example, a grid lying north of and parallel to Woodberry Avenue (Druid Park Drive) would have crossed through the rugged slopes and quarries at Cold Spring. Such plats were disregarded by the county. They frequently retained the angled rural roads that the plan recommended suppressing, such as Merryman's Lane (now University Parkway) and Joppa Road. The exceptions were the corporate ventures—the Canton Company and the Patapsco Company—who through this exercise shifted into a truly urban style of planning consistent with Baltimore's urban experience. The Canton Company in 1872 employed Simon Martenet to review all its land records and prepare an atlas showing the grades and drainage for all future improvements on a thousand acres. He ran the levels for forty-four miles of streets and avenues and drew profiles showing the depth of fill or cut. The city engineers later admired the fact that the Canton Company had proceeded to carry out its own plans.

As with the Poppleton plat, the results contributed chiefly to marketing of land. Three sections on the west were returned in April 1872, showing Edmondson Avenue 100 feet wide, through land A. S. Abell had recently purchased, and other lands of Charles Shipley, Hugh Gelston, and Thomas Winans.

The work of the street commissioners is now producing something tangible for those who have been croaking. There is scarce any doubt but these plats will have a marked influence in the sale of property in their limits, as those who buy will very likely have in view these streets as laid down . . . and this fact ought to have a considerable influence also upon the price of land.[50]

A Centerpiece

As the city built up its "inside" land on advances and "belt" landowners speculated in a future market, new expectations also ripened for the downtown area. In the center, reconstruction was undertaken to match the new intensities of exchange. The intensification of commercial activity increased the market values of downtown property. Less spectacular than on the fringe, they were, nevertheless, an impressive amount, roughly proportioned to the city's total growth. At the height of the boom, the *Sun* reported discussions of the lease of a plot of land in London at a value that would be capitalized at $7.5 million an acre. The *Sun* reporter figured that the highest valued land in New York, on Broadway, might bring under half that, or $3.2 million, and the best situated lot on Baltimore Street would bring about $1.2 million an acre.

If New York is to become another London, as her citizens fondly believe, in magnitude, in commerce and in population, there is ample room for appreciation in city real estate. And it will also be observed that when Baltimore shall become another New York—a consummation which may be accomplished before the end of this century—the concurrent advance in the highest present values of city property will be nearly in proportion to the increase in population.[51]

The new values and expectations of rents were translated into new architectural forms. New specialized buildings, new functional concentrations, and new monumental clusters were aligned on the arteries leading directly from the heart. Along Baltimore Street a large number of business houses were rebuilt. The *American* commented on the novelty of the "pretensions to architectural beauty" in business houses: "Let anyone call to mind the appearance of Baltimore street five years ago, and then take a stand at the Eutaw House and look down as far as the Maryland Institute. He will be amazed at the change."[52] The *American* took some of the credit, having built for itself a five-story "graceful grouping of iron columns, pediments, and arches." Howard Street was also rebuilt with new pretensions. It was no longer a mere workaday street of millers and farmers, but a shopping street with a wide range of goods, thanks to the pull of Camden Station, which attracted the wholesale buyers from the south, regular customers from Washington, and visitors from the West. At the north end of Howard Street the combined market and armory was rebuilt "attractive and solid-looking," with three-foot-thick walls, four rows of immense iron columns, and novel latticed trusses to support its arched roof. The hall of the armory, over the market, was designed for either drilling exercises or large soirées, the peacetime functions of the gallant Fifth. Nearby were the new City College at Howard and Centre and the Academy of Music, the city's most massive hall. It seated three thousand. This building, like others that remain on lower Howard Street, proclaimed the taste of the moment by a stripped effect of red brick and white marble or granite trim and an eclectic solid geometry of ornament. Lexington Market continued as a magnet attracting customers from North and Northwest Baltimore into the Lexington Street and Howard Street axes. The Great New York Tea Company cultivated a merchandising strategy still new in Baltimore, selling on a narrow margin with a large turnover. It opened its third "large and elegant" Baltimore branch store on Eutaw Street opposite the Lexington Market. "The entire front is painted green and fancifully ornamented with red, yellow, orange and blue, making it decidedly unique and imposing."[53]

The increase of railroad travel and Baltimore's role as purveyor to the South also fostered a new generation of hotels and banks. The most substantial was the Carrollton Hotel on Light Street. Enoch Pratt and William Keyser were among the original backers, with Niernsee and Nielson as architects. The new banking houses were also built in the original mercantile district, but with a new lavishness and a new solidity. A good example was the Safe Deposit Company of Baltimore in South Street at the east end of German Street (Redwood). The National Farmers and Planters Bank, with which Enoch Pratt was also associated, was at South Street and Lovely Lane. The Savings Bank of Baltimore was renovated. The United German Bank moved out of Raine's Hall, leaving it to the societies of workers, and built a modern banking house opposite, in Baltimore Street. Uphill near St. Paul's other monumental groups were planned. A new

In a role similar to that of the Lexington market, the Broadway market was the centerpiece of commercial life for Fells Point. The market structure included a meeting hall on the second floor.

U.S. courthouse was built at the end of the war, and a Gothic turreted post office in 1875. The Garretts and the Browns contributed heavily for a triangular YMCA building (Niernsee and Nielson, architects) at the northwest corner of Charles and Saratoga streets. A Masonic hall was built opposite, and A. S. Abell built the Morse Building.

Most important, most expensive, and longest in gestation was the city hall. Projected soon after the city's rechartering and divorce from the county (1851), but stalled by the civil war, it was finally dedicated with great fanfare in 1875. It cost a quarter of a million dollars. Streets were opened to improve access to it: Park Street was put through from Saratoga to Fayette, Liberty Street was sewered, and Lexington Street was opened eastward. New hotels, the Rennert House and the Lavelle House, moved in close to city hall. The fire alarm telegraph was completely redeveloped, and the wires connecting the engine houses and street corners with its city hall switchboard were signs of municipal efficiency extended to the municipal limits. The architect, George Frederick, designed a work to rival the handsome public buildings of the federal government. Washington had suddenly swelled to half the size of Baltimore, with a good deal of help from Baltimore builders, materials men, and mechanics. Just as the Smithsonian and the Treasury building symbolized the centralization of the national government, the mass and the dome of city hall provided Baltimore with an urban centerpiece. Reporters were taken through the construction site under a ponderous derrick worked by steam engines. They found themselves "within the subterranean depths of a huge pile of stone and bricks." They climbed a temporary staircase to admire the magnificent view from the half-finished dome—the shipping and trains "fluttering about," marked by the smoke trail of the engines. "Workmen seem as careless tramping around as on terra firma. A gang of colored hodcarriers marches around the wall in single file, singing in a cheery voice, 'Tramp, Tramp, Tramp.' "[54]

Social Adjustment

The boom economy, with its new technology and new scale of enterprise, required a reorganization of work and produced a host of social problems. Successive labor crises were geared to the Biblical succession of seven fat years and seven lean years. As the boom swelled in 1872, skilled workers organized to reduce competition among themselves and the competition of new machinery that was sapping their bargaining positions. All the growth industries were in the throes of technological change—shoes, clothing, oyster packing, cigar making. All experienced "movements" of labor. The horse shoers for the horsecar companies met "to induce the company to maintain the prices they agreed to some weeks ago." The draymen, white and black, sought to arrange a scale of prices like the hackmen. A Workingmen's Assembly was formed from delegations of other associations, including the caulkers. But the depression that set in the next year stifled the combinations of labor. In each industry the competitive position of Baltimore workers was related to the competitive position of their employers in the national economy.

Thousands of workers described themselves for the 1870 census as tailors and shoemakers. Many were still running their own shops, but a majority were skilled workers in factories. In both industries the factory work had already been subdivided into a vast array of specific tasks. It was already dull and very different from the older crafts. The range of weekly wages in a shoe factory was wide, from $4 to $40. The average wage was $22 for men, $12 for women, ten hours a day, eleven months a year.

But a rapid introduction of machinery now changed the workers' situation. Clark, Perry & Co., the largest firm, installed the McKay sewer and cabler at the end of the war, and by 1873 twenty-six shoe factories in town were using it. The same company also introduced the McKay heeler, which allowed a man and boy to do the work of five heel nailers. The net effect of a large number of different machines was concentration and a decline in the numbers employed. The more skilled machine operators obtained slightly higher wages than before, but they were fewer, while the boys and women were more numerous and remained at the lowest wage level (fifty to seventy-five cents a day). The boys were no longer apprentices who could expect promotion in the firm. In 1873 thirty shoe factories in Baltimore employed 4000 hands; in 1890 eighteen factories employed 846 hands. The value of their output remained about the same, but other cities were capturing the growth in the national market. The full impact of the mechanization of the fat years can only be seen at the end of the lean years.

The timing of labor's effort to organize was governed by the business cycle squeeze. The shoemaker Knights of St. Crispin had a lodge in Baltimore by 1868 and eight hundred members by 1871.[55] In April 1871 the women shoe fitters organized a branch. The seventy-five proprietors of the shoe establishments objected and formed an association, the Shoe and Leather Board of Trade, which locked the workers out and fired the union members. They offered to rehire them on probation if they promised not to join any society. As the employers saw it, the "superabundance of female labor rendering it procurable at very low wages," the women had no right to "exclude" others. Twelve hundred shoe workers went on strike. One employer agreed to the society so long as they would not "exclude him from controlling his own work room," and within a week the strike was settled: the employers agreed they had anticipated events, and recognized the union without making any other concessions to it. In 1872 the Knights claimed a thousand members in five lodges. But the economic crisis of 1873 produced layoffs and wage cuts. Resistance collapsed and the organization disappeared. In 1877 they reorganized with only two hundred or three hundred members.

Cigar making was becoming a sizeable industry in Baltimore, and the introduction of machinery, as in shoemaking, favored the employment of more women and young boys, and raised questions about the meaning of apprenticeship. Female workers—sorters and strippers—and boys and girls in the packing rooms were paid fifty to sixty cents a day (sometimes dropping as low as eighteen cents in hard times), while the men cutters, casers, and laborers were paid $1.20 to $1.60, and packers $1.00, varying with the state of the economy. The men and boys also received a ration of smoking tobacco. In 1873 one hundred out of the seven hundred men workers in the city formed a union "to correct the evil of admitting apprentices as breakers and fillers of cigars for the packing machines." But the trend continued, nevertheless. The long stogee that was formerly made on southern plantations had become popular in Hungary and was preferred by the Kaiser. To manufacture the stogees in Baltimore, Kremelberg imported his factory superintendent directly from Vienna, and one hundred teenage Bohemian girls adept at the work. They produced fifteen thousand cigars a day.[56]

The crisis in the garment industry resembled that in the shoe industry. Clothing cutters were the most skilled and the highest paid group in the industry, and they had the closest communication among themselves because theirs was "in house" work. (Much of the other work was subcontracted to small shops or homes.) They organized the Germania Lodge, with two hundred members, of the National Order of the Sons of Adam, and they consulted the Crispins on their experience. The clothing cutters felt that as skilled journeymen who had done long apprenticeships, they had the right to unite, to say who had learned the trade, and—a crucial issue—how much cutting should be regarded as a day's work. The clothiers (Wiesenfeld, Hamburger, Sonneborn, Gutman, Strauss, Greif) responded just as the shoemakers had, by organizing a Clothiers' Board of Trade and discharging all union members. The clothiers, like the shoe manufacturers, were immigrant entrepreneurs who had learned the trade as craftsmen, come up through tough competition and hard work, and were prepared to exact the same of their employees. Their employees could not, however, expect to

The YMCA and the city hall were two ornate Victorian symbols of civic pride. The towers on the YMCA were so elaborate that they had to be removed to accommodate the flow of traffic on Charles and Saratoga streets. Both structures have been substantially renovated and continue in use today as office buildings.

become factory owners. The cutters resisted and obtained gifts of $1000 from their fellows in New York and a strike benefit tithe from Philadelphia cutters. They objected that the employers had formed an association, yet refused the cutters the right to do so. "Capital is always aggressive against labor, and how are we to meet it? By combination." Nevertheless, little by little, the workers drifted back, and in 1873 the union collapsed.[57] The competition was ferocious among the immigrant workers, among the several firms, and between Baltimore and other manufacturing centers.

The cotton mills were different.[58] All were rebuilt or refitted with machinery within a year or two after the war. (The *Sun* figured the investment at $8 million in the region.) The population of Woodberry tripled in the seven fat years.[59] Mr. Hooper doubled the capacity of his Clipper mill, had an investment of $200,000 and an annual product of about four times that. He rebuilt Mill No. 1 in 1873 (after a fire), and built the Meadow mill in '77. Gambrill built Druid mill in '65 and enlarged it in '73. Using steam power, he processed twenty-five bales of cotton a day, producing a million-dollar yearly output of duck, seine netting, and other cottons. He also built seventy-five neat frame cottages for his 400 operatives and a boardinghouse for 250 girls. Poole and Hunt, the machinists at Woodberry benefited from the expansion. They reequipped the local cotton mills and exported similar equipment: engines, Leffel's patent water wheels, and equipment for cotton mills, linseed oil works, and white lead works elsewhere in the nation.

Baltimore's mills continued to dominate the national markets for duck and netting. The entrepreneurs and managers of those firms were the same people as in the 1850s. The same families had been involved as owners, managers, and foremen since the late 1830s—the Hoopers, the Carrolls, the Gambrills, and the Kennedys. Despite faster machinery and a higher throughput, the work was essentially more of the same, and there were few changes in the way of life or work organization of these villages, except the greater ease of going to town or to Sunday school picnics by the horsecars. The lowest paid were women and children, who minded the locally designed spooling machines that cleaned cotton and wrapped it on bobbins. They earned about fifty cents per ten-hour day. Children six to twelve years old worked as long as twelve or thirteen hours a day. Pickers, warpers, dressers, and balers earned $1.50 to $1.75 a day, and the carpenters and machinists or "outside men" earned more. The industry experienced cyclical demand and cut wages at least 10 percent in 1875 and again 10 percent in 1878. James Hooper publicly opposed child labor, and legislation limited children to a ten-hour day. But the employees were housed, and the mechanical inventions did not disturb the traditional division of labor or ranking among the groups in the mill village.

The oyster-packing industry presents a still different pattern. Baltimore was the only big oyster-packing port of the country, and by its geographic advantages Baltimore canners could aspire to national monopoly. This was the generation of its greatest growth. The packing sheds became the dominant feature of the landscape in Fells Point, and overshadowed shipbuilding in Canton and around the inner rim of Locust Point. Other industries became close woven with the canneries: can making, bottles and glass, wood packing boxes, the fitting and repair of small boats, and the operation of the coastal steamers. Baltimore firms patented important innovations in cooking and canning vegetables as well as oysters. The most important was the use of calcium chloride to shorten the time of cooking and increase the throughput.[60] The work system became finely tuned to the seasonal rotation of truck crops and shellfish. The packers even introduced a fleet of small schooners to bring pineapple from the Bahamas to fill one slack period.

In 1868 Baltimore packers associated to fix prices of canned oysters. They made handsome profits for about a year "until outsiders secretly began to enter." Meanwhile, the Can Makers Mutual Protective Association pressed to get its share of the windfall. The can makers, like other workers who organized unions, were the best paid, most skilled craftsmen in their industry; their strikes could bring the entire packing industry to a halt. Their wages moved up from $2.50 to $5.00 a day. Some men cut their work week to three days, while others made remarkable weekly wages. The employers tried combination again in 1878, and again their stock organization, estimated at $25 million capital, made 100 percent profits but broke up after a year.[61] This phenomenon resembled the pooling strategies of the railroads and oil men. It gives some idea of the powerful incentives to combination and the value of geographic concentration to combination.

The harvest of the oysters and fish packed in Baltimore was sometimes romanticized: "Like the fruits of tropical regions we have only to wait for the seasons, nature has done everything—only the fruit has to be gathered."[62] In fact, the expansion of the industry aggravated its viciously competitive character. There were six hundred or seven hundred oyster boats on the Chesapeake in 1872, possibly double this in 1880 if one counts the smaller log canoes not required to register at customs.[63] It was possible to translate years of experience on the bay into the small capital necessary; half the boats were built by their owners or by very small builders on the necks. This encouraged strong individualism and new entrepreneurship. A number of blacks became large owners of oyster boats. Improved machinery "for taking the greatest quantity of oysters from the beds in the least possible time" began to have effects on the ecology of the oyster, and conservation legislation was debated, inhibited by the rivalry between Virginia and Maryland. The state established an oyster police with an iron sidewheel steamboat of five feet draw so that it could enter the shallow creeks and rivers of the bay to enforce the season of seven months and regulations requiring small oysters to be thrown back. The *Sun* interpreted the conservation problem as a conflict between the educated and the uneducated, and described the oystermen as hardy and daring but unintelligent and improvident.[64] In fact, the oystermen, like the clothiers, were in the grip of structural competition. In the competitive struggle, cheap labor, black and immigrant, was shanghaied and often swindled of wages. Their isolation on small bay craft in winter contrasts with the cooperation possible among can makers or clothing cutters.

A similar ecologic crisis occurred at the same time in the bay fisheries. The new technology of the gill net, which was drifted behind a boat, provided an opportunity for the small entrepreneur, by the hundreds, to move in "and with his boat and net to follow the fish as they travel in search of food or to spawn." But while the fishermen increased in numbers and the demand increased, the catch did not. This produced a fierce political struggle with the long-established seine haulers. Seine nets were stretched across a river at a fixed location, and had always been controlled by "the wealthy riparian proprietors," that is, the land holders. A seine fishery was worth several thousand dollars a year. "The seine hauler cannot fish each his own shore; the giller cannot drift on one side of the river only, but follow the current."[65] The competition between them was, therefore, reflected in the geopolitics of the Potomac River boundary between Maryland and Virginia.

Even though modern techniques could increase food-processing production, oyster shucking remained a hand labor trade.

Germania Enfolds Baltimore

Such technological reorganizations affected all social groups and the relations among them. One can try to unravel these relations among the various classes of workers and ethnic groups by looking at the situation of the large German and black communities.

This was the heyday of German Baltimore. Nearly all the immigrants coming through the city by the new steamship lines were German-speaking, and their numbers exceeded all earlier rates, reaching twelve thousand in 1868. Perhaps two-thirds went west, but those who stayed nourished German language and traditions. The traditional Bremen-Baltimore ties in shipping and tobacco were maintained. Baltimore was represented at the great target-shooting festivals at Bremen, while the Bremeners were represented at the annual target-shooting in Baltimore. But the German community in Baltimore was much broader, and immigrants came from all parts of the new German union and the Austro-Hungarian empire. Bavarian Catholics began coming in 1871 to flee Bismarck's Kulturkampf. Polish Catholics arrived in modest numbers about 1870. The Bohemian Catholic community grew suddenly, and the Redemptorists through their Vienna headquarters were able to supply Bohemian and Polish priests.

Reports of the persecution of Jews in Rumania and Poland occurred simultaneously with the founding of the first Litvak, Pekroer, and Bialystok congregations in Baltimore. They were later referred to as the "Russian Hebrews." Benjamin Szold, rabbi to a decidedly German congregation, Oheb Shalom, in Hanover Street, was born in Hungary and educated in Russia. All of these groups were initially regarded as peripheral elements of a core German community.

Meanwhile, the earlier generations of German immigrants to Baltimore had become firmly established, with a complete cross section of social classes, including entrepreneurs, industrialists, schoolmasters, and doctors. Albert Schumacher, Baltimore representative for North German Lloyd, agent of the Allen line and a crony of Garrett on the board of the B&O, was also a director of the four German banks and the Zion school. He lived on Mount Vernon Place and left an estate of $1 million. The clubs marked out class alignments. In West Lombard Street the wealthy tobacco men from Bremen played billiards and chess at the Germania Club, while the Concordia produced its greatest cultural performances and operas in this generation and gradually became identified more as a Jewish club. The Eden Street schul was enlarged and renovated with a hundred gas chandeliers; the Hanover Street synagogue vied with it for elegance. The proliferation of societies and associations among the Germans even outdid the old American tendency Tocqueville had observed a generation earlier. There were the Schiller Grove of Druids, the Red Men's Saengerbund, and the Osceola tribe of German "Red Men." "Of late years, however, the numbers, wealth, and importance of our German fellow citizens have increased to such proportions that their institutions and influences are sensibly felt by the community at large."[66]

The most important influence, perhaps, was that the German community introduced new enjoyments and popular festivals. The great events of the Christmas season of 1872 were Mozart's Twelfth Mass at the Cathedral and Haydn's Mass no. 2 at St. Vincent's, the huge "Christmas Bush" at the German Orphan Home, and the dancing and prize shooting at the Schuetzen associations.[67] The other months were marked off by their masquerades, picnics, operas, gymnastic contests, and singing contests. The Liederkranz at their masked ball in January 1869 carried pasteboard towers and a bridge between, "the dance representing a manner of saving people from any further overflow of the Falls."[68] The Germania Maennerchor ball in February 1872 programmed a Grand National Bottle Dance—a quadrille of French champagne bottle and glass, German Rhine wine, Swabian white wine, and Irish whiskey.[69] In June the Maennerchor triumphantly brought home to Lombard Street a grand piano they had won in New York. At their August picnic the fifteen hundred employees of Knabe's piano factory applauded poems about pianos, lager beer, music, and limburger. The Schuetzen tournament lasted several days and featured German brass bands, dancing to string orchestras, street organs, and flying horses. The young men climbed greased poles. There was scissor cutting, crock breaking, and ten-pin rolling. The chief event was the rifle marksman competition: one man would be king for a year.

That extraordinary blend of village fair and urban spectacle was an Old

World style. One could scarcely distinguish between the patriotic holiday, the annual factory outing, the saint's day or Sunday school picnic, the camp meeting, or the family reunion. It permitted a very powerful welding of solidarities of experience and ethnic recognition that cut across and humanized the hostilities of class, politics, and religion. Theological debates subsided somewhat in all groups, and religion became more intensely sociable, a matter of kinship and shared emotional experiences. Politics, too, became more sociable, reverting to bull roasts and parades. The Germans were less tortured by the Civil War: they had espoused the winning causes earlier and more consistently, and the martial enthusiasms of parade and target practice matched the rediscovery of Germanic mythology. German-American zeal, well lagered, smothered the contradictions that divided Europeans. At the national Saengerfest held here on Bastille Day 1869 the prize composition sung by the nine Baltimore choirs concluded, "Give us, O Wodan for leaders such men, and Germania the world will enfold." They then sang the Marseillaise, and the orators praised Wodan and Charlemagne, Luther and Cromwell, Franklin and Jefferson.

Despite the incongruities, the German community added a deep current to contemporary social thought. The first aspect was a practical solidarity, broadening the sense of responsibility. The entertainments were increasingly a means of providing secular support for homes for the aged and orphans. The pattern was imitated by the Oblate Sisters, the Boys' Home, and other non-German societies. The German Workingmen's Relief Association had an annual budget of $50,000 and the Hebrew Benevolent $7500. The Jewish community founded Sinai Hospital on Wolfe Street and a Hebrew orphans home. When a new city paupers' grave was proposed, Rabbi Szold objected from the pulpit. Rich and poor, he said, ought not to be separated for eternity.

The solidarity of Knabe's or Wilkens's employees was easily translated into the solidarity of employees' relief and protective associations. The Germans were at the core of most of the organizations of labor—the Crispins, the clothing cutters, the can makers, and the cigar makers. Mechanics' Hall on Fayette Street near Eutaw, the Arbeiter Hall on Frederick Street, and the Vorwaerts Hall on Fayette near Frederick were meeting places for both German societies and other trade unions. Ethnic solidarities cemented bonds between the skilled craftsmen and the unskilled. In other generations the "aristocracy of labor" had been divided from the newcomers by ethnic differences as well as work-force position. The German shops also received an infusion of European ideas on the working-class struggle.

A second influence was German resistance to the temperance movement and the Sunday laws. The Turners, in particular, with their tradition of '48ers, opposed both Catholic and Methodist strategies for imposing their morals on the community. While the Germans danced and bowled at Darley Park, the Sunday school movement was singing, "The Temperance Ball is Rolling." The Redemptorists and the Passionists ran parish missions much like the Methodist camp meetings. But while the Sunday schools, including the German United Brethren, contemplated a picture of a felon on the gallows and sang "Away with the Wine Cup," other Germans were consuming their lager beer and limburger.

These philosophical differences occasionally burst into political rows over Sunday concerts and Sunday beer. In February 1872 the Arion Singing Society was prosecuted for its Sunday evening entertainments at Arbeiter Hall. The incident led to massive demonstrations of German groups "to uphold their social rights." Their stubborn cultural streak persisted, preparing Baltimore to become a national center of resistance to prohibition.

Having planted their institutions close to the center—the four German-American banks, the German newspapers, the clubs and halls and opera houses—the Germans also built and developed German neighborhoods in new sections of the city and expanded old nuclei of German settlement. The breweries illustrated on Sachse's 1869 map had sought good water and country sites on good wagon roads. Their beer garden entertainment and the coming of the horsecar lines fixed this locus of German settlement. Highlandtown was one such center, where the Redemptorists from St. Michael's now founded the parish of the Most Sacred Heart of Jesus. The strongest thrusts were toward the northeast and the southwest, along the old farmers market routes toward Belair and Frederick. To the northeast, St. Joseph's hospital was built at Caroline and Hoffman streets by the four original Redemptorist parishes. Nearby at St. James a new church and school were built. Farther out, the Schuetzen bought Darley Park on Harford Road, with ten acres and some of the grandest old trees in the state, beyond city taxes and firearms laws, on a horsecar line, and close to a group of breweries. The Redemptorists founded St. Joseph's parish for settlers from Hesse-Darmstadt, along Belair Road, and St. Bernard's on Hillen Road. For the Bohemians they organized the parish of St. Wenceslaus; its first home was a secondhand German Lutheran church on Central Avenue above Baltimore Street.

Toward the southwest, the new German parish of Fourteen Holy Martyrs was founded at Mount Street near Lombard. It was another offshoot of St. Alphonsus. West Baltimore Germans purchased the Carroll estate for a second Schuetzen park. William Rayner's fiefdom—his personal estate, real estate subdivisions, building activities, and gift of land to the Hebrew Orphan Asylum—created a suburban German Jewish community. Adjacent was the factory of William Wilkens, who employed hundreds of German immigrants. "You don't start to be an American till you've worked at the hair factory."[70] He built housing for worker families, donated land for churches, and subdivided real estate, in particular, Wilkens Avenue between Gwynns Run and Gwynns Falls.

The outward mobility represented a process of Americanizing the Germans and at the same time Germanizing Baltimore. The churches were often bilingual in their services, and so were the schools. The schools of the Redemptorists and Notre Dame Sisters reached their peak at three thousand pupils. Two German Protestant schools built new buildings: Scheib had over eight hundred pupils, and Knapp seven hundred, with a complete gymnasium. Knapp's pupils marched to class in military style. The synagogues also had day schools. But the success of the German educational institutions ironically produced their decline: by popular demand, the city in 1872 added to its public schools a network of "German-English" schools. German culture achieved recognition. Each young hyphenated American would live out his own inner tug of war between the two cultures and make his own personal compromise. The public German-English schools tended to secularize education, contributing to greater tensions between the Old World religious tradition and the New World way of life, but contributing also to a mutual acceptance and perhaps the period of least hostility among religious groups. The experience of the Szolds, who had come expecting to stay a few years and go back, was the experience of many: they found they could not uproot themselves from either of their two worlds. Henrietta Szold attended Western High School and moved directly from her graduating class to the role of acting principal. Like good beer and limburger, German-American identity had ripened in Baltimore to a brief, heady perfection.

For the black community, the sense of crisis continued after the war. Emancipation was insured, but the content and meaning of freedom were yet to be determined—rights to vote, to work, to go to school, to be heard in court. As I shall demonstrate, each of these rights depended on the others, and on them all hinged the struggle for economic survival. "My friends, the present is a critical moment for the colored people of this country; our fate for weal or for woe, it may be yet for many generations, trembles now in the balance. No man can tell which way the scale will turn."[71] With those words, Frederick Douglass, once a slave child and caulker in Baltimore, dedicated the Douglass Institute, organized in the old Newton University building, to the "intellectual advancement of the colored portion of the community." On that homecoming Douglass declared that he had modified his earlier views and that he recognized the usefulness of associations and institutions that would express black pride and solidarity.

"We Have No Prejudice"

The colored boy and girl now, as they walk your streets, will hold themselves in higher estimation and assume a prouder and more elastic step as they look up to the fine proportions of this ample and elegant building and remember that from foundation to roof, from cornerstone to coping, in purpose and in value, in spirit and in aspiration, it is all the property of the colored citizens of Baltimore.[72]

The swiftness with which Baltimore's black citizens organized new institutions was impressive, indicating a readiness of zeal and an urgency of needs that awaited only the enabling laws to free the energy. Nearly all the projects discussed here had their groundwork laid, the money raised, and buildings secured in 1865, all in spite of a wall of hostility from most of the white community. These included free neighborhood schools, a high school, the institute, an orphan asylum, an aged women's home, a seminary, a teacher's college, and, most remarkable, a cooperative shipyard.

No sooner was the war over than the white caulkers of South Baltimore undertook to move in again on the Fells Point black caulkers. The episode was strategic in the development of the position of black labor in the nation. It demonstrated the continuity of black experience, as well as the perennial connection between economic competition and issues of race. Over one hundred black caulkers were army volunteers, in addition to those who worked at the U.S.

Navy yard. As men returned from the war and wartime demand dropped off, there was a notable labor surplus in the industry, even without any direct effects of emancipation. The employers, Abrahams and Henderson's wharf, refused to fire their black caulkers, who were known for their management, workmanship, and dispatch. ("Vessels come from all ports to have their caulking done in Baltimore.") The black caulkers received some support from the police when the white caulkers tried to intimidate them. Two alley homes burned down in Fells Point on the same day, "supposed to be accidental in origin." Then the white caulkers persuaded the white joiners and ship carpenters to go on strike, and their unions resolved on stiff twenty-dollar fines for any who worked with the blacks. On 27 September 1865, the black caulkers were at work, while the white carpenters were "sitting idly by, every white workman refusing to take a tool in hand while the blacks are employed."[73] The position of the whites was, "All we ask of our employers is that they will give the white man the preference." The newspapers tended to line up behind the black caulkers, since the employers' right to hire was threatened. The black caulkers argued that "they must support themselves or become a burthen upon the community" and rebuked the whites, who threatened to "send wafting on a sea of prejudice the business interests of Baltimore to other ports, because a few colored men in this little corner of creation have a little business to themselves." Four hundred of them signed a statement appealing "at the bar of a just and impartial public opinion, trusting in the great Dispenser of Justice, that He will work out the evil purposes of men to the accomplishment of results beneficial to all mankind."[74]

The issues of 1858 were rehashed. Frederick Douglass's visit that very week must have recalled for the blacks how violence and outrage against the caulkers had marked every generation, whenever work was scarce. Now out of the ranks of the Baltimore caulkers came another leader of national stature, Isaac Myers. The trouble spread to the dock workers. By winter the employers began to cave in and hire white caulkers. Myers, together with other black caulkers and businessmen, organized a cooperative stock company, leased a $40,000 lot at the foot of Philpot Street, and started the Chesapeake Marine Railway and Dry Dock Company.[75] In four months they raised $10,000 from the black community, in $5 shares. Effective organization and the early success of this effort were part of a perceptive strategy for black workers. In July 1869 Myers called a meeting of mechanics at the Douglass Institute. Twenty-three crafts were represented, including the Colored Moulders, the Colored Engineers, painters, brickmakers, and longshoremen. They proposed to participate in the national union movement, but at the same time to organize their own local, state, and national labor organizations alongside the white unions, because they saw that they were being excluded. "If citizenship means anything at all, it means the freedom of labor, as broad and as universal as the freedom of the ballot." Nevertheless, blacks were excluded from the cigar makers, the brick layers, the railroad workers, and the Sons of Vulcan. In August, Myers, representing the caulkers, spoke to the third convention of the National Labor Union in Philadelphia. He spoke for the 9 black delegates among 128. "The whole Convention listened . . . with the most profound attention."

The white laboring men of the country have nothing to fear from the colored laboring man. We desire to see labor elevated and made respectable; we desire to have the highest rate of wages that our labor is worth; we desire to have the hours of labor regulated, as well as the interest of the laborer and the capitalist.

He struck a strong argument for all forms of cooperation by recounting the experience of the Baltimore caulkers:

After we were kicked completely out and cast upon the cold charity of the world, we formed a cooperative union, got it incorporated, raised $40,000, gave employment to all our men and now pay them, outside of their wages, fifty per cent on their investment. And is that all? No. We give employment to a large number of the men of your race, without regard to their political creed, and to the very men who once sought to do us injury. So you see, gentlemen, we have no prejudice.[76]

But Myers's cooperative enterprise, like his strategic hope for interracial cooperation in the labor movement, foundered. The wooden shipbuilding industry was in the doldrums. The black caulkers had defended their little corner of creation only to find it was an economic backwash. In the lean years after 1873 the business declined, and their lease expired. By 1880 it had only seventy employees and was mostly hauling out boats for repairs. Few such enterprises, black or white, survived ten years.

Was there a more general direct impact of emancipation on the labor market in Baltimore? Wages for unskilled heavy labor remained about the same, with the race differential unchanged. Most Baltimore blacks were already free before the war. There was some return of blacks who had once lived in Maryland, and there was some immigration from the Maryland countryside to the city. New arrivals included more men and youths, who tended to concentrate in the wards near the docks and Camden Station. But the influx was moderate, certainly less than expected. The Freedmen's Association helped sixteen hundred persons to return home to counties farther south.

A more important economic factor was fear. Slaves in Maryland were mainly agricultural laborers. Releasing a pool of black rural labor threatened to rebalance the labor system and affect the urban labor market indirectly. Former slave owners feared a shortage of labor, while the former slaves feared a shortage of job opportunities, and the rest of the labor force, black and white, skilled and unskilled, were nervous about competition for their jobs. The management of Negro labor, therefore, posed the most difficult ethical questions and evoked the meanest and the most noble responses. Farmers and landholders in Prince George's County, for example, tried to reach an agreement to hire free Negroes only by the year, at a maximum yearly wage of $120, $60 for a boy or woman. This kind of device failed in a competitive economy. A more effective mechanism was control of land, and it remained very difficult for blacks to buy land in most counties. General trends in Maryland agriculture were favorable to the employment and self-employment of free black labor. Demand for the planter crops was stagnant, while the demands of Baltimore's consumer markets and canning industry stimulated market gardening, fishing, and chicken farming along the railroad lines and waterfronts in Anne Arundel County. Many present-day small black settlements in the metropolitan area made the transition in the '60s and '70s from slave quarter to dirt-road village by gardening and marketing their produce. All the varied talents and enterprise Parkinson had observed seventy years earlier were brought into play. By building a boat, wagon, or cart, and buying a mule or horse, a man could develop considerable flexibility: he could carry his own produce to market, he could fish, he could work as a marketman or retail produce door to door, or he could sell his labor with the outfit for excavating or hauling, at about twice the wage he could earn alone. A web of personal connections allowed black entrepreneurs in several sectors to reinforce each other—the market gardeners, the marketmen, the caterers, and the skilled personal servants, butlers, cooks, and waiters in the clubs, hotels, and homes of the wealthy.

The slave labor force had always been a young population: field labor was done in large measure by young men, and the fetch and carry and chop and polish by children. Moreover, for a given current capacity for work, youth was a value that could be capitalized, the true capital asset of the slave. Therefore, the struggle over the freedman as a labor force was waged in terms of control over black youth. Slave holders attempted through the legislature and the courts to manipulate the apprenticeship laws, to have the children of their former slaves bound out to them as apprentices. Several thousand minors were in question. By the old laws, Negro children could be bound only to whites. Unlike white apprentices, they could be transferred with an estate, or sold if they ran away, without the consent of their parents. The crucial efforts of the Freedmen's Bureau in Maryland and of the committed emancipationists—Hugh Bond, Henry Stockbridge, and Richard Bowie among them—were directed for three years to the civil rights issues raised by apprenticeship. Their vital tools were the right of habeas corpus and the right of black persons to give court testimony. Bond, as a judge of the Criminal Court of Baltimore, repeatedly released "bound" youths, and used the right of habeas corpus to insure the supervisory right of parents and courts. The legislature aimed restraining laws at Bond, but wartime experiences had given Marylanders of all political persuasions an appreciation of the courts' right to order persons to be produced or freed. The state constitution of 1867 restrained the legislature: the general assembly could not take away the power of habeas corpus from the judiciary.

Entwined with the apprenticeship issue was the need for a system of free schools for black children. Parents claimed their children because they wanted them educated. The old form of apprenticeship did not require that Negro apprentices be taught the three Rs or any trade useful in later life. Here again, Baltimore citizens pressed the issue, while resistance was lodged in the countryside. The Baltimore Association for the Moral and Educational Advancement of the Colored People brought into full operation seven schools in the city, with an average attendance of three thousand children in 1865. The city council gave $10,000 to the effort. Black citizens and Friends (Quakers) in Baltimore gave $5000, and Friends in England sent £750. The participation of families such as the Stirlings, Needles, Chestons, Cushings, and Tysons recalls the founding of the first black schools and the first civil rights cases in Baltimore in the 1790s.

The state legislature refused to contribute, and none of the Christian churches responded to the appeal. Two rabbis forwarded donations from their congregations: Rabbi Szold, "mindful of the captivity of our people in Egypt," and Rabbi Hochheimer, who wrote: "Though you appeal in your circular to 'every Christian man's benevolence and kindness', you may rest assured that no true Israelite will stand back in supporting this or any other cause of benevolence and kindness."[77] In the counties seventeen schools were organized by the Baltimore Association, but they encountered much resistance. Black churches were burned. Children were stoned in Easton, teachers "blacked" at Cambridge. As Douglass said, "I expect to see the Rebels consistent with their whole past." Just as the association was collapsing for want of funds, the state constitutional convention (1867) ordered the founding of colored schools statewide on the same basis as for whites. This provided an institutional guarantee for a public school system for black children, but in a way that insured a marginal operation. The "colored schools" were to be entirely separate—buildings, budgets, wage levels, and regulations. White teachers were hired. The idea, designed to sound fair on the surface, was that the school taxes paid by whites should be allocated to the white schools and the school taxes paid by black citizens to the colored schools. This ensured that the low incomes and the lack of property among a people who were themselves yesterday property would be perpetuated by impoverished education. Even in Baltimore City, the white schools in this generation spent 50 percent more per pupil in both operating and capital outlays. A building lot rejected as inadequate for a white high school was denied to the Colored Grammar School on the grounds that it was too valuable.

The same attitude was apparent in other institutions, both private and public. Churches became more rigorously segregated than ever. The larger denominations were deeply split by the Civil War as well as older theological disputes, and their reorganizations created the opportunity for separating black brethren. One Anglican church, Mount Calvary, determined to hew to its "free for all" signs on the pews: "Gentlemen, let our religion be before our politics." But the overall trend was toward separation. The Second Plenary Council of the Catholic Church in the United States (1866), impressed with the Baltimore successes of the Sisters of Providence, their new orphanage, and the parish of St. Francis Xavier, opted to develop colored parishes and schools nationwide. The archbishop invited the Mill Hill fathers from England as missionaries to work among blacks. They founded the Josephites, who within a few years opened a seminary to train priests for black parishes.[78] Father Vaughan wrote back to Mill Hill from Baltimore, "I can give you no idea of the dislike of the Americans, Southerners as well as Northerners, to the Negroes. It far exceeds in intensity and subtlety anything I had expected. I assure you it makes my blood run cold."[79] The Methodists participated in organizing Centenary Biblical Institute (Morgan College), for the ministry. The Anglicans imitated the Catholic model, sending the All Saints Sisters of the Poor from England to Biddle Street; they soon took their first black novices.

The new institutions like Douglass Institute, Colored Public School No. 1, and the Centenary Biblical Institute were centrally located near the older churches (Bethel AME Church and St. James Episcopal) at Saratoga and Calvert streets. But the black churches were also hiving off neighborhood parishes from the old central locations, just as the white churches had done in the generation before the war. The new schools and churches were located in five ghetto nuclei: Hill Street, the Orchard-Biddle district, the neighborhood west of Camden Station, Oldtown (Chestnut and East streets), and the district west of Lexington Market. The Baptist extension society (white) helped found the South Baltimore Colored Baptist Church on Hill Street. St. Mary the Virgin, an offshoot of St. James Episcopal, first occupied a hall over a feed store on Howard Street, and later a former Swedenborgian church on Pennsylvania Avenue near Orchard. The black neighborhoods were complex, and within small areas one finds great social distinctions. On Orchard and St. Mary's, on Centre and Hamilton, and on Hill and South Howard streets were respected families, among them substantial provision storekeepers, barbers, caterers, sextons, and undertakers. On New Year's Day they called on one another, some in full dress, white vests, kid gloves, and canes. These were all narrow short streets with fifty- to seventy-five-year-old houses, but in health and prestige they were a world away from the adjoining alleys. In Biddle Alley, for example, typhus broke out in 1866. Cholera in '66 and smallpox in '72 and '73 struck chiefly at the poorest of the black population in the alleys around Camden Station.

In spite of the trials and the failures, sacrificing some children and salvaging others, the black community nevertheless rejoiced in new freedoms. Although there had been few slaves in Baltimore, the city's free blacks had lived under the "black code" that treated all blacks as slaves in some respects. The constitution of '67 permitted black testimony, essential for the survival of the new institutions and for a greater degree of protection of private persons. New rights of assembly and movement were expressed in ways sometimes decorous, sometimes disastrous. The black churches began holding Sunday school picnics at the beach and camp meetings of four or five thousand people in Haslup's Grove near Annapolis Junction, in Chew's Woods near Towson, and at Oakington in Harford County. The caulkers had their own meeting hall. The black veterans, Oddfellows, and the Lincoln Zouaves could parade in uniform to their hearts' content. Even in the penitentiary the black prisoners celebrated the Fourth by making ice cream, parading with fife and drum, playing baseball, and performing plantation jigs. By 1872 black voters were being courted and integrated into the customary rowdy politics of Baltimore. Their Grant and Wilson clubs escorted veterans through Baltimore with bands and transparencies. A rival torchlight procession in honor of Greeley's visit marked the first appearance of a black political club in that party. As usual, the parades ended in a fracas, but in court black witnesses were heard, and little white boys who threw stones and bottles at blacks were ordered flogged by their fathers. Like the German community, the black community knew how to enjoy itself. All that high purpose of moral advancement was joined with sheer fun, nourishing the sweet taste of freedom and an inner tug of war between the philosophy of the individual pulling himself up by his bootstraps and the philosophy of mutual assistance and cooperation.

The drastic changes in labor force management implied a host of new social problems. The decline of slavery, apprenticeship, and long-term contracts freed the employer from responsibilities of training a young labor force, from feeding and supporting his men in seasons of poor weather, poor markets, or poor health, and from governing the more troublesome elements—bailing his apprentice out of jail, paying damages, or fetching him back when he got drunk or ran away. Yet all of these social problems continued to exist, inherent in human nature or in the economic system. The incentive to substitute cheaper labor of youths and women created certain problems when they were employed and other problems whenever they became unemployed. This long-run change in the economy aggravated the problems that always accompanied the rhythm of construction: immigration, crowding, and accidents.

In the last winter of the war it was estimated there were three thousand vagrant children in the city. Delinquency was much talked about. In South Baltimore the Forty Thieves, a gang of white boys nine to thirteen years old, entered new houses at night and on Sundays. "They completely strip them of lead pipe, keys, locks, bell hangings, gas and water fixtures."[80] Police recovered a wheelbarrow load of chandeliers and shower baths. A well-organized gang of black youths lounged about the Lexington Market, ostensibly to carry baskets, but alert to opportunities for theft. A sharp rise in the jail population in 1868 was attributed to the large number of black children committed "for trivial offenses, no other means of restraint being as yet provided."

Problems acute in the fat years reflected a rapid increase in population, together with overcrowding and special problems of immigrants. In 1868 there was a great increase in police station lodgers, mostly homeless men. There were more and more fires, especially in woodworking and other factories. Coal oil lamp explosions became very common. These figures are closely correlated with mortality: high in 1868 and in 1873. A high wartime and postwar murder rate gave way in 1870 to a high rate of suicides. The number of houses of ill fame apparently increased: the police estimated there were two hundred houses, or about eight hundred women involved. Little Sharp Street, Crooked Lane, and New Church Street were "inhabited by colored courtesans" and "thickly studded with drinking houses of low degree."

When the downturn came, police station lodgers increased again and stayed high from 1873 to 1877. The number committed to the jail and admitted to Bay View rose likewise. "The whole country began to swarm with tramps, until in many sections, and especially along the lines of the great railways they became a veritable plague. . . . Freight trains were infested with them."[81]

The problems naturally called for innovation. As I have discussed with respect to the black and German communities, this was a period of hiving off new and more specialized social institutions, extending social services to new neighborhoods and new elements of society. Consistent with trends in business and technology, technical development in medicine favored a division of labor and more complex organization of hospitals. A new people's dispensary in Old-town offered clinics with specialists for the eyes, female complaints, etc., at

Social Problems and Social Institutions

different hours. Two eye and ear hospitals were founded (three hundred cataract operations were performed in one year), and also a lying-in hospital and an inebriate asylum.

Numerous ventures were undertaken for "saving" the children and women on the margins of the labor force and family structures. The Henry Watson Children's Aid Society in a single year placed a hundred children in country homes, operated a home for working girls, and trained a hundred girls in the sewing machine department and fifty more in cutting and fitting. Church societies organized sewing classes, a Home of the Friendless, a girls' industrial school at Orange Grove, a House of the Good Shepherd, and a Home for Fallen Women.

In wartime and postwar crises, the city began subsidizing all manner of private institutions to care for its orphans, alcoholics, and sick or insane poor, and the per diem costs continued to rise even after the courts and legislature ordered the city not to extend the practice to any new institutions (1875). The large taxpayers once again felt that charity was costing too much. State government was pressed to pick up the tab for dependent populations, and founded certain new institutions. All were specialized and adhered to strict racial segregation. An innovative $100,000 state school was organized for the deaf mute at Frederick, and a handsome school for the blind on North Avenue stood out "in its unsullied whiteness." For blacks who were deaf, dumb, or blind, a $12,000 mansion was purchased on Broadway. A magnificent Gothic pile was built on Lafayette Square for the Maryland Normal School (white), while the Baltimore Normal School (colored) occupied a secondhand building. A land grant college for whites was developed at College Park, and a college for blacks at Bowie. To respond to the crowding of jail and police stations with lodgers, the state built a house of correction at Jessup. Baltimore citizens organized a house of refuge for black children, to match the white institution founded by George Brown, and the state contributed to its support. The archdiocese also created colored orphanages and training schools to match its white institutions. Altogether, there were four or five hundred black children in these institutions at any one moment, and about a thousand white children. They were all removed from the city to an artificially sustained agricultural environment, as the alternative to the former systems of apprenticeship or slavery.

Institutions for public dependents readily lapsed into neglect or budget starvation. The grand jury of '78 described the House of Refuge as "a cheerless, dreary, uncomfortable prison." The boys were taken like cattle to watering troughs where twelve bathed in the same water. The House of Refuge for Colored Children was instantly overcrowded and had great difficulty with typhoma, an eye infection. At Spring Grove hospital for the insane, three quarters of a million dollars was spent by the time it opened (with 250 patients) but the elaborate heating system didn't work. Per capita operating cost was sliced by half. Treatment objectives were thwarted because the county almshouses would not send those "most susceptible to treatment," but preferred to send "only the most filthy, violent and refractory."

The institutional structures of social class were most evident in the schools and churches, as before. As Baltimore society became more complex, generation by generation, these two systems were elaborated. The piecemeal growth of the public schools illustrates the interdependency of the facilities for various classes of people. The total number of schools doubled. By '78 there were seventy, with seven hundred classrooms and thirty-six thousand pupils. The Germans and colored schools were installed in the old buildings of the 1840s and '50s or in rented property, while a middle-class clientele occupied most of the new buildings. Thus, the creation of the new colored schools (14 percent of all pupils) and the German-English schools (9 percent) allowed a distinct upgrading and modernization of the system for its initial user groups. The newer three-story buildings had wider stairways and half-basements, with wrought iron beams and galvanized iron cornices instead of wood. Their brick facades were slightly embellished.

To service so many distinctive clienteles there were often clusters of several schools near each other, for example, near Druid Hill and Biddle, near Fremont and Waesche, near Fulton and Hollins, and around Camden Station. To economize on land, the school board paid ground rents rather than buy in fee, and the paved schoolyards were barely large enough to assemble their pupils standing tightly packed. The average investment in a new school building rose to $15,000 or $20,000 (a total of $1.5 million in assets), but City College and Eastern Female High School were built as great monuments at over $100,000 each. Together with Western Female High School, built before the war, they defined another distinct system—the elite high schools. About 30 percent of all school-age children were enrolled in the public schools; of those enrolled, only 4 percent passed into the high schools. Even compared with other cities at the time, the Baltimore schools had a low efficiency of retention and promotion.

Among private institutions, the churches became somewhat less innovative. Their major investments were houses of worship and assembly. The number of churches increased by 50 percent, an investment of at least $2 million, and the range of spending was comparable to the public schoolhouses. The more modest churches near sea level ran $10,000 to $20,000 apiece, for example, the Welsh church built by Welsh employees at the Canton copper smelter, the Church of the United Brethren in Christ, the new Episcopal missions, and the Colored Baptist Church on Hill Street. On higher ground in West Baltimore and surrounding the site of Hopkins Hospital (near Jackson Place) the average was $45,000. On Lexington Street, for example, an Independent Methodist congregation moved from a stone chapel into a unique building of galvanized corrugated iron. The outside, with iron tower and spire, was to be painted white, the interior some color to suit "the dim religious light of churches." On the hilltop sites of Mount Vernon Place, Lafayette Square, Harlem Park, Franklin Square, and Bolton Hill were built the most expensive churches. The Presbyterians were decidedly concentrated in Bolton Hill and Mount Vernon Place. In 1872 they raised the brownstone steeple of First Presbyterian Church. The most elegant of all was Mount Vernon Place Methodist Church, built of Maryland serpentine or

Upon completion, the Peabody Institute library and school of music was the most elegant philanthropic gift to the city. It accordingly became the center of spectacular cultural events.

greenstone. It cost $325,000, and had the largest organ in the city, "a house within itself." A "brilliantly lit up" nighttime auction was held for the choice of pews.

This was a magnificent era for Baltimore in private philanthropy. The wealthiest of Baltimore's businessmen competed with each other in seeking to provide solutions and to crown the city's cheap public institutions with nobler creations. No other Baltimore generation was ever so lavish, so individualistic, or so hard nosed in its giving. Enoch Pratt endowed a public library and located it across the street from the cathedral and a block from his home. He continued until his death to supervise personally its collections and its courtesies. He also contributed to Moses Sheppard's private hospital for the insane, whose object was to cure, not merely to shelter. He gave 752 acres at Cheltenham for the house of refuge for colored children. William Rayner, once a peddler, gave the land for the Hebrew Orphan Asylum. George Peabody founded the Peabody Institute library and school of music on Mount Vernon Place. Peabody had made his first million in Baltimore, then gone to England and become very rich indeed by selling U.S. bond issues in Britain and Europe during the Civil War. Henry Walters began his magnificent art collection and operated it as a private museum (now the Walters Art Gallery), a block from his old home. Johns Hopkins, at the time he was memorializing the legislature against public subsidy of charitable institutions, himself gave $7 million in B&O railroad stock, as well as his Light Street warehouses, for a hospital and a university. His planning detail was characteristic of that generation of philanthropists, consistent with their rather limited faith in those who might come after them. Hopkins created his boards of trustees before his death. He sent Franklin T. King to Europe to examine their famous hospitals. In a masterful stroke, killing two birds with one stone, he acquired the site of the old Maryland Hospital for the Insane. By paying cash in advance, he got it at a discount price ($123,000). The cash allowed the state to finish its new buildings at Spring Grove and move out, leaving the property at Broadway and Orleans for the new Johns Hopkins Hospital. He assumed that upon his death, his own estate, Clifton, would become the site of the university.

The new philanthropic institutions were highly specific in their aims, open to people of all religious faiths but somewhat more ambiguous with respect to serving both races and sexes. All provided services to the deserving poor and more substantial services to the deserving rich. All were located on high ground, on the properties of families that were dying out. Their location and design confirmed the Charles Street and Monument Street axes of monumentality. The newly rich crowded close around the old Establishment.

July 1876

Despite problems and divisions, Baltimore gave itself seriously to having fun. There was a carnival quality to the '70s in Baltimore, perhaps more so than ever before. In addition to the traditional adaptation to Maryland summers and the enthusiasm of the German and black communities, there seems to have been a deep response to new means of travel and media of information. Fun was being part of a crowd. Steam railroads, steamboats, and horsecars made all-day mass excursions the most popular escape—camp meetings, picnic at the shore, a day in the new park. What the *Sun* called bad taste extended to all classes and took the form of sensationalism and melodrama. The *Sun* objected to lynchings (there were several in the environs), but thrilled to a legal manhunt and assigned its best reporters to trials of middle-class poisoner and lower-class knife wielder. The Holliday Street Theater was playing *Bertha, the Sewing Machine Girl*, "full of excitement, of rugged beauty and great situations," while the Front Street Theater offered Ethiopian comicalities, a fairy ballet, and feats of strength by the man with the iron jaw and the female Hercules. Baseball grounds were organized on the horsecar lines, on Pennsylvania Avenue near Chapell Street with stands for two thousand spectators, and near Waverley. The oriole black and yellow of Lord Baltimore added color to the parades and circuses of all classes of people. In the summer of 1872 the new $12,000 baseball nine were outfitted in "black and yellow striped stockings, yellow pants, white shirts, with the escutcheon of Lord Baltimore on the left breast, a black and yellow cap, and a belt of the same colors."[82] Meanwhile, the elite gathered "under the flag of Lord Baltimore" for jousting at Brooklandwood. A dozen knights contended for solid gold and silver spurs on Mr. Alexander D. Brown's well-rolled track. A "very large and brilliant crowd" arrived in hundreds of carriages and unpacked lunch baskets with much "popping of champagne corks and gay laughter of the charming divinities who presided."[83]

Each year had its spectacular. Following 1875, the dedication of city hall, with its parades and grandstands, came the year of the nation's centennial. The bunting and banners, illuminations and bell ringing, picked out the whole shape of the city—its new outlying parks, its center, and the substantial institutions that studded its surrounding hills. They announced in lights and colors the people's common aspirations, and at the same time their thousand competitions and rivalries. On the Fourth of July 1876,

Big Sam, the City Hall bell struck midnight, all the other bells of the city, including the fire bells, took up the note and reproclaimed the old liberty to all the people—The ringing was probably as vigorous for a hot summer midnight as one could wish and lasted fifteen or twenty minutes. It is not known that any of the bells were cracked.[84]

Thousands of people celebrated all night and breakfasted at dawn under the trees in Patterson Park and Druid Hill Park. Other thousands made excursions. Four hundred factory workers from Woodberry, together with their employers, took their lunch baskets on a special train, to spend the day at the Philadelphia

Centennial Exhibition. William Keyser took a party of gentlemen up to Deer Park in his special railroad car. Downtown, the *Sun* and the *American* vied with each other in lighting up their buildings. The *American* illuminated its statues and fired off Roman candles. The Sun Iron Building was lit by calcium lights.

eliciting general expressions of delight as the colors changed from white to crimson, pink or other tints produced by the intervention of gelatine sheets . . . while the whole of Baltimore street was at intervals aflame with burning nitrate of strontia, casting a lurid glare on all surrounding objects.[85]

In East Baltimore the Hebrew Orphan Asylum and the Colored Monumental Singing Club had flags in every window. The penitentiary was studded with flags at every corner and angle of the walls. On the west side, the Concordia and the Germania competed for decorations with German and American flags. The political clubs outdid themselves. Residents of Harlem Park put Chinese lanterns in the trees. "The whole city was a rage of color." South Baltimore organized a torchlight parade, street choruses, and the reading of the Declaration in Riverside Park. The babies were crying for flags. Five or six thousand persons watched a balloon ascension and pole climbing contests at Greenwood Park or aerial gymnastics at Holly Grove. The day came to a close with an illumination of the harbor:

Schooners at the wharves displayed their large signal lights of red, green and blue, and square rigged vessels of large tonnage lying at anchor off Canton and Locust Point showed hundreds of colored lanterns dangling from their yard-arms and rigging, while their projecting colored lights sent rainbow streaks of color into the darkness.[86]

July 1877

It was, perhaps, foreseeable that this period should end in a crisis of labor, its management and mismanagement. Accidents rose and machines displaced or demoted skilled labor during the fat years. The onset of the lean years swiftly suppressed unions; wages were cut and hours shortened. The colored grain carriers in Commerce Street experienced it, as well as the shoe and clothing cutters. It all ended in a bitter crisis that recalled 1861. Again trains and marching regiments were stoned in Baltimore. Again its streets were "flecked with gore" and occupied by federal troops. This time, however, the language was not of sectional strife but class warfare, "A War on the Railroad."[87]

Railroad men had suffered all the pressures. In the best of times the firemen and brakemen received $3.00 a day (engineers and conductors more), and by overtime they could make ten or eleven days a week. Accidents had, however, reached a terrible toll. In addition to the mangled hands and amputated fingers at the railroad shops and the landslides on tunnel construction, four B&O employees died in the summer of '72 on separate accidents of routine work in the yards at Mount Clare and Locust Point. Three were coupling cars, and the fourth, a youth, was unloading cars. When the lean years set in (1873), overtime ceased. A day's pay was reduced to $2.25, then to $1.75. Layoffs of brakemen made the accident risk even greater. On the road the men had to pay thirty cents a meal. The company itself appeared to be making money. It had borrowed a great deal "on short date, a dangerous mode of financeering," but paid its interest to J. P.

Morgan and annual 10 percent dividends, and reported a fictional "surplus" of millions. When the wage cut provoked protest at Cumberland, John Garrett, president and controlling stockholder, sent William Keyser, the vice-president, with a posse to arrest the ringleaders in their beds.

I confess, when I think of the poor, almost squalid cabins and the justness of the ground of the complaint, I should feel ashamed of the whole transaction, were it not that I was solely governed by a sense of duty, and the knowledge that it only required a single spark . . . to start an explosion.[88]

The spark was a second 10 percent wage cut. Wages were down to $1.58. The men were working only fourteen to eighteen days a month. This meant, all told, that their monthly wage was now only one-quarter of what it had been in 1873. The firemen refused to take out their trains. The Pennsylvania Railroad workers followed suit. Problems were nationwide. The initiation of violence in Chicago, Pittsburgh, Grafton, and Martinsburg remains controversial, although popular opinion blamed the railroad's hired guards. But what happened in Baltimore, less obscure, was a capsule form of the whole affair. Two founding generations of the B&O, Alexander Brown and Johns Hopkins, were dead. But in the city of its origin the B&O continued to cast up both riches and poverty. In its ownership, its management, and its tragedy, the B&O still belonged to Baltimore. On 20 July the newspapers were calling the nationwide strike illegal and vicious. The strikers were attempting to "coerce the company," and were "in conflict with the federal power as well as the governor of West Virginia."[89] At Grafton, Keyser had dismissed all the striking firemen, but in Baltimore the striking firemen were reported to be quiet, orderly and sober. They had succeeded in stopping all B&O freight in Maryland, with pecuniary loss to the B&O and to the coal and petroleum business, which were controlled by the same men. John Garrett wanted the governor of Maryland to send Baltimore's own Fifth and Sixth regiments to Cumberland, where a train had been stoned. Governor Carroll came in from his country place in Howard County to meet Garrett at the B&O's Camden Station offices. When the militia captain arrived with only 150 men, he and Garrett persuaded the governor to order the general alarm, a fire emergency call never before sounded in Baltimore. This was done at 6:25 p.m., the very hour when workers were leaving the factories. Crowds immediately gathered around the armories.

In East Baltimore, at the Sixth Regiment armory opposite the shot tower, the soldiers slipped into their upstairs hall. Occasionally a man in uniform was roughly handled. Toward dark, brickbats were thrown, ready to hand since the streets were torn up for laying gas pipes. When the 220 soldiers had answered the roll and started to leave the building, the crowd turned them back. The crowd sent up cheer after cheer for the strikers. "It was not the purpose of the officers to fire on the crowd, but after the first recoil . . . the soldiers seemed to lose control of themselves so far as to think only of their own defense. Firing began at the door."[90] Nine citizens were killed, sixteen severely wounded.

Meanwhile, at the Fifth Regiment armory over the Richmond Market, in a more middle-class neighborhood, two hundred men marched onto Linden Avenue with eleven drummers, and a good-humored crowd had "many pleasant bye-byes for the boys going to the wars." But as they reached Camden Street, packed with people, they were assaulted with stones and bricks. They refrained from using their weapons.

By the time both regiments reached the depot, the crowd had forced the engineer and fireman to desert the train that was waiting with steam up. They stoned and disabled the engine at the Barre Street crossing. Retreating southward, they forced the telegraph operators out of the dispatcher's office at Lee Street, burned the office, set a train going, and tore up the track along Ohio Avenue to Cross Street. Several other sections of track were breached between the depot and Gwynns Falls. To prevent the firemen from going to work, they cut the hoses and put out the fire engine.

"It being impossible to proceed," the mayor, the governor, and the railroad president decided to keep the soldiers in Baltimore. They telegraphed the president that the soldiers were more needed in Baltimore than in Cumberland, and the governor issued a proclamation deploring "a spirit of lawlessness which, if not suppressed, must end in the ruin of vast interests and the destruction of large amounts of the property of our citizens."[91] The *Sun* discerned, even sympathized with, the sense of outrage in Baltimore. The editors urged "a patient acquiescence, however, in the efficacy of legal proceedings as methods of redress." The only legal proceedings that followed were the prompt arraignments of 195 rioters in the southern district.

On Saturday everything was perfectly quiet. Two thousand federal troops arrived. Five hundred marines came on warships. A federal revenue cutter with thirty men guarded the bonded warehouses on Locust Point. That night a crowd stoned and tried to burn the foundry at Mount Clare. Dispersed, they gathered again at 2 a.m., three hundred strong, and set fire to a coal oil train belonging to the Consolidated Coal Oil Company, then attacked police and firemen from the hill above, near the Carey Street bridge.

Within the week the strike weakened in all quarters. The Baltimore workers caucused at Cross Street Market, then met for two hours at Camden Station with William Keyser. Keyser was also prominent in the control and management of the Consolidated Coal Company (a B&O subsidiary) and its coal oil company, as well as the copper smelter and the iron rolling mill at Canton. Keyser's speech to the assembly of 250 strikers and the press added insult to injury: "It will be our pleasure, after you return to work, to investigate your minor grievances." The company made no concessions and stuck to its 10 percent wage cut. He assured the workers, "that order reached the president in its effects as well as the humblest subordinate on the road." Keyser attributed the short hours and previous wage cuts to "the retention of too many men of your class in the service, thereby lessening the ability of each man to earn a competency." This he proposed to remedy by layoffs. He accused the men of having deserted their posts. As for allowing none to take their places, if that principle were accepted, he said, "all discipline, all law, and all order would be sapped at their very foundations. . . . You men whom I see before me have been the cause of this great disturbance. The whole foundation of the social fabric has been shaken

. . . and (you) will be held rigidly accountable for it."[92] The strikers listened respectfully. Some objected and cheered their leaders. Some were said to have shaken hands with Keyser. On 20 July traffic was resumed under military escorts, while the last holdouts among the strikers watched at Riverside Park.

The final episode, as in 1812, 1834, and 1861, occurred six months later, when the governor requested the legislature to tax the city to pay for the suppression. He had borrowed $85,000 at 6 percent from Alex. Brown & Co. and the Farmers and Merchants Bank to equip and pay off the troops and stores. He had also ordered a regiment to Hancock to deal with a strike of boatmen on the C&O Canal. He took the opportunity to advise workers that the only way to revive business was economy in government and policies such as would attract capital. "No political platforms can be of any use to the working man or furnish him with work. In a free country like ours, the relations of capital and labor must always adjust themselves, and are regulated by conditions which politicians cannot control."[93]

Consolidation

1878–1899

In the winter of 1893 a London reporter filed a feature story on Baltimore, noting how different were visitors' impressions depending on whether they arrived by B&O or by Pennsylvania Railroad. Those who approach by the B&O, he wrote, are "apt to think it a dirty, dreary, ramshackle sort of place. The Royal Blue trains . . . pass along scores of dirty streets with shabby little one and two story dwellings, largely inhabited by Negroes, with plentiful supplies of pigs, chicken coops, and swarming children." But arriving through the Pennsylvania's tunnels,

one emerges into the Union Station, and passes out into a fine street, full of character, and giving evidence of a luxurious population—large, massive, well-built houses with an air of solidity, suggestive of high rents, dividends and bank stock, and with a certain Southern aspect very picturesque to one coming from the more commonplace Northern towns.

From the Union Station he drove down Charles Street, over its handsome bridge, to Mount Vernon square: "Elegant ladies slip out of great spacious doorways into roomy family carriages driven by old colored servants in livery. Colored men are also sweeping the stone steps of the houses and washing the large fine windows." He drove past the Washington Monument: "A little park surrounds it, with spacious houses, some of them even approaching a certain massive grandeur, standing round. You feel that it is always afternoon here . . . thankful so quiet a city is to be found in the same country which contains New York and Chicago."[1]

Like modern travel pages and popular geographic magazines, the London *Chronicle* was satisfied to describe the incongruity, without wondering whether one image was necessary to explain the other, without wondering how such contrasts emerge or how they come to seem so natural, so solid, so timeless. In fact, Baltimore was infinitely more complicated. The reporter had not yet seen the bustling new department stores, the new garment factories that stocked them, or the new factory suburbs of Sparrows Point and Brooklyn, or the new trust and insurance buildings on South Street. The city was still possessed of a lifelike energy. The railroad station was new, the elegant bridge was new, the houses he passed along Charles Street and Mount Royal Avenue were new, the asphalt paving and the electric rapid transit were new that year. The B&O was digging its own tunnels to spare its passengers the shabbier view. The tranquillity of Mount Vernon Place was illusion: Baltimore was boiling with conflicts, and was at that moment coping with sudden massive unemployment. The reporter was in fact on his way to interview the cardinal archbishop on labor. But he scarcely realized that the cardinal's international reknown as a man of social concern was rooted in his Baltimore pastorate. From the moment he was made archbishop, on the heels of the B&O Railroad strike, the city had experienced a succession of crises, each seeming to threaten, but ultimately solidifying, the social order that impressed the man from the *Chronicle*.

The census suggests a rather steady growth, at 25 percent per decade since the Civil War. Baltimore had a population of half a million. But to see into the economic growth and the social changes taking place, one should see the city as Cardinal Gibbons must have seen it—its ups and downs, its moods and seasons. The country's best brickmakers and bricklayers erected thirty-five hundred houses a year at the peak (1885–87), as in the previous generation. Summers were a round of boisterous picnics, gorgeous parades, impassioned revivals, from Labor Day (1 May) to Artisans Day (1 September). But during the wet and cold seasons the brickmakers and construction workers were laid off, and in the slumps of 1878–79 and 1893–94 construction slowed to nine hundred or one thousand dwellings, and the charities opened their stoneyards, where men stood in line to break rocks for fifty cents a day. Just as summer and winter were inseparable parts of nature's growing cycle, so the boom and slump of building and the quicker pulse of manufacturing crises were part of the city's growth process—the ring of new houses and streets, the massing of people, and the accumulation of wealth. To grasp this rhythm of growth, I shall concentrate on three turning points: the boom year of 1886, the depression winter of 1893, and the year of business concentration of 1898. Each of these turning points of construction and trade also marked a crisis in the relations of capital and labor.

The parades in honor of Baltimore's 150th birthday (1880) showed a revival of the role of labor in municipal undertakings.[2] The assertions of pride of craft, identity of the firm, and the rights of free labor recalled the Fourth of July parade of 1809 and the B&O cornerstone laying of 1828. The reassertion crescendoed in 1886, when labor organized its own parades. Just by watching the parades go by, one can discover important changes in the economy and organization of the labor force.

The new parades were bigger. Eleven thousand marched in the eight hour demonstration on 1 May 1886. Whole new industries had been created. Five hundred B&O shop workers marched. The hundreds of canmakers, cigar makers, and piano makers were new, as well as the horsecar drivers, a hundred electric light employees, and the window-glass blowers, "strongly organized." The marchers of 1886 were no longer mainly craftsmen, but factory workers. The old-time parades highlighted shop organization—a master tailor surrounded by six journeymen at work, a complete hatshop, two master shoemakers with two journeymen and two apprentices, a master cooper with four journeymen and a

"Einigheit Macht Stark"

boy. But in 1886 the shoemakers, hatters, the cigar makers, piano makers, and can makers were all factory labor. They worked for enterprises that employed five hundred or a thousand people in a single plant. Instead of tinsmiths there were now hundreds of employees of Matthai, Ingram. Instead of independent cabinet makers like Finlay, there were some six hundred furniture makers from steam-powered mills. The box makers carried a huge wood model of a circular saw.[3]

The parades also reveal a new complexity in the division of labor, and changes in the matching of ethnic identities with particular occupational roles and ranks. The B&O shop workers were heavily Irish. The three hundred journeymen butchers were mostly German. They no longer wore their aprons and carried meat cleavers. Instead, they rode in carriages or on coal-black horses, while their black employees carried the meat cleavers in the rearguard. The new labor parades usually had a German division of at least a third of the contingent. They made up the masses of furniture makers, cigar makers, piano makers, brewers, and saloon keepers. A much remarked upon aspect of the parade was the fraternization of the two thousand black and white brickmakers. The blacks were a majority. Their union had branches in Locust Point, Mount Clare, and Canton. Said to be the hardest worked men in any trade, they were heartily cheered.

The parades reveal the trends, but there were other less visible elements in the labor force, yet unorganized, sometimes feared. Many of them were immigrants despised by the last generation of immigrants. A German-American organizer for the Knights of Labor expressed afterward a common sentiment:

I think that we owe a great deal to the class of immigrants that came over to this country—the sturdy Irish and the sturdy Germans—up to 1875 or 1880, after the war. When the lower classes—that is, the scum of society in Europe—commenced to come over here in large hordes. . . . I think that they did not add so materially to the wealth of the country.[4]

On Locust Point the Bohemians pushed coal cars on the wharves and shoveled coal down the chutes into vessels, while Irish, German, and black gangs of coal trimmers worked in the vessels: "Coal trimmers work stripped naked to the waist, covered with coal dust, the sweat pouring off them in the black holds of the vessels, where the hot air is so thick with the dust that the lights of their lamps can scarcely be discerned by the unaccustomed sight."[5]

The adjacent immigrant piers supplied labor recruits and even strike breakers. In 1882 six thousand German miners struck the Consolidated coal mines near Frostburg, to protest wage cuts. John Garrett, interested in the Consol and the B&O loss of coal traffic, shipped German immigrants direct from the Bremen steamships to guarded camps on the Consol mine property. They were known as "the boxcar hunkies." Italians were beginning to arrive, "the scourings of humanity"[6] recruited on New York piers for construction camps on the Baltimore and Annapolis Short Line, the Catonsville Short Line, and the B&O extension at Principio Creek and the Big Gunpowder. Their wage was $1.50 a day, but they kicked back twenty-five or fifty cents to the contractor. None of

Near the Pennsylvania Railroad's "Union Station," the Jones Falls flowed through Victorian gardens. The bridge carried St. Paul Street over the Jones Falls and the tracks. The flower gardens rapidly proved vulnerable to railroad smoke.

these men appeared in the labor parades. Neither did the four thousand oyster dredgers, largely blacks and Germans recruited or shanghaied directly off the wharves in New York. Abused, sometimes mutilated, or suffering from painful "oyster hand" from icy water, they were put ashore on isolated necks without pay, sometimes without water. They often ended up in the city hospital at Bay View. In the winter of 1884 a young German crewman was spiked, kicked, and beaten with a rope. The captain planted his heel on his throat, had him hauled up by the armpits, repeatedly ducked him in ice water, then unloaded him at Lower Fairmount, pounded him with an iron bar till he died, and reported him drowned. Two of the terrorized crew reached Baltimore on Christmas Eve and told their story to the German consul. That captain was convicted of murder, but new incidents occurred every winter.[7]

Also invisible were the gangs of black labor shipped out of Baltimore for fifteen-month stints at eight dollars a month to dig guano out of pits and crevices on the barren island of Navassa. They were undernourished and brutalized to a point that caused a rebellion in 1889.[8] One hundred thirty-nine black laborers dug among the coral rocks or loaded rail cars with dirt under eleven white officers, mostly Irish. The men had to walk barefoot along an inch-and-a-half-wide iron rail. "The hot sun made the work very unpleasant to the feet." "Officers were accustomed for any violation of the rules, to trice them up by rope, tied around their wrists, with the arms outstretched above their heads, and to fasten them in that position with their toes only touching the ground." Half the men had just been notified of their debts to the company store. They protested. The protest ended with the white overseers drawing guns and the

Sweatshops such as this one of 1904 offered indictment of the economic system and were targets for social reformers.

laborers throwing stones. "What do you want?" "Stop cursing us, stop working us to death, stop Mr. Roby threatening us at the mines, and give us suitable food." Five of the overseers were killed. The case was tried in Baltimore. An all-white jury condemned three blacks to hang, fifteen others to hard labor. Meanwhile a new crew was shipped, and work conditions continued as before.

The labor parades also understated the presence of women and children in the labor force because they were unorganized. Of sixteen thousand clothing workers in Oldtown and Fells Point, two-thirds were women, working twelve hours a day, "universally underpaid and overworked . . . buried out of sight in the privacy of the working people's homes."[9] The labor commissioner referred in particular to "Polish Jew labor, the most squalid and unprogressive that comes to the state."[10] Also out of sight were six thousand laundresses and twenty thousand other domestic servants, mostly black, mostly women. Although the can makers were prominent in the labor marches, the cannery labor force was not displayed. It was known as family labor—several thousand women and children, sometimes old men. They were largely Bohemian and German, some Polish and Negro and Irish, who shelled the peas and filled the cans in the great sheds at Canton.[11] The only recorded strikes of women workers were fourteen pottery decorators at the Chesapeake Pottery and sixteen chair caning girls. The only ones who marched were a group of sewing girls who called themselves the Unknown Assembly and about twenty in the Frauenbund of the Socialist Labor Party.

The changes in the pecking order at this time were geared to technological changes. The advances of machinery, capital, and productivity meant the replacement of skilled with unskilled workers, men with women, and mature journeymen with teenage boys who formerly would have been apprentices. In one industry after another these changes were taking place, and each swing of the business cycle squeezed one group or another. The female labor force in manufacturing increased fourfold (from an eighth to a quarter of the labor force), while the male labor force merely doubled. The use of the cigar mold, for example, changed the hiring pattern in cigar factories from mostly skilled German men in the mid-'80s to half women, both white and black, in 1900.

Machinery favored the introduction of women into cake and cracker baking, confectionery, and sewing straw hats. Estimates of child labor are unreliable, but all suggest that the numbers increased in this generation. The state agency figured there were several thousand, chiefly the sewing girls ten to fifteen years old, the cannery children with their mothers, a swarm of four hundred glasshouse boys in South Baltimore, and a large number over ten years old in the cotton duck mills. When machines were introduced to make common brick, more young boys were hired.

The fast-growing canning industry illustrates the way in which changes in the several social sectors were geared into the economic growth. "The Shore has become a great garden," and canning seemed Baltimore's vocation among American cities. A machine to make cans was first widely adopted in 1880, but the Can Makers Mutual Protective Association resisted vigorously. It replayed the shoemakers' scenario and moved to the forefront of organized labor. A machine for soldering the can required only one man and a boy, instead of five craftsmen can makers. By 1890 a machine could produce the whole can, and by 1896 the mechanized factories employing mostly young boys and girls outnumbered the handmade can shops. Union membership fell. At the same time, machinery was replacing the unskilled labor in the canning operations. A machine for filling cans was tried out before 1880; it had to be guarded to keep workers from destroying it. A corn-cutting machine was introduced in 1885, a capping machine in 1887, and a label machine. In 1890 the big factories were using pea-hulling machines that displaced hundreds of women and children.

The parades reflected fairly accurately, therefore, differences in the bargaining power of various branches of the labor force. As a result, over the generation, skilled workers such as window glass blowers, by their efforts to "organize, educate, and agitate," were able to increase their wage rates from about $1.75 to $3.00 a day, while unskilled labor stayed at $1.25, with boys and women still lower. In a number of industries—shoes, cigars, furniture—the skilled workers were replaced by machines or by unskilled workers to such an extent that the average wage and the aggregate number of workers in those industries declined. In spite of the greater product of canning and clothing, the number of workers did not increase. And in spite of the higher product per worker, the average worker's pay did not increase.

During 1886 the labor movement mushroomed in a way that amazed everyone. It had, as Professor Richard Ely of Johns Hopkins observed, deeper roots. It was sensed by people in many walks of life as an expression of powerful forces, and was recognized instinctively as a turning point of some kind. But fifteen years later, as J. G. Schonfarber looked back, he simply situated it as one of a series of crises. Referring to the unions, he said, "My experience as a local organizer is that it is like the tide, it has ebbs and flows; all of them do."[12] Schonfarber figured there were in Baltimore at the flood tide of 1886 twenty-four thousand full members of the Knights of Labor. As I shall show, the ebbs and flows, like the interfering solar and lunar cycles in the tides, reflect the complex rhythm of the short-swing business cycle and the long-swing construction cycle.

"Organize, Educate, and Agitate"

People were the chief cargo shipped from Bremen through the port of Baltimore over the immigrant piers at Locust Point. They were off-loaded onto the B&O Railroad, headed for the prairies.

A groundswell of the Knights of Labor movement began with 450 ship carpenters and caulkers who struck in August 1885 to protest a cut in wages, and with the German coal miners at the Consolidated mines in Frostburg. About the same time, Stieff's piano workers objected to his offhand dismissal of their grievance committee. They waited from August to December, then struck. "Very well," said Mr. Stieff, "boycott. I'll have to experience it." In March he had the police arrest strikers who were intercepting his scab workmen at the factory near Camden Station. With sixteen men, under police protection, he continued to sell and deliver pianos, although the strikers accompanied the piano wagons with their circulars.[13]

In February, the twenty-five or thirty brickmaking bosses were invited to a meeting and were "well received by their men," who wanted higher wages at uniform rates. The two groups appointed committees and scheduled negotiations "in the best of feeling." But in March, as the countryside leafed out, a spring fever of participation set in. Baltimore still loved a meeting—flights of oratory,

earthy common sense, intimate caucus, quarrelsome palaver, and delegations to Annapolis. The construction season looked promising, and the building crafts spearheaded the eight-hour movement. Many employers were willing to contemplate an eight- or nine-hour day, but at a corresponding reduction of wages. Thus, the hours issue cannot be distinguished from the wage issue. Much of the wage pressure was an attempt to restore the wage cuts of the hard years of 1884–85. "All we want is justice and our old wages," read the signs in the parades. The Central Committee of United German Working Men visited the tobacco factories to find out how the bosses felt about the eight-hour day at present wages. They were cordially received by Gail and Ax. The employers said they were glad to see the union, and they, too, opposed child labor, but competition had forced them to it. They would cooperate on lobbying for a child labor law. A crisis of competition was felt from the point of view of employers and consumers, as well as workers. It was expressed in unreliable product quality and false measures, as well as layoffs, piece rates, and working hours.

The hours movement tended to spill over beyond the manufacturing sector. The ice drivers determined to deliver enough ice on Saturday to last over Sunday, and the barbers resolved not to work on Sunday. The oyster shuckers lobbied in Annapolis for a standard measure, and the saloon keepers wanted a standard beer glass. Five hundred retail clothing salesmen met to discuss early closing for stores (6 p.m.), and the tea and provision dealers joined them. "Many employers are in favor."

The issue that mobilized public opinion and won the sympathy of the newspapers and the archbishop was the cause of the horsecar drivers, who were on duty seventeen or eighteen hours. Like Philadelphia and New York drivers, Baltimore's "Midnight Assembly" demanded $2 and twelve hours. A twelve-hour law was passed at Annapolis, but in some companies the drivers were locked out by the employers, who claimed they could not redesign their systems overnight to operate on any other shift basis. The lockouts and layoffs meant the men were working for sixty-six cents a day. A baseball game between the union men of two lines raised $700 for the strikers. Even the schoolboys near Light and Poultney streets got the fever, held a secret mass meeting, and nailed up the gates of several schools.

All the unions endorsed an eight-hour rule to go into effect on 2 May. They held a torchlight parade to announce their solidarity. The can makers sponsored a May Day holiday, parade, and picnic at the Schuetzen park. "The weather was fair. The police arrangements were perfect." But their hard-won solidarities were drenched by the front page news of 5 May: "Night of terror in Chicago." Foreign anarchists were blamed for the Haymarket explosions, and public outrage was fanned nationwide by the trial. The labor movement began to ebb; in Baltimore within a few days the carpenters had begun to settle for nine hours instead of eight. The builders were making no new contracts; some recognized the union and some locked the men out. The ship carpenters settled their twenty-month strike, and in the end did not get their old wages. The concrete gains had been limited, yet the agitation had polarized the city and marked each individual.

Certain pathological events indicate the social nightmares of 1886. The imaginings of the insane, as in 1831, mirrored a social reality. During the horsecar strike, a young and esteemed German box maker committed suicide, expressing fears, altogether groundless, that he would be thrown out of the Boxmakers Assembly of the Knights. He slashed his neck with a razor in front of his two-year-old child.[14] The newspapers reflected also a public imagination hungry for the exotic in religion and race. On the day of the Haymarket explosions, the *American* reported in melodramatic terms the taking of the veil at the Convent of the Visitation by Miss Edgar, "who is young, wealthy, and beautiful." She sang, they reported, from under the burial pall with a wonderfully touching effect, then appeared in wedding dress, and as the nuns with lighted candles chanted "weird and jubilant strains," she passed out of sight into the cloistered life.[15] Most bizarre was the fascination with the Chinese. There were between 150 and 300 Chinese in Baltimore. Half were Masons, nearly all men, operators of laundries, who had the "unAmerican habit of living within their means." They represented no significant competition in the labor force, even for the six thousand black laundresses, yet a preoccupation by black unions and white newspapers suggests that a "yellow peril" appealed to deep anxieties and racist imaginations. When Wong Chee, a young respected Chinese laundryman, died of tuberculosis, a crowd of eight thousand followed the hearse and the twenty-two carriages of Chinese mourners. The crowd climbed trees, jeered, and threw eggs and mud. The newspapers passed quickly over this embarrassment, but recounted every detail of the "heathen funeral in a Christian land"; how the face was washed with rice paper wetted with whiskey and five coins were put in his mouth, how his countrymen produced "music of doleful and unmelodious character," and how they burned all of Wong Chee's belonging on his grave. "After the fire was burning, nearly every one in the group lighted a cigar or cigarette and began to smoke."[16] Several weeks later the police raided an alleged opium den at Calvert and Saratoga streets and marched the company to the station house. "Their complexions were of a pale and yellow hue."[17] A month later "distinguished residents" of Harlem Square, including the proprietors of two newspapers, demanded the eviction of Tong Sing's Chinese laundry from a back building of the handsome row known as Latrobe Place.[18]

The labor movement in Baltimore forced the development of the social thought of men of national stature, Richard Ely and Cardinal Gibbons. Ely, who had studied in Germany and come to teach at the young Johns Hopkins graduate school, had been an enthusiast of the Knights in their aim to promote all of the labor force. Ely in 1886 published an account of the great national labor movement; he perceived it as part of the process of urbanization, and Baltimore events marked every strain of thought and every stage of the struggle toward a national movement. The ten-hour day, he reminded us, originated in the shipyards of Baltimore in the 1830s.[19] In 1850 the Baltimore Turnverein was the first large group in the nation to espouse socialist principles: "Organized labor is labor in its normal condition. Association is so natural to man, and its benefits so great, that it is ever sought, and, indeed, more and more sought with the progress of civilization. Isolation is weakness, but union is strength."[20] Ely rejected anarchism and radical socialism; he also rejected as un-American the paternalism of Pullman, Illinois. He explored the Rochdale community and argued strongly for cooperative enterprise. His most telling examples of cooperation were also Baltimore experiences: the women's cooperative shirt factory, the blacks' cooperative shipyard, and the cooperative commission house of the Maryland Grange, "a brilliant success" grossing half a million dollars a year. "Yet the ground is strewn with the fragments of wreckage." Deeply disappointed in the ebb of the labor movement, Ely directed his attention toward the analysis of wealth and the political privileges that preserved wealth and constrained labor. The relation between wealth and political privilege was visible and personal in Baltimore, and Ely found a key to the relation between those different social landscapes that baffled the *Chronicle* reporter. Pigtown, Locust Point, and Mount Clare were B&O fiefdoms. Directly and through the B&O, John Garrett owned the coal lands in western Maryland and West Virginia. He bought townhouses on Mount Vernon Place for himself and his heirs, where it was "always

Mechanical toys enticed
passers-by in the Christmas
season of 1897, as hucksters,
street hawkers, and vendors
vied for street space.

afternoon." He died leaving $5.6 million, the largest estate in his generation
(1884). The ownership of all these properties structured the relation of Garrett
to the inhabitants of those landscapes.

Meanwhile, the archbishop was in a more influential position, in fact,
caught in the middle. The week of the Haymarket crisis, in a letter to the
archbishop of Cincinnati, the archbishop of Baltimore described his own personal style and what might be called his Baltimore strategy: "A masterly inactivity and a vigilant eye on their proceedings is perhaps the best thing to be
done in the present juncture."[21] The expression, "a vigilant masterly inactivity"
was a phrase he had used before with respect to secret societies and labor
organizations. James Gibbons believed the Knights should be rebuked for their
persecution of nonunion men and their custom of boycotting. "But we should
be careful not to be too hard on them, otherwise they would suspect us of siding
with the moneyed corporations & employers. . . . Labor has rights as well as
capital. We should not condemn labor and let capital go free."[22] As the archbishop of Quebec had just persuaded the Holy See to outlaw the Knights of
Labor in Quebec, the archbishop of Baltimore was determined to do all he could
to prevent a similar turn of events in the United States. On 28 October in his
Charles Street residence the archbishop met with Terence Powderly, the national
leader of the knights, and then drafted his position for Rome. He would regard
condemnation of the knights as disastrous to the church: "We have a controlling
influence over them; if they are condemned, a secret organization will follow in
their wake, and over that we will have no control."[23] This position, effectively
lobbied in Rome, identified the archbishop with the Catholic social movement in
Europe. Gibbons perceived the connection between the Holy Name societies with
their parish banners and the German Workers Central Committee. Not only did
he know Powderly, but he knew the Baltimore knights—their generosity, their
reasonableness, and their dependability. It was the German workers who were

most affected by mechanization and the demotion of craft into factory labor. Thanks to the church they also possessed instruments of solidarity, through their massive participation in the Catholic men's societies, the German parish beneficial societies, and the new building and loan associations. Beyond the parish there were the workers' choral groups, a reactivated Turnverein, and gymnastic societies. Their awareness of the social insurance legislation of Bismarck and European working-class political movements provided them with a common set of ideas for unions.

Born in Ireland, James Gibbons is more often remembered for his concern for the new immigrant nationalities. In 1880 he had created an Italian parish, St. Leo's. He was building a larger church for the Bohemian parish of St. Wenceslas. He dedicated three new Polish churches in East Baltimore: Sacred Heart, St. Stanislas Kostka, and Holy Rosary. But it was the German experience in Baltimore that stamped his views of American society. As he watched the rapid expansion of Redemptorist churches (St. Michael's, St. Alphonsus, St. James, and Holy Cross), he saw their German parish schools become Americanized. Both his social concern and his intense patriotism were part of the loyalty and development of East and South Baltimore.

The swell and ebb of union activity, its popular emotion, its action in the streets, were followed by an equally sudden physical transformation of the city in 1893. A belt of twenty-three square miles on the north and west of the city was annexed in 1888, and cable railway companies were incorporated. These events jointly provoked a wave of speculation and a sharp increase in the sales of real estate, which bore fruit in 1893. The horse railways were rapidly shifted to electric rapid transit. Housing was developed in the belt and the new suburbs beyond it. There was a reshuffling of elements in the population, and at the center a recrystallization of the downtown area for the greater metropolis.

The Electrification of Baltimore

The reconstruction in 1877 of the fire alarm telegraph with its 169 miles of wire running over the housetops to city hall was a preview of electrification—its centralizing property and its extension of tentacles. The same year an experimental telephone "concert" was presented at Masonic Temple. Despite interference from rain, the audience heard sung "Sweet Bye and Bye" and a cornet rendition of "Old Folks at Home" from New York and Philadelphia. Baltimore's first telephones allowed the mayor and two coal dealers to talk to their offices, the police chief to call the station house, and Mr. Booz to call his shipyard on Thames Street. The *Sun* installed a phone and was the first business house lighted by electricity. The first electric arc street lamps were installed. Within five years of these pilot operations, the modern structure was in place. The phone company and Brush Electric were organized, messenger boys were supplanted by women operators, and national technological monopolies were assured. AT&T, by controlling the patents and long distance lines, began taking a tribute from local telephone companies that enabled it to pay 15 to 18 percent annual dividends for the rest of the century.

Overhead wiring immediately created serious problems for firefighters. In the sleet storm of 20 December 1884, telephone wires fell across the fire alarm telegraph wires and shorted out alarm boxes. The B&O telegraph line to Bay View Station interfered with the fire department phone line to the Bay View asylum. On 30 April 1886, a business block at the corner of Howard and Baltimore streets became a "colossal furnace." Awnings were consumed. Barrels of china on sidewalks in the next block cracked to pieces. Firefighters threw out smoldering rolls of carpet, which fell across telegraph and electric light wires and burst into flame. Brush Electric had the current cut, then cut all the wires to relieve firefighters of danger.[24]

In rapid transit, Baltimore was at once first and last. Leo Daft's experiment on the Baltimore & Hampden, between 1885 and 1889, is considered the first successful electric railway operation in the country. He used a third rail and operated on grades up to 6.5 percent. The B&O was the first steam railroad to operate an electric locomotive. (This simplified ventilation problems in the mile-long Howard Street tunnel.) But before Baltimore entrepreneurs finally adopted electric streetcars and overhead wires, they first plunged into cable railway technology. In 1893, Baltimore was among the last cities in the country to bring into operation new cable lines, which within three or four years had to be converted to electric overheads.[25]

Either system, cable or overhead, required sizable new capital and intensification of operations. Therefore, electrification involved financial consolidation of companies and fostered the entry of Philadelphia and New York capital. Mergers and acquisitions were as devious, as intensely political, and as much talked about as the original horsecar franchises before the Civil War. But they involved much larger sums of money. The investment in electrification amounted to $15 million (1889–95).

The new Baltimore Traction Company was capitalized at $5 million, from mergers of Citizens and Peoples, under the presidency of James McLane. It began operating cable systems along Gilmor Street and Druid Hill Avenue on 25 May 1891, and took in nickels faster than anyone could count them. The cars were heavy—seventeen thousand pounds—and the company had to lay heavier rail, more like steam railroad, modify the grades, rebuild gutters and sewers—indeed, virtually rebuild the streets. Its two hundred cars were built in Philadelphia.

McLane was also involved in the Lake Roland Elevated, which built the North Avenue railway and the Guilford Avenue elevated between Lexington and Chase. Their "ride in the sky" was devised to avoid the stretch where the Northern Central tracks ran at grade in Guilford Avenue. The technology of steel was essential for the viaducts, built by the Pennsylvania Steel Company, parent company of the new Maryland Steel works at Sparrows Point. Lake Roland Elevated eventually merged with City and Suburban Railway (made up of the older Union Passenger or Perin lines) and was involved in the York Road turnpike company. It had a Gilmor Street route and overhead electrics on York Road. It added lines in Wilkens Avenue, Maryland Avenue, and Eastern Avenue to Highlandtown.

Bowie's line, City Passenger, built a cable system. Its blue, red, and white lines all opened in 1893. Rope speeds were calculated at six, eight, and eleven miles per hours in various parts of the system depending on grades and traffic,

This architectural rendering shows in cutaway the proposed power plant for the Gilmor Street cable car.

which cut running times over horsecars by half. The *Sun* recounted "baby's evening ride": "The cars whirl past and create a fine breeze, which seems to put new life into little forms drooping under summer's heat. They want to see the wheels go round."[26] At the end of the summer there were thirty-three miles of cable lines and eighty miles of overhead electrics. "The horse-cars looked lonely and deserted." Unable to compete, they were rapidly converted to overhead electrics, and the cable cars were in turn converted in 1895 and 1896.

Electricity created new environmental hazards, to which people were not accustomed. In the first year the *Sun* recorded forty transit fatalities. While coal oil and gasoline accidents had been significantly reduced by inspection acts, electrical accidents appeared.[27]

William Brown, colored, was accidentally killed at Brush Electric when he stepped on a live wire with his heel, at the same time touching an iron water pipe.

George Gamble, colored, was killed at Fayette and Green, by a "dead" electric wire which had crossed a live one.

New applications of electricity were nevertheless all the rage: "A patient at City Hospital before an audience of 400 students swallowed an electric light bulb . . . floating in water, to light up the stomach wall, for diagnosis."[28] William Keyser built the Electric Refining Company at Canton in conjunction with his copper rolling mill. By importing copper from Cuba, then from Anaconda, purifying it of gold and silver, and selling a high-quality product to Europe, Keyser made himself a millionnaire.[29] The operation was predicated on the demand for copper electric wire, as well as the technology of electrolysis.

The stringing of wires continued to transform the town. By 1893 the phone company had four thousand phones, by 1899 seven thousand. There were 1338 arc street lamps. The streets were lined with plantations of nineteen thousand electric poles. The fire commissioners complained bitterly about "the network of all kinds of wires which festoon the streets, electric, telegraph, trolley and telephone." Engelhardt described the city as "a dull red maze of roofs and towers, domes, pinnacles and steeples, flagstaffs, fire walls, chimney pots; and all, Gulliver-like, bound down in meshes of electric wires."[30]

The City Expands

Baltimore's expansion was channeled by the combination of electric transit with annexation. One can distinguish three rings of growth. I shall deal first with the more distant suburban ventures developed on the car lines. Then I shall discuss the belt or annex, often referred to as "outside property," where dramatic growth took place from the year of annexation, 1888. Last, I shall focus on the "inside property," inside the old city limits: how was it affected by the annexation? I shall show that changes in the three zones were related.

The Suburbs

Suburban communities were small. The largest concentrations were still the mill villages along the falls, such as Woodberry. But the modest suburbs of this generation were models for a new way of life for a hundred years to come. They were of two principal types, the commuter village and the industrial suburb. One was associated with the piedmont, the other with tidewater.

On the rolling hills of the piedmont north and west of the city were created comfortable middle-class suburbs of single-family homes, frame or brick. Electric or steam railways permitted conversion of communities of summer homes into year-round commuter villages. By the mid-'80s Mount Washington had a population of two thousand; Catonsville was slightly larger. Electric rapid transit enabled others to develop in the '90s. Engelhardt described Roland Park, Walbrook, and West Arlington as "large and stylish." Sudbrook, on the Western Maryland Railroad, was small and stylish. They were invented hand in hand with rapid transit schemes, and entrepreneurs hoped to profit from both land sales and the farebox. But a village with full services was an expensive proposition, designed for an upper middle class. All development costs—water supply, street building and lighting—had to be planned and financed by the development company. The difference between profit and loss depended on the rapidity with which lots could be sold off to home owners. West Arlington, for example, was "a model suburban town" accessible by Western Maryland Railroad and the Edmondson Avenue electric cars. Its 257 acres were to be sold on the installment

The *Lord Baltimore*, developed
as a promotional symbol of
corporate boosterism, was one
of the plushest streetcars. As
shown in this photograph, it
was pressed into regular
service after the 1904 fire.

plan. The houses were individually designed and built, with streets laid out in
curves. Lurman commented in 1892 that wide straight streets were "a blot on
the landscape."

Roland Park was Baltimore's important suburban model for the future.
Financed by English capital (the Lands Trust Company), the Roland Park Company was incorporated in 1891 and assembled some hundreds of acres by buying
Woodlawn, Oakland, and other large estates. The panic of 1893 bankrupted the
Kansas City management firm, but did not interrupt development. The local
manager, Edward Bouton, involved the firm in the financing and construction
of the North Avenue electric and the Lake Roland Elevated, and sold its bonds
to Baltimore investors, notably McLane, Bartlett, Semmes, and Carey. Bouton
offered free transit tokens and went into building houses, priced at $2600 to
$3000, in order to hasten the sale of lots. Harry G. Schalck claims the company
was never a great financial success, but Bouton had both a grand vision, "to
catch the whole of the better class suburban development of the city" by gradual
land acquisition and an incredible attention to detail that has made Roland Park
to this day a suburban ideal.[31] The first portion was designed by George Kessler,
with curving streets following the contours of the land. In 1897 Bouton brought
in the Olmsted sons as planning consultants, and thus involved them in the
whole planning of the Baltimore region, leaving a profound mark on the city of
Baltimore (see chapter 10). Bouton touched base continually with his consultants,
his Kansas City bosses, his residents, neighbors, and local bond holders, even
on such details as the form of gutters, the street names, and the oiling of the
roads. His relatively modest advertising, discreet landscaping, house exteriors
that fit into the landscape, and the new golf club and country club, were consistent with the creation of a whole new style of living for the elite—a low
public profile, exclusive, and secluded.

On the low-lying coastal plain south and east were laid out industrial
suburbs such as Brooklyn and Sparrows Point. Their populations were self-
contained, but they required efficient transport of industrial materials. Here, too,
town building was undertaken by a corporation, with no investments or services
from the county. The corporation created joint values and profited from them
in various ways, on the model of the Canton Company. They were conceived
in relation to steam railways to insure the industrial metabolism, but promptly
added electrics to connect them with downtown Baltimore.

The city bought the rights to the privately owned Light Street bridge (1878), eliminated the tolls, and rebuilt it. It was nearly a mile long, on wood piling, with a steam draw. This caused a rapid increase of population and business on the county as well as the city side of the river. It set the stage for the first important expansion of Baltimore capital and enterprise into Anne Arundel County. The South Baltimore Harbor and Improving Company bought the old Patapsco Company lands at Brooklyn, which had about five hundred residents (1882), and the B&O built its Curtis Bay branch. The same capitalists involved in the Improving Company and the B&O created the South Baltimore Car Works to build cars for the B&O. Chappell's fertilizer company abandoned its Hughes Street plant after a fire and built the nation's most modern fertilizer factory (later Davison Chemical) near Hawkins Point. The electric cars ran to Brooklyn in 1892. Construction of the Baltimore and Annapolis Short Line and a scheme for the Drum Point Railroad allowed another group of investors to acquire three thousand acres and lay out Glen Burnie.

Sparrows Point was the most swiftly developed and complete example of a new-type company town.[32] This time the object was not to sell or develop real estate but to make iron. The eleven-hundred-acre site was fourteen miles out of Baltimore and originally accessible only by boat, but it was ideal, since the Pennsylvania Steel Company, incorporated here as the subsidiary Maryland Steel Company, wanted tidewater shipment of ore from its Cuban iron mines. The company planned to send the pig iron up to the parent works near Harrisburg. It first built a causeway and a settlement of fifteen hundred employees. By 1892 it had a $10 million investment: four blast furnaces with a capacity of three hundred tons a day, rail and bloom mills, and a coke plant and shipyard, with fourteen miles of internal railroads.

The layout of the residential districts of Sparrows Point reveals the company's conception of the relation of the various classes of workers. It described the labor force as one-third black, one-third recent immigrants, and one-third "of a mixed character." A residential village was designed with streets 60 and 70 feet wide, lots 125 feet deep, and "neat frame and brick structures." The village was equipped with underground sewers, sidewalks, electric lights, and piped water from deep wells. By 1904, eight hundred houses had been built. Trees and hedges were planted. For the supervisory employees, office and technical staff, and school teachers, there were two dozen "commodious" detached frame houses on lots 28 feet wide. Such houses had seven rooms, bath, furnace, and cellar, and were plastered inside. The construction cost ran $2500 to $3100 each, comparable to the first group of Roland Park homes. For skilled workers there were three hundred "comfortable cottages" of duplex type, also on 28-foot lots, and several hundred row houses, 14 feet wide, of brick ($1350) or frame ($1100). They had six rooms, stove heat, and cold water. A village of similar homes for black workers was separated by an 800-foot bridge across Humphrey's Creek.

But this was not the whole labor force. Half the workers in the plant commuted from Canton by electric car or steam railway, and about two thousand of the unmarried, unskilled immigrant and Negro labor lived in the barracks.

One group of barracks was in back of the Negro section of the town, inside a high barbed-wire fence with a guarded gate. The other set of barracks was inside the yards, entirely surrounded by the iron works. These sections had dirt streets. The barracks were built of rough pine boards roofed with tarpaper in rows of ten one-room shanties. Each room was ten feet by fourteen feet and had two double bunks, arranged so a man of ordinary size could "crawl in." The shanties cost fifty dollars each to put up, and when fully occupied by four men, their rent paid for the shanty about three times over in the year. The men provided their own mattress, stove, and fuel, and brought their water from outside hydrants. After 1904 a shower house and cookhouse were supplied to the barracks.

Overall, the town was not a profitable operation. It was run on a break-even policy whose object, as expressed by the company in 1891, was to insure a settled labor force, whose wage averaged $1.75 a day. Pullman, Illinois, was a model of the general strategy of creating a total environment consistent with company goals. Sparrows Point had a free kindergarten, a clubhouse, and a manual training school. Sites were offered for churches and a savings bank. The only store was the company store, cash only. "If a man wants a glass of beer, he must go to Baltimore to get it." The company collected the garbage, provided fire and police protection, plants from their hothouses, and prizes for family gardens. It prohibited the keeping of animals. "We own everything. The men have better homes, better comforts, greater happiness."

A third type of suburban site consisted of recreational environments, the "parks" and "shores" to which electric transit brought a great flux of city people on summer evenings, Sundays, and holidays. The private amusement parks were created at the ends of the car lines. The North Avenue railway was extended beyond Walbrook to Ridgewood amusement park, near Mount Holly Casino. City and Suburban Railway developed Riverview Park beyond Canton. Baltimore Traction organized Shore Line Park and a special rail line from Westport.[33] The Baltimore & Curtis Bay electric line extended from Brooklyn to Jack Flood's Curtis Creek resort. The Lake Roland Elevated terminated at its own Lakeside Park, fourteen acres of wooded ground with pavilion and merry-go-round, seven miles or thirty-five minutes from city hall. The whirlwind ride added to the attractions, and the nickel fare allowed the development of new recreation habits. Families joined gay but anonymous people-watching masses, and no longer depended on organized picnics and festivals of close-knit groups. Courting habits changed with the new range of cheaper entertainment for young adults.

The electrics and commuter railways made the camp meetings a yet more popular activity. The summer of 1893 was a high-water mark of combined fervor and sociability. All the nuances of class, identity, and life style in Baltimore were expressed in the tent geography. Emory Grove, twenty miles out on the Western Maryland Railroad, used by the Methodist Episcopal churches, was said to be the largest and most prestigious. The *Sun* published its annual list of "tent holders." At Wesley Grove (Dorsey's Station), fourteen miles out on the B&O, the Southern Methodists had 130 tents and a hotel. Their central

Worker housing provided a bed and blanket but few other conveniences.

tabernacle held fifteen hundred. "A straw floor makes kneeling easier for the worshiper." The *Sun* reporter described the "cozy interior" of a tent assigned to six young ladies:

At the entrance are lounging chairs, circular Japanese mats and hassocks, with birds and flowers hanging outside. Further inside are parlor tables, upon which are Bibles, hymnals, the SUN, and magazines. Pinned around the white canvas walls or fastened to the fall in the center of the tent are autumn leaves and ferns, Japanese fans, silken tidies, artistic groups of cattails, and colored Japanese lanterns.[34]

At Summit, a thousand resided in the tents and thousands more came out daily by special train. In addition to prayer meetings, the young men and maidens played tennis and strolled in the woods. "Baseball was played," and families spread the "snowy cloth." Washington Grove, twelve hundred acres on the B&O, had "more pretentious habitations." One had to be a stockholder in the association to buy one of the comfortable summer cottages. At Wildwood Park near Mount Airy, an eleven-day Methodist Protestant camp meeting was thronged with six or seven thousand people and declared "a religious and financial success." The annual convention of the prohibition and cold water party was held at its own circular tabernacle at Glyndon. The black community held camp meetings at Asbury Grove on the Western Maryland Railroad and Greenwood Park near Catonsville. The Colored Union met at Calverton Grove. At Hurley's Grove the Allen African M.E. Church and Carroll circuit laid out twenty-four tents in the form of a horseshoe, and more people arrived by the Wilkens Avenue electric. "The singing was spirited. Within the meeting-tent the flickering lights at night made grotesque shadows of the swaying bodies and nodding heads of the penitents or worshipers."[35] The *Sun*, always ready to amuse at the expense of the colored community, reported the preacher's text, "Arise, Peter, kill and eat," along with the consumption of chickens, watermelons, and ice cream. For Baltimore in 1893, the eating, drinking, making merry, and repenting were all electrified and suburbanized. An innovation was the trolley party. The employees of City Passenger Railway made it a tradition. With their wives, sisters, and sweethearts, eight hundred strong, they rode over the city, with a brass band in the first car. All the cars blazed with electric lights concealed under flags and bunting, "an immense fiery serpent creeping up the track."[36]

The annexation urged for ten years was accomplished in 1888. A referendum was held by districts, and the east border of the city—Highlandtown and Canton—refused, but a broad band was added on the north and west. The twenty-three squares miles nearly tripled the area of the city and added only 8 percent (forty thousand) to its population. By the turn of the century the annex population rose to sixty thousand, or one-eighth of the city total.

The Annex

Annexation "boomed" land in the annex. The year after annexation the number of real estate transactions doubled. The massive transfer of property was a sign of the scramble to capture the sudden increase of land values. It provided commissions for more middlemen, with legal, financial, and sales skills and inside information. The new Real Estate Exchange had a hundred members who met daily. Naturally, they interested themselves in portfolios well balanced among the three zones of property. One of the largest, Graham and Co., dealt in ground rents and mortgages, in the sale and subdivision of large estates; they developed several tracts themselves, and managed the suburb of Mount Washington. Smith & Schwarz developed fashionable rows on North Calvert and West Baltimore streets; that was "outside property." Twenty-eight acres in East Baltimore and an expensive row on Mount Royal Avenue were its "inside property." In the suburbs it acquired Venture Gwynn Oak, 486 acres, formed the Walbrook, Gwynn Oak, and Powhatan electric railway, and assigned 25 acres to the Gwynn Oak amusement park.[37]

Public streets and public parks defined the locus of housing development. In the northwest, terraces were built on Auchentoroly, and the Mount Royal area was rapidly built up near Druid Hill Park. Development of the northwest was described as "superinduced" by construction of the North Avenue electric to Walbrook and the extension of Fulton Avenue northward into the annex. To connect Druid Hill Park with annex property to the east, the Cedar Avenue bridge was built, as designed by C. H. Latrobe, and developers instantly put up a hundred houses. On the southwest the city purchased the old Schuetzen Park, redeveloped it as Carroll Park, and renovated the Mount Clare mansion. To eliminate grade crossings in the approaches to Carroll Park, it built the Russell Street bridge and the Monroe Street bridge over the B&O. Again private construction followed immediately. On the northeast, the city bought Clifton Park, Johns Hopkins's estate, from the university, and the university acquired Homewood. On the southeast, Patterson Park was extended. The four parks in the four corners of the city were embellished in this period thanks to the park tax on the transit nickels. Thanks also to electric transit, they were intensely used.

Annexation was a critical political event. In the several waves of growth between 1816 and 1888, as the city gradually filled its large territory, the redistribution of property values seemed a simple matter. The line of direct taxation was moved outward every few years: people inside the line received more city services, chiefly fire and police protection, and paid a higher property tax rate. City water was paid from water rents on connected houses, and pumps and repaving were assessed on the fronting owners. But the annexation of 1888 posed the explicit problem of the role of public investments in creating wealth. Public services had become capital-intensive and highly visible. The questions had to be faced: who would benefit from the land values created? Who would pay the interest and sinking funds? How would older parts of the city be affected?

Under the Maryland constitution, annexation had to be negotiated, and in order to annex, the city had to sell out its tax privilege. It agreed to a twenty-two-year grace period on raising taxes in the annex. In other words, the county rate of 1887 was to apply until 1910 in the annex. No reassessment of land value was made in city or county for twenty years (1876 to 1896), so that the city tax basis did not change much. These two political "nonevents" generated an ever wider gap between tax rates in city and annex—sixty cents on $100 of property in the annex, $2.25 in the old city. Taxes collected in the annex were earmarked for improvements in the annex only. The annex taxpayer couldn't lose. In fact, spending in the annex often reached as high as twice the level of annex tax receipts, without counting water board investments.[38]

Indeed, the annex needed everything. Many of its wells were polluted, and there was no adequate water supply for putting out fires. The county volunteer fire departments were ineffectual, and city fire fighters had long complained of the "good neighbor runs" they made out of town because of wear and tear on their horses and steam engines: they had to race uphill over rutted roads and draw silty water from farm ponds. Baltimore inherited nine country schoolhouses and seven firehouses, plus certain bridges, culverts, and roads "most unsafe, all in need of repair," and built to low standards. It had actually paid $100,000 compensation to the county for this endowment. Improvements were urgent. The school budget illustrates the importance of the shift toward a more capital-intensive city-building process. By 1897 the school commission was spending 14 percent of its operating budget in the annex, in proportion to its pupil population, but half of its capital budget. It built eleven schools in the annex. Walbrook got a firehouse and a schoolhouse. The neighborhood between North Charles Street and Greenmount Avenue got a new storm sewer. The city built the Guilford high-service reservoir, so that the Gunpowder water supply could be distributed to higher elevations in the annex.

Included in the special tax regime was a privilege for the street railways: in the annex they were not subject to the park tax. They were even allowed to calculate their ratio of tax relief on the basis of mileage in annex or city, rather than their farebox receipts or passenger volume. Not only did this deprive the park board, but it skewed corporate balance sheets, making extension of the electrics into the suburbs seem profitable. It favored building up the annex rapidly, and offered a hidden subsidy to the rise of annex land values. In other words, the growth process had a feedback, insuring a stream of benefits from the public to the private sector and from overtaxed residents of the old city to undertaxed residents of the annex.

Tax structure also fostered a tendency to invest in buildings rather than manufactures. Ground rents and municipal bonds were privileged, untaxed investments. Baltimore was not keeping pace with the industrial growth of other big cities of the nation, especially in its ability to attract manufacturing capital. To counter this, the city government began chasing its own tail: it removed municipal taxes from manufacturing inventory and machinery, and lowered industrial water rates. This threw a yet greater burden on the older districts, which paid the full city property tax. An important but hard-to-measure effect of annexation was the diversion of public investment from the old city. The fire department was nervous because no new fire stations were built in the inner city in this era. Private construction in the city peaked in 1885 to 1887, and the municipal investment that should have followed was diverted into the annex of 1888.

The generous favors to certain classes of land holders stimulated development, and the high rate of investment in house construction had certain economic and social advantages. Forty thousand houses were built in this generation. The total number of houses in the city nearly doubled. Tax benefits favored a wave of building in the annex in 1898 and 1899, and Baltimore suffered less of a drop in construction than other cities in the '90s; at the end of the century it had the most favorable housing supply conditions of any large city in the country. The number of persons per house fell to 6.5, the lowest of the large cities. Baltimore had no multistory tenements such as were built in New York and Chicago in the 1880s. It had a higher percentage of home ownership and a lower average rent than other cities. The housing advantages benefited a much larger "middle class" than formerly, including most skilled and steady labor. More than two-thirds of new construction consisted of two-story row houses, twelve or thirteen feet wide, "respectable working class homes," whereas in the last generation less than half were of this type. House building employed a large force, most of whom could afford this type of housing for themselves. There were at least 1900 carpenters, 2500 bricklayers, and 850 stonecutters, earning $500 to $850 a year.

The scale of construction, its standardization, and new techniques cheapened and improved the row house. A high standard of excellence was reached that lasted till World War I. Baltimore brickmakers and bricklayers were world famous. (A particularly fine example of their skills was the Bryn Mawr school near the Richmond Market.) All woodwork was delivered from the mechanized sash and door mills, no longer carpentered on the site or in the shop. Whitecoat finish on plaster became less fashionable, and it was customary to paper the walls of new houses. Most houses had cold water, only a fifth had bathtubs— enough to provide a growth market for McShane's—and few had water closets. Most were built with dirt floor cellars.

The shift to a mass market in good housing depended on effective financing. Advance or bonus building was still prevalent in the '80s. Meanwhile, ground rents became a favored form of investment, as they were safe and tax free.[39] While ground rent originally meant the right of the landowner to collect an annual rent on the land from the developer or owner of buildings on it, the market value of the ground rent rights was generally greater than the actual market value of the land. This meant the ground rent owner was, in fact, making a loan to the owner of the house (leaseholder). The house owner had to pay the property taxes on both house and land, and the ground rent owner was well secured: if the house owner failed to pay either ground rent or taxes, the ground rent owner could claim the house. The leaseholder could not demolish his building or rebuild without permission from the ground rent owner. Houses were sometimes built "ahead of demand" merely to create these ground rents or loans. The financing incentives stimulated building and brought ownership within the reach of more people.

While it hastened and facilitated new development of urban land, the ground rent tended to hinder or retard its *re*development. This was recognized in the '80s with respect to downtown property. As buildings depreciated or became obsolete, the fixed charge seemed "disproportionately great." Confusion of land titles arose as ground rents were divided among heirs. Reconstruction was trammeled in a web of legal technicalities, with numerous parties to a single lot. Leasehold owners found it hard to sell their buildings subject to these handicaps on redevelopment. To ease the problem in the future, laws of the '80s required that all new ground rents created could be "redeemed" or bought out by the leaseholders after five years. These redemption acts fixed the relation between the annual rent and the amount that would have to be paid to buy it out: ground rents were to be capitalized at 6 percent. The ground rent remained attractive for seventy-five years, so long as 6 percent was well above the market interest rate.

While an investor class and institutions such as churches held the ground rents, the working class contributed the largest share toward financing the houses, through the building and loan associations. At least half the houses put up in this generation were financed by them, by 1895 two-thirds. The societies were incorporated in waves that matched the building cycle, peaking in 1886–88.[40] About this time the savings banks of the city reduced their interest rate to 3 percent, and many of their hundred thousand depositors withdrew their savings to pay for small houses. (The average deposit was $300, compared with $1025 for the twenty-one thousand depositors of the large banks.)[41] By 1899 a thousand societies had been incorporated, of which 250 or 300 were active. The typical association had fifty to two hundred shareholders and made loans of $100 up to $1500. Their capital was entirely local and often very small. Their members were chiefly artisans and mechanics, mill and factory hands, sometimes laborers, often women. Some associations were based on ethnic solidarities: there were several dozen in the chains of German-American building and loan societies, especially the Germania and the Bohemian (St. Wenceslas), and there were several Polish and Hebrew associations organized in the '90s, and curiosities such as the "William Tell" and "Our Fritz." Some were associated with a craft or shop, as the employees of the B&O and the Northern Central. Others were organized by developers to encourage mutual financing of home buyers on a certain street of East or South Baltimore. Organizations like the South Bond Street Bohemian Workingmen's Building Association Number One were the cornerstones of a hundred neighborhoods. The building and loan societies reconciled the contradictory goals of different classes of society: an improved standard of living for a majority, expansion of capital, a stable labor force, and preservation of the elaborate system of social classes and ethnic groups. Their names reflect the ideology of the movement: Perseverance, Harmony, Enterprise, the Bee-Hive, the Log Cabin, and all of the Permanents, Perpetuals, and Progressives.

Street Space

City space can be divided into building space and street space, the one essentially private, the other public. Frederick J. Brown set forth a vigorous argument in 1894 against certain street-opening projects, on the grounds that they would produce "overstreeting," or small blocks and buildings of small value. He argued the importance of what he called municipal geography, "the *wastefulness or economy of space* with which a city is laid out, the shape and size of the blocks, the proportion which the area of the streets bears to the area of blocks."[42] Washington, D.C., Brown claimed, was laid out "very extravagantly" as the nation's show place, but Baltimore must strive for a golden mean. His notion locates for us the growth stresses of his generation: maintaining a certain ratio in the development of building space and street space, of private and public enterprise. In the private space, private values could be captured or capitalized by private persons, but they could only be developed to the extent that street space was improved and furnished with services such as street railways, gas mains, water mains, wires, and drains. Extension of streets and services raised land values in the belt. In the center city likewise, raising private land values required a higher degree or greater efficiency of downtown streets and services. The amount of business activity in the streets was increasing dramatically, in particular, livery stables and delivery of milk, bread, and beer to homes and corner stores. To some extent flows or speeds could be increased; this was the meaning of electric transit and telephone lines. As these channels multiplied, people began to see the streets as three-dimensional spaces. Just as private owners built taller buildings with passenger elevators and pneumatic mail chutes for more intense vertical circulation, so the public corridors became three-dimensional labyrinths. The city commissioner complained in 1894, "Nearly all the space under the surface of the streets is now occupied. This is particularly true of the immediate center of the city."

Accelerated investment in street spaces was politically important in three ways. First, it meant that the municipality became involved in franchising and contracting to private corporations to build and supply street services. Second, new problems arose in the coordination and integration of the new functions. The sudden growth was often ill managed, and larger-scale inefficiency provoked demands for reform. Third, a redistribution of income occurred (as with annexation), depending on who could manipulate public investments, who could capture the private values generated, and how those private values were taxed for public investments. Most of the political disputes of this period were expressed in terms of street-space privileges.

As total residential construction was about equal to that of the last generation, one should find at least a comparable increase in the public utilities. In fact, it exceeds expectation, because the interactions tend to multiply, increasing faster than the population or area of the city. I have already noted the $15 million investment in rapid transit. In much the same way, gas service expanded, by alternate periods of competition and consolidation. The original Gas Light of Baltimore had come under the control of Brooklyn, N.Y., interests. People's had built a coal gas plant at the foot of Scott Street and drawn a line separating their territories. Consumer's Mutual introduced the water gas (Lowe) process in 1878 at Lancaster Street and Harris Creek. In 1880 the three were consolidated (and named the Consolidated Gas Company of Baltimore) and reorganized at a new level of plant efficiency. But a new set of competitors came in with New York capital. Equitable built at Severn and Bayard streets, and the Chesapeake Company built nearby on Bayard Street at Wicomico. In 1888 there was consolidation once again. The several companies had built more than two hundred miles of gas mains, which had to be reintegrated into a single network. The volume of gas sold had tripled, and the price was cut in half.

The same argument can be extended to nonresidential activities. Accelerated investment in private industrial spaces in this generation also required new public investments in the connecting utilities, railways, and ship channels. Over the same five years when rapid transit was created, the B&O spent at least $7 million on its Curtis Bay branch, its belt line, and the Howard Street tunnels (see below), and the city made direct loans of $8 million to the Western Maryland Railroad. In the harbor, the enlarged Brewerton Channel stimulated sizeable private investments in warehouses, piers, and elevators on the waterfront. It tended to silt rapidly, so in 1881 the federal government began work on the $1.25 million Craighill Channel, which followed the natural channel and was deeper (27 feet) and wider (450 to 600 feet). In the '90s another $2 million worth of work was done on the channels.

Meanwhile, Baltimore borrowed $15 million for making new streets, mains, and drains. Municipal employment reached 4700 in 1898, and annual construction contracts and purchases indirectly employed thousands more, varying from year to year. The council attempted to impose local contractors and union labor. As the municipal sector grew, there were more and more defects of coordination among municipal departments. A city schoolhouse had no city water and an infected pump. The new city hall drained its sewage illegally into the Jones Falls. Inadequate garbage collection on Harrison Street meant that the offal was being removed by dredging the falls and basin. Many of the interferences appeared in the form of public nuisances in street spaces. The introduction of the Gunpowder water supply (1881) favored the installation of plumbing fixtures in houses and an increase in water consumption. A plumbing law was promptly passed, and four hundred plumbers were licensed. New dwellings were ordered equipped with bathrooms. But most of the new bathrooms and kitchen sinks simply emptied into the gutters. Interior water closets of elegant homes were discreetly connected to the city storm sewers or to streams. In other words, the Gunpowder water supply was used, dirtied, and turned into the streets of Baltimore, producing a demand for attention to sewers.

As usual, that comedy of errors, Harford Run, provides examples of the

In the 1970s a $15 million storm sewer was the most recent attempt to control flooding in Harris Creek, now buried under Kenwood Avenue.

chain reaction of public improvements. In 1828 the "wash" had been diverted from Ann Street and Washington Street into Harford Run by rearranging the street grades, and in the last generation Harford Run had been canalized along Central Avenue. In the 1870s it was covered. It tended to flood because of the rapid building up of its watershed. In 1879–81, Harford Run itself was diverted, near Ann and Eager streets, into Harris Creek. This one-mile drain cost $150,000. The consequences were unfortunate in every part of the system. The Ann Street diversion sewer itself proved too small and overflowed, requiring a new ten-foot diameter sewer. The old channel, which ran through private property and then under Bond Street and Central Avenue, became more dilapidated; diversion of the water made it stagnate and stink all the more. Finally, the extension of the city eastward and the development of Patterson Park required that Harris Creek in turn be properly graded and covered. Thus, the charade of Harford Run was repeated at Harris Creek. When the commissioners began sewering the section between Lancaster and Boston streets near the Abbott iron works at the waterfront, they found that to get a large enough capacity drain, "the arch crops out the tops of the streets." They would have to raise the grades of Hudson and Patapsco streets at least three feet and relocate numerous water and gas mains. Much of the investment in Patterson Park extension consisted of a transformation of the swamp into a lake and esplanade, an attractive solution after sixty years of moving the problem.[43] Flash floods were still a subject of complaint in the area in 1975, as the drainage proved inadequate to carry the storm water from the streets and rooftops that replaced the green areas to the north of Patterson Park. The Lakewood Avenue Drain Project currently under way to eliminate flooding in the Patterson Park area by increasing the capacity of the underground drain for Harris Creek is the largest storm drainage project in Baltimore's history. It is expected that by the time the project is finished, it will cost about $21 million. In addition, because the old streets are narrow and the excavation is large, adjacent homeowners contend that the project is causing walls and foundations to crack.

It was difficult to distinguish between incompetence, a lack of vision or system, and sheer greed. In Jacob Hollander's estimation, Baltimore in the '80s and '90s was not the target of wholesale graft or election fraud as in the '50s, nor the sleight of hand and systematic robbery that characterized New York City in the '80s. But he felt that inefficiency and torpor were just as costly because they lulled the voters, and it took fifty years for inefficiency to become a public issue. One can interpret the demands for reform as a response to the growth of the enterprise and its new scale of inefficiency. In each public enterprise were introduced new levels of management, parallel with what was happening in large corporations such as the B&O and Standard Oil.[44] Fire, police, and water departments had been rationalized and professionalized in the 1850s. Now new levels of middle management were introduced into the schools, the courts, and the fire department, in private charities and public welfare services. Even in the structure of politics itself, one sees the enhanced roles of professional intermediaries like Isaac Rasin, Sonny Mahon, Frank Furst, and the "b'hoys" who held no elective office. In the public construction sector, the first step was the reorganization of the harbor board in 1876. A full-time engineer was hired and bids required. Dredging costs were miraculously reduced to a third of their former level. This indicates the scale of inefficiency at stake. Street cleaning became a burning issue in 1886: "The people are inexpressibly aggravated." The health commissioner had a yearly budget of $250,000, but no control over hiring. Costs of paving and repaving also became an issue. The municipal reform of 1895 (defeat of the Gorman-Rasin machine) permitted a degree of professionalization of paving, grading, repair, and cleaning of streets.

The uproar over the condition of the streets was an expression of a more fundamental dissatisfaction with the redistribution effects—who paid and who benefited. Despite the public interest rhetoric, there was little information about the redistribution achieved by the various policies and franchises in the streets. These were the questions to which Richard Ely and Jacob Hollander addressed themselves. Ely participated in the taxation commission of 1888 and pointed out the relation between the development of private capital and public finance:

Taxation may create monopolies or it may prevent them; it may diffuse wealth or it may concentrate it; it may promote liberty and equality of rights, or it may tend to the establishment of tyranny and despotism; it may be used to bring about reforms, or it may be so laid as to aggravate existing grievances and foster dissension and hatred between classes.[45]

Ely recognized that taxation was a rather new phenomenon, and municipal taxes were rising because of the need to provide new municipal services, just as state taxes had been introduced (1841) to provide canals and railroads. But taxes were resented and avoided, and Ely recommended instead municipal ownership of all the natural monopolies—streets, bridges, railroads, canals, ferries, gasworks, electric-lighting works, waterworks, harbors, and streetcar lines.

Private monopolies are odious. They are contrary to the spirit of the common law and of American institutions, and wherever or whenever they exist, are a perpetual source of annoyance and irritation. Public monopolies, on the other hand are productive of vast benefits, when confined to their own proper sphere.[46]

Above all, private entrepreneurs should be offered no perpetual rights, which "squander the rights of those who are to come after us." They might be offered fifteen-year leases. Mayor Swann's horsecar franchises were to expire in 1889, and Ely suggested that the street railway franchises be auctioned to the highest bidder for another short period.[47] The object would be "to exact from every natural monopoly using public property full compensation." After all, if a private citizen owned absolutely the streets of Baltimore, how would he manage the streetcar business? Certainly not by a perpetual grant.

Ely also recognized land as a natural monopoly, whose increases of value arose from the growth of the whole city.

Wealth is only possible in a community, and in this community no one lives for himself alone. . . . There are certain fundamental conditions of our future prosperity which no individual as such can supply, but which must be provided by us in our organic capacity as a city and as an important part of a commonwealth, or not at all. Society lives in a condition of solidarity.[48]

Ely urged, therefore, that Baltimore, like Savannah, acquire the acreage around the city, annex it, provide streets and services, and lease the lots for twenty-five-year terms. Municipal ownership of land would thus provide a future revenue to the city; the public would own the ground rents. This would be a more elastic and less resented source of revenue than taxation. To Ely's regret, the city ignored his tax proposals and his suggestions for auctioning streetcar franchises and for a municipal land bank and ground rents. Ely left for the University of Wisconsin, but many of his ideas bore fruit after his departure, influencing the reform campaigns of the '90s, and the leaders of the business elite in the Progressive party.

The basic issues of redistribution were, like all political issues in Maryland, clouded by being expressed as a conflict between the city and the rest of the state. "Baltimore should have full control over its own streets" was the refrain. In 1884 the argument was over telegraph poles, "an almost unendurable nuisance on our sidewalks; where the extraordinary legislation obtained at Annapolis some years since enables telegraph companies to locate them at pleasure." In 1885 there were objections to a gas company, "a foreign corporation," tearing up the pavements. The state legislature permitted incorporation of new utilities and took over the entire privilege of awarding franchises. Exgovernors appeared as presidents of assorted gas and transit companies. The city was not paid anything for the use of its streets, and the street railway tax of Mayor Swann's time was whittled down from 20 percent to 12 percent, then to 9 percent. With the cable cars and electrics the nuisance became more acute. The streets were continually dug up. Egged on by the bicycle craze, people began demanding the new "smooth paving." It created wonderful entrepreneurial opportunities. In 1895 Isaac Filbert had three hundred men and one hundred teams of horses at work. Only forty-nine miles of city streets were laid with improved pavements (granite block, sheet asphalt, and asphalt block), about three hundred miles were cobbled, and another three hundred miles unpaved.

The trends toward public investment in street space and its greater engineering complexity can be seen in the transformation of a stretch of the Jones Falls valley near North Avenue. Today it is an archaeologist's puzzle of footings, bridges, tunnels, and sewers. The physical labyrinth is an accurate representation of the inextricable public and private interests. Since the Civil War, the B&O had been using the Philadelphia, Wilmington and Baltimore Railroad to send passengers and goods from Washington and Cumberland on to Philadelphia. They were ferried from Locust Point or hauled by horses through Pratt Street to the President Street Station and north over the PW&B. In 1881, when the Pennsylvania bought the PW&B from its Boston owners, Garrett saw the threat. Bold as ever, he proposed to counter the Pennsylvania by creating a competing main line through from Washington to New York. By 1886 the B&O had built a ninety-five-mile track from Baltimore to Philadelphia. By 1889 it reached New York harbor, but it had yet to be threaded through the developed parts of Baltimore, to connect the Washington branch with the line to the north. The B&O management considered an elevated connection parallel with Pratt Street, and even began buying private property for such a scheme. Then it reached an understanding with the Baltimore Belt Railroad Company (originally intended to serve the Lehigh Valley) for a system of tunnels. Samuel Rea was appointed engineer and contracts awarded in 1890; the Royal Blue trains began running over the whole New York to Washington line in 1895.

The scheme to traverse Baltimore had three distinct parts. The first was a 7341-foot tunnel under Howard Street from Richmond Market to Camden Station. It would be a steady grade, so southbound trains could coast downhill through a masonry tube 21 feet tall and 27 feet wide. The second part was the Baltimore Belt rail line, which would connect the B&O from Bay View junction through open cuts along Twenty-sixth Street with short tunnels between Oak and Charles streets and between St. Paul and Calvert streets. The third part, connecting those two, was a curved grade running on a viaduct and partly through tunnels. This "crossover" had to be threaded across the Jones Falls and the Northern Central tracks, under North Avenue, and across the Pennsylvania's line (the B&P) in the very mouth of its tunnel. Negotiation with the rival Pennsylvania line was toughest. The curve had to be introduced, and ideas for a principal station at Maryland Avenue were abandoned because the PRR would not let the B&O cross right at its new Union Station. A peculiar bridge arch construction had to be devised so that the Belt line would not rest its weight directly on the B&P tunnel.[49]

To complicate the negotiations further, the city was undertaking the North Avenue sewer[50] and a new North Avenue bridge.[51] The bridge would have to be raised higher and cost more, to cross over the Belt Railroad's crossover! The one-mile sewer had to run under the Belt line's railroad and bridge pier. The sewer, "one of the most valuable and intricate public works in the city's history," was a $200,000 project running from the old Druid Hill Avenue sewer, through Laurens Street, Park Avenue, and North Avenue to the Jones Falls. The project was essential to the development of Bolton Hill and Mount Royal, the vicinity of the new Friends' School at Park and Wilson, and the terraces in Park

Avenue. It was a fine example of the new sophistication of civil engineering under C. H. Latrobe (the third generation of his family to work for Baltimore City) and of the technical problems of coordinating the new public and collective works in three-dimensional street space. The grade of North Avenue itself was so steep that for the sewer under it they introduced several drops or waterfalls of 6 feet, 18 feet, etc.: "If the surface grade had been followed, it is said the water would have attained such a great velocity as to tear the sewer to pieces in a few years." Half the work was done by tunneling. A shaft was sunk 40 feet below the level of the Northern Central railway, and the last 179 feet were tunneled from the bottom of that shaft to the Jones Falls, while trains were constantly passing above. The sewer also ran under the passing ten-ton cars of the Lake Roland Elevated. The tunnel bore the weight of the western abutment of the Belt Railroad bridge over the falls. Farther west it would support the future retaining walls for the western approach of the North Avenue bridge. "At such points the sewer looks as if it would bear a mountain on its back."

In 1889 these Mount Royal Avenue rowhouses, between Charles and St. Paul streets, were not yet occupied and the street was unpaved.

The next phase in rationalizing the three-dimensional street space got under way just as the B&O tunnels, the North Avenue sewer, and the electric elevateds were completed. Two sensible proposals were sketched out under Mayor Ferdinand Latrobe and pursued vigorously under the reform administration that followed: the electrical subway commission and the topographical survey. The electrical subway was a solution to the problem of overhead wires. The plan was to place under the streets a system of channels in which the city would lay a complete set of fire and police telegraph alarms, with additional channels for the private telephone and telegraph companies to lay their circuits. The scheme addressed itself to the problem of coordinating public and private monopolies. Topographical Survey was the offspring of the Sewerage Commission. The storm drainage plan of 1862 was implemented very gradually, piecemeal. A major defect was the failure to prevent its use for sanitary disposal. A new sewerage commission in 1880 recommended a dual system of separate storm drains and sanitary sewers.[52] An 1893 plan was more elaborate, considered all of the engineering alternatives, and recommended a dual system with pumping station to permit draining the harbor areas and disposal of the human wastes into Chesapeake Bay. The plan naturally appeared costly, but the real political stumbling blocks were the objections of the oyster industry and the night-soil contractors, who talked up the dangers of typhoid from pollution of the oyster beds. So the construction of a sewer system was postponed for another twenty years. Nevertheless, enough momentum was developed to do the three-dimensional map, postponed since Poppleton's time. It was the first step to building sewers, and it would provide a thoroughly new planning perspective.

In its earliest deliberations, the survey abandoned the hope of reviewing or adjusting the Poppleton plat as a base map. By rigorous triangulation, accounting for error, they discovered the extent of previous errors in both private and public spaces. Private land surveyors had taken little account of variations in the departure of magnetic north from true north. Therefore, streets laid out at different times were out of line. The difference of angle between Charles Street and its extension, Charles Street Avenue, is a measure of the extent of this accumulated difference. A perceptible curvature of Edmondson Avenue is an indication of how gradual block-by-block extensions of a street reflected the gradual divergence of the magnetic declination.

With the consultation of the U.S. Geological Survey, the U.S. Coast and Geodetic Survey, and the young and ambitious Maryland Geological Survey, the Baltimore Topographical Survey selected a base line and made elaborate preparations for measuring it along Fort Avenue with a specially manufactured steel tape in the light of the moon, to minimize its expansion from the heat of the sun. The selection of highly visible points for triangulations gives us some idea of the landmarks of greater Baltimore: the head of George Washington on his monumental pedestal, the cupolas of Hopkins Hospital and Bay View. At last the city had recognized the three-dimensional character of its municipal geography.

The Crisis of 1893

The summer of 1893 was the kind of summer that must have given the Gay Nineties their name. The newspapers reported day after day, weekend after weekend, a succession of camp meetings, picnics, and parades. But the good-natured crowds and Old Country and workers' solidarities did not include everyone. The same summer there was another rash of suicides, mostly by Germans. One died of opium poisoning, two took laudanum, another drank chloral. A woman lay down in front of a locomotive at Sparrows Point. Two men shot themselves. One swallowed Rough on Rats in Patterson Park, and still another plunged a six-inch shears into his abdomen. Troubles afflicted whole communities. Even in good times men in the building trades could put in only 200 working days a year. The black brickmakers in the clay field could work only 155. Some turned to oyster packing in winter. Women made ends meet by working at the needle trades in winter and the packing houses in summer. Even at the height of the construction boom of 1892 and the summer of 1893 the Bay View almshouse and hospital were overflowing. The trustees attributed it to the "sequels of prosperity." Eighteen ninety-three turned out to be a bad year, a year of financial panic, spreading outward from bank crashes to railroad bankruptcies and layoffs, the collapse of farm prices, and foreclosures nationwide. In Baltimore the winter was colder than usual: oyster catching shut down at Christmas, and construction workers were laid off. Men on city contracts begged to be kept at work and take their pay later. By 28 December observers estimated that seventy-five hundred residents were out of work. The most careful estimates suggest ten thousand by New Year's Day, then thirty thousand.[53] Several of the craft unions had unemployment benefits, but their resources ran out quickly. A quarter of the cigar makers were unemployed, a third of the carpenters, bricklayers, can makers, and store clerks, half the musicians and shoe lasters, and three-quarters of the painters and iron molders.

The institutions were overwhelmed. Three hundred destitute were housed in the police stations every night. Instead of the floral tribute traditional for New Year's, the postal workers offered their chief five hundred loaves of bread to distribute in the station houses. A Central Relief Committee was formed. "It is the resident poor whom we wish to reach, and the best way to relieve them

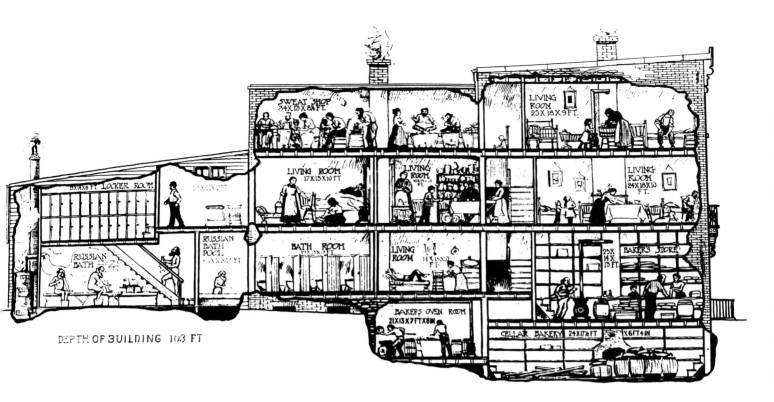

Labels in the illustration: SWEAT SHOP 34X15X8½FT., LIVING ROOM 25X18X9 FT., 15X8X8 FT. LOCKER ROOM, LIVING ROOM 17X13X10 FT., LIVING ROOM, LIVING ROOM 24X18X10 FT., RUSSIAN BATH POOL, RUSSIAN BATH, BATH ROOM, LIVING ROOM, 25X14X13FT, BAKER'S STORE, BAKER'S OVEN ROOM 21X13X7FTX8IN, CELLAR BAKERY 24X17½ FT, X6FT4IN, DEPTH OF BUILDING 103 FT

is providing work for them."[54] The committee opened a stoneyard on Edmondson Avenue and another on Falls Road. Next morning there were nine hundred applicants, half skilled workers, half unskilled laborers. "They were all respectable-looking." The committee organized a second Friendly Inn with adjoining woodyard, "to sift the professional vagrant from those who want to work, by offering work as part of the relief."[55] The city's Light Street paving project was hastened, and hundreds stood around city hall, waiting to learn who would be the fortunate ones hired.

Among the hardest hit were the clothing workers in Oldtown. Here the depression of the market was reflected in the drop of piece-work prices. There were three to four hundred sweatshops between Central Avenue and the Jones Falls, on both sides of Lombard Street. The majority were Jewish, with a number of Catholic Lithuanians and Bohemians. Master tailors (at one time many were Irish) were less necessary than formerly, and the contractor system had reached its peak. Before the business crisis, the task or day's work of a sewing machine operator was $3.00, the baster $2.50, the presser $1.00, and "the girls" from fifty cents to $1.00. Among the Lithuanians the workers were paid a cut, subcontracting down the line through the shop: of whatever the wholesaler paid for the finished shirt or pants, the contractor paid his tailor 24 percent; the tailor paid the baster 33 percent from his share, and the baster in turn paid his assistant 40 percent. But during the season of 1893–94 prices fell by half, and all wages accordingly. Operators were working fifteen or sixteen hours a day, six days a week. There was not so much unemployment as extreme exhaustion.

A large proportion of these people are upon the verge of starvation, and were it not for the well known benevolence of the Hebrew people, many would be constantly slipping over it. They have reduced their standard of living to such a point that any further reduction involves death.[56]

A *Sun* reporter walked through Albemarle, Front, Exeter, High, Lombard, Fayette, and other streets where clothing shops were numerous. "Outside there is little, if anything, to indicate the destitution within." The Hebrew Relief Committee organized a food distribution center in what was once an elegant parlor in Lombard Street. The sign outside read, "Who is short of food shall come inside

A cross section of a 1903 Lombard Street rowhouse shows a sweatshop on the third floor, a Russian bath at the rear, a cellar bakery, a bakery shop in the front, and five "living rooms." The house is about 18 feet wide, the back building 13 feet wide, and the full depth of the building 103 feet.

and get it." The shelves were piled with loaves of bread, and the mantle laden with packages of tea, sugar, and coffee. In a corner was a big pile of small sacks of flour. Smoked and fresh meats were on the table.[57]

The working environments were investigated by health officers and indicate the acute competition in the industry. In David Harris's small shop on Low Street, six persons were employed in a room ten by twelve by nine feet, rented at $3.00 a month: "Cooking, washing, and in fact, all the domestic work is carried on in close proximity to the tailoring work. A terrible odor pervades the whole house, and the only entrance is through a filthy alley." Coats that formerly paid $1.25 now pay only fifty cents. "It is of such shops as these that so much complaint is heard and which, so it is complained, tend to bring down prices."

It was an exceedingly complex industry. "The conditions prevailing among the pants and vest makers are much worse than that of the coat tailors," evidently associated with a larger share of female labor. Wages were reduced more severely. Some workers lost their tools or furniture. The contractors were "little, if any, better off" while there was little work. They paid for the fuel, thread, and rent, and furnished the sewing machines, which they bought by weekly installments. "It is only by constant self-denial and hard labor that they can even live." Andrew Rochuba was making letter carriers' uniforms at 1631 Shakespeare Street. "It would be difficult to conceive a more filthy and unwholesome place." Simon Silbert, 622 South Charles, carried on trade in two third-floor rooms, with eight persons. He paid $13 a month for the whole house. "Bags of clippings are standing about, and the floor is literally covered with those which they have not taken time to gather up. The smell of gasoline pervades the whole house. . . . The paper on the wall hangs in shreds." At Simon Schapiro's in North Exeter Street eleven persons worked in one room. Altogether six families lived in the house. Each hallway was filled with baby carriages and furniture. "None of them appeared to pay any attention to their surroundings, but seemed to think that their very life depended upon the speed they exerted while at work."[58]

The solution to the cut-throat competition and environmental horrors of the small sweatshops was already sketched in the arrangement of the large clothing factories by 1895. Among the earlier factory-style operators, Sonneborn employed as many as two thousand in Hopkins Place, Wise Brothers a thousand in a new six-story building in West Fayette Street. Wise also participated in the Chesapeake shirt factory (six hundred employees) in West German Street. Langfeld and Holzman had five or six hundred employees each. Together they defined a garment district close around the University of Maryland. The buildings, of massive and elegant exterior with plenty of window area, required several lots. They were several times larger than the warehouses of 1851 or 1871. They competed for the large contracts (Rosenfeld, for example, made police uniforms), and increasingly dispensed with subcontractors. The factory was more vulnerable to labor organization. In 1889 Ulman's factory was struck; the cutters demanded a nine-hour day: "Take your scissors and go home." Ulman brought strikebreakers from New York. They joined the strikers, but the movement petered out, and little was accomplished. In 1893, however, the bitter depression in the clothing industry generated organization, in much the same way as the wage cuts had produced a railroad strike in '77, a coal miner's strike in '82, a shipbuilders' strike in '85, and the horsecar drivers' strike in '86. Prosperous conditions generally favored union gains, as in 1886, but the depths of depression set the stage for a terrible resistance, usually ending in demoralization. The crucial issue in the clothing strike was the blacklist: the shirt manufacturers attempted to exclude agitators from the industry by sharing blacklists among firms.

The clothing workers' crisis illustrates the interplay of class conflict and ethnic estrangement emerging in the Jewish community. While cut-throat competition in the garment shops brought the east European immigrants to the verge of starvation, an older generation of German Jews, who had peddled and pinched and starved in the '50s, owned the large garment factories and department stores on Lexington and Howard streets. Hutzler's new building of 1886 was the height of elegance. The Friedenwalds, the Sonneborns, Greifs, Hutzlers, Hochschilds, Kohns, and Gutmans all moved out of Oldtown and Southwest Baltimore to Eutaw Place, newly embellished, halfway between downtown and Druid Hill Park, admirably served by the new electrics. Naturally, they took with them their synagogues. The four principal German congregations over three years moved into a six-block radius.[59] The competition for handsome and opulent buildings was a status competition, rehearsing the religious and political disputes of the '50s. They sold off their temples in Oldtown to the new struggling congregations of east Europeans. In 1891 Baltimore Hebrew Congregation built at Madison and Robert streets, and sold its Lloyd Street temple to Shomrei Mishneres. In '93 Oheb Shalom built in Eutaw Place at Lanvale. The prominent church architect of the moment, J. E. Sperry, designed it, and the pews were sold at several hundred dollars each, much to the distaste of retiring Rabbi Szold. Its old Hanover Street temple was sold to a Litvak congregation. The new Har Sinai, also designed by Sperry, at Bolton and Wilson, had steam heat and electric light. The next year Chizuk Amuno built at McCulloch and Mosher, and sold its Lloyd Street temple to the B'nei Israel or "russische shul."

The moves of the synagogues are a design in stonework of the transformation of a value system, struggling between tradition and adaptation, and of a much larger struggle between values of class and kin. In this sense, what was happening within the Jewish community was a microcosm of what was happening in the adjoining Bolton Hill community along Park Avenue and Bolton Street, and also within the Catholic and Methodist communities. The stresses in the Jewish community—the debate over Yiddish, Jewish education, and the reception of Russian refugees—point to problems of education and welfare in the larger community.

In November 1881 seven refugee families from Russia arrived in Baltimore. Eight months later the Benevolent had sheltered 450 and exhausted its $3000 fund.[60] It raised another $3000 and resolved to "make known to the New York Committee that the Baltimore Hebrews have their hands full. . . . No more should be sent hither from New York."[61] But still they came. The just ones of their time, who tried to reach across the gap in various ways, are the only human measure of the aching contradictions of Baltimore. Henrietta Szold, the rabbi's daughter, met the immigrant boats and attempted to find jobs, twenty-five-cent pieces, and food for newcomers. She organized the Russian Hebrew Literary Society and then the Russian night school, usually considered the original immigrant night school. Seven thousand passed through it. It was imitated by the Bohemians in 1898, and the idea was carried on thenceforth by the public school system. Samson Benderly founded a Hebrew kindergarten, and a Hebrew Free School (Talmud Torah) was organized to combat the raids of Protestant Sunday school missionaries.

Under the pen name of Sulamith, Miss Szold also criticized the older generation for their "ultraconservative life, so far as intellectual activity is concerned."[62] Of the arts and sciences "only music distracts them." She argued the need for public institutions to train "susceptible youth" through Jewish schools and a Young Men's Hebrew Association, by pointing to the drastic changes in Jewish life. For a first generation raised in the European ghetto, home was a sanctuary and Friday night a transfiguration, "all that was dearest combined." But since then, "the high walls of the ghetto have fallen. They have plunged themselves into a vortex of pleasure and business."[63] Her indignation was kindled by the charity banquet custom of "amusing one's self thoroughly, of dancing, of eating, of feasting" to tide the poor over winter. Givers' names were pompously read and applauded. "Is there not something intensely egotistic, no, more than that—something barbarous in this wide-spread custom?"[64]

Miss Szold was not only "her mother's daughter" and "her father's daughter," but a child of Baltimore. Charity reorganization was a larger movement. Reverend Lawrence moved into Parkin Street to pursue his settlement work among slum dwellers, and Mary Richmond was moving the Charity Organization Society toward a new thrust of professional social work, structuring the benevolence of volunteers. Miss Richmond, like Sulamith, wanted "humble, unobtrusive charity," a charity "purified and enlightened." She preached against "unwise philanthropy."[65] The society urged regrouping and redistricting the dispensaries for efficiency's sake, creating industrial celibate colonies for the epileptic and feeble-minded, and reducing Baltimore's "attraction" to crippled beggars. The Charity Organization movement emerged in precisely the same conditions as the Society for the Prevention of Pauperism and the Friends of the Poor in 1804 and 1822: on the heels of a severe depression with sharp increase in the cost of welfare. City costs for the care of the poor had tripled while population doubled. City subsidies were distributed to a miscellany of private organizations. The Trustees of the Poor were now replaced by Supervisors of City Charities, whose object still was "to assure the kindest possible treatment to the city's dependents with the least possible waste of the city's money." They founded Rosewood, created a system of juvenile probation, and returned to the plan of placing small children in foster families rather than orphanages: they were more likely to survive, and it cost less. The old contradictions inevitably surfaced: the preoccupation with classification and the distinction between deserving and undeserving. New ironies appeared in the efficient processing of the poor. The supervisors hired a permit clerk, a female clerical assistant, and a female investigator. "The result has been the adoption of suitable books of record and blanks, the accumulation of much valuable experience and data, a well indexed mass of facts, and a remarkable diminution of the number of inmates usually supported by the city at this time of the year."[66]

What distinguished the new charity organization from that of Thomas Griffith's time was the shift toward a strong faith in education and new roles for educated women. Miss Szold graduated from Western High School for Girls, Miss Richmond from Eastern. Szold participated actively in the demand for more education for women, as well as in the development of Jewish schools and free night schools. She joined forces with Mary Garrett (John's daughter) and Martha Carey Thomas in raising $100,000 for the Hopkins medical school, on the condition that qualified women would be admitted. With them she protested the continuing discrimination of The Johns Hopkins University against women and supported the founding of John Goucher's Woman's College.

Within the black community a resegregation was also taking place, similar to that in the Jewish community. Already visible in the '80s were new aspirations and new forms of degradation. This apparently reflected an in-migration of rural blacks and a promotion of the Baltimore born. The city had developed into a single elaborate plantation with its house niggers and its field niggers. Geographically, the resegregation produced ghettos, or neighborhoods of thousands, much more extensive than the alley environments of the '70s. The sharpest contrasts were between Pigtown and Northwest Baltimore. Pigtown, at the foot of Fremont Avenue, altitude twenty feet, was the home of the greatest number of country blacks. Around Camden Station, the market houses, and produce docks, black immigrants from the counties of Maryland and Virginia adjoined clusters of white immigrants, especially Russian Jews and Italians.

Open drains, great lots filled with high weeds, ashes and garbage accumulated in the alleyways, cellars filled with filthy black water, houses that are total strangers to the touch of whitewash or scrubbing brush, human bodies that have been strangers for months to soap and water, villainous looking negroes who loiter and sleep around the street corners and never work; vile and vicious women, with but a smock to cover their black nakedness. . . . That's Pigtown.[67]

The other extreme was northwest of St. Mary's Seminary, where the "respectable" class moved from the alleys out onto streets such as Biddle Street, altitude one hundred feet. On New Year's Day 1886 "a swell colored reception" was given on West Biddle Street at the home of Mrs. L. W. Lee, "assisted by about half a dozen young belles. The parlors were lighted dimly with gas, the shutters tightly closed." Celery and winter delicacies were served.[68] Another society event was a wedding at North Street Baptist Church. The bride's hairdo was decorated with a single ostrich plume, but she was upstaged by a light brown girl in a rich black dress, cut décolleté, and a black silk lace fascinator with orange dots.[69]

Between these extremes lay an elaborate system of social status, which felt every ripple in the job market or the housing market. In the job market, certain individuals and restricted classes of the black community were promoted, but

Moving Uphill

the mass was not. Each unemployment crisis squeezed the unskilled blacks. In 1885 the Italians squeezed them out: "Great gangs of labor drifted from New York have dispossessed the colored and Irish labor on the railroads and water-front, and filled the streets with fruit vendors, retailers of peanuts, and per-formers on harp and organ."[70] The black hod carriers lost their lawsuit to retain union shop rights with contractors for the North Avenue bridge in 1893. They were replaced, apparently, by white laborers. In 1898 "white help" displaced some of the "colored help" in the class of low-skilled servants.[71] During good times the black community acquired a little leverage in employment and the professions. For example, when street cleaning was reorganized, two colored brigades were added.[72] The city wage of $1.66 a day was higher than other common labor.

All the black professionals listed in the census of 1890 amounted to perhaps 250 people, certainly under 1 percent. Twenty or thirty black doctors practiced in the black community and participated in public health efforts, and Dr. Whitfield Winsey was admitted to the Medical and Chirurgical Society, but they could not practice in the new hospitals. E. J. Waring and Joseph S. Davis were admitted to the Maryland bar; Waring took part in a constitutional test of racial clauses in the state's bastardy laws,[73] and both were among the legal defense of the Navassa guano laborers. Associated with them in prestige were the more successful dealers or businessmen and the best situated of the fifteen thousand domestic servants. Experienced servants had skills and job security, and they patterned their standards, aspirations, and manners on the wealthiest members of Baltimore society. Richard Macks, for example, born a slave in Charles County, came to Baltimore when Grant was elected and served four or five employers, each wealthier and more demanding than the last. Toward the end of the century, after being Tom Winans's and then Robert Garrett's butler for many years, he founded his own catering business.[74]

Semiskilled black workers formed assemblies of the Knights of Labor—the brickmakers, the Fells Point wagoners, three hundred grain trimmers, and the Montgomery Street stevedores.[75] Isaac Myers founded a newspaper, the *Colored Citizen*, and organized a Colored State Industrial Fair to set before the public the skills and development of the black community. But Isaac Myers had already lost his battle, outweighed by the divisive strategies that pitted the interests of race against the interests of class. In a speech at the Sharp Street Methodist Church, for example, at the height of the eight hours movement,

Mr. Waring advised the colored laborers not to join the white trades unions or take part in the present struggle of labor against capital. Until recently, the trades unions had refused to receive the colored men in their organizations, but now that they need all the forces they can muster they are asking them to come in. The speaker said the colored laborers were not interested in the fight. If the white laborers were worsted, the colored laborers could expect to be preferred by the capitalists.[76]

The effective exclusion of blacks from most of the skilled crafts had its reflection in the housing market. The building of extensive home owner neigh-borhoods of German and Bohemian mechanics had a corollary: the exclusion of the black community. Despite the proliferation of corporations, beneficial societies, and unions among blacks, they had only one building and loan society by the turn of the century. They were effectively prevented from obtaining real estate or credit. Consequently, there was scarcely any new housing built for blacks in this period, there were only a handful of black home owners, and the rural immigrants aggravated a severe housing shortage.

What was within reach of hundreds, and soon thousands, of black families, was the expansion of the secondhand neighborhoods in St. Marys, Orchard, and Biddle streets, and in Jefferson and Caroline streets. These neighborhoods grew, pushing from the narrower streets to the wider ones, uphill, block by block. Critical events in the search for a path of upward mobility were the creation of the Colored High School (1887) and the employment of black teachers in a new colored primary school at Carrollton and Riggs (1888). The effects were swift, analogous to the breakthrough of the 1840s, when women were hired as teachers. Black school enrollments began to rise.

Schools of the 1840s in Druid Hill Avenue near Biddle Street, and Fremont near Lombard, had in the '70s become English-German schools; in the '90s they became colored schools. Other older schools were changed to colored schools "due to decreasing white populations," and the white pupils moved to new school buildings in newer neighborhoods—from Jefferson and Caroline streets to Patterson Park Avenue and McElderry, and from Mulberry near Fremont to Harlem Avenue and Monroe Street. Each community in turn—the Bohemians, the German Jews, the German Catholics, the blacks—followed a radial path, uphill, along the car line, outbound.

The simplest motive for all the reshuffling in this period was survival of the young of the species. Changes in social status can be evaluated in terms of infant survival. The process was ruthless: the family able to move left a vacancy; newcomers to the city filled the vacancies. In this generation both death rates and birth rates began to fall. Smallpox in 1882–83 was the last of the great epidemics. The 1881 Gunpowder Falls water supply made a real difference; it was relatively unpolluted and offered more people adequate volume and pressure. But the general progress conceals a selection of places and persons. The smallpox epidemic, for example, could be described in the same terms as in 1821–22: there were 1184 deaths, confined to the lanes and alleys where the poor lived. Of the white victims, 85 percent were minors, mostly children of recent immigrants—Polish Catholics and Germans, with a scattering of the poorest of the Bohemians, some Norwegians, Hungarians, Italians, and Russian Jews. More than half of them lived in two wards of the city, Fells Point and Canton. Similar conditions prevailed on the rim of Federal Hill and Locust Point, but their total numbers were smaller. Of 294 black victims of smallpox, two-thirds were minors, and more than two-thirds lived in South Baltimore between Camden Station and the waterfront.

The smallpox outbreak is a fair indicator of the general pattern. John S. Billings calculated death rates from all causes for 1886–90, with attention to differences of race and age.[77] He found infant death rates a sensitive barometer of environmental conditions. Infant mortality in Fells Point and parts of South

The prestige once accorded the water system is illustrated by the Mount Royal Pumping Station, at the west end of the North Avenue bridge. The elegant pumphouse, built in 1899, was removed in 1957 for the construction of the Jones Falls Expressway.

Baltimore was three times the city average. Black mortality ran nearly double the white average. Net growth of the black community occurred thanks to the high rate of immigration from rural Maryland and Virginia. The stream of immigrants and the housing squeeze aggravated environmental conditions, especially the risk of tuberculosis. In Billings's terms, "Making all due allowance for errors in the census data, these conclusions may be accepted as correct, and they point distinctly to bad sanitary conditions in and about the homes of the colored population, which conditions have become worse in 1890 than they were in 1880." In response, the black community began moving uphill into Northwest Baltimore, where death rates for colored and white were close together —twelve to fifteen per thousand as compared with thirty-five to forty in East Baltimore and forty-five to sixty in South Baltimore. Doctors and social workers were scandalized at the blacks' infant mortality and the apparent "negligence" of mothers, but the black community attached prestige and status to environments in exact proportion to their survival records. Except for a tardy vaccination campaign in 1882, there was no public attention to the environments occupied by blacks or by the new white minorities.

Since the water supply provided the chief cause of the general progress of health, one might also expect differences of water supply to explain the differential rates of survival. If we map the water supply options of various parts of town, we find the geographical matrix of the chances of dying young.[78] When the newer and safer external water supplies were introduced, especially the Gunpowder water in 1881, they were effectively provided to the newly developed areas—the high ground and the outer rim of the city. Water was piped to private properties on the streets (not the alleys), for a rent. In addition, two hundred free public fountains "for man and beast" were installed, chiefly in the new districts, in the public markets, and the east-west business streets of the downtown. But the inner city—Fells Point, Oldtown, and the sections west and south of Camden Station—still depended on public pumps from shallow wells, vulnerable to pollution from privies and street drainage. The infants of the black community of South Baltimore and the Polish community of East Baltimore were dying from acute intestinal disease, as in the cholera epidemic of 1832, because they were still dependent on the defective water supply of 1832. For want of collective action to solve the hydrologic problems of the low-lying areas of the city, the people continued to move uphill. Where Wynne figured a seventh of the population was living above the one-hundred-foot contour in 1850, Billings figured a quarter in 1890. The black community had shifted even more, in response to the more severe differential of death: a third were living above one hundred feet. For want of collective organization to isolate the sick and interrupt the spread of disease in the urban community, households and sub-communities struggled to isolate themselves one from another. An upper middle class began to consider the single-family dwelling attractive, and racial segregation appeared at a new scale of whole neighborhoods.

The general progress in containing epidemics meant that the public health no longer consisted of seasonal or sudden emergencies and threats of catastrophes, hasty clean-up campaigns and repentance. The Grim Reaper became more predictable than the oyster harvest, the coal trains, or the B&O dividends. This required a decided shift in the whole conception of public health and a reorientation to targets of endemic disease, in particular, typhoid, pneumonia, and tuberculosis. The opening of Johns Hopkins Hospital in 1889 was an important step. It was founded on new principles of organization. John Billings, with his thorough experience of army hospital organization in the Civil War, laid out the pavilions with attention to engineering detail and materials. A system of flues, vents, and ducts, an aspirating chimney, and basement ventilating chambers supplied a scientifically calculated flow of air and prevented the exchange of germs.[79] When Dr. William Osler agreed to take charge of operating the new hospital, D. C. Gilman, the president of the university, met him at the Fifth Avenue Hotel in New York, where they spent a couple of days examining the hotel management. Gilman assured him, "There is no difference really between a hospital and a hotel." Everything was arranged in departments with responsible heads and a director over all. "The clinical unit of a hospital is the exact counterpart of one of the subdivisions of any great hotel or department store."[80] Good nursing care made differences of life and death, and nurses' training was wholly reorganized. Dr. Welch and Dr. Osler organized the Maryland Public Health Association, and tried to dramatize the steady sacrifice caused by the defects of the water system, the lack of sewers, and the lack of an infectious-disease hospital for isolating the sick.[81] Eight hundred and twenty-nine cases of typhoid were treated at Hopkins in its first ten years. Referring to typhoid, Osler said, "The penalties of cruel neglect have been paid for 1896; the dole of victims for 1897 is nearly complete, the sacrifices will number again above 200. We cannot save the predestined ones of 1898, but what of the succeeding years?"[82]

Going, Going, Gone!

As in 1851, the growth of the urban organism meant changes in form and functioning—higher rates of exchange with its environment, more rapid circulation of materials within the organism, and the development of new specialized organs within it. In 1851 the swift growth was coupled with a new political status and sense of self-determination. But in 1898 the sudden expansion of industry and its metabolism destroyed the city's internal mechanisms of adjustment and threatened its identity.

From the bird's-eye views of 1869 and 1889 one can readily see the great chunks of capital built into the landscape in this generation: the Eutaw Street garment district, the great elevators on Locust Point, the post office and city hall. Just over the horizon were the massive works of civil engineering at North Avenue and the Jones Falls, the scores of buildings at Sparrows Point, and the expanded shops of the B&O and Bartlett-Hayward at Mount Clare. The 1889 Friedenwald view also conveys the relation of the concentration of capital to a quickened exchange with other cities. The angled railroad piers, the steamboats trailing smoke in the wind around the harbor rim, are part of that intense circulation. There was a radical increase in the bulky industrial raw materials shipped into Baltimore. By the turn of the century the copper refinery was bringing sixteen thousand tons a year of smelter copper from Anaconda, twenty-five hundred miles by rail. Export tonnages of copper tripled. The steel company brought a million tons a year of iron ore from Cuba. Monumental Sulfur works brought fifteen thousand tons of pyrite ores by rail from its mines in Virginia, and the fertilizer companies fifty thousand tons of phosphate rock from South Carolina and twenty-five thousand tons of ammonia from the Chicago slaughterhouses, as well as the schooner loads of guano from Navassa and potash from Germany. They exported half a million tons of fertilizer. The railroads brought down 10 million tons of coal to Locust Point for export or fueling steamships. Through Baltimore's heroic effort to develop its railroads, its seaport, and street system, it had overcome the underdevelopment Parkinson complained of in 1799. Baltimore was now an excellent location for cheap inland shipping as well as cheap ocean shipping. Labor, too, had become cheap, through the importation of human ballast, insuring job competition of black, immigrant, and native-born workers.

The physical lumps of capital were visible signs of financial concentration. Incorporation was the first step beyond the traditional family firm or partnership. In 1881 there were only thirty-nine industrial corporations in Baltimore; by 1895 there were two hundred, and by 1905 the corporations were producing half the value and employing half the manufacturing workers. The second step was cooperation or combination among corporations. In 1878, twenty-three canners formed an oyster-packing pool with $300,000 capital, to abolish competitive price cutting and to guarantee quality and weight. For a year or two they were successful: their profits doubled. But such pools collapsed whenever one individual withdrew or started a new firm.[83] The third step, therefore, was permanent consolidation through corporate merger or through holding companies and trusts.[84] This occurred in a halting, experimental way in the '80s, then in a sudden flood in the winter of 1898–99. The American Can Company assembled the fourteen can factories. Sixteen of the twenty breweries in town were marshaled (Gottlieb-Bauernschmidt-Strauss) with $14 million capital. The Baltimore Brick Company absorbed all the large brickmakers of the city. Mount Vernon–Woodberry cotton duck mills were brought under a trust agreement, together with several southern cotton mills; their owners aimed at an international monopoly of cotton thread as well. The rival utility companies were gathered into unified monopolies: the United Railways, the United Electric Light and Power Company, and the Consolidated Gas Company. The new powerhouse of United Electric on Pratt Street in the inner harbor in 1899 was a massive and even elegant symbol of the new technology and the new corporate monopoly.

Local mergers characterized the industries whose national production was concentrated in Baltimore, such as canning, can making, and cotton duck, or whose market was confined to Baltimore by peculiarities of transport or distribution, for example, brewing, brickmaking, mass transit, gas, and electricity. Although they paid a tribute to New York or Philadelphia financiers for capital and patents, Baltimoreans were able to retain control of their local monopolies, knowing that Philadelphia or New York producers could not supply Baltimore markets for beer and bricks and gas. Other Baltimore industries, however, competing in national markets, were absorbed into national pools and trusts.

"Baltimore in 1889," a lithograph by Isaac Friedenwald, records the enormous growth of the city and represents the related industrialization with dozens of smoke plumes.

Standard Oil was the model. By thwarting the pipeline to Baltimore in 1877, Rockefeller had succeeded in merging all the independent refineries of Baltimore into the United Oil Company. He and Gould then developed Western Union into a monopoly, and in 1887 bought out the last holdout, the telegraph company of the B&O Railroad. They paid Robert Garrett $5 million in Western Union stock plus a fifty-year rental. As the nationwide mergers accelerated, more Baltimore businesses were absorbed. The moment of truth came in 1898–99. Within the space of two years the industrial base of Baltimore was sold out of town—lock, stock, and barrel.

Baltimore had been a most old-fashioned town in terms of family ownership of industry. It was the last of the city-states of the East. Its diversified manufactures had grown out of local resources, family talent, regional demand, ingrown linkages, and the internal accumulation of capital. Over eighteen months Baltimore was converted, once and for all, into a branch-plant town. American Tobacco bought out both Marburg and Gail & Ax. American Sugar Refining, a national trust, bought a controlling interest in the Baltimore Sugar Refining Company. American Type Founders absorbed all the type foundries, and a New York company (later Nabisco) bought out Mason Bakery, the oldest and largest bakery south of New York City. American Agricultural Chemical Company bought out the eight big fertilizer companies in Baltimore. Matthai, Ingram was sold to a new $30 million corporation, National Enameling and Stamping.[85] McShane and Regester, two of the city's largest foundries, were absorbed by Central Foundry Co., known as the soil pipe trust. The enamel and soil pipe trusts were relatively effective monopolies in their sectors of the economy. Produce merchants from Baltimore, New York, Philadelphia, and Boston organized a tropical fruit combine (United Fruit) with sugar, coconut, and banana plantations.[86] B. N. Baker's Atlantic Transport Line and Baltimore Storage and Lightering Co. were the backbone of J. P. Morgan's international shipping trust, which split the market, dividing European and American ports of call with the major German steamship lines. The Old Bay Line steamers, largest in the regional network, were purchased by the railroads in the Morgan group. Cochran-Oler sold out to the ice trust (Knickerbocker of Maine), Monumental distillery to the whiskey trust (Standard Distilling), Knabe to the American Piano Company, and Keyser's copper refinery to Rockefeller's Anaconda.

What made this swift sellout possible? The roller-coaster business cycle offered a toehold to outside financiers. An enterprise that needed capital urgently to take advantage of the boom economy in the early '80s or early '90s mortgaged its physical assets to New York bankers, chiefly banks associated with J. P. Morgan or John Rockefeller. In the depression years (beginning in 1893), the mortgage holders foreclosed or forced corporate reorganizations favorable to themselves as bondholders. In 1898 a higher tariff lessened foreign competition, but "just in proportion" it increased domestic competition. At that moment the Spanish-American War provided immense market opportunities—the sale of cans, ships, and shipping services to the army and navy, and the purchase of land in Cuba for iron ore, copper ore, sugar cane, and asphalt. The war also generated huge increases in the money supply and commissions on unprecedented war loans. Morgan's syndicate floated the federal war loans. The war boom thus allowed it to capture new enterprises and new sectors of the economy, forming gigantic national monopolies, the so-called industrial trusts. The legal trusts, developed out of the old family law protecting widows and orphans, was yet further developed in this generation. A trust was designed to protect the interests of several parties with different time horizons and risk preferences, that is, different conceptions of the relative values of income this year versus income ten or twenty years in the future. The trust was used to preserve wealth from generation to generation by limiting its dispersion or waste. It could also be used to concentrate control of the wealth of many individuals or corporations in the hands of a few, in particular, to insure control by mortgage or bond holders (financiers) in the management of railroads and industrial corporations. In the industrial trust, stockholders exchanged their stock for trusteeship certificates, leaving control of the corporation in the hands of two or three trustees. Such a trust could be set up to harmonize the management of competing corporations and achieve monopoly in a branch of industry. Again, the model was Rockefeller's Standard Oil trust. Used in this way, the trust was a mechanism of redistribution, designed for the concentration of wealth, both immediately and in the long run.

The formation of nationwide trusts to supply national markets from strategic large-scale plants depended, of course, on cheap, efficient transportation. Investment in railroads—more powerful engines and vast switchyards—made possible the intensification of exchange. The success of John Pendleton Kennedy's idea that Baltimore must extend its lines like the spider now made it possible to integrate the national economy and to rationalize production into

The massive generating plant that powered much of the electric street railway system reflected a complex technology that still coexisted with the watermelon boats of the bay.

larger units. Kennedy had visualized a web by which the whole southeast and midwest would become tributary to Baltimore, but the traffic ran two ways. Some enterprises in Baltimore grew large, like the Sparrows Point steel plant and Bartlett-Hayward. Sparrows Point imported Cuban ore and manufactured a huge floating dry dock for Manila Bay. Bartlett-Hayward began exporting gasholders and sugar processing plants to Montana, Chicago, Cuba, and Venezuela, as well as to cities of the southern United States. Meanwhile, other Baltimore plants were sacrificed: the sugar refinery and McShane's and Regester's foundries were shut down soon after they were absorbed by the trusts. Local ties were loosened or broken as nationwide linkages were tightened and woven together. The Atlantic Transport Line ordered its ships built in Belfast, inside the trust group, instead of in Baltimore. United Fruit had its steamships built in Boston, the old Bay Line in Wilmington. The tin-plate trust, wholly outside Baltimore, succeeded in raising the price of tin plate, thus raising costs to the Baltimore can makers and the Baltimore-based canneries.

Financial centralization was also founded on the financial cohesion of transport. Just as Rockefeller had monopolized oil markets by his grip on railroads and pipelines, the other industrial trusts were also founded on privileged relationships with railroad and steamship lines. The great industrial trusts were all associated with the great railroad groups, aligned principally with either Rockefeller or Morgan. The depression of '93 bankrupted 210 railroads. Reorganizations engineered by Morgan allowed most of them to become solvent and self-directing again by 1899, but they were in new hands, paid higher tribute,

A crippling snowstorm in 1899 prompted men of Fire Company No. 1 to devise a makeshift sled to get through the snow-choked streets.

and worked in closer cooperation with Morgan. In 1898–99 Morgan got control of all of the southern railroad systems, in particular, the Atlantic Coast Line, the Seaboard Air Line Railroad, the Southern, and the Central of Georgia. The tug of war among New York capitalists meant wresting control from Baltimore and other southern financial barons such as Henry Walters, John Cowan, and J. Skelton Williams. These events were followed closely by Baltimore investors, but strictly in dollar-and-cents terms or in individual fortune and prestige. Only one chain of events dealt a blow to their morale as Baltimoreans—the embarrassment of the B&O Railroad. Here Baltimore's men of wealth as a group seemed to sense a loss of identity and self-determination.

Events on the B&O reveal how Baltimore's identity was submerged in the demand for greater capital, the intensified exchange in the whole economy, and the rhythm of financial crisis. The B&O had refinanced in 1875 and 1877 through the house of Morgan. Then, to compete with the Pennsylvania Railroad (closely connected with Rockefeller), the B&O built its lines to New York and Chicago and its tunnels through Baltimore. These projects were gluttonous of capital. A "car trust" and mortgage allowed the company to buy Mogul engines and coal cars to handle the increased traffic of the boom years. But each boom was followed by a depression that cut back railroad revenues, while the interest on the immense loans had to be paid steadily. Like the municipal corporation, the B&O began depending on short-term loans, putting more and more debt-service strain on the operation and cutting down its flexibility for the next crisis. In 1890 the city sold its share in the B&O. So did the state. So did Alexander Brown. The university was constrained by Johns Hopkins's wishes and by Robert Garrett's presence on the board not to sell its B&O stock, but the board was unnerved enough to accumulate a building fund from the income. When the B&O failed to pay any dividends in 1887, 1888, and 1889, the university survived by paying salaries out of the building fund. The panic of 1893 was the last straw. It was precipitated by the failure of the house of Baring in London, who had been bankers to the B&O. The railroad ceased to maintain its tracks and buildings and its efficiency declined, till it mortgaged even its magnificent Central Building at Charles and Baltimore streets. Finally, when a New York bank foreclosed on a loan in February 1896, the New York courts appointed receivers.[87]

The B&O was bankrupt. The reorganization, planned by John Cowan (earlier involved in reorganization of the Seaboard Air Line Railroad), was approved by J. P. Morgan and by Alexander Brown II, who had a large interest in the Belt Line bonds. The receivers generated a miniboom in Baltimore and Cumberland by ordering $12 million worth of labor on track and equipment. Not all of this money was spent in Baltimore: the steel rail was manufactured by the U.S. Steel trust, and the two hundred engines by the locomotive trust, in Philadelphia and Lima, Ohio. Baltimore was no longer in a position to insist on its right to home investment. When the receivership ended (30 June 1899), the capital value of the B&O was restored. In fact, it was magnificently increased. But Baltimore had lost control of it. The new owners were a Chicago group— Armour, identified with Chicago beef; Field, with the Chicago department store; and Hill, with the northwestern railroads. The railroads Baltimore had built to make a region tributary to itself now made Baltimore and its region tributary to Chicago and New York.

The financial roller coaster stirred great changes of mood. Crisis gave way to euphoria. The mood of 1898 was that of a great "bubble." Nationalism and distant excitements fermented in all sections of society. The phosphate owners protested because Navassa Island had been seized by the Haitians. Landowners agitated for a navy yard. The saddle and harness merchants of Baltimore wanted to make the city a port of embarkation. Large and small lenders elbowed each other to buy government bonds. At Grace Methodist Church amid a profusion of flowers four hundred children dressed in white unfurled small flags and waved them high over their heads as they sang, "Then conquer we must."[88] The Colored High School graduates in their dress suits or white gowns and bouquets gave school yells while they waited for the curtain of Ford's Theater to rise:

> Cuba, Cuba, bow, wow, wow!
> Libre, libre, chow, chow, chow!
> Vengeance, vengeance, down with Spain!
> Yankee, Yankee, remember the Maine![89]

The sudden tide in national mood was the climate for the sellout of Baltimore industry. "The owners of great manufacturing establishments were seized with a mania for consolidation as if it were the true and only panacea for the ills under which they imagined themselves to be suffering."

The same national excitement influenced the style of reinvestment. As outside capitalists bought Baltimore industries, they paid off the Baltimore owners or stockholders. This meant a sudden conversion of wealth in Baltimore. The former owners often took as much as two-thirds of the payment in the form of common stock in the new or merged corporation. Their control was diluted in the trust or holding company. For many years Baltimoreans continued to hold large blocks of National Enamel and Stamping, American Agricultural Chemical, and American Tobacco. But they took the other third or two-fifths in cash. These windfalls of cash at the turn of the century had to be invested. Baltimoreans sowed large sums in real estate, and overnight created a new superstructure of local trust companies to invest their ready money. Thirteen trust companies, with capital and surplus of $40 million, were organized in this generation, half of them in a single year (1898/99).[90] Their stock was oversubscribed, and the shares sold at a premium of 50 percent "before even the office furniture had been procured." Through these financial holding companies, as well as directly, Baltimoreans consolidated their local monopolies and invested in similar enterprises in the South—streetcar, gas, and electric companies.[91] The *Manufacturers Record* estimated that Baltimoreans had $100 million invested in the southeastern United States, half accumulated in that magic year. The Baltimore trust companies also favored bonds rather than stocks and saddled their utilities with heavy bonded debt and heavy fixed costs. Mercantile Trust (founded by John Gill and the Hambletons) participated in the B&O car trust, the related South Baltimore Car Works, and later the Baltimore brewery combine. The Realty Trust made loans to the Baltimore Brick Company, the suburban development of Walbrook, and a coal syndicate. Union Trust participated in street railway bonds and the cotton duck mortgage. Founders of Continental Trust, with $2 million capital and $2 million surplus, were the Warfields, Alexander Brown, George Jenkins, and Isidor Rayner. Local trusts like the brewery combine and the cotton duck and brick merger were also speculative: "The common stock was wind and the preferred three-quarters water." Within a year or two they had to be reorganized, "both wind and water being drastically pumped out of them."[92]

The new financial groups naturally invested part of their resources in monuments to finance, designed by the more distinguished church architects. The Mercantile Trust was one of the earliest. Farmers and Merchants National built a five-story brownstone building at South and Lombard streets. Joseph E. Sperry designed the Maryland Life Insurance Company building in South Street (1893), and Baldwin and Pennington the Merchants' National bank at the corner of Water and South streets. Seven stories high, it was in Renaissance style, with the interior of "variegated marbles, all handsomely carved and polished." It featured the ultimate in modern communications, three high-speed passenger elevators "enclosed by ornamental bronze screen work," and a Cutler mail chute. Uptown, the Equitable and the Fidelity trust companies built office buildings and located on high ground close to the new city hall and the courthouse. The buildings of the windfall of 1899 rose even higher, and introduced "fireproof" construction of steel and concrete, such as the Continental Building. Realty Trust built the Belvedere Hotel. George A. Fuller of Chicago built the ten- to twelve-story buildings of Atlantic Trust, Guardian Trust, and the Calvert Building. A massive courthouse was undertaken with immense marble columns.[93]

In spite of the new downtown monuments, in 1899 Baltimoreans looked at the city and felt it had not completed its superstructure. It was "the steeple without the spire." Its old-fashioned skyline and its business streets bound down with electric wire worried its businessmen. The spires and pinnacles of finance were in New York and Chicago.

The Art of Urban Landscape

1900–1918

The whistle and bell of a locomotive mean far more than the undisturbed trill of a singing bird. The rumble of a freight car is prosperity's favorite music. The rush and din of whirling machinery are the melody that thrills a business man's soul. . . . That which produces is of more importance than that which adorns.[1]

There was plenty of rumble, whistle, and bell in Baltimore, in a crescendo from 1900 to 1918. The Pennsylvania Railroad was running four hundred trains a day past Union Station, ten times the number of 1890.[2] In spite of the priorities suggested by Mayor Preston's comment in 1913, Baltimore managed to achieve an exceptional harmony of planning. In no other period was so much done to acquire woodlands where the trill of the bird and the ripple of the run could still be heard. The city made or captured magnificent investments in port and rail facilities. It hired a forester and grew six hundred thousand goldfish in its parks. City projects were a happy mix of adornment and practicality. The sewage pumping station on Pratt Street and the water filtration plant at Montebello were elegant works of municipal architecture. Several blocks of park on St. Paul Street, all marble and floral display, combined efforts at slum clearance and traffic flow. There was a new awareness of the landscape in three dimensions. The tentacles of asphalt conformed to the contours of the land. There was a powerful exploration of all aspects of "the municipal geography." How does one explain the coherent planning? How does one explain the new sensitivity to the natural landscape, and certain blind spots in perceiving the social landscape?

The interlocking of several projects was already evident in Mayor Hayes's thinking early in 1903, when he announced his "Greater Baltimore" strategy. He had just sold the city's stock in the Western Maryland Railroad for $5 million. He intended to use the money to build a sewer system. "Following the construction of the sewers in each street, and as fast as it is completed, will come the improved pavement." Paving and street-opening priorities were sketched already in a plan to make the valleys of the Gwynns Falls and Stony Run into parks, and to connect them and the older parks by parkways. The city and federal governments would complete the thirty-five-foot channel. The well-capitalized buyers of the railroad had agreed to complete its route, develop piers near Ferry Branch, and bring down coal from West Virginia and Cumberland for manufacturing development. "Manufacturing industries are the true source of municipal prosperity."[3]

The mayor's strategy reflected fairly accurately the thinking of the reform government and the national Progressive movement. It also reflected his conception of the municipal government as go-between, brokering investments in the city, ordering and synchronizing a city-building process that had many centers of action and many sources of initiative. The structure of government that had grown up in Baltimore, somewhat streamlined in the reform charter of 1898, favored such a view of the mayoralty. The city still did not possess the home rule powers it desired or the legislative representation it merited on the basis of population. The mayor was further limited by a fragmentation of powers. Agencies such as school board and harbor board had their independence reinforced. Police, elections, and liquor boards were still under state control. The water board and park board were financially independent thanks to privileged revenues from water rents and the streetcar tax. The coordination of municipal energies in this era appears all the more remarkable in such a framework.

The Fire

The agency most rigidly confined in the mayor's fiscal reforms was the fire department, and he was highly pleased with his success at reducing its operating budget over three years. He did not point out that the number of fires had increased and losses reached $400,000 a year. Ironically, it was fire that interfered with his grand plan. The great Baltimore fire of 1904 destroyed the whole of the town laid out in 1730. The $5 million fund became the working capital for a swift reconstruction. But even during this interlude Baltimore did not lose sight of its priorities.

The immediate cause of the Baltimore fire is a much-discussed but meaningless detail. What was decisive for its magnitude was the weather—a weekend of high winds and freezing temperatures, like the terrifying fires of the eighteenth century. A catastrophic fire might even seem predestined, the outcome of that procrastination Thomas Buckler railed against. Since the reorganization of a professional fire department before the Civil War and its equipment with steam engines, there had been little new investment. Since Buckler's time the fire department had pleaded, year after year, for resources and regulatory powers to cope with the new building technology and functions of the downtown area: "We cannot deal with two major fires at the same time." The fire chief observed in the 1880s the construction of bulky close-built warehouses where kerosene, cotton, fertilizer chemicals, and grain were stored side by side, and in the 1890s the garment factories, tall buildings, extensive lumber and coal yards, and tiers of electric wires. Horses were housed in multistory stables, and hay was kept in lofts. There was no regulation of floor loadings, elevators, storage of packing boxes, or wiring.[4]

On Sunday morning, 7 February, fire companies were called from Washington and Philadelphia, but found they could not connect their hoses to city hydrants. Individuals of courage, folly, and loyalty tested themselves against the natural enemy. They carried land and probate records out of the courthouse and plats out of city hall, as the fire lapped at Fayette Street. They flooded store roofs with water. Hundreds stamped out cinders and brands falling on their housetops, prayed at the edge of the falls, and bedded down children on the

The extent of damage of the 1904 fire is shown by this photograph taken the morning after. The shadow in center right is a building that may have fallen as the time exposure photograph was taken. Note the cast-iron columns in the foreground and the steam fire engine in the center.

pavements beyond. The Maryland Trust building, the Continental Trust, the Union Trust, the Atlantic Trust and Guardian Trust, the Calvert Building, the Equitable, all the "fireproof" symbols of finance and power, burned like torches. A number of lower buildings, apparently caught in pockets of lesser draft, survived—the Alexander Brown firm, the Mercantile Bank building, the Safe Deposit and Trust Company. An ice warehouse produced rainbows as it burned.

Over a 140-acre district, 1545 buildings were destroyed. Poles stood in the rubble staking out the streets. The burnt district corresponded roughly to the original 60 acres of Baltimore Town, plus its eastern filled-in margins to the falls. The city immediately launched a relief committee, but there were no deaths, few injuries, and few homeless. The district had become so fully commercial that the personal problems were chiefly those of small business owners. Hundreds lost equipment and inventory. The merchants and bankers had to wait till the safes cooled, so that their bills and contracts wouldn't char instantly when opened.

The reconstruction problem underscores the fundamental importance to the brick-and-mortar city of a legal and financial substructure. The problem of municipal government was to "find" the property lines, to "locate" the street levels, to reconstruct and mark on the landscape those visible tokens of mine

The fire-proof station was one of the buildings left intact after the devastating 1904 fire.

and thine. Plats were made of each block, the lines surveyed and marked on the ground with copper bolts five feet from the building line. The surveyors were literally blazing roads and staking claims in a new wilderness. In July ten thousand were at work removing debris.

Meanwhile, private individuals and corporations went after insurance claims and mortgage money to finance the rebuilding of the private spaces. The financial operation is difficult to evaluate. Twenty-nine million dollars in insurance claims was paid. The situation differed sharply from the 1790s and 1820s, when virtually all of the insurance was paid locally. The integration of Baltimore into the national economy meant that the risk had been spread nationwide. Fourteen hundred brick buildings assessed at $13 million before the fire were replaced by eight hundred buildings assessed at $25 million—about double. Assessments are generally an understatement, but an updating process might account for a large part of the difference. The city government acquired ten acres of additional street space and twenty-eight acres of docks and markets, and spent over $7 million on public improvements, rebuilding streets and docks. It took in $1.1 million from 2200 fronting property owners for the benefits of these improvements.[5] Land valuation was believed increased by 50 percent. The fire created a capital crisis for numerous central enterprises. United Railways, already hampered by a 45 percent burden of interest since the consolidation deal, needed to borrow huge sums for downtown reconstruction and new rolling stock. A "car trust" was created that issued $8 million bonds to buy equipment they would lease to United Railways. This mode of financing, modeled on the B&O, has since extended to ships, airplanes, and fleets of trucks and cars. It allowed modernization, but at the price of overextension of credit and greater vulnerability in subsequent financial crises.

Inevitably a prompt response to the great fire was a good deal of fire prevention. The numbers of fire fighters and horses were increased 50 percent. Alarm boxes and hydrants were installed to cover the larger urban territory being developed. A high-pressure water service was brought into operation over seventy acres. The fire insurance business increased dramatically, and recognition of the risk of fire gave a powerful impetus to the adoption of a building code. Even then, it required seventeen nights of hearings and several reviews in council. United Railways, stung by another serious fire in 1906, which demolished the Waverly car barn and fifty cars, built a series of seven steel and concrete carhouses that proved nearly indestructible. The school commissioners began bracing themselves for the idea that it would cost 25 to 30 percent more to build "fireproof" schools. On the west side of Baltimore, the garment factories and department stores still punctuated the skyline with reminders—an ominous rooftop forest of wooden water tanks.

Physically the city was rebuilt much as it was before. As one can see from "before" and "after" skylines, or the bird's-eye views of 1889 and 1911, the changes were discreet. The steel-frame skyscrapers were rebuilt. The major changes in plat were the widening of Pratt and Light streets bordering the inner harbor. The important resculpturing was the cutting down of St. Paul Street between Baltimore and Lexington and a paring off of Fayette Street by five feet to correspond. Private firms tended to rebuild their business houses on the same sites or to enlarge their sites by throwing together two or three lots. Over half the new buildings were three and four stories high. Both public and private acquisition programs encountered enormous legal obstacles in attempting to clear land titles, because of the old irredeemable ground rents dispersed among many heirs and trustees.

The new buildings aspired to a solid and imposing style, and the new downtown had an ordered appearance, modern and comfortable, but overstuffed. In what is now Charles Center, the core of new buildings created after the fire illustrates a tightening of the web of financial power. On the southeast corner of Lexington and Liberty streets, the newly consolidated gas and electric company built its twenty-story million-dollar landmark, with eight high-speed elevators and showrooms for new appliances. On the four corners where Baltimore Street crosses Charles Street were the *Sun* building, the B&O building, the marble Savings Bank of Baltimore, and the Hub department store. At Light and German streets the C&P Telephone Company built its ten-story headquarters. In the rebuilt Continental Trust Building were the offices of United Railways.

The men who preserved the continuity and interlocking of enterprise in Baltimore in this generation were Alexander Brown II and S. Davies Warfield. Brown was a leading stockholder and broker for Consolidated Gas and United Electric, and a principal bond holder in the Belt Railway Company. He was the fourth generation to preserve the interlocking of his banking house, the board of the B&O, and the Savings Bank of Baltimore. Brown and the Jenkins family owned the largest shares of United Railways, and J. E. Aldred held "the balance of power" between them. Warfield had built Continental Trust and created a holding company of telephone and telegraph. With the Jenkins and Black families, Warfield held local shares of the Consolidated Coal Company. Together, Brown and Warfield engineered the consolidation of United Railways (1899)[6] and the union of gas and electric companies (1906). The investment of the Savings Bank of Baltimore in the consolidated enterprise rose to $500 million. The personal fortunes of Brown and Warfield were thus founded upon consolidating and solidifying those natural monopolies Ely had described twenty years before. But they felt the hemming in of Baltimore's political economy. As Baltimore industries were absorbed into the nationwide trusts, all that remained as a power base for the business elite of Baltimore was their local monopoly of land, improvements, and utilities, the physical core of a disarmed city-state.

Once reconstruction was under way, the city could get back to its unfinished business—the sewers. If Baltimore was the nation's last city of its size to have proper sewers, it would be the most modern, scientific, and creative in its engineering. Intellectually as well as physically, the operation tied into everything that was done in Baltimore in this generation. As proposed in 1880, and as proposed again with more elaboration in 1893, it was to be a dual system—two complete and independent systems of storm sewers and sanitary sewers. The sanitary (or rather, unsanitary) wastes would be conducted to a treatment plant on Back River (out Eastern Avenue). Its massive stone trickling filters are still

A Work of Art

in use today. The sludge would be dumped into Chesapeake Bay off Moore's Island.

The new sewerage commission made up for lost time. A small pilot plant was built at Walbrook in 1906; in 1909 the full-size Back River plant was functioning and the mayor and city council drove ceremonially through the interceptor sewer in the city's tiny fleet of automobiles.[7] By the end of 1914 there were twenty-one thousand houses connected, and about that many drop privies were abandoned. There were a like number of washbowls and bathtubs, and twice that many water closets and sinks. Sewering made possible a rapid transformation of urban environments, in particular, the alleys. It put an end to

Edward W. Spofford's bird's-eye view of Baltimore in 1911 showed the city as it was rebuilt after the 1904 fire but before construction of the Fallsway.

board fences, to bluing and laundry drainage in the alleys. It ended the incredible build-up of ice in alleys, sidewalks, and streets during cold snaps. In the severe winter of 1903/4, for example, cold weather had lasted for a hundred days. Where large amounts of water were used, as in the case of church organ motors, cellar drainers, and beer pumps, ice built up daily four to five feet thick. When ice and snow made the alleys impassable for horses, garbage and trash piled up, amounting to as much as 200 cartloads in a block.[8] As these nuisances were eliminated, over the next ten years the women's clubs led a movement to pave the alleys, cover the garbage cans, and attack flies and mosquitoes.

There were other less obvious effects of the sewer work. The technical

This is Light Street in 1910 after the completion of an early widening. The view is south from Pratt Street. The site approximates the location of Harborplace, a redevelopment begun in the late 1970s.

demands of building sewers made them a privileged element of the municipal geography. The sanitary sewers had to be essentially one system, watertight. Every dwelling was supposed to be connected. The sewers had to operate as far as possible by gravity flow. A pumping station on Pratt Street forced the drainage of the low-lying land around the inner harbor. (Only small outlying and low-lying areas were neglected.) They were to run under public property, in alleys where possible. In a lyric moment, the engineer described the layout as a tree: "the Disposal Plant being the roots, the Outfall Sewer the trunk, the large intercepting sewers throughout the City the branches, small laterals the twigs, the houses the leaves, and the people the birds in the trees."[9]

The demands for storm sewers were less rigorous, and the natural stream valleys functioned as trunk lines—the Gwynns Falls, the Jones Falls, and Herring Run. The thirty miles of old sewers and some privately built drains were incorporated into the storm drainage, and the old built-over streams were "tunneled" with concrete arches or conduits.

In the burnt district and surrounding downtown, the combined effort of rebuilding the streets, sewering, and laying a high-pressure water system and electrical conduits meant total reorganization of the underground. Water and gas mains were often relocated: because they operated under pressure, they could be threaded through greater variations of grade and curvature. The sewer engineers prepared block by block, as they dug, an underground map of the city. The water department replaced all its six-inch mains with mains ranging from ten inches in diameter up to forty inches in Lombard Street. One hundred and fifty miles of new gas mains were laid, of sizes up to forty-eight inches in diameter, and steam pipes were extended through the business district. The entire city was turned into a construction site. In 1904 the city engineer issued eight thousand permits to dig in the streets to lay pipes, tracks, mains, and poles. In 1914, eight hundred blocks were still "open" and two thousand people were at work on the sewers.

With its electric power lines Baltimore was linked electrically and financially. The fire alarm telegraph ran over the rooftops to the new city hall in 1876. In 1895 the city was bound down "Gulliver-like" with electric wires. Here in 1911 the Harford Avenue powerhouse was part of the United Railways system.

The epitome of the three-dimensional multichannel street was the Fallsway. The mayor, the Municipal Art Society, and the sewer engineer (Calvin Hendricks) began promoting the idea in the summer of 1906. The Jones Falls was canalized in a cement channel or storm sewer, and a road was built on top of it. The "Fallsway" or "tradeway" would take advantage of nature's only graded route for new road transport efficiency, and would add elegance in its proportions and details. The double-decker drainage and transport would lace together the harbor and the Union Station. Woven into this project were the long-nursed memories of the Jones Falls in flood and drought, the long-frustrated schemes for thoroughfares, brought to a focus by debates over the burnt district, the perennial appeals for system-conscious street grading, and the irrepressible idea of a "union" station for the several passenger railroads. Voters approved a loan in 1911. The Jones Falls conduits were ready, and the Fallsway could be built immediately. It was raised on a viaduct, allowing railway tracks to pass under it, and numerous streets that had formerly bridged the Jones Falls joined the Fallsway at grade. But the plans for a union station and an extension of Howard Street once again foundered on the rivalries of the railroads. The B&O was satisfied with its handsome Mount Royal Station uptown and its downtown Camden Station. The Pennsylvania Railroad rebuilt adjacent to its old site in 1912.

The sewer project forced new planning concepts into every part of the municipal territory. The essential engineering prerequisite was the topographical survey. To make water or sewage run downhill, one has to know where the hills are. The long postponement of topographical mapping (notably in 1816 and 1876) had created a thirst for this kind of information. Each street opening, railroad scheme, water or park development, and private subdivision entailed a "survey." The demand of all municipal agencies for maps and surveys placed the Topographical Survey Commission in a key position in municipal administration despite its limited budget for direct spending. Under two successive engineers of imagination, Colonel H. T. Douglas and Major Joseph Shirley, the survey became the broker of ideas, a comprehensive planning agency able to relate all manner of public and private projects.[10] Their conception of the municipal geography as a circulation in three dimensions led them to relate the various interests of a neighborhood, to relate a particular neighborhood to the whole organism, and to formulate priorities and sequences of projects. Out of the Topographical Survey grew the annex street plan, a street paving commission, a factory site commission, and finally a commission on city plan. Although actions were simultaneous on both fronts, one can sort out the development strategies into the two distinctive topographical regions—piedmont and tidewater.

Developing the Piedmont

"Digesting" the annex of 1888 was the planning preoccupation for the piedmont landscape of rolling country, steep valleys, and graveled plateaus. A street plan for the annex was prepared by the Topographical Survey and enacted into law in 1898. It was still the conventional grid, piecing together past development. In 1902 the survey began requiring developers to submit plats of proposed subdivisions, which until then had been "entirely isolated, having no interconnections, and devoid of any element allowing a check on their accuracy." The survey's next target was the creation of an overall street-grading plan. The logic of street grading and interconnection of subdivisions gradually forced reconsideration of the 1898 plan. By 1908 the survey recommended significant departures and proposed a set of priorities in openings and pavings. It sent forward lists of "grade establishments" consistent with these priorities, as common sense had pleaded a hundred years before.

The logic of street grading in a piedmont landscape forced the abandonment of the "unsightly gridiron method"[11] and the substitution of a kind of urban contour plowing. The city had already adopted a policy of expensive "permanent" bridges rather than timber trestle. These structures meant long-run economy of maintenance, but a high capital investment. Street extension implied the extension of all the new understreet utilities. Consequently, the two great valleys were crossed only at a few strategic points: the Gwynns Falls by Edmondson Avenue, Baltimore Street, and Wilkens Avenue, and Stony Run by Huntingdon Avenue and University Parkway (Merryman's Lane).

Meanwhile, the Olmsted plan fostered a new reading of the landscape. The Municipal Art Society fostered in Baltimore the Progressive nationwide city-planning movement. Carrere & Hastings were invited to submit plans for a plaza, through routes, and traffic circles, and the Olmsted Brothers, consultants at Roland Park, were invited to make a plan for municipal parks and parkways to develop the annex. The Baltimore park commissioners had already introduced romantic European ideas into aristocratic Druid Hill Park and Clifton Park— winding carriage drives and walkways conforming to the topography, alternations of groves and lawns, vistas and copses, cascades and still waters, in a maze of movement offering the inhibited city dweller a sense of freedom and spaciousness. But the application of such ideas to the scale of the annex offered a new perception of overall urban development that changed Baltimore's vision forever. Olmsted Brothers envisioned all the stream valleys—Gwynns Falls, the Jones Falls, Herring Run, and the Patapsco—as parkland, each with its distinctive relief and its unique forest, meadow, or boulder landscape. These and the older parks would be connected by parkways or landscaped drives through the smaller stream valleys, for example, Ellicott Driveway, Hilton Street, Stony Run Parkway, and Wyman Park Drive. The new parkways were instantly recognizable by their landscaping: Thirty-third Street, Gwynns Falls Parkway, the Alameda. Some had separated drives at different levels, such as University Parkway and Druid Park Drive, which "diverge and converge with the contour of the ground."

One of the monuments to civic pride was the 1909 sewage pumping station on Eastern Avenue at the mouth of the Jones Falls. Its design included a brass-railed, multifloored central gallery and massive coal-fired, steam-driven pumps.

The entire urban landscape of the piedmont would become a park—a labyrinth of drives and walks, a harmony of man and nature.[12]

While the 1851 Boundary Avenue Plan was also a scheme for developing a periphery, combining carriage drive and greenspace, a radical change of perspective had occurred. First, the Olmsted plan of 1903 is all curves. It abhors the straight line, a change apparent in all street making. Second, where the boundary commissioners were enamored of the long vistas and high places dear to chapel builders and the owners of country seats, Olmsted turned the landscape of values inside out, admiring, photographing, and beautifying the streams and valley floors, the vales and glens. For example, to protect the view of the Gwynns Falls meadowland, he recommended relocating the Western Maryland Railroad line and rebuilding the Edmondson Avenue bridge. Third, where the Boundary Avenue Plan was tied to an artificial and short-lived political boundary, Olmsted's idea, rooted in the piedmont landscape, cut across political boundaries. It would be extended to the 1918 annex and ultimately to the six-county metropolitan region.

Most of the parkways were developmental street openings, that is, they prepared new territory for private residential construction and were, therefore, self-financing. This strategy reinforced the power of the Topographical Survey as an intellectual or planning arm of the city. The romantic view of the landscape and the "country life" movement appealed to a community that had always looked back upon the life of the country gentleman with nostalgia.[13] Masses of people, unable to aspire to servants and trout streams, were nevertheless attracted by countrified environments with city conveniences. In the spring of 1913, the *Sun* featured the Herring Run Valley near Harford Road as "nature's respite." A walking tour, although "not an American exercise," offered "a strenuous and thrilling adventure, over huge boulders, along angled pathways, up and down steep banks." The walker would find swimming holes, mossy rocks, arched passageways, and "the coolth and hum of the breeze."[14] Three years later, Frank Novak had four hundred or five hundred semidetached houses under construction in this section.[15]

By cooperation between the Topographical Survey and the new State Roads Commission (Shirley assured the link), the old turnpikes were redeveloped— Reisterstown Road, Washington Boulevard, and Harford Road. Differences of philosophy and planning horizon in the several rings explain present variations

256

Sewers were added to an already built-up city at enormous expense, effort, and engineering skill. Officials often formally toured the sewers before completion of the system.

of standards of width, grade, and development along these routes. Park Heights Avenue had been laid out as a development axis by the county (1874), and the city now created Park Circle as a connecting point.

The radial routes and radial stream valley parks structured the development of the annex along a system of wedges like pieces of pie, a pattern that was later extended into the region beyond. As estates changed hands and tracts were subdivided, the social differentiation of the wedges was confirmed. A series of strategic operations defined for several generations to come the boundaries of a Jewish wedge west of Falls Road. The Roland Park Company and the Baltimore Country Club controlled the land on the east and practiced rigorous exclusion. On the west, the Suburban Club of the Jewish elite was located at Park Heights and Slade avenues. Mayor Preston sold his country home, the Colonies, near Pikesville to Mrs. William Levy. The Friedenwalds had a twelve-hundred-acre estate near Glyndon.

Property transfers occurred within a framework of the social order. The piedmont locus of the elite, together with the new romantic view of the piedmont landscape, matched a social regulation. Instant indignation forced the steel company to resell the Cockeys's land in the Worthington Valley, where they had hoped to take limestone for steel making, and the usually arrogant Pennsylvania Railroad backed away quickly from a plan to build a "cut-off" line around Baltimore, cutting across the valleys, through the green wedges and country gentlemen's backyards.[16]

The most elaborate weaving together of institutions occurred in the northern wedge. The development axis of Charles Street was planted with lindens and carried to the new city line. Connecting routes were opened to the parks (Thirty-third Street and Twenty-fifth Street), and a paving program knitted over the land of the Peabody Heights Company toward Waverly and Guilford. Meanwhile, the Maryland and Pennsylvania narrow-gauge railroad was built through Stony Run valley, The Johns Hopkins University campus was laid out at Homewood, and the Gilman School was organized in the Homewood mansion. The Olmsteds' role as consultant for the development of Hopkins campus, Wyman Park, and Roland Park harmonized these physical plans. It is indicative of the close connection among the parties who generated the green wedge. When the boundary line between Wyman Park and Hopkins campus was negotiated and surveyed, each tree was mapped and protected, Wyman Park Drive was engineered, and a full-dress debate was staged over the esthetics of the stone bridge that would carry University Parkway across Stony Run. The Guilford Company, a subsidiary of the Roland Park Company, was permitted to modify the street plan on the 1400-acre Abell estate to a "series of reverse curves." It began home building in 1913 with Chancery Square: "twin houses" grouped around a private park, built in an exotic style with a brick first story and half-timber with stucco above. In Homewood the company built a dozen three-story dwellings at $4000 each, and continued to add tracts to its property along the northern edge of the city.

Among those who took up residence in the green wedge of Guilford and Roland Park were many leaders of the Progressive movement and the Municipal Art Society. Roland Park had 250 homes in 1904 and nearly 500 in 1910. The residents tended to belong to the Baltimore Country Club on Falls Road, and they insured the full integration of the wedge. They worked in its old center near South Street and the courthouse square, they belonged to the clubs near Mount Vernon Place, and they supported the institutions in the new connecting districts: the Woman's College, Sts. Philip and James Church, the university, the Episcopal cathedral, and University Baptist Church. They began to buy cars, and to combine into one suburban life style the dual advantages of the traditional "townhouse" and "country house."

Only for the rich and only in the green wedge were apartment houses built. They cost more per unit than ten-room homes, $5000 to $10,000 each, and commanded views of the new parks and access by the new parkways. The apartment-house districts of the city were fixed for several generations. Among the largest was the Marlborough, facing the Eutaw squares. A ten-story apartment was built at Charles and Reed streets. Smaller ones were clustered in Homewood or Peabody Heights; for instance, architect John Forsythe's building at Calvert and Thirtieth streets, where each of the twelve apartments had a jewel safe and a servant's room in the basement. Smaller ones clustered along Druid Lake Drive, Linden, and Eutaw Place at the entrances to Druid Hill Park. The most impressive was the eight-story Emerson Italian Gardens designed by J. E. Sperry. Each of the twenty-eight units had four bedrooms, three baths, three large living rooms (15 by 20 feet), a suite of two rooms and bath for two maids, a walk-in linen room, five porches, and a kitchen balcony. The design was intended to reproduce a vertical image of the suburban home, so it had a "vertical street" with front entrances, porches, and flower boxes, and a "vertical alley," that is, a freight elevator, for servants' entrance, deliveries, and garbage collection. There was a spiral fire escape: "You run, seat yourself inside it, and slide to the ground floor."[17] Its eccentric developer, Captain E. E. Emerson, illustrates the mix of balanced real estate investments, and his creations cover the mix of conveniences and pretensions of his time. In addition to the Bromo-Seltzer Tower, 290 feet tall with a 61-foot blue bottle revolving on top, and the Emerson Italian Gardens, he built the Emerson hotel with five hundred rooms, at

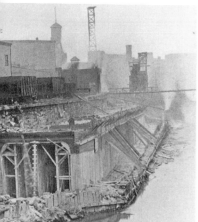

The Jones Falls was finally confined in 1912. Floods such as the one shown here were controlled through a system of conduits. Coffer dams were used during the construction, which employed the most modern equipment and techniques. Ultimately the Falls was buried, the Fallsway developed, and the Fallsway Viaduct constructed over the railyards.

Calvert and Baltimore streets. He bought a glass factory to supply blue bottles, and to supply the hotel with milk and eggs he converted Brooklandwood, his Green Spring Valley estate, into a model dairy and an attraction for the Sunday drive. All worked together to enhance the suburban idyll.

In spite of the effort to conform to the topography, development of the annex demanded large investments and provoked debate over taxation. Although the special tax privilege of the annex was scheduled to cease in 1900, it took nine years more of debate and litigation before the pill was swallowed. The principles that determined the tax status of various properties as "urban," "suburban," or "rural" were density and streeting—that is, the development of at least six houses on a block and the bounding of the block by "improved" streets, properly paved and curbed. Some developers, such as the Park Land and Improvement Company in Mount Royal Avenue, had retained "private" streets to keep the taxes low. The city's street opening priorities were therefore influenced by the need to complete blocks in the annex and insure their transfer to the higher tax rates. Except for the burnt district, most of the growth of municipal revenues in this era came from the reclassification and development of the annex. Once the tax principles were firmly established and development was proceeding at a rapid pace, the matter suddenly ceased to be an issue, and city delegates began submitting bills for a new annexation.

Development on Tidewater

"A man is as old as his arteries," argued the *Municipal Journal*, summarizing the strategy for "rejuvenating" Baltimore.[18] More important than streets as the arteries of the tidewater landscape were ship channels, railroads, pipelines, and power lines. Keeping the arteries healthy demanded coordination among corporate interests—the rival railroads, utility companies, and land developers. Here again, city government functioned as negotiator and broker. The low-relief landscape of tidewater was malleable, a matter of dredging here and filling there. Instead of conforming the streets to the landscape, as in the piedmont hills and valleys, the engineers rearranged the landscape, creating the typical cogged edge of the harbor, with its fans of rail spurs, its long pier warehouses, and its slips angled into the river. The amount of dirt moved in this generation, from 1900 to 1918, was much greater than what Buckler had proposed to move by shoveling Federal Hill into the inner harbor.[19] The federal government invested

$3.3 million. River and harbor investment was its chief input to public works and urban competition. In 1905 it developed the 35-foot channel 500 feet wide from the Lazaretto Light down the bay to the Atlantic. It also dredged the Quarantine anchorage, a parking lot for deep-draft ships. The city invested $16 million for local access to the new channel. In 1901 only the Canton docks and the B&O wharves at Locust Point were served by deep channels (27 to 30 feet), but by 1911 there was deep draft access to the rebuilt inner harbor docks, the old city block, and the south side of Locust Point as well.

A yet more expensive, technically impressive, and remote channel, the Panama Canal, was also perceived as part of Baltimore's new highway of opportunity. "DO MILLIONS AWAIT US?" ran the front page headline: "each wide-awake American port will endeavour to reap as much benefit for itself as possible."[20] The *Sun* advocated a new steamship line to west coast South America, and offered a lesson in the new geography: Baltimore was two thousand nautical miles from the canal, forty-five hundred miles from Valparaiso, and fifty-four hundred miles from Buenos Aires. From these points the Trans-Andean railroads were being built inland to tap areas of South America rich in rubber, tin, and copper. Baltimore already had its railroads into the heartland and the coal land of North America. Since freight would seek "the shortest rail haul and the longest water route," Baltimore was ideally situated.[21]

The threading of new arteries in tidewater Baltimore provides an accurate image of the metabolism of its political economy: coal, steel, gas, and electric power. The industrial revolution was only now stamped into the landscape, visible in the great mountains of coal outside the new electric generating plant at Westport and outside the gas plant at Spring Garden, whose new gasholder was big enough to hold the seven largest downtown buildings. A two-foot-diameter gas pipeline was run twelve miles across Bear Creek. Barges plied the harbor, loaded with coal, and car floats ferried railroad cars across Curtis Bay. The three major railroads all built coal piers and bought several thousand coal hopper cars. The rim of the harbor was studded with coal yards. Production of western Maryland coal peaked in 1907 at 7 million tons a year. Maryland coal provided more heat for the ton than other grades of bituminous coal, so that it was shipped longer distances and came more nearly into competition with anthracite. The U.S. Navy preferred Georges Greek coal and purchased it to fuel Admiral Dewey's fleet at Manila Bay and the new classes of dreadnoughts. It was sold in Canada in competition with Nova Scotia coal, and shipped to the river Plate. This was the clue to the new geographical meaning of Baltimore's location in the world economy: six thousand miners dug Appalachian coal at an elevation of 2000 feet above sea level, while world trade in coal took place at sea level. The link, of course, was the railroad. The rail haul was a much larger item in the cost of coal to the consumer than mining the coal or moving it on the ocean. This was, therefore, the period of peak development of Maryland railroads, their greatest demand for acreage in the city, and their maximum contribution of noise and smoke.

Major components of Baltimore's coal-hauling system changed hands but the New York financiers were still following the basic Garrett strategy: the joint

This Spring Garden gasholder was under construction in 1912. Built by Bartlett-Hayward, it was 222 feet high, 219 feet in diameter, and 6 million cubic feet in capacity.

capture of coal land and railroad right of way. Federal antitrust actions from time to time signaled a reshuffle. The Chicago financial group resold the B&O to the Kuhn-Loeb banking group who owned the Pennsylvania Railroad. Baltimoreans shuddered again at this threat to competition. The state sold its stock in the B&O Washington branch. In 1906, in the face of an investigation, the B&O sold off the Consolidation Coal Company. Who bought? The Rockefeller interests, who had meanwhile acquired control of the Western Maryland Railroad from the Gould group to whom the city had sold it. The Rockefellers bought the Wheeling and Lake Erie Railroad as part of the same grand coal-mining plan. Just as Rockefeller replaced Johns Hopkins and John Garrett in railroad and banking control, his largesse displaced local philanthropy. The Rockefeller Foundation created The Johns Hopkins School of Hygiene and Public Health, endowed the medical school, compensated the university for losses in the fire, and sent a Baltimore builder to Peking and Shanghai to build hospitals on the Johns Hopkins model. In 1909 the Pennsylvania, faced with an antitrust hearing, sold off the B&O to the Union Pacific Railroad. "B&O presidents are made and un-made in New York." The combinations and recombinations generated pressures to keep coal miners' wages down, increase their productivity somewhat, raise the freight rates on coal substantially, and raise the price of coal at tidewater.[22]

Looking at tidewater coal users, one can see other dimensions of the network. Production of electricity soared between 1900 and 1914. This growth sector depended on coal. United Railways phased out its powerhouse and purchased its power from the electric company. Another top customer was the electrolytic copper refinery of American Smelting and Refining, the world's largest, solidly in the hands of the Rockefeller interests by 1907. The copper industry was doubly linked with the electric industry: not only did the copper refinery buy lots of electricity, but the copper it produced was used largely to provide copper wire for distributing electricity. In other words, the copper industry had both "backward" and "forward" linkages with the electrical industry. The entire complex of gas, steel, copper, coal, electricity, and streetcars was woven together by these cross products, so that each fed on and nourished the growth of the other.

In 1914 a power crane and steam engine were used for the construction of a power plant.

The Maryland Steel Company, owned by Pennsylvania Steel, which was in turn owned by the Pennsylvania Railroad, was expanding steadily. As its Cuban ores began arriving (1906), the company went into integrated steel making at Sparrows Point. The demand of the steel company and United Railways for electricity grew steadily and justified the introduction of hydroelectric power in 1915. The Holtwood Dam on the Susquehanna was one of the earliest large low-head dams of its type, and the power line led directly to a Highlandtown sub-station that integrated the steel company power plant and Consolidated's metropolitan system. To fuel the new furnaces, the steel company built rows of beehive coke ovens. The by-products of making steel and coke reinforced the industrial network. By-product tar and slag supplied roofing materials for the building boom and smooth-paving materials for street making. Demand for these materials tripled. In 1913 the steel company again made a $3 million investment, extended its beehives, and contracted to sell coke oven by-products to the Koppers Company to recover benzol. By-product methane was piped from Sparrows Point to the Consolidated Gas Company works at Canton. By World War I, the steel company was supplying half to two-thirds of the gas that the gas company in turn distributed to the rest of the city. This helps explain why Baltimore politicians resisted several successive schemes for bringing in natural gas. The triangular trade in gas, electricity, and steel also gave more meaning to the consolidation of gas and electric monopolies into a single corporation.

The Consolidated Gas and Electric Company sponsored new enterprises to stimulate demand for its products. It displayed, sold, and financed gas appliances, electric fixtures, and home wiring. It introduced cheap rates for large users, and began publishing a pictorial magazine to highlight uses and users of gas and electricity. The company's backers—Aldred, Griswold, Brown, and the Jenkinses —participated in the Baltimore Gas Appliance Company, which made gas stoves and water heaters. Gas Appliance in turn helped organize the Baltimore Tube Company and the Baltimore Enamel Company. Drawn brass and copper seamless tubing were used for gas fixtures and water heaters. The enamel company used gas in its new techniques of baking enamel finishes on kitchen ranges and water heaters. The gas company bought its ever larger gasholders from Bartlett-Hayward, which was also its largest customer for gas.

Geographically, the coal metabolism and the triangular trade of gas, electricity, and steel defined a potential in Baltimore that would be developed rapidly in World War I. In the local landscape, it confirmed the industrial vocation of tidewater Baltimore, fixing the pattern for seventy-five years. Industrialists, developers, utilities, and the municipal government collaborated to connect the entire waterfront by railroads, to give value to new industrial sites, and to make easy the transfer of intermediate goods—coal, steel, gas, acids, slag —between industries. They looked forward to developing both sides of the whole magnificent Patapsco River.

On the north shore, the Canton Company extended development to the tip of lower Canton, where it built a modern pier warehouse—six stories high, "fireproof," with loading bays at all levels to load directly from ships on either side. The Pennsylvania Railroad purchased a half-million-dollar site for a terminal and yards in Canton. The Canton Company built a thirty-two mile terminal railroad to connect the three trunk lines (B&O, PRR, and Western Maryland). It also built specialized bulk-shipping facilities—ore pier, sulphur bins, and nitrate shed—and began unloading foreign ores for Pittsburgh. It organized subsidiaries to provide stevedoring and warehousing. The Canton company sold sites for industrial expansion to Electrolytic Zinc, American Agricultural Chemical, and Standard Oil. Most important was Friedenwald's Crown Cork & Seal, on a backland site close to the Highlandtown and Canton labor force and convenient to the rebuilt packing houses and can makers on the Boston Street waterfront. American Can Company remained very strong, despite antitrust suits. As Judge Rose said, he couldn't set things back to where they were in 1901; "I am reluctant to destroy so finely tuned an industrial machine."[23] The hundreds of new jobs stimulated residential building. A thousand houses were put up in Canton in the years 1914–16. The company seized every opportunity: it sold twenty acres to the city for parkland to extend Patterson Park, while selling off its own Canton Park to row-house developers for five hundred homes. It deeded free to the city a right of way for the outfall sewer, but was allowed to lay a road on top, and was given a construction contract for the sewage disposal plant.

To the south, the city was limited by its boundaries to a field of action along the undeveloped south rim of Locust Point, between Fort McHenry and Ferry Bar. When the city sold the Western Maryland Railroad, the negotiations insured development of a tidewater terminal, Port Covington, in this vicinity. The railroad ran a drawbridge across Spring Garden, built a huge grain elevator, an open pier, and a two-million-gallon treacle tank. Baltimore's $16 million port loan was a boon to the railroad, and by 1914 the city was already planning a next step, the development of municipal piers along McComas Street east of Port Covington, or on the Patapsco mudflats opposite.

Beyond the city limits, development was modest. At Curtis Bay the B&O, secure in its monopoly of access, built a $1.5 million mammoth coal pier that would operate by gravity flow and electric controls. The old-fashioned timber pier was replaced with reinforced concrete, the first on such a scale. Davison Chemical built the first sulfuric acid factory of concrete and steel (1909–15). It

The scale of the power plants
is reflected in the Westport
plant fire room.

used three thousand tons of lead to line its tanks. (Acid plants were formerly
built of timber, and were perennially rebuilt.) Davison subsidiaries shipped
phosphate rock to Curtis Bay, and other subsidiaries adjoining the acid plant
manufactured complete fertilizers. Baltimore remained the fertilizer capital of
the nation.

Otherwise, the southern perimeter of the harbor remained a mere alley
gate to Baltimore. Traffic under the Light Street drawbridge was large, but it
was mostly mud, dirt, ice, manure, and garbage. Of lesser volume were coal,
oil, hay, fertilizer, building sand, and brick. These low-grade materials were,
however, the stuff of city building and offered opportunities for political enterprise. An informal web of such alliances gave coherence to municipal activity
in this generation, despite apparent fragmentation and changes of administration.
In the planning of Baltimore the alley-gate entrepreneurs were as essential as the
creative engineering imaginations—Olmsted, Shirley, Hendricks, etc.—and the
financial elite—Brown, Griswold, Aldred, and Warfield. The alley-gate entrepreneurs managed to bring into collaboration imagination and power, and to
harmonize a thousand venal interests, great and petty, national and parochial.
Of them all, the most remarkable was Frank Furst. After retiring from a career
of forty-five years at the Northern Central grain elevators, Furst launched into
political entrepreneurship based on manipulation of the tidewater landscape. His
power as political broker in Baltimore rested in large measure on the political
muscle of South Baltimore. The working-class coastal plain districts had been
neglected as residential neighborhoods: drainage problems were hard to solve
on low ground, and the railroads had created irritating bottlenecks to street
traffic. By 1909 the public "clamored justly for relief." Collaboration between
working-class voters and manufacturers made South Baltimore the strongest
component of a neighborhood improvement movement and a citywide congress
of neighborhoods.[24] A plan was made to remove the garbage reduction plant and
create several new parks in South Baltimore. Isham Randolph was brought from
Chicago to reconcile the B&O and the South Baltimore populace with respect

to grade-crossing elimination. Another "arterial" element of the plan was Key Highway. Like the Fallsway, it would be an easy-grade route suitable for industrial hauling. Onto it was grafted a municipal belt railway that, like the Canton Railroad, would connect the B&O, the Western Maryland, and the docks all the way around the Locust Point peninsula.[25]

Furst built an economic base from the interface of political monopoly and city-building enterprises: dredging, sand, gravel, ballast, and real estate. About 1910 he merged his half-dozen firms into the Arundel Corporation, which held land along the tidewater rim, exploited the sand and gravel deposits, and in the Maryland tradition used its dredging spoils to "make" more land for industrial sites. By 1917 Furst had broken into a larger market. As founder and president of the Atlantic and Gulf Coast Dredge Owners' Association, he arranged the price fixing and assignment of government contracts.[26] His company, Maryland Dredging, had contracts at fourteen cents a cubic yard, others at nine cents. He was awarded a navy contract to build at Philadelphia an 1100-foot $3 million dry dock, large enough to handle dreadnoughts. He also had the dredging contract for the B&O coal pier at Curtis Bay. As the B&O extended its Curtis Bay line from the asphalt plant at Brooklyn to Sea Wall, it crossed four hundred acres owned by Arundel, opening them up as prime industrial sites.[27] Arundel had acquired part of the property from the city: the city had walled and filled the old quarantine grounds in the interest of industrial development. Arundel had a city contract to barge downtown street-cleaning refuse from the back basin to this site. Furst was also involved in the Baltimore Sanitary Contracting Company, the night soil contractors. They used the former Pratt Street powerhouse of United Railways as a stable. When the sewer system displaced the night soil men, they shifted into garbage disposal. Taken singly, these enterprises were modest, but they were political franchises, secure monopolies, and they allowed Furst to hand out laboring jobs and fill the coal hods of the poor, reinforcing his political base.

Furst's activities expose the close cooperation between reformers and old-style politicians, between the financial elite and newspaper publishers, between immigrant Catholics and "blue ribbon" Presbyterians. Furst was active in all the local monopolies: he was vice-president of United Railways (1906–19), a director of the Pennsylvania Railroad and the Big Vein Pocahontas Coal Company. He operated from an office in the Continental building, built by Continental Trust. It was the home base of the Warfield interests, the offices of United Railways, Consolidated Coal Company, and Big Vein. Furst was also close to the Fidelity Trust Company, founded by Warfield, in which Van Lear Black was active. The Blacks were involved in the Consolidation Coal Company and the *Sun* papers. Warfield was governor. Fidelity Trust financed the jitney business, Davison Chemical, important tidewater builders Keelty and Knott, and the brewery syndicate. The breweries began to have influence with the state liquor control agency. They controlled most of the saloons in the city through their influence on licenses, the premises they leased, and the beer contracts. The $100,000 Riverview Park improvements were made jointly by United Railways

The Inner Harbor already
sparkled with incandescent
illumination by 1915.

and the brewery monopoly. The Fidelity trust enterprises reflect a Catholic social
milieu. Furst himself was German born; he immigrated as a young child, and
went to school at St. Michaels. Several of the families of original owners of coal,
brewery, utility, and streetcar companies were prominent Catholics, and their
drivers, miners, carters, and laborers were the original German and Irish labor
force whose solidarities offered political capital. The local enterprises—gas, electricity, United Railways, Arundel, and the breweries—continued to hire in
Catholic neighborhoods and to recruit managers among Loyola graduates for
several generations.

Furst's popular base and his understanding with entrepreneurs extended
into Anne Arundel County, and he played a prime role in two of the great
landscape-molding operations in tidewater: the sale of ten thousand acres of
farmland for Camp Meade (1917) and the annexation of Curtis Bay to Baltimore
City (1918).[28] When Furst died, he left $1 million—modest beside Garrett or
Abell, but impressive in terms of his beginning from nothing.

Washing the Great Unwashed

The coordination of municipal energies and the new harmony of planning in both piedmont and tidewater landscapes had been triggered by the building of the sewers. Baltimore's reengineering was essentially composed of sanitary engineering. But it involved new kinds of social engineering, directed toward social goals. The motive that led Baltimoreans to give top priority to sewers affected their perception of the social landscape as well as their perception of the natural landscape. That motive was simply a grasp of germ theory. Chlorination of the water supply was adopted in 1911, the same year the sewers were hooked up. The typhoid fever rate dropped. Introduction of the Gunpowder water had already reduced the incidence of typhoid and cholera somewhat. Declining rates of scarlet fever, whooping cough, and tuberculosis were perceptible, although unexplained. All these factors contributed to a substantial reduction of deaths in this generation, most visibly infant deaths. Once the process was well under way, people began to regard infant survival or "child saving" as feasible and morally compelling.

The disease that demonstrates the day-by-day, year-by-year struggle was tuberculosis, the white plague. Like cholera in 1832, TB was regarded as the disease of the poor, the alcoholic, and the ignorant, the great threat to the rich, the decent, and the well scrubbed. At a public meeting early in 1902, Dr. Osler shook his finger in the mayor's face: "What are we doing for the ten thousand consumptives who are living today in our midst? We are doing, Mr. Mayor and fellow-citizens, not one solitary thing that a modern civilized community should do."[29] But by 1916 one could discern that germ theory was affecting social habits, personal self-discipline, and mutual regulation. A modest symbol of the attack on contagion was the Walters Bath. William Walters, who had made his million by rebuilding southern railroads and organizing the Atlantic Coast Line Railroad, was a great traveler and collector. His art collection was already regarded as a public treasure. Impressed with the filth of Egypt while he was on a collecting trip, he made inquiry at home, and discovered that there was filth in Baltimore as well. So he decided to create a system of public bathhouses.[30] The idea was extended to add laundry rooms, bubble drinking fountains, public comfort stations in the squares, swimming beaches in the parks, and summer street showers.

That movement matched the thrust of public works—the filtration plant in Montebello Park, the raising of Loch Raven Dam to a new height, and the great revolving fountains of the trickling filters on Back River. Sanitary engineering reached into all aspects of life. The city put litter baskets on the corners and arrested men for spitting in streetcars. Cow stables in the city limits were shut down. Dairies began pasteurizing milk. The industrial school and the jail installed shower baths. Medical students slept on screened porches in winter, and the aseptic shave became popular: "There is nothing in the form of instruments that are not sterilized and given aseptic baths before being applied to the face, and the towels, barbers' coats, and aprons are kept in a glass case, in which a formaldehyde lamp is kept burning, thus thoroughly fumigating them."[31] The tools of epidemiology were applied to everyday problems. Like the street

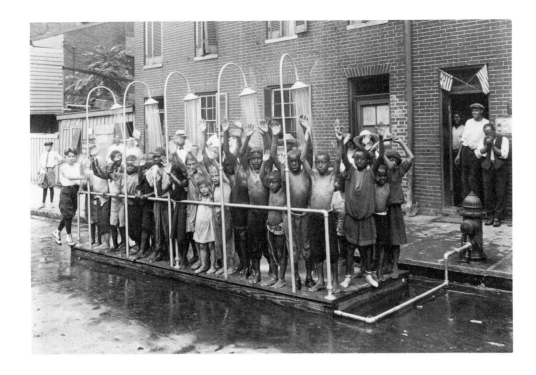

In the summertime, the public bathhouse system was augmented with open showers attached to hydrants.

planners, the health authorities began publishing and exhibiting maps of tuberculosis and typhoid.

In 1910 the tuberculosis commission proposed a strategy of prevention based on benefit-cost analysis. Figuring that half the population was under twenty-five and half over, that people's productivity in the work force was fixed by the age of twenty-five, and that the "unfit" were already "marked" by twenty-five, they aimed at a mass target population of the young

which streams through the schools into the city's working population. . . . Above that age, the profits which we are able to foresee will be secured at relatively high cost, by dealing with the *separate instances* and the *declining* values of adult life. Below that age, on the other hand, we may deal with the great numbers and the growing values of childhood.[32]

In the fall of 1906 a compulsory school law and child labor law came into effect. Twenty thousand work permits were issued in the first quarter for children twelve to sixteen, and three thousand more were refused: the children were supposed to speak and read simple English. Mount Vernon mills dismissed all children under twelve. Issuing the permits produced dramatic polyglot scenes day after day, underscoring the evidence that it was the children of the foreign born who were working in the factories. School enrollment had leveled off in about 1900, but from 1910 the application of the new laws produced a surge of enrollments that continued into the next generation. Truant officers began raiding the movie matinee parlors.

Public schools, originally designed for mass processing of the poor, rediscovered their vocation. They organized to clean up the unwashed. Annual school medical inspections of sixty-six thousand children were carried out. A third were reported sick and disordered. Inspections in the Catholic schools led to mass vaccinations. Vermin slips were handed out in several languages. In 1911 the doctors reported 381 cases of extreme filth and begged milk and eggs for several dozen cases of malnutrition and debility. In 1912 they tested vision and attempted to survey the scholastically retarded. The compulsory mass operations created shock waves for school personnel. They suddenly had to organize classes for epileptics, a class for "adenoids," in Lombard Street fresh air classes for children showing signs of TB, and summer schools and night schools for the pottery and glass-house boys of South Baltimore. They attempted to define norms of age and grade, but then had to organize ungraded classes and kindergartens to deal with those who did not fit the norms.

Unfortunately, the facilities did not keep up with the surge of enrollment or the new demands made on the schools. Schools were built at the rate of one per year, mostly additions in the annex. Classes of fifty children were common, and none of the older schools could be abandoned, despite the pleas of the health department. Most buildings dated from the 1870s or 1890s, and were out of line with new standards of hygiene.

As in earlier generations, mortality had to be politicized. The equations had to be established between tax dollars and personal risks. Whose dollars? Whose risks? In this process, which naturally produced tension and anxiety, H. L. Mencken managed to vent the outrage of the man in the street and to introduce the necessary comic relief.

> Laugh, suckers, laugh!
> Down goes the tax rate!
> Oh, say, can you see —!
> Up goes the death rate!
> —by the dawn's early light![33]

Mencken regularly published the scores of the National Typhoid League. Baltimore always led, well ahead of Panama. "A million dollars for a new bridge to the Brooklyn poolroom, but not one cent for typhoid!"[34] Mencken personified the ambivalence of his generation. He resented the streetcar company and the police for disciplining and regimenting the people of Baltimore. He despised the blue laws. In the Baltimore German tradition he demanded beer and concerts on Sunday. If people wanted to take the streetcar to the resorts in Brooklyn or Back River, where the police were less efficient, why interfere? "Now and then, of course, a drunken man rolls overboard and is drowned—but is the world so idle that it can waste time mourning drunken men who drown?"[35]

When his own convenience or health was at stake, however, Mencken was prepared to promote discipline. Throughout 1911 and 1912 he inveighed against the carrying of "freight" on the streetcars, and he zealously supported the campaign against the housefly. He reviewed the twenty-five-year history of the antispitting campaign and the current war on the mosquito. "The propagation of any such new and anarchistic idea in Baltimore is always an enormously slow and tedious business." At that rate, the campaign against flies had scarcely begun. By 1914, he reckoned, the city council would begin to discuss the matter. By 1920 "all the humor will be out of it, and a preliminary and ineffective ordinance will be passed." The fly, he supposed, would begin to disappear about 1935.

> Swat the fly!
> Boil your drinking water!
> Throw a rose into the harbor!
> Watch the City Council![36]

This 1915 street-washing machine, shown near the front of city hall, was pulled by a chain-drive tractor.

Isolation Wards

A corollary of germ theory was isolation of the contaminated. This was an important aspect of the management of tuberculosis to protect families and the public. A new facility for contagious diseases was built at Bay View. Each bed was in a separate room that opened directly to the outside. Several TB sanatoriums were opened: Sabillasville, Eudowood, the Jewish Home, and a ward at Bay View. Together they had seven hundred beds, for advanced cases, whites only. But since Osler had organized the "immaculately clean" Phipps clinic at Johns Hopkins and introduced home visiting, cases were being diagnosed much earlier, with no place to send them.

The fear of contagion reinforced the old ideology of isolation and classification in the hospitals, jails, and asylums. At Bay View, the City Hospitals held 1700 persons on the average day. In the jail there were 750, while the state was supporting 1200 "city insane." They still amounted to only 1 percent of the population, but as the institutions overflowed, there were always new gaps, new needs discovered that could not be satisfied. "Scores of feeble-minded children disturb whole neighborhoods." In 1913 the state opened a hospital for the colored insane at Crownsville, and agreed to finance a school for feeble-minded (white) children at Owings Mills.

City officials appeared baffled by the perennial increase of "disordered lives." They offered no long-range plan and no integrative thought. The eleven hundred delinquent or dependent minors were largely "contracted" for care in various private and Catholic institutions—St. Elizabeth's, House of the Good Shepherd, St. Mary's, and St. Joseph's industrial schools. Only the large numbers of religious vocations among Catholics made this possible. In 1908 there were three thousand inmates, patients, or pupils in the Catholic charitable institutions, and five hundred religious involved in caring for them. The church received sizeable bequests of land, and by its selfless "cheap labor" and the day-by-day generosity of Catholic market men and mechanics, it fed and housed most of what Alexander Brown called "all that broken wreckage of industrial society."

In spite of official and officious efforts to sort people into appropriate slots, in the public mind the problems fused. Fear of contagion aggravated the horror of the poor and reinforced segregation along lines of income and ethnic group, the traditional interpretations of otherness. Contagion was part of the threat of outsiders, other races, other tongues. The housing investigator of the Charitable Organization Society defined two types of slums: the tenement houses of the recent immigrants and the alley dwellings of the blacks.[37] All the ills of society were attributed to these slums. The mayor urged a close watch on such "blotches" or "dark spots":

Debasing environments like these are the ones from which creep forth the pinched bodies and pinched souls which make our criminals and disturbing elements. These wretched abodes are menacing to both health and morals. They are the breeding spots from which issue the discontents and heartburnings that sometimes spread like a contagion through certain ranks of our laboring element.[38]

The housing investigators found it difficult to distinguish between characteristics of houses and the habits of people who lived in them. They contrasted "a remnant of the colony of clean, hard-working, thrifty Germans" with the black tenants of Biddle Alley and Hughes Street: "It is impossible to observe these gregarious, light-hearted, shiftless, irresponsible alley dwellers without wondering to what extent their failings are the result of their surroundings, and to what extent the inhabitants, in turn, react for evil upon their environment."[39] The school doctors reinforced the association: "Among the foreigners and negroes the degree of filth is indescribable. . . . Filth is most marked among Italians, Poles, and negroes."[40] Race fears were nourished by the new "eugenics" as well as the fear of contagion. The whole ideology of hygiene buttressed a systematic effort to segregate blacks. TB was increasingly defined as a problem of the Negro race, whose death rates were double those of whites. The Municipal Tuberculosis Commission recommended that the city provide a special hospital for blacks with tuberculosis. "The colored population, with its special susceptibility, furnishes the distinctive feature of the local problem of tuberculosis in Baltimore." It argued for "superior as well as separate" facilities because "the colored population carries a larger hazard; the colored consumptive is a more serious menace."[41] The *Sun* commented:

Many negroes are servants for white families and those who suffer with tuberculosis are likely to spread it among the families that give them employment. A State sanatorium for negroes suffering from consumption is demanded not only by considerations of humanity, but as a measure of protection for the white race.[42]

The argument for solidarity was ambiguous, easily transformed into an argument for segregation. In fact, though, the resources assigned for treatment of tuberculosis remained principally for whites. At City Hospitals there were repeated recommendations that a new building be built for whites and the old one handed to blacks. Every instance of segregation made clear the implicit second-class status. In the general hospitals, the city's subsidy patients received second-class accommodations. Like many hospitals, St. Agnes accepted white patients only. City (Mercy) had a "poorly ventilated" railroad ward, an "absolutely unventilated" ward for immigrants, and for colored patients an old building "inferior" to those. At the homeopathic hospital the colored patients were housed in "a slightly remodeled stable." "Only at Johns Hopkins Hospital and Bay View are the two races treated equally well or badly, as the case may be."[43] Mencken unleashed his savage pen on this blind spot.

Why is Baltimore such a pest-hole? . . . The niggero is to blame. Wherever he lives and has his being, there the death rate soars. . . . In brief, more than three per cent of all the darkies in town die every year. And no wonder! But who cares? The negro is an unwelcome citizen. Let him climb his golden stairs.[44]

In the harsh light of self-interest, Mencken pinpointed the consequences:

But who ever heard of a plan for the decent housing of negroes in Baltimore? When the darky tries to move out of his sty and into a human habitation, a policeman now stops him. The law practically insists that he keep on incubating typhoid and tuberculosis— that he keep these infections alive and virulent for the delight and benefit of the whole town.[45]

He even suggested that the "Mount Vernon Place issue" might make as good an election issue as the perennial "nigger issue," and proposed an Association for the Suppression of Prominent Baltimoreans. "Why not a public trial of them one by one?"[46]

As poverty was defined by filth, working-class success was defined in terms of cleanliness. Scrubbing differentiated the modest but respectable from the unwashed. The goal was to scrub one's own marble steps. In spite of what seemed a great reservoir of the poor, there was a distinct current of movement into a "middle class" of home owners. Construction stayed around a thousand dwellings a year till 1904, when the fire touched off a relatively steady level between two and three thousand. Public-works investment matched closely. Despite the national business crisis of 1907, Baltimore maintained a high rate of sewering, paving, and home building until World War I brought it down with a wrench to a few hundred homes in 1918.

The Well Scrubbed

The overwhelming majority were solid, modest houses, two stories tall, with six rooms—a well-built product for the mass market. As early as 1901, virtually all new houses were being built with hot air furnaces and water in the house. A typical row in Wilkens Avenue had electric wiring, gas, complete plumbing, and full basements. In 1915 the gas company was installing a thousand water heaters a month, and there was a gas range for every building in the city. Layouts became more diverse. Builders contrived to fit in a hall passage and bathroom, and to introduce some light into the center dining room. (The center bedroom could be lighted with a skylight.) Built by the block, on paved streets with concrete sidewalks, they were the image of respectability. Touches of sober elegance were anonymous—the stained glass light in the door and window and the resident's white curtains defiant of coal smoke. The builder signed his work with his personal finial or urn in the parapet. The developers worked hand in hand with the improvement associations. Edward J. Gallagher, for instance, was active in the East End Improvement Association, which promoted street openings and paving projects (Luzerne, Fairmount), demanded a car line on Wolfe Street, the beautification of Patterson Park, a new gym, and the Ogier Run storm sewer.[47]

A somewhat more comfortable class in North and West Baltimore favored porches—the continuous veranda along the row, as on Abell Avenue, Poplar

E. J. Gallagher built these houses at Linwood Avenue and McElderry Street about 1910. The brown brick houses sold complete with stained glass over the front windows and doors; marble steps, lintels, and sills; tiled entry halls; and imitation fireplaces.

Grove Street, and East Thirty-third Street. Houses in the north and northwest cost about double the houses in East and South Baltimore. By 1917 almost all the new houses were porch fronts. They featured solid cement steps, porches of blue cut stone with pressed brick columns, and mosaic tile floor set in cement. The rage was iron-spotted brick. They had enamel tubs and sinks, hand-painted ceilings, and tiled vestibules. On Park Heights Avenue the fronts were terraced and the lawns made, shrubbery was put in, and the rooms were papered.

The mystique of home ownership was something everybody agreed on— clergy, politicians, employers, and mechanics. It was the solution to heartburnings. After the mayor had described the threat of dark blots, he praised the laboring element of Baltimore:

We have few strikes. We have comparatively no disorder. This I believe is due very largely to the domestic or home qualities of the Baltimore laborer. There is little or no inclination to crowd into large and noxious tenements. The individual home for each individual family is the rule. And the effect is wholesome.[48]

This ideology was associated with many other conservative feelings in Baltimore. The cardinal said a woman's place was in the home. Neighborhood solidarity was identified with the 100 percent home-owned block, the parish, the political club, and the pitcher of beer from the corner saloon.

The agreement on home ownership was the closest the generation came to an integrated social system, but even this idea was bedeviled by inconsistencies. One of them was the ambivalence toward property rights, brought out in an article in the *Municipal Journal* entitled "Should a Man Do as He Pleases with His Own Property?" The broadening of home ownership reinforced the sacredness of property, but the new sensitivity to conflagration and contagion created pressures for regulating "the other fellow." The health department began to quarantine and placard houses for scarlet fever and diphtheria. The fire department demanded regulation of commercial properties as hazardous, and the police counted twelve thousand buildings where people were dwelling over stores. The housing survey photographed chickens roosting in Lombard Street basements and protested the nearly complete coverage of Thames Street lots with buildings. On North Avenue, home owners sued a builder (unsuccessfully) for putting up exceptionally narrow dwellings, on the ground that it would injure their property values. All of these were the issues of zoning regulation and property law, as raised by Richard Ely's book of the same year. He defined property as "a set of relations between men, defined in terms of the relations between men and things." The editor of the *Municipal Journal* proceeded, like Ely, to argue that while downtown Baltimore was as sterile as the Sahara, it was much more valuable land. "Who wants a thousand acres or even a thousand inches of land in some distant isolated spot? What value is field, mansion or barn if it is standing upon a lonely island with no means of communication?"[49] This was the "quivering nerve."[50] Because the community gives value to property, the property owner must consider the rights of the community.

He comes in contact with a seething current of human beings and human rights on all four sides of his property. There is not an inch of it that isn't intertwined with the multi-farious relationships of community life. The very market value of the property itself is due to its connections with this community life.[51]

The other problem surrounding home ownership as an integrated social strategy was the question of access to home ownership. Who would be the home owners? As one might expect from the mechanisms of the savings and loan associations created in the last generation, a large proportion of the new houses and neighborhoods were sold to householders of German descent—again that "colony of clean, hard-working, thrifty Germans." The Bohemians were able to outrun that track record. Of white families to whom a baby was born in Baltimore in 1915, about a quarter owned their homes; of American-born parents, a third; of German-born parents, half; and of Bohemian-born parents, three-quarters.[52]

But now from the ranks of the great unwashed there emerged several streams of upward mobility based on the ideology of home ownership and hard scrubbing. Each group—black, Russian Jewish, and Polish Catholic—adopted a distinctive strategy, determined in part by preference and tradition, in part by an economic situation and a matrix of discrimination by other segments of society.

Colored Streets

The black community was a hydraulic system that siphoned a very small number into higher income and status. In the competition to enter these higher social circuits, the key strategies were complete economic adaptability, home ownership at any price, and schooling. These were the signs of ambition and status. In each circuit, the white community was able to control the valves regulating the flow and pressures. It is impossible to grasp the situation of black leaders without continual reference to the pressures of a tide of people below. The smallness of the group, the rigors of the competition, and the inconsistencies among these strategies produced conflicts, personal and social, that survive to the present.

Of a thousand successful families, there were the professionals and entrepreneurs—thirty doctors, a few lawyers, more preachers, more teachers, undertakers, an increased number of rental agents and real estate dealers, and wagon owners who did moving and hauling or who dealt in coal, ice, rags, bottles, and junk. The majority of grocers and retailers in the black neighborhoods were, however, whites, often Jewish. Most successful financially were the caterers who served the lavish entertainments of the wealthy and suburban residents. Richard Macks, Garrett's former head butler, went into the catering business at this time. Black middlemen also catered to the demands of other classes of society for food, sex, entertainment, and cocaine. At the Marsh Market dance halls the black piano players made their reputations, among them Eubie Blake, Baltimore's great ragtime improvisor. Labor recruiting and travel imposed by the job provided large clienteles looking for liquor and women in Baltimore. The dance halls were frequented by sailors, steamboat hands, and cattlemen. On a single night 500 blacks were vaccinated in a mass operation when a recruit from Rochester broke out with smallpox. At Sparrows Point a thousand black men were living, recruited from Virginia without their families. Red-light districts existed in black neighborhoods, such as Raborg Street, certain blocks of Paca Street, and the 700 blocks of Mulberry and Franklin streets, for the convenience of white patrons and traveling salesmen who would not be recognized. Readily exploited were young girls recruited from Virginia by the boatload to work as domestic servants in Baltimore. Among blacks in the city there were perhaps 117 women for each 100 men.

Blacks were continually forced to readjust their vocations. As technological and competitive forces demanded adaptation of the Baltimore economy, the greatest adjustments and risks were shifted onto that part of the labor force with least power. Changes in the assignment of jobs by race involved legislation, violence, or other forms of coercion or exercise of power outside the "free market." Barbers, for example, were forced out by the creation of the barbers examiners board, presumably for sanitary regulation. Alongside the several thousand black laundresses who did washing at home, whites operated the new steam laundries, and the politicians delivered to them the contracts of hospitals and restaurants. Most other black women were servants. The new ten-hour law for women was not applicable to domestic work, where fourteen or sixteen-hour duty was common, for a dollar a day. Employers still gave food and clothing to their servants because they couldn't make ends meet without them, "but many feel the colored should be able to live cheaper, because they don't need new clothes, but can depend on what is given to them."[53] Black women, therefore, were eager to get factory work, to escape the more personal form of domination. Some moved into the lowest-paid and filthiest jobs in the cigarette factories, replacing old men and cripples as tobacco strippers. At least one shirt factory, Wise Brothers, organized a separate shop, later a separate floor and entrance to their large factory, with a hundred black women as sewing machine operatives. They were paid less than white workers. Other garment factories used them as pressers, the least-paid job.

In the building trades a caste system was also well entrenched. This was one of the side effects of the collapse of the Knights of Labor and their replacement by Federation craft unions and the Baltimore Labor Council. John Ferguson, organizer for the Labor Council, observed, "The skilled colored worker works largely among his own people, and is willing to work at a lower rate than the white worker. This is a source of feeling against him on the part of the whites."[54] The largest black union was the stevedores' union, with thirteen hundred members. The best paid were the hod carriers who worked with the white bricklayers and plasterers; they earned $2.50 to $3.50 in an eight-hour day. But the other building crafts excluded blacks. Relatively mild to employers, their unions effectively protected the masons and carpenters against competition from black craftsmen. Employers continued to exploit ethnic rivalries in labor disputes. When the black cellar diggers and shovellers union of nine hundred went on strike for $1.50 and a nine-hour day, white scabs were hired on jobs such as Kernan's theater. There is no evidence that the other craft unions expressed solidarity with the cellar diggers. Likewise, when 125 Locust Point drivers, mostly foreign born, struck the B&O, asking $1.60 plus twenty cents an hour overtime, the B&O brought seventy-five or eighty Negroes from Philadelphia and paid them the extra overtime to break the strike. There is no indication that B&O skilled workers protested.[55]

Job struggles were followed by campaigns to disfranchise colored voters (1903, 1905, and 1908) and impose stricter forms of segregation (1911 and 1913). All the voter campaigns failed because other political groups joined the opposition of black voters. The Colored Law and Order League was assisted by the Foreign Born Voters League, who opposed literacy tests, and by Charles Bonaparte's Progressive organization, which objected to grandfather clauses smacking of "hereditary honors." Bonaparte participated in many aspects of reform in Baltimore, but was by this time attorney general in Teddy Roosevelt's administration. Party bosses also recognized that understanding clauses that required a would-be voter to demonstrate his understanding of the constitution would allow great latitude to state voter registrars and might be used against any party out of power.[56] Baltimore wholeheartedly voted against the disfranchisement schemes, while the rest of Maryland voted for them. These were mere incidents in the Maryland political tradition, but they sustained inflammatory rhetoric, kept the black community continually on the defensive, and diverted white class frustrations into racial conflicts.

In the housing market a pattern emerged that was repeated in subsequent waves of black immigration at the end of World War I and World War II. The block-busting pattern was not altogether new, but it was for the first time organized into an effective commercial operation. The handful of blacks siphoned to the top continually pioneered new housing opportunities, while masses pressing on behind them created a "slum" image, which strengthened the resistance of whites to admitting any blacks to their neighborhoods and at the same time strengthened the determination of blacks to escape the ghetto at any price. This vicious circle was profitable to a small group of realtors who operated on the margin of turnover, but it is essential to recognize the total context of supply and demand in a dual housing market to see why such profiteering was possible. The collusion of the community was necessary to block busting.

An essential factor was the rural black immigration of the late 1890s and early 1900s. In addition to insuring the scramble for bottom-of-the-heap jobs, immigration insured an increased demand for housing, the presence of large numbers of the malnourished and illiterate, and a wave of tuberculosis with each wave of immigration. TB is often assumed to be a disease of crowded cities, but it is associated more precisely with the urban crowding of recent immigrants from the countryside. By 1904 half the black population of the city was living in the northwest. This half still included most of the home owners, the professionals and dealers, and the highest share of literate and youthful. The northwest ghetto, chosen for its healthfulness, became packed close around Pennsylvania Avenue and Dolphin Street. Between 1900 and 1910 this seventeenth ward changed from 8 to 60 percent black, and elected the city's first black council member.

The other essential was the restriction of total housing supply for blacks. No new streets or subdivisions were built for black residents, and no new land was allocated. The only suburb "strictly for colored people" was Patapsco Park. There were also shanties built by industry or tolerated on industrial land adjoining the fertilizer and chemical factories as at Fairfield. But it was virtually impossible for black dealers to buy land or for white developers to buy land to build houses for blacks. The only option was secondhand housing, and any expansion of the total housing supply for blacks depended on some turnover of communities. By containing and manipulating this rate of turnover, realtors could control the total supply and the prices that could be extracted from blacks for housing. The economics of ghetto expansion, as described by a colored real estate dealer for the 1200 block of Druid Hill Avenue are still recognizable sixty years later. As black residents "removed near," values depreciated for whites and houses were rented to whites at nominal rates (phase one). "As soon as the colored tenants came in (phase two) these depreciations did not count for them, and the rates again went up. . . . Houses for colored tenants generally speaking are kept in poorer repair than for whites, and the city takes poorer care of colored streets." Consequently (phase three) the rents went down again "due to general depreciation of the neighborhood. . . . The colored paid less than white people had done in earlier days. Houses in this district which now rent for $30. had been as high as $75. a month."[57] On the ground that the black residents depressed prices, segregation ordinances were passed. They were written with elaborate attention to their "equal" application to whites and Negroes: neither would have the right to buy or rent in a block occupied by the other race. Such ordinances constricted the supply further. In general, whites could rent small houses in all-white working-class neighborhoods for $2.00 or $2.50 a week, while blacks had to pay $3.00 or $4.00 for larger houses of a middle-upper class who were moving out farther. To pay the rents for houses "too expensive and too large," they had to double up. Subletting suddenly became widespread, and many damp basements were occupied. Demolition aggravated the scarcity. B&O expansions at Camden Station, first the long warehouses on the west, then on the east the widening of tracks, took two hundred black dwellings. The number demolished from the St. Paul Street squares was never reported, but removal of Negro dwellings was an objective of the project. Such property was always regarded as a public nuisance. These additional constraints on supply pushed up rents paid by blacks and ensured a higher return to their landlords. Several slumlord dynasties well known in Baltimore in the 1940s and even the 1970s were initiated by investment in alley housing during the era when the segregation ordinances were in effect (1913–1917). Three different studies all confirm that black families paid more rent than whites for the same accommodations.[58] Roughly a third of their earnings went for rent, while the average in the white community was a fifth of the budget.

How did they make the rent? First, mothers and youths continued to work, and families tended to take in country relatives and boarders, so there were more members of the household bringing in some income. They economized on the food budget by eating cornmeal and pig meat, with little beef or dairy products. "Soul food" was an economic strategy as well as a rural southern tradition. As their incomes rose they bought more sweet potatoes. Thus, the lower income of black workers was siphoned off, a third of it directly into the hands of a small class of white property owners who were creating capital assets. The city's upper class depended on the blacks to scrub their marble steps and their new bathrooms and kitchens, while the white working class depended on them to dig the cellars, make the bricks, and mix the mortar and cement for their new homes.

In the schools segregation was complete, and there was no pretense of equal accommodation. The new school and work permit laws were not enforced for black children. There was not a single new colored school built between 1898 and 1915. All were hand-me-downs. At Pennsylvania Avenue and Dolphin Street, a German-English school "unfit for use" was turned over to house the Colored High School, while "the best" colored families on Druid Hill Avenue occupied the homes opposite Western High School, "the best" white-only public girls' school. Overcrowding in the colored schools was severe, and from 1905 most of them held half-time classes. Black teachers and principals were at last given complete control, but they had no proper salary and promotion schedule. In the white schools a civil service had been the basic reform of 1901, and wages had been raised to compete with the jobs offered white women in other sectors of the economy.

In education as in home ownership, advancement was restricted to a small class. There were on the order of eight hundred black home owners in Baltimore in 1904, nine hundred in 1913. Of seventy-three southern cities, Baltimore ranked seventy-second in black home ownership rate.[59] This is striking in contrast with its top rank for white home ownership. This tiny minority, trying to increase the chances of its children for survival and education, continued to move along the northwest axis. "Dissatisfied in alley homes, they saved their money and purchased nearly the whole length of Druid Hill avenue. . . . Then they began to expand into parallel streets, one of which was McCulloch. They had been told that 'money talks.' "[60] In these terms W.E.B. Dubois described Druid Hill Avenue as "one of the best colored streets in the world." Amanda Bowen, for example, who grew up in Montgomery County, then taught school in Howard County in the '70s and married Charles Carroll (he had learned to read and write as a slave in the home of the Signer's descendants), in 1903 bought a house at 1134 Druid Hill Avenue. Her seventh child, Lillie, began teaching public school in Baltimore and became the leader of a stubborn generation who saw a relationship among neighborhood improvement, education, and racial justice. Black home owners had great difficulty defending their neighborhoods against both white commercial interests and the pressure of larger numbers of black tenants for housing. Home owners and churches protested the city's toleration of vice districts and the state's willingness to issue liquor licenses in their neighborhoods. Black home owners were perceived as a threat by white neighbors, but they worked to separate themselves from the contaminating image and habits of other sections of the black community. This reinforced a sharp sense of ambition and achievement, a strong individualism. Their institutions were always caught between the ambitions of their leadership and the needs of large numbers. The Colored YWCA on Druid Hill near Dolphin ran an employment service. A colored teacher training school was founded, later Coppin College. Provident Hospital was organized in the abandoned building of the Union Protestant Infirmary.

A critical initiative to break out of the ghetto of West Baltimore was the move of Morgan College from Edmondson and Fulton avenues to Hillen Road. After several years of effort, the mobilization of the mayor's blue ribbon commission on health problems of the black community, and the patronage of Goucher College, Morgan College managed to obtain the land, sixty-seven acres known as the Ivy Mill tract. The object was to create a community, "scientifically sanitary and with the best conditions for housing some 300 families," adjoining the college. "The mayor said he had made it a meeting of practically all white people because they were, to a large extent, the owners of the property under consideration. . . . It is largely a problem for the property-owning class to solve."[61] He wanted to work along "practical" lines and not attempt "impractical" ones: "Any change in the segregation would meet with very great opposition from our white populations and bring about friction and hostility between the races which would be very much to be deplored."[62] Despite the mayor's caution, opposition arose. Delegations from Hamilton, Clifton Park, Montebello Park, and beyond gathered to protest. They publicized the names of the realtors, brokers, and attorneys concerned in the deal. "Lauraville has blood in its eye for any invasion of its 99 per cent pure white community by a negro institution, colony or settlement of any kind or character."[63] The president of the improvement association concluded with a definite statement "that he preferred to live near a community of ignorant and tractable negroes than one of 'educated' negroes."

The Morgan College episode is one of dozens that show how the threat of violence lay behind all forms of housing discrimination. Rumor was both a symptom of tension and a tool for manipulating people. The segregation ordinance was passed after a "disturbance" on McCulloch Street. Rumors spread that black bidders were "well supplied with money." A black home buyer had his windows broken. In West Baltimore, the Harlem Park Association objected to a colored orphan asylum and spread rumors of other colored bidders on property in the neighborhood. "We will give hundreds or even thousands of dollars for prosecution and defense, but not one cent for tribute."[64] In Bolton Hill a mass meeting was held to prevent a black family's taking possession of a house they had bought in Eutaw Place near Lanvale Street. The headline read,

"Eutaw Place Threatened by Negro Invasion Now."[65] Again rumors circulated suggesting a larger threat; money "from Washington" would finance an apartment house for blacks. At Canton rocks were thrown to prevent a black family's moving from Hudson Street a block over to Elliott Street. At Arlington there were rumors of a race riot if more black families moved onto Denmore or Patapsco avenues. Residents expected a repetition of what had happened a few years earlier: "Practically every window in the house was broken and things grew so warm for the occupants that they waved a white tablecloth from a window as a truce signal, and later shook the dust of Arlington from their feet."[66] In 1915 there was a similar stoning of the first black family in a block of Stricker Street.

These incidents invariably followed publicity of more remote incidents of violence, such as a month-long manhunt for a murderer in Baltimore County, a Christmas morning lynching in Anne Arundel County, or a race riot in Chicago. The *Sun* disapproved of lynchings and riots, but found minor local episodes amusing. Its reporting was consistent with a national image of the black as brute. The Baltimore papers gave wildly enthusiastic reviews of the racist novels *The Clansmen* and *The Leopard's Spots* and the film version of *Birth of a Nation*, whose author, Thomas Dixon, had been a student at Johns Hopkins. Such films were shown, of course, to white-only audiences. Indeed, no first-run pictures were shown in Negro theaters; they obtained worn-out films from the cheapest white theaters. In this context the black churches in Baltimore and a Baltimore woman, Dr. A. W. Marchant, pioneered in creating several films featuring family themes, such as Booker T. Washington's reception in Baltimore and the history of several churches. Dr. Marchant was a homeopathic physician trained in the city. Her two young daughters began acting. From chaperoning her daughters, she moved into producing films, innovative because the actors were colored people "not made by burnt cork, but the real thing."[67]

J ewish immigration continued till the war. The Jewish population of Baltimore rose to sixty-five thousand, half the present population. Most arrived with no property or resources, but by 1915 the income distribution of the Jewish community roughly matched that of the native white population. The basic split remained between the comfortably off "uptown" German Jews who spoke English and whose six synagogues espoused various shades of reform, and the "downtown" East Europeans who spoke Yiddish and whose twenty-five "Russian" shuls were orthodox. But in the course of this generation individuals marked out certain paths of moving up, and the promotion of the whole group was evident. It was a process involving intense conflict within the community, but also a remarkable capacity for containing and resolving conflict. In exploring the nature of their success, one has to look at the interplay of economic and cultural factors, or, more precisely, a cultural economy.

First, the Jewish community was remarkably successful in protecting its children. Environments of Oldtown and South Baltimore were not favorable. Crowding was severe. Thousands worked feverishly at tailoring in poor light and gasoline fumes. Tuberculosis was common. The shul also kept them indoors.

A Strategic Place

Advantageous for the infants were cultural preferences: most of the infants were nursed at the breast, many of their mothers were employed helping in their husband's business rather than in factories, and after the third child, births were spaced farther apart. But the health experts remained mystified: these factors did not adequately explain why Jewish infants had the lowest death rate of any group in the city. Apparently they survived thanks to the orthodox attachment to ancient rules of diet, child raising, and family life.

Second, the Jewish community had a solid economic base. Despite the presence of Bohemian and Lithuanian Catholic sweatshops and Italian workers in the larger firms, the clothing industry was rather solidly Jewish. It employed twenty-three thousand persons, over a quarter of the manufacturing labor force. Perhaps 70 percent of the Jewish community lived directly from the clothing industry, while the rest—the grocers and the carpenters—serviced the clothing workers. For the clothing industry, markets expanded and productivity increased. More power machinery was introduced. This generation made the transition from the sweatshops (450 at the turn of the century) to factories of ever larger size. Schloss, for example, had a thousand employees in a seven-story building at Baltimore and Paca streets, and perhaps twenty-five hundred in a six-story, "perfectly equipped" building near Exeter. The clothiers were tied economically and socially to the department stores who sold to all of Baltimore and to dry goods jobbers and mail order establishments who sold in the southern mass markets. Jacob Epstein's Baltimore Bargain House had a thousand employees and sold in both markets. The Jewish community collectively acquired both the return to labor and the return to capital in this industry. The black community had no comparable economic base.

Third, on this economic base the Jewish community built its own system of recirculation. It captured the profits made from its workers, who hired, rented, bought, and borrowed within the family. They saved and they gave, within the community. It was not uncommon for a twelve-dollar-a-week worker to save a tenth of his earnings. Successful relatives invested in the education of a nephew, or made loans to a brother-in-law's business. Despite the conflicts and exploitation within the community, there was a strong tendency for good times and bad times to be shared, for risks to be spread farther. Giving was phenomenal, widely admired, each as he was able—Jacob Epstein and William Levy in the thousands of dollars, down to the pennies for the strike funds. For these mechanisms of solidarity to succeed in promoting the entire group, the ratio must be reasonable between rich and poor, established and newcomers. The presence of a large, well-established, well-financed, well-educated class of grandchildren of the '48ers meant that a great many problems could be handled and resolved within the community. If the black middle class had shared as fully—giving, saving, lending, investing within the community—it still could not have promoted the whole mass so rapidly in a generation. They were too few.

Fourth, the larger community, strongly German, permitted more upward mobility to the Jewish community, in proportion to its Germanness. German Jews had first passed through the sieve and were, like other Germans, largely assimilated. The Jewish community experienced discrimination, but not in the same degree as the black community. The effective differences were in property and education. Jews were restricted to buying residential property in specific areas, and were rigorously excluded from certain new developments such as the Roland Park Company suburbs. But prior investments of the Rayners made available considerable land, and a normal range of housing types was developed at a normal rate relative to demand. The wealthiest families continued to filter northwestward, from one block of Eutaw Place to the next, to Lake Drive. Jews were allowed to invest in commercial property and investment shares, and in Negro alley dwellings. The Sunday laws were rigidly discriminatory, and continued to pressure the orthodox to prefer self-employment, the professions, or the Jewish garment factories rather than other trades, reinforcing the cultural economy. Likewise, in the schools, the Jewish community did not have to accept a separate administration and financial starvation as the colored schools. Beginning from the "German-English" schools, Jews could profit from the best of the public high schools. The Johns Hopkins University, thanks to both its German model and the coincidences of its initial staff, was open to Jewish students and had distinguished Jewish faculty members, although it remained nearly impervious to blacks and women. The Jewish community also exercised initiative in creating new institutions in this generation. The Talmud Torah had nine hundred children. Hans Froehlicher's Park School was modeled on a "country day" principle. In this domain also, cultural tradition provided a critical choice of paths. The logic of the law fostered respect for books, teachers, learning, and reasoning, in their deepest, most individual, and most critical forms.

Because both the workers and owners of the garment industry were part of the Jewish community, intense conflict continued within the community. But one should situate the dialogue between the German Jewish owners and the Russian Jewish workers in the context of labor conflict in the city as a whole and in the nation at large. All the important strikes in Baltimore in this generation were part of nationwide movements of labor. The issues are familiar: the eight-hour day and the right to organize. A new aspect was the struggle to solidify national organizations. Disputes between unions complicated the politics. As Baltimore's industry was integrated into the national economy, so naturally the conditions of labor were determined in the national arena, and the need was felt in Baltimore to belong to national organizations of labor. Union activity gathered strength in 1902 and 1903, for the first time since the '80s. All the skilled craft unions flexed their muscles. The Hebrew, Bohemian, and German bakers obtained better working conditions: they were used to working eighteen-hour days in cellars. Building craftsmen made remarkable gains by a strike in 1904 because of the building boom in the wake of the fire. The plumbers, steamfitters, gasfitters, and plasterers all obtained the eight-hour day.[68] After the nationwide recession of 1907, nationwide strikes followed in which gains were less and repression was more severe. Violence and private police activity were intense on the railroads and the coal mines. In Baltimore the Mount Clare shops were on strike, and newspapers reported a series of bizarre dynamite plots.[69]

The garment workers' struggle involved all these elements. Since Baltimore had the largest garment industry next to New York and Philadelphia, it was a critical spot for the unionization of the industry nationwide. Within the Baltimore factories, solidarity was imperfect between the cutters—men, often German-American and Jewish, paid by the hour—and the rest of the workers, principally Jewish immigrants from Eastern Europe, paid at piece rates. Most of the employees worked longer and more variable hours and earned less than the cutters. Women were employed most often in the lower grades of labor, as coat basters, finishers, and buttonhole makers. A woman worker averaged $175 to $200 a year.

The story can be simplified by noticing that most of the action revolved around the extremes of the largest manufacturers—Sonneborn's and Greif's. Sonneborn's was unionized as an open shop in 1904. Sigmund Sonneborn was himself a '48er and "very advanced" in his ideas. Other firms resisted bitterly. In December 1909, two thousand workers in three large shops went on strike: Sonneborn's, Schloss's, and Silverman's. Schloss had refused to reinstate a union worker charged with spitting in the face of a loyal and faithful employee.[70] The critical issue was the attempt of the Clothiers' Board of Trade to eliminate union members from the industry. The clothiers created an employment bureau and agreed among themselves not to rehire anyone not registered. Baltimore was one of the first chartered locals of the International Ladies Garment Workers Union (ILGWU), associated with the American Federation of Labor (AFL), and Samuel Gompers arrived to manage the strike. Addresses were made to a thousand strikers at once, in English, German, Hebrew, Italian, and Russian, warning the workers, "The object is to index every garment worker in the city so that union men and labor agitators will be refused positions." The stress was intense, marked by a rash of suicides among strikers. Ultimately their demands were met, and they did not register.

The next breakthrough was Baltimore's selection as "a strategic place" when Sidney Hillman's Amalgamated Clothing Workers seceded from ILGWU in 1913. To organize Baltimore, they strategically selected Sonneborn's, already the best organized and best paid work force. Many of the tailors were socialist Bund members, and the Labor Zionists used to pass the hat at lunchtime. The union and Sonneborn quickly reached an agreement to organize a system of arbitration: they appointed Jacob Moses, judge of the new juvenile courts and Sonneborn's own company legal adviser, as arbitrator. Sonneborn formulated an internal Plan of Organization for his factory that sought to reconcile a patriotic conception of American constitutional democracy and free-enterprise capitalism.[71] The grievance committee drew members from a "cabinet" of owners of the firm, a "senate" of department heads or management, and a "congress" of workers. The employees' mutual association was more democratic then earlier ones such as on the B&O: all employees belonged, voted, and could stand for election. Workers outnumbered management on the grievance committee, and settlements required nearly the unanimity of a Quaker meeting. Sonneborn introduced the best features of the B&O savings and loan and pension plan, ordered fire drills, and a medical department with oculists and a trained nurse on duty at all times. Nevertheless, piece work and a take-home pay of twelve dollars a week remained.

By 1916 the ACWA had 9,000 members in Baltimore, and determined to unionize Greif's. Greif's paid wages as low as $4.50 a week, and discharged twenty ACWA members. The ILGWU and the ACWA were struggling for control. The ILGWU had the reputation of being easier on management. On 2 February the ACWA called out 2,000 workers from Sonneborn's and 700 from Strouse's for a demonstration at Greif's at Milton and Ashland streets. The crowds poured out from ten blocks around. More than half were women. "Jeering, unfavorable comment and fist-shaking were freely indulged in." The police chief said, "Get these people moving and keep them moving. . . . If any one kicks, take her in." They arrested 87 women, including a houseful of people chanting, "We will never give up." The next week, at Westheimer's factory at Preston and Gay streets, the police arrested 24 Bohemian women who were shouting, "Scab! Scab! Scab!" and following scabs home. Greif's agreed to reinstate the 20 ACWA members, but failed to do so, and trouble broke out again. On 3 March police refused to let 500 Sonneborn workers picket at Greif's. The workers allegedly threw stones at the police, and 111 were arrested.[72] However, the brutality of the police, whose chief was appointed by the governor, outraged the larger community and stirred the sympathy of Baltimore clergy. John Ferguson, the AF of L representative in Baltimore, tried, unsuccessfully, to split off Bohemian, Lithuanian, and Italian workers. Inside Sonneborn's, the cutters (ILGWU) refused to go out with ACWA, and the hostility resulted in a fight on the floor with cutting shears. But the ACWA won, and attributed its national survival to the courage of the Baltimore tailors. A thousand workers participated in family celebrations of Sonneborn's ninetieth birthday.[73] The workings of a labor court or board of arbitration were now extended to the entire industry. Work stoppages were practically eliminated. Jacob Moses settled some 900 cases, and Frank Goodnow, president of The Johns Hopkins University, was frequently involved in the mediation process.

The talent for containing conflict was a remarkable example to Baltimore. Jewish culture had embodied the tug of war between faith and reason, the law and the spirit, individualism and solidarity. The European Jews had struggled for centuries already with the moral problems posed by the coexistence of rich and poor. Therefore, in spite of the argument and agitation on the surface, there was beneath it a process of reflection and a cultural foundation that could embrace contradiction and survive conflict. Tradition provided mechanisms for labor mediation; they were outgrowths of millennial effort to keep disputes within the Jewish community and within the framework of Jewish law. In Baltimore, a Jewish Court of Arbitration was functioning by 1912 for a wide range of criminal, civil, and domestic cases.

Simultaneous with the labor conflicts, and closely related, there had appeared a variety of other conflicts. In 1915 the number of domestic cases brought before the courts increased. The pressures of poverty on the lives of families and children were severely felt. The community expressed anxiety about the number of delinquent Jewish children, pickpockets, wayward girls, drug habits, and boys committed to the Maryland Training school. Again they exercised imagination and deployed their resources. They founded a Big Brothers League, a home for girls, a street club for boys, and the Jewish Educational Alliance (JEA), which offered "settlement house" programs—dances, recreation, and club activities in the heart of Oldtown.

The educational and charitable organizations remained paternalistic, consistent with both Jewish tradition and Baltimore tradition. William and Julius Levy built the JEA building on East Baltimore Street (1914), and the "uptown" Jews maintained and largely staffed it. Charity was proportionate to wealth, and certainly Levy, Epstein, and Friedenwald were generous beyond measure. They were Baltimore's greatest philanthropists in their generation. They reveal once again how philanthropy was linked with capital: theirs were among the last remaining home-owned industries. "There was, naturally, a great deal of unhappiness among the immigrants, because the charities were in the hands of the German Jews, and at the same time the German Jews were also their employers."[74] The "uptown" organization, the Federated charities, adopted a new style of "efficient" giving, with "the application of skilled intelligence and thorough-going business methods" of the older Charity Organization Society. They gave up bazaars and ticket peddling. The "downtown" community organized the United charities, and proceeded to assert their identity. In politics, East Baltimore refused absolutely to have a *goy* candidate imposed upon it with the support of uptown Jews. Instead, it elected Seidenman to the city council (1903), which had the effect of sensitizing the political parties to the "Jewish vote." Through the cooperation of both uptown and downtown, Jacob Moses was elected to the state senate.

The very things that separated the Jewish community also drew it together. Divided with respect to the kind of adaptation they would make to non-Jewish society, Baltimore Jews were united by the discrimination they experienced. The terrible import of the Russian pogroms and the revolutions in Russia reverberated in Baltimore, raising the question of a home for the Jewish nation. Zionist associations, active in Baltimore since the '90s, committed to the creation of a Jewish state in Palestine, came into conflict with the socialists (the Bund and the Workman's Circle). The Labor Zionists (Poalei Zion) reconciled the two sets of ideas by proposing a workers' state in Palestine. The young Labor Zionists, like Dr. Herman Seidel, stood on a soapbox at Baltimore and Exeter streets on Friday nights, arguing the cause. Their youth organization, in white uniforms with the Star of David, periodically marched down Front Street. They, too, considered Baltimore a strategic place.[75] These little organizations, scrapping and speaking in tongues, opened Baltimore to currents of thought and international events. The people who looked so parochial, so out of date and out of step, were tuned into the current of ideas and had antennas for the world. In the anguish of their response to the Kishinev massacre and the Easter massacre in Russia, in their outpouring of relief for the starving in Poland in 1915, even in their confrontations with the Baltimore police, they alerted the clergy and the Christian establishment of Baltimore to the labor movement in New York City and to the Russian revolution, to French domestic politics, and to British military affairs in the Middle East. In many ways the Jewish community—Russian and German Jews together—had picked up roles played earlier in Baltimore by the Germans

—German Catholics and German Jews together. They were the conduit for new ideas from the Old World; they asserted the cultural ties of family, religion, and language, and made them the basis for reclaiming justice for workers and individual human rights.

Catholic Communities

The cardinal reported in 1912 that his twenty thousand Poles, eight thousand Bohemians, and twenty-five hundred Lithuanians were all easy to care for because they lived in compact parishes. The two thousand Italians caused him more trouble because they were scattered. He regarded the Germans and the Irish as assimilated, and their schools were English speaking.[76] Like the Jewish immigrants, the Catholic immigrants—Polish, Bohemian, and Lithuanian—maintained a rather ambivalent relation with the older German community of Baltimore. For the Italians, there was a similar relation to the Irish community. They inherited jobs, neighborhoods, and institutions, and, most important, they observed a model of the aspiration and strategy of home ownership.

Polish homes and neighborhoods were notorious in this generation for being the most crowded and filthiest, and for having the highest infant mortality. Of the Polish mothers of newborns in 1915, half had already borne four children, a quarter seven or more. Like the Italian and Lithuanian mothers, many of the Polish mothers could not speak English or read, and many worked outside the home. The mixed family labor force of the canneries became solidly Polish. The men often took German forms of their names, and those who spoke German found it easier to get jobs, working for the shippers and the fertilizer companies. "Responsible posts" were filled by politically well-connected German and Irish, while the unskilled and dirty jobs were done by the Polish and blacks. The Polish fathers' incomes averaged $500 to $550 a year, comparable to that of the Italians and Lithuanians. But their infants died in numbers not explained even by the handicaps of low income and crowding.

However, a careful reading of school medical reports and other studies suggests that signs of changes were already apparent by 1911. In Fells Point and Canton, by 1914 the school doctors reported a smaller proportion of "defects" in both public and parochial schools. Although Locust Point was still described as "isolated and filthy," there was rapid response to parent education and the translation of hygiene into Polish. The community adopted gymnastics and sports from the neighboring Turnvereins and Sokols, and took advantage of the new Patterson Park facilities. A tradition of neighborhood sports teams was launched. The Polish community had economized stringently on housing in the first generation—Poles paid only a third of the rents most people paid. Then they pooled their savings and bought themselves whole neighborhoods, some old, some spanking new. They spent the second generation working overtime, and working their wives and children, to pay for them. Mortgages were generally written for five-year terms. Through a building and loan association a family could undertake a variable number of shares, paying a quarter a week on each outstanding $100 share, plus the 6 percent interest, taxes, and ground rent. By 1914 there were twenty Polish building and loan associations, notably the Polish National and the White Eagle. Most were located on Eastern Avenue. (In 1970 there remained seven of them, distinctly Polish, with over $25 million in assets.) In Canton they took advantage of the new districts of solid working-class housing, and the new job base, and founded St. Casimir's parish. In South Baltimore, Holy Cross Church became a Polish National Catholic parish, and a Polish Presbyterian chapel was across the street. There was a Polish parish in Curtis Bay, St. Aloysius.[77]

The other nationalities followed much the same pattern of solidarity focused on the parish, but with variations of their job base, location, and child-raising habits. The purchase of new homes by German families and the settlement of German and Italian families at Calverton and of Bohemian and Italian families in the northeast led to the creation of several new suburban parishes: St. Ambrose, Blessed Sacrament, St. Cecilia, and St. Katherine of Sienna. Building and loan associations were still being organized at the rate of thirty-five a year.

A large portion of the Italians were from Cefalù, and had come recently. There were communities living near all of the markets, quarries, stoneyards, and cemeteries, as well as in St. Leo's parish, once an Irish neighborhood where the cathedral had first been proposed. St. Leo's had undergone an "unparalleled and wonderful transformation."[78] The cardinal considered his Italians hard to educate, and doctors at the public schools at Fayette and Green streets (near Lexington Market) noted many problems of malnutrition and debility. More infants survived because the mothers nursed their babies and by taking boarders managed to work at home while the babies were young. In this generation were formed numerous social corporations among Italians—saving and loan associations, the society of fruit vendors (die Mutuo Socorro), and a protective association for manufacturers of ice cream waffles. Skilled masons and stone cutters often worked for the Irish contractors and pavers and rapidly became independent in contracting. Italian produce vendors associated themselves with the butchers in the city market stalls. Contractors and market men were part of a well-buffered network of Irish and German Catholic politicians.

The Individual Home

Each community in Baltimore sought to develop home ownership as a means of protecting its children and its identity. Compared with other cities in the United States and elsewhere, Baltimore homes were cheaper, and more workers owned homes. British investigators of working-class living conditions were impressed with the savings and loan societies and the neighborhoods they had built, with streetcars, well-distributed parks, and low rents. But they noted the weakness of the trade unions, and their interviews fill in the details of working hours and family budgets. When these are matched with the infant mortality study, one finds a more complete and consistent picture of the pecking order of work and survival.

Of the infants born in 1915, 6 percent were from homes with over $1050 a year income—professionals, public officials, manufacturers, proprietors, contractors. Altogether, a third were from homes that earned over $850. Printers, skilled building craftsmen, brewery workers, and public service employees were in this "aristocracy of labor." They worked forty-eight hours a week or less. All were strongly unionized. Half owned their homes—a figure as high as the professional and business class. Six percent of their infants died in the first year. In the next third were the infants of boiler makers and clothing cutters, who worked fifty-four hours a week and earned between $650 and $850. A quarter owned homes. Brickmakers, drivers, shipping labor, and waiters worked sixty hours and earned around $600. Ten percent of their infants died. In the bottom third were the oyster shuckers, cannery workers, coal stokers, and servants, who worked seventy or seventy-two hours a week and earned less than $550 a year. Only 7 percent owned homes. Fifteen percent of their infants died.

In other words, those with the longest hours earned least money and were more often laid off for bad weather or hard times. They had less housing space and ate less meat. It was more often their infants who died, and the surviving children went to work at twelve or thirteen. Those differences of class were so matched with differences of color and language that they were easily confused. Most blacks were in the bottom third, a plurality of recent immigrants in the middle third, and more native-born whites and people of German origin in the top third. Even the imperfections of the caste system—the individual exceptions —undermined solidarities by individual competition. Many thoughtful people in Baltimore perceived the vicious circle of poverty and ethnic status, as did the tuberculosis commission. But there was no way to integrate human relationships within the context of the competitive economy and the extreme range of economic inequality. Physical planning could be harmonious—the circulation of drainage and vehicles could be coordinated—but there was no such easy reconciliation in the circulation of income. The infant mortality study of 1915 (not published until after World War I) was the best attempt to untangle numerous factors of habit and way of life, and therefore the interplay of labor force and ethnic group. From ten thousand interviews, they concluded:

Isolation of a group from the life of the community as a whole, may or may not affect the physical welfare of the babies of the group. If it deprives men of economic opportunity, because they cannot pass barriers of language or of color, the babies born into their homes will pay with a high mortality the price of the fathers' poverty.[79]

On the eve of World War I Baltimore still did not give the impression of a highly mechanized city. Introduction of dozens of mechanical, electrical, and automobile devices excited a sense of futuristic changes and visions of comfort, speed, and youth. But the quality of urban life, for better and for worse, was essentially human and animal, rather than mechanical. It was this quality—the human tempo—that after the war became the object of nostalgia.

Labor was still mainly muscle power, and the rhythm of human teamwork structured the job, however inhuman the pressures. The million-dollar payroll for stevedoring was assisted only by the old-fashioned steam hoists. The Canton Company introduced its first electric crane on the piers in 1913. The massive labor of public works and home building was still handled by pick and shovel, man and mule. In 1899 there were only four steam rollers in the state. By 1915 the city had introduced a snowplow and weed killer, and the city engineer designed and built 150 mechanical trench diggers, which cut excavating costs by

Mechanization and
the Future

Hand labor was still used exclusively in this 1923 cable-laying operation.

two-thirds. (They were copied by the Russian ordnance department.) One of the biggest builders in town, McCullough, described how they excavated the basements for the long block on Wilkens Avenue: A line of men with spade-tipped steel bars broke off chunks of earth; a line of men with picks broke up the chunks; behind them were teams of three men shoveling left-handed, three right-handed—"scoop and pitch, scoop and pitch." From ten feet down the workers heaved earth to the five-feet level; another team pitched it up to the surface. This was ten-hour, $1.65 a day labor. Mortar was mixed in the street bed.[80] McCullough bought his first steam cement mixer after 1913. The gas and electric company introduced a steam shovel and air compressor on its 1913 construction site, and celebrated the completion of the project with an oyster roast. The company brass and city fathers attended in a fleet of thirty-three sidecar motorcycles. The city introduced several experimental motor vehicles as well as a dozen ceremonial automobiles: the Bay View ambulance, the first garbage truck in the nation, and a $5,000 electric truck. The fire engine fleet was rapidly built up to thirty-five electric and gasoline vehicles.

Despite those previews of things to come, Baltimore was still a horsey town. Five thousand buildings were used as stables, and seventeen thousand horse-drawn vehicles were licensed. The B&O Railroad was still using horses in Pratt Street. Sixteen hundred teams a day drove over the Light Street bridge, four hundred over the Block Street drawbridge. As late as 1910 the city built a central stable at Pratt Street and Central Avenue for 350 horses and vehicles, and leased a thirty-acre farm out Liberty Road for their sick, run-down, or overworked horses. The gypsies camped every year near Brooklyn to sell horses and mules. Catholic children's societies took a special interest in the protection of horses from cruelty, and the grand event for Baltimore youngsters in May 1913—while their elders buzzed about the women's suffrage marches—was the workhorse parade.

While the horses still did the work, the automobile was gaining rapidly as the vehicle of luxury and pleasure, and auto owners began redesigning the city. Baltimore's first auto show was held in 1906, and the 700 auto owners in the city were invited to participate. On the great day twenty cars were in line, mostly dealers'. "Honk! honk! honk! The cars all behaved beautifully." That night the mayor bought a Rambler touring car. A car owner not only had to lay out in cold cash for a car ($650 to $3,500), he had also to maintain a chauffeur at $15 a week and a mechanic at $25.[81] The 1906 crowd was enthusiastic because the speed limit had been raised from six to twelve miles per hour and the governor announced plans for a new cement boulevard to Washington (Route 1). By 1910 there were four thousand cars in Maryland, by 1917 fifty-five thousand, plus four thousand motor trucks. The "truck farmers" began buying motor trucks, and Consolidated began selling and using electric trucks. Accidents were reported every day. In 1916 20,000 new operators were licensed, 1,700 drivers were arrested, and 150 had their licenses revoked for driving under the influence.[82] A cabaret performer and party joy riding in a seven-passenger rented car drove into the harbor. Police commandeered a car and a taxi to chase a stolen car through the downtown streets. Mass transit began to feel competition. Unlicensed automobile "jitneys" forced United Railways into experimenting with a motorbus service and its own subsidiary jitney service. The Maryland and Pennsylvania commuter railroad complained of competition from private automobiles but reassured its stockholders, "We are confident that the bottom has been reached."[83]

Sharp entrepreneurs began adapting the urban landscape to the new form of locomotion. Charles Street, Cathedral Street, and Mt. Royal Avenue, convenient to the elite of Mount Vernon Place and Bolton Hill instantly became an auto-oriented district, and the dealers created new types of display. Mount Royal Avenue featured Peerless, Chalmers, the Hupmobile, the Locomobile, the Riordan, Hudson, Pathfinder, the Kissel-Kar, Packard, and Cadillac. Shopping for less swell models was better along North Avenue. By 1917 fifty dealers handled sixty-five different makes. The most elegant Automobile Club in the nation—it cost $100,000—confirmed the auto dealers' hub at Mount Royal and Cathedral streets. The fire department chafed at the presence of three thousand gas pumps on the sidewalks in front of grocery stores. Jacob Blaustein, who had begun delivering kerosene in a horse-drawn tank cart, now created the first drive-in filling station, the Lord Baltimore, on Cathedral Street. He set the ten-gallon glass jar on top of the pump: "You see what you get. You get what you see." Robert Garrett's banking firm underwrote Grimes and Duncan's creation of the Commercial Credit Corporation, a financial adaptation to the auto age. They offered working capital to manufacturers and dealers, and bought "open accounts receivable" on the "confidential nonnotification plan." That meant you didn't know your overdue bill was now owed to Commercial Credit instead of your dealer. When the corporation began financing installment sales of pleasure cars, their business began its swift climb to national rank.

The rural landscape, too, began its transformation. At the beginning of the century, the Maryland Geological Survey, the State Roads Commission, and the Federal Bureau of Roads made Maryland the pioneer for experiments with road materials nears Kingsville, Baltimore County. The county had a thousand miles of road, only a third of which was graveled or shelled, the rest dirt.[84] Hauling

Officials and notables attended an oyster roast at the dedication of the Woodbrook Electric Station. A fleet of "dainty taxicabs" brought many of the honoraries to the celebration.

costs were no different from a century earlier. By 1917 the county was spending half a million a year to grade, gravel, and oil the roads, and had hired an engineer to reorganize the operation, but the public was still dissatisfied. At the state level, with the Automobile Club and the "good roads movement" behind him, Governor Austin Crothers initiated a $5 million program, acquired the private turnpikes, and built Route 1 to Washington. As in all aspects of state politics, the ambiguity remained between private and public enterprise. In 1904, when the Pennsylvania Railroad built a double-track bridge across the Susquehanna, it offered its obsolete 1873 single-track bridge at Havre de Grace (thirteen feet wide and thirty-three hundred feet long) free to any taker, so the company would not have to remove it. A group of seven private citizens accepted the offer and put in $100 each to convert it to a highway bridge. They were, in fact, all connected with state politics (e.g., the governor's brother, Omar). Over thirteen years they made $370,000 profit from tolls, then in 1923 sold the bridge to the state for $585,000. It became known as the gold mine bridge.[85]

Excitement over the "auto-picking" season of January 1917 shows how completely the pattern was set for automobile civilization, and the euphoria with which it was viewed.[86] By means of thousands of electric lights and hundreds of powerful nitrogen lamps "the grim armory was magically changed from a big void to a huge bower of beauty. An orange sky, soft and mellowy, covered all, and big canopies of brilliant white and black and yellow fluttered from the walls." Columns surmounted by palms, smilax, and chrysanthemums marked off the floor into booths "wherein a wealth of mechanical beauty—a king's ransom in motorcars—lay gleaming, glowing, fairly blooming in prismatic splendor." The auto show was a society event and fashion show as well. Women in décolleté wore strings of pearls, diamond lavalieres, and their "favorite flashing ear pendants." They danced the waltz and the one-step, patronized the ice cream parlor, or sat and chatted, finding an "irresistible lure in the comfy seats of the cars." Apparently the wealthy and the influential in Baltimore agreed with *Sun* editorial writer, "Art and utility have met together, science and grace have kissed each other, in the latest realization of the auto-mechanic's dreams. . . . May the day soon come when no well-regulated family can afford to do without one!"

Torpedoes and Thunderbolts

World War I differed in tempo from Baltimore's previous experiences of war. For two and a half years America remained neutral while war in Europe continued on an unprecedented scale. This allowed a build-up of the Baltimore economy and a deepening but many-sided emotional involvement. The city climbed back to its rank as the nation's seventh largest industrial center and stayed there. The climate remained one of tolerance. Then there followed a year and a half of full participation in the war—short, total, intolerant. The war became a crucible in which intense heat and pressure hastened all chemical reactions. Gradual social and economic changes were accelerated. The processing of the great unwashed was intensified. National patriotic symbols were elevated, hastening a destruction of some elements of a Baltimore identity. The opportunities and sacrifices of war fueled antagonism between classes, while the logic of defense contained its expression. One can look at the war effort first in terms of the economic expansion of Baltimore, then in terms of its social meaning, always bearing in mind that over six or eight weeks early in 1917 there was a great wrenching of ideas and feelings from neutrality to total participation. This critical period is most revealing.

In 1915 and 1916 the city responded to constant appeals for aid. Paderewski played the piano for starving Poland, Mischa Elman fiddled for tubercular French soldiers, and the Mary Magdalen of Oberammergau sang for German war relief. The cardinal appealed in the churches for Ireland, while the United solicited the garment workers, "Bread for the Living, Shrouds for the Dead," and "We Have Our Own Belgium." Jacob Epstein offered a thousand dollars a month for the duration of the war, and Yiddish East Baltimore brought nine thousand dollars to a sobbing rally at the Academy of Music. Twenty-five Lithuanian organizations representing ten thousand people in the neighborhood of the

Hollins Market joined hands to send aid to the old country. The largest effort was the "Allied Bazaar" at the Fifth Regiment armory. The prominent socialites and business leadership of the city were by mid-January 1917 publicly committed to the Allied cause. They promised that along with a monkey and pony circus, Serbian and Bohemian folk dancers, "healthful and innocent amusements" would be provided such as moving pictures of the great battles of the Marne, Verdun, and the Somme. Laborers spent a month digging two hundred feet of trenches on the Preston Street lawn of the armory. In the trenches a visitor, "having left the brilliantly lighted, music-filled bazaar behind," would come upon an officers' dugout, a Red Cross station, a wicked-looking machine gun, an ominous stretch of barbed wire entanglement, and a twenty-foot British caterpillar.[87]

Covering all those diverse sympathies with a cloak of unity, the fourths of July were celebrated with all the zeal of Spanish-American War days. Children were spangled with stars, stripes, gold buttons, and sailor collars; backyards were decked with tables of steamed crabs and beer kegs; and the red brick and white marble neighborhoods of Canton, Highlandtown, South Baltimore, and the point were spread with bunting. The German bands played brassy music. The kids put "torpedoes" on the streetcar tracks and tossed "thunderbolts" into the storm sewers.

The War Economy

The closer America came to entering the war, the more clearly industrial and financial leaders recognized the value of Baltimore as a location for steel making and shipbuilding. It was well placed for labor, fuel, and freight rates. The harbor's superb, thirty- and thirty-five-foot channels were adequate; its industrial rim was elastic. Close to Europe by sea and close to the U.S. heartland by rail, it also had the unique advantage of being 100 miles west of the seacoast and relatively defensible against submarines. Charles Schwab, the tough financial collaborator of Andrew Carnegie and J. P. Morgan (he managed to outwit them in succession), acquired the Sparrows Point plant for his Bethlehem Steel Company. The real prize of this $25 million maneuver was the company's holdings of Cuban iron ore. Bethlehem Steel promptly undertook massive expansion at Sparrows Point. It built a tin-plate mill (by taking over Aldred's plant) and invested $15 million in a mill for rolling steel plate for tanks and battleships. The Cunard line ordered two big freighters from it, the first orders of British companies to American shipyards in fifty years. The U.S. Navy contracted for fifty steamers. To fill these orders, Bethlehem Steel bought the 535-acre Numsen property on Humphrey's Creek, and built a second big shipyard adjoining: "Ship-building is more of a money-maker now than steel-making." Other new shipbuilding ventures selected Baltimore. Baltimore Drydock and Shipbuilding bought the McLean property next to Fort McHenry on the south side of Locust Point, for a $3 million plant. (McLean contractors moved to a site at Canton.) The Maryland Shipbuilding Company, incorporated locally by Aldred, Jenkins, and Griswold, acquired a million-dollar 1800-acre site on Marley Neck. It planned to hire two thousand employees and make steel. The steel and shipbuilding investments had the stunning virtue of offering an industrial base with

Wooden shipbuilding was revived briefly in 1918 at Fairfield.

potential for generating future peacetime industrial growth. Bethlehem Steel became the kingpin of the regional economy.

Bartlett-Hayward founded its extraordinary expansion on industries geared more exclusively to war needs. It had several early million-dollar ammunition contracts for the Russian and French governments. When America entered the war, its employees swelled from four thousand to twenty-two thousand, a scale of operation never seen in Baltimore. Experienced in the swift erection of huge gasholders, the company put up industrial buildings with astonishing speed. On fifty-five acres at Sollers Point (Turner Station) it built fifty-nine buildings and hired six thousand workers, mostly women, girls, and country boys, for manufacturing munitions and processing toluol and light oils from methane for high explosives. On Washington Boulevard it redeveloped a forty-nine-acre dump. On Bush Street it built a plant for shell loading and steam blowers (now the Koppers piston ring plant). It rebuilt and expanded its original Mount Clare site by removing dwellings on Ramsay Street.[88]

Poole Engineering, owned in Delaware, expanded along the same lines. It had several million dollars worth of Allied contracts for mine cars, gun carriages, and aircraft guns before the United States entered the war. As the war approached, hundreds of special police were sworn in, and a detail was assigned to guard the Prospect Hill overlook in Druid Hill Park, which gave a view of the Poole plant at Woodberry. It doubled its labor force and built a long cold-frame type factory back into the valley; it also tested shrapnel at Texas, Maryland, and manufactured airplanes at Hagerstown.

The prime locus of investment was the outer harbor: Curtis Bay, Canton, and Patapsco Neck. Military installations and utilities complemented the investments of private industry in each district. Consolidated Gas and Electric enlarged the Westport plant and introduced natural gas by pipeline. The Pennsylvania Railroad invested $10 million, the B&O $4 million. At Curtis Bay, on the site of the old sugar refinery, U.S. Industrial Alcohol created a $5 million enterprise, a vinegar factory and the world's largest alcohol factory. American Refractories built a plant on twenty acres, near Brooklyn, to supply Bethlehem Steel with firebrick. Davison Chemical added a machine shop. There were soon five thousand workers at Curtis Bay, and a large Ordnance Department storage depot. At Canton an acid plant was built for Baugh Chemical, and the Quartermaster built rows of warehouses for shipping war material to France. On Sollers Point the Aldred group developed a $3 million aluminum ore company on the former site of the McShane foundry, adjoining the Bartlett-Hayward munitions plant. Beyond the Sparrows Point steel mill and shipyard, the military invested $4 million in Fort Howard defense works at North Point.

The outlying industrial locations required a vast labor force. United Railways improved its service to Curtis Bay and Sparrows Point. Real estate values soared. On Patapsco Neck over five years the prices rose from $30 to $1000 an acre. During the fifteen months before the United States came into the war, 90 percent of the land changed hands. The largest single development was a $5 million project of the Eastern Land Company on a thousand acres. It had the financial backing of Frederick Wood of Bethlehem Steel and the management expertise of E. H. Bouton of the Roland Park Company. They translated the curves of Roland Park into a working-class model neighborhood and projected it onto the coastal plain landscape of Dundalk, Gracelands, and Schwab City. Formulas for ground rent financing and home ownership were borrowed from the Canton experience. Cheap, instant, and institutional housing was built on Sollers Point for workers of the munitions and aluminum plants. The Emergency Fleet Corporation bought back some Eastern Land Company property on St. Helena to put up "convertible" houses for shipyard workers.

Industrial development began to threaten the vulnerable tidewater environment, but this attracted less attention. Beginning in March 1917, frequent fish poisonings were recorded at Curtis Creek: "Hundreds of fish have taken three gulps and died." There were complaints of smells and air pollution in the same district, and the city experienced an invasion of rats. Even in the '90s, industry at outlying sites depended entirely on ground water from the Patapsco formation, a geologic layer of sand and gravel underlain by clay. Rain falling on outcrops adjacent to the piedmont trickled down under Baltimore, and around the rim of the harbor two hundred wells were sunk. The volume pumped has been estimated at 5 or 10 million gallons a day in 1900, 15 million in 1915. Acid contamination of the wells resulted from surface pollution, especially seepage through the stockpiles of copper ores, sulfur, and slag. A drop was noticed in artesian head in the '90s. The drop in pressure of the mass of ground water resulted from too high a rate of pumping, and it allowed brackish water from the harbor to move in. Deep dredging in the harbor may also have contributed to salty water entering the geologic fresh-water layer. These problems were not troublesome during the sluggish period between 1900 and 1914, but were aggravated by wartime industrial production. Where acid or salt content was too high, wells were abandoned, and the abandoned wells acted as sources of further pollution of the ground water.

Baltimore's industrial recovery was achieved by a great leap of productivity: "The city has put on seven-league boots." Over five years (1914–19), the labor force in manufacturing increased by a third, manufacturing capital doubled, and the value of manufactured products and exports tripled. The war effort demanded that everyone get the greatest possible output from each hour of labor, each square foot of space, each pound of steel or cotton. Wartime labor shortage tended to overcome the old tendency of Baltimore manufacturers to be wasteful of labor because it had been relatively cheap. Bethlehem introduced the bonus system that Frederick Taylor had designed at the Bethlehem, Pennsylvania plant, pushing up the productivity of labor at numerous tasks. In fields already unionized, the labor force won its goal of an eight-hour day. The clothing industry, making uniforms for the U.S. and Italian armies, went on an eight-hour basis and obtained a pay raise of 7 to 15 percent. The shorter work day was associated with an intensification of labor—a faster pace, piece-work pressure, a more complete adaptation to the machine, accelerated mechanization, and also a longer trip to work.

Labor shortages had other effects on social behavior and ideas. In the first month of the war three thousand Marylanders enlisted in the navy. By the end of the war sixty-two thousand were serving in some branch of the armed forces. This produced exceptional labor force turnover. Ten percent of B&O employees enlisted, and perhaps a quarter of the employees of city government. The outflow to the military meant the city had to draw in newcomers. Bartlett-Hayward sought to recruit country boys, and Bethlehem continued to absorb black workers from its Virginia recruiting grounds. The shortage of labor hastened the acceptance of women into new types of work, a trend already under way with the mechanization of clerical tasks: the typewriter, the telephone, and stenography. Seventy-five daughters of the elite bobbed their hair and went to Chevy Chase to learn first aid. The gas company hired women to clean and repair stove parts and gas fixtures, United Railways hired 150 women to drive streetcars, and the B&O Locust Point shops hired women in "men's jobs" such as laborer, foreman, dope reclaimer, or operator of the pipe-threading machine and drill press. Some picked up old iron or swept the shops. The crisis gave social value to rather meaningless jobs because the women workers released men for more important jobs "over there." The color line was more strict than sex roles; it hardly budged. There was no apparent visible change in the black participation in the civilian labor force, although within the black community symbolic importance was attached to military participation.

The official idea was that everyone pulled together. The entire population

The Social Economy

World War I created a shortage of traditional male factory labor and led to expanded opportunities for training and employing women.

was being processed, young and old, rich and poor, to conform to the moral discipline of war. Fifteen thousand public school children weeded their home gardens. The women's clubs canned vegetables. The young men at Hopkins learned to handle Krag rifles. The Goucher women gave up between-meal snacks and plowed up their tennis courts at Twenty-fourth and St. Paul streets. A cadet corps of two hundred boys drilled twice a week at St. Mary's industrial school. "Brother Paul, the director, is intensely patriotic; he is constantly impressing upon the minds and hearts of the boys that religion and patriotism are inseparable."[89] In May 1917, two hundred men of Baltimore's elite were selected for officer training at Fort Myer and began raising mustaches and learning to use brooms and sew on buttons. On the weekly society page in the *Sun* "Betsy Patterson" wrote to "Dearest Girl":

Eleanor Sweringen, who binds books so exquisitely, is getting up a shooting club. We will practice at the Maryland Rifle Range at one-half cent a shot. . . . Perhaps you know that there are already more women than men in Baltimore, but, gracious me! pretty soon there won't be any men at all. They're all going off to Fort Myer and they seem so horribly cheerful about it . . . a real masculine lark.[90]

Other people had other concerns. Staple food shortages appeared, not based on "real" scarcity like the scarcity of labor. Grain prices were rising. Gambrill shipped 500,000 bushels of wheat from Minneapolis to Baltimore to forward to the Allies, and reportedly made $500,000 profit. There were 3.5 million bushels of grain in Baltimore elevators. Because they didn't move into the market, people jumped to the conclusion that they had been purchased by the Germans. Potatoes and onions disappeared from the markets. The "onion special," a thirty-six-car train from St. Louis destined for Baltimore, simply vanished. The Salvation Army hadn't put an onion in its soups for six weeks. The price of admission to the Purim ball for Jewish War Relief at the Phoenix Club was three potatoes, to be distributed in East Baltimore. The price of greens soared, yet the newly built cold storage warehouses were full. What did they hold? What was the turnover? Who was hoarding? Nobody knew. A car shortage was blamed: railroad cars hauling material eastward for shipment to Europe "piled up" in the yards, docks, and factory sidings in the east. As prices rose, the whole newly developed and finely tuned system of circulation was being used as a holding system by speculators. They were "making a warehouse of the cars." Goods were "consigned and reconsigned a dozen times to different places without being unloaded, the owners or consignees finding it more profitable to pay the freight charges and the car demurrage than to unload and sell their contents. Railroad officials say they are powerless."[91] Money circulated faster than goods, and profits were generated while others tightened their belts. Farmers began calling the mayor to tell him about potatoes "hid in the city." At last he sent twenty-five city trucks to buy potatoes direct from the farmers and sell them in the city markets at cost. Potato prices fell. "On some dining-room tables in Baltimore last night there were sights that have not been seen for two months. Potatoes were there, mashed, fried, boiled, barbecued, garbed in gravy, with jackets and without jackets. But there was no potato salad. You need onions for potato salad."[92]

Despite the mayor's gesture, the family budget squeeze continued. Wages had not yet begun to rise. For the first time since '94, steady workers were standing in bread lines. The Salvation Army was distributing a thousand loaves a day in South Baltimore. In Pigtown, the Volunteers of America began offering breakfasts to five hundred school children who had only coffee and hard bread. Workers who earned $10 to $12 a week—carpenters, teamsters, longshoremen, clothing workers, factory hands, laborers—were spending a quarter of their budget for rent. A 50 percent increase in the price of coal,[93] the highest price ever experienced in Baltimore, was forcing them to cut back their food budget by 30 percent, while food prices rose. They were substituting hominy, rice, and cornbread for potatoes and bread, molasses for sugar. White folks were turning to soul food. "Eggs and meat have been wiped clear from the small wage-earner's board." Meat was a little liver or tripe or soup. "Fish has become more expensive than meat." Their luxuries were fruit pies and cabbage on Sunday. A federal grand jury indicted a West Virginia coal combine that had arranged to double the price of soft coal again. A thirteen-year-old girl was killed by a passenger train while she and her sister were picking bits of waste coal from the tracks between West and Ostend streets. A hard winter pushed the cost of fuel still higher in the family budget. Factories shut down, electricity was cut off frequently, people burned furniture.

Initial propositions for financing the war also presented the image of people tightening their belts together: there would be munitions taxes, excess profits taxes (8 percent on profits above 8 percent of capitalization), income taxes ranging up to 50 percent for millionnaires, and estate taxes up to 15 percent for estates over $5 million. The instant plan to borrow a staggering $7 billion was, however, intended at "passing a part of the burden along to the next generation."[94] To make the bonds easier to sell, they were tax free. The new government tax bite plus the huge tax-free bond issues produced a reshuffling of financial assets among various classes of people.[95] The *Sun* emphasized that the government needed the small man: "The small men are coming in grandly in Baltimore."[96] A Bohemian delegation from Curtis Bay brought in $500, the boys at St. Vincent's orphan asylum $200, and the children at Friends School—once it was explained to them—$3,000. Nevertheless, the bulk came from the big men. People with incomes over $4,000 were interested in tax shelters, and the larger their incomes the more appealing were Liberty bonds. When Henry Walters died in 1931, his estate included $2 million worth of first Liberty loan bonds. In addition to the tax advantages of the Liberty loans, the federal government agreed to redeposit all the money used to buy bonds in the coffers of the banks where it lay. The banks were allowed to relend these sums (until the government needed them), not subject to the usual 18 percent reserve requirements. Therefore, the money correctly channeled would pay 3.5 percent interest—tax free—from the federal government plus 5 or 6 percent from short-term loans, often more. This situation, coupled with the urgency of war contracts, offered remarkable profits on short-term financing. Bethlehem, in March 1917, to fill its contracts for British ships issued $15 million in new stock and $50 million in twenty-five-year 5 percent notes, which in turn were "secured" on $37 million worth of British government notes due in two years. American investors bought in notes of the British investors in American railroads, utilities, and real estate. With the cooperation of the Marines, they replaced German investors in the Dominican Republic. "Quick turn" was the strategy of the hour. The land sales in Patapsco Neck were known as quick turn. "New high-priced automobiles are appearing all over the peninsula, and the old buggies and daytons have been sent to the discard."[97] Davison Chemical was sued by certain stockholders for having issued new stock, manipulating its price to make $5 million worth of assets appear worth $12 million, and reducing the subsequent market value of their shares.[98]

A climate of uncertainty and swift change also created special opportunities for short-term speculation. For example, as prohibition gained counties and then whole states and the national temperance lobby gained ground, fantastic ups and downs could be generated in the price of shares of U.S. Industrial Alcohol. At the time the company was building its $5 million plant in Baltimore, the stock had never paid a dividend, but through manipulation of the market, the "Standard Oil crowd" was believed to have made "a killing on the long side."[99] Baltimore opened up a lucrative mail-order business in monthly quarts of "horn," "third-rail," and "fourth dimensional distillation." A hundred firms were organized, most of which simply wrapped up the goods, stuck tags on them, mailed them to Virginia or West Virginia, and cashed postal money orders. Wholesale liquor dealers were moving their headquarters to Baltimore.[100] After a debate as strenuous as the defense bill, Congress passed a "bone dry" bill that forbade use of the mails for shipping liquor from wet into dry states.[101] But this was a challenge Baltimore entrepreneurs relished. Baltimoreans were solidly in favor of prohibition—everywhere except in Baltimore. The city would be an oasis in the desert. The watermen turned from the dwindling oyster catch to new activities. Captain Ike Bozeman, a seventy-year-old oysterman from Somerset County, and his Negro mate, Horace Jones, were notorious. They loaded 250 cases of whiskey in Baltimore and made the rounds of the wharves in the dry counties of Virginia. Bozemen was eventually cornered by the state cutter in the Rappahannock; he was shot by the "revenuers" and died in jail.[102]

Eliminate the Germans

In late January 1917, as German U-boats began attacking shipping in wider areas of the seas, a sharp wrenching of public opinion began. Maryland's prominent leaders petitioned the president for universal military training: "No people who have preserved their sanity will neglect to provide itself with adequate means of defense. We have practically no army at this time available for our defense."[103] They were rebuked by the president for their "intemperate" language. A panic period of two months followed. The level of anxiety can be gauged by the level of rumor. The rumors allowed people to test their ideas against all sorts of "unthinkable" possibilities. Three steamers supposedly cleared for the river Plate ports and took out several million dollars in gold, in American coined eagles and half-eagles. The gold was rumored destined for Germany, as German raiders were operating off the coast of South America. But it was later learned that the gold was shipped by Allied and American wool manufacturers to pay for South American wool.[104] A week later, three German steamers lay in port, unable to sail for fear of raiders. It was rumored that their crew had wrecked the machinery so the vessels would be useless to the United States if seized. "Locust Point was highly excited." In fact, the crew were "scattered around the Point saloons drinking their beer and trying to be cheerful."[105]

Anxiety in the face of rumor and uncertainty allowed buried hostilities to surface. The regimentation and bending of social efforts to wartime goals tended to smash other values and to curb deviations savagely. The primacy of national goals fit the trend of diminishing Baltimorean identity.

The first target was, of course, the sense of identity of the German community. The war put an end to the German-American era in Baltimore. The schools were already "Americanized." Pledges to the flag and patriotic singing had been introduced during the Spanish-American War. The connection between Catholic faith and German language was no longer an issue, since the parochial schools were all English speaking. The public "German-English" schools had become less German and were reputed chiefly for their strong college preparatory orientation and high intellectual standards; they were frequented by many Jewish children. But America's entry into the war dramatized the heartbreak of hyphenation. "U.S. Eye on Hyphens," shouted the *Sun*. Frank Furst, "in many respects the first citizen of Maryland, a native of Germany," was quoted, "The hour has come when every American must be an American to the exclusion of all else."[106] Other prominent citizens such as Judge Rose and the editorialists called for understanding: "The German elements will be loyal, although their hearts will bleed." German-born persons rushed to take out citizenship papers. In the schools, confusion and tension broke out. Youths acted out the apprehensions of their elders and played games with old-fashioned signs of authority. The German teacher at Poly was accused of having given vent to unpatriotic utterings. The girls at Western High School refused to sing "Deutschland Uber Alles," and the German Club disappeared. The Sons of the Revolution mistakenly protested against compulsory German, although, in fact, the courses had not been compulsory for some years. Again rumors circulated. Mystery ships were reported. The German consul's car was stolen. An unnamed "John Doe," fertilizer expert and music lover, was arrested as an agent for German chemical firms. Telegraph wires "to the north" were reported cut by saboteurs. A Russian agent was mysteriously shot in his room at the Baltimore Country Club. The first official act of war in Baltimore was staged as a cloak and dagger affair. The three German merchant ships that had been lying off Locust Point for two months were taken as contraband. Deputies with high-powered rifles and hand lanterns full of oil sat by the telephone, awaiting a flash from the custom house to go get 'em. When the word came from the *Sun* at 3 a.m. that Congress had voted the declaration of war, off went the collector of the port and the surveyor of customs in big sightseeing cars. Streetcars carried a company of the fourth regiment, eighteen city police, and a Coast Guard platoon of twenty. They took the twenty German officers to the Hotel Junker, and marched the sixty-one sailors through the early morning crowds on Locust Point to the police station: "The Germans' heads were bowed and the crowd was silent. Not a comment was heard, not a cheer, not a greeting. It was almost an American tribute to an American enemy."[107]

Unnaturalized Germans were now classed as enemy aliens. The police searched their homes for wireless equipment, cipher code, weapons, and explosives. They were excluded from within a half-mile of defense plants and military installations. Levi Goldenberg, for example, a department store owner for thirty-five years, was under $10,000 bond and allowed to move about only in the vicinity of his home or his store, and to make the trips between only by streetcar. Little by little, German symbols were rooted out. German Street was renamed Redwood. The German-American Bank retitled itself simply "The American Bank." The Concordia opera house was turned into a straw hat factory. In 1918 the last touch was the prohibition on drinking beer.

In sharp contrast, the identity of the Polish community was reinforced. Poles had immigrated to Baltimore in large numbers just before the war and established organizations such as the Polish Falcons, which expressed fierce loyalty to both Poland and America and considerable militarism. Several hundred had already gone to Canada to enlist in the British army, along with a hundred Baltimore Labor Zionists who had joined to wrest Palestine from the Turks.

In addition to anti-German feelings, there was a resurgence of antipacifist, antiinternationalist, antiforeign, and antisocialist feelings. On the eve of the president's asking Congress to declare war, a pacifist meeting in the academy was broken up by a "great patriotic demonstration" of several thousand people of all ages led by a number of prominent citizens.[108] Outside the hall Miss Gill, a Baltimore socialite, mounted a soapbox and called for three cheers for the president, then led the singing of "The Star-Spangled Banner" and "Hang Billy Bryan to a sour-apple tree." Jacob France mounted the wall and recited a patriotic poem. Then the crowd rushed forward into the hall, up to the orchestra pit, and shoved the flag in the face of the speaker. Forty police swept toward the crowd outside with clubs. They beat several wealthy persons. In the papers, the pacifists, including clergy, Quakers, and internationalists, were described as frightened specimens, corpulent and ashy pale, the police as brutes or at best "country constables." The cartoons showed "pacifist and pacifistess" running away from Uncle Sam piping "Yankee Doodle." On Sunday the preaching in the churches was everywhere on the Prince of Peace. "The Divine call," said the Episcopal bishop, "has been most clearly revealed to us by the medium of human wrath." The German pastors came out "like men, honest and unflinching." In the Irish parish of St. John's at Valley and Eager streets, eight hundred men of the Holy Name Society went to early communion to prove their "manhood, their Americanism, their Catholicism." Five boys who refused to salute the flag, "a high and holy symbol," and one who left the room during the singing of "The Star-Spangled Banner," were suspended from school, and their parents brought before the school board. The newspapers published long poems on flags in churches. "What seems most singular . . . is that three of the five boys who do not consider the American flag good enough for them were born in Russia."[109] The *Sun* commented,

We are not advising persecution, but it is essential that we should be vigilant, that we should know where we stand. To believe in certain economic and political theories is not treason, if they do not involve disloyalty. But socialism which is in conflict with patriotism is only another way of spelling treason.[110]

Next day a cartoon appeared of Columbia as a young lady in her nightie, a Secret Service candle in her hand, searching, while the feet of Foreign Plotter stuck out from under the bed—"They're Lurking Everywhere."[111]

Every ancient nightmare or protest suddenly appeared in the garb of treason and every repressive tradition took on a patriotic aura. A black man from Georgia was arrested in a fertilizer plant in Curtis Bay, suspected of working with German agents to stir up Georgia Negroes to refuse to serve.[112] A federal court test of the segregation ordinance was blamed on a Minnesota senator whose speech "stirred them up," and who had been delaying the vote to defend American rights at sea. The city solicitor claimed, "there probably would not have been any test case brought if our colored people in Baltimore had been left to themselves."[113] The president of the B&O, faced with a strike for an eight-hour day, raised the question, "I hope it will never be said that B&O employees at a time like this took any action which gave satisfaction, aid and comfort to those opposed to the welfare of the United States."[114] The next day's cartoon showed the railroad workers striking "A Foul Blow" at Uncle Sam. At Canton, where two hundred longshoremen of the IWW and one hundred freight handlers on the PRR were on strike, the police department dispatched a like number of officers for fear of sabotage, and an incident followed promptly in which a black striker was shot.[115]

Once war was declared, the processing of the population became very thorough. People were scrubbed, vaccinated, registered, pledged, and drilled. A thorough cleansing was moral and ideological as well as physical. At the telephone company, twenty-three hundred employees were asked to sign a pledge of patriotism. Ten refused. A law was finally passed against spitting. Dr. Howard argued that pointing a cough or a sneeze at someone was just like pointing a revolver at him. Mencken had always deplored the United Railways as an instrument of discipline invented for the regimentation of everyone. This discipline was heightened: thousands were moved daily on hour-long trips to Curtis Bay or Sparrows Point, and the unpopular "skip-stop" service was introduced to make the flow smoother. During the flu epidemic the streetcar tokens were bathed daily in antiseptic solution. Regular bathing was urged: "It will better fit the men to eliminate the Germans as a menace to the world—because cleanliness certainly improves efficiency."[116] The final step was registration of the fifty-five thousand young men of Baltimore.[117] By order of the mayor, the city hall bell was to boom out one hundred times at 7 a.m., and be taken up by all the church bells and steamboat and factory whistles. Each man after registration was decorated with a khaki band on his left arm.

A Place to Move About In

1919–1934

Baltimore emerged from World War I with its ego wonderfully mended. The city was launched as a modern industrial complex, vital to the American economy, to whom all the world owed money and brought a tribute of raw materials. Its area had tripled: the annexation of 1918 extended it from thirty square miles to ninety-two square miles, and most of the new belt was as empty and green as Druid Hill Park. As a result of these two changes, Baltimore's self-image took a new turn. Its buoyancy matched the national mood of the '20s. From a population of 729,000, the city expected to reach 1 million by 1930. What Mencken called "the boosters, boomers, go-getters and other such ballyhoo men" were hard at work promoting new product lines in manufacturing and new speculations on the fresh land. In the green annex the factory city and the park city no longer seemed to be in conflict. Industry would be set in a park; workers and neighbors would enjoy "daylight houses" and clean air. The whole city, well planned and well ordered, would be spacious, healthy, and productive. Skyscrapers and smokeless stacks would reach up to where sunshine burst through the clouds. Dirigibles would hang in its skies. European flights would land at a municipal airport built out of the harbor mud off Dundalk. Seaplanes, built in Baltimore, would land in the harbor itself.[1] Streams of traffic would flow uninterrupted over handsome viaducts, along elm-lined parkways, and in canyons between sleek rows of skyscrapers. Even when the boosting, the booming, the go-getting, and the ballyhoo suddenly quieted, when construction stopped and the factories laid off workers by the thousands, Baltimore pursued its agenda, like a mirage on the horizon, while more and more Baltimoreans echoed Mencken's question, "In what way, precisely, has the average Baltimorean benefitted by the great growth of the city during the past ten years?"[2]

Decompression

Annexation came with a whoosh. The pressure for Lebensraum in the old city could be released into the new territory. The city was suddenly rich in space. In the new annex there were two thousand people per square mile, whereas in the 1888 annex there were already twelve thousand per square mile, in the old city limits thirty-four thousand, and in the pre-1816 core (Fells Point, Oldtown, the inner harbor) there were fifty thousand—twenty-five times the density. At first nothing happened. War priorities were followed by shortages

City Hall Plaza before the
construction of the War
Memorial to the east was the
site of this peace celebration
following World War I.
The temporary decorations
included potted plants and
brilliant strings of lights.

of materials, erratic prices, and land speculations.[3] But in the mid-20s construction hit a peak of 6,000 houses a year, double any previous peaks. By the time it dropped back down (only 119 houses were built in 1934!), the effects were substantial. Population had doubled in the new annex and had dropped by half in the core. A clear pattern was visible that would be repeated in the next generation: thinning the old city and filling the new. But the filling would never reach previous densities.

Lower-density development permitted changes in the types of houses built. Frame houses were allowed in the annex. Builders, pressed by the city code, adopted wider frontages, which would admit daylight into all houses, whether rows, semidetached, or detached. Two-story porch-front rows were developed in new sections of West Baltimore. By 1930 there were several thousand in Rosemont and in the Hilton Avenue section, between Edmondson and Frederick Road. The average price of new houses doubled, and the builders aimed at a broad middle-class market, including the best-paid manufacturing workers. The price of land began to represent a larger share of the cost of a home, while the average household was smaller than before. Middle-class areas had wider lots, and the alleys were lined with garages. The most elegant neighborhoods had driveways and curving streets. The Roland Park Company opened Homeland on the Perine estate, and George R. Morris developed Ashburton on the 165-acre Gittings estate. Apartment houses were promoted between Guilford and the Johns Hopkins campus: the twelve-story Greenway, the Warrington Apartments, and the Ambassador.

The wealthy were moving out. From Eutaw Place old Mr. Strouse moved into the Riviera to die, and Manuel Hendler, the ice cream magnate, took his paintings six blocks up to a mansion on Lake Drive. Shaarei Tfiloh congregation built on Auchentoroly Terrace facing Druid Hill Park. Before the war, 60 percent of Social Register or "black book" families still lived on Mount Vernon and Bolton Hill, 8 percent in Roland Park, and most of the others somewhere in between. By 1932, only a third lived in Mount Vernon and Bolton Hill; nearly

The scale of Baltimore rowhouse construction in the 1920s is exemplified by this panoramic photograph. Extensive grading was necessary even when a grid pattern was not strictly adhered to. Note the two technologies in use: dump trucks and steam cranes were augmented by horse-drawn wagons.

half lived in the Roland Park Company suburbs of Roland Park, Guilford, and Homeland, or along University Parkway. "It is no idle jest that Baltimore Society is moving farther and farther out and from all signs soon there will be no more Baltimore society, literally speaking, as everyone will live in the country."[4] Green Spring, Worthington, and Dulaney valleys were the most popular, according to the *Sun* society editor. The way of life there was described as health giving, and the children of the Obers and Ridgleys "can sit a horse as well as their parents by the time they are eight or nine." Ironically, however, the car was essential to the "horsey" set; "Most of the people who live out there have two or more cars."[5]

Institutions moved as well. The Sulpicians removed their younger seminarians from the "blighted district" of St. Mary's to Roland Park. The "March violets" of St. François de Sales moved their convent and Academy of the Visitation. As investment sought the annex, property in the old city tended to depreciate. "The three-story houses of the last generation grow shabbier and shabbier. . . . Nearly everywhere speculators are converting them into walk-ups."[6] Commercial uses squeezed out downtown residents, and where residents left a vacuum, businesses sprouted. The car dealers' yards crept northward. "With the invasion of Charles Street, above the Monument, by store fronts of protean and appalling hideousness, the old Baltimore bids us goodbye." The "crest, apex, and masterpiece" of this, in Mencken's eyes, was the filling station at North Avenue.[7]

Industrially, Baltimore grew in the '20s by capturing its share of the nation's new branch plants. The strategy devised in about 1913 by Griswold, Warfield, Wood, and Aldred—the bankers, steel men, and utilities directors—was to attract outside capital and pursue a full integration of Baltimore into the national economy. The Industrial Factory Site Commission had published maps of sites and rail spurs, a guidebook, an interindustry analysis, a bird's-eye view, a model, and even a movie of the port of Baltimore. All of this paid off in the 1920s in new large manufacturing plants. Lever Brothers Gold Dust Twins built a soap factory at Canton, while its rival, Proctor and Gamble Ivory, built at Locust Point. In the inner harbor, Coca-Cola built a bottling plant and McCormick Spice built at Light and Barre streets. Their rivals, Crosse and Blackwell, built at Canton. Montgomery Ward purchased a site across Monroe Street from Carroll Park for a mail-order operation. Stieff Silver built at the Cedar Avenue bridge. All were substantial sites of ten to twenty acres, and were built on a standard plan of reinforced concrete with walls of glass windows in metal frames. All were relatively clean industries, and the outsides had a whitewashed look. Montgomery Ward and Stieff's were built to face on public parkland. In floor space they were as big as the garment factories of the last generation. Montgomery Ward was a solid eight stories tall, 340 by 400 feet, McCormick's was eight stories, Coca-Cola twelve. But in terms of labor force, these companies operated at only a third or half the density of garment factories. They ran 500 to 1200 workers, or only 50, 100, or 200 people per acre of land,

comparable to the new residential densities. The decompression of industrial sites arose from the attempt to save labor. Baltimore's new plants in the mid-20s were investing $2,000 for each job created, while the older firms, trying to raise productivity and reduce their work force, invested $6,000 for each job they added. The substitution of power machinery for human labor implied deployment in larger spaces. The larger the sites needed and the lower the density of workers on the site, the more appealing were sites farther away from the center, on cheaper land. Consequently the Canton Company, whose land stretched east beyond the city line, was the industrial matchmaker. In this, the company's fifth generation, it finished selling off the industrial land that it had originally reserved. The Canton Railroad was the spine for extension east of Sixteenth Street. The company sold 47 acres to Standard Sanitary, 66 acres to Eastern Rolling mill, and land for expansion of older enterprises. Crown Cork and Seal and Standard Oil, for example, each had a site of 125 acres. The most important new site was Western Electric's 125 acres, planned in one fell swoop. It was formerly the Riverview amusement park, on the waterfront between Canton and Sparrows Point. The fifty buildings, $22 million worth, from one to eight stories high, were grouped in a parklike setting. Western Electric was the epitome of the clean, ultramodern, spread-out industry.

Industrial development spread still farther. At Curtis Bay the work force did not grow in the '20s, although buildings were added at Davison, Glidden, and U.S. Industrial Alcohol, and the industrial spaces there formed an imposing landscape. At Sparrows Point (2200 acres) the work force was reduced after World War I, while production rose. A new rod and wire mill supplied Anchor Fence, and a larger tin mill supplied the can companies. City representatives were trying to bring the Glenn L. Martin Company of Cleveland into a 200-acre site beyond Riverview, adjoining the proposed airport on the Dundalk waterfront. Offended by high-pressure selling tactics, the volatile Martin selected a vast site of 1200 acres (nearly two square miles) at Middle River. There, beyond any municipal meddling, he could develop his own airport and spread out some of the world's most gigantic one-story industrial buildings.

Services, private and public, had to spread out to follow the people. Personnel had to be deployed over a larger area, and capital investment had to be increased to save labor. The fire department had doubled the number of companies and tripled the staff since the great fire. A fleet of ambulances was added. A scavenger vehicle drove 100 miles a day collecting dead animals. A hundred public health nurses pounded the pavements to make home visits. There were thirty-six thousand streetlights to service. Inspectors of food stores had to cover 92 square miles. Charitable institutions sought greener sites farther from the center and adopted the cottage system for housing their patients. Consistent with the idea that the whole city was a park, public services landscaped their property or located new facilities in the parks. Swimming pools were built in Druid Hill and Riverside parks, with night lighting and a sand beach. A stadium was built in record time to hold the army-navy game of 1922. A million-dollar art museum was built on land donated from the Hopkins campus and overlooking Wyman Park. Six buildings were laid out for a million-dollar hospital for communicable diseases on water department land overlooking Lake Montebello. The new municipal office building, central police station, and fire department headquarters were grouped round a plaza or "civic center" in front of the War Memorial hall. All of these projects, including the landscaping ideas and grand Greek facades for the art museum, stadium, and civic center, were conceived by the Municipal Arts Society a generation earlier.

The schools were disgracefully backward, and an impressive school-building program was likewise based on the perceived lag. The new educational philosophy and program adopted in the prewar generation had not yet been translated into brick and mortar. In 1921 the city commissioned the Strayer School Survey.[8] Its three volumes comprise the most important single planning document of the generation. It had the virtue, unlike other public plans, of a powerful shock to the public conscience through its photographs of grim basement toilets, shedlike wooden "fire escapes," and hundreds of children packed into standing-room-only schoolyards. The report put into words the smell of outdoor privies, the memory of ill-ventilated classrooms heated by coal stoves, the eyestrain of classes facing windows or dependent on gaslight at midday. The study put Baltimore "on the educational map." The National Education Association cooperated in the study and publicized the results as a model of self-criticism that other cities should imitate. The shock waves produced public support for three large school loans in the '30s, totaling $32 million. Fifteen new schools were built. Operating budgets and salaries were increased, and resignations checked. Citizens like Mrs. Marie Bauernschmidt, through organizations such as the Public School Association, pressed the bosses to rid the schools of politics. "Mrs. B," who had known the Padgetts, Sonny Mahon, and Frank Kelly in her husband's brewery business, moved from traditional charitable work—the babies' milk fund and children's hospital—deeper into politics, and took on the bosses. She employed radio appeals on election eve, and, occasionally, blackmail.

The new schools, like the new factories, were larger and more spacious. The new junior high or combined junior-senior high schools were designed for 2000 to 2500 pupils, elementary schools for 850. These norms survived into the 1970s. An ornamental staircase, a marble trim course, or finials embellished what was otherwise the contemporary three-story, brick and reinforced concrete factory building. The new schools had built into them the philosophy of health and productivity. Playgrounds were added, and lawns, landscaping, and the flagpole. Several were set in parks, notably Montebello School, Clifton Park High School, and Forest Park High School. Frederick Douglass High School was of great symbolic importance as the first colored high school built to contemporary standards. All the new buildings were fully modern in terms of electricity, daylight design, central steam heat, and multiple stairways for quick egress.

The design for the new school on Locust Point embodied the strategy of processing the great unwashed and Americanizing the foreign-born worker. It

was situated opposite Latrobe Park and designed to be convertible for light manufacturing. The standard twenty-four classrooms occupied only a third of the building. An equal portion was occupied by new kinds of space for newer programs—kindergartens, auditorium, shops for wood and metal working. The children would be prepared to transfer to the factory when they finished grade 6. The other third of the building was devoted to the healthy body—a suite for doctor, dentist, and nurses, the lunchroom, gymnasium, health classroom, and showers for boys and girls, with flush toilets and drinking fountains throughout.[9]

Thanks to child labor and school laws of the last generation, school population increased faster than the total population. From ninety-seven thousand in 1919, the pupil population reached a peak of one hundred twenty-eight thousand in 1934, then leveled off. The number of high school pupils doubled. Consequently, the construction of fifteen schools plus substantial additions and repairs did not allow the school commissioners to retire the backward facilities featured in the Strayer report.

The Catholic schools went through the same revolution. Michael Curley, archbishop between 1921 and 1939, is chiefly remembered for his school program. Parochial grade school enrollments rose from thirty-two thousand to fifty-four thousand, and their high school enrollment increased fivefold. (They had formerly depended upon private Catholic high schools for the small percentage who continued.) The archbishop raised $30 million, comparable to the public school investment: Catholics paid twice. Catholics were represented on the public school board, and there was a tacit understanding that the two systems would not undercut each other. The archbishop and Governor Ritchie both opposed federal aid to the schools; they were for local control and local financing. As the archbishop argued in every parish, in every public meeting, at every choice point, "God wants the school."[10]

The trends in education matched the trends in work and home: more space per person and more capital per person. Space embodied capital. By 1934 the accumulated per-pupil investment in the public schools was $380, or four times the level of 1918. Like the factory buildings and the homes, it was all borrowed money. The social order of debtor and creditor relationships was translated into grass, concrete, and marble. "Nowhere else in the world, at home or abroad, have I ever found so many shades of green, or so much lushness, or so caressing a rural quiet and peace, or so eloquent an invitation to lie down under a tree and snooze away an afternoon."[11] Baltimore had rediscovered its Maryland landscape, but wanted to furnish and reorganize it, to spread out under the trees. Even the new police headquarters in the center of town included an immense gymnasium on its top floor, and the lions in the Druid Hill Park zoo were transferred from their smelly, cramped, wooden cages into spacious, easy-to-clean, cement lairs.

The Self-Aligning Coupling

The spread of urban activities onto more generous spaces, coupled with larger scale and more intense specialization to get higher labor productivity, meant there had to be decided increases of traffic. Within the factory the flow of goods had to be speeded up, and more space had to be assigned to moving things between work stages, between buildings, and between plants. Investments had to be made in hauling capacity, communications systems, and regulatory mechanisms to keep flows synchronized. New levels of supervision had to be introduced, and a larger share of personnel assigned to moving things, scheduling, meshing the larger number of specialized operations, and resolving the "jams" produced when things got "out of sync." The smooth flow of traffic became the governing principle of planning: adjusting capacities of new facilities to one another and minimizing resistance, obstruction, or turbulence.

Several of the solid technical achievements and money makers of Baltimore industry in the '20s illustrate the overriding importance of smooth flow. Jacob Blaustein in 1923 began selling his new Orange Gas. Most manufacturers added tetraethyl lead to prevent knocking, but American instead added one-third benzol. Benzol was a by-product of the Bethlehem coke ovens, processed at the Koppers plant. In order to insure smooth flow of his product to the market, Blaustein contracted with Pan American Petroleum and Transport Company (Edward Doheny) for supply from Venezuela via a refinery on Aruba Island. American Oil also built substantial refinery in Baltimore to make asphalt from Mexican crude oil, and acquired control of Crown Central Petroleum and moved its offices to Baltimore.

Bartlett-Hayward, the country's biggest manufacturer of gasholders, bought patent rights to the waterless gasholder.[12] An old-fashioned gasholder was like a huge cup upside down in a pan of water. It was on "lifts" so that the cup could be extended or telescoped according to how much gas was being stored, but the pressure varied. In the waterless device, pressure could be held constant, as it

In the 1920s, crowds celebrated the opening of a swimming pool in Patterson Park.

should be to maintain a constant-pressure flow of gas to metropolitan consumers. It was an instant success; the company sold one hundred in the first ten years and made new improvements in 1932. The articulation of parts was refined with the object of maintaining the most perfect constancy of pressure and flow. On the strength of this patent, the Koppers Company of Pittsburgh, already producers of coal, tar, gas, and pistons, bought Bartlett-Hayward.

The other great success of Bartlett-Hayward in this generation was the Fast Self-Aligning Coupling.[13] The mechanical problem was to connect shafts that were not in perfect alignment. The coupling device, a sleeve with gear teeth that meshed with the teeth on the two shafts, solved the problem for tiny machines as well as for the huge power drives found at Westport generating station or in diesel ships. The mesh took place in an oil bath. Power was transmitted through the film of oil, so that in spite of the misalignment or varying alignment of the rotating shafts, there was little wear on the teeth, and the couplings lasted for years.

More power required moving materials, and to increase material flows and make them more reliable, more power had to be consumed. The Standard Oil

Montebello School, under construction in 1921, was typical of the siting of schools in parklike settings.

pier at Baltimore could discharge six thousand barrels of crude oil per hour. It received a steamer of Mexican crude oil each day, and loaded 100 tank cars of refined products. It had its own distribution fleet of oil trucks and a fleet of Chesapeake Bay oil boats. The new B&O grain elevators used a loop of track: the empty cars rolled downhill, 115 a day. The grain, dumped automatically into pits, was carried by belt conveyors to twenty "elevator legs," where it was raised 206 feet to run down into storage tanks. When it was reloaded into ships, it was carried on grain galleries, or overhead belt conveyors 4 feet wide. Next door, at the new sugar refinery, a reverse flow of traffic was developed: each day a steamerload of sugar cane arrived, and 70 railroad cars of sugar were shipped inland. The volumes were all mechanically weighed and measured; "No human hand touches the sugar."[14] The recipe for a pound of refined sugar called for a quarter pound of coal and a gallon of clean water. So the refinery became the city's largest single consumer of water (2 million gallons a day), and the mains had to be rebuilt. At the Westport electric generating plant, cooling water was pumped directly from the harbor (30 million gallons a day), while coal was supplied by a system of 240-foot towers, much like the grain galleries. Traveling cranes could unload three hundred tons an hour (a four-ton coal car was dumped in four seconds), and automatic scales and stokers fed the coal into the furnaces while automatic regulators and pumps fed the water to the fifty-two boilers. The various water, steam, and hot water pipes were color coded for quick repair, and critical feed systems were duplicated to increase reliability of the overall system and insure flow.[15]

The continuous flow of gas and electric energy required large spaces and intense capitalization at specialized production sites like Westport and the Canton gasworks, but it allowed users to economize space, capital, and labor. Hutzler's converted its former boiler rooms and coal bins into a bargain basement. The Belvedere Hotel modernized its kitchens. The *Sun* used gas to melt typemetal for stereotype plates on new high-speed rotary presses. Smaller enterprises adopted the electric candy pot and the electric enameling furnace. Cleanliness was made possible by getting rid of the coal dust, so by about 1924 there was a visible change in the style of work places. Basements and industrial shops were redone in white tile and electric lighting. Granaries were designed with smooth surfaces and no ledges. Dust control reduced the hazards of explosions and fires, and there were sliding poles for workers to escape.

The feedback is apparent: the more effectively and cheaply flows were sustained, the greater could be the decentralization of enterprise in the urban space. And the more people and activities were spread out, the greater the flows became, and the greater the demand for their reliability. One can also see the interaction of the several subsystems—water supply, electric power, railroads—carloads downhill and ships outbound, ships inbound and carloads uphill. The whole region can be seen as a single system, operating with as much gravity flow as nature would permit. Oliver Evans's gravity-flow flour mill was expanded to the scale of the metropolitan region. In each subsystem the attempt was made to bring the operation into balance, to maintain reciprocal flows or circuits. The electric power grid, for example, was improved in this generation. The two major power stations were functioning during the war: at Holtwood dam a share of the immense flow of the Susquehanna River was converted into electric power transmitted at 70,000 volts to Highlandtown. In the early '20s the "ring" was completed around Baltimore, so that all parts of the metropolitan region could be supplied through underground cables and cables under the harbor. Power generated from water and from coal were complementary sources. With the cooperation of Governor Ritchie, Frank Furst, and the Baltimore *Sun*, the Consolidated Gas and Electric Company of Baltimore arranged with its Philadelphia counterpart a division of territory confirming the system boundary. The Pennsylvania Railroad interests built the Conowingo Dam on the Susquehanna. Consolidated was protected by an agreement that none of the power would be distributed to Baltimore consumers for fifty years. The Pennsylvania Corporation did not pay any taxes to the State of Maryland, but the state received a toll-free bridge on top of the dam, Furst's Arundel Corporation got a $20 million construction contract, and the Union Trust Company received a share of the deposits.[16] Simultaneously, the state bought the older "gold mine" bridge upstream and generously paid off the capitalized value of projected future tolls. (Its owners had originally invested $700 capital.)[17]

Gas distribution was improved in much the same way, by adding gas mains across the Patapsco to Brooklyn and Curtis Bay. A line was run to pipe byproducts from the Continental Oil refinery at Curtis Bay to the Spring Garden gas plant. The municipal water system was expanded and integrated. The Loch Raven dam of 1915 was raised from 188 feet to a height of 240 feet, drowning the villages of Warren and Phoenix and increasing storage tenfold. A "balancing reservoir" was added to equalize the pressures on the tunnel between Loch Raven and Montebello.

Plans to expand port facilities led to discussions of the total gravity system of flows and the problem of coordinating rail and steamship traffic. The new harbor development commission (1920) emphasized the port itself as coupling. "A port may be considered a mechanism for accomplishing the interchange of freight between land and water carriers."[18] Baltimore was known as a "railroad port" since most of the docks were owned by the three major railroads, which provided free ship terminals to attract freight. The city envisioned a new group

In 1922, the completed American Sugar Company refinery complex showed the coordinated transportation advantages of the water, rail, road, and streetcar. The site, directly south of Fells Point, was convenient to the labor supply.

of piers in McComas Street as a "union terminal" of the three railroads jointly. The choice among expansion at McComas Street or filling the Patapsco mud flats or developing lower Canton eastward involved a tug of war among the three railroads as well as among the several sets of landowners. The upshot was that the city invested $8 million in McComas Street piers and then leased the piers to the adjoining Western Maryland Railroad. The most pressing need, recognized but not achieved in this generation, was "Unification of the Control and Operation of the Port."[19] The city hinted that it would force the B&O and the Western Maryland into reciprocal switching "between the yards or tracks of one railroad to the piers and terminals of another railroad." A related management problem was the need for an outer belt line or cutoff with sorting yards. If through rail traffic could be diverted, the Howard Street tunnel could become a backbone of a rapid transit system. This scheme, too, foundered on the stubbornness of the railroads. Their rivalries and external considerations were a perennial obstacle to joint operations.

Plans for a municipal airport were tied to harbor development. Logan Field, the existing airport, belonged to a real estate subsidiary of Bethlehem Steel at St. Helena, and sufficed for the two or three flights a day in 1928. But Mayor Broening's vision of international flights, dirigibles, and an airplane industry called for a more ambitious plan, a starlike pattern of landing strips 2500 feet long in eight directions on 1000 acres off Dundalk. Half would be built up on submerged land from dredging spoils. A new Riverview anchorage would require dredging 8 million cubic yards, and more ambitious plans for deeper channels would require dredging 27 million yards at federal expense. Charles Goob, Broening's engineer, considered the anchorage spoils to be good fill material with 20 percent moisture content. "This material becomes very hard very quickly when exposed to the air, and when placed in a large fill will become firm within a reasonable length of time."[20] Airport costs were figured between $3 million and $6 million for land acquisition, fill, and bulkhead. Technical problems and costs were grossly underestimated, and Baltimore's gigantic mud pie became an embarrassment, along with the Orleans Street viaducts proposed by the same administration. Mencken fumed, "All of these projects have three things in common: they were all launched by real estate speculators, they are all completely unnecessary, and they will all cost a great deal more in the long run than they seemed likely to cost at the start."[21]

But what about the banana peels, the crabshells, and the clinkers? The solid waste disposal system had been neglected. Garbage, ashes, and street dirt increased somewhat faster than population. The city was annually collecting half a million cubic yards of ashes and rubbish, plus the "wet" garbage. The radial growth of the city and the lower density of settlement increased the distances garbage had to be hauled in collection, the distances to which it had to be removed to satisfy public sensibilities, and consequently the costs. The city had experimented with feeding, burning, and cooking garbage. It had switched back and forth between public and private management. Each contractor promised the city a cheaper solution, but each was after a larger profit. The improvements of the early '20s were intended to take advantage of economies of gravity and natural recycling. Seven hundred city employees with mules carted the refuse downhill to assembly points, where they transferred the garbage to motor trucks that hauled it down to the harbor. From the docks the garbage was barged to Graveyard Point (Bodkin Creek), eleven miles downstream. There it would be fed to fifteen thousand pigs. The solution had financial appeal: the piggery contractor would pay for the garbage, and the city would turn a profit. The city bought the 160 acres, built the wharf, handled the barging, and employed a veterinarian. The pigs were housed at about the same density as people in the center city, sixty thousand per square mile. They were served on concrete feeding floors by an oil locomotive dump car. Each hog could convert twenty-five pounds of garbage to a pound of pork a day. The price of the garbage was pegged to the price of pork. This happy rural solution delighted the urban taxpayers until the piggery contractor reached the first slaughter season, abandoned the piggery, and disappeared with fifteen thousand dollars.[22]

In 1924 a steam shovel speeded construction of the Tyson Street Electric Substation.

The next solution, "more permanent," involved the national garbage syndicate. The contractor built a reduction plant on Bodkin Creek, cooked the garbage into grease, and sold it to the soap companies. The city used the ashes to fill in ravines and built two incinerators to handle rubbish.

$a = \pi r^2$

The increase of automobiles was more impressive than any other type of traffic. Cars ran on roads, and in spite of their speed, their adaptability to moderate grades, and individual ownership and operation, auto traffic in the '20s added up to a rigid, specialized, and integrated subsystem with many of the properties of the rail, cable, and pipeline systems. The automobile was a marvel for covering the generous distances of the spread-out city, but it nevertheless aggravated congestion and competition for space.

The number of automobiles in Maryland tripled, from a hundred thousand in 1920 to three hundred thousand in 1940. At least half were in the Baltimore region. By 1930 there were only five thousand horses left in the city limits. The horseshoers and livery stables had been eliminated. Wagon peddlers were down to fifteen hundred and were confined to the inner city, essentially their old radius of operation. The horse was not efficient for long distances and low densities of population. The piedmont landscape provided strenuous rolling terrain, and in the tidewater landscape the branching roads onto the necks exaggerated the distances to be covered. The fire department sold its last horse in 1919. The post office substituted motor trucks for both horses and streetcars, and installed drive-up mail boxes at curbs. The gas and electric company built a garage for three hundred company cars. Apartment houses built garages: the Ambassador housed two hundred cars for its 125 apartments. Cars were used for trips to the beach, and the city developed Fort Smallwood bathing beach. In 1930 the city had 929 miles of streets, about 50 percent more than at the end of the war, and virtually all of it was smooth paved: there were only twenty-four miles of cobblestones left.

Congestion was, as always, most acute at the center. A downtown area brand new in 1906 did not yet need to be rebuilt. But the decompression of the city—its more rapid expansion in area than population—aggravated the traffic problem downtown. The central business district had a much smaller residential or nighttime population than before, but continued to pack in higher densities in the daytime. A few prestige skyscrapers and highly specialized buildings were added. One of the first was the fourteen-story Southern Hotel on the site of the old Fountain Hotel on Light Street. Some moved away from the original and most congested district, creating new small centers of congestion around them. Mutual Life Insurance moved from South Street to a five-story building at Charles and Chase streets near the Belvedere Hotel, and Maryland Casualty moved out to Roland Avenue and Fortieth Street. Standard Oil moved up St. Paul Street, its towers facing Preston gardens. The tallest and most solid was the $3 million thirty-two-story Baltimore Trust Company building, bounded by Light Street, Baltimore Street, and Redwood Street. Its internal circulation was a micromodel of the downtown problem itself. All had the finished sobriety and incised or chiseled look of the best factory buildings—smooth, avoiding dust.

This northward view shows the results of a 1915 renewal effort. Preston Gardens relieved the congestion of buildings, while a modern street system accommodated increased traffic.

They were modeled after New York City. Mencken remained skeptical, feeling that skyscrapers were a mistake: "There was never any need of them here. . . . Wasting millions on such follies is a kind of confession that Baltimore is inferior to New York, and should hump itself to catch up."[23] No true Baltimorean, he said, believed that. He knows the difference between a provincial capital and a national metropolis. "He lives in Baltimore because he prefers Baltimore. One of its greatest charms, in his eyes, is that it is not New York."

The problem of parking cars in the central district became urgent. In 1923 Charles Scull, chairman of the board of U.S. Fidelity & Guarantee Company, proposed the solution preferred for the next fifty years: stacking the cars.[24] His design for four-story cement parking garages already incorporated the esthetic contradiction of garage design: the problem of combining sloping ramps with the rectangular framing of horizontal floors and vertical structural supports. It also incorporated the economic contradiction: a parking space would cost about $800, roughly the value of the car itself. The absolute values have changed, but the equivalence remains in the 1970s. A thousand-car garage appeared self-financing, but the more effectively garage building solved the parking problem, the more cars would come downtown, and the more land value would increase. The very success would add to the cost of another garage, and to congestion in the streets.

Most intractable was the effect of the automobile on public transit. Again a vicious circle was apparent. Immediately after the war, patronage began to drop, while inflation pushed up wages. Raising fares to seven cents caused patronage to fall further. The transit company tried "trackless trolleys" on Liberty Road, double-decker buses on Charles Street, and a line of buses on East Fayette Street. It retired the funeral car, the post office cars, and the payroll car, and closed Riverview Park. The form of the street railway system, traced on the form of the city's street space, reflected the differences of density. Service in the suburbs was sparse, with few routes and infrequent cars or skip-stop service, and therefore unattractive to the residents, who had plenty of space to house their automobiles. Lines to suburbs like Guilford and Homeland operated at a loss, and were subsidized by inner-city riders. But dense and frequent service in the center was impeded by the flood of automobiles that poured in from the lower-density surroundings. The streets were "clogged up" with passenger vehicles parked all day. Consultants in 1923 argued that space essential for commercial vehicles, the city's "lifeblood," had been "usurped," and congestion was worse than before the fire and the widenings.[25] In the morning rush hour, ten thousand people arrived in five thousand cars, while fifty thousand people arrived in a thousand streetcars. "Whose convenience then should be first considered, the fifty-four riding in a streetcar or the two riding in an automobile?"[26]

The physical squeeze and a capital squeeze worked together. The company was burdened by exceedingly high fixed costs, and declining revenues forced it to try to save on labor. The Brill cars in the basic fleet were usually operated by two people, motorman and conductor. The company now bought a hundred streetcar "trailers" so that a motorman and a ticket taker on the rear platform could together handle a double carload of passengers. The next innovation was the articulated unit or double streetcar. The company also tried the Birney cars, which had no rear doors: the motorman took tickets and made change, but the congestion in entering the car increased the time it took to discharge and load passengers at each stop, adding to congestion in the downtown streets. Gradually the capital squeeze grew worse. Because the Public Service Commission allowed a return no higher than 6.26 percent on the streetcar monopoly, the bonds were "watered," and 6.26 percent was paid on "paper assets" or face value of more than $100 million. When in 1928 the courts evaluated the real assets at only $75 million (still generous), the market value of the stock dropped, and new capital became scarce.

The city's advisory engineers at the end of this period pointed to the chief source of urban problems as a mathematical formula most citizens learned in the

The municipally owned Preston Street Industrial Building, known as "the bee-hive," housed a second-floor clothing factory in 1932.

seventh grade: the area of a circle equals πr^2. As the radius of the urban circle was extended, its area was extended much more rapidly, proportionate to the square of the radius.[27] Because the streetcar and the automobile had each in turn shortened the time it took to travel a mile, vast areas had been brought closer to the center, and the effective radius of a reasonable trip to work or a trip down-town had doubled or tripled, and the area opened for development grew four-fold or ninefold. When the legislature passed the Annexation Act of 1918, it fired the starter pistol in a race to realize this potential. But the runners had to run faster and faster: the spreading city required more intense traffic, congestion was felt in all systems of movement, most acute at the center—in the smallest circle—and demands were again generated to cut travel time and travel cost, extend the radius, and spread the city further.

The discovery of bottlenecks to proper flow led to a demand for planning. The two aspects of planning required for the war effort were recognized as essential to the postwar metropolis: a larger role for municipal and state govern-ment, and an ordering of priorities. Baltimore had always had fierce discussion of its large projects and a wish book of unfulfilled projects for the future. But these projects were not ordered or scheduled in relation to one another. Since the major changes in the city were lower-density city building and increased traffic flow, one might expect that city planning would focus on these two problems.

The theory and rhetoric of urban planning in Baltimore unfolded out of annexation. The Topographical Survey was set to work to provide a detailed relief map of the annex.[28] On that map the survey would then develop a street plan. Water mains, sewers, gas mains, and electrical conduits would be built into the streets. For the first time, forecasting was emphasized. Efficiency and economy in providing the services depended upon an accurate forecast of population densities.[29] The city was, in fact, experiencing difficulties maintaining water pressure in tall buildings on high ground. It had had to replace water mains to service a seven-story apartment on Upland Avenue. Lot coverage affected the

Setting Priorities

Riverview Park and Pier had already passed its heyday in this photograph. The complex was demolished in 1928 for the Western Electric plant.

design of storm sewers and the branching of streets. Efficient systems of sewers, gas and water mains, and wires implied a consistent ordering of sizes. Control over density of population would yield the essential data for calculating the sizes of sewers and mains.

Making a plan for the annex led to more comprehensive planning. A City Plan Commission, a Public Improvements Commission, and a Port Development Commission were appointed. Within two years the procedure and main features were framed. A zoning ordinance was passed and a general street plan adopted. The Strayer school survey was reported, a traffic study was made for the first time, and a new recreation study was commissioned from the Olmsted firm. These studies provided an orderly agenda for two generations of public improvements.

The objective of the zoning plan was to regulate densities. Following the lead of other cities, Baltimore mapped the city according to a triple classification: building height zones, land use zones, and zones for the number of dwelling units permitted per residential acre. A characteristic feature of planning was hierarchy, or a system of nested restrictions. The "highest" class of land, for example, permitted only single detached dwellings, the second class allowed those and also row houses, a third class allowed all of those types and apartments as well. The height zones created an interesting hierarchy of design, because heights were expressed in terms of the relation between building height and street width. The "2½ Times" district coincided with the downtown high-pressure water service for fire fighting. (Fire protection was the legal basis for zoning.) The "2 Times" district matched existing apartment neighborhoods on wide streets like Eutaw, Charles, and University Parkway, facing parks. "1½ Times" districts allowed loft factories, and "1 Times" districts were generally three-story neighborhoods, but might allow buildings to run up to five stories on wide streets. The lowest "forty-foot" zone was much like the city's ancient fire-ladder rule, permitting two to three and a half stories. The law did not, therefore, forbid mixing various uses or heights or densities of development. Dwellings could be built in business zones, and businesses in industrial zones, but the reverse was not allowed: industries could not be built in business zones, nor business in residential zones. In theory, this protected the highest *use value*—the home—against the encroachment of business and industry. The Zoning Commission was definitely opposed, for reasons of fire hazard, to homes over groceries. A tenth of the buildings in the city were of this type. "People should live in the country or suburban parts of town for the sake of health."[30] But in practice, industry and business were mapped out very generously. Whole neighborhoods were classified for industry and thereafter left without sewers, storm drains, or code enforcement on the assumption that they would sooner or later be torn down for industrial expansion. Since industry could pay more for land than most home buyers, the hierarchy of *market values* was quite the reverse: industry chose first, business second, and home builders third.

The Zoning Commission had no mandate to change the developed city. Its job, like Poppleton's a hundred years earlier, was to define and coordinate future improvement, in order to permit development of the highest possible

To maximize street space, the Guilford Avenue streetcar lines operated on elevated tracks. This remarkably steep incline is at the north end near Eager Street.

property values. That meant a cautious, legalistic, and politically acceptable juggling of present and future interests in property. The owner of a store or stable in a residential zone was allowed to keep operating his business as a zoning exception. To protect his future interest in the property, he could sell the business for the same use, indefinitely. The purpose of public zoning, like the private zoning of the Roland Park Company or the Canton Company, was to confirm and protect the existing structure of property values.

The other concern of city planning was traffic flow. The mayor's charge to the Annex Plan Commission was to develop "a connected community." "Cities have spread, pushing their existing street systems over hills and valleys with a magnificent disregard of man and nature."[31] The new theory was to develop the city as "a place to move about in," truly a marketplace. "To say that city planning is a traffic problem is as truthful a generalization as may be made."[32] As in zoning, there would be a ranking imposed: several classes of streets with different capacities. Projects would be scheduled in relation to one another. The plan gave first importance to arteries radiating from the city. Because widening the built-up radials was so expensive, new ones were opened: Walther Avenue, Hillen Road, Loch Raven Boulevard, and The Alameda. Most were designed without car tracks. Their curves indicate the changed esthetic, conformity to piedmont topography, the capabilities of the automobile, and above all the difficulty of threading new roads through districts already developed. Of next importance were laterals to connect the arteries, for example, the Cold Spring Lane "inner belt" and an "outer belt" formed by Lake Avenue, Belvedere, and Northern Parkway.[33] Branching off from the radials and laterals was a fine network of minor streets. To make the plan adaptable over a long future, "elastic streets" were proposed. Wide rights of way would be acquired: "Grass, hedges, flower beds and trees may be used to beautify the right of way or to screen in car tracks and wires." In ten or twenty years, when repaving would be necessary, the parks could be removed and the full width developed. "Then the metamorphosis will be gradual and economical. During the changing process, such streets will be attractive. After the transition they will be adequate and highly

The Age of Viaducts

Fashions of the Twenties date this Flower Mart of the Women's Civic League on Mount Vernon Place. Its move to Charles Center in recent years indicates a displacement of the center of gravity of the "Monumental City."

efficient. . . . At all times their property values will be stable and thereby conserved."[34]

Highway planning spilled over municipal boundaries. Developing the radials required cooperation with surrounding counties and state government. The automobile offered a springboard for extraordinary growth of state government. It offered, as city street making had in the 1890s, opportunities for state spending and patronage hiring. More wonderful, it also offered revenues such as gasoline and motor vehicle taxes and tolls to support the operation, sufficiently elastic to secure massive loans. The state developed the planning initiative of which the counties were incapable, and created structures for obtaining their cooperation through state matching funds. Road making provided new windfalls for private profit and permitted the revival of the Maryland tradition of close-woven private and public enterprise. An automobile ferry across Chesapeake Bay got under way with the backing of a former governor and New York financiers: they then stood in the way of bridge proposals. To satisfy political pressures from all parts of the state, the tendency was to develop secondary roads for local traffic and neglect primary roads for through traffic. Crain Highway was the first wholly new primary route laid out. U.S. 1 toward Washington and Philadelphia was modernized. It was a good example of the impulse to growth: the more roads were improved, the more cars they carried, and the more roads were wanted. In 1925 the road to Washington, twenty feet wide, was carrying six thousand cars a day. Ten years later, twice as wide, it was carrying three times as many cars, and a plan was hatching to rebuild it again. But the greater traffic raised land values and pushed up the cost of the next widening. Where formerly land-owners had donated rights of way, it now became necessary for the state to pay for land.[35]

The convergence of all these streams of traffic on the city center refocused attention on the old intractable problem of downtown thoroughfares. A $6 million loan was authorized for the extension of Howard Street and an east-west viaduct. Both illustrated the problem of redevelopment. Threading new streets through intensely developed property could only be done at great expense and "in 3-D."

The viaduct idea was seized upon as a solution. Howard Street would have to be threaded east of Richmond Market and west of Mount Royal Station; it would have to go under Mount Royal Avenue and over the Jones Falls, the B&O, and the Pennsylvania Railroad. It would meet North Avenue with both streets on the viaduct, and continue north by way of Oak Street. Oak Street (now Howard Street) would have to be widened. The alignment was expensive but not much disputed, as it would clearly benefit "the Howard Street interests," that is, the downtown merchants and the produce wholesalers, and it suited the residential convenience of the city's leaders in the northern suburbs. But the viaduct to connect eastern and western sections of the city turned out to be the most hotly debated issue of the generation. As it was finally built, in 1930, a viaduct 2200 feet long sprang from St. Paul at Bath Street, over Preston gardens, the Calvert Station tracks, the Guilford Avenue elevated, and the Fallsway, past the old Brush electric plant and Consolidated's new garage, south of Belair Market, to descend into Orleans Street. Traffic from the high-capacity viaduct had to be distributed into the older system of inelastic streets. Ensor Street was widened at great expense. Under the viaduct, a wide entry was created from Calvert into the Fallsway. At the west end of the viaduct, an underpass was built for through traffic on St. Paul Street, and a Y or plaza shunted westbound traffic into Franklin Street and received eastbound traffic from Mulberry Street.

The controversy surrounding the Orleans Street viaduct foreshadowed the problems of expressways in the next generation. Each of several alternative routes offered advantages for different pieces of property and different parts of town. The critical decision was whether the viaduct would angle north or south of Belair Market. The Monument Street merchants wanted it to come north. Expensive properties such as the new Standard Oil building could not be touched, and the route had to fit into the plans of the Pennsylvania Railroad. On the other hand, weeding out black slums was considered desirable. The chosen route would "eradicate a large group of small unsightly buildings" between Gay and Forrest streets and a tracery of alleys south of Belair Market. Certain property owners, such as the Fairfield–Western Maryland Dairy, were eager to be bought out. In 1930, scandal exploded when it was learned that the city had paid out $1 million for property without professional appraisals, normal procedures, or public scrutiny.[36]

Completed in the '30s, the viaduct provided a breathtaking approach to downtown Baltimore. The Baltimore motorist coming home from Philadelphia might swell with pride as he drove onto the viaduct with the cathedral apse before him. But the Philadelphia motorist hurrying to Washington cursed Baltimore as he stopped at each light on Orleans Street and then Franklin Street. Baltimore could not be bypassed by automobile any more easily than by railroad. Anyone merely driving through added to the ever more intense traffic flowing across the high ground on either side of those great oases of calm, the old cathedral and the new Pratt Library. The flood of traffic battered the liveability and the property values of all the streets into which it poured—Franklin and Mulberry, Fulton and Monroe, Paca and Greene, McCulloch and Druid Hill. The problem of crosstown traffic was not yet solved.

Efficiency and
Economy

Expansion of government functions forced a streamlining of government itself. The demands of business and industry for new public services were consistent with new forms of participation of businessmen in government. In the late 1920s a whole philosophy of businesslike methods in government was pushed forward by Mayor Jackson and Governor Ritchie, as well as presidents Coolidge and Hoover. The city now had eleven thousand employees in forty-five departments and a payroll of $17 million a year. Departments were consolidated and internal services were centralized—for example, receipts, purchases, payroll, vehicle repair, and complaints. The city's telephone switchboard was reorganized. An elaborate physical inventory was made. City employees tagged the office furniture, posted city land, redrew the tattered maps, indexed the deeds, and insured it all. A civil service commission and a retirement plan were introduced. Businessmen from the large firms—Bartlett-Hayward, Bethlehem Steel, Yellow Cab, Gas and Electric, United Railways, the B&O, the phone company, the sugar refinery, and Continental Trust—offered the services of their accountants, statisticians, and actuaries to the mayor's Commission on Efficiency and

A panoramic view from the
city jail in the 1920s illustrates
the multiple use of
transportation corridors. The
streetcar lines were elevated
above Guilford Avenue,
and the Fallsway crossed railroad tracks that in turn crossed
the Jones Falls.

Economy. The city built a handsome office building to new generous space norms
of the telephone company: 60 square feet for clerks and stenos, 100 square
feet for engineers and draftsmen, 300 for executives.[37] In the same vein, Governor Ritchie called a State Reorganization Committee of 108 Democrats who
consolidated state agencies into nineteen executive departments and introduced
central purchasing and "merit" provisions.[38] One of his efficiency measures,
resisted tooth and nail, was the Fewer Elections Act, a conservation measure that
confined the state sport of campaigning to designated hunting and fishing
seasons. The city was still an enterprise of greater scope than the state: its
budget of $65 million was about double that of the state.

Businesslike methods did not interfere seriously with political methods.
Mayor Jackson channeled a third of the new $12 million insurance payments on
city property into his own insurance firms. The bonding business was handed
to Fidelity Trust, the instrument of Furst and the Blacks. State deposits remained
concentrated in the same banks, and the same brokers and brokerage attorneys
continued to handle municipal and state bonds. Following the gold mine bridge

affair, the chartering of the bay ferry, and the Conowingo power deal, a $375,000 scandal broke in the State Roads Commission: several employees were sent to the penitentiary. States' rights were consistent with the protection of local fiefdoms. "Curly" Byrd was developing another semipublic monopoly at the University of Maryland in College Park.

The drive for businesslike organization was, nevertheless, necessary, and it contributed significantly to the caliber of professionals the city was able to retain. The systems view of the city and its hardening into concrete demanded a much larger role for professional civil engineers. Their broad perspective came from their initial base in the city topographic survey and the state health department before the war. The essence of planning was coordination, and the effective coordination of projects among municipal, state, and federal agencies in this generation was insured by the continuity and rotation of the engineers. Major Shirley moved from the Topographical Survey to the State Roads Commission to chairmanship of the City Plan Committee and Annex Plan Commission. B. P. Harrison, trained at the B&O, worked for the wartime Patapsco River survey, became harbor engineer for the city, then went to the State Roads Commission. John E. Greiner, bridge engineer on the B&O, was chairman of the Port Development Board in 1920 and the Railroad Commission in 1928; he consulted on the Orleans Street viaduct and the state primary bridge program. Ezra Whitman served the water department and chaired the Public Service Commission and the Commission on Economy and Efficiency. Nathan Smith was engineer to the State Roads Commission, the city highway department, and Baltimore county in turn. Abel Wolman moved from the state health department to the role of federal public works coordinator and then advisory engineer to the city. This rotation of personnel was favorable to imaginative and well-integrated solutions, consistent with the philosophy of the earliest city plan report: "The railroad problem is bound up with the harbor. The harbor development is bound up with the street layout. The real solution can be found for the one only in finding it for the other."[39]

The technical nature of engineering decisions made it more difficult, however, for citizens to evaluate projects like the east-west viaduct or the airport scheme, and to impose their views on their representatives. Land appraisal and cost estimating became highly specialized and technical matters, difficult for citizens to verify directly. The decompression of the city had set distances between citizens and their government. Only the planners or engineers could familiarize themselves with the whole spread-out city, its growth tissues, and its circulation systems. Often in their highly personal mix of discretion and indiscretion lay the secret of their staying power and of the city's surge of energy. They developed in the '20s the agenda from which Baltimore was still working in the '70s.

Lebensraum

The sudden decompression of Baltimore was not shared equally by all parts of society. The sharpest cleavage was between black and white. Traditional differences of environments allotted to black and white, rich and poor, were translated into differences in density of habitat. The competition of Lebensraum produced distinctive race spaces in Baltimore.

In a long and gradual process, by which the suburban counties have shifted from 40 percent black (1810) to 3 percent (1970) while Baltimore City went from 12 to 15 percent to over half, there had been a period of stability and parity—15 to 20 percent black in both city and countryside between the Civil War and World War I. But the trend set in again decisively in the 1920s, as blacks continued to enter the city and whites began to exit to the suburbs. White immigration from Europe virtually ceased with the new national quotas after World War I. This affected the age structure. The white birth rate began to fall, and match the low black birth rate in the early '20s. Infant deaths were still twice as high among blacks, but were falling more rapidly. As a consequence of all these factors, the city's black population grew 50 percent (from 1920 to 1940), compared with 25 percent for whites.

The redefinition of race spaces occurred within the city as well. Rings appeared in the city's social arrangement. In 1920 blacks made up 20 percent of the old city, 10 percent of the old annex, and 4 percent of the new annex. But over the years the differences were aggravated. The old city became 30 percent black, the old annex 14 percent, while the new annex was down to 3 percent. The new low-density habitat was reserved for whites. Although the segregation ordinances had been found unconstitutional, a selection system operated through the collusion of realtors, developers, mortgage institutions, and suburban residents. Most of the newly developed annex homes were built by large-scale developers. The Roland Park Company employed the restrictive covenant in individual deeds. In areas of modest homes, large builders such as Novak and Keelty worked closely with the savings and loan associations. As mutuals and instruments of white churches and white work organizations (e.g., United Railways and B&O), they did the bidding of their membership in excluding blacks.

The selection process was rigorous with respect to race, and very precise with respect to religion, national origin, and income. In the '30s Julius Levy was the only Jew with a house in Guilford, and the newspaperman, the breadman, and the milkman wouldn't deliver to him. But population groups other than blacks all experienced decompression by moving outward along certain radials or wedges of the city, as defined before the war. In 1920 the foreign born were still concentrated in the core of the city, but by 1930, they were redistributed fairly evenly in all rings of the city, and their children likewise. The children of "native whites" remained at the top of the heap. Two-thirds of them were concentrated in the two annexes, where they formed two-thirds of the population.

The old city had an average density of thirty thousand per square mile, ten times that of the new annex. If one looks more precisely at the bounds of black space, one can find concentrations as high as fifty thousand to one hundred thousand per square mile in the seventeenth ward and just west of Hopkins Hospital, as high as the immigrant clusters around the harbor had been in the late nineteenth century. These densities did not, however, imply crowding of houses. Most people, even in narrow lanes like Greenwillow and Union streets (the "lung block" notorious for tuberculosis cases) lived one family to a house, and less than one person per room. Popular assumptions about congestion, breathing space, and promiscuity were not borne out by studies of the Urban League. But because the traditional high-density urban habitat was identified with black space, crowding was blamed for all the problems of the black community, and a negative view was taken of high-density environments. For the first time, "urban problems" were identified with "the Negro problem," and the "slum" was associated more with blacks than with immigrants. The same districts stuck out on new maps made of violent crime, juvenile delinquency, and family service case loads. Social problems were identified with crowding and "dark breeding places." In 1934 a housing study by W. W. Emmart for the Real Estate Board designated a belt of half a dozen neighborhoods as a ring of "blight" around the commercial heart of the city. He recommended that such areas, the locus of crime, delinquency, and dependency, be demolished or at least thinned out.[40] One such thinning project was the construction of a large, modern colored school on half of the lung block, over the objections of the black community. The perception was fixed for the next generation of urban renewal as a series of targets for black removal.

Compared with the complete neglect of the Progressive period before the war, the planning of the '20s did begin to create and invest in spaces for blacks. The new spaces were always restricted, and overwhelmed by numbers. When a swimming pool was built for whites in Druid Hill Park, a smaller pool was built for blacks. The state at last built the 100-bed Henryton Sanatorium for black TB patients. The death rate was very high at first because of the backlog of acute cases, but conditions improved. The same differential can be seen in the decompression of the schools. Nearly the whole increase of pupils enrolled in the public schools in the '20s was among black pupils; their numbers doubled. The school board fixed an investment quota: 10 percent of the capital budget for colored schools, to match their 10 percent of enrollment. This was a step forward, but it did not overcome the accumulated gap in facilities. Douglass High School was the symbol of improvement: a third of its graduates went on to college or normal school. There were ten new buildings, three additions, with several playgrounds, cafeterias, gyms, and showers. Eleven hopeless buildings of the 1850s and '60s were abandoned, and for the first time (1934) all the children enrolled in the colored schools were reported to be full-time pupils. However, their thirteen hand-me-down buildings were all buildings recommended by the Strayer report for immediate demolition.

The peculiarities of vocational training in the colored schools hint at the more fundamental discrimination in the job market. Ira Reid reported in 1934 that the progressive idea of vocational education had been developed "subjectively," as the school board stepped cautiously between the demands of the black community for marketable skills and the demands of white elements to keep blacks in their place. "A public school must be careful not to train pupils for such skills, and in such a way as to upset a usually neurotic labor market." Consequently, no construction skills were taught except carpentry, no new crafts

Black employees of the gas and electric company gather at a 1924 union meeting.

like radio and automotive work were taught, and the only subjects for girls were trade cookery and cafeteria service.

That was the basic problem: for a fast-growing young population of blacks, the economic space was not increasing fast enough. The constraint of poverty forced half of black women into the labor force, compared with only 17 percent of white women. Ira Reid classified the job market into four parts, according to the way race space was assigned.[41] Blacks had a near-monopoly of certain strenuous and dirty jobs—labor in the fertilizer plants, coalyards, lumberyards, digging jobs, porters in stores, and personal service (servant, waiter, laundress). These jobs were confirmed as theirs, since federal quotas cut foreign immigration to a trickle. Second, there was a white space clearly staked out in the job market, including city fire fighter, police officer, railroad fireman, accountant, nearly all the construction crafts, the professions, and the public services. (Less than 2 percent of municipal employees were black, aside from teachers.) The boundaries of this white space had not changed. Third, there was a small but growing black space, the jobs Reid called "racial service" jobs. Negro public employees and private businessmen served other Negroes in separate institutions, such as schools, hospitals, funeral parlors, and hairdressers. Reid figured that the purchasing power of Baltimore Negroes was $45 million a year, but he could identify only a few hundred thousand dollars worth captured by Negro businessmen. For example, Negroes paid insurance premiums of $360,000, most of which went to white companies. There were perhaps seven hundred black businesses in all. A fifth were barbers and hairdressers. Only a handful hired more than six people: the Afro newspaper, the American Bottling Company, Druid Hill Laundry, Dunbar Theatre Amusement Company, Metropolitan Finance, and Harry O. Wilson, banker. The larger Negro entrepreneurs were hampered by discrimination in lending, bonding, and insurance, as well as real estate. The crumbs were left for enterprises like those on the Pennsylvania Avenue side of the lung block. The people "massed in the little runaways" of Greenwillow, Union, and Numsen alleys, supported a picture parlor, a soft drink parlor, seven pool parlors, sixteen clothing shops, several restaurants, and two pawnshops. As the number of horsecart peddlers and scavengers diminished, these marginal businesses were left to blacks, while whites began driving trucks.

The fourth category was a zone of competition between race spaces. It was regulated by unwritten rules within white firms and white unions. One such zone was the unskilled but unionized jobs tied in with the white craft unions: the longshoremen, hod carriers, postal clerks, and post office laborers. Another such zone was in the mechanical and manufacturing industries. Here jobs for blacks had risen from 4 to 18 percent, but three-quarters were jobs without opportunity for further advancement, and their presence depended on the ups and downs of total employment. Blacks were threatened by every layoff. When the overall economic space contracted, the economic space allotted to blacks contracted even more.

The growth of the racial service sector coincided with the growth of leadership and a stronger voice pleading for equity. Symbolic gains were essential in all social classes. The new colored schools were named for Benjamin Banneker, Frederick Douglass, and Paul Lawrence Dunbar. The Easter parade on Pennsylvania Avenue and the live music in its night spots created a backbone for "soul." There were some four hundred social and political clubs in the Negro community. The Urban League and the Maryland Interracial Commission were founded. The Negro churches remained the institutional basis for community, and their distribution shows the residential pattern.[42] Of 216 churches, half were Baptist. They were concentrated in three clusters. The largest was within a one-mile radius of Lanvale Street and Fremont Avenue, the second largest just west of Hopkins Hospital, and the smallest near the tracks south of Camden Station. The older churches were self-supporting with their own paid-off permanent buildings; others were weaker, with mortgages or leases, and the store-front churches "rarely lasted three years." The very names of these Baptist churches imposed a pilgrimage of the spirit on the dense brick rows of Baltimore. Down the alley, around the corner, to Jerusalem, Bethlehem, Nazareth, Antioch, and over into Macedonia and Abyssinia, they preached and they sang and they shouted. They drowned out the trolley cars on Fremont Avenue and Caroline Street in their search for the mountaintop experience: Mount Zion, Mount Carmel, Mount Sinai. I will lift up mine eyes unto the hills—Mount Moriah, Mount Calvary, Mount Lebanon. The mountains shouted for joy—Mount Nebo, Mount Ararat, Mount Hebron—and the little hills clapped their hands. Under the coal smoke, the neon light, and the July thunderstorms shone out Morning Star and Shining Star, Fountain, White Stone, and Shiloh, Little Ark, Sweet Hope, Rose of Sharon, and New Vine.

The Beer Tap and the Breast Pump

Just as the decompression was not equally shared, the benefits of intensified flows were not shared equally. Just as there were traffic jams, there were also social bottlenecks and breakdowns. The mayor's goal of a connected community was realized only in part. Some system failures were short-lived and brought quickly under control, such as a sudden increase in the number of fires (from three thousand to four thousand a year in 1920 to 1923) and an epidemic of asphyxiations by gas: 145 deaths in the winter of 1922/23 from gas heaters and stoves. But other system problems became aggravated, such as the traffic squeeze. The one hundred thousand cars were owned by half the families in the city—a tremendous increase in their living standard. But as the trolley parks closed down one by one, as industry decentralized and the trip to the job lengthened, the modest differences of wage or credit required to buy a car created a gulf between two ways of life. The man in the automobile had more time and more space, while the man who rode the streetcar had less time and less space. Every municipal dollar, every parking privilege or right of way for the automobile, protected the time and space of half the people at some expense to the other half.

In such a context, stopping a smooth flow of traffic or goods was a weapon. A well-integrated, delicately balanced system was vulnerable to malfunction or sabotage. The interconnection of so many subsystems meant that a breakdown might invade all society. As a result, a strike was perceived as an immense threat to public order, the public welfare, and the American system. A terror of total breakdown led to severe forms of repression like the "red scare" of 1919 and 1920. The labor movement was identified as "un-American," and the sense of patriotic emergency carried over several years after the armistice. The specific issue in most of the strikes of the early '20s was the union shop. Nearly all these battles were lost. The broader issue was that of who would bear the costs of change—the readjustment to a peacetime economy, the impact of technological change, adjustment to international inflation and debt. The labor movement weakened steadily. AF of L membership dropped throughout this period. Industries with skilled labor, unionized or ripe for unionization, were weakened by the adjustment to peacetime: steel, shipbuilding, and building. As they recovered, by the mid-'20s, the introduction of more machinery, more space, and more capital increased the productivity of workers, and selected groups improved their hourly wage. But factories could cut back on the total number of workers needed, weed out presumed troublemakers, enforce job competition, and prevent labor from claiming its share of further increases in productivity. Unemployment had reached alarming levels by 1927 and 1928.

These trends were reflected in the violent conflict of the early '20s followed by "stabilization" in the late '20s. In the first three months of 1920, six thousand workers at Maryland Drydock went on strike for a union shop. By 1 April they had given in: violence had sown division. In May 1921 the longshoremen were on strike, and the violence included incidents betwen races. The U.S. Navy appeared on the scene, on the grounds that vessels of the U.S. Shipping Board were threatened.

Three submarine chasers, machine guns mounted on their deck, entered Baltimore harbor shortly after dark last evening. The craft were stripped for action. . . . Crowds of strikers continued however to go around the harbor in launches in their attempt to halt all shipping through the port of Baltimore.[43]

In August, four hundred shipyard workers were laid off by Baltimore Drydock, and the rest had their wages cut back 10 percent, as the corporation adjusted to the peacetime reduction of shipbuilding contracts. From April to December 1922, five thousand coal miners were on strike in Western Maryland, protesting similar cutbacks. Consolidated Coal again imported strike breakers. Hundreds of disillusioned miners quit and went to work for the B&O or Kelly Springfield Tire, the only other big employers in the region. Losses were estimated at $5 million to the company and $4 million to the workers. Governor Ritchie let the companies hire their own guards, but consistent with his concern for the rights of the states, he refused to invite "federal bayonets" into Maryland.[44] During the same period B&O shopworkers and Western Maryland Railroad workers went on strike. The U.S. Railroad Board upheld the workers' view, but to no avail. So long as the coal strike went on, the coal-carrying railroads were satisfied with lockout. Among the last of these prolonged and fruitless struggles was the strike of cotton mill workers in the Jones Falls valley. Their wages had been cut by a third to meet competition of new deep south mills. Half were women. "In almost every house there was either a deserted wife left with small children or a separated husband and wife." Many were very old, 15 percent had worked in the mills thirty-five years or more. They still worked fifty-four hours, averaged $15 a week, and lived in company houses. Low rent helped the mills retain their workers, and evictions helped break the strike. The strike petered out, the union dwindled, and "curiously, the union officers are no longer mill workers."[45] The companies began selling off mills—for tire, paper cup, vinegar, and raincoat factories. The company was reorganized under Baltimore ownership (1915) but after the strike it relied increasingly for its profits on its own southern mills. It also began selling off the company houses in the valley to the workers, who welcomed the notion that they would henceforth be safe from eviction in case of future strikes. This was consistent with the trend throughout Baltimore toward home ownership among factory workers. Each worker was tied to home and mortgage. Hampden and Woodberry, like Canton and Locust Point, in the '20s got a reputation for stability, and put tremendous energy into their baseball clubs.

The improved circulation in the system as a whole created new moral quandaries. One problem was solved, only to raise others. It became more difficult to see how the whole system functioned. Efficient flow was achieved at the cost of some human relationship. The health department, for instance, discovered how to save foundlings (white) by keeping them at the shelter for unwed mothers (white) and feeding them mother's milk, by breast pump and bottle. New mechanisms also sanitized the flow of money, so that the way nourishment was extracted and fed to the big spenders was intricate, artificial, and invisible. Actual spending by the very wealthy was still much in public view. In the younger generation of Garretts, for example, John collected Oriental art and rare books, and his wife, Alice, embellished Evergreen House with a theater and Leon Bakst's gorgeous red and yellow Russian stencils. They embellished the Baltimore social season with the visits of the Musical Art Quartet and great dancers. Robert threw the discus in the Olympics of 1896, founded the Public

Athletic League in Baltimore, and chaired the Public Improvements Commission, which allocated the city's spending. The production of wealth, likewise, was in the public view: the sewing machine operators and steel workers paced themselves to new faster machines, all-electric conveyors moved the grain into storage, and no human hand touched the sugar, while the coal miners and longshoremen took their wage cuts. Yet the financial coupling was invisible, so that there was no apparent connection between Baltimore's rich and Baltimore's poor or unemployed. The highly visible large industries were great national firms that extracted wealth from Baltimore to "outside," while the highly visible spenders had inherited their wealth and added to it by quietly clipping coupons at the bank or trading their shares in the broker's office, receiving regular infusions of interest from "outside." Henry Walters's estate in 1931 consisted of $3 million in government bonds, $7 million in railroad securities, and $4 million in other stocks and bonds.

The question was raised, from time to time, as to the advantages of the continued growth of these outside industries in the city. Mencken put the question sharply: "In what way, precisely, has the average Baltimorean benefitted by the great growth of the city during the past ten years? So far as I can make out, in no way at all."[46] He argued that the real improvements of paving, sewers, fire protection, and schools were initiated before the industrial boom, and not to be credited to it, and he saw no source of pride in a rising population. "Everytime they bring in another glue factory, with another trainload of slaves to work it, they fill the newspapers with hosannahs. Well, what is the good of another glue factory? What is the good of bringing in another trainload of slaves?"[47]

Much of the population was preoccupied with maintaining the flow of alcohol. Baltimore was a center of resistance to prohibition. Governor Ritchie expressed the formal states' rights view of federal prohibition, and Mencken expressed the gut feeling of German Baltimore that individual freedom was freedom to imbibe, and social rights revolved around beer and concerts on Sundays. The "drys," led by Bishop Cannon, were numerous in the rural counties of Maryland, especially on the Eastern Shore. When national prohibition came in, Baltimoreans bent their efforts to circumvent it. The city's forty-two-mile shoreline was convenient for smuggling Cuban and Canadian liquor. Some breweries were sold, converted, or shut down, but others survived by manufacturing "near beer." They were allowed to produce the real thing, age it, then (supposedly) reduce it to near beer by lowering the alcohol content to the legal limit. Likewise, at the U.S. Industrial Alcohol plant, the world's largest and most modern, installed at Curtis Bay at the onset of prohibition, alcohol was again produced in the normal way, then (supposedly) denatured by adding chemicals to prevent human consumption. In fact, a steady supply was diverted to Glidden's adjoining paint factory, from there to the "cracking plants" of a fictitious lacquer thinner company, and into retail trade. (U.S. Industrial Alcohol was later sued by the federal government for $8 million in back taxes on a part of the company's illegal output.)[48] Smaller operations moved frequently. On North Avenue, a motor car company produced several hundred gallons a day in a $100,000 Jack

Pal's Lunch was established in the 1930s as a philanthropic act. It assured adequate meals for 15¢ or less.

column still three stories high. The thirsty public was most interested in the more personal retail circuits, and was ready to defend them. Crain Highway was known as bootleg boulevard, and U.S. 1 was spotted with speakeasies. The daughter of Harry Jung, tavernkeeper at Fell and Wolfe streets, told his secrets a good while afterward. He kept his stock of hard liquors hidden behind a sliding wall. He had two beer taps, one for near beer and one that was supposed to be out of order. It was, in fact, connected by tubes concealed behind water pipes to a stock of real beer in the basement under a pile of coal.[49] Federal arrests rose from four hundred to a thousand a year, but agents complained that state and city police did little to protect them from hostile mobs. A mob of five thousand besieged eight prohibition agents inside a saloon near St. Peter and Barre Street for two hours. "If the man we were raiding had not protected us, we never could have got out alive."[50]

Paralysis

The great breakdown did not come, however, from the feared halt of labor or a failure in the delicately balanced materials flows. It came, instead, in the circulation of money. It did not last three days like Baltimore's mass disorders of 1812, 1834, 1861, or 1877. It did not last three months like the bitter winter of 1893 or the fatal summer of 1832. This crisis deepened for five years and persisted for ten. The headlines announced the stock market crash of 29 October

1929, a distant event in New York City. Closer to home, the Chesapeake Bank closed in 1930, and in the summer of 1931 an $8 million bank closed in Frederick, together with fourteen smaller farmers' banks. Farm loan defaults were blamed on the drought. On 31 September 1931 the Baltimore Trust Company closed the great bronze doors of its thirty-two-story skyscraper. A year later the Park Bank failed, and anxious rumors provoked a run on the Union Trust Company. In February 1933 the Title Guarantee and Trust Company closed, and deposits were being withdrawn from a dozen banks in the city. Panic threatened. Thirteen million dollars were withdrawn within a few days; on 25 February the governor closed all Maryland banks till order could be reestablished. "Actually there is no sense at all in this local banking crisis," he said.[51] Nevertheless, the same thing was happening in other states. The papers reported the "grim and ominous inauguration atmosphere" of 4 March 1933, and Franklin Roosevelt's first act as president was to declare a national bank holiday. "The great financial mechanism of the United States stood still today."[52] This prolonged the bank closings in Maryland till 14 March, altogether three weeks.

Between financial spasms, the game was to keep up appearances, and there were few hints at the stubborn paralysis of capital. Statements of public officials and bankers offered no reliable clues to the gravity of events. They filled the newspaper columns with reassurances, just as in the cholera epidemic the board of health had buried the dead secretly at night. Monthly figures for relief payments by the charitable associations appeared in fine print. The largest, the Family Welfare Association, spent $200,000 in 1930, $600,000 in 1931, and $3,400,000 in 1932, while Catholic and Jewish charities also distributed money, food, and layettes. At Christmas 1931 there were eight thousand families unemployed and dependent on relief, at Christmas 1932 eighteen thousand.[53] In February, as the bank holiday began, the society page reported a whirl of Sunday aperitif parties at which only "chiff chaff" was discussed, while in one block in Hampden every family was under the care of Family Welfare. In two blocks of West Mulberry Street there were 150 families. "Morale is deteriorating." In March, gay Lenten parties were held. "The country clubs are in great favor, with duets, quartets and choruses, the conversations interrupted by numerous deflections toward the tea table, which usually has small glasses—not used for tea."[54] As the bank holiday ended, thirty-seven hundred opera lovers turned out "in a grand gesture" to welcome Lily Pons and Ezio Pinza starring in *Rigoletto*. Baltimore was the only city in the country that had invited the Metropolitan opera that year. The crowd at the Lyric "came as brilliantly dressed as in many former years. . . . The story was told in the lobby about a certain jewel-laden dowager who used the last of her available cash to pay the servants' wages last Saturday, then borrowed from them enough money to pay for her opera tickets."[55] At Arbutus the Methodist church begged the use of a horse so their unemployed could plow gardens. By Christmas 1933 one family in six was on relief—twenty-three thousand families. The Baltimore office of the Home Owners Loan Corporation said three-quarters of the applicants for federal loans were desperate, on the verge of insanity or suicide, without food. They mentioned a widow with

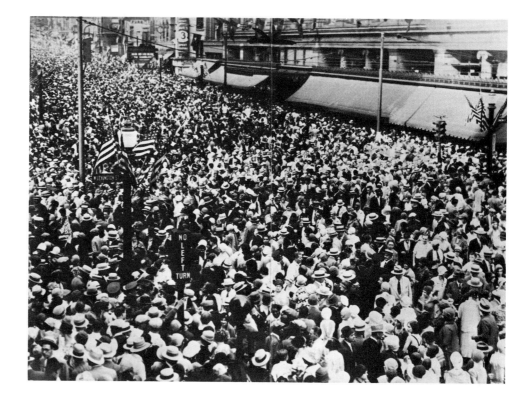

In 1929, the 200th anniversary of the founding of Baltimore was the excuse for enormous gatherings. This one at Howard and Lexington streets took place in the heat of the summer.

thirteen children, two mortgages, served with an eviction notice. "All they have is an equity in their home."[56] The Christmas fashion pages featured chinchilla and "the humble bunny" as favorites with the college set.

Baltimore congratulated itself from time to time on being better off than other cities. Its diversified economy resisted layoffs a little longer. The large proportion of paid-off homes and the existence of ground rents (which did not have to be paid off) meant a somewhat lower rate of foreclosures and evictions. Fewer of the big banks failed, apparently because of their ingrown and conservative history and their large holdings of city and federal bonds. The Savings Bank of Baltimore gained customers and discreetly reorganized the interior so that deposits and withdrawals were made at the same counter "to avoid panic." But most observers agreed that Baltimore arrived eventually at the same point, at the bottom of the depression in 1934. There were twenty-nine thousand registered unemployed in the city, another four thousand in Anne Arundel County. The fifteen hundred taxi drivers were working heroic hours but only taking home $8 or $9 a week. Women and girls at Schoeneman's garment factory were earning between $4 and $20 a week for sixty hours. The sugar refinery closed, throwing three hundred more out of work; it had been paying twenty-eight cents an hour. The price of tobacco was below the cost of producing it, and fifteen hundred farms in Anne Arundel County were under the red flag of the auctioneer.

An autopsy of the more spectacular local bank crises is essential because it reveals the connections between the national economy and the Baltimore economy, between the investments of the '20s and the liquidations of the '30s. The Park Bank was a medium-sized operation at Liberty and Lexington streets. Its clientele, mainly women who used the Lexington Street shopping district, had on deposit $3 million. The bank had borrowed more than banking laws allowed, and had made loans to its own officers and directors on worthless "securities." In this way the officers and directors had used $1 million worth of the depositors' money to buy stock in the bank for themselves. They had continued to accept deposits and to declare dividends to themselves when the bank was no longer solvent. Criminal charges were brought against the officers. One shot himself during the trial, and the bank president was brought "in prison gray" to recount the "silent run" by which they had siphoned out money.[57]

The Union Trust Company weathered the storm. In a first crisis (August 1932), precipitated by the Park Bank failure, it was bolstered by a federal loan. A fleet of armored cars was assembled overnight from Washington, New York, and Philadelphia to truck in the $20 million loaned by the federal Reconstruction Finance Corporation.[58] "Having mobilized huge cash resources, the Union Trust Company today met all the demands made upon it."[59] It was brought under federal rules of reserve and insurance, and its real estate assets were gradually liquidated, restoring liquidity, making it possible to allow the sixty-five thousand depositors to dip into their deposits normally, and gradually paying back the RFC loan. In the more general bank crisis of February 1933, Union Trust closed again. It reopened in December, salvaged by the same interests that had been supporting its growth for some years. Union Trust was the bank favored with deposits by Governor Ritchie's administration. The president was state treasurer, and during the February banking crisis state agencies had on deposit in Union Trust at least $3 million. The Baltimore and Philadelphia power companies (the Aldred group) also favored this bank, and at the critical moment increased their deposits. This kind of high-level solidarity could either make or break a bank. Bank runs, ostensibly caused by panicky depositors lining up for their small savings, were, in fact, generated by sudden cash flows in the accounts of the large depositors. In the wake of the bank holiday, a thousand prominent names were read to the legislature of those who had made withdrawals of more than $10,000 in the critical week of the run, altogether $13 million. It took hours, while *Sun* reporters stretched out on a skylight to listen.[60] But only the little socialist paper, the *Leader*, printed the list, at the top of which were the city ($3 million), the B&O Railroad ($2.5 million), the Baltimore Gas and Electric Company, and the state (over $1 million each). Close behind were the archbishop, the private banking houses, Garrett's and Brown's, and several large department stores.

The Baltimore Trust Company made the biggest smash.[61] By early 1929 it had become an $85 million bank, second in the city, with nineteen branch offices and a thirty-two-story skyscraper. But it had pursued growth without administrative control. It had bought other banks without checking their assets closely. Nineteen vice-presidents all had the power to make loans independently, with no effective checks on the value of the collateral offered. Of the $19 million invested in this way, half was lost. The board of directors included prominent men in Baltimore, all of whom knew something about how to run a bank. But they had simply left the operation to the president. They were on the board in order to attract the deposits of their firms (about a fifth of all deposits) and to get financing for their own ventures. The trust company lent a great deal to its directors, who were not watching each other. Many of their pet projects were so remote from Baltimore that a close watch was difficult. Baltimore Trust lent several million dollars to C. Wilbur Miller, head of the Davison Chemical Company, after other banks had ceased to extend credit to him. They poured $1 million into a Puerto Rican sugar company to buy fertilizer from a Davison subsidiary, Miller Fertilizer, and still more into a Puerto Rican bank formed by the sugar company. Most of this was lost, the sugar company having already suffered hurricane loses. In the same way, Baltimore Trust was the sole source of capital for another of its directors, C. B. Gillet. The bank lost $1 million on his ventures in hotels in Houston, land development in Miami and Tampa, and a cold cream factory. Some speculations originated as far back as World War I. A group of Quaker investors, Edwin and Philip Poe and Holden Evans, had organized a shipbuilding company (Baltimore Drydock) on the Skinner family's shipyard and a steamship company for South America, to buy the ships the company would build; it would survive on a U.S. mail contract subsidy. The house of cards collapsed. Poe was also a Baltimore Trust director. Still other unprofitable investments were made in Florida cypress farms, Alabama coal mines, and a sand and gravel monopoly on the Mississippi River. "These enterprises did not build Baltimore; they impoverished many Baltimoreans by taking millions of dollars out of the city."[62]

Baltimore Trust had to be closed and reorganized. "The winding up of an organization, Mr. Baetjer explained, consists of two functions. One is to distribute the assets to creditors, and the other is to conserve the assets in such manner that their highest value will be realized."[63] The federal Reconstruction Finance Corporation (RFC) bought stock in a new corporation, the Baltimore National Bank, and supplied it with working capital in cash. The new bank could receive deposits, while the old bank gradually liquidated its real estate and began paying off the depositors. An investigation was made. The courts managed to shake $225,000 out of its directors, deemed "inexcusably reckless" in their administration. When the judge ordered them to divide the sum among them, "the defendants, who included some of the richest men in Baltimore, started squabbling." The lawyers took a hundred thousand. By 1936 the depositors had got a third of their money back. Payments were made every few months, at 1 or 2 percent. By Pearl Harbor Day, they reached half, and at the end of 1942 70 percent.

As in the banks, so throughout the economy, redistribution took place over the whole boom-and-bust cycle. There were losers in every class of society. A bank manager shot himself, and an unemployed Italian immigrant jumped off the Calvert Street bridge into the Jones Falls. Mrs. Jacobs (Mary Frick Garrett) stopped adding to her art collection, and The Johns Hopkins University stopped subscribing to journals. But a person's chances of weathering the crisis or even winning in this poker game depended heavily on his initial position as debtor or creditor and the timing of when those debts fell due. As the ma and pa groceries failed, the chain stores grew. By 1933 the three largest chains had 630 stores with forty-three hundred clerks in Baltimore.[64] The two thousand independent grocers rarely employed even one person outside family help. Smaller and shakier banks were absorbed by larger ones. Maryland Trust Company was consolidated out of Drovers Bank and Continental Trust. Equitable Trust Company doubled in size between 1932 and 1938. Standard Oil captured Pan American Petroleum and began to squeeze Blaustein for control of American

The Municipal Office Building was nearing completion at the time of the 1931 Armistice Day celebration at the War Memorial Plaza.

Oil Company. (He successfully resisted in the courts, but it took twenty years.) Consolidated Coal went into receivership.

The B&O Railroad had to be refinanced in each generation. Each crisis was a brush with catastrophe for its creditors, and required rearranging the financial structure, extending debts to a larger amount and a longer future. After the receivership and reorganization of 1899, its $126 million in bonds came due in 1925; it was refinanced at $350 million, providing new capital and new equipment. By laying off employees and skimping on maintenance it continued throughout the depression to pay $29 million a year interest to its bond holders. But it had half its debt in short and medium-term loans that came due in the late '30s. To keep the B&O from falling into receivership again, the RFC lent it a total of $88 million, more than any railroad in the country. The B&O debt structure was put "on a long-term basis." Ultimately the loans of the RFC ran until 1965, and the B&O had paid interest comparable to the full amount of the loans.

United Railways was in a worse situation. Its financial position was already weak before the stock market crash, and it had $8 million of bonds due between November 1929 and 1 March 1932, when refinancing was impossible. General Electric, its creditors, forced it into receivership and reorganization. Since Brown's consolidation in 1906, the finance of United Railways had been based largely on bonds rather than common stock, and its paper capital obligations of $75 million or so ran "far in excess of the actual value of the property." In other words, the bond holders had been getting a steady annual return ($3 million) regardless of earnings, and the return was about twice the rate it appeared to be. During the receivership their interest payments were suspended, and after reorganization the bondholders were forced to accept debentures and preferred stock instead of bonds, meaning that their future income would depend on the net earnings of the company. The total capitalization was reduced to $50 million, somewhat more realistic, and the company was renamed Baltimore Transit Company.[65]

The luck of timing also determined the fate of real estate. Paid-off neighborhoods, including whole communities of German, Bohemian, and Polish, despite bitter unemployment and hunger, kept their homes. Such neighborhoods as Locust Point, Patterson Park, and Canton, and parts of Hampden and Highlandtown, remained at home ownership levels of 80 or 90 percent. The thousand savings and loans performed feats of solidarity, as parishes rallied to save their neighbors' homes. The St. James Savings Bank, one of the largest and oldest, originally identified with the Redemptorist parish, in many cases foreclosed reluctantly, but rented the home to its original owner and afterward remortgaged it to the same family. In new, more comfortable neighborhoods of the '20s, still trammeled by mortgages, foreclosures were more common, and refinancing often implied social turnover. Ashburton, a development built by George Morris in 1919 under restrictive covenants that excluded Jews and Negroes, became 50 percent Jewish in the '30s. Among investment owners, likewise, those loaded with debt in the early '30s caved in, while others, able to borrow from relatives or keep their savings liquid, picked up properties cheaply at auctions and tax sales. The Needles and Merowitzes amassed property in the black ghettos of South and West Baltimore. For the first time since 1822 the city experienced wholesale abandonment of property. There was a pattern to it: tax abandonment was concentrated in the oldest sections.[66] The squeeze followed the same logic as the earlier expansion: in the '20s while the new suburbs were pumped with new capital producing highly visible growth, the black housing market, black businesses, and black institutions were starved for capital and suffered invisible stagnation. In the '30s suburban growth ceased, and the physical meaning of disinvestment became visible at the center, as paint flaked, roofs leaked, brick fronts bowed, and back porches sagged. The city razed a substantial number of dilapidated houses, leaving a missing tooth in blocks west of Lexington Market or in Hill Street and south of Hanover Market. This was consistent with various proposals for "thinning" overcrowded black neighborhoods, but the thinning was illusory. Alongside the vacant houses and bare lots were "converted" homes where families doubled up with relatives or sublet. A proposal to use federal funds to build a Negro housing project provoked opposition. George R. Morris, now president of the Real Estate Board, recommended that the city "plow under" the slums, like the surplus potato crop, and convert the land into parks and playgrounds but not build new housing "until the present supply of good housing at fair prices is absorbed." The problem in the housing market, he argued, was like the market for food and coal; there was a surplus, not a shortage. "Congestion which is due largely to inadequate rent-paying capacity is generally conceded to be the greatest contribution to slum conditions."[67] In the black community, rent-paying capacity was certainly squeezed. Negroes were half of the relief rolls, and their unemployment rate rose to 40 percent, among whites to 13 percent. Just as they were expected to make do with lower wages in normal times, blacks were now expected to make do with lower relief payments, about six dollars a week for a family.

The Federal Resource

I have shown how governments, first municipal, then state, were called upon to play ever larger roles in developing the city and keeping its economic mechanism well greased. But the city-state economy of Baltimore had been absorbed into the national economy. Sooner or later, there would be a corresponding enlargement of the role of national government. Except in wartime, the federal presence in Baltimore had generally been discreet, confined largely to sorting and stamping the mail in its Gothic post office, looking down the throats of immigrants on the Locust Point pier, and appraising packages and collecting cargo duty in the custom house. From time to time the federal government paid for deeper dredging of the ship channels. Occasionally the federal court interfered in commercial disputes, admiralty cases, or prosecuted murderous oyster captains or riotous guano diggers. Wartime experience reinforced local resistance to any enlargement of federal power, and the image of the federal government was especially negative in Baltimore in the '20s thanks to the "revenooers" who enforced prohibition. But the financial crisis created an emergency of national dimensions; local agencies called for help, and despite the rhetoric of states' rights, the federal government became a powerful agent of city building and a factor to reckon with in all urban conflicts. The pulling and hawing over contracts and wages, over road locations and building sites, was symbolized in the travels of officials around the Baltimore-Annapolis-Washington triangle. Baltimore had experienced this during the Civil War, but this triangle of negotiation now became a permanent feature of urban development.

The earliest federal priority was to take care of the creditors and restore confidence. Under President Hoover, the Reconstruction Finance Corporation (RFC) made the massive loans that saved Union Trust Company and salvaged the assets of Baltimore Trust. RFC disbursed $66 million to reorganize Baltimore banks, $50 million to shore up Maryland Casualty, $4 million for U.S. Fidelity and Guarantee, and $88 million to the B&O Railroad. These were among the largest and longest commitments RFC made anywhere.

Relief, on the other hand, was supposed to be primarily local: food, clothing, and fuel for the unemployed must spring from a warm human charity among neighbors. Baltimore had always relied upon private institutions for this, providing meager reimbursement afterward, with minimal supervision. The private charities were overwhelmed by the numbers, and the governor refused to allow the city to borrow money for relief payments. The philosophy of efficiency and economy in city and state government provided no guidance for dealing with the crisis. The swelling burden of "unemployment relief" increased the clamor for "work relief." Private construction had dropped to nothing, and public construction would have to take up the slack. The federal government moved forward certain scheduled projects, such as dredging the Riverview anchorage and building a new post office. Already under President Hoover the RFC proposed to lend money for public or private enterprise to create jobs, so long as such projects were self-liquidating through tolls or fees, not taxes.

Once President Roosevelt adopted the idea of pump priming by budget deficits, the money began to flow. The federal government would borrow, then lend or grant money to state governments, cities, private institutions, or private enterprise, to put people to work.[68] There were two distinct phases and administrations. The first was the Civil Works Administration (CWA). It was supposed to tool up fast. Workers were hired from the relief rolls. By Christmas 1933 the CWA had ten thousand people at work in Baltimore. This was its high-water mark and about a third of the goal, but even to employ this number the CWA had to "spread the work." A man was allowed to work only twenty-four hours a week and earn $11 or $15. Work projects not only relieved hungry households, they relieved local emergency budgets. Over the next few months the state ordered the relief rolls trimmed of single men without dependents, then of domestic servants (pressing hardest on the black community), then of all "employables." The CWA was criticized for "make-work" of low productivity and repressive character. Work relief was supposed to preserve human dignity more effectively than the dole. Five hundred "high-type men" were hired to trap millions of rats, deliver them alive to the quarantine station on Leading Point, chloroform them, comb their bodies, count and classify the vermin in glass jars, and dissect the rats.[69] Most of the tasks were less ingenious, simply pick and shovel work, the same as work relief in 1894. Broadus Mitchell watched from his window at Johns Hopkins the landscaping and lighting project of a hundred CWA workers digging for several weeks in the frozen earth with pick and shovel and sledge. "I venture to say that a steamshovel could do it all in ten hours. Now, why must this Government use sweat instead of steam."[70] Nevertheless, because of its strategy of putting men to work, and even because of its disregard of steam-engine efficiency, the CWA performed a rather special city-building function. It provided landscaping, preservation, and artwork on public sites and public buildings. It restored the Carroll mansion and landscaped the new Philadelphia Road. In seventy-nine schools, always starved for common maintenance, it replastered, repointed brick, repainted, and refinished desks. The CWA was followed by the WPA (Works Progress Administration), which spent $40 million in Maryland (1934–39) along the same lines. The WPA took 88 percent of its labor, chiefly unskilled, from relief rolls.

The second strategy, the Public Works Administration (PWA), selected projects for their value as future public assets, as well as for their potential for

A public works project on
Calvert Street employed
extensive work teams for ice
removal in the winter of 1936.

employing people and their chances of getting started quickly. It was this stream
of resources that made the depression a city-building period. The criteria were
consistent with the City Plan, and Baltimore was in an exceptional state of readiness with its agenda of the '20s. The PWA in Maryland was headed by a civil
and sanitary engineer, Abel Wolman, and housed in the vacant Baltimore Trust
Company skyscraper. It spent $100 million over four years (1934–37), and
reached a peak employment level in August 1934 of 12,500 men. The unskilled
labor, 35 percent of the PWA's workers, was taken from relief rolls. For each
person it hired, the PWA figured private enterprise hired two or three more to
provide materials and transport services.[71] PWA funds allowed the city water
department to complete a ten-year program in four years: Prettyboy Reservoir, a
second water tunnel from Loch Raven, a "high service" reservoir and pumping
station at Ashburton, and a siphon under Curtis Creek. Sewage treatment
facilities were expanded at Back River. The city completed plans for the annex
using PWA funds. The Herring Run valley was developed: a retaining wall
along the run, Mount Pleasant Park and golf course, buildings for Morgan
College, the extension of Loch Raven Boulevard, Edison Highway, the Brehms
Lane fire house and school, and several streets crossing the run. PWA funds
enabled the school board to finish the Eastern High School campus. The city
added a wing to the art museum to house Mrs. Jacobs's collection of modern
paintings. PWA funds allowed the city to finish its viaducts: Howard Street,
Orleans Street, Hilton Street, Twenty-ninth Street, and Cold Spring Lane. Their
clean lines, stone work, lightness of cement work, and landscaping mark them
as PWA projects, which contrast with massive works of the 1950s alongside.
The PWA also contributed to the "$4 million dump" at Dundalk: the fine liquid
mud from the harbor refused to settle, and even the two planes that were
scheduled each day couldn't land on a bowlful of jelly. Citizens proposed ingenious schemes for drying up the airport, as wild and wonderful as their
grandfathers' solutions for the basin. An "otherwise sane" structural engineer
suggested drying it up with millions of candlewicks. Several private projects
received PWA loans. The Pennsylvania Railroad at last undertook its $22 million
electrification program—2500 jobs—announced with such fanfare in 1907. The
city shared half the bill for grade-crossing eliminations.[72]

Highway projects led the agenda of state government. The State Roads Commission was able to provide about half the jobs in the first year of PWA in Maryland. The most controversial was the alignment of the new Philadelphia Road (Pulaski Highway). The most important, because it fixed an agenda for thirty years to come, was the Maryland Bridge Program. Following the lead of New York and the initial philosophy of RFC grants, the bridge program was designed to be self-liquidating. Revenue bonds would be issued, to be repaid from bridge tolls. The bridges were conceived as of part of a total traffic system and a total financial program: they would be scheduled so that each bridge need not repay its cost, but repayment was spread over the whole set of bridges. The earliest was the bridge over the Susquehanna at Havre de Grace. (The "gold mine" bridge was finally abandoned.) The Harbor Tunnel and Chesapeake Bay Bridge were not completed till after World War II.

Because it was important, economically and politically, to spread funds widely over the state, the federal money accomplished a great deal outside the city and prepared the communities around Baltimore to receive suburban influx after World War II. In addition to the State Roads Commission, Mr. Morse of the state health department also had an agenda, with which Abel Wolman was thoroughly familiar. The state leaped fifteen years ahead in sewer and water-works construction. Services of urban standard were provided in Towson, Annapolis, Bel Air, and Frederick. Administration of public construction was professionalized in the counties and the state, reining in small fiefdoms such as Curly Byrd's at College Park. The Civilian Conservation Corps built trails and fire breaks in its work camps in the Patapsco state forest. This provided impetus to the joint effort of federal, state, and municipal agencies to acquire and "park" the Patapsco valley, consonant with the Olmsted stream valley plan. Reservoir projects did much the same thing for the Gunpowder Falls valley. Together, they provided a framework for recreation for what would a generation later be a metropolitan area.

Thanks to the PWA and CWA, institutions long starved for state funds were developed with modern buildings: Spring Grove, Springfield, Crownsville, and Sykesville mental hospitals, Rosewood training school, the House of Corrections at Jessup, and the Montrose School. The investments crystallized a certain institutional style for a generation to come: isolated campuses ringing the metropolitan area. In the city, substantial additions were made to several hospitals. The federal government made sizeable investments in its own property at Aberdeen proving ground, the Chesapeake and Delaware Canal, the agricultural experiment station at Beltsville, and the coast guard station and ordnance depot at Curtis Bay.

The combined effects of the devalued dollar and federal pump priming taught Baltimore to think big, in millions and tens of millions of dollars, and to juggle the political interests of several levels of government. As federal administrator for Maryland projects, Abel Wolman rode to Washington with the mayor and made the rounds of the federal offices; they came home one night with Harold Ickes's check for $3 million. The negotiations worked right down to the neighborhood level. Another night, when they were negotiating to buy the land for the Reedbird incinerator, the mayor and Wolman went to see the parish priest, who reckoned they would get their land if they would reroute the trucks through South Baltimore. The contractors also learned to think big. Bartlett-Hayward began building dam gates for the Tennessee Valley Authority and the Bureau of Reclamation. The Commercial Credit Corporation, which had narrowly extricated itself from a $5 million venture in aviation finance, now went into FHA receivers, that is, Commercial Credit operated as a collection agency for federally insured mortgages.[73] Locally, the dredging, hauling, paving, and brick companies waxed fat. The largest purchases for PWA projects were building materials, including steel and cement, then machinery and transportation equipment. The Arundel Corporation got contracts for widening Curtis Creek channel. Bethlehem Steel benefited from the deepening of Sparrows Point channel to thirty-seven feet for its ore boats, and a PWA loan to its Sparrows Point railroad. The engineering firm of John E. Greiner had been discredited in the city for its involvement in the scandalous land acquisition and costing of the Orleans Street viaduct, but continued as engineering consultants to the Pennsylvania Railroad (with which the Orleans Street viaduct was "perfectly coordinated") and undertook the engineering work for the Maryland Bridge Program, a relationship good for a generation.

The money was all borrowed. The U.S. government marketed bonds through special consortiums of bankers, then reloaned the money to the state, the city, or the railroads. The RFC channeled $124 million into Maryland (1932–35), most of it in the form of loans at 3 percent interest. Some were loans to the state government for its share of relief and work projects, to be "repaid" as credits on federal highway funds in future years. The private loans to shore up Maryland banks, insurance companies, and railroads amounted to another $200 million. In addition, the federal Home Owners Loan Corporation refinanced sixteen thousand mortgages in Maryland, or $50 million worth. Four out of five of the families managed to save their homes, but they still owed the money. Instead of owing it to the bankers, they now owed it to the federal government, which in turn owed it to the bankers. The Federal Land Bank of Baltimore did the same thing for farm properties, and B. H. Griswold (of Alex. Brown) organized an investment syndicate to sell its bonds. Griswold was also chairman of the Chesapeake Bay Bridge Commission and organizer of the Maryland Primary Bridge Program; he assured the federal government that the bridge revenue bonds could be sold, and organized the syndicate that sold the first $6 million worth. The need to protect holders of the revenue bonds regulated the schedule and location of bridge construction into the 1970s. Overall, the borrowing strategy of the thirties prepared a new set of debtor-creditor relationships, a vise of public debt that would perpetuate the bond holders' grip on the future of the city.

The federal investment strategy was a continuation of the city and state planning of the '20s. In the '20s, private capital flowed into automobile manufacture and sales credit, and public capital into viaducts and highways, while the streetcar system stagnated. In the '30s, the bankruptcy of the streetcar company gave it sudden prominence, but the implacable logic continued: more public resources were put into viaducts, highways, and bridges. In the '20s Baltimore's private investors put money into English race horses, Puerto Rican sugar plantations, and Houston hotels, while corporations owned in Pittsburgh, New York, and Chicago invested in labor-saving equipment in their Baltimore factories: the number of jobs in Baltimore did not increase substantially. In the '30s federal funds put people to work temporarily, but were not investments that created permanent jobs. Over the '30s the potential labor force grew by fifty thousand, but available jobs grew scarcely at all, and in 1940 there were still people seeking work.

What was the climate of opinion in Baltimore? Bankers and business leaders were very much afraid of riot. Stories were still told of how one hundred years earlier the mob burned the furniture and smashed the wine cellars of the trustees who were trying to untangle the affairs of the insolvent banks. The Savings Bank of Baltimore set an example in 1931 by giving $30,000 to the Unemployment Emergency Relief Fund "to prevent riots," and in 1932 $20,000 to the Baltimore charities campaign. The other banks followed suit. Baltimore was close to Washington, and hungry people in Baltimore knew that hungry people in Washington had been driven out of their camps by the army. "Give a Job! Share the Work!" people were urged, and invited to take part in Self-Denial Day. The socialist paper suggested instead, "On Your Way Take Home a Brick." Norman Thomas, Emma Goldman, and Margaret Sanger spoke in Baltimore. Ten thousand voted for Norman Thomas and a like number for Broadus Mitchell, the outspoken Hopkins professor who for years had been taking his students through the lung block and to the bachelors' cotillion. Meanwhile, the CWA hired musicians for the park casinos "where the people can gather and dance their blues away."

The federal government attempted to enforce a minimum wage, maximum hours so as to spread the work, and the right of workers to organize their own unions. But the bitter competition for jobs was not a climate that fostered solidarity among workers or among the unemployed. The PWA observed the market wage differential of $1.10 an hour for skilled labor and forty-five cents for unskilled, which split the labor force. The fear of violence kept authorities on edge, and repressive measures worked against labor solidarity. In the summer of 1934 there were strikes in a dozen different industries. Most were not widely reported, and nearly all failed either through outbreaks of violence or the collapse of solidarity. At Canton, five hundred longshoremen massed to impress officials and nonunion stevedores. The longshoremen wanted seventy-five cents an hour. But each time the steamer was brought to the pier, four hundred to five hundred police filled the pier, to prevent the longshoremen from reaching the ship. The police refused to let representatives board the ship to negotiate. They used tear gas, clubs, and the city fireboat to drive the longshoremen off the pier.

Mount Vernon Mills introduced piecework and speeded up the production line under federal rules; a year later the workers joined the United Textile Workers of America. Eastern Rolling Mills laid off 400 workers and tried to go on piecework. This plan might allow the mill to pay five or six dollars instead of the fifteen-dollar minimum wage, so the workers struck. Twelve hundred meatpacking workers asked for twenty dollars a week, and the shoe workers wanted twelve dollars. Five thousand Amalgamated clothing workers walked out because the factories had "chiseled down the wage" to twelve dollars a week. The evolution at Sparrows Point was typical of a national pattern. By March 1933, Bethlehem Steel had discharged 1231 workers into the arms of city charity. At its shipyard "peach trees were growing in the ways." But Bethlehem testified against legislative proposals for unemployment insurance by state government.[74] By fall a speed-up had raised the accident rate, and workers were signing up with the union. The company fired several hundred steel workers suspected of being union members. Crown Cork and Seal hired armed guards to prevent union organizers from talking to its workers. The scenario on the B&O was also typical. The B&O had borrowed $4 million from the PWA for construction work in this region. At the Mount Clare shops, it laid off, rehired, and again laid off its 2800 shop workers, according to the flow of PWA loan funds. To force its Paw Paw, West Virginia, work gangs to accept thirty cents an hour instead of the legal minimum of forty-five cents, the B&O brought up workers from the Salvation Army Transient Home in Baltimore. They were promised two months of work and put up with ropes around them to grade the mountainside to prevent landslides onto the tracks. Next day, when local workers appeared ready to go to work at thirty cents, the transients were shipped back to Baltimore.[75]

Much frustration was turned inward or directed against easier targets. Alcohol deaths increased. The number of "domestic cases"—suits for divorce and abuse—soared. There were fewer marriages and many fewer births. A larger share were illegitimate, and more infants were abandoned. In addition to the larger numbers of tramps, the Salvation Army and Travelers Aid despaired of the appearance of "the woman hobo" who rode the freights or hitchhiked, "an almost hopeless social problem."[76] On the Eastern Shore several Negroes were lynched; a man was burned and his ear cut off.

Just as in the '20s people had been diverted from the workaday world by their preoccupation with maintaining the illicit flow of beer, now they were diverted from the grim world of no work by the sideshow *Beer Is Back.* In his campaign, Roosevelt had promised an end to prohibition, and the repeal of state and federal laws began soon after his inauguration. As Hitler took full control of Germany, as reports began coming in of atrocities against the Jews, as the Baltimore unemployed signed up to comb rats, as the bank holiday drew to an end and the Park Bank case came to trial, the thirst for beer captured the headlines. No sooner had the state legislature passed the beer bill than "there is enough beer on hand right now, they said, to flood the city, figuratively speaking, within two hours, and a number of breweries which have been shut down since the prohibition law was passed, are ready to open up on a moment's notice."[77] The breweries fenced in adjoining lots to prepare loaded trucks. Three thousand applied for first-night licenses, and got out New Year's Eve noise-makers. The clubs and hotels created beer gardens. The Germanic touch was all schmaltz and nostalgia, and the price had doubled to ten cents a glass. A city police officer who had vowed never to raise the flag during prohibition built a flagpole on his house in Potomac Street. On 1 April at one minute past midnight at each brewery the government inspector called "Time!" "As the inspector dropped his hand, the whistle of the brewery sounded, the doors in front of the loading platform swung open, and beer-truck drivers shoved their vehicles into gear and shot away."[78] Gunther's sent the first load to the Germania Turnverein, and forty-six more trucks sped out of Conkling Street, escorted by motorcycles and cheered by a thousand people. A crowd of fifteen hundred roared as sixty trucks dashed out of the Globe brewery on South Hanover Street. Another fifteen hundred mobbed the Southern Hotel. Traffic was "hopelessly tied up" around the Emersonian. Two thousand Negroes collected on Pennsylvania Avenue. At the Rennert Hotel, Mencken drank the first glass, and a case was sent by motorcycle to Frank Furst.

Hemmed In

1935–1979

Ever the stubborn rhythmic continuity of eleven generations, the growth of Baltimore was geared to the tempo of the world economy. As in the eighteenth and early nineteenth centuries, Baltimore's economic motor purred at any outbreak of war and stalled at any threat of "disasters of the peace." The long stagnation of the great depression was broken and a new tide of industry and population rolled in: glue factories and trainloads of workers. From a population of 1.2 million in 1940 the metropolis grew to 2 million in 1970.

Continuity was also preserved in the spatial pattern of growth: population packed into the center, then spilled beyond the city limits into a suburban ring. The city population declined gradually, by about a thousand a year, while the counties mushroomed at a rate of thirty thousand a year. First industry, then housing pushed out into Baltimore and Anne Arundel counties, and then to Howard, Carroll, and Harford counties.

Once the second world war was over, housing starts began to climb, never dropping below three thousand dwellings a year. Construction crested at seven or eight thousand after the Korean War (1954–55), swelled again at the height of the Vietnam War (1965–68), and reached fifteen thousand in the mid-1970s. The metropolitan areas of Washington, Philadelphia, Wilmington, and Harrisburg reached out to touch the Baltimore suburbs. Washington grew faster, concentrating in itself the federal instruments for managing a war economy and leading the way toward the postwar service economy.

The remarkable transformations of the production engine of Baltimore in this generation stemmed from World War II. Out of them grew radical changes in the metabolism of the city: a higher exchange of materials with the world economy and an insatiable appetite for energy. One can see these changes, like those of earlier generations, as changes of scale. Larger lumps of capital were amassed and incorporated into the fabric of Baltimore, thereby channeling and accelerating energy flows and restructuring human relations within the metropolitan area.

Rearmament and the industrial step-up began before the United States entered war. By February 1937 the steel, aircraft, and shipbuilding industries were expanding. Bethlehem Steel's biggest customer was the emperor of Japan. "World Is Building Warships," ran the headline. The junkman collecting

The Logistics of World War

Although the site and the designs change, the rowhouse has remained a popular style of construction to the present. In 1939 the 1500 block of Lockwood Road won a prize for design and construction.

old flat irons and radiators from the alleys of Baltimore did his bit for the Japanese war effort.[1] By the time the Japanese invaded China and Hitler annexed Czechoslovakia, the Martin Company had $70 million of British aircraft orders. By August 1941 $1 billion of U.S. government contracts had reached Maryland and fifty thousand people were working in defense plants, about half of them at Martin aircraft. Japanese buyers were no longer allowed to visit the plant. The strategic advantages that had favored Baltimore in World War I made it once again the place to build ships and airplanes. After Pearl Harbor, decisive changes in scale of enterprise were achieved in a matter of months. Martin increased its employment to thirty-seven thousand. Bethlehem Steel achieved the same record. Western Electric peaked at nine thousand, Maryland Drydock at forty-five hundred, and others operated at levels of two or three thousand workers.[2] As the defense industries grew, relief and WPA employment dwindled.

Federal finance was the key. The Reconstruction Finance Corporation, converted from fighting the depression to fighting the war, provided $70 million for construction of defense plants in Maryland.[3] Among them were a sixty-acre Lansdowne site for Westinghouse Electric, "scrambled" facilities (only partly government owned) for steel production at Bethlehem, a tax-free shipyard site at Fairfield, and $2 million capital to Davison Chemical, whose silica gel technology was strategic to the synthetic rubber program. The RFC also siphoned working capital and materials such as scrap iron and chrome ore into Baltimore. In the rubber program it bought up raw materials for industrial alcohol—potatoes and Cuba's entire output of sugar and molasses—and stored them at a tank farm at Morgantown. Virtually all home construction during the war (roughly thirty thousand dwellings) was "defense housing." At Aero Acres, near the Martin plant, streets were named Right Wing, Aileron, Fuselage, and Dihedral. Whole communities were built at Turner.

Federal defense investments had a tidewater suburban locus. The new industrial plants and defense housing were built on the tidewater necks toward Bear Creek, Back River, Middle River, and Curtis Bay. Military bases employed large numbers of civilians and construction workers at coastal plain sites farther from the city: Fort Meade, Edgewood Arsenal, and the coast guard depot at

Curtis Bay. New peninsular highways were built. During the war eight hundred fifty thousand people were carried daily on the streetcars, only 40 percent to the downtown. Most of the rest moved through the downtown area out to the new industrial sites on the necks. The new geography of war industry prepared the way for massive blue-collar suburbanization, as at Essex, and the collapse of central mass transit after the war. All these efforts were financed by expanded federal taxing and borrowing, setting a pattern for a generation to come.

Wartime production spaces had new properties that foreshadowed postwar development in size, assembly-line organization, the one-story floor plan, and cleanliness. The Martin Company built the largest aircraft assembly floor in the world, 350 by 450 feet, with 40 feet headroom and fluorescent lighting. Manufacture was speeded by introducing auto assembly techniques into aircraft assembly, and thence into shipbuilding. Baltimore built more than five hundred Liberty ships and Victory ships. Materials and parts were supplied at one end of a 1540-foot-long building at Fairfield; the ship emerged onto the ways at the other end. In April 1942 the company was launching two a week and it took 110 days to build one.[4] By August it had cut the time to 52 days. A swifter pace required smoother linkage along the assembly line, not only within the plant, but between plants in the harbor area. Bethlehem Steel supplied flat plate steel from the Sparrows Point mill by rail to the Fairfield shipyard. Ellicott Machine was building the engines near Federal Hill, and Bartlett-Hayward was producing the bronze propellers and main propulsion gears.[5]

Baltimore's specialized war production role—building ships and planes— had implications for its economic future. The logistics of world war demanded a worldwide transport revolution. After the war this required total readaptation of the port, the airport, and the metropolitan space. Baltimore initially grew faster than the national average, as its industrial plant shifted into high gear. But the nationwide impact of federal defense investments tended ultimately to cramp Baltimore industrially and to develop regions of competition elsewhere in the nation. The demands of the Pacific theater favored growth of Pacific Coast seaports. Defense strategists consistently favored industrial sites between the Appalachians and the Rockies. A critical decision was made, for example, to locate a world-scale tin smelter at Longhorn, Texas, instead of Baltimore.[6] The strategic demands of lightning warfare forced the concentration of federal investment on oil, synthetic rubber, light metals, and aircraft engines, and the choices also favored gulf coast or midcontinent locations. Even housing investment flowed more heavily into California and Utah, Los Angeles, Detroit, and Chicago.

In July 1945, Baltimoreans watched the war wind down with mixed emotions. Ads appeared, "Gas, Yes We Have It." "Watermelons are beginning to arrive in force at Long Dock and the lights are on again on the Washington Monument. Painters again are at work redecorating homes, and venturesome dealers are risking the display of popular-brand cigarettes."[7] But what would happen in the job market? By October, forty-five thousand war workers were laid off, and thirty-five thousand veterans had arrived. A massive turnover occurred in jobs, through conversion of land, industrial plant, and machinery.

The groundwork had been laid during the war, in terms of new product technologies. The sacrifices of wartime, forced savings, and a "baby boom" prepared the way for a "consumer economy." Backlog orders and expectations of home building stimulated massive investments in telephone equipment, gypsum, titanium oxide paints, chain link fencing, home power tools, and bathtubs. An airplane parts foundry began casting soil pipe for home builders. The recycling of equipment created curious reversals in the flows of materials. For example, Bethlehem Steel transformed a shipbuilding site into a "ship-breaking" operation, which supplied steel scrap to Sparrows Point. Morris Schapiro also made a specialty of scrapping ships, streetcars, and ferry boats. Wrecking entrepreneurs flourished on slum clearance projects.

The technological basis for future changes in Baltimore production was generated through wartime problem solving. Westinghouse bought its federally built Lansdowne plant, and converted from x-ray inspection of armor plate to industrial uses of x-rays. Immediately after the war, Westinghouse and the Martin Company launched development work on StratoVision, airborne TV and FM radio transmitters. Western Electric was manufacturing coaxial cable for TV at Point Breeze by 1951. Davison Chemical's methods for packaging whole planes and tanks had industrial uses. Grease coating was replaced by packing with silica gel, a chemically inert substance that absorbs water on an enormous internal surface. Davison's granulation techniques were then applied to its fertilizer. Its related war work on fluid catalytic cracking for aviation fuels was applied to gasoline manufacture at the Baltimore Esso refinery, and later to emission control agents.[8]

Successive waves of federal investment in weapons systems and aerospace continued to generate waves of industrial technology and construction in Baltimore. Westinghouse Air Arm was involved in radar and automatic pilots for night fighter planes in Korea. It became the Aerospace Division and "spun off" a Molecular Electronics Division, which built a "clean room" of one hundred ten thousand square feet at Friendship Airport, for the manufacture of integrated circuits. Their Ordnance Division, whose torpedoes left no visible wake and sank 2 million tons of Japanese shipping, devised new generations of submarine weapons and submersibles. It grew into the Westinghouse Environmental Center and the Ocean Research and Engineering Center near the Bay Bridge.

Baltimore industry remained intensely interconnected. As some webs were unraveled, others were knitted together. There were two powerful reintegrating forces in this process. One was the technical complexity of the new weapons and aerospace systems, which required an elaborate planned integration of design, timing, and assembly through federal contracts and subcontracts to hundreds of firms. By 1972 the aerospace industry was contributing $1 billion a year to the Maryland economy, and what Eisenhower called the "military-industrial complex" had its characteristic spaces in the Baltimore landscape. The sites were linked together by highways in the Baltimore-Washington corridor and beltways around the two metropolitan areas. A second integrating process was the growth of the firm. As in 1898, when accumulation and diversification occurred by merger of firms at the national scale, in the 1960s

The pressure on port-related rail facilities resulted in the continued use of coal-fired steam engines into the 1940s. This photograph shows an engine coaling at the Riverside yards.

firms merged into great corporate families that ringed the earth. Their corporate genealogies, their internal exchange of goods, their internal accounting, and their global communications by telex and computer were invisible to consumers. For example, when W. R. Grace merged with Davison Chemical, internal vertical integration became more elaborate among the divisions: ocean transport, Latin American trade, advertising and brokering, organic chemicals, rare earths, and scrap recovery of nonferrous metals. The worldwide strategies of the superfirms were not visible to most Baltimoreans, but the role of the largest Baltimore plants belonging to "transnational" firms can be inferred from cargo movements through the port.

The port of Baltimore felt every round of expansion of world trade. After lendlease and firepower for Eisenhower, Baltimore shipped Marshall Plan cargoes to rebuild Europe, then military supplies to Korea and Vietnam. A world trade boom was felt from 1970 through 1973. In boom years the port of Baltimore handled 30 million tons of cargo. The level of activity from year to year still depended largely on world trade in four bulk cargoes: exports of grain and coal and imports of iron ore and oil.[9]

Changes in the structure of the world economy appeared in the metabolism of the port of Baltimore, as new frontiers and new centers of world trade emerged. Highly specialized products such as coke, specialty steels, and engineering goods moved among U.S., European, and Japanese ports. Japan

A World-Scale Port

bought metallurgical coal from Baltimore, purchased and built dredges under license from a Baltimore firm, and brought Toyotas into Baltimore for distribution on the east coast. Japanese ships also brought Canadian potash from Saskatchewan via Vancouver, and Japanese trading firms shipped goods made in Korea and Taiwan to U.S. department stores. In 1976, $12 billion worth of goods was imported to the United States from Japan via Baltimore, and somewhat more was exported.

Baltimore was connected with a new frontier of mushrooming cities that performed as it had once performed, as collection points from inland resource frontiers. In 1962, Baltimore was receiving 10 million tons a year of Venezuelan iron ore from the brand-new city of Ciudad Guayana. In 1965 Bethlehem Steel began bringing iron ore from Quebec and Labrador, via Sept-Iles. The port of Baltimore received Chilean copper. These new cities were also a market frontier for American goods: Baltimore periodically shipped grain to Calcutta and Bombay, and bridge steel, soap, fertilizers, and bottle-washing machinery to Mombasa and São Paulo. As new outposts of rapid capital accumulation, these cities attracted migrants from their backlands, and they became rivals to the Baltimore labor force. Baltimore had struggled to protect and develop its manufactures of shoes, cotton goods, and nails in the 1820s and succeeded in exporting these goods in the world trade boom of the 1870s. Now Baltimore consumers again became importers of shoes, textiles, dishes, and clothing—from Singapore, Hong Kong, Taipei, Seoul, Lisbon, and Port-au-Prince. Earlier frontier cities also emerged as centers competing with Baltimore. Its investors had helped rebuild Atlanta and connect Atlanta and Norfolk with the northeast. Now it found Atlanta a rival, attracting corporate headquarters and regional sales and insurance offices, and Norfolk, Newport News, and New Orleans functioned as rival ports. Baltimore capital was being invested on the frontiers, and Baltimoreans received dividends, but the headquarters for channeling and managing these investments were not found in Baltimore. Decisions were made in a small number of more central places: New York, London, Frankfurt, and Tokyo. Thus, Baltimore was neither frontier nor center, and its growth was hemmed in globally, in much the same way it had been hemmed in regionally in the 1840s when New York and Philadelphia had skimmed the cream of commerce with the nation's inland frontier, leaving Baltimore the "blue milk."

Ships built in Baltimore provided an example of the larger lumps of capital. The Liberty ships were 515 feet long. In 1954 Baltimore shipyards launched the first converted containerships or "sea trains" for McLean, and specialized in "jumboizing" oil tankers. Ships 883 feet long were built for the Alaska oil run. In 1973 an 1100-foot "oilberg" built at Sparrows Point was too large for the port of Baltimore, indeed too large for any American port at the time, and in 1975 they were building five supertankers 1200 feet long. The industrial might of the city had outgrown its commerce. Meanwhile, home-grown commerce had also outgrown local industry. McLean's Sea Land, now a subsidiary of RJR and a major container line on the North Atlantic, ordered "supercontainerships" from German shipyards.

The weight, carrying capacity, and cost of these ships increased more than their length. The Liberty ships weighed 10,000 tons. Atlantic Richfield's ships for Alaska were 120,000 tons deadweight, able to carry a million barrels of oil. The 1975 supertankers of 265,000 tons could carry two million barrels. Coupled with the new belts, blowers, and containers for handling mixed cargo, the superships allowed quicker turnaround of the ship, the freight, and the capital they embodied.

The new scale of ships and cargo corresponded to changes of scale in other features of the landscape. The channel would be deepened from 42 to 50 feet. Faster unloading and greater flow of goods across the docks required much larger back-up working spaces. At the 550-acre Dundalk marine terminal, Volkswagens and Toyotas could be driven off the ship into parking lots, inspected, washed, loaded onto car carriers, and delivered within five days. Seven giant bridge cranes were installed at Dundalk to handle containers. New barges for cement were as big as Liberty ships, and a group of sixteen cement silos at Curtis Bay were 190 feet tall, like the Washington Monument. At Sparrows Point a novel shipbuilding basin replaced traditional dry docks, a thousand-foot mechanized ore pier was built, and the blast furnaces of the "world-scale" steel mill were 320-foot skyscrapers. Smaller copper refineries were shut down, and in effect replaced by Kennecott's "world-scale" refinery at Hawkins Point. Such installations had one-story floor plans and required large tracts of land, comparable in size to the original land grants of Maryland in the 1650s. Bethlehem Steel bought 1300 acres for linked industries and future expansion, then evacuated and scrapped its old company town to make room for the electric furnaces. An 1100-acre site was purchased for General Electric's Appliance Park at Columbia, and the overall town plan for Columbia required an assembly of 15,000 acres, five times the initial tract for Canton, an 1830 project with much the same mix of ideas.

In the drive to promote the city's growth from the world trade boom, Baltimore came up against a handicap of its own making. In its perennial zeal for developing trade to the hinterland, the city had allocated most of its waterfront to railroads. The several railroads had provided shipping piers and warehouses and had specialized the port in the handling of coal, grain, ore, and oil. But the railroads had become moribund, inefficient monopolies, short of fresh capital, and were interested only in the "captive" commodities, coal and grain, not likely to move by truck or pipeline. Baltimore's three great railroads, the Baltimore & Ohio, the Chesapeake & Ohio, and the Western Maryland, all came into a single vast "Chessie" system in 1965, devoted primarily to moving coal, and managed from Cleveland. They paid little in taxes, but controlled most of the tidewater sites available for industrial development, notably five hundred acres of Marley Neck and five hundred acres in Fairfield. Like Ellicott's wharves in Cheapside in 1818 and Johns Hopkins's Light Street warehouses in 1859, the railroad piers had become obsolete. Each agent of developed land became a vested interest and in its turn an obstacle to growth.

Once again, public investment was essential to break the barrier and allow a new spurt of private enterprise. Developable waterfront land was largely downstream, outside the city limits, and beyond the city's fiscal reach and its

The state of Maryland reinforced Baltimore's "world scale" viewpoint when the Port Authority opened its World Trade Center in 1977. The five-sided, thirty-story building perched on the waterfront but its working aspects were minimized, since the original docks were made into promenades, shops, and marinas and the warehouses were pulled down and replaced by hotels, a science center, and an aquarium.

investment horizon. The solution was to create a state agency, the Maryland Port Authority, to overcome the constraints of the "railroad port." In 1967 the Port Authority launched Decade for Progress, an investment plan on the order of $90 million. (A second "decade" may reach ten times that investment level.) Its priorities were to create public land, raise productivity, coordinate all modes of transport, and develop the neglected potential for attracting high-value general cargo. The key strategy was to promote container handling. The federal government would dredge a hundred million cubic yards of muck, to deepen the channel from Baltimore to the Virginia Capes to handle the iron-ore super-carriers. The problem of where to dump the muck, contaminated with chemical wastes, delayed the project for several years. Public investment was also needed for the metropolitan airport. At the end of the war the city abandoned the $7 million mud pie at Dundalk and built a $15 million airport on a 3200-acre site at Friendship, between Washington and Baltimore. Like the port, the airport was taken over by the state for operation, and a State Department of Transportation was created to coordinate public investments and manage the entire transport revolution in Maryland.

Even the so-called world-scale plants in Baltimore were only modest links in the worldwide corporate metabolism of the '70s.[10] The Kennecott copper refinery at Hawkins Point, with a rod-casting mill and a sophisticated plant for recycling metals from "black slimes," had a work force of only seven hundred. But the overall growth of Kennecott as a transnational firm occurred primarily outside Baltimore. Kennecott's growth in the '70s arose from transforming and connecting resource spaces at opposite poles of the earth; its profit level depended on variations in foreign exchange, international tax differentials, and prices of copper and gold. The company mined Australian coal with a dragline bucket that took two hundred-ton gulps and shipped it to Japan, five thousand miles away. It did the start-up engineering for brass and tungsten plants in Japan and Singapore, explored for ores in Papua and Indonesia, and participated in a joint venture with power companies to mine Wyoming coal, turn it into gas, and ship it to Indiana; another with Bethlehem Steel, Rio Tinto Zinc, and Mitsubishi to mine manganese nodules from the ocean floor.

Another giant, the Martin Company, recycled its Baltimore real estate. It demolished the world's biggest factory floor at Aero Acres, redeveloped the region's largest industrial site of the last generation, and built and leased an office tower at Friendship. After merger with Marietta cement, Martin Marietta contributed to building runways, highways, and bridges in the Baltimore landscape. But overall, the corporation has become a diversified and tightly interwoven structure, producing aluminum, chemicals, and aerospace and data systems, and its growth frontier is outside Baltimore, in the southern and western rim of the United States: Charlotte, Atlanta, Tulsa, Orlando, and Denver. Its highest profits have come from an ocean periphery of world growth much like Kennecott's: chemicals from Australia to Indonesia, bauxite from Guinea to a Caribbean refinery and a smelter in the Pacific Northwest. The Baltimore region of the 1770s was a congeries of plantations. In the 1890s it was a single well-integrated plantation. In the 1970s it appeared to be one "quarter" or subsystem in a world-scale plantation.

The All-Electric County

The new metabolism of Baltimore involved a new scale of energy exchange. While its population doubled in thirty-five years, electrical energy consumed in its homes and industries increased fivefold, the amount of natural gas used tripled, and the amount of gasoline burned rose sixfold. As one might expect from clues of the 1850s, 1870s, or 1920s, the shift of scale was associated with important changes—technical, managerial, financial, and geographic—in the production and consumption of energy.

The size of electric generating units rose from sixty megawatts—which could keep a hundred-watt lightbulb burning in each home in the metropolitan area—to fifteen times that size. Energy was transported much longer distances. A grid of high-tension lines was built to connect power plants farther from Baltimore: Calvert Cliffs nuclear generating plant and mine-mouth coal-burning plants at Conemaugh and Keystone, Pennsylvania. The high-voltage power lines took the form of a beltway, a coastal plain corridor, and stream-valley radials. The scale of management was boosted accordingly. By 1956, Baltimore Gas and Electric Company was participating in the largest power pool in the country, known as the Pennsylvania–New Jersey–Maryland Interconnection. It shared load diversity and introduced automatic load controls. The service area of Baltimore, a few hundred square miles, was plugged into a vast interconnection from the Appalachian backbone to the Atlantic. It in turn exchanges power with other systems of the continent: the Northeast New York–Canadian Interconnection, an Allegheny group, and the Southeast.

Changes in the choice of fuels to generate electricity show how Baltimore was plugged into the world and how vast complementary spaces of oceans and continents were connected, to tap Mesozoic pools of oil and gas and Paleozoic deposits of coal. At the end of World War II, 1 million tons of coal were burned annually to make electricity in the Baltimore region. Volume peaked at 5 million tons in 1968, roughly equal to the amount exported through the port. But the Baltimore Gas & Electric Company began converting its power plants from coal to low-sulfur oil, and abandoned its regional energy base in coal. Coal was cut back to less than 2 million tons. In 1974 consumption of oil peaked at 16 million barrels, the equivalent of sixteen trips by one of the oilbergs under construction at the time. Oil was providing three-fifths of the region's electric power, and most of it came from Venezuela, eighteen hundred miles by sea. It was refined at Curaçao or in Delaware Bay. Refining in Baltimore ceased. Meanwhile, the Appalachian coal was sent ten thousand miles by sea, to make steel in Japan. As conversion was completed and the coal-handling equipment was scrapped, the price of oil tripled (1973), and nuclear power was substituted to produce three-fifths of the region's power.

In the same manner, natural gas was supplied from Columbia Gas System over the Big Inch pipeline from Texas, and in 1978 Columbia was building a new terminal at Cove Point to receive liquefied natural gas (300 million cubic feet per day) from Algeria, forty-six hundred miles away. Like the delivery of electric power, the supply of gas to Baltimore was merely a small excrescence on a larger wholesale system. The Columbia System in turn was a minor participant in an investment pool with other large companies, to bring Arctic gas from Prudhoe Bay and the Beaufort Sea, to pump gas from 370 feet deep in the Gulf of Mexico, to explore offshore Labrador, and finally in a new venture with Exxon to make gas from coal at the mine mouth in West Virginia.

The hum of high tension lines, the snore of the power plant stacks at Wagner Point, and the rush of warm water returning to the bay were signs of a financial circulation. The Baltimore Gas and Electric Company was investing $25 million to $30 million a year from World War II through 1965, then moved up to a level of $250 million a year in the '70s, about tenfold.[11] By 1974 the company was hungry for capital, paying interest rates of 10 percent, and novel ways had to be found to finance power development. In preparing to operate the Calvert Cliffs nuclear plant, for example, the company had bought some nuclear fuel, but then to raise capital, it resold its nuclear fuel and arranged to lease it, paying over some years as the fuel was consumed. Likewise, federal income tax rules permitted deferrals on the massive investments at Calvert Cliffs, to be repaid over the future "life" of the property. In other words, the energy push of the 1970s followed the rule by which the B&O pushed over the mountains in the 1830s:

"This generation can afford to pay interest; let the next generation pay the principal."

Since the energy was supplied from a worldwide resource base, and from a national or transnational managerial and financial base, naturally the scale of public regulation was boosted to federal and diplomatic levels. The Atomic Energy Commission regulated design and fuels for nuclear plants. The regulator of natural gas pricing was the Federal Power Commission. The Environmental Protection Agency affected plant location, design, and the choice of technical alternatives. Decisive elements of tax structure were federal: the corporate income tax, depletion allowances, depreciation rates, investment deferral, and foreign tax credits. Back in 1906 Alexander Brown had consolidated gas and electricity as the last productive monopoly of Baltimore investors, to be kept in check by state incorporation laws, municipal franchise, and a state power commission. Now the power company had outgrown Baltimore as surely as the B&O Railroad before it, and the arena of control had outgrown the city-state.[12] Local management and local government expressed the same sense of powerlessness as local consumers in response to remote events such as high diplomacy in the Near East and the Byzantine politics of the oil companies. Extremes of natural hazard, as in former times, coupled with human error and managerial risk (as in gas storage and reservoir levels) found the population vulnerable: in a cold winter schools were closed to save gas; coal cars, sprayed for dust control, froze solid and piled up in the yards. In a hot summer, electrical "brown out" threatened to stall elevators and immobilize sweltering office workers. Power failures in New York demonstrated the threat of total blackout.

Massive changes occurred in the "consumption" of energy, as well as its "production." Increases in the overall energy metabolism of the Baltimore region were matched by increased energy metabolism of each individual household: a threefold increase in its use of gas and a sevenfold increase in its use of electric power. Population growth did not begin to explain the thirst for energy. The number of households rose faster: as more grandparents, more youths, more students, and more divorced people established separate households they installed more water heaters and stoves. More important to this energy revolution was a geographical transformation of the city: the suburban life style. As people spilled into new single-family homes in the suburban counties, the population of cars tripled. In 1964, a boom year in housing, the gas and electric industry launched a program to coordinate the marketing of appliances through the design of dwellings. Manufacturers, sales outlets, and utilities intensified their promotion, and developers featured appliances in their advertising. More households began purchasing color televisions, dehumidifiers, air conditioners, dryers, and frost-free refrigerators. By 1974 the strong sell was the "all-electric home," as at Red Fox Farms in Baltimore County: central electric heating and air conditioning, the built-in dishwasher, the electric range, water heater, and garbage disposal. Newly built homes were twice as likely to have these appliances as homes built twenty years ago.

The accumulation of little lumps of capital in households was geared to the accumulation of great lumps of capital in power plants and supertankers. As the household enterprise substituted labor-saving appliances, domestic servants disappeared from the labor force and more women went to work to buy the appliances, consolidate the debts, or contribute to the mortgage. Households went deeper into debt. Consumer credit expanded to match the expansion of credit for power generation. In the all-electric home, appliances were covered into the home mortgage itself, and young families undertook heavier burdens of mortgage debt. The new thirty-year debentures of the gas and electric company were paralleled by the extension of home mortgages from the traditional fifteen years to thirty.

The strategy of building energy consumption into the landscape and the mortgage implied a geographic pattern. Baltimore County, with a third of the region's population, uses two-thirds of the electric power. In the new structure of life-style differences, the important boundary was between the city and the gas-guzzling all-electric counties. Air conditioning in the all-electric counties and the central office spaces governs the peak loads and design capacities of the power system.

The productivity achieved in such a system seemed remarkable. From the outbreak of World War I until 1973 natural gas prices were held constant. Electric rates fell by one-fourth, and the number of people employed by the Baltimore Gas and Electric Company did not change (about eight thousand). All this occurred in a period when wages rose fourfold, more than enough to cope with a tripling of consumer prices. This kind of growth also characterized the telephone company and the city's world-scale steel, copper, and chemical industries. But paradoxically, the growth added up to stubborn unemployment and equally stubborn inflation, with especially strong pressures toward rising prices for land and rising interest rates in the 1970s and a race to develop yet more distant and more capital-hungry resource frontiers.

The frenzied metabolism also implied immense energy losses in the long hauls of fuels and in local heat wasted to generate 500,000 volts for long-distance transport and then step the power back down to the users' 120-volt level. The big power plants and steel furnaces used water for cooling and radiated heat to the atmosphere, affecting the temperatures experienced in various parts of the city.

The boost in the levels of energy circulated through Baltimore thus produced a boost in the circulation of money. The effects of waste heat and overloads were concentrated in some parts of Baltimore, and the cooling effects and savings of human energy were concentrated in others. But the influences on price and supply and the management and investment decisions came from outside Baltimore. The step-up in the circulation of money was most apparent in the growth of the financial system. While employment remained constant in the gas and electric company itself and at the steel plant, the fastest-growing sectors of the metropolitan economy were the "FIRE"—finance, insurance, and real estate, which indeed grew like wildfire. The deepening of capital could be seen on the night skyline in the thrusting up of a tight cluster of thirty-story buildings on the original sixty-acre site of Baltimore: the Arlington Federal, a Hilton hotel, One Charles Center, the Blaustein Building a shade taller, the pentagonal World Trade Center, and the forty-story U.S. Fidelity and Guarantee Company.[13]

Like all the transport revolutions that changed Baltimore's situation in the world economy, this one also required changes in the internal form of the city. When the shortages of rubber and steel ceased, households bought automobiles in startling numbers. The mass transit system disintegrated. Streetcar ridership plummeted after VJ-day. The Baltimore Transit Company collapsed financially, and was bought out by a Chicago group, indirectly connected with General Motors, who converted the transit system to diesel buses and sold out to the city.[14] The ferries were eliminated. Trains and electric commuter lines sold off their rights of way. Pennsylvania Station became a half-deserted hulk, smelling vaguely of diesel fuel, marble urinals, and the cigar smoke of vestigial ticket agents. Mount Royal Station auctioned its high-backed rocking chairs and was converted into an art school. Camden Station virtually closed when passenger service was taken over by Amtrak and it was no longer possible to go west by train.

In the '50s the capacity of the street system was stretched by ingenious management to accommodate the cars. The "elastic streets" of the '20s were stretched by eliminating the green medians. Henry Barnes created pairs of one-way streets, automated the traffic signals, and introduced a pedestrian crossing interval known as the "Barnes dance." But management was not enough. The mass switch to the automobile required massive investment in new roadbed and the allocation of new spaces. The entire urban landscape had to be readapted. The great public works of the generation were highways and bridges. In style they ran to massive, angular, long, and low slung. Highway investments created a new "hard" landscape. The concrete poured annually in Maryland rose fivefold. It averaged 3 million cubic yards, enough to fill the inner harbor every year, according to Buckler's century-old scheme. Over the whole generation it amounted to 130 million cubic yards, more than equal to all the muck to be dredged to deepen the channel from Baltimore to the Virginia Capes.[15] For the parallel Bay Bridge, concrete was poured continuously for six days and five nights, as a fleet of tank trucks shuttled cement from Martinsburg. Continuous casting allowed the core of the U.S. Fidelity and Guarantee Building to rise one foot per hour. The new suburban landscape, whether seen from the air or from the expressways themselves, is a skein of ribbons and bows of bright concrete and green. Standard banked curves, vetch-covered slopes, and wide-angle vision replaced the meanders in schist or limestone, the piedmont roller coaster, and the gentler cuts and curves in the red clay, sand, and gravel of tidewater. All modes of transport were integrated and connected by highly specialized limited access routes. The higher speeds and intensities of traffic reflected an acceleration in the circulation of goods, people, money, and information. The human connecting rod in this system was the driver of the tractor-trailer who hauled his

The Pinball Game

piggyback container from ship to railyard on orders from a computer terminal or radio service, and kept abreast of accidents or speed traps on his Citizen's Band radio.

The plans for such a system and the direction of landscape change were already clear by 1937, thanks to bottlenecks recognized in the '20s and the engineering zeal of the depression. The trend toward wider ribbons of concrete, more permanent engineering works, and higher investments per mile was carried out in several bursts of energy. The first surge, prewar, was to construct three-lane highways and bridges to connect all the awkward appendages of Maryland, put stop signs on rural roads and traffic lights in the city, and build high-capacity roads to eliminate "stop and go" driving on the great corridors. Ritchie Highway was built to Annapolis and a dual highway to Frederick.

In the '50s the entire secondary road system was rebuilt to reduce curves and grades. At the same time, the state embarked on a set of major improvements to handle traffic through Maryland: the four-lane Harbor Tunnel, the Bay Bridge on two hundred-foot piles, and the Baltimore-Washington Parkway, which had grade separations, 3.5 percent grades, three-degree curves, and cost $1 million a mile.

A third generation of projects was the interstate highway system.[16] A six-lane Baltimore beltway opened in 1962, thirty-three miles around, with one exit and two bridges per mile. Radial roads followed. The road-making strategy resembled the public improvement strategies of earlier generations, as highway engineers followed the 1834 advice of John Pendleton Kennedy: "Baltimore must imitate the spider and spread out her lines in all directions." They rediscovered and redeveloped the basic lineaments of the Maryland landscape. New radial toll routes replaced the old post roads and mill roads. Robert Mills's canal plan of 1820 sought to connect Baltimore with the Susquehanna and Potomac water-level routes across the Appalachians. Now Interstate 83 was built from the Susquehanna valley at Harrisburg down the Jones Falls toward the inner harbor, and branches of Interstate 70 came from the Ohio River and the Potomac valley through Frederick into the Gwynns Falls valley. The interstate from Washington entered on stilts through the Spring Garden of the Patapsco. The vocation of the stream valleys had changed from gristmills to cotton mills to water supply to a green network and then to a highway network. On tidewater, limited access roads were braided down the necks to connect with new harbor crossings.

The modern road builders resembled the railroad-building generation in their financial strategy. They assumed that the transport system would pay for itself—tomorrow—and they depended upon the credit of the state. Families and firms passed on from generation to generation their roles as surveyors, engineers, bankers, and brokers. In 1828 Alexander Brown had arranged for the city to borrow money to purchase stock in the B&O Railroad. His successor in the firm's fourth generation, B. H. Griswold, Jr., arranged state revenue bonds for the new toll bridges of the 1940s. His successor, Charles Garland, in the firm's fifth generation, handled state loans for the Harbor Tunnel, the Bay Bridge, the outer harbor crossing, and a second Bay Bridge parallel.

As the railroad makers had found in the 1830s, the great difficulty lay in

By 1972 a large regional shopping center was under construction at the interchange of I–70 and I–695, near the Social Security Administration headquarters.

threading a way through the developed central city and connecting with the "streets of bustle." From 1942 to 1972 engineers repeatedly proposed crosstown routes, while neighborhoods passed the ball back and forth from year to year to resist demolition, isolation, expropriation, or environmental nuisance. While the beltway and radials, built first and located rather easily, cost $2 million a mile, connecting links within the city limits cost $50 million a mile. At that price, they were distinctly unpopular with city voters, so that the bonds were issued on the credit of the state, and 90 percent of the money came from federal highway trust funds. Baltimore citizens, as in 1784 and 1804, contended fiercely, and complained that their "perverse stars" still submitted them to the whims of an unresponsive legislature.[17]

Like the railroads before them, the expressways provided the prime basis for land speculation—a struggle to capture prize sites as springboards to private wealth. Whose property would be irrigated by this great watering pot? A sketch map of the expressway system shows where land values ripened, where real estate activity was most intense, and where geopolitical strategies were directed. Roadbuilding gave value to the suburban county ring, then to the great corridors, and above all to the nodal properties where they crossed. Baltimoreans, never averse to mixing their metaphors, began to sense an encirclement, to see the city as the "hole in the doughnut," and to speak of the "noose" around their necks. Suburban housing developments of six hundred to one thousand units moved outward by rings in the '50s between the city line and the beltway, in the '60s astride the beltway, and in the '70s into the more distant counties, onto one-acre and half-acre lots—about the size of the original lots of little Baltimore Town. Apartment and townhouse developments, packaged by the thousand dwellings, followed the new radials that crossed the beltway. Industrial parks were strung along the Harrisburg expressway, the Baltimore-Washington corridor, Pulaski Highway, and the Kennedy expressway. Industry, once confined to waterfront locations, dispersed somewhat, and eighteen thousand acres were rezoned for industry in Baltimore County. A land use pattern of alternating wedges emerged.

At the crossings of radial highway and beltway where land values rose most, developers competed fiercely and investments were made in shopping centers, office complexes, and mixed-use developments. Here the spotlights played on the circus acts of county zoning politics. Baltimore County remained an astonishing throwback to that litigious, property-conscious society of the eighteenth century. Even in the process of transforming its landscape, a confusion three centuries old persisted between the public weal and private wealth. Baltimoreans enjoyed a court case as in old times, and the hothouse ripening of land values through public investments resulted in the mid-1970s in the indictment or imprisonment of the chief executives of the state and several suburban counties. When Spiro Agnew resigned from the vice-presidency and pleaded no contest in such a case, he argued from history: "This is the way business has always been done in Maryland."[18]

In the 1940s Route 1 between Baltimore and Washington was lined with "one-armed bandits" like Silver Sally, the slot machine that blinked and beeped and gobbled quarters, and occasionally spat them out. Now the expressways with their strings of peach-colored sodium vapor and bluish mercury vapor lights, at a hundred thousand watts per mile, and their streams of white head lights and red tail lights, insured a redistribution of dollars, and turned the city itself into a giant pinball game.

Pink, Blue, and White Collars

The work force, as in earlier generations, had to adjust to the alternation of war and peace and revolutions in transport and technology. Between 1940 and 1970 the Baltimore labor force doubled. The number of paid workers grew faster than the population as a whole, and they were able to support larger proportions of babies, youths in school, and retired people. This was accomplished by substituting new sources of power for manpower, and by reallocating womanpower. The share of women rose from 30 to 40 percent of the paid labor force. The change was swiftest in the 1960s, when the number of working women grew 40 percent, of working men only 13 percent. Short-run stresses of the roller-coaster economy were absorbed by hiring or firing women workers, as in defense plants or government contract work. More women in the labor force meant more day-to-day flexibility: a large share worked evenings, Saturdays, or the Christmas rush, or filled in for other people's vacations. High turnover in jobs seemed to satisfy the needs of family changes and household investment, as well as changes in production.

The shrinkage of some job sectors and the growth of others was absorbed primarily by reassigning young black women. As power machinery raised productivity in factories and on construction sites, there were no new "blue-collar" jobs. The number of craft workers doubled, proportionate to the whole labor force, but operatives increased less, and there was zero growth of laborers. Likewise, as power machinery entered households, the number of servants dropped by half. Laundresses were made obsolete by the automatic home washing machine. Instead, three types of employment grew. "Pink-collar" workers tripled —to clean offices and hotel rooms, serve lunches, or mind other women's children. Black women filled these jobs. The clerical force tripled. This sector, virtually closed to blacks in 1940, now offered work to twenty thousand young black women, as large as the entire domestic service sector before the war. The numbers of professionals and technicians (chiefly nurses and teachers) grew fivefold, providing the springboard for the rapid growth of a black middle class. Professional and technical jobs for blacks rose eightfold, from two thousand to sixteen thousand.

As in the past, some changes were cushioned by immigration. Foreign immigration was small: survivors of the holocaust in the 1940s, Hungarians in 1956, Cubans in 1962, Indian, Filipino, and Chinese doctors and engineers in the late '60s, Russian Jews in the 1970s. Highly skilled workers, managers, and professionals moved from the rest of the United States into the jobs created by NASA and Westinghouse. Migrants from distant regions leapfrogged over local migrants in social space: they settled in the suburban counties, southerners more often in Anne Arundel County, northerners more often in Baltimore County. Most important in numbers was the flow of rural Americans into Baltimore. Blacks moved in as machines displaced them from sharecropper farms in North Carolina and Virginia. They were joined by four thousand Lumbee Indians from Robeson County, North Carolina,[19] and by whites from small towns and from the coal-mine regions of western Maryland and West Virginia. Like the German and Irish immigrants of the 1830s and 1850s, the newcomers, white, black, and Indian, lived side by side or back to back in East Fayette Street, Pratt Street, and South Baltimore, sharing the lead poisoning, the tuberculosis, and the threat of the bulldozer. The several ethnic groups who competed for the more crowded housing spaces were, as always, competing in the cramped sectors of the economy. Pressures for change produced social tensions among those in closest competition.

When World War II began, only one Baltimore factory worker in a dozen was black, and nearly all the black factory workers were employed in the hot spots at Bethlehem Steel. Wartime demand for labor opened more factory jobs to them. "Colored Defense Schools" held training classes in aircraft riveting, industrial sewing, and small part assembly. Some ironies were evident to the black community, but had escaped notice in the white. On 23 May 1943, as the Allied TRIDENT conference in Washington fixed the strategy of global war, the shipyard at Fairfield launched one more Liberty ship. A black opera singer

The juxtaposition of street "Arabs" with modern streets and automobiles has not changed the role of such hucksters in supplying services such as selling fresh fruits and vegetables and scavenging.

christened it the *Frederick Douglass*, and they celebrated with a lunch at a Negro hotel, while black laborers scraped the grease off the ways to ready them for the next launching.[20] The newspapers, in reporting the day's events, made no reference to Douglass's experience as a caulker in Baltimore, where in 1836 he had been stoned by white carpenter's apprentices. Nor did they mention that the ship was built in part at the Key Highway yard, the site of William Skinner's shipyard: in 1858, white gangs had stoned Skinner's men in a renewed attempt to displace black caulkers. Two months after the *Frederick Douglass* was launched, the shipyards were shut down by a strike that resembled the events of 1836 and 1858. Bethlehem Steel had agreed to train 15 blacks as riveters, and 125 white riveters walked out in protest. The company removed the black trainees from the class, and 600 black employees walked out. When Bethlehem reinstated the trainees, 7,000 white employees walked out. After this escalation and several days' shutdown, while the Air Force bombed Rumanian oil fields and the Marines were landing in the Solomons, the company and the white-controlled union agreed on a compromise. They agreed to principles of seniority and no racial discrimination. Openings would be filled by length of service in the department. Riveters would be chosen from among the "holders on" of longer service, holders on from among the heaters, heaters from passers. "No skilled men from the outside will be hired as long as there are qualified men in the department."[21] Thus, change could be contained, and the inertia of the past could be preserved. At industries as large and complex as Bethlehem Steel, this strategy resulted thirty years later in a structure of hundreds of watertight compartments of personnel. Seniority rules maintained the segregated structure of promotions, work environments, lines of authority, and pay scales. The caste structure of the factories, which seemed fluid during the war, hardened like concrete.

In the autumn a similar episode occurred at Western Electric. There had been no black employees at Point Breeze, but now seventeen hundred were hired among the seven thousand. The company interpreted presidential fair employment orders as requiring the elimination of all separate accommodations, and took the signs off the toilets. Twenty-two white women walked off the job, claiming they feared venereal disease. The Point Breeze Employees Association, to which black workers also paid dues, backed the Jim Crow demand. It argued that the city's plumbing code required separate facilities, that there had been hundreds of "incidents," and a "race riot" threatened. The War Labor Board disagreed, and the white workers struck. Five hundred black workers crossed the picket lines to work, in the presence of five hundred police. The week before Christmas the army seized the plant.[22] In the aftermath, more sanitary facilities were installed, the "company union" was displaced by nationally affiliated labor unions, and seniority rules were tightened.[23]

At the end of the war, the black community had to absorb the readjustment to a peacetime economy where services were the growth sectors. The Enoch Pratt Library rejected, one after another, two hundred black applicants for librarian training school. Batteries of lawyers solemnly contended whether it was a public or a private institution. The Public Service Commission, after long deliberation, agreed to license a black cab company, since white drivers were passing up blacks who hailed them. In 1952 the telephone company agreed to hire a few switchboard operators, the streetcar company some motormen, the gas company some meter readers, and the fire department its first black trainees. Within a generation all of these became sectors of opportunity for blacks, but every step was hard won.[24]

In the 1960s the State Employment Service and the newspapers were forced to drop the racial tags for job openings. Political organization at the national level created counterpressures for "fair employment." Now half the city's population, blacks organized politically to demand their share of jobs in the police force, the courthouse, and city hall, and their share of the jobs generated by city demolition, construction, and purchases. On balance, the changes in occupational roles raised the purchasing power of the black community, and raised the aspirations and visibility of younger black workers and black women. Afro hairdos were a symbol. Older people, whites, and men felt they were "invaded" while younger workers, blacks, and women sensed resistance and hostility to their presence. Consequently, labor force adjustments tended to take the form of conflicts between races, sexes, and age groups.

The arena for strike and boycott changed. The labor movement, as in earlier generations, grew strong when there was plenty of work. "Real" unions replaced company unions in wartime. National steel strikes and dock strikes followed the national business cycle. But union strength ebbed when work was scarce. Consistent with this pattern, strikes occurred in the growth sectors of the economy, that is, the service sectors, rather than the shrinking manufacturing sectors. Hospital workers unionized in the 1970s. School teachers, police, and musicians held long drawn-out strikes. In these sectors women workers and black workers began to organize. The civil rights movement provided new models for labor and a sense of militancy, just as the labor movement had earlier provided models for civil rights groups. The city's black fire fighters formed the Vulcan Association, a union within the union. As black women replaced retiring Jewish workers in what was left of the city's garment industry, the Amalgamated responded to their demands for day care centers. But competition between black and white labor reduced the credibility of the unions with blacks, and weakened union bargaining power. For example, the construction industry in Baltimore was only half-unionized.

Worst off were the unemployed. In the late 1960s, ten thousand families in Baltimore were receiving surplus cornmeal and dry milk, or using federal food stamps to stretch their food budgets, which took half their income. Unemployment was continually nipping at the heels of the work force. The "normal" turnover of technical advance sifted workers into heaps. At each lurch in the economy, more dropped into permanent unemployment. Unemployment stalked those made obsolete in their fifties. It stalked those disabled by hazardous work. It stalked women who had dropped out of the labor force to raise children. It stalked children who failed in school, truants the schools chose to forget, and products of obsolete "vocational" programs. And it stalked both the youths who had not yet done their military service and those who returned from it.

In phases of economic expansion, unemployment was concentrated in the inner city, but in economic downswing the effects were felt more widely. In the "energy crisis" and disturbances of world trade and money supply beginning in 1973, the whole world tightened its belt. As in all previous world crises, shrinking markets for copper, grain, steel, and coffee were felt in the port of Baltimore. But much more devastating effects were experienced in other parts of the world. Famine this time around was most severe not in Baltimore, but in the African savannas and the caatinga of northeastern Brazil. Cholera was confined to India, Africa, and Italy, and yellow fever to Colombia. Wage cuts ground down copper miners in Chile, as they had the Baltimore railroad workers in 1877. The hours lengthened among garment workers in Hong Kong and Singapore, as they had in Baltimore in 1893. Migrant workers were shipped out of Switzerland, France, and Belgium, back to Turkey, Algeria, and Greece. Baltimore was somewhat insulated, but eventually even its "world-scale" plants had to lay off workers. At New Year's Day 1975 Black and Decker shut down. Thirty-seven hundred were laid off, from the $140,000-a-year president to the newest assembly worker at $7,000. Western Electric laid off eleven hundred, about one worker in eight. Some of the city's oldest large plants were shut down for good: Mount Vernon Mills, the Mutual Chemical bichromate plant, and the copper refineries of Revere and American Smelting & Refining Company. Kennecott shut down its copper refining operation and laid off half the work force for six weeks. Bethlehem Steel cut its white-collar staff by early retirements, stopped overtime work, then laid off workers with least seniority. In 1975 and 1977, Sparrows Point was working at only two-thirds capacity and the pinch was felt throughout Baltimore. In general, women, youths, and blacks experienced higher unemployment rates: last hired, first fired. The gains of the fat years were eroded in the lean years.

Separate and Unequal

Over the generation, the growth sectors in the job market demanded longer schooling, and people with less education were confined to shrinking sectors. People of North Baltimore and Northwest Baltimore sent their children

Well-maintained rowhouses
such as these in the 2500 block
of East Baltimore Street serve
to define the character of
neighborhoods.

to graduate and professional schools. The salesman, manufacturer, and small businessman spoke of "my son, the doctor," "my daughter, the social worker," and "my son, the programmer." These children were members of high-mobility professions, and a large share left Baltimore. In East Baltimore and South Baltimore, skilled craftsmen, unionized operatives, and laborers clung tight to seniority rules, union rules, and nepotism to provide niches for their sons in the slow-growth sectors of factory or waterfront. Newcomers to the city struggled for unskilled jobs in the shrinking sectors, but saw that schooling might allow their children to get a toe hold in the growth sectors. In the schools, therefore, were determined the future productivity and adaptability of the labor force, and Baltimore's ability to compete in the world economy. The futures of individuals, families, social groups, and neighborhoods depended upon their schools. The future of the black community and the white, together, was forged in the schoolhouses.

From deep roots in Baltimore, black leaders drew a sure sense of strategy. Schooling was the pathway to freedom and economic independence, the churches were the rallying points, and the courts were the battle ground. It was a strategy recognized in the 1790s, built on by Reverend William Livingstone of St. James Episcopal, by Elisha Tyson and Joseph Townsend and the pastors of Sharp Street church. The Oblate Sisters built on it in the 1830s. Nine-year-old Frederick Douglass and his master, Captain Auld, both knew it: "If you teach that nigger how to read, there will be no keeping him." The Civil War was followed by a round of legal battles for the custody of Maryland children, and from that struggle were founded the Baltimore colored schools. Now a new round of battles had to be waged on behalf of "infant appellants."[25]

In the civil rights movement, just as earlier in the struggle of the Jewish garment workers, Baltimore was a strategic place. It was a great frontier city, an outpost of the North in the South. Northern in the size and wealth of its educational system and in the values and hopes placed in public education since the 1840s, Baltimore was critical in the civil rights strategy of the 1930s as a beachhead in the legal segregation of the South. After a lull, Baltimore again became a strategic place in the late phase of the 1960s, as a beachhead against the de facto segregation typical of metropoles of the North. Baltimore's nearness to Washington also made it strategic. Along Route 1 traveled the African diplomats between the U.N. headquarters in New York and the nation's capital. They stopped to eat in Maryland's Jim Crow diners. Baltimore's middle-class blacks kept close social ties with Washington's, and each breakthrough in federal jobs —from the post office to the army to Health, Education, and Welfare—was an opportunity seized in Baltimore. The rate at which the Mitchells, the Murphys, and the Marshalls shuttled between Baltimore and Washington was a barometer of civil rights storms over the generation. Thurgood Marshall, raised in West Baltimore, went to Sunday school at St. James. When he was excluded from the University of Maryland law school in Baltimore because of his race, he commuted to Howard University in Washington. Back in Baltimore in the '30s, he filed strategic lawsuits. In the 1950s, while Baltimore marked time, he helped forge the array of "separate is unequal" cases from Topeka and Wilmington, Virginia and North Carolina. When he obtained the Supreme Court order to integrate the schools of Washington, D.C., he brought that revolution back to Baltimore. When Baltimore again became a strategic place in the '60s, Thurgood Marshall was himself a justice of the Supreme Court.

Lawyers for the National Association for the Advancement of Colored People had laid out in 1931 a long-term nationwide strategy for the legal battle for integration. They would press first for the admission of blacks to the graduate and professional schools. At that level it would be easiest to prove the inequalities evident in the education offered to black and whites. The absurdity of the legal fiction "separate but equal" would be made clear. Any attempt to duplicate equal facilities at that level would raise the costs of a segregation policy. Because the number of individuals involved was small, public reaction would likely be limited, and the operation would affect only the most highly educated and cosmopolitan populations. Then the pressure would work back to the undergraduate colleges, the high schools, and the grade schools. In such a program, Baltimore was a natural starting point. The University of Maryland's graduate schools in Baltimore—law, medicine, dentistry, and pharmacy—were closed to blacks. In 1935, too late for Thurgood Marshall and for Lillie Jackson's daughter, Juanita, Judge O'Dunne of the Baltimore City Court ordered Donald Murray admitted to the law school. The state proceeded to expand its Negro higher education, to develop a college at Bowie and extend public funding to Morgan College. Marshall was the NAACP's roving adviser to the counties of Maryland where teachers were demanding equal salaries. In 1939 Anne Arundel County was ordered to comply, and the governor and state board of education accepted the principle of equal pay for teachers in the white and colored schools.

Lillie Jackson's five-member NAACP chapter grew to two thousand by the end of the war. Her rasping voice kept on. The black community of Baltimore marched and preached and whined and signified. "God opened my mouth," said

Mrs. Jackson, "and no man can shut it."[26] For fifteen years, however, the situation deteriorated in the colored schools of Baltimore. Between 1943 and 1953 the number of children increased 50 percent. Buildings were dangerously over-crowded. Thousands of children went to school "on part time." Of fifty-eight city schools recommended for demolition by the Strayer Commission in 1921, thirty-five were still in use—as colored schools. Century-old schools with wooden fire stairs, basement toilets, and little paved yards were being used by "opportunity classes" and "special curriculum." More and more of the black children were sorted, often by bureaucratic whim, into these sinks of educational inertia. They were a lumpen proletariat of children.

On 13 September 1952, a decision was taken by the Baltimore City school board, without court action but after unprecedented silent prayer for guidance, to admit a dozen Negro students to Polytechnic High School. The alternative, discussed "on a high plane," was to create a comparable school for blacks. This was testimony to the wisdom of the NAACP strategy of raising the costs of "separate but equal" schools beyond what taxpayers would consider. In the words of Rob Roy, a Hopkins engineering professor on the board, "Segregation is a luxury."[27] A token integration of education had filtered down from the graduate schools of the University of Maryland, as far as the elite high schools. The school board's recognition that a matching "colored Poly" was an absurd idea, a contradiction in terms, marked the critical shift of NAACP lawyers, jurists, and the Baltimore establishment toward recognizing that segregated education was everywhere inherently unequal. The Poly case also showed the delicate relation between the civil rights struggle and social status. Four remarkable college preparatory schools of Baltimore were providing an elite public education for a small number of white students. The school board decision meant upward mobility for a handful of blacks.

In July 1954 the D.C. school board, the express target of the Supreme Court decision, ordered the assignment of teachers and pupils without regard to race and according to the most efficient use of space and personnel. The Baltimore school board simply ordered "desegregation in compliance with the law." Baltimore was one of several hundred districts in the nation that announced prompt compliance, under united civic leadership. Eighteen hundred black children out of fifty-seven thousand transferred into the white schools—2 percent among the eighty-seven thousand white children. The city congratulated itself for several years afterward on the lack of violence. But there was resistance and it was strong and subtle. The school board rejected "deliberate race mixing" and continued to open schools with all-Negro teaching staffs. Nothing was done to compensate for the legacy of ninety years of unequal investment in school buildings, or for fifteen years of inertia in the face of growth.

The consequences of those "economies" of the 1940s and early 1950s produced predictable responses to desegregation. The school board tolerated "freedom of choice" plans: "No child shall be required to attend any particular school." It left to principals the authority to permit or refuse transfers between schools. It located new high schools in the outer fringes of the city. Families who could afford it moved in response. From 1954 to 1970, white children withdrew from the city schools at the rate of ten thousand a year to enter schools in the suburban counties. "The bulk of the educational investment in Baltimore has traditionally been made in the white middle-class child." They were the children who moved out. By 1958, half the children in the city schools were black; in 1978, two-thirds. The resegregation of the region by race, age, and income was accelerated. The city council slashed school board budgets. Teachers' salaries fell relative to the counties. A third of the teachers in the city schools were "provisional." These responses produced the de facto segregation characteristic of northern cities.

As this situation was grasped in the mid-1960s, Baltimore again became a strategic place, a target city. In 1962 the Baltimore Activists documented the grievances of de facto segregation, and in 1967 the National Educational Association picked Baltimore as a symbol of the problems facing large cities: underpaid teachers, undermaintained buildings, understaffed schools, an underfinanced system facing a shrinking property tax base and children with urgent needs. The NEA found the Baltimore school system "not uniformly bad."[28] Good things were happening: some children attended superior facilities, some received foreign language instruction and imaginative science and physical education programs. Some had access to fine libraries, cafeterias, gymnasiums, pools, and home economics and science laboratories. Some were getting advanced college preparatory programs or technical training. "On the other hand, some children in Baltimore City are not receiving these things. These are the majority of children." On the whole, they were poorer children, and they were the black children. "The poor in Baltimore are overwhelmingly Negro, and the affluent in Baltimore are overwhelmingly white." Both the advantaged and the disadvantaged were responding to the differential of educational privilege. Ten thousand children were dropping out of high school each year, risking unemployment and low pay. The children who stayed in the city, the NEA observed, "become its assets or liabilities—whichever the community has chosen."[29]

New leadership appeared. Constitutional issues and courtroom theater gave way to tactics of financial and political power and displays of naked force. The issue of equality was pushed back from the graduate school, the high school, and the elementary school to kindergarten, the Head Start nursery school, the day care center, and nutrition for newborn infants. A school building program was initiated. The black community demanded community control, parent participation, and decentralization of decision. The new Dunbar High School became a symbol of these desires. But it became evident, year by year, that with all the juggling, the perennial recarving of districts, and the reshuffling of children into buildings, the readjustment of building sites and building designs would not greatly alter the new segregation, which was grafted on a segregated housing market and a county boundary. When Mr. Justice Marshall issued his dissent in a Supreme Court case in 1974, he might have been talking about his home town: "In the short run, it may seem to be the easier course to allow our great metropolitan areas to be divided up each into two cities—one white, the other black—but it is a course, I predict, our people will ultimately regret."[30]

The block of West Lexington Street developed by Lewis Pascault in the 1820s showed signs of decline in the 1930s but was still commercially active.

"Two cities—one white, the other black." The reorganization of metropolitan space was much more complicated. In some ways it resembled the transformations of past generations. But Marshall expressed a stark political reality, an unprecedented polarization of the city-state.

Growth in one part of the city was associated with stagnation or disinvestment in another. Baltimore had experienced eleven successive suburban fringes and eleven reconstructions of its downtown and harbor. In between these visible frontiers of physical change were rings of social change, rolling out like ripples in the pond—turnover of landowners, of home owners, of tenants. Each population boom that ran ahead of construction, as in World War II and the late '60s, transformed whole neighborhoods from nine-room row houses to triple deckers of misfit three-room apartments. In other periods, such as the early '50s and early '60s, building and home finance surged on the suburban frontier and some neighborhoods raised their home ownership rate, while other inner-city neighborhoods experienced a thinning of population, higher vacancies, falling property values, and tighter mortgage money. Thus, changes took place on the several frontiers, one in relation to another. The tidal wave of white population that rolled over the suburbs in the '50s was matched in tempo by a tide of black migrants arriving in the center, and an intermediate line of breakers where black families replaced white families.[31]

There were two new features of the spatial reorganization of the city in this generation. The first was the jurisdictional rivalry between the city and the surrounding counties. A new ring of growth had always meant redistribution of investment. The frontier between investment and disinvestment had once been the "line of direct taxation," extended in 1817 and 1831. The annexations of 1888 and 1918 provided such a frontier between the old city and its new annex. But capital flows had each time occurred inside the expanded city, allowing the surrounding counties to remain largely rural and undisturbed. Now, for the first time, the line between city and county divided the zones of investment and disinvestment.

The other major feature was resegregation by race, income, and age, at an unprecedented metropolitan scale. There had always been strong contrasts at the

Two Cities

scale of the block or the neighborhood, between the point and the town, between uptown and downtown. Racial segregation had always existed in Baltimore in a fine-grained pattern enforced by legal power, greenback power, and violence. The nineteenth-century street-and-alley segregation gave way about 1900 to sizeable hemmed-in ghettos in East Baltimore, West Baltimore, and South Baltimore. Now, as the Jim Crow laws were eroding, a Jim Crow space was coalescing, growing larger and more formidable. Other ethnic groups moved outward along traditional wedges, mixing along the fringes, but the black community was locked in. Its space expanded grudgingly, explosively, block by block and year by year.

Age differences were also projected onto spaces. The old and the young, fast-growing groups, were sorted out spatially. The "rising values of childhood" were concentrated in the new family-centered environments of the suburbs, while the elderly stayed on in areas of elderly houses and elderly trees. Poverty, also confined to the center, was again perceived as it had been during the cholera epidemics, as an intractable mass: criminal, contagious, immoral. This was the perception of the modern plagues that victimized the inner city: tuberculosis, venereal disease, heroin overdose, illegitimacy. As the process of resegregation moved forward, the confusion, already present in 1934, became more insistent between poverty, black skin, and the inner city. What the genteel Baltimore of 1822 called "pauperism," what prominent Baltimoreans of 1915 called "the Negro problem," the establishment of the 1960s called "the urban problem."

And so the two new structural features of the city were closely related. Suburban growth and inner city decay fed on each other, as they always had. But because people and capital moved across a political boundary, the process was perceived as a political process, a struggle for power. A rival "noncity" emerged. The suburban frontier became the frontier of investment, youth, and higher energy use, the frontier of land grabbing, and the frontier of social exclusion. Thus, all the old intractable problems of ring-by-ring redevelopment, obsolescence, and fiscal squeeze were redefined and perceived as phenomena of race: white flight or black invasion. The presence of the political boundary meant that race space was perceived as a political space.

Government: The Left and the Right Hand

In the polarization of the metropolis, what would be the role of government? As in earlier generations, one must situate Baltimore in a government of tiers—the metropolis, the state of Maryland, and the nation. The trend of several generations was toward enlarging the sphere of government and shifting the action to higher tiers. One also has to situate new conceptions of planning in the old tug of war between haves and have nots. It was the job of the city government to devise strategies to develop property and pile up wealth. It was also the job of city government to devise strategies to contain poverty and cope with the costs, the dissatisfaction, and the hostilities generated in the process. This was the same tug of war as in the generation of Raymond, Griffith, Tyson, Poppleton, and Smith.

The clearest trend was the expansion of government at all levels—the federal role above all, then state functions, and municipal functions next. This can be seen in the numbers hired or the dollars spent. Spending by governments rose from a fifth of the national product in 1940 to a third in 1976. Throughout the nineteenth century, Baltimore City had spent more locally than either the state or federal governments. But by 1976 federal spending in Maryland reached $6 billion a year, the state budget rose to $2 billion, the city budget to $1 billion. The budget of Baltimore County rose from a trivial amount to half a billion, with a tax base equal to that of the city. From a fiscal point of view, Baltimore was split: the city's tax base and borrowing power were confined. Deprived of initiative and the fiscal room to maneuver, it became dependent on state and federal governments for piggyback taxes and revenue sharing.

As in Poppleton's time, the city prepared land for subdivision and industrial sites, to develop property values. The county government followed the old street-making strategy, with opportunity to borrow on the strength of its rapid growth and youthful population. The county made a much stronger investment in human resources than earlier generations: nearly two-thirds of county employees were in the schools. Investment came from higher tiers of government. The state invested in the port, the airport, and highways. Half of the federal billions spent in Maryland consisted of the salaries and contracts of federal installations such as NASA, Fort Meade, Social Security, and the National Institutes of Health, all at suburban sites.[32] "Impacted" areas also received grants to build schools for children of federal employees. The federal government invested in highways, water and sewers, and home mortgage insurance. The locus of most of this investment was the suburban belt. Channeled by the planning in the counties, such federal investments were massive subsidies to segregation. In Baltimore County, the new high schools and highways, even the very symbols of home rule—courthouse, municipal building, and school administration building—were situated to demolish or hedge in the small, long-established, black communities of Towson and Turner.[33] In 1978 there were only 12 percent black children in the Baltimore County schools.

But another ancient logic of local government also operated. As in Thomas Griffith's time, provision had to be made for the afflicted, and suffering could not be permitted that "might render doubtful the disadvantages of the savage state or the benefits of civilization." Doubters reappeared. Daniel Raymond's old-fashioned phrases on pauperism applied to the "war on poverty" in the 1960s: "The laws of justice, as well as the laws of the land, require the rich either to furnish the poor with labour, or support them without labour."[34] But the geographical division between poverty and wealth meant that the city itself was hamstrung as a dispenser of relief. Redistribution from rich to poor could take place only through higher levels of government. City dwellers were eager to promote the sharing of wealth across the city line. The federal government paid out $1.5 billion a year in "income maintenance": social security and benefits to veterans, the elderly, the disabled, dependent children, the "medically indigent," and the unemployed. Those transfer payments went heavily to the inner city: in some neighborhoods up to a quarter of all households depended on them, in the suburban ring 1 or 2 percent.

The internal order of Baltimore city government gradually took on a dual character, reflecting the tug of war between wealth and poverty. Seven "physical development" agencies concerned themselves with the renewal of street spaces and public works, to add value to the taxable property base, while seven "human resources" agencies concerned themselves with day-by-day spending: putting out fires, carrying heart attack victims to hospital, drying out drunks, and keeping children off the streets. The head of municipal finance was on both teams, between the horns of a dilemma. Physical development was limited to a fixed territory and the taxable base could only be raised 1 or 2 percent a year, yet the need for human resource funding seemed a bottomless pit. The city charter and the state constitution were made of "the same patched-over materials" Niles fumed at in the 1820s, and sober attempts at political reconstruction failed.

The city's urban renewal program also reflected the tension between the two strategies of government. A conception of the relation between physical development and human resources, already explicit in the Emmart report in 1934, reappeared in the MetroCenter/Baltimore report of 1970.[35] To maintain the tax base, the city must embark on massive physical redevelopment of structures and a transport revolution. To retain and attract private investment at the core, it must design a distinctive district of skyscrapers, sanitize and enliven the old waterfront, and still preserve a human-scale streetscape. To protect the core property and allow the polis to survive, a surrounding ring of blight must be razed and the city's "human resources" must be renewed.

The slums were unproductive liabilities, Emmart had argued. He staked out a belt of redevelopment projects—the inner harbor, the vicinity of Camden Station and Calvert Street Station, the vicinity of St. Mary's Seminary and Richmond Market, Belair Market, and Lafayette Market. He proposed to eliminate alley dwellings, to consolidate larger lots in central areas, to separate commercial from residential districts. Like Brown in 1894, Emmart wanted a "correct" block dimension and visualized city blocks as self-supporting residential neighborhoods with their own automobile parking and recreation spaces. A hop, skip, and jump through the city's succession of "target blocks" will provide a view of the strategies for juggling physical and human renewal.

In 1939 the city condemned a house in St. Johns Court, in Oldtown, as unfit for human habitation. The Citizens Planning and Housing Association was organized. Like the local NAACP, it grew in a generation from seven members to two thousand. A new housing code was passed, and fifty thousand houses were found in violation. In 1945, city block number 1 on Sharp Street was chosen for testing a law enforcement strategy against blight. City agencies tried to coordinate their efforts to enforce the tangle of laws—plumbing code, fire laws, housing code, health laws. Police sanitarians fined tenants for littering, and school teachers enlisted their pupils for clean-up. By 1947 the block was again deteriorating, and the lessons drawn from the experience were to take a larger area than a pilot block, something less difficult than a "rock-bottom slum," and to work with people as well as houses.[36]

In the next round, therefore, a twenty-seven-block pilot area was chosen in East Baltimore in 1951.[37] A hearing board and housing court were created, and a central corps of housing inspectors was trained who devoted their energy

Even in the mid-1950s, slum
properties were seen as legal
problems that called for police
action.

to issuing "multiple violation notices." The "battle of the slums" demanded
the coordination of municipal agencies and private social services. A private
Fight Blight fund was created to finance repairs. In some cases, slumlords sold
homes to their tenants to escape responsibility for the violations. Baltimore
formalized its unique style of responsiveness, with praise and rage alternating in
strong doses.

The city's efforts ran consistently ahead of national legislation. Federal
urban renewal assistance increased, often building into federal incentives the
latest "Baltimore Plan." Mencken might have snoozed away the summer
afternoon in the green of the Maryland countryside, and the *Afro-American*'s
society editor escaped the "deep purple humidity" by going to the beach. But
in the inner city, summer was the season for painting old tires white and planting
geraniums in them, for hosing the marble steps, for leaving dead rats on the
landlord's lawn, for sending for the mayor, "the man," or "the man from headquarters." Volunteers—the Brethren, the Jesuits, the Lutherans, VISTA, HOPE,
CORE—discharged their zeal, a weekend, a year, or a lifetime of commitment
to a block here or there. Out of each pilot block emerged half a dozen salt-of-
the-earth residents to add savor to city politics. They organized rat hunts, tore
down board fences, and eliminated twenty thousand outside toilets and the
unvented and explosive oil stove for heating homes. But in 1960 there were still
fifty thousand "defective dwellings."

In 1956 the Baltimore Urban Renewal and Housing Agency (BURHA) was
formed, and chose a pilot block in an area surrounding Harlem Park.[38] Poppleton
could not foresee the days when "block clubs" would rework his basic design.
In each block, alley dwellings were demolished, backyards evened off, and a park
was built in the center of the block, with a basketball court, picnic table, concrete turtles, or spaceship junglegym. Manufacturers devised an all-aluminum
face lifting for a hundred-year-old façade. Window frames were reduced to a
suffocating modern standard. Public estimators worked out renovation budgets
for owners. Rents went up, and the poorest tenants moved. Thirteen years later,
when the last of twenty-seven blocks was completed, the city recognized already
that the official assumption of renewal as forty years' lease on life was an
illusion.

At Pennsylvania Avenue and Biddle Alley the old "lung block" was torn
down to expand the school; the school children and two property owners turned
a vacant lot into a park. Its population had grown old. For forty years the most
investigated block in the city, it was replaced by the 1600 block of Eutaw where

This alley was typical of the small rear yards developed in the 1850s. Most alleys were paved about 1915, but the board fences and outbuildings survived into the 1950s. After the clearance efforts, agencies pointed proudly to the rediscovered rear yards with sunny expanses. In most cases, the success was short lived and people returned to the front steps.

in 1956 several children burned to death. A multiple dwelling ordinance was passed to insure secondary egress. Nevertheless, in 1962 five more children died in another fire in the same block. They could not escape because fire exits were nailed shut.

When the 1800 block of Linden Avenue was scheduled for demolition, it was invaded by a platoon of social workers. They tracked a dozen cases of tuberculosis to an old man who was everybody's babysitter. They inquired into the birth control habits of women from Virginia and North Carolina. They introduced neighbors to each other and measured participation in basketball teams and Sunday schools. But by 1965 the people were all evicted. Some kept moving a block ahead of the bulldozer: some children made ten or eleven moves in an elementary-school career. Most moved a few blocks north into the Experimental Conservation District, set up in 1962. An addition had to be built to the school. Tenants demanded a crackdown on unvented gas heaters and a "rollback" of dwelling units in excess of legal densities. Ten years later the school was overcrowded again, and the pilot block of the experimental district was found more crowded and more rundown than before. New demands for code enforcement resulted in a block of renovated cooperative housing in Callow Avenue.

As reconstruction of Gay Street, Pennsylvania Avenue, and Fremont Avenue proceeded, housing of the 1830s and 1840s was demolished. Stirling Street, originally condemned as worn-out "negro dwellings," received a late reprieve and became an experiment in urban homesteading. The city gave away houses for a dollar to citizens who could undertake a federal mortgage for their rehabilitation. But all the pre–Civil War neighborhoods of Baltimore were at risk. The core of all three turn-of-the-century ghettoes was flattened. The dozens of pilot blocks, remnants of the salty politics and home-grown ingenuity of a generation, surrounded an inlay of public housing projects: the plain dense rows of the 1940s brightened by their wash lines, the cagelike towers of the mid-'50s with yellow and turquoise balconies, midrise housing for the elderly of the 1960s, and the townhouse groupings of the 1970s.

There were several tense moments in this tightrope act. The spatial concentration of poverty had suggested, as it did to the yellow fever and cholera doctors, causes in local environments. Could blight be eradicated by tearing down the neighborhoods of the poor? The rate of demolition rose from six hundred households a year in the '50s to eight hundred in the early '60s. It leaped to twenty-six hundred households a year in the late '60s, as sites were being cleared for expressways, new schools, and public housing projects all at once. The people evicted were mostly poor, often elderly, and nine out of ten were black.[39] They saw urban renewal as "Negro removal" and painted URBAN RENEWAL GO HOME on the hoardings. The demolitions also produced a fiscal crisis, as property was removed from tax rolls and the land lay fallow ten to fifteen years, waiting for investor consensus. The planning process created risk. The numbers of buildings abandoned for taxes reached one thousand a year; the official count of vacant dwellings reached five thousand. A vacant house coordinator was appointed, and read the inventory into a computer. In 1970 the city undertook a program to renovate fifteen hundred vacant homes. The genial vandals of the 1860s reappeared, able to strip a dwelling overnight; they stole the sinks, kitchen cabinets, and copper gutters, or smashed fixtures by sheer destructive whim.

Neither federal transfer payments nor the demolition of twenty-five thousand dwellings nor the construction of fifteen thousand units of public housing could arrest the polarization of the metropolis. Supermarkets, bank branches, and physicians fled the dry milk and tear gas belt and resituated themselves at expressway nodes near the green valleys. Because the costs were redistributed through higher tiers of government, evaluation became ever more difficult. As welfare costs accelerated in the '60s and '70s, and the social services caseload rose sixfold, the rhetoric of idleness and stimulants reappeared as in 1804 or 1822. But redevelopment was no longer planned by a half dozen property owners who walked over the ground and assessed the costs among themselves in relation to their direct benefits. The complexity of taxing and spending at three

Gay Street, a declining commercial strip before the riots of the 1960s, became a showplace of community revival within a decade.

levels of government made it impossible for citizens differently situated in income and jurisdiction to discover the extent of their contributions or their benefits. The average county resident paid twice as much income tax as the city dweller, while the city dweller paid twice as much property tax.[40] Each simply looked around him, trying to read the landscape. New towers of federal and state government rivaled the new towers of private finance. On the horizon were four massive clumps of hospital buildings and four massive clumps of public housing. At Towson the county built a marble courthouse. At Annapolis the state built a "colonial" brick library. For the nation's bicentennial, Baltimore put up scaffolding and refurbished the dome of city hall.

A Money-Making Moses

Despite the feverish rate of change, a system of social relations persisted. Over each building boom the growth process tended to regenerate differentials of wealth, such that a basic structure of inequalities was maintained. Each generation in Baltimore cast up a few millionnaires, larger numbers of upwardly mobile and hopeful people, and large numbers of the poor and vulnerable. In this generation the old wealth became invisible. The older millionnaires retired to Gibson Island and the Eastern Shore; their children preferred to live in New York and California. In the confrontation politics of the 1960s they abdicated the traditional leadership roles of Charles Carroll and Samuel Smith. The school boards, the task forces, and the blue ribbon commissions became arenas of combat for a wide assortment of parents, lawyers, activists, and neighbors. The politicians and engineers came to depend on a new species of professional "flak catcher." New wealth was often "small potatoes," but more visible and more talked about. Two rags-to-riches examples show how the city's transformation continued to generate profits through the manipulation of its social structure and the reconstruction of its spaces.

When Morris Goldseker died in 1976, his assets were over $10 million. The dollar no longer being what it was in Hopkins's or Garrett's day, he was a small-time millionnaire, insignificant next to Alonzo Decker, Robert Merrick, or Henry Knott, but important nevertheless because his strategy characterized a number of entrepreneurs. Of seven thousand black families who became home owners in the 1960s, a third dealt with speculators following the same strategy of neighborhood turnover in a particular ring of the city. Goldseker himself bought seventeen hundred homes in Baltimore in the '60s. On the average he bought a home for $7500 and resold it for $13,000, a markup of $5500.[41] People who managed to buy directly from former owners or to get veteran loans paid $10,000 for homes in the same block. The $3,000 difference was known to black buyers as "the black tax." Had they been organized in the same way, elderly sellers might have referred to the $2500 difference as "the gray tax."

Speculators and buyers were also engaged in long-term financing relationships. Goldseker's practice, for example, was to create a ground rent, worth perhaps $1500. A savings and loan company provided the family with a mortgage for $8500, while Goldseker held a second mortgage of $4500. Under his installment contract, the buyer earned no equity in the house till he had paid off 40 percent of the purchase price. Then the savings and loan company would "refinance" the house, consolidating the mortgage and adding new settlement costs. Paying off such a double mortgage often took thirty years instead of fifteen. The initial "buy like rent" contracts were not even recorded in the courthouse.[42] The buyer's risk under such contracts was so great, his equity so slow to accumulate, and the congeries of creditors so tangled that families tried hard to save rather than borrow, and many black home buyers were people in their fifties. One grandmother burst into tears on discovering that she was dealing with Goldseker.

By that mechanism, whole neighborhoods were simultaneously refinanced and turned over to younger populations—for example, 1,000 homes in Edmondson Village in the early 1960s, 750 in Montebello in the mid-1960s. The new residents had incomes comparable to the former residents, but were paying higher sales prices and higher finance charges, roughly double normal housing costs. Thus, the neighborhoods were drained of money and little was available for maintenance.

In 1968 Goldseker became the symbol of the turnover of white neighborhoods to black. Activists picketed and chanted outside his downtown real estate office for four months. But they did not regard him as the real target. He could operate only with the collusion of powerful institutions and powerful fears. Financial institutions were perceived as the enemy, and the activists launched a year of research into his sources of credit. Each residential community in the city had its own precise set of financial institutions, and each investor or creditor group in the city was identified with one or another.[43] Just as the home appliances were plugged into the electric power grid, so were individual home buyers plugged into the financial grid, and the financial institutions were the inner city's transformers and switching stations. Equitable Trust loaned Goldseker $1 million in personal credit to buy houses for resale to people to whom they would not lend directly. Uptown Federal Savings and Loan loaned $2 million to Goldseker's buyers, depending on him to absorb the risk of accumulating the down payments. He provided the ground rents, the second mortgages, and management, when the Federal Housing Authority, local government, and local mortgage bankers were "doing virtually nothing." Goldseker's operations filled a gap where other investors refused to venture. Some building associations like St. Casimir's stuck to tradition and still made small direct loans for modest homes in East Baltimore, but most were financing the exodus. They offered home mortgages to young white families to purchase new housing in the counties, while they refused direct loans to black families and elderly couples and "red lined" the inner city. The city's municipal pension fund was typical of such institutional investors as the churches. The fund had invested the savings of city employees, both black and white, three-quarters of them city dwellers, in a thousand mortgages in Baltimore County, but none in the city. Jesuit volunteers picketed Loyola Federal Savings and Loan in the attempt to open to blacks the opportunities that the Redemptorists had created among the German, Bohemian, and Polish Catholics a century earlier. Two dozen other savings and loan associations, like Uptown Federal, Jefferson Federal, Ashburton, Northeastern Bohemian, and Slovanstvo, had become captives of speculators and politicians. In 1968 alone they made available over $4 million to the buy-like-rent speculators.

In the century-old tradition of Baltimore's home-grown millionnaires, Goldseker left his wealth "to help people help themselves." The black tax and the gray tax were converted into a capital fund whose income supports legal counseling for the elderly, scholarships, and the diagnosis of iron deficiency among inner-city children. It pays for vocational rehabilitation and housing rehabilitation, and helps "the working poor," black and white, become home owners.

Goldseker's was only one facet of the complicated encounter between the Jewish community and the black community. The Jewish community moving out of Oldtown, Eutaw Place, and Forest Park provided exceptional values for the black community, often by tolerance and a recognition of common experience: they transferred buildings, resources, legal services, financing, and schools. About 1960, as in 1893, the whole set of synagogues got up and moved. The older, originally German, Reformed and Conservative congregations sold off their temples to the Prince Hall Masons, the Baptists, and the Seventh-Day Adventists, just as they had once sold off their temples in East Baltimore to the Orthodox congregations from Eastern Europe. Baltimore Hebrew Congregation removed to Park Heights and Slade Avenue. Har Sinai, the Strengthening of Faith, the Lovers of Peace, and the Remnants of Israel followed. As in 1893, they rivaled in the elegance of their architecture and the prominence of their international architects; they featured cement curves, circular spaces, and stylized tablets of the law. The younger congregations, principally orthodox or "modern orthodox," established in Forest Park in the 1920s, moved out, too, some along Park Heights Avenue, some along Liberty Road. The institutions moved as well: Sinai Hospital and the Jewish Community Center. Apartment houses and nursing homes were built. It was harder and harder to find a minyan in Oldtown or Mount Royal.

But once again the newcomers, the elderly, and the indebted were caught in the middle, and looked at their mess of pottage with bewilderment. Middle-aged children in the new "golden ghetto" no longer knew what to do with the four-story shell of Uncle Nate's once respectable apartment house, and feared to venture where Aunt Rose's purse was snatched and a rent collector was stabbed. An immigrant couple bearing the scars of the Nazi prison camp bought up a dozen houses one by one at auctions and tax sales for $3500 apiece, and "rehabbed" them by slopping lead paint on the walls and selecting toilets, tubs, shutters, and radiators from the wreckers' depotoir in South Baltimore, a vast acreage guarded by German shepherds. A delicatessen parking lot became the meeting place of drug peddlers, and the aging partners finally sold out in bitterness to urban renewal. A man of Vilno, survivor of the Dachau camp, lost his delicatessen to urban renewal. A survivor from Chelm suffered five holdups in his little grocery. The two became partners and attempted to buy a new site at auction: their downpayment disappeared into the complicated divorce suit of a Greek immigrant in the state mental hospital. One pharmacist continued to serve his old neighborhood faithfully, but suffered a series of holdups; another adapted his enterprise to selling liquor, "nerve tonics" for the winos, and codeine cough syrup by the quart.

Meanwhile, another millionnaire, diminutive in stature but a bundle of energy, hopscotched through the squares marked out for black players. He was "Little Willie" Adams. Born in North Carolina, he had spent the depression in Frederick Douglass's old neighborhood at the foot of Caroline Street, sorting old leather and canvas and spoking bicycle wheels. His real springboard was the numbers racket. The public placed bets under a quarter at five hundred to one odds, six hundred to one for "big book" from twenty-five cents to $1. A thirty-cent hit, for example, would pay $180. The writer earned a commission of 15 to 20 percent. When Adams "retired" in 1951, he testified to Senator Kefauver's crime investigating committee that he had an average daily play of $1000; he was then sued for nearly $1 million in taxes on unreported income. His profits from the numbers, his whiz-kid arithmetic, and a combination of stinginess and generosity allowed the young sportsman to expand into legitimate businesses. At eighteen, he bought a $300 candy store on Eager Street. He sold snowballs, shined shoes, and added a barbershop. By buying the Sugar Hill Tavern and a Democratic club, he moved into West Baltimore, and from there he extended into fashions, soft-drink bottling, a music company, an amusement park, and the clubs. He became known as the Prince of Pennsylvania Avenue, and admitted, "The height of my ambition is the sky."

Adams was looked to as philanthropist and fund raiser for the NAACP court cases, Provident Hospital, and St. Peter Claver Church. Most important, he became the backer for other black businessmen who moved into the wider economy—meatpacking, food processing, parking lots, retailing, contracting. "Our salvation is in business." He pioneered northwest to a home where his nearest black neighbor was a mile away, although others soon followed. In the white community he gained the respect of contractors, banks, race track owners, liquor interests, and insurance companies, "the people and corporations who bankroll elections."

Adams's economic base rested in the black community, and he was a conduit for the purchasing power and voting power of the black community in the structure of white power. Earlier millionnaires had found ways to exploit consumer groups in the larger community, even where they exploited workers within their own ethnic group. But the black entrepreneur was still operating in a confined economic space. The black community could not support a large number of such men, and looked with fascination and ambivalence at its "money-making Moses leading his people from economic bondage."[44]

Saturday Night

In each generation there has been present a substantial hostility, outrage, and mutual fear among factions of Baltimore society. These feelings have generally been deflected from class conflict toward ethnic otherness, turned inward to self-destruction by suicide or alcohol, or diffused in domestic or street-corner violence. The new generation followed the old pattern, with much the same timing as in previous booms. The combined rates of murder and suicide rose rapidly in the late 1960s to a thousand per year, or one death in eleven in the city. Pills and chemical products offered escapes for more people, primarily the young, and the illegal drug industry invited entrepreneurship among dock workers, truck drivers, and politicians, as well as street-level pushers in jails, high schools, and neighborhoods. A new geographic pattern of deaths from an overdose of heroin was traced over the old geography of cirrhosis and TB. As endemic violence rose, the city was again perceived as a place of personal fear and risk to property. It was a return to the Know-Nothing Baltimore of the 1850s, although modern home owners and businessmen preferred guns to ice picks. Police retreated into automobiles and armed themselves with spray cans, space shields, and a helicopter with searchlight. Households in high-density areas acquired larger and fiercer dogs. Where Baltimore citizens had earlier bemoaned the nightly baying of retrievers, they now endured the howls of one hundred thousand nervous watchdogs.

Once again scapegoats were sought, and racial tensions mounted. In the 1830s rumors of conspiracy and repression of blacks were associated, however irrationally, with bank scandals, factory layoffs, and arson. In the 1850s party politics polarized into antiforeign and antiblack factions. In 1886 and 1917 cartoons and letters blamed labor troubles on "foreign anarchist plotters," but shifted their focus among Russians, Jews, Reds, and Orientals. All of these ideas now reappeared: the forms for expressing tension were influenced by episodes elsewhere in the world. In the 1930s anti-Semitism festered in Baltimore. In the 1940s racism directed at the Japanese enemy spilled over into domestic racism. When World War II ended, anxieties about foreign spies and dupes were not extinguished. Rumors of treason and oaths of loyalty reemerged. In the 1960s "outside agitators" were held responsible for civil rights demands, for student unrest, and for resistance to the draft for the war in Vietnam.

As in other cities, the hostilities had a geographic expression. A zone of tension ran around the town between blue-collar neighborhoods, black and white, roughly along Broadway, Twenty-fifth Street, and Fulton Street. The old roads of the country trade—Gay Street, Greenmount Avenue, and Pennsylvania Avenue—had become corridors of suburban movement and urban displacement, visible ribs of white commercial exploitation in the black ghettoes. While the overall economy of the Baltimore region was still swelling with prosperity in 1968, the inner-city economy was in a depression as deep as 1934.

On Thursday, 4 April 1968, Martin Luther King—the symbol of constitutional and peaceful struggle—was shot in Memphis. Washington, Baltimore, and a hundred smaller cities began to writhe in grief, anxiety, and rage.[45] The event recalled the senseless, the unexplained, the irrational of John F. Kennedy's assassination in 1963. It recalled the trigger events of "hot summers" in Detroit, Newark, Los Angeles, and Cleveland. The "enormities of the old world" cast their shadow over Baltimore. The sequence of events resembled those of 1812, 1835, 1861, and 1877. Rates of arson and false alarms had been rising steeply for eight months. On Friday afternoon in the black ghetto of East Baltimore, small gangs along Gay and Aisquith streets began attacking businesses. They broke windows and tossed Molotov cocktails. Holiday crowds, who knew the difference between looting and scavenging, waited for the police, then gaily carried off cases of whiskey, canned foods, and their neighbors' dry cleaning. On Friday evening the governor declared martial law and sent in fifty-five hundred National Guard to assist the twelve hundred exhausted city police. On Saturday morning the News American could have reprinted Niles' Register of 133 years before: "The state of society is awful. Brute force has superseded the law." On Saturday night troubles spread into West Baltimore along Fremont Avenue, Pennsylvania Avenue, and Whitelock Street. The night was filled with red skies and sirens.

On Palm Sunday morning "sunlight crackled." In the outer city the air was scented with new grass. The News American writer continued toward town: in the inner city the sun sparkled on broken glass, and the wind swept up cinders and smoke. Police cars darted everywhere like waterbugs on a pond. "They had brushed each other, these two cities that make up Baltimore." A young man in a purple suit wheeled home a shopping cart piled high with hams. Crowds grown sullen immobilized a passing automobile, a police car, and rained bottles on fire fighters. The firemen, tired and angry, crouched under their trucks and let a block burn while the National Guard tried to flush the people out of the buildings. On Sunday evening the president sent in five thousand regular soldiers. Tents bloomed again overnight like century plants in the city parks.

By Monday there was a "general, but gloomy, resolution" to restore order. The downtown department store district was cordoned off by four hundred state police. Routes to the suburbs were cut off, and early-morning commuters from the counties were stopped at the border. Lines of bayonets swept surly crowds, one by one, from Gay, Aisquith, and Whitelock streets, North Avenue, and Pennsylvania Avenue. Sleepless street people of CORE and U-JOIN were everywhere, "That's enough baby, you've taught 'em a lesson, now let's calm things down." Major Gelston's credibility and experience in Cambridge, Maryland, provided a basis for confidence. Six deaths were considered riot connected; rumors of sniping were never confirmed. Five thousand were arrested. Twelve hundred fires had burned. Most of the thousand burnt-out stores were white owned, many Jewish owned, some owned by "soul brothers." Some were the same corner bars and package liquor stores Mrs. Jackson was fighting in the 1940s. Some were places that had refused to serve blacks in the 1960s. Governor

Spiro Agnew addressed a monologue of reprimand to urgently assembled middle-class black leaders; they walked out. For four days, Mayor Tommy D'Alesandro roamed the streets in anxious dialogue with fire fighters, police, street people, and crowd watchers. The governor and the mayor reflected the respective attitudes of state and city governments that had surfaced in the face of every Baltimore mob for two hundred years.

On Wednesday, twenty-two thousand Baltimoreans, black and white, trooped out to cheer the Orioles' opening day game. The mayor threw out the first ball. That was normalcy. The fires dropped to two hundred, only a third over an average day. A convoy of city dump trucks and an army of sweepers moved down Gay Street. A parade of sightseers crept down Pennsylvania Avenue bumper to bumper, with black "do rags" tied to their aerials. For eight or nine months afterward, arson and false alarms continued at relatively high levels in the city, as children and teens continued to act out what they had witnessed. The rhythm of mounting tension, sudden release, and gradual grim restoration resembled the model of history. Citizens were as baffled as Niles had been in his time as to "whether the effect is *periodical* or belongs to certain accidental causes—the foundations of which are deeply laid."[46]

Coming to Terms with the Past

Thus, the Baltimore landscape of the 1970s, the dull red maze of the inner city and the infinite greens of the outer city, the beaded string of viaducts over stream valleys, the ribbons of concrete, and the geometry of the inner harbor, came to reflect a set of human relationships. The urban landscape is a history book, a readable set of social relations. Just as it was for Daniel Raymond and James Gibbons, Baltimore has remained a model of the political economy and a mirror of the human condition.

Generation after generation, observers in Baltimore looked at the city around them, at the cancers of mortality, at the heartburnings, at the dens and hovels, and they recognized the succession of events. Inequalities of property and of opportunity in the city were built into its Lebensraum. Investment, public and private, functioned as a transmission belt from past to future, imposing the constraints of one generation on the next. Each new wave of investment transformed the landscape, recycled the assets, created new debts, and regenerated new debtors and new creditors. Each observer drew his own conclusions as to how the transmission belt might be interrupted, and each chose his mode of persuasion: the printing press, the soapbox, the hustings, the plaintiff's box. After John Woolman mourned the "inward desolation" of the slave-holding economy, the next generation of Quakers developed an alternative economy. Elisha Tyson filed suits to adjust the laws to allow it to operate. Daniel Raymond, considering that a great portion of the evils in society arose from the unequal division of property, challenged the inheritance laws. Richard Ely, perceiving that real property was the source of monopoly, proposed preserving future options by auctioning only short-term franchises in the use of the city streets. Ely, and after him Jacob Hollander, testified on tax reforms and urged fiscal responsi-

Baltimore's neighborhood re-
vitalization in the 1970s reflects
a strong commitment to
maintaining the physical
integrity of a built environment. The greater challenge is
the sensitive restoration of
the social structure.

bility, that each generation should pay its own bills. Broadus Mitchell invited his
students to look around at the city: he took them to the lung block and the
bachelors' cotillion. Another generation of lawyers and parents took its children
to court as plaintiffs, and to picket lines. Their children, in turn, celebrated
Earth Day and with graceless accuracy concluded, "There's no free lunch."

Coming to terms with the past has always meant coming to terms with
one another and with the situations the past has handed down, and taking
part in structuring the situation the next generation will inherit. Looking over
our shoulders are Elisha Tyson and George Presbury, some assorted Carrolls,
Howards, Browns, and Bucklers, Miss Szold, Father Dolan, Brother Alex, Isaac
Myers. Portraits on the walls, faces at the windows, they stare from the bricked-
up windows of cotton mill and brewery or off the marble steps, watching the
children play hopscotch on the sidewalk. Spirits echo through the empty railroad
stations. Ghosts are evicted from their churches or dispossessed of their market
stalls and horsecarts. Locked-out specters parade through the streets: mourners
follow caskets, pickets hop streetcars, matrons carry violets and laundresses their
baskets of dirty linen, brickmakers, stonecutters, hodcarriers, brass bands, and
Shriners on minimotorcycles, Fourth of July following Fourth of July, one
Armistice Day after another. Behind them march generations of frustration, the
pea hullers and tobacco girls, the men with round-pointed shovels, and the boys
with bayonets, portraits never painted, the embarrassments of history. They
pour gin into the gutter, they demolish a printing press, they break into the
jail, they make a bonfire of the law books, they throw the fire engine off the

dock, they stone a regiment, they stop a locomotive. Their chants bounce off brick walls, "Scab! Scab! Scab!" "Take Home a Brick." They repeat slogans scrawled on board fences, Kill Jim Crow, Off the Pusher, Justice Now. They echo the voice of the madman in the almshouse, "Don't come near me!" and the caulkers' appeal for a little corner of creation.

Notes

The Empty Century

I have freely used Baltimore's great chroniclers and interpreters: Thomas W. Griffith, *Annals of Baltimore*, 2d ed. (1824; Baltimore: W. Wooddy, 1833), and J. Thomas Scharf, *The Chronicles of Baltimore* (Baltimore: Turnbull Bros., 1874). The *Archives of Maryland* are volumes of documents published by the Maryland Historical Society over many years.

1. Griffith, *Annals of Baltimore*, p. 288.

2. Baltimore is located at latitude 39°12′, has a growing season nine months long, "abundant" sunshine, and a rainfall of forty-two inches rather evenly distributed throughout the year. Maryland Geological Survey, *Baltimore County* (Baltimore, 1929), p. 368, contains meteorological data and a more detailed account of the geology of piedmont and coastal plain "provinces" and "the fall line." (The B&O Railroad track can be said to demarcate the fall line.) See also *Maryland Soils*, University of Maryland Cooperative Extension Service bulletin 212 (May 1967).

3. Maryland Toleration Act of 1649, as transcribed by Isaac M. Fein, *The Making of an American Jewish Community: The History of Baltimore Jewry from 1773 to 1920* (Philadelphia: Jewish Publication Society, 1971), pp. 245–46.

4. Bliss Forbush, *A History of Baltimore Yearly Meeting of Friends* (Sandy Spring, Md.: Baltimore Yearly Meeting of Friends, 1972), p. 4.

5. Baltimore City Council journal, 1835.

6. Winthrop D. Jordan, *White over Black: American Attitudes toward the Negro, 1550–1812* (New York: Oxford University Press, 1974), pp. 71–82.

7. Silvio A. Bedini, *The Life of Benjamin Banneker* (New York: Scribner's, 1972).

8. Griffith, *Annals of Baltimore*, p. 23. See also Avery O. Craven, *Soil Exhaustion As a Factor in the Agricultural History of Virginia and Maryland, 1606–1860*, University of Illinois Studies in the Social Sciences 13 (Urbana: University of Illinois Press, 1925), p. 51; Jacob M. Price, "The Economic Growth of the Chesapeake and the European Market, 1697–1775," *Journal of Economic History* 24 (1964): 496–511; and Pauline Maier, *From Resistance to Revolution* (New York: Knopf, 1972).

9. For information on large landowners, see Clarence P. Gould, *The Land System of Maryland, 1720–65*, Johns Hopkins Studies 31 (Baltimore: The Johns Hopkins Press, 1913), p. 59; idem, *The Economic Causes of the Rise of Baltimore: Essays in Colonial History* (1931; reprint ed. Freeport, N.Y.: Books for Libraries Press, 1966); Aubrey C. Land, "Economic Base and Social Structure: The Northern Chesapeake in the Eighteenth Century," *Journal of Economic History* 25 (1965): 639–54; idem, "Economic Behavior in a Planting Society: The Eighteenth Century Chesapeake," *Journal of Southern History* 33 (1967); and Jack Mowll, "The Economic Development of Eighteenth Century Baltimore" (Ph.D. diss., The Johns Hopkins University, 1956).

10. Dr. Charles Carroll of Annapolis to his son, Charles Carroll (later barrister Carroll), "Correspondence of Dr. Charles Carroll," *Maryland Historical Magazine* 25 (1930): 284–89.

11. L. C. Gottschalk, "Effects of Soil Erosion on Navigation in Upper Chesapeake Bay," *Geographical Review* 35 (1945): 219–37; and idem, "Sedimentation in a Great Harbor," *Soil Conservation* 10, no. 1 (July 1944): 3–5, 11–12.

12. St. George L. Sioussat, "Highway Legislation in Maryland and Its Influences on the Economic Development of the State" (Ph.D. diss., The Johns Hopkins University, 1889), in *Maryland Geological Survey* 3 (1899): 105–89.

13. Scharf, *Chronicles of Baltimore*, p. 21.

14. Griffith, *Annals of Baltimore*, pp. 18–20, 101.

15. Ibid., p. 23.

16. Ibid., p. 28.

Rhythms of Growth

In addition to Thomas W. Griffith, *Annals of Baltimore*, 2d ed. (1824; Baltimore: W. Wooddy, 1833), sources used frequently are the *Maryland Gazette* or *Baltimore Daily Advertiser*, published in Baltimore between 1783 and 1786, and Frank A. Cassell, *Merchant Congressman in the Young Republic: Samuel Smith of Maryland, 1752–1839* (Madison: University of Wisconsin Press, 1971).

Conversations of Tocqueville with John Latrobe and other Baltimoreans, 29 October–5 November 1831, are found in Alexis de Tocqueville, *Oeuvres complètes*, ed. J.-P. Mayer, vol. 5, *Voyages en Sicile et aux Etats-Unis* (Paris: Gallimard, 1957), pp. 97, 108, 121, 185, 236, 242, 247.

Records of the City of Baltimore consist of several volumes compiled by Wilbur Coyle, City Librarian. For this period, see vol. 1, *First Records of Baltimore Town and Jones Town, 1729–1797* (Baltimore: King Bros., 1905).

1. Griffith, *Annals of Baltimore*, p. 35.

2. Governor Sharpe to Lord Calvert, 9 July 1755, *Archives of Maryland*, 1: 240; to John Sharpe, ibid., 1: 497; to Lord Calvert, ibid., 1: 512.

3. John Woolman, *The Journal and Major Essays of John Woolman*, ed. Phillips P. Moulton (New York: Oxford University Press, 1971), p. 64.

4. Griffith, *Annals of Baltimore*, p. 43. They also often held lots elsewhere in Baltimore County.

5. *Records of the City of Baltimore*, vol. 1.

6. Cassell, *Merchant Congressman*, and Everstine, *A History of the Ancient and Honorable Mechanical Company of Baltimore*.

7. Douglas Carroll, Jr., and Blanche D. Coll, "The Baltimore Almshouse: An Early History," *Maryland Historical Magazine* 66 (1971): 135–52. They ascribe the history to the same Thomas W. Griffith, ca. 1821.

8. For information on the Revolution, see Charles A. Barker, *The Background of the Revolution in Maryland*, Yale Historical Publications 38 (New Haven: Yale University Press, 1940); Ronald Hoffman, *A Spirit of Dissension: Economics, Politics, and the Revolution in Maryland* (Baltimore: The Johns Hopkins University Press, 1974); and Thomas O'Brien Hanley, *Charles Carroll of Carrollton: The Making of a Revolutionary Gentleman* (Washington, D.C.: Catholic University of America Press, 1970).

9. On the activities of the Sons of Liberty, see Pauline Maier, *From Resistance to Revolution* (New York: Knopf, 1972), p. 109.

10. Cassell, *Merchant Congressman*.

11. *Archives of Maryland*, vol. 48, passim. I noted letters of marque and reprisal issued by the State Council of Maryland, as indexed from Baltimore, 1781–84.

12. Griffith, *Annals of Baltimore*, p. 80.

13. The lawsuit involving Oliver Evans, the Hollingsworths, and other Baltimore millers was reported in *Niles' Register*, annual addenda of March 1813 and March 1814. See also Silvio A. Bedini, *The Life of Benjamin Banneker* (New York: Scribner's, 1972).

14. State Council of Maryland to Honorable Robert Morris, Esq., *Archives of Maryland*, 48: 212 f.

15. John Adams, *The Works of John Adams*, 10 vols. (1856; reprint ed. New York: AMS Press, 1971), 3: 433, diary entry of 6 February 1777.

16. On the estate tail, see Laws of Maryland, Act of 1786, ch. 45, and Tocqueville's conversation with Latrobe, *Oeuvres*, 5: 108.

17. George Whitefield, *Journals, 1737–1741* (1905: reprint ed. Gainesville, Fla.: Scholars' Facsimile, 1969), p. 362.

18. Question 42, Proceedings of the Methodist Christmas Conference, in *Minutes of the Annual Conference of the Methodist Episcopal Church, For the Years 1773–1828* (New York, 1840), 1: 20–21. See also Lucius Matlack, *The History of American Slavery and Methodism, From 1780 to 1849* (New York, 1849); H. Shelton Smith, *In His Image, But . . . : Racism in Southern Religion, 1780–1910* (Durham: Duke University Press, 1972); and Donald G. Mathews, *Slavery and Methodism: A Chapter in American Morality, 1780–1845* (Princeton: Princeton University Press, 1965).

19. Dieter Cunz, *The Maryland Germans: A History* (Princeton: Princeton University Press, 1948), pp. 179 ff. See also L. Hennighausen, "History of the German Society in Maryland," *Maryland Society for the History of the Germans in Maryland* 1 (1909).

20. *Maryland Gazette*, 6 December 1785.

21. Griffith, *Annals of Baltimore*, p. 55.

22. Robert Hunter, Jr., *Quebec to Carolina in 1785–1786*, ed. Louis B. Wright and Marion Tinling (San Marino: Huntington Library, 1943), p. 180.

23. John Pendleton Kennedy, in Edward Spencer, ed., *Celebration of the 150th Anniversary of the Settlement of Baltimore* (Baltimore, 1880).

24. Among the wharf owners and merchants who were port wardens were Samuel Purviance, Samuel Smith, John Sterrett, Daniel Bowley, Thomas Ellicott, and William Patterson.

25. *Maryland Gazette*, 27 August 1784.

26. Magnetic declination is the angle between the true north-south line and the magnetic north-south line as pointed out by a compass needle. Its secular variation was discovered in 1634, and the change varies in magnitude, at greatest about one degree in twenty years.

27. Rules and Orders for the Direction of Surveyors, 15 April 1782, *Archives of Maryland*, 48: 132.

28. Ibid. The Maryland rules were old-fashioned, in contrast with the federal orders for the Northwest Territory: "Geographers and Surveyors shall pay the utmost attention to the variation of the magnetic needle, and shall run and note all lines by the true meridian, certifying with every plat what was the variation at the time" (*Maryland Gazette*, 24 May 1785). A Baltimore surveyor, Robert Gibson, discusses variation in magnetic amplitude in *A Treatise on Practical Surveying*, 3d ed. rev. by John D. Craig (Baltimore: F. Lucas, 1822): "But a true meridian line is seldom to be met with."

29. An example of an error recognized is the Lancaster Alley case: *Records of the City of Baltimore*, vol. 1, 3 July 1788, p. 66.

30. Griffith, *Annals of Baltimore*, pp. 115–16, 150–51.

31. Letter of Civis, *Maryland Gazette*, 26 October 1784.

32. Griffith, *Annals of Baltimore*, p. 114.

33. Letter of Civis. See also *Maryland Gazette*, letters of 27 October 1784 and 6 February 1786.

Order and Disorder

Newspaper sources are the *Baltimore Daily Repository*, April–July 1793, the *Baltimore Daily Intelligencer*, October–December 1793, and the *Federal Gazette and Baltimore Daily Advertiser*, January 1797.

Also used extensively are: Richard Parkinson, *A Tour in America in 1798, 1799 and 1800*, 2 vols. (London: J. Harding and J. Murray, 1805); Wilbur Coyle, ed., *Records of the City of Baltimore*, vol. 2, *City Commissioners, 1779–1813* (Baltimore: King Bros., 1906); Stuart Weems Bruchey, *Robert Oliver, Merchant of Baltimore, 1783–1819*, Johns Hopkins University Studies 74, no. 1 (Baltimore: The Johns Hopkins Press, 1956); and Richard H. Townsend, Diary, transcribed by Works Progress Administration of Maryland, 1937, in the Enoch Pratt Free Library, Baltimore, Md.

1. Bruchey, *Robert Oliver*, p. 190.
2. Parkinson, *Tour in America*.
3. Cunz, *Maryland Germans*.
4. Peter K. Guilday, *The Life and Times of John Carroll, Archbishop of Baltimore, 1735–1815* (New York: Encyclopedia Press, 1922).
5. *Baltimore Daily Intelligencer*, 10, 11, 13, 15, and 26 July 1793. More refugees arrived in June 1804.
6. My estimate of French population is based on French names in the city directory of 1804.
7. Parkinson, *Tour in America*.
8. For entertainment, theater, and dance, see Chrystelle T. Bond, "A Chronicle of Dance in Baltimore, 1780–1814," *Dance Perspectives 66* (Summer 1976): 1–49.
9. Townsend, Diary, and *Federal Gazette*, 7 July 1797.
10. Parkinson, *Tour in America*, pp. 75–76, 214.
11. Ibid., p. 456.
12. Ibid., p. 428–29.
13. All Negroes were presumed to be slaves and subject to the slave's legal handicaps until either descent from a free ancestor or manumission according to the law was proved (Paul S. Clarkson and R. Samuel Jett, *Luther Martin of Maryland* [Baltimore: The Johns Hopkins Press, 1970], p. 165).
14. *Negro Cato v. Howard*, 2 Harris and Johnson (1808), p. 167, as cited in ibid.
15. John S. Tyson, *Life of Elisha Tyson, the Philanthropist, by a Citizen of Baltimore* (Baltimore, 1825). John S. was Elisha's son. Townsend, Diary, confirms Tyson.
16. Protection Society cases were reported in *Niles' Register* and the *Federal Gazette* years later when they reached the Court of Appeals.
17. William Pinckney, speech at age twenty-five, cited in Tyson, *Elisha Tyson*, p. 20.
18. *Federal Gazette*, 23 December 1797. Maps in the Baltimore Courthouse refer to litigation between Edward and Samuel Norwood (*Niles' Register*, 23 November 1833).
19. *Records of the City of Baltimore*, vol. 2. On insurance rates, see *Federal Gazette*, March 1797, and Baltimore City Council journal, 15 February 1836.
20. Moreau de Saint-Méry, *Voyage aux Etats-Unis de l'Amérique, 1793–1798*, ed. Stewart L. Mims (New Haven: Yale University Press, 1913), as translated in *Maryland Historical Magazine* 35 (1940): 229. John H. Powell reports the epidemic in Philadelphia and the role of French immigrants from Santo Domingo in doctoring and nursing the population: *Bring out Your Dead: The Great Plague of Yellow Fever in Philadelphia in 1793* (Philadelphia: University of Pennsylvania Press, 1949).
21. John B. Davidge, *Physical Sketches* (Baltimore: W. Warner, 1814), p. 71.
22. Ibid.
23. Dr. Nathaniel Potter, *Federal Gazette*, 13 November 1797.
24. Ibid., 25 November 1797. The epidemic occurred in October.
25. Montebello was built in 1796, and Willow Brook in 1799. Beyond three miles from the city center, subdivisions ran 50 to 100 acres for farms; beyond ten or fifteen miles, 200 to 500 acres, except for mill seats.
26. Griffith, *Annals of Baltimore*, p. 155.
27. Money was raised for Santo Domingo refugees in 1793, and for victims of the Norfolk fire in 1797.

28. On the resurvey at Pratt and Charles streets, see the testimony by George Presbury, 2 July 1810, *Records of the City of Baltimore*, 2: 165–69.

29. Saint-Méry, *Voyages aux Etats-Unis*, p. 227.

30. Parkinson, *Tour in America*.

31. *Federal Gazette*, 2 September 1797.

Commerce Is the Mainspring

Niles' Register, ed. Hezekiah Niles, was published weekly in Baltimore from 1810 to 1837, and is supplemented by dailies, the *American* and the *Federal Gazette*.

Annual messages of the mayor were delivered, usually in January, to the city council, for the year ending 31 December. Other city documents are found in the Baltimore City Council journal (city hall library) and in *Records of the City of Baltimore*, ed. Wilbur Coyle (Baltimore: King Bros., 1905), vol. 4, *Special Commissioners*, and vol. 5, *Eastern Precincts Commissioners* (1812–17) and *Western Precinct Commissioners* (1810–17).

Many important public works documents are found classed as "canal pamphlets" or "railroad pamphlets" in the Peabody library and The Johns Hopkins University library.

1. Useful comments on the varying intensity of building activity are found in *Niles' Register*, 1 May 1813, 29 April and 3 June 1815, 1 June 1816, 5 July 1817, and 2 July 1818; for examples of magnificent private houses, see the entry of 19 September 1812.

2. *Niles' Register* reported much detail of manufactures.

3. On this influential circle of intellectuals, see John E. Uhler, "The Delphian Club," *Maryland Historical Magazine* 20 (1925): 305–12; James W. Foster, "Fielding Lucas, Jr., Early 19th Century Publisher of Fine Books and Maps," *Proceedings of the American Antiquarian Society* (October 1955), pp. 166–91; John E. Semmes, *John H. B. Latrobe and His Times, 1803–1891* (Baltimore: Norman, Remington, 1917); and Charles H. Bohner, *John Pendleton Kennedy: Gentleman from Baltimore* (Baltimore: The Johns Hopkins Press, 1961). I located their residences and those of patentees from Baltimore city directories.

4. Niles's economic philosophy and the "American system" of Mathew Carey and Daniel Raymond are discussed by Broadus Mitchell in *Dictionary of American Biography*, ed. D. Malone, 20 vols. (New York: Scribner's, 1934), 15: 406–7 and 13: 521–22.

5. On Latrobe's architectural work in Baltimore and rivalries with Robert Mills and Maximilian Godefroy, see Thomas Hamlin, *Benjamin Henry Latrobe* (New York: Oxford University Press, 1955), pp. 483–504. See also R. H. Howland and E. Spencer, *The Architecture of Baltimore* (Baltimore: The Johns Hopkins Press, 1953); and Carolina V. Davison, "Maximilian and Eliza Godefroy," *Maryland Historical Magazine* 19 (March 1934).

6. "A Letter from General Harper, of Maryland, To Elias B. Caldwell, esquire, secretary of the American Society for colonizing the Free People of Colour in the United States, with their own consent" (Baltimore: E. J. Coale, 1817). Penelope Campbell, *Maryland in Africa: The Maryland State Colonization Society, 1831–1857* (Urbana: University of Illinois Press, 1971). On Harper's national political significance, see David H. Fischer, *The Revolution of American Conservatism* (New York: Harper & Row, 1965). On the relation to the national colonization movement, see George Frederickson, *Black Image in the White Mind* (New York: Harper & Row, 1971).

7. *Niles' Register*, 20 June 1818.

8. Stuart Weems Bruchey, *Robert Oliver, Merchant of Baltimore, 1783–1819*, Johns Hopkins University Studies 74, no. 1 (Baltimore: The Johns Hopkins Press, 1956).

9. Ibid., pp. 218, 222.

10. Ibid., p. 229.

11. Ibid., pp. 265–99. Ouvrard was the French banker; the Dutch bankers were Hope & Co.

12. *Niles' Register*, 24 October 1812 and 20 February 1813; John P. Cranwell and

William B. Crane, *Men of Marque: A History of Private Armed Vessels out of Baltimore during the War of 1812* (New York: W. W. Norton, 1940).

13. Charles C. Griffin ("Privateering from Baltimore during the Spanish American Wars of Independence," *Maryland Historical Magazine* 35 [1940]) discusses the American concern and recounts the exploits of John O. Chase. See also Jared Sparks, "Baltimore," *North American Review* 20 (1825); and Laura Bornholdt, *Baltimore and Early Pan-Americanism*, Smith College Studies in History 34 (Northampton, Mass.: Smith College, 1949).

14. *Federal Gazette*, 10 January 1804; see also ibid., 3, 5, and 6 July 1804.

15. Ibid., 14 February 1804.

16. Ibid., 10 January 1804.

17. Thomas W. Griffith, *Annals of Baltimore*, 2d. ed. (1824; Baltimore: W. Wooddy, 1833).

18. Maryland State Roads Commission, *A History of Road Building in Maryland* (1958), cites J. Thomas Scharf, *History of Western Maryland*, 3 vols. (Philadelphia: L. H. Everts, 1882), 2: 1331, with respect to profits of the Cumberland Turnpike Company.

19. On water company subscriptions, see *Federal Gazette*, 5 May 1804; see also ibid., 8–12 May 1804, and Nelson M. Blake, *Water for the Cities: A History of the Urban Water Supply Problem* (Syracuse: Syracuse University Press, 1956).

20. *Federal Gazette*, 14 April 1804.

21. City Spring is now the site of the Mercy Hospital garden.

22. John Davis worked for the Philadelphia waterworks about three years. He was solicited by Baltimore in fall 1804 ("Autobiography of John Davis, 1770–1864," *Maryland Historical Magazine* 30 [1935]: 11–39.)

23. Robert Mills was chosen as architect for the monument in 1815, and as water company consultant in August 1816 ("The Daily Journal of Robert Mills, Baltimore, 1816," *Maryland Historical Magazine* 30 [1935]: 257–71).

24. North Street was also called South Street Extended, then Belvidere Street, and now Guilford Avenue.

25. Drawings of Waterloo Row are found in publications of the Baltimore Museum of Art. See also *American*, 3 June 1818.

26. *American*, 11 August 1817, and *Niles' Register*, 16 August 1817.

27. Robert Mills, "Report on the Survey of Jones Falls," was published in full but without maps in the *American*, 3 October 1817; see discussions of 29 and 30 October.

28. Baltimore City Council journal, 29 September 1817.

29. Benjamin Latrobe's alternate plan was described in reports on the flood of 1868 (see notes to chapter 8) and mentioned in *Records of the City of Baltimore*, vol. 4, 15 March 1819; Baltimore City Council journal, 1st branch, 15 March 1830 and 29 March 1832.

30. On death rates and epidemics, I have relied heavily on William Travis Howard, Jr., *Public Health Administration and the Natural History of Disease in Baltimore, Maryland, 1797–1920* (Washington, D.C.: Carnegie Institution, 1924).

31. John B. Davidge, *Physical Sketches* (Baltimore: W. Warner, 1814).

32. *Niles' Register*, 5 January 1822. See also *Federal Gazette*, 2 May 1804.

33. *Niles' Register*, 25 January 1822. See also ibid., 5 January and 23 February.

34. *Federal Gazette*, 14 February and 6 April 1822.

35. Griffith, *Annals of Baltimore*, pp. 172–73. Howard opines that vaccination had little effect on the epidemics.

36. Davidge, *Physical Sketches*.

37. *Niles' Register* gives weekly reports on the epidemic from 17 August to 16 October 1819.

38. Topographical accounts and ideas about putrefaction are found in *A Series of Letters and Other Documents Relating to the Late Epidemic of Yellow Fever, Published by Authority of the Mayor* (Baltimore: William Warner, 1820). The letters are from the doctors of the Second Dispensary.

39. Ibid., p. 96.

40. Ibid., p. 101.

41. *Niles' Register*, 11 August 1821 and 26 October 1822.

42. Davidge, *Physical Sketches*.

43. *A Series of Letters*.

44. *Federal Gazette*, 23 February 1822.

45. *A Series of Letters*, p. 46.

46. *Records of the City of Baltimore*, vol. 4 (1818).

47. Hampstead Hill is the high ground on the west side of Patterson Park. Effects of reorganizing drainage from Hampstead Hill and from Hughes Street at the foot of Federal Hill are discussed in chapter 5.

48. Lewis Brantz describes his survey in a torn manuscript fragment in the Enoch Pratt Free Library, Baltimore, Md.

49. On the Poppleton plan, see *Federal Gazette*, 1 January, 25, 28, and 30 March, 6 April, and 3 and 12 September 1822. Thomas Griffith was one of the citizens who wanted a true topographical survey.

50. Richard H. Townsend, Diary, transcribed by Works Progress Administration of Maryland, 1937, in the Enoch Pratt Library, Baltimore, Md.

51. North Street in Oldtown is now known as Hillen Street; the new York turnpike is Greenmount Avenue. West of the falls, North Street was known as Belvidere, now Guilford Avenue. Lewis Wernwag built the Belvidere bridge; he also bridged the Schuylkill in 1812 and the Susquehanna in 1818. The Centre Street bridge was authorized in 1809, and the Saratoga Street connections in 1811. At the mouth of the falls, the drawbridge ran from Chase's wharf, now West Falls Avenue, to the City Block.

52. John Skinner, *American Farmer* 1, no. 1 (1819): 6.

53. *Federal Gazette*, 30 March 1822.

54. Christian Mayer's and Edward Ireland's estates (*Federal Gazette*, 24 January and 15 March 1822).

55. *Niles' Register*, 20 June 1818.

56. Henry-Marie Brackenridge, *Recollections of Persons and Places in the West* (Pittsburg: J. I. Kay, 1834), p. 45.

57. *Niles' Register*, 8 August 1812, 18 January 1813 (legislature's report), and 6 February 1813.

58. Ben Stoddert to James McHenry, 15 July 1812, cited in Bernard C. Steiner, *The Life and Correspondence of James McHenry* (Baltimore: Burrows Bros., 1907), p. 582.

59. *Niles' Register*, 17 April 1813.

60. Ibid., 14 August and 10 September 1814.

61. Ibid., 8 June 1816 and 31 January 1818.

62. Ibid., 1 March 1817.

63. Ibid., 31 January 1818, 16 December 1820, and 9 March 1822.

64. Ibid., 25 November 1820. See also 13 October 1821.

65. Mayor's messages, January 1807 and January 1811. The mayor and council also discuss the misery of chimney sweeps (ibid., January 1820), and foreign mendicants and superannuated slaves (Baltimore City Council journal, 24 January 1833).

66. *American*, October 1817.

67. *Niles' Register*, 5 and 26 June and 23 October 1819.

68. Frank A. Cassell, *Merchant Congressman in the Young Republic: Samuel Smith of Maryland, 1752–1839* (Madison: University of Wisconsin Press, 1971).

69. *Niles' Register*, 3 November 1821 and 2 November 1822.

70. *Niles' Register*, 26 June 1822.

71. *American Farmer*, 8 October 1819.

72. *Federal Gazette*, 20 August 1822.

73. Ibid., 9 February 1804.

74. Blanche D. Coll, "The Baltimore Society for the Prevention of Pauperism, 1820–1922," *American Historical Review* 61 (1955): 77–87.

75. Thomas Griffith, as cited in Douglas Carroll, Jr., and Blanche D. Coll, "The Baltimore Almshouse: An Early History," *Maryland Historical Magazine* 66 (1971): 135–52.

76. Ibid.

77. Ibid.

78. Special Report of Council Joint Committee, *Federal Gazette*, 24 January 1822.

79. Letter of Trustees of the Poor House to the Legislature, ibid., 1 January 1823.

80. John M. Duncan, *Travels through Part of the United States and Canada in 1818 and 1819*, 2 vols. (Glasgow: The University Press, 1823).

81. Reports of Baltimore Grand Jury on conditions in the jail, *Federal Gazette*, 9 February 1804 and 15 March 1822; and Board of Visitors to the City Jail, *Annual Report*, 1830.

82. Letter of O. B. (probably Thomas Griffith), *Federal Gazette*, 31 October 1822. O. B. published other letters on the subject in October and November.

83. John S. Tyson, *Life of Elisha Tyson, the Philanthropist, by a Citizen of Baltimore* (Baltimore, 1825).

84. Paul S. Clarkson and R. Samuel Jett, *Luther Martin of Maryland* (Baltimore: The Johns Hopkins Press, 1970).

85. Tyson, *Elisha Tyson*.

86. Ibid.

87. Daniel Raymond, *The Missouri Question* (Baltimore: Schaeffer S. Maund, 1819), p. 7.

88. Idem, *Thoughts on Political Economy* (Baltimore: F. Lucas, 1820), p. 436.

89. Idem, *Missouri Question*. On the character of freed slaves, Raymond takes issues with General Harper, "Letter."

90. Raymond, *Political Economy*, p. 448.

91. Ibid., p. 456.

92. Raymond's labor theory of value is developed in *Political Economy*, pt. 1. Charles Patrick Neill attributes to Raymond a decided influence on Friedrich List, who in turn influenced Marx and Engels. Thus, although he was reprinted a few times in Baltimore and then forgotten, and never translated in Europe, Raymond belongs to the mainstream of economic theorists. See Charles Patrick Neill, *Daniel Raymond*, Johns Hopkins University Studies 15, no. 6 (Baltimore: The Johns Hopkins Press, 1897). For biographical data, see Charles J. MacGarvey, "Daniel Raymond, Esquire, Founder of American Economic Thought," *Maryland Historical Magazine* 44 (1940): 111–22.

93. Raymond, *Political Economy*, p. 453.

94. Ibid., p. 452–53; see also p. 220.

95. Ibid., p. 253; see also pp. 233, 248–49.

96. Idem, *The Elements of Political Economy*, 3d ed. (Baltimore: F. Lucas, Jr., 1836).

97. Idem, *Political Economy*, 1st ed., pp. 258, 302.

98. Ibid., p. 294. See also p. 302.

99. *Federal Gazette*, 29 December 1819.

100. *Niles' Register*, 19 May and 21 July 1821.

The Grand Civic Procession

Newspapers used are *Niles' Register*, the *Federal Gazette*, and the *Genius of Universal Emancipation*, published in Baltimore by Benjamin Lundy from 1825 to 1828.

Published annual reports of city agencies include those of city commissioners (on public works), port wardens, jail visitors, and trustees for the poor. Annual reports of the Canton Company are for the year ending 1 June.

Works I have used throughout the chapter are James Silk Buckingham, *America: Historical, Statistic and Descriptive* (London: Fisher, Son & Co., 1841); Edward Hungerford, *The Story of the Baltimore and Ohio Railroad, 1827–1927*, 2 vols. (New York: G. P. Putman's Sons, 1928); and Jacob H. Hollander, *The Financial History of Baltimore* (Baltimore: The Johns Hopkins Press, 1899).

1. *Niles' Register*, 1828.

2. Robert Mills, *Treatise on Inland Navigation* (Baltimore: F. Lucas, 1820). For more information on canals, see Albert Gallatin, "Report of the Secretary of the Treasury on the

Subject of Public Roads and Canals," Washington, 4 April 1808, reprinted by *Niles' Register*, 29 August, and 5 and 12 September 1818; Harry N. Scheiber, *Ohio Canal Era: A Case Study of Government and the Economy, 1820–1861* (Athens: Ohio University Press, 1968); Carter Goodrich, ed. *Canals and American Economic Development* (New York: Columbia University Press, 1961); Walter S. Sanderlin, *A History of the Chesapeake and Ohio Canal*, Johns Hopkins University Studies 64 (Baltimore: The Johns Hopkins Press, 1946); and Joshua Gilpin, *A Memoir on the Rise, Progress, and Present State of the Chesapeake and Delaware Canal* (Wilmington: R. Porter, 1821).

3. "Report by the Maryland Commissioners on a Proposed Canal from Baltimore to Conewago," 25 November 1823.

4. "Report of the Commissioners Appointed by the Mayor of the City of Baltimore to Explore and Survey the Route for a Canal and Stillwater Navigation from the City of Baltimore to the Head of Tidewater at Port Deposit," 11 February 1825. The commissioners were John Glenn, Robert Cary Long, and James Mosher, with William F. Small, engineer, and Jehu Bouldin, surveyor.

5. Ibid.

6. John E. Semmes, *John H. B. Latrobe and His Times, 1803–1891* (Baltimore: Norman, Remington, 1917), pp. 400, 444.

7. "Proceedings of Sundry Citizens of Baltimore, Convened for the Purpose of Devising the Most Efficient Means of Improving the Intercourse between This City and the Western States" (Baltimore, 1827).

8. *Niles' Register*, 17 March 1827, reprinted from the *American*.

9. Canton Company, *Annual Report*, 1835.

10. Semmes, *Latrobe*.

11. Lt. Stephen H. Long and Capt. William Gibbs McNeill, *Narrative of the Proceedings of the Board of Engineers of the Baltimore & Ohio Railroad Company*, (Baltimore: Bailey & Francis, 1830), Resolution of 28 May 1828.

12. Report of 4 September 1828, in Long and McNeill, *Narrative*, p. 4.

13. Document E, letter of 23 June 1828, ibid., p. 41. For general principles of railroad location see Stephen H. Long, *Rail Road Manual* (Baltimore: W. Wooddy, 1828), p. i.

14. Lexington Street crossed Chatsworth Run at Division Street. The site adjoining the city dock became the President Street Station.

15. George Winchester, President, Baltimore and Susquehanna Rail Road Company, in Baltimore City Council journal, 2nd branch, 27 August 1829.

16. Ibid. See also "Report of the Joint Committee of the City Council, Appointed to Examine the Baltimore and Susquehanna Rail Road" (Baltimore, 1837).

17. Semmes, *Latrobe*.

18. Baltimore City Council journal, 2nd branch, 19 March 1835, p. 159.

19. Ibid., p. 160. See also 1st branch, 12, 15, 17, 18, 19, and 30 March, and 2nd branch, 13 March.

20. John Pendleton Kennedy, *Letters of a Man of the Times* (Baltimore: Sands & Nielson, 1836), originally letters to the *American*.

21. Ibid.

22. Canton Company, *Annual Report*, 1835, p. 7. See also "Report of Committee of Stockholders," 13 June 1838.

23. John Pendleton Kennedy, *Quodlibet* (Philadelphia: Lea & Blanchard, 1840), p. 35.

24. Mayor Jacob Small, *Message*, 22 January 1828, p. 134.

25. Kennedy, *A Man of the Times*.

26. Hollander, *Financial History*.

27. Ibid.

28. [John H. B. Latrobe], *Picture of Baltimore* (Baltimore: F. Lucas, 1832), p. 78. See also *Niles' Register*, 1 and 8 March 1823, 17 September, 12 November, and 3 December 1825.

29. Calverton millrace was at 185 feet elevation, Hockley mill reservoir at 190 feet, and Tyson's millrace at 150 feet (Report of Water Committee, Baltimore City Council journal, 1st branch, 16 June 1830).

30. Ibid., 2 March 1835.

31. Ibid.

32. Letter of John Randel, ibid., 21 April 1836.

33. Baltimore City Council journal, 1st branch, 8 April 1830 and 29 March 1832.

34. Richard H. Townsend, Diary, transcribed by Works Progress Administration of Maryland, 1937, in the Enoch Pratt Free Library, Baltimore, Md., p. 201. He lived at 18 Baltimore Street.

35. Mayor's message of January 1823; see also 1825, 1828, and 1829.

36. Niles' Register, 4 November 1826.

37. Thomas's steam sugar refinery burned in 1829, and the planing mill in 1833 (Thomas W. Griffith, Annals of Baltimore, 2d ed. [1824; Baltimore: W. Wooddy, 1833]).

38. Owners of powder mills and shot towers were Lorman, Beatty, and Jameson. The tower on Gay Street was built in 1823, and the Phoenix shot tower in 1828. The coal company was incorporated in 1829. Other details of factories are largely from Niles' Register.

39. Niles' Register, 4 October 1828.

40. Ibid., 26 April 1828.

41. On the law of succession, see Alexis de Tocqueville, Oeuvres complètes, ed. J.-P. Mayer, vol. 5, Voyages en Sicile et aux Etats-Unis (Paris: Gallimard, 1957), chapter 2; and Daniel Raymond; Thoughts on Political Economy (Baltimore: F. Lucas, 1820), pp. 232–33.

42. Semmes, Latrobe, pp. 290–93. His grandson, Charles Carroll, lived at Homewood; one daughter, married to Robert Goodloe Harper, lived at Oakland, and another daughter, married to Richard Caton, lived at Brooklandwood, now Catonsville. See Kate Mason Rowland, Life of Charles Carroll of Carrolton, 1737–1832, with His Correspondence and Public Papers, 2 vols. (New York: G. P. Putman's Sons, 1898).

43. The estate of James Carroll can be documented from wills, etc., at the Mount Clare Mansion.

44. Poppleton's survey for the division of the John Eager Howard estate is in the Hall of Records, Annapolis.

45. Niles' Register, 16 and 23 October 1824.

46. Ibid., 19 July 1826.

47. John S. Tyson, Life of Elisha Tyson, the Philanthropist, by a Citizen of Baltimore (Baltimore, 1825).

48. Niles' Register, 12 July 1828.

49. Ibid., 19 November 1825.

50. My estimates of occupational structure are from the city directory of 1827 and the U.S. census of 1830. Free blacks made up 13 percent of directory listings.

51. Niles' Register, 23 January 1830, 23 April, 30 July, and 20 August 1831, and 5 October 1833.

52. Karl Bernhard, Duke of Saxe-Weimar Eisenach, Travels through North America, during the Years 1825 and 1826 (Philadelphia: Carey, Lea, and Carey, 1828), p. 167.

53. Harold A. Williams, History of the Hibernian Society of Baltimore, 1803–1957 (Baltimore, 1957).

54. Niles' Register, 15 September 1832. See also Dieter Cunz, The Maryland Germans: A History (Princeton: Princeton University Press, 1948), pp. 159, 236, 241.

55. Niles' Register, 23 April 1831.

56. William Travis Howard, Jr., Public Health Administration and the Natural History of Disease in Baltimore, Maryland, 1797–1920 (Washington, D.C.: Carnegie Institution, 1924).

57. Horatio G. Jameson, "Observations on Epidemic Cholera, As It Appeared at Baltimore, in the Summer of 1832," Maryland Medical Recorder 2 (1831): 393. On social psychology and the class impact of cholera, see Charles E. Rosenberg, The Cholera Years: The United States in 1832, 1849, and 1866 (Chicago: University of Chicago Press, 1962), and Louis Chevalier, Le Choléra, la première épidémie du XIXième siècle (La Roche sur Yon: Imprimerie Centrale de l'Ouest, 1958).

58. "Journal kept by Th. H. W. Monroe, during the Raging of that Awful Plague, the Cholera, in the City of Baltimore, 1832," Maryland Historical Society, Baltimore, Md. See also daily reports in the *Federal Gazette*.

59. Jameson, "Epidemic Cholera," p. 446. Wells may have been an informal student of Jameson's at Washington Medical College. *Rev. Lewis G. Wells* is elsewhere mentioned as a participant and memorialist at a meeting of the free people of color at Bethel Church, Sharp Street, 7 December 1826, to promote colonization.

60. *Annual Reports* of jail visitors. See also M. Demetz and Abel Blouet, *Rapport à Monsieur le Comte de Montalivet sur les pénitenciers des Etats-Unis* (Paris: Imprimerie Royale, 1837); and David J. Rothman, *Discovery of the Asylum: Social Order and Disorder in the New Republic* (Boston: Little, Brown, 1971).

61. *Picture.*

62. Frederick Douglass, *Narrative of the Life of Frederick Douglass an American Slave, Written by Himself*, ed. Benjamin Quarles (1845; reprinted ed. Cambridge, Mass.: Belknap Press, 1960), p. 59.

63. *Genius of Universal Emancipation* (New Series), 12 July 1828.

64. *Niles' Register* 44 (1835): 72; and *Picture*, p. 165.

65. The early history of the Oblate Sisters of Providence is movingly told in manuscript diaries in the archive of the order in Baltimore.

66. Ibid., 2 July 1830.

67. Ibid., 15 April 1835.

68. *Genius of Universal Emancipation*, 5 September 1825.

69. Ibid., 16 September 1826.

70. Tocqueville, *Voyages.*

71. Ibid.

72. *Federal Gazette*, 17, 22, and 23 March 1832.

73. Ibid., 3 April 1832.

74. Moses Sheppard is cited in Penelope Campbell, *Maryland in Africa: The Maryland State Colonization Society, 1831–1857* (Urbana: University of Illinois Press, 1971), n. 19.

75. Buckingham, *America*, p. 455.

76. Douglass, *Narrative*, pp. 127–33.

77. Thirty suicides were recorded in 1835, about three times the normal reported level. Suicides are generally understated.

78. *Niles' Register*, 22 August 1829. On later B&O Railroad riots, see ibid., 14 March 1835, and Hungerford, *Baltimore and Ohio Railroad.*

79. W. David Baird, "Violence along the Chesapeake and Ohio Canal, 1839," *Maryland Historical Magazine* 46 (1971): 121–34.

80. *Niles' Register*, 1 February 1834.

81. Ibid., 26 April 1834.

82. Ibid., 9 September 1826.

83. Ibid., 19 September 1835.

84. Townsend, *Diary*, p. 60. On the relation of the Union Bank, the Bank of Maryland, and local and national party policies, see Frank Otto Gatell, "Secretary Taney and the Baltimore Pets: A Study in Banking and Politics," *Business History Review* 39 (1965): 205–27.

85. *Niles' Register*, 26 April 1834.

86. Ibid., weekly, 7 February to 9 May 1835.

87. Ibid., 8 August 1835.

88. Ibid., 15 August 1835.

89. Mayor Samuel Smith, messages of 4 January and 3, 13, and 17 March 1836, in Baltimore City Council journal, 1st branch.

90. *Niles' Register*, 22 April 1837.

91. Baltimore City Council journal, 1st branch, 18 February 1835.

A Lifelike Energy

Newspaper sources: the *Baltimore Sun* began daily publication in 1837. Phoebe M. Stanton read and made available her notes on the *Sun*, 1837 to 1852. The *American* frequently carries more detail of labor conflicts.

I also used annual messages of the mayor, commissioners of health, school commissioners, commissioners for opening streets (from 1841), city commissioner (public works), and chimney sweeps.

A useful source is Ferdinand C. Latrobe, *Iron Men and Their Dogs: A History of Bartlett, Hayward* (Baltimore: I. R. Drechsler, 1941). Ferdinand Latrobe, son of John H. B. Latrobe, was the mayor of Baltimore for seven terms between 1875 and 1895. The company, depending on dates of partnerships, is variously called Hayward, Bartlett; Bartlett, Hayward; Bartlett-Hayward; or Barlett, Robbins, and is now a division of the Koppers Company.

James Wynne, *Sanitary Report of Baltimore: Extract from the First Report of the Committee on Public Hygiene of the American Medical Association* (reprinted in annual report of the Baltimore Commissioners of Health, 1850).

1. *Sun*, 25 March 1850. On other locomotives, see ibid., the *Tiger*, 12 November 1850; the *York*, 18 September 1850; and 29 June 1849, 19 October 1846, and 25 March 1851.

2. Ibid., 28 August 1849.

3. Ibid., 19 February 1849.

4. Ibid., 23 April 1849; see also 10 June 1851.

5. See Brinley Thomas, *Migration and Urban Development: A Reappraisal of British and American Long Cycles* (London: Methuen, 1972); Richard A. Easterlin, *Population, Labor Force, and Long Swings in Economic Growth: The American Experience* (New York: National Bureau of Economic Research, 1968); Walter Isard, "A Neglected Cycle: The Transport-Building Cycle," *Review of Economics and Statistics* (November 1942), pp. 149–58; idem, "Transport Development and Building Cycles," *Quarterly Journal of Economics* (November 1942), pp. 90–110. Construction cycles in Baltimore are discussed in relation to national and regional cycles in John R. Riggleman, "Variations in Building Activity in United States Cities" (Ph.D. diss., The Johns Hopkins University, 1934). Construction figures appear in the *Sun*, 1 February 1844, 31 October 1845, and 13 March 1847.

6. Factory descriptions are primarily from John C. Gobright, *City Rambles, or, Baltimore As It Is* (Baltimore: John W. Woods, 1857), and idem, *The Monumental City* (Baltimore: John C. Woods, 1858). These two volumes provide details of factory operations, employment, and organization. The Knabe piano works was located in the block bounded by Eutaw, Cross, Warren, and West streets.

7. Curlett's was at Holliday and Saratoga streets.

8. Whitman's farm tool factory was in Canton, on the block bounded by Cambridge, Essex, Burke, and Concord streets (*Sun*, 23 January 1849). On the copper companies at Canton and Locust Point, see *Sun*, 1 October 1846 and 22 March 1849.

9. On the Mason bakery, see *Sun*, 8 March and 25 October 1847. Numsen's pickle works was on Jackson Street, south of Cross Street.

10. *Sun*, 17 August and 21 September 1852, and 6 May 1851.

11. Ibid., 15 March 1845.

12. The city invested $1.5 million in the Northwestern Railroad through Virginia to Parkersburg, $0.5 million in the Susquehanna Railroad to connect Bridgeport and Williamsport, and $1 million in the Pittsburgh and Connelsville line to Cumberland and the Cumberland Valley line to York.

13. *Sun*, 23 January 1849.

14. Ibid.

15. Information on rolling stock and bridge material has been compiled from annual reports of the B&O Railroad and the B&S Railroad. On railroad finance, see Edward Hungerford, *The Story of the Baltimore and Ohio Railroad, 1827–1927*, 2 vols. (New York: G. P.

Putman's Sons, 1928), and Jacob H. Hollander, *The Financial History of Baltimore* (Baltimore: The Johns Hopkins Press, 1899).

16. On the roles of Bollman, Fink, and C. H. Latrobe (all B&O bridge engineers) in railway bridge design, see John E. Greiner, "The American Railroad Viaduct: Its Origin and Evolution," *Transactions of the American Society of Civil Engineers* 502 (October 1891): 349–60.

17. John H. White, "James Milholland and Early Railroad Engineering," *Contributions from the Museum of History and Technology*, no. 69 (Washington, D.C.: Smithsonian, 1968), pp. 1–36. For Milholland's local activities in Baltimore, see also the *Sun*, 19 October and 7 December 1846, 3 May and 24 June 1847, and 9 March and 8 July 1848.

18. *Sun*, 21 September 1852. Camden Station was not built until 1856 and was never completed fully according to the design.

19. Calvert Station was demolished for the Sun Papers building; the freight station still stood in 1973.

20. *Sun*, 27 April 1849 and 28 June 1850.

21. Ibid., 1 April 1851.

22. Gobright, *City Rambles*.

23. Baltimore had three cast iron bridges over the Jones Falls in 1847 (*Sun*, 23 January and 12 February).

24. The popular Latrobe stoves were from a patent of John H. B. Latrobe, lawyer for the B&O and brother of Benjamin H. Latrobe, Jr., their engineer. The Cathedral portico was designed by John (John E. Semmes, *John H. B. Latrobe and His Times, 1803–1891* [Baltimore: Norman, Remington, 1917]).

25. Peter L. Payne and Lance E. Davis, *The Savings Bank of Baltimore, 1818–1866*, Johns Hopkins University Studies 72 (Baltimore: The Johns Hopkins Press, 1954). See also the manuscript compiled by Richard Cluster for 150th birthday of the Savings Bank of Baltimore, which can be consulted in offices of the bank.

26. Avery O. Craven, *Soil Exhaustion As a Factor in the Agricultural History of Virginia and Maryland, 1606–1860*, University of Illinois Studies in the Social Sciences 13 (Urbana: University of Illinois Press, 1925).

27. Thomas Swann, "Address Delivered at the Opening of the Maryland Institute," (pamphlet, Baltimore, 1851). Swann became the mayor in 1856.

28. Frank R. Rutter, *South American Trade of Baltimore*, Johns Hopkins University Studies, 15th series, no. 9 (Baltimore: The Johns Hopkins Press, 1897).

29. *Sun*, 27 April 1852.

30. Gerald W. Johnson, Frank R. Kent, H. L. Mencken, and Hamilton Owens, *The Sun Papers of Baltimore* (New York: Knopf, 1937).

31. Ibid., p. 80.

32. Ibid., pp. 85–86.

33. Gobright, *City Rambles*, p. 83.

34. Ibid., p. 46.

35. *Sun*, 2 September 1851. Similarly, Cortlan's, *American*, 5 July 1858.

36. *Sun*.

37. Ibid., 31 March 1851.

38. James Silk Buckingham, *America: Historical, Statistic and Descriptive* (London: Fisher, Son & Co., 1841).

39. *Sun*, 10 October 1850 and 8 August 1851.

40. Albert Schumacher's home, built in 1850, now Asbury House, belongs to Mt. Vernon Place Methodist Church.

41. The proportions of houses of two and three stories can be estimated from annual reports of the chimney sweeps.

42. *Sun*, 7 March and 17 April 1850.

43. Ibid., 1 September 1849.

44. On the returns of the water company, see ibid., 2 and 30 August 1848.

45. Wynne, *Sanitary Report*.

46. *American*, 1835, and *Sun*, 12 June 1839.

47. *Sun*, 11 April 1850 and 6 May and 11 June 1852, 30 September 1851 and 24 March 1852.

48. Buckingham, *America*.

49. Board of Health, *Annual Report*, 1858.

50. *Sun*, 29 July 1847.

51. Gobright, *City Rambles*.

52. *Sun*, 8 and 24 September and 7 October 1847, 29 January 1848.

53. Canton Company, *Annual Report*, 1850.

54. On property speculation near Mount Clare, on Ramsay, Fulton, McHenry, and Mount streets, see *Sun*, 11 April 1851 and 1 December 1858.

55. Information on B&O employees is drawn from published payrolls of 1848 and 1852.

56. On the West Baltimore subdivisions of Riddlemoser, Shirk, and Bolton, see *Sun*, October 1840 and 18 August 1847; in East Baltimore, ibid., 11 June 1839, 18 April 1843, 12 June 1850, and 26 May 1852.

57. The earliest state charters for mutual-type building associations, in 1850 and 1851, were the St. James Building Association, the Baltimore German Building Associations nos. 2 and 3, the Pius Building Association, Metamora Building Association, the Building Association of St. Joseph, the Baltimore City Domicil Society, the Baltimore House Building Association no. 1, the Central Building Association, and the Baltimore German Homestead Association.

58. The city commissioner's annual report for 1860 contains an index of streets, giving their length and width.

59. Board of Health, *Annual Report*, 1858.

60. Immigrant arrivals at the port of Baltimore are accounted from the city's head tax, names on file in city hall.

61. Mathew Carey, *Sun*, 14 September 1838.

62. Ludwig Beutin, *Bremen und Amerika* (Bremen: Schunemann Verlag, 1953). See also Dieter Cunz, *The Maryland Germans: A History* (Princeton: Princeton University Press, 1948).

63. Harold A. Williams, *History of the Hibernian Society of Baltimore, 1803–1957* (Baltimore, 1957).

64. M. Ray Della, Jr., "The Problems of Negro Labor in the 1850's," *Maryland Historical Magazine* 66 (1971): 14–32.

65. John Latrobe, "Address to American Colonization Society," 24 January 1851.

66. *Sun*, 14, 18, 21, and 25 May 1858.

67. Ibid., 3, 4, and 7 June 1859.

68. *American*, 8 July 1858; see also ibid., 12 February and 11 October 1858, and *Sun*, 28 and 29 June, 8 July, and 4 November 1858 and 29 June 1859. Events of 1858 are reviewed, with new testimony, in *American*, letters of 7 and 9 October 1865.

69. W. David Baird, "Violence along the Chesapeake and Ohio Canal, 1839," *Maryland Historical Magazine* 46 (1971): 121–34.

70. *Sun*, 20 January 1838.

71. Ibid., 14 November 1850.

72. Ibid., 8 October 1837.

73. Ibid., 8 October 1839.

74. Ibid., 9 September 1850.

75. Ibid., 28 January 1851.

76. Ibid., 15 June 1852.

77. Ibid., 12 October 1852.

78. Noah Davis, *A Narrative of the Life of Rev. Noah Davis, a Colored Man*, 2d ed. (Baltimore: J. F. Weishampel, Jr., 1866).

79. Cluster, manuscript. Experiences of several Baltimore area blacks in this period (Macks, Foote, Hammond, Wiggins, and Williams) are recounted in reminiscences of the

1930s: George P. Rawick, general ed., *The American Slave: A Composite Autobiography* (1941; reprint ed., Westport, Conn.: Greenwood Press, 1972), vol. 16.

80. Residential patterns of the several ethnic groups and of the occupancy of alleys in 1828, 1850, and 1880 were worked out by students at The Johns Hopkins University and me, from city directories and original schedules of the U.S. census (microfilms in Maryland Historical Society) for sample blocks. Residential geography of the rich can be traced from ward lists of taxpayers with incomes over $1,000, published in the *American*, 10–18 August 1865.

81. *Sun*, 16 August 1838 and 18 December 1839.

82. Ibid., 14 December 1839.

83. Ibid.

84. Ibid., 19 December 1839.

85. Ibid., 25 September 1843.

86. Ibid., 3 July, 26 August, and 9 September 1852.

87. Ibid., 12 August 1852.

88. On several victims of poverty, see ibid., 8 October 1839, 28 May 1849, 20 December 1851, and January 1858.

89. Ibid., 19 July 1839.

90. Ibid.

91. On the early history of the mission societies, see Edward John Hickey, *The Society for the Propagation of the Faith, Its Foundation, Organization, and Success, 1822–1922* (Washington, D.C.: Catholic University of America, 1922), and Benjamin J. Blied, *Austrian Aid to American Catholics, 1830–1860* (Milwaukee: By the author, 1944). Baltimore had received some $20,000 from the Leopoldine Foundation by 1860, as well as a large share of the foundation's direct contributions to the Redemptorists, plus sizeable travel allowances for the Redemptorists. Contributions from the Ludwigsverein and from the Society for the Propagation of the Faith were probably larger.

92. On the Redemptorists in Baltimore, see Michael J. Curley, *The Provincial Story: A History of the Baltimore Province of the Congregation of the Most Holy Redeemer* (New York, 1963); John F. Byrne, *The Redemptorist Centenaries* (Philadelphia: The Dolphin Press, 1932); and St. James Church, *Centenary* (Baltimore: Lewis A. Gorsuch & Co., 1934). St. Michael's Church was built at Pratt and Register streets and rebuilt at Lombard and Wolfe; Holy Cross was on West Street at Light; St. Anthony's orphanage was on Central Avenue near Madison Street.

93. Sister Mary Gilbert Kelly, *Catholic Immigrant Colonization Projects, 1815–1860* (Washington D.C.: U.S. Catholic Historical Society, 1939), pp. 122–29.

94. See Joseph Salzbacher, *Meine Reise nach Nord-Amerika im Jahre 1842* [My trip to North America in 1842] (Vienna: Wimmer, Schmidt, and Leo, 1845).

95. Manuscript journal in the archive of the Oblate Sisters of Providence, 30 June 1846. Father Joubert died in 1843. Another talented Redemptorist, Father Joseph Neumann, was in Baltimore from 1840 to 1844, and again as superior from 1847 to 1852, when he became bishop of Philadelphia; he was canonized in 1977.

In 1857 the Jesuits replaced the Redemptorists as chaplains. They founded the chapel of St. Peter Claver in the basement of St. Ignatius Church, then bought the old Universalist Church for a colored parish, St. Francis Xavier.

96. Isaac M. Fein, *The Making of an American Jewish Community: The History of Baltimore Jewry from 1773 to 1920* (Philadelphia: Jewish Publication Society, 1971).

97. George E. Bell, "Emerson and Baltimore: A Biographical Study," *Maryland Historical Magazine* 65 (1970): 343.

98. On Baltimore church buildings, the role of Robert Cary Long, Jr., and Niernsee and Nielson, see Phoebe M. Stanton, *The Gothic Revival and American Church Architecture: An Episode in Taste, 1840–1856* (Baltimore: The Johns Hopkins Press, 1968), and R. H. Howland and E. Spencer, *The Architecture of Baltimore* (Baltimore: The Johns Hopkins Press, 1953).

99. The uptown moves of the Pennsylvania African Methodist Episcopal Zion and Madison Avenue Presbyterian churches occurred in 1848.

100. Buckingham, *America*.

101. H. Shelton Smith, *In His Image, But . . . : Racism in Southern Religion, 1780–1910* (Durham: Duke University Press, 1972).

102. School enrollment figures were mapped from special censuses of the school board. Annual reports of school commissioners contain the occupations of fathers of high school pupils, as well as data on buildings and ground rents.

103. *Sun*, 5 January 1843.

104. Wynne, *Sanitary Report*.

105. William Travis Howard, Jr., *Public Health Administration and the Natural History of Disease in Baltimore, Maryland, 1797–1920* (Washington, D.C.: Carnegie Institution, 1924).

106. Thomas H. Buckler, *A History of the Epidemic Cholera As It Appeared at the Baltimore City and County Alms-house, in the Summer of 1849* (Baltimore: J. Lucas, 1851).

107. *Sun*, 27 January 1852.

108. Wynne, *Sanitary Report*.

109. Ibid.

110. Mayor's message, January 1852; City Council journal, 1st branch, 1852, p. 745; Board of Health, *Annual Report*, 1858.

111. *Sun*, 12 June 1839.

112. *Sun*, 5 January and 8 March 1848, 29 July 1845, 5 December 1846, and 9 October 1850.

113. Deep artesian wells were also introduced as permanent sources at Fort McHenry (145 feet), Fort Carroll (247), and Smith's distillery (132 feet).

114. Board of Health, *Annual Report*, 1851 and 1856.

115. City Commissioners, *Annual Report*, 1852, See also *Sun*, 8 June 1849.

116. City Surveyor, *Annual Report*, 3 January 1857.

117. Board of Health, *Annual Report*, 1856.

118. *Sun*, 11 January 1850.

119. On the relation between summer freshet and winter fill, see the mayor's messages of January 1847 and January 1859.

120. Ibid., Mayor Hinks, January 1856; Mayor Swann, January 1857, 1862, and 1863.

121. Baltimore City Council journal, 1st branch, 23 February 1843.

122. Buckler, *Epidemic Cholera*.

123. Jean Baker, *The Politics of Continuity: Maryland Political Parties from 1858 to 1870* (Baltimore: The Johns Hopkins Press, 1973).

124. Baltimore City, *Report in Reference to City Property Made by the Register, on the 2nd of May, 1851* (Baltimore: J. Lucas, 1851).

125. Baltimore City, *Report of the Board of Commissioners to the Mayor and City Council Relative to the City Boundary Avenue* (Baltimore: J. Lucas, 1852). (A copy is filed with the map in the Library of Congress Map Division.)

126. Mayor's message, January 1853.

127. Baltimore City, *Report upon a Supply of Water for the City of Baltimore, by Commissioners . . . together with Reports Made to the Commissioners by Thomas P. Chiffelle and James Slade, et al.* (Baltimore, 1854), pp. 90, 101.

128. Ibid.

129. Thomas H. Buckler, *Baltimore: Its Interests, Past, Present, and Future, A Letter* (Baltimore, 1873). See also Thomas H. Buckler to editor, *Sun*, 11 December 1875.

130. As cited by Nelson M. Blake, *Water for the Cities: A History of the Urban Water Supply Problem* (Syracuse: Syracuse University Press, 1956), n. 113.

131. Thomas H. Buckler's address to city council, *Sun*, 24 November 1858.

132. Benjamin Latrobe, Jr., "Report of 23 May 1859," in Enoch Pratt Free Library, Baltimore, Md.

133. Buckler, *Baltimore*.

134. "Report of the Special Commission Appointed to Investigate the Matter of Sewerage," 1862, manuscript, in Baltimore City Department of Public Works.

135. Ibid. The extent to which the plan was followed for storm drainage can be

evaluated from consultant studies to Department of Public Works, 1952, containing maps of older storm drains.

136. Mayor Jerome's messages of January 1850, 20 November 1850, and 19 June 1851. See also the mayor's message of 15 January 1849.

137. Ibid.

138. Charles Frick, *Annual Report of the Physician, Baltimore City Jail,* 1857.

139. Baltimore House of Refuge, "Laying of the Cornerstone," 28 October 1851 (pamphlet, Baltimore, 1851). See also George Brown, "Memorial to State Legislature," 5 February 1852 (pamphlet, Baltimore, 1852).

140. Statistics of inmates are found in House of Refuge annual reports.

141. Antiforeign comments of Mayor Swann can be found in his messages to council, 15 November 1858 and January 1860.

142. Baker, *Continuity.* The American party held a parade and an anti-Catholic meeting, "Eternal Separation of Church and State," when Bishop Kenrick attempted to collaborate with the city council for a reform of public schools and a share for Catholics in the school fund (City Council journal, 1st branch, 1853, p. 545; *Sun,* 19 August 1853).

143. Masakiyo Yanagawa, *The First Japanese Mission to America (1860), Diary,* ed. M. G. Mori, trans. Fukuyama and Jackson (Kobe, 1937).

144. *Sun,* 9 June 1860. On the first steam engine, see ibid., 18 May 1858.

145. Wartime party politics in Maryland can be followed in Baker, *Continuity,* and Charles Wagandt, *The Mighty Revolution: Negro Emancipation in Maryland, 1862–1864* (Baltimore: The Johns Hopkins Press, 1964).

146. J. Thomas Scharf, *History of Baltimore City and County* (Philadelphia: J. H. Everts, 1884), and original newspaper accounts.

147. John Pendleton Kennedy to S. P. Chase, 24 April 1861 (Chase papers, as cited in Wagandt, *Mighty Revolution,* p. 11).

148. Bernard C. Steiner, *Life of Henry Winter Davis* (Baltimore: John Murphy & Co., 1916), p. 195, as cited in Wagandt, *Mighty Revolution,* p. 13.

149. Frederick Bernal, British Consul, to Lord John Russell, 29 April 1861, in Public Record Office, as cited in Wagandt, *Mighty Revolution,* p. 13, n. 34.

150. Thomas Swann to Salmon Chase, 28 January 1861, Chase papers, cited in Baker, *Continuity,* p. 51.

151. Samuel Harrison, journal manuscript, Maryland Historical Society.

152. Hecht, memoir.

153. Harry L. Albrecht, "An Economic History of the Wilkens Hair Factory at Snake Hollow" (paper for Broadus Mitchell, The Johns Hopkins University, 1939, in Enoch Pratt Free Library).

154. Hecht, memoir.

155. The meeting of free colored men was held on 29 February 1864.

156. *Sun,* 24 September 1864.

157. Camp Cattlegrounds was actually Camp Bradford, located on the state fairgrounds at Remington.

158. *Sun,* 31 October 1864.

159. Ibid., 22 September 1864.

160. Ibid., 15 September 1864.

161. Ibid., 24 October 1864.

162. U.S. Christian Commission of Maryland, *4th Report of the Committee* (Baltimore, 1866).

A Rent in the Social Fabric

Newspaper sources used are the *Sun* and the *American.* The best all-around document on demography, schools, and labor in this period is Charles Hirschfeld, *Baltimore, 1870–1900: Studies in Social History,* Johns Hopkins Studies 54, no. 2 (Baltimore: The Johns Hopkins

Press, 1941). See also William Keyser, "Recollections of a Busy Life," 3 vols., Maryland Historical Society, Baltimore, Md.

1. *American*, 26 September 1865.
2. Ibid.
3. Ibid.
4. *Sun*, 14 August 1872.
5. Ibid., 15 November 1872.
6. Industrial accidents compiled from the *Sun*, summer of 1872.
7. Ibid., 10 September 1872.
8. *American*, 27 September 1865.
9. *Sun*, 19 July 1876. On Garrett's operations, see Sister Mary Anne Dunn, "The Life of Isaac Freeman Rasin" (M.A. thesis, Catholic University of America, 1949), and Keyser, "Busy Life," pp. 228, 330.
10. Keyser, "Busy Life," p. 250.
11. Loans and purchases of the B&O Railroad Company are documented from B&O annual reports.
12. Canton Company annual reports.
13. *Quodlibet*, a satire by John Pendleton Kennedy (Philadelphia: Lea & Blanchard, 1840) (see chapter 5).
14. Col. Joseph D. Potts, President of the Empire Transportation Co., cited in Ida M. Tarbell, *The History of the Standard Oil Company* (1925; reprint ed. New York: P. Smith, 1950), p. 199. On pipeline objectives and survey, see Hermann Haupt papers, box 17, Sterling Memorial Library, Yale University, and Haupt's letter, *American*, 13 February 1878.
15. *Sun*, 16 August 1865.
16. Ibid.
17. Ibid., 13 September 1872.
18. Ibid., 11 March 1872.
19. Ibid., 11 December 1871.
20. *American*, 9 January 1869; *Sun*, 27 November 1872; *Baltimore Engineer* (February 1976), pp. 4–5, 15.
21. *Sun*.
22. Ibid., 14 December 1871. See also *American*, 9 January 1869.
23. Canton Company, *Annual Report*, 1872. The Union Railroad embankment and tunnel are now part of the usual approach of Amtrak trains to Baltimore station from Wilmington. The Baltimore and Potomac tunnel is part of the usual approach to Baltimore station from Washington. They were long operated as part of the Pennsylvania Railroad, now the Penn Central, and are a bottleneck to modern rail traffic. The B&O Howard Street tunnel, through which trains passed between Camden and Mount Royal station, is now rarely used for passenger trains. Its construction is discussed in chapter 8.
24. Charles Latrobe was the son of Benjamin H. Latrobe, Jr., and the nephew of John H. B. Latrobe.
25. *American*, 11 August 1871 and 26 and 27 June and 4 September 1872.
26. *Sun*, 23 February 1872.
27. Ibid.
28. Ibid., 10 January 1890; Maryland legislature 1876, ch. 159.
29. *American*, 15 January 1878.
30. *Sun*, 30 October–5 December 1872, *passim*.
31. Richard H. Townsend, Diary, transcribed by Works Progress Administration of Maryland, 1937, in Enoch Pratt Free Library, Baltimore, Md.; *Report of the Joint Standing Committee on Jones Falls to the First Branch of the City Council of Baltimore, 7 October 1870* (Baltimore: Kelly, Piet & Co., 1870).
32. *Sun*, 25 July 1872.
33. Mayor Joshua Vansant, message, 3 September 1872. See also the mayor's message, January 1876, and Baltimore City Council journal, 1st branch, 8 February 1876.

34. "The Plan for the Improvement of the Channel of the Jones Falls," 8 April 1869; "Report of the Engineers upon Changing the Course of the Jones Falls," Baltimore, 1868.

35. The disagreements of the engineers over the Jones Falls improvements appear to reflect their business rivalries and personal alliances more accurately than any engineering logic. Bollman was involved in the Western Maryland Railway project and was earlier in business with J. H. Tegmeyer, City Commissioner and member of the Jones Falls Improvement Commission. Henry Tyson, their consultant, also President of City Passenger Railway and former head of the Sewerage Commission, was determined to manage the flood control operation and supervise contracts personally. Ross Winans kept the controversy alive. He urged filling or raising the flooded district instead of dredging out the falls. His son, Thomas Winans, had participated in Buckler's 1859 plan to fill the basin. Tyson was aligned with Tom Winan's brother-in-law, Hutton, on the plan to create a current in the basin. (Ross Winans, *The Jones Falls Improvement* [Baltimore, 1872].)

36. Thomas Buckler, *Baltimore, Its Interests, Past, Present, and Future, A Letter,* 12 September 1873 (Baltimore, 1873).

37. Lake Clifton has been filled and is presently the site of a high school. The churchlike pumphouse has been preserved.

38. *Sun,* 22 November 1877.

39. Ibid.

40. City Health Commissioners, annual reports; Board of Health, *Annual Report,* 1875; Baltimore City Council journal, 2d branch, 25 January 1875; Mayor's message, 21 January 1878.

41. C. A. Leas, "On the Sanitary Care and Utilization of Refuse in Cities" (Address to the American Public Health Association, 1872), reprinted in Donald Worster, ed., *American Environmentalism: The Formative Period, 1860–1915* (New York: John Wiley, 1973), pp. 150–61.

42. *Sun,* 9 September 1872.

43. Ibid., 31 July 1872. On improvements in northwest Baltimore, see ibid., 9 August 1865 and 4 December 1872.

44. Ibid., 17 June 1867.

45. Ibid., 14 June and 8 July 1876.

46. Ibid., January 1872, *passim.*

47. Ibid., 27 July 1872.

48. Ibid., 1 May 1872.

49. Ibid., 17 November 1874; City Council journal, 2d branch, June 1875.

50. *Sun,* 30 January 1872.

51. Ibid.

52. *American,* 24 January 1878.

53. *Sun,* 20 December 1871. It was later the Atlantic and Pacific Tea Company, or A&P.

54. Ibid., 22 November 1872; see also 23 July.

55. Hirschfeld, *Baltimore,* p. 66. See also *Sun,* 6 March and 13, 17, 18, and 19 April 1871; 7 March and August 1872; and 22 November 1877.

56. *Sun,* 9 October 1872 and 24 March 1873.

57. Ibid., 15, 22, and 25 October 1872. See also Hirschfeld, *Baltimore.*

58. George W. Howard, *The Monumental City: Its Past History and Present Resources* (Baltimore, J. D. Ehlers & Co., 1873, with addenda to 1889).

59. *Sun,* 29 July and 8 August 1872.

60. Baltimore patents for canning include Isaac Solomon's use of calcium chloride in 1860 and A. K. Shriver's kettle in 1874.

61. *Sun,* 5 January 1872 and 25 March 1869. H. F. Going, canmaker, testimony in *Report of U.S. Industrial Commission* (Washington, D.C.: Government Printing Office, 1900), vol. 1.

62. *Sun,* 5 January 1872.

63. Henry Hall, "Report on the Ship Building Industry of the United States," in U.S., Bureau of the Census, *Tenth Census* (Washington, D.C.: Government Printing Office, 1880), p. viii.

64. *Sun*, 5 January 1872.

65. Ibid.

66. *American*, 22 August 1865.

67. Ibid., 16 August 1865.

68. *Sun*, 26 January 1869.

69. Ibid., 21 February 1872.

70. Harry L. Albrecht, "An Economic History of the Wilkens Hair Factory at Snake Hollow" (Paper for Broadus Mitchell, The Johns Hopkins University, 1939, in Enoch Pratt Free Library).

71. *American*, 30 September 1865.

72. Ibid.

73. Ibid., 2 October 1865.

74. The conflict of the white and black caulkers can be followed blow by blow in the *American*, 28 September–2 October 1865.

75. Bettye C. Thomas, "A Nineteenth Century Black Operated Shipyard, 1866–1884: Reflections upon Its Inception and Ownership," *Journal of Negro History* 59 (1974): 1–12.

76. *New York Times*, 19 August 1869, cited in Philip Foner, ed., *Organized Labor and the Black Worker, 1619–1973* (New York: Praeger, 1974), p. 26.

77. "First Annual Report of the Baltimore Association for Education and Moral Advancement of the Colored People," 6 November 1865. See also Richard Paul Fuke, "The Baltimore Association for the Moral and Educational Improvement of the Colored People, 1864–1870," *Maryland Historical Magazine* 66 (1971).

78. John T. Gillard, *Colored Catholics in the United States* (Baltimore: The Josephite Press, 1941). See also John M. Slattery, "Twenty Years Growth of the Colored People in Baltimore," *Catholic World* (January 1878).

79. Father Vaughan, letter of Christmas 1871, cited in Peter Edward Hogan, *Catholic Mission Efforts for the Negro before the Coming of the Josephites* (1974), p. 60.

80. *Sun*, 24 March 1869.

81. Keyser, "Busy Life," p. 270.

82. *Sun*, 4 April 1872.

83. Ibid., 26 and 27 September 1872.

84. Ibid., coverage of 4 July 1876.

85. Ibid.

86. Ibid.

87. Ibid., headline, 20 July 1877.

88. Keyser, "Busy Life," p. 253.

89. The account of the mob is from *Sun*, 21, 22, 23, 28, and 30 July 1877.

90. Ibid., 21 July 1877.

91. Ibid., 28 July 1877.

92. Ibid. See also Keyser, "Busy Life," p. 276.

93. *American*, 3 January 1878.

Consolidation

Sources used on the crises of 1886, 1893, and 1898: *Sun* papers. The *American* often contains more detail on labor. Annual reports of city agencies now include those of the Topographical Survey and the Commission on City Charities. State publications are useful: Maryland Bureau of Industrial Statistics reports (biennial, then annual, beginning in 1885) and reports of Maryland school commissioners and commissioners of health. See also U.S., Commissioner of Labor, Carroll D. Wright, *Seventh Special Report: The Slums of Baltimore, New York and Philadelphia* (Washington, D.C., Government Printing Office, 1894). See also Michael R. Farrell, *Who Made All Our Streetcars Go?* (Baltimore: NRHS Publications, 1973).

1. *London Daily Chronicle*, as reprinted in *Sun*, 6 January 1894.

2. Edward Spencer, ed., *Celebration of the 150th Anniversary of the Settlement of Baltimore* (Baltimore, 1880).

3. *American*, 30 April and 2 and 5 May 1886.

4. J. G. Schonfarber, testimony to *U.S. Industrial Commission*, 30 vols. (Washington, D.C.: Government Printing Office, 1900), 7: 436.

5. Maryland Bureau of Industrial Statistics, *3rd Biennial Report*, 1888–89, p. 85.

6. Idem, *1st Biennial Report*, 1884–85, p. 144.

7. L. Hennighausen, "History of the German Society in Maryland," *Maryland Society for the History of the Germans in Maryland* 1 (1909). On other such incidents, see newspapers of December 1886, December 1889, February 1892, and December 1892; federal hearings of February 1906; Maryland Bureau of Industrial Statistics, *3rd Biennial Report*, 1888–89, p. 67; and Trustees for the Poor, *Annual Report*, 1888.

8. *Sun*, 16 November to 30 December 1889, 8 May 1894, and 4 July 1898; *Sun Magazine*, 22 October 1972.

9. Maryland Bureau of Industrial Statistics, *2nd Biennial Report*, 1886–87, pp. 86–87.

10. Ibid., p. 16. See also Edward K. Muller and Paul A. Groves, "The Changing Location of the Clothing Industry," *Maryland Historical Magazine* 71 (1976): 403–20.

11. *American*, 23 May 1886.

12. Schonfarber, *Industrial Commission*, p. 420.

13. *American*, 8 and 10 April 1886.

14. Ibid., 14 April 1886.

15. Ibid., 5 May 1886.

16. Ibid., 29 March 1886.

17. Ibid., 13 May 1886.

18. Ibid., 15 June 1886.

19. Richard T. Ely, *The Labor Movement in America* (New York: T. Y. Crowell & Co., 1886), p. 56.

20. Ibid., p. 34.

21. Gibbons to Elder, cited in John Tracy Ellis, *The Life of James Cardinal Gibbons, Archbishop of Baltimore, 1834–1921*, 2 vols. (Milwaukee: Bruce Publishing Co., 1952), pp. 447, 494.

22. Ibid., p. 503.

23. Ibid., based on a draft of minutes of the meeting at the cardinal's residence, 28 October 1886.

24. *American*, 30 April 1886.

25. Farrell, *Streetcars*.

26. *Sun*, 21 August 1893.

27. Ibid., 3, 4, 6, and 10 July 1893.

28. Ibid., 12 January 1894.

29. William Keyser, "Recollections of a Busy Life," 3 vols., Maryland Historical Society, Baltimore, Md., pp. 393, 414.

30. George W. Engelhardt, *Baltimore City, Maryland: The Book of Its Board of Trade* (Baltimore, 1895). Other useful details on turn-of-the-century industrial and commercial buildings can be found in *A History of the City of Baltimore, Its Men and Institutions* (Baltimore: *American*, 1902).

31. Harry G. Schalck, "Planning Roland Park, 1891–1910," *Maryland Historical Magazine* 67 (1972): 419–28. See also *Sun*, 26 September 1893.

32. G. W. W. Hanger, "Housing of the Working People in the United States by Employers," in U.S., Bureau of Labor, *Extension Bulletin*, no. 54 (1904), pp. 1191–1243. Leifur Magnusson, "Housing by Employers in the United States," in U.S., Department of Labor, Bureau of Labor Statistics, *Bulletin 263*, miscellaneous series (1920): 164–72. Maryland Bureau of Industrial Statistics, *2nd Biennial Report*, 1886–87. Report of the eighth national convention of bureaus of labor statistics, Maryland Bureau of Industrial Statistics, *Annual*

Report, 1891, pp. 124–25. J. Thomas Scharf (commissioner of Land Office of Maryland from 1 December 1885 to 1 January 1888), "Report to the Governor" (Annapolis, 1888).

33. Riverview Park is now the site of the Western Electric plant; Shore Line Park is the site of South Baltimore General Hospital.

34. *Sun,* 29 July 1893.

35. Ibid., 8 August 1893.

36. Ibid., 15 July 1898.

37. Engelhardt, *Baltimore City.*

38. Jacob H. Hollander, *The Financial History of Baltimore* (Baltimore: The Johns Hopkins Press, 1899).

39. Maryland Bureau of Industrial Statistics, *6th Annual Report* (Baltimore, 1897), pp. 82–89. See also Henry N. Bankard, "Some Mistakes in Taxation," *Addresses before Landlords Mutual Protective Association* (Baltimore 1889), pp. 22–42.

40. Building and loan association lists and lists of incorporations are found in Maryland Bureau of Industrial Statistics annual reports.

41. Francis T. King, cited in Richard T. Ely, *Taxation in American States and Cities* (New York: T. Y. Crowell & Co., 1888).

42. Frederick J. Brown, *Streets and Slums: A Study in Local Municipal Geography* (Baltimore: Cushing, 1894). Of the annual city budget, about a quarter was spent on streets and their maintenance, a quarter on schools, a quarter on water, and the last quarter on the traditional fire and police services. For an analysis of public investments, see Alan D. Anderson, *The Origin and Resolution of an Urban Crisis: Baltimore, 1890–1930,* (Baltimore: The Johns Hopkins University Press, 1977).

43. On the sequence of problems in Harford Run, see Baltimore City Council journal, 1st branch, 31 January 1843; *Sun,* 3 and 12 February 1848; 5 April, 30 May, and 8 June 1849; 22 January and 25 February 1851; and July 1852; annual reports of the city commissioner for 1877, 1878, 1881; annual reports of the board of health for 1854–56, 1860, 1861, and 1877; and mayor's messages for 1816, 1829, 1849, 1862, and 1879. On the diversion to Harris Creek, see city commissioner's annual reports, 1881–86, and "Report of the Sewage Commission, October 19, 1911," on storm of August 25.

44. Alfred D. Chandler, Jr., *Strategy and Structure: Chapters in the History of the American Industrial Enterprise* (Cambridge, Mass.: M.I.T. Press, 1962). Professional management was introduced in the reform of the Baltimore schools in 1880, the judges' campaign in 1882, the fire department in 1892, and private charities and welfare in 1895.

45. Ely, *Problems of To-Day* (New York: T. Y. Crowell, 1888), p. 55. The articles on tariffs, taxation, and monopoly originally appeared as articles in the *Sun.* See also Ely, *Land Economics* (reedited with George S. Wehrwein, 1940; reprint ed. Madison: University of Wisconsin Press, 1964).

46. Ely, *Problems of To-day,* p. 138.

47. Ibid., pp. 173–74.

48. Ibid., p. 160.

49. *Sun,* 21 November and 2 December 1889.

50. Ibid., 3 August 1893.

51. City Commissioner, *Annual Report,* 1894.

52. C. H. Latrobe, "Report to the Mayor and City Council upon a Plan of Sewerage for Baltimore City, and Its Probable Cost" (Baltimore, 1881).

53. Maryland Bureau of Industrial Statistics, *Annual Report,* 1894.

54. *Sun,* 28 December 1893.

55. Ibid., 25 January 1894.

56. Ibid., 26 September 1893.

57. Ibid.

58. Maryland Bureau of Industrial Statistics, *3rd Annual Report,* 1894. See also idem, *10th Annual Report,* 1902, pp. 139, 152–67; *11th Annual Report,* 1903; *13th Annual Report,* 1904; and *17th Annual Report,* 1908, p. 243.

59. *Sun,* 17 August and 25 December 1893. The last to move was the latest created: the

union of two small Orthodox congregations in 1879 founded Shearith Israel; in 1903 they moved to McCulloh Street, near North Avenue. See Isaac M. Fein, *The Making of an American Jewish Community: The History of Baltimore Jewry from 1773 to 1920* (Philadelphia: Jewish Publication Society, 1971); Joseph A. Feld, "The Changing Geography of Baltimore Jewry" (Paper, The Johns Hopkins University, 1968); and *Jewish Social Register* (Baltimore, 1904).

60. *Jewish Messenger* (New York), 25 November 1881 and 30 June, 18 August, and 3 November 1882.

61. Ibid., 16 June 1882.

62. Ibid., 21 January 1881.

63. Ibid., 27 December 1878 and 28 February 1879.

64. Ibid., 25 February 1881. See also Rose Zeitlin and Henrietta Szold, *Record of a Life* (New York, 1952).

65. Mary E. Richmond, *The Long View* (New York: Russell Sage Foundation, 1930). The group of articles includes "What Is Charity Organization?" from *Charities Review*, January 1900.

66. Trustees of the Poor, *Annual Report*, December 1896; and Commission on City Charities, *Annual Report*, 1897.

67. *News*, 20 September 1892, as cited in James B. Crooks, *Politics and Progress: The Rise of Urban Progressivism in Baltimore, 1895 to 1911* (Baton Rouge: Louisiana State University Press, 1968), p. 20.

68. *American*, January 1886.

69. Ibid., 7 April 1886.

70. Maryland Bureau of Industrial Statistics, *1st Biennial Report*, 1884–85, p. 144.

71. *Sun*, 18 October 1898.

72. Commissioner of Street Cleaning, *Annual Report*, 1896.

73. *American*, 6 June 1886.

74. George P. Rawick, general ed., *The American Slave: A Composite Autobiography* (1941; reprint ed. Westport, Conn.: Greenwood Press, 1972), 16: 56.

75. *American*, 24 February and 29, 30, and 31 March 1886.

76. Ibid., 2 April 1886.

77. John S. Billings, *Vital Statistics of the District of Columbia and Baltimore Covering a Period of Six Years Ending May 31, 1890* (Washington, D.C.: Government Printing Office, 1893). See also the biographical article on Billings by Debra Shore, "John Shaw Billings: Hopkins' Forgotten Soldier," *Johns Hopkins Magazine* 26 (1975): 21–34.

78. I compiled maps of wells (groundwater) and fountains (Gunpowder water) from annual reports of city commissioners and commissioners of health, which list locations of new installations and removals.

79. American Institute of Mining Engineers, *Guide to Baltimore* (Baltimore, 1892).

80. Harvey Cushing, *The Life of Sir William Osler* (Oxford: Oxford University Press, 1925), p. 303.

81. Ibid.

82. Ibid., p. 464.

83. Charles Hirschfeld, *Baltimore, 1870–1900: Studies in Social History*, Johns Hopkins Studies 54, no. 2 (Baltimore: The Johns Hopkins Press, 1941); Schonfarber, *Industrial Commission*; H. F. Going, canmaker, testimony in *Report of U.S. Industrial Commission* (1900).

84. Ida Tarbell, *The Nationalizing of Business, 1878–1898* (New York: Macmillan, 1936). John Moody, *The Truth about Trusts* (New York: Moody Publishing Co., 1904).

85. *American*, 30 January 1899.

86. *Sun*, 6 October 1898.

87. Edward Hungerford, *The Story of the Baltimore and Ohio Railroad, 1827–1927*, 2 vols. (New York: G. P. Putnam's Sons, 1928); B&O annual reports; *Sun*, 21 and 23 June 1898; *American*, 28 January 1899.

88. *Sun*, 9 June 1898.

89. Ibid., 23 June 1898.

90. Information on local trust companies is drawn from newspapers, corporate annual reports, and miscellaneous histories and pamphlets in the vertical files of the Enoch Pratt Free Library.

91. *American,* 26 and 31 January 1899.

92. Keyser, "Busy Life," pp. 13–14.

93. *Sun,* 9 and 21 June and 18 July 1898.

The Art of Urban Landscape

Newspaper sources are the *Sun* and the *American;* the *News* is also useful. Citations from H. L. Mencken are largely from the *Evening Sun,* but come directly from manuscripts in the Mencken Room of the Enoch Pratt Free Library, Baltimore, Md., not from the published papers. Municipal reports of special value include annual reports of the Topographical Survey and police censuses of housing, school attendance, and special population groups by age or race.

Isaac Fein placed valuable interview manuscripts in the Jewish Historical Society in Baltimore while preparing his book. Leonard Rea, "The Financial History of Baltimore, 1900–1926" (Ph.D. diss., The Johns Hopkins University, 1928), picks up where Jacob Hollander stopped.

An essential source that situates Baltimore in a nationwide political and intellectual movement is James B. Crooks, *Politics and Progress: The Rise of Urban Progressivism in Baltimore, 1895 to 1911* (Baton Rouge: Louisiana State University Press, 1968). It is usefully supplemented by Eleanor S. Bruchey, "The Business Elite in Baltimore, 1880–1914" (Ph.D. diss., The Johns Hopkins University, 1967).

Useful sources on living standards and health are Janet Kemp, *Housing Conditions in Baltimore* (Baltimore: Charity Organization Society, 1907), and U.S., Department of Labor, Bureau of Children, *Report on Infant Mortality in Baltimore* (Washington, D.C.: Government Printing Office, 1922). This remarkable sociological study is based on the total population of infants born in Baltimore in 1915. The original documents, in the U.S. National Archives, Record Group 102, boxes 216 and 220, contain a wealth of reports on social and housing conditions of the black community. Baltimore was chosen for the study because it contained a population large enough to permit statistical analysis of infant mortality rates by race.

Many details of industrial ownership and enterprise are found in *A History of the City of Baltimore, Its Men and Institutions* (Baltimore: *American,* 1902), and E. V. Illmer, *Industrial Survey of Baltimore: Report of Industries Located within the Baltimore Metropolitan District* (Baltimore, 1914).

1. *Municipal Journal,* 11 April 1913.

2. *American,* 14 December 1905; *Sun,* 7 June 1909.

3. Mayor's message, 1 February 1903.

4. *Fire Department, Annual Report.* Clarence H. Forrest, *Official History of the Fire Department of the City of Baltimore* (Baltimore, 1898). Harold A. Williams, *Baltimore Afire* (Baltimore, 1954).

5. Burnt District Commission reports, 11 September 1904 and 11 March 1905. Records and memorabilia exist at the Equitable Fire Insurance Society, Baltimore, Md.

6. Michael R. Farrell, *Who Made All Our Streetcars Go?* (Baltimore: NRHS Publications, 1973); *Sun,* 1 and 25 March and 5 April 1906, 4 February 1916, and 29 January 1917.

7. Calvin W. Hendricks, "Colossal Work in Baltimore," *National Geographic* 20 (April 1909): 365–73.

8. Commissioner of Street Cleaning, *Annual Report,* 1904.

9. Sewer Commission, *Annual Report,* 1911.

10. A similar connection was created among doctors and public health agencies through the medical and chirurgical faculty of The Johns Hopkins University Medical School.

11. Topographical Survey, *Annual Report,* 1910.

12. Olmsted Brothers, *Report on the Development of Public Grounds for Greater Baltimore* (Baltimore: The Lord Baltimore Press, 1904).

13. Peter J. Schmitt, *Back to Nature: The Arcadian Myth in Urban America* (New York: Oxford University Press, 1969).

14. *Sun*, 18 May 1913.

15. Ibid., January 1916 and 1 February 1916.

16. Ibid., 17, 20, and 28 March 1906 and 25 May 1917.

17. Ibid., 8 February 1916.

18. *Municipal Journal*, 19 June 1914.

19. Buckler and Latrobe had proposed moving 3 million cubic yards (see chapter 6).

20. *Sun*, 15 December 1909.

21. Ibid.

22. Ibid., 16 and 29 December 1909 and 5 January 1910; Katherine Harvey, *The Best Dressed Miners: Life and Labor in the Maryland Coal Region* (Ithaca: Cornell University Press, 1969), pp. 60, 62. Reorganization of Pennsylvania Railroad property within the central part of the city was the subject of perennial study and negotiation throughout this period. See *Sun*, 29 and 30 May 1913 and 26, 27, and 28 February and 1 March 1917; *Municipal Journal*, 27 April, 11 May, and 9 November 1917. On the taxation of the Pennsylvania Railroad, see *Sun*, 23, 24, 27, and 28 February and 13 and 18 March 1906.

23. *Sun*, 4 February 1916.

24. See *Addresses Delivered at the First City-Wide Congress of Baltimore, Maryland, March 8–11, 1911* (Baltimore, 1911).

25. *Municipal Journal*, 14 March 1913, 3 September 1915, 11 August 1916.

26. *Sun*, 23 January 1917.

27. Ibid., 27 January 1917.

28. Ibid., 2 June 1917, and 4 February 1916.

29. Harvey Cushing, *The Life of Sir William Osler* (Oxford: Oxford University Press, 1925).

30. Free Public Bath Commission, *Annual Report*, 1901.

31. *American*, 1 December 1905.

32. Municipal Turberculosis Commission, *Annual Report*, 1910.

33. Mencken, 9 December 1911.

34. Ibid., 9 April 1912.

35. Ibid., 19 July 1911.

36. Ibid., 16 June 1911.

37. Kemp, *Housing Conditions*.

38. Mayor's *Message*.

39. Kemp, *Housing Conditions*.

40. School inspectors, Health Department, *Annual Report*, 1906, 1908, and 1911.

41. Municipal Tuberculosis Commission, *Annual Report*, 1910.

42. *Sun*, 6 August 1911.

43. Supervisors of City Charities, *Annual Report*, 1907, p. 27.

44. Mencken, 7 December 1911.

45. Ibid., 26 October 1911.

46. Ibid., 4 October 1911.

47. *Evening Sun*, 3 March 1906.

48. Mayor's message.

49. *Municipal Journal*, 3 December 1915.

50. Ibid.

51. Ibid. See also Richard T. Ely, *Property and Contract in their Relation to the Distribution of Wealth*, 2 vols. (New York: Lord, 1914).

52. U.S., Department of Labor, Bureau of Children, *Infant Mortality*.

53. National Archives, Record Group 102, boxes 216 and 220, records relating to *Infant Mortality*, interview with Anna Herkimer, 28 June 1916.

54. Ibid., interview with John Ferguson, 28 June 1916.

55. Maryland Bureau of Industrial Statistics, *12th Annual Report*, 1903–1904.

56. On Progressivism in Baltimore, see James B. Crooks, *Politics and Progress*.

57. National Archives, Record Group 102, boxes 216 and 220, records relating to *Infant Mortality*, Interview with William L. Fitzgerald, 28 June 1916.

58. Kemp, *Housing Conditions*; U.S., Department of Labor, Bureau of Children, *Infant Mortality*; Great Britain, Board of Trade, *Cost of Living in American Towns: Report of an Enquiry by the Board of Trade into Working Class Rents, Housing and Retail Prices* (London, 1911), pp. 73–84.

59. Police Census of Negroes, 1904, published in Maryland Bureau of Industrial Statistics, *13th Annual Report*, 1905; and Police Housing Census, 1913.

60. W.E.B. Dubois in *The Crisis* 1 (1910), as cited in Aptheker's documentary history, *The Negro People in the United States, 1910–1932* (New York: The Citadel Press, 1951).

61. *Sun*, 22 and 24 February 1917.

62. Ibid., 3 March 1917.

63. Ibid., 1 May 1917.

64. Ibid., 5 April 1906.

65. Ibid., 12 and 15 May 1913.

66. Ibid., 2 February 1917.

67. *Sunday Sun*, 4 March 1917.

68. Maryland Bureau of Industrial Statistics, *Annual Report*.

69. *Sun*, 1, 2, 3, and 5 January 1910.

70. Ibid., 15 December 1909.

71. Manuscript memoir at Jewish Historical Society.

72. *Sun*, 2, 4, 15, and 24 February and 3, 6, and 10 March 1916. *Official Souvenir*, Third Biennial Convention of the Amalgamated Clothing Workers of America, Baltimore, Md., 13 and 19 May 1918.

73. *Sun*, 17 February 1916.

74. Jacob Moses, interview by Isaac M. Fein in Jewish Historical Society.

75. Herman Seidel, interview by Isaac M. Fein, in Jewish Historical Society.

76. Cardinal Gibbons, Report to the Holy See, 1912, in John Tracy Ellis, *The Life of James Cardinal Gibbons, Archbishop of Baltimore, 1834–1921*, 2 vols. (Milwaukee: Bruce Publishing Co., 1952).

77. Mary L. Swanson, "A Study of the Polish Organizations of Baltimore" (M.A. thesis, The Johns Hopkins University, 1925).

78. Sara Jean Reilly, "The Italian Immigrants, 1920–1930, in Baltimore" (M.A. thesis, The Johns Hopkins University, 1962).

79. U.S., Department of Labor, Bureau of Children, *Infant Mortality*.

80. *Sun Magazine*, 3 June 1973, p. 2.

81. *Sun*, 5 April 1906.

82. Ibid., 21 January 1917.

83. Ibid., 2 March 1917.

84. *Maryland Geological Survey* 3 (Baltimore, 1899).

85. Maryland, State Roads Commission, *A History of Road Building in Maryland* (1958), p. 132.

86. *Sun*, 20, 24, and 26 January 1917.

87. Ibid., 24 January 1917.

88. Ferdinand C. Latrobe, *Iron Men and Their Dogs: A History of Bartlett, Hayward* (Baltimore: I. R. Drechsler, 1914). The industrial might of Baltimore in World War I can be traced in its geographical location by the official restricted areas (*Sun*, 9 May 1917) and by the volumes of ground water used and problems of ground water contamination (John C. Geyer, "Groundwater in the Baltimore Industrial Area" [Ph.D. diss., The Johns Hopkins University, 1944]).

89. *Sun*, 26 March 1917.

90. *Sun*.

91. Ibid., 26 February 1917.
92. Ibid., 2 March 1917.
93. Ibid., 21 February 1915.
94. Ibid., 4 April 1917.
95. Ibid., 21 February and 4 and 30 April 1917.
96. Ibid., 22 May 1917.
97. Ibid., 16 March 1917.
98. Ibid., 24 March 1917.
99. Ibid., 20 February 1916 and 17 May 1917.
100. Ibid., 5 March 1917.
101. Ibid., 4 March 1917.
102. Ibid., 2 March 1917.
103. Ibid., 26 January 1917.
104. Ibid., 24, 28, and 29 January 1917.
105. Ibid., 2 February 1917.
106. Ibid.
107. Ibid., 5 April 1917.
108. Ibid., 1 April 1917.
109. Ibid., 1, 9, and 10 March 1917.
110. Ibid., 10 March 1917.
111. Ibid., 11 March 1917.
112. Ibid., 16 May 1917.
113. Ibid., 9 March 1917.
114. Ibid., 16 March 1917.
115. Ibid., 7 March 1917.
116. Ibid., 24 May 1918.
117. Ibid., 31 May 1917.

A Place to Move About In

Newspapers used are the *Sun*, the *American*, and the weekly *Maryland Leader*, 1933–35. The *Municipal Journal* contains maps and reports of the City Plan Commission, the Municipal Factory Site Commission, Topographical Survey, etc., as well as booster articles; it ceased in 1931. Items of industrial technology and new industry appear in *Baltimore Gas and Electric News*, monthly, beginning in 1912, and *Power Pictorial* (new title) from 1925.

H. L. Mencken citations are from manuscripts in the Mencken Room, Enoch Pratt Free Library, Baltimore, Md. The Maryland Bureau of Industrial Statistics becomes the Office of the Commissioner for Labor and Statistics.

Public works are inventoried and priorities are outlined in Abel Wolman, Gustav J. Requardt, and Nathan L. Smith, *Report to the Commission on City Plan of the City of Baltimore on Present and Proposed Physical Facilities: Report of the Advisory Engineers* (Baltimore, 1942).

1. Mastheads, *Municipal Journal*; *Sun*, 1 and 12 February 1925; Norman N. Rubin, "From the Sea with Wings: Maryland and the Flying Boat," *Maryland Historical Magazine* 72 (Summer 1977): 277.
2. *Evening Sun*, 10 September 1923.
3. Real Estate Board of Baltimore, in cooperation with Police Department of Baltimore City, *A Survey of Housing Conditions* (Baltimore, August 1921).
4. *Sun*, 21 December 1924. The analysis of residences of families in the *Social Register* was made by Mark K. Fleeharty, a student at The Johns Hopkins University, in 1970.
5. *Sun*, 21 December 1924.
6. Mencken, *Evening Sun*, 3 October 1927.

7. Ibid., 22 July 1929.

8. George D. Strayer, *Report of the Survey of the Public Schools System of Baltimore, Maryland, School Year 1920–1921*, 3 vols. (Baltimore: Board of School Commissioners, 1921).

9. *Municipal Journal*, 6 August 1920. On the school investments that followed, see Wolman, Requardt, and Smith, *Report of the Advisory Engineers*.

10. Archbishop Curley, cited in Dorothy M. Brown, "Maryland between the Wars," in *Maryland: A History, 1632–1974*, ed. Richard Walsh and William Lloyd Fox (Baltimore: Maryland Historical Society, 1974).

11. Mencken, 13 June 1921.

12. Ferdinand C. Latrobe, *Iron Men and Their Dogs: A History of Bartlett, Hayward* (Baltimore: I. R. Drechsler, 1941).

13. Ibid.

14. *Municipal Journal*, 2 December 1921.

15. Ibid., 21 July 1922.

16. *Sun*, 19 December 1924; 4, 28, and 31 January, 1, 3, 4, 6, 10, and 12 February and 9 and 12 March 1925.

17. See chapter 9, note 85.

18. *Municipal Journal*, 7 April 1922.

19. Ibid., 24 March 1921. For full illustrations of plans for the port, see original manuscript and photographs entitled "Plan of Baltimore, Maryland," dated 24 March 1921, in Enoch Pratt Free Library, Baltimore, Md., and published version, *Port Development Plan of Baltimore, Maryland* (Baltimore: Hoen, 1922).

20. *Municipal Journal*, 24 September 1928. See also ibid., 13 February and 8 October 1928 and 29 March 1929.

21. Mencken, *Evening Sun*, 22 August 1932.

22. *Municipal Journal*, 21 February and 19 December 1919 and 22 April 1921.

23. Mencken, 11 June 1934.

24. *Municipal Journal*, 26 October 1930.

25. Kelker, DeLeuuw & Co., *Report on Street Railway Routing and Improvement of Traffic Conditions in the City of Baltimore* (1926), and Michael R. Farrell, *Who Made All Our Streetcars Go?* (Baltimore: NRHS Publications, 1973).

26. United Railways and Electric Company of Baltimore, *Annual Report (25th) to Stockholders for Year Ended Dec. 31, 1923*.

27. Cited in Wolman, Requardt, and Smith, *Report of Advisory Engineers*, p. 1.

28. *Municipal Journal*, 8 November 1921.

29. Ibid., 5 November 1920, p. 5.

30. Ibid., 7 April 1922.

31. "Report of the City Plan Committee on the Development of the Territory Added under the Act of 1918 . . . ," 1 May 1919, in Enoch Pratt Free Library, Baltimore, Md.

32. City Plan Committee, *Municipal Journal*, 19 May 1919.

33. Ibid., 21 February 1930.

34. Ibid., 5 November 1920.

35. Maryland State Roads Commission, *A History of Road Building in Maryland* (Baltimore, 1958).

36. *Municipal Journal*, 10 and 31 May, 18 October, and 22 November 1929 and 27 July 1931. "Report of Mr. F. L. Olmsted on East and West Viaduct, Baltimore, Maryland, to Municipal Art Society," 2 December 1929, Maryland Historical Society, Baltimore, Md.

37. *Municipal Journal*, 25 June 1924 and 25 April 1927.

38. Joseph B. Chepaitis, "Albert C. Ritchie in Power, 1920–1927," *Maryland Historical Magazine* 68 (1973): 383–404. See also Brown, "Maryland between the wars."

39. City Plan Committee, "Report," 1 May 1919.

40. W. W. Emmart, *Report on Housing and Commercial Conditions in Baltimore Constituting Studies Prepared for Mayor Howard W. Jackson, Oct. 1934* (Baltimore, 1934). See also "A Report on Slums," *Baltimore Engineer* 8 (January 1934): 6–10; John Edward Semmes,

Jr., "Baltimore Fights the Slums" (Thesis, Princeton University, 1940), in City Hall Library; and Postal Survey, *Real Estate News*, August 1934.

41. Ira DeA. Reid, *Summary Report: The Negro Community of Baltimore* (Baltimore: Urban League, 1934). See also *Sun*, 15 December 1929; "The Lung Block," Urban League Study no. 2 (Baltimore: Urban League, 1925).

42. "The Negro Church in Baltimore" (Baltimore: Urban League, 1934); and Ralph L. Pearson, "National Urban League Comes to Baltimore," *Maryland Historical Magazine* 72 (Winter 1977): 522–33.

43. *Sun*, 6 May 1921. The strikes are documented in Maryland Commissioner of Labor and Statistics, *Annual Report*, 1919, 1920, 1921, 1922.

44. Chepaitis, "Albert C. Ritchie."

45. Maryland Commissioner of Labor and Statistics, *Annual Report*, 1922, pp. 143–45. See also Elizabeth D. L. Otey, *The Cotton Mill Workers on Jones Falls* (Baltimore: Christian Social Justice Fund, 1924).

46. Mencken, *Evening Sun*, 10 September 1923.

47. Ibid.

48. *Sun*, 14 and 16 January 1934.

49. *Sun Magazine*, 18 October 1970.

50. As reprinted in *Sun Magazine*, 8 October 1972. On other raids, see *Sun*, 15, 16, and 19 December 1924, and 1, 12, 13 February and 17 March 1925.

51. Ibid., 25 February 1933.

52. Ibid., 5 March 1933.

53. Ibid., 22 February 1933. See also Baltimore Committee on Unemployment, "Report," mimeographed, 1932 (copy in Library of Congress); Municipal Commission on Stabilization of Employment, "Report," in *Municipal Journal*, 12 September 1930.

54. *Sun*, 19 March 1933 and 19 February 1933.

55. Ibid., 14 March 1933.

56. Ibid., 30 December 1933 and 6 January 1934.

57. Ibid., 26 and 28 March 1933 and 5 January 1934.

58. On the role of the Reconstruction Finance Corporation, see Jesse H. Jones, *Fifty Billion Dollars: My Thirteen Years with the Reconstruction Finance Corporation* (New York: Macmillan, 1951).

59. *Sun*, 19 August 1932; see also ibid., 20 March and 17 and 19 December 1933.

60. Taped reminiscences of Thomas D'Alessandro, *Evening Sun*, 28 January 1976.

61. *Sun*, 14 March 1933.

62. Simon Sobeloff, report, cited in *Sun*, 7 June 1936.

63. Edwin Baetjer, cited in *Sun*, 20 March 1933.

64. The three largest grocery chains in Baltimore in 1933 were American, A&P, and Sanitary.

65. Farrell considers that if Storrs had not been hampered by such tight credit, he could have bought more Peter Witt steel cars, run the company in the black, and restored appeal to the Baltimore public.

66. Margaret Wolman, "Real Property Tax Delinquency in Baltimore" (Ph.D. diss., The Johns Hopkins University, 1937).

67. George R. Morris, quoted in *Sun*, 14 January 1934.

68. Broadus Mitchell, *Depression Decade: From New Era through New Deal, 1929–1941* (New York: Rinehart, 1947).

69. *Sun*, 10 January 1934.

70. *Leader*, 17 February 1934.

71. Figures on spending and employment come from monthly reports of the PWA, copies in the possession of Melvin Scheidt, of The Johns Hopkins University.

72. *Sun*, 31 January 1934.

73. William H. Grimes, *Commercial Credit Corporation, 1912–1945* (Baltimore, 1946). Other new financial institutions are discussed in Joseph Lilly, *Helping America Buy What It*

Wants, 1912–1952 (Baltimore, 1952). Clark J. Fitzpatrick and Elliott Buse, *Fifty Years of Suretyship and Insurance: The Story of United States Fidelity & Guarantee Co.* (Baltimore, 1946). Frank R. Kent, *The Story of Alex. Brown & Sons, 1800–1900* (Baltimore, 1950). *Sun,* 4 January and 26 December 1924 and 4 February and 10 March 1925.

74. Ibid., 20 and 24 March 1933 and 10 January 1934.

75. *Leader,* 26 January, 15 September, and 13 October 1934; *Sun,* 29 December 1933.

76. *Sun,* 7 January 1934.

77. Ibid., 15 March 1933.

78. Ibid., 7 April 1933.

Hemmed In

Published documents and mimeographed reports of the Baltimore Urban Renewal and Housing Agency (BURHA) and its successor, the Department of Housing and Community Development, have been used extensively. Documents of the Community Action Agency and the Model Cities Agency contain comprehensive material on poverty and inner city demands. My perspective on the relative importance of events in Baltimore in the years 1960 to 1973 has been influenced by participation in the Neighborhood Action Group in Reservoir Hill.

1. *Sun,* 22 February 1937.

2. On Bethlehem installations, shipbuilding, sizes of ships, and technology at Westinghouse and Western Electric plants in Baltimore, see newspaper clippings in the vertical files, Enoch Pratt Free Library, Baltimore, Md., by corporate names.

3. Jesse H. Jones, *Fifty Billion Dollars: My Thirteen Years with the Reconstruction Finance Corporation* (New York: Macmillan, 1951).

4. *Sun,* 18 April 1942.

5. *Bartlett Hayward Presents This Pictorial Review of Its Industrial Activities* (Baltimore: Koppers Co., Bartlett Hayward Division, 1945).

6. Jones, *Fifty Billion Dollars.*

7. *Sun,* 7 July 1945.

8. Davison Chemical Co., *Prospectus,* 1952 and 1953; *Chemical and Engineering News,* 25 December 1943.

9. Maryland Port Authority, annual reports and handbooks. Baltimore Bureau of Harbors, annual reports, 1932 to 1948, contain dredging figures. Wallace McHarg Roberts and Todd, Inc., for Maryland State Department of Planning, "Maryland Chesapeake Bay Study: Report" (1972). Knappen, Tippets, Abbott Engineering Co., "Report on the Port of Baltimore on Behalf of the City of Baltimore and the State of Maryland, for Baltimore Association of Commerce" (New York, 1950). Martin L. Collins, "An Evaluation of Baltimore Harbor Land Use Potentials" Report for the Maryland Environmental Service, Regional Planning Council (February 1973).

10. On the far-flung activities of W. R. Grace, Martin Marietta, Kennecott, Crown Central, Black & Decker, Bethlehem, and Columbia Gas System, see corporate annual reports of the 1970s.

11. On energy use, see Baltimore Gas and Electric Company publications: annual reports; residential electric and gas appliance surveys (1972 and 1976); *Power Pictorial* (1946–49); and *Power and Fuel Pictorial* (1959). The company supplied summary statistics, copies of reports, and maps.

If annual investment figures are deflated to "real" dollars, there has been roughly a fivefold increase of Baltimore Gas and Electric Company investment levels, rather than tenfold. A fivefold increase closely parallels the physical growth rates of electric power produced and fuels and cement consumed in the region. New industry and construction projects are recorded in monthly newsletters of Baltimore Association of Commerce, Industrial Services (former Industrial Bureau).

12. The city's financial institutions and business elite and their limited spheres are

indicated in Chaloner B. Schley, "Baltimore's Role in International Banking," *Baltimore Magazine* (December 1971), pp. 24–32; and Frank DeFilippo, *News American*, 17 and 18 December 1967.

13. Martin Millspaugh, *Baltimore's Charles Center*, technical bulletin 51 (Washington, D.C.: Urban Land Institute, 1965).

14. *Sun*, 17 and 26 April and 9 July 1945. Maryland Commission to Study and Report on the Transportation System Operated by the Baltimore Transit Company, "Report to Governor McKeldin, under 1951 Act of Maryland Legislature." See newspapers during transit strike, 30 January–5 March 1956, for discussions of transit company finances.

15. Portland cement shipped into Maryland rose from 1.5 million barrels a year in 1935 to 8 million barrels in 1973 (U.S., Bureau of Mines, *Yearbook*). About 1.5 barrels, or 550 pounds, of cement are used for a cubic yard of concrete in expressway construction. The yearly energy requirement to produce the cement alone would be about a million barrels of oil plus 100 kilowatt hours of electricity.

16. *Sun*, 4 April 1945; *Evening Sun*, 14 November 1952 and 20 November 1955; *Power and Fuel Pictorial* 85, beltway edition (December 1962); *Sun*, 29 August and 18 November 1971 and 27 August 1972. Marc Reutter, "The Thirty Years War" (Paper, The Johns Hopkins University, February 1972). Douglas H. Haeuber, *The Baltimore Expressway Controversy* (Baltimore: The Johns Hopkins University Center for Metropolitan Planning and Research, 1974). Urban Design Concept Associates, *Segment Area Reports* (1 November 1968) and *Point III Reports* (July 1970), prepared for Maryland State Roads Commission and Interstate Division for Baltimore City. On the highways and parks, see James Dilts, *Sun*, 29 September 1968; "A Study and Recommendations for the Recreational Development of the Patapsco River Valley Park" (Report to Mayor T. R. McKeldin, May 1946, in Enoch Pratt Free Library); BURHA, "Jones Falls Valley Woodberry-Hampden Study" (Baltimore, 5 April 1963); and "Plan of Municipal Art Society and Greater Baltimore Committee for a Jones Falls Valley Park" (Baltimore, n.d., ca. 1963).

17. See chapter 2, note 25, on the road building controversy of 1784, and chapter 4, note 16, on the controversy of 1804.

18. Joseph Albright, *What Makes Spiro Run* (New York: Dodd, Mead, 1972). See also Franklin L. Burdette, "Modern Maryland Politics and Social Change," in *Maryland: A History, 1632–74*, ed. Richard Walsh and William Lloyd Fox (Baltimore: Maryland Historical Society, 1974), pp. 881–83.

19. *Evening Sun*, 22, 28, and 29 September 1970; *New York Times*, 13 September 1970.

20. *Sun*, 23 May 1943; see also 13 November 1943.

21. Ibid., 31 July–2 August 1943.

22. Ibid., 18 October 1943.

23. Ibid., 11 August 1944.

24. Joseph P. Healy, chairman, *Report of the Governor's Commission on Problems Affecting the Negro Population* (Baltimore, 1943). *Sun*, 12 February 1950. Baltimore Community Self-Survey of Intergroup Relations, *An American City in Transition* (Baltimore, 1955).

25. To situate Baltimore school integration in the national context, I relied heavily on Richard Kluger, *Simple Justice* (New York: Random House, 1977). The term "infant appellants" is attributed by Kluger (p. 645) to Charles Black, 1953. For Baltimore reactions to Supreme Court cases, see *Afro-American*, 14 November and 5 December 1953, and 29 May and 5 and 12 June 1954.

26. On Lillie Jackson and Thurgood Marshall, see vertical files, Enoch Pratt Free Library, Baltimore, Md.

27. *Afro-American*, 13 September 1952.

28. National Education Association, *Baltimore, Maryland, Change and Contrast: The Children and Public Schools* (Washington, D.C.: NEA, 1967).

29. Ibid., p. 57.

30. *Milliken v. Bradley*, 94 S. Ct. 3112 (25 July 1974) applied to Detroit, as cited by Kluger, *Simple Justice*, p. 773.

31. Sherry H. Olson, *Baltimore* (Cambridge, Mass.: Ballinger, 1976). For population redistribution, see Center for Metropolitan Planning and Research, The Johns Hopkins University, *Metro News, Occasional Papers,* and *Census Notes* (1971–72).

32. Office of Economic Opportunity, *Federal Outlays in Summary: A Report of the Federal Government's Impact by State, County, and Large City* (Miscellaneous Publication PB–219, 463, 1972). *Federal Outlays in Maryland* (OEOOSL–73–21). Advisory Commission on Intergovernmental Relations, *Significant Features of Fiscal Federalism* (M–106, Washington, D.C., June 1976). In the mid-1920s, the city budget was $65 million a year, still double the state government budget. In the generation 1919–34 the city floated $60 million of loans, including the public schools loans. Municipal property was valued at $300 million.

33. U.S., Commission on Civil Rights, Maryland State Advisory Committee, "Transcript of Hearings, Baltimore, Maryland, January 1971."

34. Daniel Raymond, *Thoughts on Political Economy* (Baltimore: F. Lucas, 1820), p. 452.

35. W. W. Emmart, *Report on Housing and Commercial Conditions in Baltimore, Constituting Studies Prepared for Mayor Howard W. Jackson, October 1934* (Baltimore, 1934); John Edward Semmes, Jr., "Baltimore Fights the Slums" (Thesis, Princeton University, 1940) in City Hall Library; Wallace McHarg Roberts and Todd, for Regional Planning Council and Baltimore City Department of Planning, *Metro Center/Baltimore, Technical Study* (Baltimore, 1970).

36. Citizens Planning and Housing Association, mimeographed press releases, 1942–73; "Unvented Gas Heaters," *Baltimore Magazine* (September 1970), pp. 30–34.

37. Martin Millspaugh and Gurney Breckenfeld, *The Human Side of Urban Renewal,* ed. M. L. Colean (New York, 1958).

38. Baltimore Urban Renewal and Housing Agency (BURHA), "A Demonstration of Rehabilitation, Harlem Park" (Baltimore, 1965). The pilot block, no. 314, borders Harlem Park on the east.

39. "Displacement and Relocation, Past and Future, Baltimore, Maryland," BURHA stage one staff monograph 5.4, mimeographed (March 1965). Constance L. Barker, "Relocation and the Housing Market in Metropolitan Baltimore, 1968–1975," mimeographed (Maryland Regional Planning Council, 1968).

40. Interviews with Abel Wolman and Janet Hoffman, *Metro News,* 15 September 1974, pp. 6–11.

41. *Sun,* 2 October 1971 and 15 January 1972; *Afro-American,* 28 February 1976; The Activists, *Stop Black Tax* (pamphlets, Baltimore, 1970).

42. There are three distinct types of "buy like rent" contracts; the scale of such activity is indicated for 1950s in Baltimore Community Self-Survey of Intergroup Relations, *An American City* (Baltimore, 1955).

43. On housing and financial institutions, see Lata Chatterjee, David Harvey, and Lawrence Klugman, *FHA Policies and the Baltimore City Housing Market* (Baltimore: The Johns Hopkins University Center for Metropolitan Planning and Research, 1974); David Harvey, *Class-Monopoly Rent, Finance Capital and the Urban Revolution,* University of Toronto Papers on Planning and Design no. 4 (March 1974); and M. G. Wolman, David Harvey, Lata Chatterjee, Lawrence Klugman, and Jeanne Newman, *The Housing Market and Code Enforcement in Baltimore* (Baltimore: City Planning Department, 1972).

44. *Afro-American,* 20 March, 29 May, and 5 and 19 June 1954; *Sun,* 11 March 1971.

45. *News American* and *Sun,* 4–14 April 1968.

46. *Niles' Register,* 8 and 15 August 1835.

Index of Subjects

Road making: by State Roads Commission, 255, 289, 319–20, 324, 342, 360; by turnpike companies, 8–9, 18, 47–48, 49. *See also* Bridge(s); Street making

Roland Park Company, 212, 213, 256, 281, 294, 303–4, 319, 325

Row houses. *See* Dwelling types

Rumors, 96, 298–99

Saint Mary's Seminary, 29, 43, 44, 82, 95, 304

Schools, 94–95, 256, 299, 306–8; Catholic, 64, 66, 129, 307–8; colored, 186–87, 190–91, 235, 243, 370; German, 182–83, 191; investments in, 128–29, 307–8, 370; private, 64, 66, 124, 125, 129, 304; segregation in, 277; and social class, 128, 370; surveys of, 306, 370. *See also* Black community, schools in; Women, education of

Seafood, 110, 132, 145, 179. *See also* Oysters

Sedimentation, 6, 8, 21–22, 222; at foot of Ann Street, 55, 82; in Hughes Street, 55, 132–33; in Jones Falls, 55, 133

Segregation, racial, 121, 269; in churches, 187; in factories, 364–65; in hospitals, 270; in housing, 275, 287, 301, 372; in state institutions, 190. *See also* Schools

Servants. *See* Labor

Sewage disposal, 92, 131, 162, 227, 264; by odorless excavating, 166

Sewers, sanitary, 245, 249–53, 262. *See also* Drainage

Shipbuilding, 26, 28, 83, 98, 119, 150, 204, 207, 292, 336, 347–49, 352–53, 363–64. *See also* Caulkers; Cooperatives; Labor; Steamboats

Skyscrapers, 244, 248–49, 314, 335, 341, 358–59

Slavery: 12, 18, 66–67, 120; abolition of, 34–35, 96–97, 127, 146; and African colonization, 45, 67–68; extension of, resisted, 70; in rural economy, 4, 6, 11, 34. *See also* Friends, Society of, members of; Religion, Methodist

Slaves, in city: conscripted, 146; emancipated, 147, 186; hired out, 34; jailed, 64, 146; manumitted, 45, 68; protected in rights, 34–35, 45, 67; purchase freedom, 120

Slums. *See* Urban renewal, and slum clearance

Solid waste. *See* Garbage removal

Sparrows Point, 198, 213, 214–15, 261, 274, 292, 305. *See also* Iron and steel companies, Bethlehem Steel Company

Speculation: in currency, 58; in foodstuffs, 296; in franchises, 137, 160, 166; in housing, 47, 116–17, 275, 278–79; in land, 79, 116, 154, 167–70, 172–73, 209, 212, 217, 294, 361–62 (*see also* Land); in stocks of Canton Company, 78, 243, 297; in ventures, 151, 154–55; in wartime, 296–98

Squares, 114–15, 132, 135–36, 167, 191. *See also* Parks

State government. *See* Maryland, state of

Steamboats, 102, 150, 151, 259

Steam engines and power, 84, 150–51, 200, 203, 287

Stenches, 131–32, 148

Storm sewers. *See* Drainage

Strategic location of Baltimore, 127, 143–45, 159–60, 183–84, 259, 282

Street: cleaning, 131, 224; extensions, 49–50, 56–57, 82–83, 163; grades, 54, 55, 58, 132–33 (*see also* Drainage; Planning; Surveys); paving, 20, 166, 222, 224, 314; widenings, 83, 111, 122

Streetcars. *See* Electric transit

Street making, 7, 8–9, 18, 20, 54–55, 56–58, 221–22, 341; in Canton, 116, 172, 262; on city boundary, 136; developmental, 55, 167, 172, 255, 258; on viaducts, 253, 254, 313, 320–21, 343. *See also* Alley(s); Planning; Road making; Surveys

Street railways. *See* Electric transit; Horsecars

Streets: Fallsway, 253, 264; Fort Avenue, 113; Key Highway, 263; Mount Royal Avenue, 159, 165. *See also* Alley(s)

Street space, 166, 221, 248; elastic, 319–20, 359; franchised, 224–25; for railroads, 74, 75, 76, 83, 113; for wiring, 212, 227, 244. *See also* Congestion; Monopolies

Strikes: by canal labor, 197; by can makers, 178, 181; by carpenters, 38; by coal miners, 200, 204, 330; by cotton mill workers, 330, 344; by dry dock workers, 329; by garment workers, 176–77, 181, 230–31, 281, 345; by guano diggers, 201; by longshoremen, 301, 329, 344; by piano makers, 199; involving racial disputes, 275, 329, 363–64 (*see also* Caulkers); by railroad workers, 194–97, 330; by steelworkers, 344

Subdivision. *See* Land, subdivision of

Suburbanization, 167, 169–70, 212–17, 347, 348, 361–62

Suburban life style, 257–58, 357

Sugar refining, 239, 310

Suicide, 40, 139, 189, 206, 228, 382

Sulpicians. *See* Religious orders, Sulpicians

Surveys: of burnt district, 247; of harbor, 55; of Howard estate, 86; techniques of, 22, 71; topographical, 58, 163–64, 227–28, 253–54,

Index of People

THE JOHNS HOPKINS UNIVERSITY PRESS

This book was composed in Linotype Palatino text and Photo-typositor Palatino display type by Maryland Linotype Composition Co. from a design by Susan Bishop. It was printed on 70-lb. Paloma Matte paper and bound by The Murray Printing Company.

LIBRARY OF CONGRESS CATALOGING IN PUBLICATION DATA

Olson, Sherry H
  Baltimore, the building of an American city.

  Includes bibliographical references and index.
  1. Baltimore—Economic conditions. 2. Baltimore—
Social conditions. 3. Baltimore—History. I. Title.

HC108.B2047   975.2′6   79–21950
ISBN 0–8018–2224–6